INTERNATIONAL ENCYCLOPEDIA

OF

Population

INTERNATIONAL ENCYCLOPEDIA

OF

Population

EDITOR IN CHIEF

JOHN A. ROSS

Center for Population and Family Health,
International Institute for the Study of Human Reproduction,
Faculty of Medicine, Columbia University

VOLUME TWO

THE FREE PRESS
A Division of Macmillan Publishing Co., Inc., New York

Collier Macmillan Publishers, London

THE FREE PRESS
A Division of Macmillan Publishing Co., Inc.
866 Third Avenue, New York, NY   10022

Collier Macmillan Canada, Inc.

Library of Congress Catalog Card Number: 82-2326

Printed in the United States of America

printing number

3 4 5 6 7 8 9 10

Library of Congress Cataloging in Publication Data
Main entry under title:

International encyclopedia of population.

   Includes bibliographical references and index.
   1. Population—Dictionaries.   I. Ross, John A.,
1934–   .   II. International Institute for the Study
of Human Reproduction. Center for Population and Family
Health.
HB849.2.I55   304.6′03′21   82-2326
ISBN 0-02-927430-3 (set)   AACR2
ISBN 0-02-927440-0 (v. 1)
ISBN 0-02-927460-5 (v. 2)

Some of the articles included herein are based on previously
published materials. Acknowledgments of sources, copyrights,
and permissions to use these materials are gratefully made in
a special listing at the back of volume 2.

LABOR FORCE

The labor force, or the economically active population, is conventionally defined as those individuals who furnish the supply of labor for production of economic goods and services. In peasant or "primitive" economies, participation in work activities is constrained mainly by health, nutrition, family size, sex roles, the rhythm of the seasons, and the demand for income. It is when the economy changes, when agriculture becomes commercialized, when wage labor becomes a dominant feature of agriculture, and when urbanization and nonagricultural employment expand that other social and economic factors have a greater effect on the level and pattern of labor-force participation. This article reviews concepts and methods of measurement of labor supply and utilization; labor force participation patterns and trends associated with economic growth and industrialization; factors that in particular influence the participation of women; and the relationships between migration, urbanization, and labor force participation.

Labor Force Concepts. Indexes of labor force participation have two complementary functions; the first is to provide a measure of labor supply, the second is to indicate the extent of actual labor utilization. All concepts used for measuring the labor force have been controversial, and there has been a continuing debate on the most appropriate concepts for low-income environments. The difficulties stem largely from the rather hazy notion of labor supply.

Methods of measuring labor supply and underutilization can be classified basically as behavioral or normative. The principal behavioral method is the conventional labor force approach, which has various extensions and may be compared with a variety of normative approaches.

Labor force approach. The conventional approach is to multiply the "working-age population" by the "economic activity rate," or "participation rate," which is supposed to provide an approximate measure of aggregate labor supply. Whereas the working-age population is usually regarded as a socially determined demographic measure, the activity rate is calculated by dividing the sum of the employed and unemployed by the total working-age population, which by definition consists of the employed, unemployed, and economically inactive.

This approach was initially adopted in the United States at a time when there was a widespread desire to generate data on the extent and incidence of unemployment in the slump conditions of the 1930s. For that purpose the previously accepted "gainful worker" approach was found to be seriously deficient, essentially because censuses and sample surveys that relied on that procedure gave information only on an individual's gainful occupation without referring to his or her current activity. As a result it was not possible to estimate the number of workers who were employed, unemployed, ill, retired, or not able or willing to work for some other reason. Moreover, all first-time job seekers were effectively excluded from the labor force because by definition they had no gainful occupation. As an attempt to remedy these deficiencies, the labor force method laid stress on current activity and in particular on whether an individual was employed, unemployed and seeking work, or economically inactive.

By 1970, and in many countries long before, the superiority of the labor force approach over previous methods had been generally accepted and was given what amounted to an international seal of approval when the International Labour Organisation (ILO) formally recommended its use in all population censuses done in or around 1970. The approach is behavioral in the sense that labor supply and underutilization are measured on the basis of past or current behavior. However, there are difficulties with this method, particularly when applied to conditions typical of many low-income countries. Essentially the criticisms are of two types: those concerned with distinguishing between each of the separate categories, and those concerned with the usefulness and validity of the classification as a means of measuring the degree of labor underutilization and aggregate labor supply.

Activity rate and gainful employment. The labor force approach is based on the notion of economic activity, which in turn is based on two criteria: the distinction between economic and noneconomic uses of time, and the distinction between the active and the inactive. Neither distinction has been easy to make. Some critics contend that in low-income countries, particularly in rural areas dominated by subsistence agriculture, the concept of economic activity is effectively meaningless because it is either impossible to have any clear conception of what is work and what is not, or absurd to distinguish between labor force work and other forms of work that are typically excluded from the term "economic activity." When the specialization of activities has not been developed, work, leisure, and consumption tend to be intermingled, without any sharp distinction of one from the other. Social activities essential in some societies may be casual leisure pursuits in another.

In practice, economic activity is based on the notion of gainful employment, usually defined as any occupation by which the person who pursues it receives compensation in money or in kind, or in which he or she assists in the production of marketable goods and services. But the economically active have also included those wanting gainful employment. This had caused further difficulties, for it is hard to distinguish between the unemployed and the economically inactive. Usually, to be counted in the labor force, individuals must have been actively job-seeking during a specified period, usually the "past week." There is no clear justification, however, for selecting any specific period; moreover, in rural areas, or where there is no unemployment registration, or where there is mass unemployment, many of the unemployed are unlikely to have been actively seeking work. Consequently, many "discouraged workers" have been excluded from the labor force and from measurements of labor underutilization.

Time-use surveys. Because of the inherent difficulties in drawing meaningful distinctions between economic and noneconomic activities in low-income economies, many researchers feel that at least in rural areas it is more appropriate to collect information on the allocation of time to all types of activity. A number of detailed time-use surveys along those lines have been carried out; in the present context their principal advantage is indeed that they make no *a priori* judgment about what is and what is not economic activity. They also give a realistic estimate of the actual work schedules of certain population groups in societies where culture inhibits the admission of economic activity, as seems to be true of married women living in Muslim Arab countries. There is little doubt that important insights into the patterns and determinants of the allocation of time can be gained from comprehensive time-use studies, and in fact they represent a logical extension of the behavioral, labor force approach. Their drawbacks are that they tend to be expensive, require highly trained and competent interviewers, and take a great deal of time; and their results may contain measurement and sampling errors because responses will tend to be highly sensitive to such factors as the weather, the respondent's health and mood, the availability of complementary people and goods, and the interviewer's perceptions, probings, and character.

Alternative approaches. A number of alternative approaches have been suggested that are at least partially normative, some almost purely so, some combining both behavioral and normative elements. The emphasis of normative approaches has been on measuring labor underutilization. A major objection to the labor force approach as typically applied is that treating the employed, unemployed, and economically active as three clearly defined homogeneous groups is inappropriate for measuring the extent and incidence of the underutilization of labor in low-income economies where underemployment is a more widespread symptom of underutilization than open unemployment.

A widely discussed method for overcoming some of the shortcomings of the labor force approach to the measurement of labor underutilization has been suggested by Gunnar Myrdal (1968). Perceiving a need to take account of variations in labor efficiency as well as labor constraints, Myrdal proposed that the level of labor utilization be expressed as the product of three ratios:

$$\frac{\text{working numbers}}{\text{labor force}} \times \frac{\text{man-hours}}{\text{working numbers}} \times \frac{\text{output}}{\text{man-hours}} \equiv \frac{\text{output}}{\text{labor force}}.$$

Several extensions of this approach have been suggested, but all have been criticized, partly because of normative judgments required to devise empirical indexes of underutilization and partly because it is recognized that the size and composition of the labor force are not constant (Standing, 1978, pp. 41–42). More disaggregated approaches, notably the ILO scheme based on distinguishing different types of underemployment, have been criticized on similar grounds.

Another approach is one based on the classical Marxian distinction between productive and unproductive labor. A Marxist set of concepts for measuring labor surplus would consist of one component that would conform to the standard categories covered by most other approaches to labor underutilization, and a second that would consider as a special category of underutilized labor all those employed in socially unproductive labor. These and other approaches are reviewed critically elsewhere (Standing, 1978, chap. 2). They have been based upon a recognition of the failings of the gainful worker, conventional labor force, and time-budget approaches, and it seems likely that further refinements will make some of the new alternatives more operational and theoretically justifiable. Given the multidimensional nature of labor supply and utilization, however, it also seems likely that statisticians and social scientists will come to rely upon a variety of complementary approaches rather than upon any single method.

Patterns of Participation. The size of the labor force is a function of three sets of factors—the demographic composition of the population, the extent to which different groups in the population participate in labor force activities, and what might be briefly labeled as "statistical ambiguities."

Labor force measurements. Most experts would agree that the size and age structure of the population are the two most important substantive factors determining the size of the labor force, but they do not necessarily override other influences. In many instances observers have regarded statistical ambiguities as of such importance as to render labor force totals not only unreliable but misleading. Concepts and methods of measurement have varied, certain groups have been excluded or included in totals for different reasons, and qualifications have been introduced in ways that make comparability of one set of figures with another problematical or impossible.

The size of the labor force is also determined by the extent to which various population groups participate in it. Some have challenged the importance of this factor, believing that in the aggregate the activity rate is fairly constant. Certainly it is remarkable that in the United States the overall labor force participation rate fluctuated over a very narrow range during much of the twentieth century, being 54.8 percent in 1900 and 55.3 per-

cent in 1960. But the constancy of that figure was the result of offsetting trends—a rising rate of participation by women, particularly among the middle-aged groups, as against falling participation by men in both the oldest and youngest age brackets. There was no adequate reason to expect these offsetting trends to continue or to cancel one another out; indeed overall participation rates have differed markedly from country to country, and in many parts of the world have fluctuated around either declining or rising trends.

Activity rates and economic growth. With economic growth and industrialization two trends are fairly clear, and in the post-1945 period both have encouraged a fall in the crude or aggregate activity rates throughout the world. One trend is that the participation rates of children and youth in the labor force decline; the other is that the elderly tend to withdraw from the labor force at an earlier age.

In low-income countries economic growth has been typically associated with expanding schooling facilities and with a rise in the income of male family heads (so-called prime-age males) relative to the income-earning opportunities of other family members. These developments have coincided with the gradual substitution of adult male labor for that of family dependents and with an increased willingness and ability to keep children in school. If expected lifetime earnings are significantly augmented by additional schooling, and if expected future earnings of educated children increase relative to current expected income from their working, it becomes rational for parents to encourage their children to remain in school longer and thus postpone their entry into the labor force. This is the principal reason for the declining activity rates of children, teenagers, and young adults in the course of economic growth. Another reason has been the changing pattern of employment by which child labor has been reduced.

Economic growth is also associated with declining participation rates of men over the age of about 60, though the apparent relationship is attenuated because in some low-income countries a reduction in employment opportunities has depressed the participation rates of older workers. They contribute more to production where the subsistence economy is important and where the extended family is the dominant productive unit, and both of these situations diminish with economic growth. In particular, the decline of subsistence farming contributes to the declining participation rate of the elderly. They may also retire earlier because of rising incomes. Their position in the labor market may deteriorate for various reasons—as employment becomes more determined by market demand, as technological change makes skills obsolescent, as the intensity of labor increases, and as working arrangements are formalized and standardized.

But equally, the greater prevalence of pensions and institutionalized retirement ages, as well as the greater ability of workers in high-income countries to accumulate personal assets to cover retirement, have contributed to the declining levels of participation by older age groups in the labor force.

Within industrialized countries, including the socialist countries of eastern Europe, levels and age patterns of male activity rates are fairly similar, although there are differences in the average age of entry into the labor force and of retirement. On average, age-standardized male activity rates have been relatively low in the socialized countries of eastern Europe because of late entry into the labor force and fairly early retirement. But in general the pattern is for men in all parts of the world to spend their adult years as participants in the labor force.

Levels and Trends of Female Participation. Any generalization about the participation of women in the labor force is apt to be misleading, since levels, patterns, and trends vary widely between and within countries. Overall, in the context of economic growth and industrialization a logistically declining trend in the crude participation rate (fairly rapid fall followed by much slower decline) is not found with women as it is with men, if only because of the very low rates recorded in some low-income countries. Even in the industrialized countries, where differences in male activity rates are small and largely reserved to the two ends of the age spectrum, differences in female participation rates are considerable. One interesting feature, however, is that the socialist countries of eastern Europe have consistently high, age-standardized rates of female participation, higher on average than in other industrialized countries or in low-income countries although some of the latter have registered higher rates.

Some observers have suggested that in the course of economic development there is a U-shaped pattern of female participation, with declines occurring in the early stages of industrialization that are later counteracted by the increases in the relative size of the service sector and the growth of clerical and white-collar occupations. According to this hypothesis, in the early stages women are pushed out of jobs by competition with men as unemployment increases, while rising levels of family income are supposed to relax the pressure on women to act as supplementary earners. Later the trend is reversed as employment opportunities for women improve. The ILO used the hypothesis of a U-shaped curve for the labor force projections it computed for the 1965–1985 period (International Labour Organisation, 1973).

Despite the intuitive appeal of the simple relationship involved, this is not a hypothesis that can sustain detailed scrutiny, not least because any relationship based on aggregate cross-national data may involve serious errors of misaggregation. Changes in female participation will depend in part on the traditional economic roles of women in agricultural and nonagricultural occupations, as well as on the changing sectoral distribution of employment and the degree to which female workers are substituted for male and vice-versa. Accordingly, a simple U-shaped pattern is unlikely.

Ethnographic and agricultural-labor survey data do suggest that in peasant economies most family members work, to some extent, if they are physically capable of doing so. But even so, relating women's participation to a particular stage of development is surely invalid. Indeed the most salient characteristic distinguishing the labor forces of different low-income economies is the variation in the economic role of women. These countries may be classified into four distinctive groups—those where female participation rates are low in both villages and towns, those where they are low in villages and high in towns, those where they are high in villages and low in towns, and those where they are high in both rural and urban areas. In other words, there is no pattern typical of low-income countries in general. Census and sample survey data gathered in recent years, including local time-use studies in various agrarian economies, suggest the approximate classification shown in Table 1, although some countries within each of the groupings will come close to being in another category, and changes in definitions of economic activity from census to census, as in India, for example, will arbitrarily shift one country from one category to another.

It may be tempting to explain this pattern in terms of varying statistical practices and the influence of predominantly cultural factors, emphasizing religious and other social attitudes to women working for pay. Cultural factors may play a part, but they should be treated cautiously. Muslim opposition to women working, for example, is contradicted by Indonesia, a predominantly Muslim country with a relatively high rate of female participation. And in the Sudan, questions about "secondary" as well as main activity led to a massive upward revision of the estimated participation rate.

Urbanization. Given the diversity of rural patterns, the level of female participation in the rural economy will help explain changes occurring during economic growth,

TABLE 1. *Female participation rates*

Area	Rural	Urban
Arab countries	Low	Low
Latin America	Low	High
Africa and India	High	Low
Southeast Asia	High	High

industrialization, and urbanization. As it is, women have played a relatively minor economic role in urban areas of Arab countries, India, and sub-Saharan Africa, although at least in the last instance they have played a prominent role in trade. In urban areas of Southeast Asia, female participation has also been high but often no higher than in rural areas. In Latin America women have been largely relegated to domestic work in rural areas, although their contribution to agricultural production has surely been greater than is implied by official labor force statistics. As a result of this low level of participation, many young, single women have moved to the town where they have been used as low-paid domestic servants or have worked in factories or in various personal service occupations.

At present, partly because severe data limitations make the identification of patterns and trends difficult, explanations of international differences remain somewhat speculative. But it is possible to draw at least one tentative conclusion; with economic growth and urbanization in nonsocialist countries, female participation rates tend to converge towards a medium level within the wide range of rates recorded in various parts of the world. This is simply because urbanization and economic growth tend to reduce the very high rates observed in countries where women have played a major role in traditional agriculture, and to raise the rates in those countries where women have played an insignificant role in agriculture. Thus the convergence is produced by the elimination of extreme values. In the case of male labor force participation there is also a convergence, but of a different type; as noted earlier, crude activity rates of males appear to decline logistically during industrialization. For women, average activity rates may not decline because of the very low initial rates of some low-income countries.

Age patterns. Age distributions of female participation also vary considerably. In some countries the female participation rate reaches a peak in the 15–19 age group; in some the peak is in the 20–24 age group; in others the 50–54 age group; and in some countries there are two peaks, one before the onset of childbearing and one some years after the period of childbearing. Although there is no single pattern, in industrialized countries the most common feature has been a sharp peak in activity rates for women in their early twenties. Other patterns are associated with differences in the life cycle of marriage, average age at first pregnancy, average number of children per woman, and the structure of the labor market.

As an example of the pitfalls of comparative analysis of patterns, it is useful to consider a study conducted for the United Nations some years ago (United Nations, 1962). Comparing average age-specific activity rates from a group of fourteen industrialized countries (de-

fined as having less than 35 percent of the male labor force engaged in agriculture), this study concluded that "the most striking difference was the much greater participation of young women aged 15–30 in economic activities in low-income countries." However, the small sample of countries classified as underdeveloped contained Arab, Latin American, Asian, and African countries with disparate rates of female economic activity. Consequently averages for the group of underdeveloped countries depended arbitrarily on the selection of countries, making comparative conclusions unreliable or misleading, even if the statistics of the individual countries were accepted as reasonable. Nevertheless, if census data are at all reliable, they suggest that young women have had higher rates of labor force participation in industrialized than in low-income countries, a pattern quite unlike the equivalent one for men.

Trends. Since 1945, female participation rates have risen substantially in industrialized countries, conspicuously so in a few countries, such as the United States and the United Kingdom. Such rises are generally expected to continue. According to the Statistical Bureau of the International Labour Office there has also been a small net decline in low-income countries taken as a group, a trend that is also expected to continue (International Labour Organisation, 1973).

Few trends, however, can be clearly and reliably identified through the study of international aggregative data, in part because the concepts and measurements have varied between countries and over time, and in part because of the inherently hazy and multidimensional notion of labor supply.

Fertility and female employment. The constraining influence of fertility and the associated demand for time for child care have often been considered as the principal determinants of female labor force participation and as such have figured prominently in the recent empirical and theoretical research on female labor supply. Correspondingly, a considerable body of research has been devoted to the study of the impact of female labor force participation on fertility, the most usual assumption being that an expansion of female employment would lower fertility. Among planners in low-income countries the possibility that female employment would slow the rate of population growth has led to widespread enthusiasm for policies designed to accelerate the growth of the female labor force. Many academics, as well as international organizations and governments, have accepted that an inverse relationship does indeed exist and have accordingly advocated policies to increase female employment. In doing so certain problems have been glossed over. The most important of these is that more-recent research has cast doubt on the general validity of the inverse relationship, while several studies have emphasized that if there is a relationship it depends crucially on the type of employment.

The evidence is mixed. Although much of the empirical analysis is methodologically questionable and based on inadequate data, the general conclusion is that the demand for time for child care acts as less of a constraint on female participation in rural areas and where domestic employment predominates. In urban and industrial areas an inverse relationship is more likely, although it is still unclear whether or not the effect is greater for women with relatively low opportunity wages.

One factor that might contribute to a U-shaped curve of female participation rates in the course of industrialization is the changing effect of fertility. In preindustrial societies fertility is likely to have little or no effect, whereas in urbanizing and industrializing societies its effect could increase until alternative forms of child care are developed to replace the extended family system. Perhaps significantly, in recent years the constraining influence of fertility has appeared to decline in the United States; and analysis of Puerto Rican data from the 1950 and 1960 censuses suggested that although there was an inverse relationship in both years, in 1960 young children had become less of a constraint on female participation. But if the influence of fertility does increase in early industrialization and become less important in highly industrialized economies, few studies have attempted to determine whether or to what extent that is true, or what factors might account for it. In low-income, predominantly rural societies, work and fertility tend to be compatible, and the extended kinship system allows the child-caring roles to be shared. If middle-class women work in the growing urban areas, they can obtain cheap domestic labor, so that for them too children are rarely an effective constraint. But even if the constraint of child care is reduced by the existence of a large pool of young women workers—typically migrants to urban areas resigned to working for low wages—the constraint is not entirely removed. Indeed, the process of industrialization and the unemployment that has usually accompanied it tend to strengthen that constraint. The growing premium put by employers on a stable, committed work force no doubt induces discrimination against women who have young children or are likely to have them. This discrimination spills over into the provision of schooling and training, so widening the male-female opportunity wage differential, and encouraging an intrahousehold division of labor whereby women concentrate on raising children.

In highly industrialized economies, on the other hand, the male-female opportunity wage differential has shrunk somewhat, and employers and the state have been inclined to assist in the provision of institutional facilities for child care. More important, the small number of children has not only encouraged greater commitment to the labor force by women but has also lessened discrimination against women workers in general. In these circumstances fertility is likely to decline as a factor constraining female labor force participation.

Migration and Urbanization. If the level and pattern of participation in the labor force depend primarily on employment opportunities, the labor market structure, and the demand for income, then the pattern of population mobility is likely to be an important factor. Migration reflects in part a population's capacity for adjustment, and economically it is a process by which population resources are reallocated from areas of lower to higher opportunity. That in itself should mean that the degree of mobility would be positively related to levels of economic activity. In fact though, the relation between migration and labor force participation is somewhat more complex.

Microbehavioral relationships between migration and participation in the labor force need not correspond to macrolevel relationships. Empirically, migrants might have a higher propensity to be in the labor force than nonmigrants, although an area in which a high proportion of the population consisted of migrants might have a low rate of labor force participation. Indeed, there are three separate issues. First, do migrants have higher or lower rates of labor force participation than nonmigrants? Second, is in-migration to an area associated with rising or falling rates of participation? Third, what is the effect of out-migration on the size of the labor force and the division of labor?

In each instance the expected relationship will depend on the nature of migration and the interaction of the socioeconomic or labor market structures in areas of in-migration and out-migration with the behavioral responses of migrants and their families. Thus to explain the relationships between migration and participation, both the nature of migration and the relationship with socioeconomic or labor market changes must be analyzed.

The nature of migration. Since the motivations and pressures inducing migration determine its relationship to participation in the labor force, at least at the individual level, it is significant that most migration appears to be undertaken as an attempt to improve status and income. This is not always true, of course, since migration is also undertaken by youths becoming students and by elderly workers going into retirement. But the bulk of migration consists of moves from areas of low levels of economic opportunity to areas of better expectations.

Even if migration is predominantly the result of economic factors, the incidence or selectivity of the migration process means not only that some groups will be more inclined to move than others, but that the composition of the population in both the sending and receiving areas will change.

Three aspects of migrant selectivity should be noted. First, although they may be largely due to differences in educational and work opportunities, there tend to be differences in the migration propensities of men and women, although these vary from country to country, and in particular vary systematically among different regions of the low-income part of the world. In Africa, at least until recently, males have been heavily predominant. In Latin America and the Caribbean, rural-urban migration has been greater among women. Unlike either Latin American or African countries, the most common form of migration in Southeast Asian countries seems to be family migration, in which neither males nor females predominate. Even there, however, in several countries at least, there are signs that recent migration has been slightly selective of women. The migration of men, other than of those moving to retire or for education, can be expected to be a function of relative employment opportunities, but the widespread tendency for women to migrate independently of their families indicates that migration serves a similar function for them, perhaps more so because female employment opportunities have been more unevenly distributed among different areas. Thus in Latin American and Caribbean countries employment is the major reason for migration by women, and in Africa various studies have found that work-related reasons have also been important.

A second aspect of selectivity is that migrants tend to be young, in their teens or early twenties. A third aspect is that they tend to be more educated than their peers in the sending area, although often migrants on average have educational qualifications that are intermediate between those prevailing in the sending and receiving areas.

Migration: A microview. Insofar as migration shifts those wanting to become or remain economically active from areas of lower opportunity to those of greater opportunity, it could be expected to increase aggregate levels of labor force participation. But are there grounds for also arguing that migrants will have a greater propensity to participate in the labor force than nonmigrants, controlling for such factors as age, sex, and level of education?

For men the move itself may affect the likelihood of participation, but relative to other urban men of similar age there is unlikely to be any great difference in labor force behavior, at least as compared with the relative positions of migrant and nonmigrant women. The factors that might produce some differential behavior between migrants and nonmigrants, and which might particularly affect their relative supply of time and effort in labor force work, are as relevant to women as to men.

According to Ester Boserup, women's participation in nondomestic economic activities is likely to decline after rural-urban migration (1970). This view is based in part on the implicit assumption that bazaar and service employment, the work traditionally done by women, would be limited and declining in urban areas, when in fact many such activities have been concentrated there. And indeed there is little evidence to support Boserup's view.

To the extent that migration is associated with rising levels of urban unemployment, there might be indirect effects of migration on urban participation rates through the impact of unemployment. Empirically, however, any impact depends on the relative strength of, first, the effect of induced labor force entry by members of the families of migrants working for low wages, and second, the discouragement effect of high unemployment on labor force participation.

Similarly, the effects of migration through its relation with changes in the family or kinship structure need to be carefully investigated. In many countries migration has been associated with a growth in the number of "female-headed households", and in such circumstances the women directly concerned have very high rates of labor force participation.

Theoretically, the arguments for expecting migrants to have a higher rate of labor force participation than nonmigrants in urban areas seem stronger than those suggesting the opposite. Above all, to the extent that migration can be regarded as an act of personal investment in terms of expected increases in income, migrants should have a high propensity to be economically active. This assumption applies to women as well as to men. Empirically, a review of the limited and fragmented evidence generally supported the expected positive relationship, particularly in Latin America, migrants having a relatively high rate of labor force participation.

Aggregate relationships: A macroview. Migration may have effects on the labor market, wage patterns, and related behavior that could raise the aggregate female labor-force participation rate. Two plausible factors deserve mention. First, where women rural-urban migrants outnumber men, the ratio of women to men in towns clearly will be high, as has become the case in many Latin American and Caribbean cities. As a result, not only will young women have a lowered expectation of male financial support but employers will become less inclined to discriminate against women, both of which factors will increase the labor force commitment of women. Second, an influx of young women migrants, often relatively poorly educated and resigned to work for very low wages, not only means a high labor force participation rate among such women but encourages that of urban married women who can substitute cheap domestic labor for their own time in domestic and child-care activities while taking relatively high-paying jobs with favorable social status.

Out-migration could reduce rural participation rates insofar as the selectivity of migration means that those with a relatively strong attachment to the labor force leave in search of income-earning opportunities. But some studies are more consistent with the opposite outcome; much of the migration in Latin America and elsewhere has evidently involved a departure of nonactive females from the rural areas, thereby elevating the rural production and the division of labor in several ways. For instance, it has sometimes been observed that the mass withdrawal of young adult males leaves the rural area without a particular type of labor; in extreme instances the decline of agriculture, and with it rural labor force participation, have been attributed to the withdrawal of those workers. Yet elsewhere it has been observed that the emigration of young men has tended to alter the division of labor in agriculture by raising women's participation, even to the extent that much of the rural economy has become dominated by women. In India it was observed that villages classified as having high rates of out-migration had significantly higher female participation rates. In those instances out-migration may have led to a higher level of female economic activity both directly and indirectly, since there is some evidence that the out-migration of men leads to delayed marriages and later and fewer births, situations that in themselves tend to raise the female participation rate. Finally, return migration, and even information sent by migrants, tend to widen the horizons for consumption and increase the demand for cash income in the rural area, effects that are likely to encourage labor force participation. Moreover, return migration in several contexts has been observed to lead to the initiation of cash crops, acting as a stimulant to rural economic activity. Thus migration brings several possible long-term positive effects on rural economic activity, in addition to the expected one arising from the adjustment in the relative numbers of workers and jobs.

In sum, at both the microlevel and macrolevel the relation between migration and labor force participation is complicated. On balance, migrants seem to have a relatively high propensity to participate in labor force activity, while migrant households are also likely to have a relatively high household labor force participation rate. At the macrolevel no general conclusions are possible, as the factors likely to produce changes will vary in significance from country to country. There are several reasons, however, for supposing that the general phenomenon of migration, insofar as it diffuses information of new patterns of consumption, tends to raise the demand for monetary income in a large proportion of the population. To that extent it will tend to reduce "withheld labor" and, in the language of economics textbooks, to increase the utility of income. It will thus induce greater attachment to the labor force and a greater quantity of labor supplied at any given wage rate.

By shifting groups that in the sending areas are marginal to the production process to areas where they are less marginal, migration may facilitate higher rates of economic activity in general. And insofar as migration shifts labor from areas of low opportunity to areas of greater opportunity it is reasonable to conclude that, other things equal, a population with a high level of population mobility will have a relatively high level of labor force participation.

Guy Standing

See also AGING POPULATION; FERTILITY AND MIGRATION; INTERNAL MIGRATION.

BIBLIOGRAPHY

Boserup, Ester. *Woman's Role in Economic Development.* New York: St. Martin's Press, 1970. London: Allen & Unwin, 1970.

Durand, John D. *The Labor Force in Economic Development: A Comparison of International Census Data.* Princeton, N.J.: Princeton University Press, 1975.

International Labour Organisation. *Labour Force Projections, 1965–1985.* Part 4: *Methodological Supplement.* Geneva, 1973.

Myrdal, Gunnar. *Asian Drama: An Inquiry into the Poverty of Nations.* 3 vols. New York: Pantheon, 1968.

Standing, Guy. *Labour Force Participation and Development.* Geneva: International Labour Office, 1978.

United Nations, Department of Economic and Social Affairs. *Demographic Aspects of Manpower.* Report 1: *Sex and Age Patterns of Participation in Economic Activities.* Series A, Population Studies, no. 33. New York, 1962.

———. *The Determinants and Consequences of Population Trends.* Rev. ed. Volume 1: *New Summary of Findings on Interaction of Demographic, Economic, and Social Factors.* Series A, Population Studies, no. 50. New York, 1973.

LACTATION
See BREASTFEEDING.

LATIN AMERICA

"Latin America" is the term most frequently used to designate the twenty countries south of the Rio Grande that, early in the nineteenth century, achieved their independence from Spain, Portugal, or France. With a total population of more than 350 million, these countries represent about 15 percent of the earth's land area and 8 percent of its inhabitants. Most of the nations can be categorized as "developing"; most of the people profess the Roman Catholic faith; and most of the governments can be characterized as having highly concentrated decision-making processes. Although more of the region's people speak Spanish than any other language, about one-third speak Portuguese, and as many as 30 million speak Amerindian tongues.

Population Characteristics. Several demographic features are peculiar to the region: high ratios of women in urban areas, high proportions of out-of-wedlock births in a number of countries, and, until recently, high rates of European immigration. Of greater significance are the region's population growth and urbanization rates. Over the last several decades, Latin America has provided the world's most spectacular example of population growth. Between 1920 and 1960, while the population of developed nations increased by 40 percent and those of the less developed by 70 percent, Latin American population grew by 138 percent. In the third quarter of this century its growth averaged 2.7 percent annually, compared with 2.2 among the developing countries as a whole.

Latin America is at once one of the least densely settled and the most crowded areas of the world. While its 16 persons per square kilometer (42 per square mile) is only about one-half of the world average, most Latin Americans live in areas of high population density. In 1975, close to two-thirds were classified by the United Nations as urban dwellers, compared with only one-quarter in less-developed countries generally. Urban life, moreover, is heavily concentrated in the capital cities, which account for one-half or more of the urban population in ten countries. Large cities are a relatively recent phenomenon. Toward the end of the last century, Rio de Janeiro had a population of one half million, Mexico City one-third million; Lima and Bogotá were large towns of little more than 100,000. Today, Latin America has twenty-one cities of more than 1 million in population (the number has tripled in the last twenty-five years), and by the end of the century São Paulo and Mexico City may have reached populations of 25 and 32 million, respectively. [See URBANIZATION.]

Such massive urbanization could imply rapid modernization, but few other economic or social measures have kept pace. Agriculture still occupies about 38 percent of the labor force. Nevertheless, it is clear that by several socioeconomic measures, Latin America falls between the developed and the developing regions. The proportion of the labor force engaged in agriculture (Table 1) is far below that of the developing countries in general (63 percent) and is closer to that of Europe or the Soviet Union (18 and 20 percent, respectively). Similarly, according to UNESCO statistics, Latin America is ahead of most developing countries in terms of education: 75 percent of the children of primary school age were attending school in the late 1960s, compared with only 55 percent in Asia and 40 percent in Africa.

The social and economic advantages that Latin America has over other regions are to some extent reflected in its low death rates, but they are only beginning to be seen in its birth rates (Table 2). With young age distributions that are favorable to low mortality, and with considerable control over infectious diseases facilitated by urbanization and by health ministries that foster preventive medical techniques, the region's crude death rates are now under 10, and life expectancy at birth was 61 in the first half of the 1970s. Again, the latter figure falls between the fifty-two years for developing areas generally, and the seventy-one for the developed countries. The causes of death, however, make it clear that there is still a qualitative difference between mortality in Latin America and in the developed countries. In a careful study of cause of death in a sample of cities in the western hemisphere, the Pan American Health Organization found that nutritional deficiencies were an underlying or associated cause in only 10 to 20 percent of the deaths in North

TABLE 1. *Economic indicators, selected Latin American countries*

Country	1977 GNP per capita (US$)	1975 adult literacy rate	Percentage of 1977 labor force in		
			Agriculture	*Industry*	*Services*
Argentina	1,730	93%	14%	29%	57%
Brazil	1,360	76	42	20	38
Chile	1,160	88	21	27	52
Colombia	720	81	31	23	46
Ecuador	790	74	47	24	29
Guatemala	790	46	57	19	24
Honduras	410	57	63	15	22
Mexico	1,120	76	34	25	41

Source of data: World Bank, 1979.

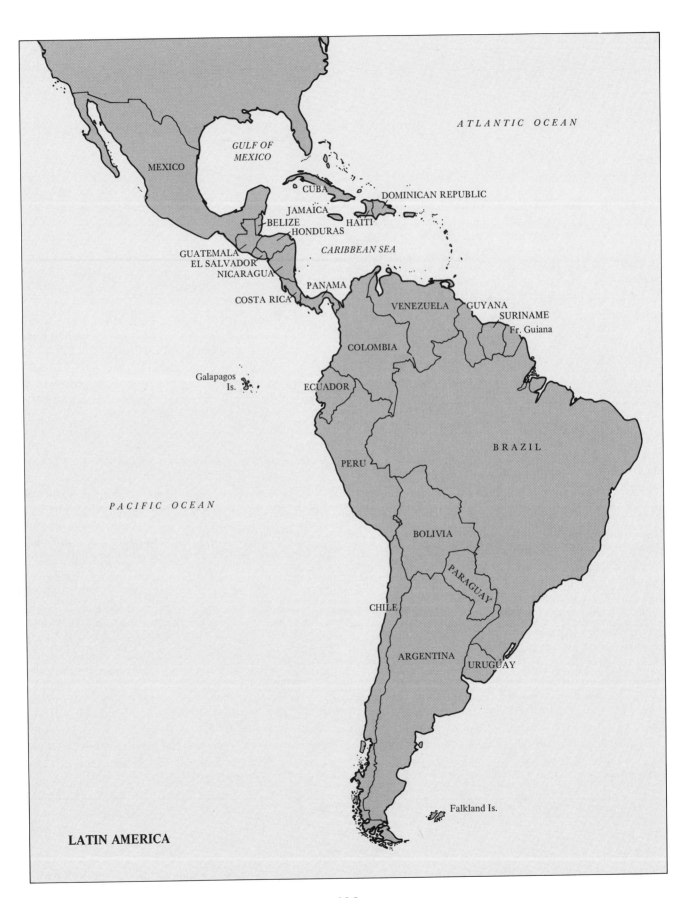

ATLANTIC OCEAN

GULF OF
MEXICO

MEXICO

CUBA

DOMINICAN REPUBLIC

JAMAICA

BELIZE
HONDURAS

HAITI

GUATEMALA
EL SALVADOR
NICARAGUA

CARIBBEAN SEA

PANAMA

COSTA RICA

VENEZUELA

GUYANA
SURINAME
Fr. Guiana

COLOMBIA

Galapagos
Is.

ECUADOR

PERU

BRAZIL

PACIFIC OCEAN

BOLIVIA

PARAGUAY

CHILE

ARGENTINA

URUGUAY

Falkland Is.

LATIN AMERICA

400

TABLE 2. *Demographic indicators of Latin American countries for various years, 1972–1977*

Country	Total population estimated for 1980 (thousands)	Crude birth rate per 1000 population	Crude death rate per 1000 population	Infant mortality rate per 1000 live births	Rate of natural increase
	(1)	(2)	(3)	(4)	(5)
Argentina	27,056	22.9	9.4	59.0	1.4%
Bolivia	5,572	46.6	18.0	77.3†	2.9
Brazil	126,377	37.1*	8.8*	n.a.	2.8*
Chile	11,107	23.9	7.7	54.7	1.6
Colombia	26,907	34.1*	9.0*	46.6*	2.5*
Costa Rica	2,213	31.1	4.3	27.8	2.7
Ecuador	8,023	42.2*	12.1*	65.8*	3.0*
El Salvador	4,801	41.7	7.8	59.5	3.4
Falkland Islands	2	19.4	15.5	n.a	0.4
Guatemala	7,262	42.6	13.1	76.5	3.0
Honduras	3,693	48.6*	13.7*	31.4	3.5*
Mexico	69,994	42.0*	8.6*	54.7	3.3*
Nicaragua	2,737	48.3*	13.8*	37.0	3.5*
Panama	1,897	35.1*	6.9*	22.7	2.8*
Canal Zone	47	14.8	2.0	14.3	1.3
Paraguay	3,067	39.8*	8.9*	38.6*	3.1*
Peru	17,773	41.0*	13.6*	70.3*	2.7*
Uruguay	2,925	20.9	10.2	45.9	1.1
Venezuela	14,914	36.2*	7.1*	40.4*	2.9*

*Estimates for 1970–1975. †For 1978. n.a. = not available.

Sources of data. Column 1: United Nations, 1979c. Columns 2–5: United Nations, 1979b. Estimates for 1970–1975 were prepared by the Population Division of the United Nations. In column 4, the statistic for 1978 is from Inter-American Development Bank, 1978.

American cities, but in a number of the Latin American cities they were an underlying or associated cause in about 65 percent of the deaths. Similarly, while infectious diseases were an underlying cause in less than 5 percent of the North American deaths, they figured in 50 to 67 percent of the deaths in cities in Brazil, Bolivia, Colombia, El Salvador, and Mexico (Puffer and Serrano, 1973).

When it comes to fertility, Latin America falls squarely in the developing area category, with crude birth rates averaging 37 per 1,000 population between 1970 and 1975, about the same as those for developing countries in general. Sustained high birth rates in combination with rapidly declining death rates have produced Latin America's extremely high rates of natural increase and ratios of economic dependents to productive members of society. Thus, there were 2,210 noneconomically active persons for every 1,000 who were economically active in 1975, a figure twice as high as that in the developed nations (1,180) and 44 percent higher than in the less developed nations generally.

Regional and National Variations. If Latin American countries share common European ancestors, who, through colonial economic patterns, intermarriage, and religious conversion set a tone for the region's architecture, commerce, religion, literature, and family life, it is also true that each country has gone its own way since the independence movements of the early nineteenth century. A certain homogeneity has been produced through similar types of external trade relations, but this economic orientation toward the north, combined with intellectual and artistic links with Europe, tended to discourage communication within the region. Further, differences in proportions of indigenous Americans (heavy concentrations in Bolivia, Guatemala, Mexico, Ecuador, and Peru) and African slaves (especially in the Caribbean and circum-Caribbean nations) have been important in establishing cultural variability. A number of regional organizations have attempted to foster hemispheric, regional, or subregional cooperation and communication. Among these are the Organization of American States (OSA, which includes the United States and several of the English-speaking Caribbean nations), the Pan American Health Organization, the Latin American Free Trade Association, the Central American Common Market, the Andean Pact Nations, the Economic Commission for Latin America, the Inter-American Development Bank, and the Inter-American Statistical Institute. Despite such efforts, Latin American countries continue to interact more with, and possibly to care more for, nations outside than inside the region, and a number of serious disputes have occurred between such neighbors as Haiti and the Dominican Republic, El Salvador and Honduras, and Argentina and Chile.

It is common practice to divide the area into three subregions: temperate (Argentina, Chile, and Uruguay);

Central or Middle America (Mexico, Panama, Nicaragua, Costa Rica, Guatemala, Honduras, and El Salvador); and tropical, which includes the other nations of South America, along with the Caribbean islands of Cuba, the Dominican Republic, and Haiti [*see* CARIBBEAN REGION]. The three temperate-zone countries are fairly homogeneous and are quite distinct from countries in the tropical zone and Middle America. The populations of temperate-zone countries are characterized by large proportions of European migrants, high educational levels, low rates of population growth, small proportions engaged in agriculture, and low fertility and mortality.

Countries within each of the other two regions, however, have much less in common, beginning with size of population. In tropical America, Brazil's population (126 million) is four times as large as that of the next-largest country, Colombia, which, in turn, has five times the population of Bolivia. In Middle America, Mexico's population of 70 million people is ten times that of Guatemala; which, in turn, is 3.5 times that of Panama.

Within these two regions, differences are not confined to population size. There are major differences even among the six small Central American nations whose combined population is less than 20 million. El Salvador's population density is more than ten times that of Nicaragua; Panama's per capita gross national product (GNP) is three times that of Honduras, and its number of telephones per capita nine times that of Guatemala; Costa Rica has no indigenous populations, while at least half of Guatemala's population is Indian. Differences are no less in the tropical area. The proportion of illiterates in Bolivia is three times that in Colombia; per capita income in Venezuela is three times as high as in Ecuador; Venezuela's proportion of illegitimate births is twice that of Colombia; Peru has twice as high a proportion of its population living in cities of 20,000 or more as Paraguay.

Latin American intellectuals are acutely conscious of such differences, and they resent the lack of discrimination implied and encouraged by reference to "Latin American problems." International regional meetings have repeatedly stressed the diversity of demographic conditions among Latin American countries, ranging from underpopulation to overpopulation, or from excessive to inadequate population growth rates.

The point could be taken one step further. As a legacy of colonial patterns and a consequence of more contemporary trade relations, variation within countries of Latin America is at least as great as variations among them. For example, as a whole, Latin America has made astonishing strides in the reduction of mortality: between 1955 and 1975 tropical America has added nine years to life expectancy and Middle America has added twelve—

the latter, an achievement that took about 150 years for England and Wales. But within Middle America, intercountry and intracountry differences are huge. Around 1970, infant mortality in Costa Rica was only half of that of El Salvador's. Despite this low level, and in a country blessed with good communications, high literacy, and a better than average distribution of income, child mortality among families in which the mother had no formal schooling was *four times* that of families in which the mother had reached tenth grade. In El Salvador, where mortality is considerably higher than in Costa Rica, the comparable ratio was five to one (Behm, 1979).

Fertility also shows very large differentials, usually by urban and rural residence and invariably by education. As an example, in Panama, a country in which fertility is lower than the average for Middle America, women over 40 who had less than four years of schooling had 6.3 births, while those with 10–12 years of schooling had only 2.9 births.

Compared to the situation in more developed countries, where social and economic differences between urban and rural areas are moderate, rural and provincial areas in Latin America are heavily underprivileged. In terms of such a basic commodity as drinking water, for example, more than three-quarters of urban households but less than one-third of rural households in most Latin American countries have running water. Access to private medical services is another indicator of the gap. For example, El Salvador had only 2.8 physicians per 10,000 population in 1974, and in one major province only 0.3, but in the metropolitan areas there were 10.

Demographic Trends. Two of the variables that affect the region's population growth—mortality and migration—cannot be expected to change greatly before the end of this century. Infant mortality can diminish substantially, and life expectation, according to United Nations projections, might increase by an additional nine years; but in most countries, since overall death rates are already under 10 per 10,000, further change will not greatly affect population growth.

International migration into the region has slowed to a trickle. The three main sources of migration to the region—Spain, Portugal, and Italy—sent 869,000 in the first half of the 1950s, but only 77,000 in the first half of the 1970s. Out-migration, largely to Canada and the United States, has increased markedly over the same period. Canada, which received only 10,000 immigrants from Latin America in the early 1950s, received 116,000 in the early 1970s; the United States received 174,000 in the earlier and 769,000 in the later period. This is a large proportional increase, but its significance for the region's population trends is not great, given an annual natural increase of more than 1 million persons per year. In a number of individual countries, however, illegal migration across borders can be of sufficient magnitude to alleviate demographic problems but to exacerbate political ones; for example, Mexicans to the United States, Salvadorans to Honduras; and Haitians to the Dominican Republic. There is also a serious loss of professionals to the more-developed countries—nearly 13,000 engineers, physicians, and scientists to the United States alone in the decade of the 1960s. The number of physicians that migrated to the United States was greater than the size of the entire medical profession in the four Central American republics in the mid-1970s.

Fertility is the variable most critical in future population trends, and throughout most of this century it has seemed impervious to change. According to CELADE estimates for the latter half of the 1950s, birth rates were 45 or more in fourteen of the twenty countries. In a number of them, birth rates seemed to be rising; and, with few exceptions, the high and possibly rising rates were sustained in the face of low death rates, high urbanization, moderately high literacy, and rising per capita products. Impressive post–World War II economic gains and moderate social progress in the ten largest countries appeared to have no impact on overall fertility levels, leading to speculation that Roman Catholic resistance to birth control and a Luso-Hispanic culture favoring large families make Latin America an exception to the theory that economic modernization eventually leads to low fertility.

On the other hand, sample surveys since the late 1940s have shown consistently that the average Latin American woman does not favor large numbers of children and rarely opposes family planning for religious reasons. The degree of religiosity seems only weakly related to beliefs about family planning and family size, and theories about the role of *machismo* in sustaining high fertility, though still popular, have gone unsubstantiated. Insofar as Catholicism has been a factor in sustaining high levels of fertility, it has done so through formal, informal, or imagined pressures by the hierarchy on governmental decision makers. These pressures at first inhibited governments from initiating national family planning programs or from making them effective once they were organized.

There have been other ideological streams as important as Catholicism in inhibiting family planning programs. Nationalism coupled with the belief that a nation's economic and military power is enhanced by a large and rapidly growing population has been characteristic of the political right, while the Marxists' traditional opposition to Malthusian doctrines has been salted with the notion that population pressures are a useful precipitant of revolution. Both left and right have been vociferous in identifying family planning with North American imperialism. U.S. President Lyndon Johnson's

dictum that "five dollars invested in population control is worth a hundred dollars in economic growth" was widely interpreted as proof that pills at worst were being substituted for imperialist bullets, or at the very best were to be a cheap substitute for economic assistance.

In such an atmosphere, the pioneering efforts of private family planning organizations were critical. Spearheaded by organizers from the International Planned Parenthood's Western Hemisphere Branch, local footholds were established before 1960 only in the English speaking Caribbean and Puerto Rico, but by the mid-1960s they were in nearly all the Latin American nations. The later private programs met much less opposition from governments than the earlier ones, for the international climate had become favorable to family planning. Also, policy makers had available, in many instances for the first time, two consecutive decennial censuses that conclusively demonstrated extraordinary rates of population growth. Usually led by distinguished physicians, the private programs served the governments as trial balloons, which provided convincing evidence both of public demand for services and of relatively weak opposition from the church. By the early 1970s, most governments had added family planning to Social Security and Health Ministry services, usually rationalized as anti-abortion or maternal and child health programs. By the mid-1970s, some countries were evidencing case loads of a magnitude sufficient to effect substantial reductions in birth rates. In Colombia in 1977, 50 percent of all married women aged 15–44 were enrolled in a public or private clinic; in Panama, 44 percent; in Costa Rica and the Dominican Republic, about 33 percent; and in Chile and Mexico, about 20 percent. Moreover, despite restrictive legislation against abortion (most countries at best allow it only if the mother's life is actually endangered by the pregnancy, and two countries forbid it unconditionally), rates of illegal abortions probably continue high, except in Chile and Cuba where abortions are available on broad medical grounds.

It is in most instances too early to ascertain the extent to which such programs have affected fertility, but one thing is clear. If fertility was rising in the 1950s, it ceased doing so by the mid-1960s and began to decline in a few countries by the early 1970s and in several more by the late 1970s. Certainly improving economic and education levels, better contraceptive technology, and the efforts of family planning programs have contributed to the decline; but how much and in what sequence is still largely unknown. Now that declines have been initiated in a number of countries, it may be easier for family planning programs to accelerate them. On the other hand, although Latin American countries generally moved farther and faster on population issues than could have been predicted two decades ago, the ideological issues to which we have alluded have left their stamp on programs and policies that often appear to lack commitment, when compared, for example, to Asian programs.

A few countries wish to increase growth rates so that they can better exploit their resources and settle underpopulated areas. Thus, Argentina, like Uruguay and Paraguay, considers its rate of increase (0.6 percent annually) too low. Its policy is to increase fertility by direct incentives and by discouraging the distribution of contraceptives. Bolivia, with a growth rate of 2.8 percent, is similarly inclined and has closed the nation's family planning clinics to expedite its policy. A series of questionnaires sent to governments by the United Nations in 1974, 1976 and 1978 show a trend toward recognition of population growth as a problem. In 1974 only seven of 25 nations considered their growth rates as excessive, in 1978, 13 out of 27. However, between 1976 and 1978 three countries (Colombia, Ecuador, and Panama) moved from the "excessive" category to the "satisfactory"; and Bolivia changed from "excessive" to "insufficient." Most of the Caribbean and Middle American countries considered their rates too high; but Brazil, the temperate zone countries, and a number of others still felt their rates were acceptable or too low (United Nations, 1980, pp. 14–15).

Under such conditions, family planning programs cannot be expected to receive high priority. Existing programs often receive a small proportion of the budget of the Ministry of Health, which is often small. Since the 1974 World Population Conference, however, all Latin American governments appear to have an enhanced awareness of the importance of demographic variables and the need to integrate them into other aspects of socioeconomic planning. What varies is how seriously this concept is regarded, what direction it takes with respect to population growth and distribution, and how vigorously and directly the policies are translated into programs. The severity of population problems and the velocity of population change can be expected to depend in part on the answers to these questions.

Population Problems. Of the many problems that can be aggravated by population growth and distribution, there is one that will be increasingly severe in Latin America: employment. Between 1970 and the year 2000, Latin America's labor force is expected to grow by over 100 million or by roughly the size of the United States population in 1920. It took the United States from 1900 to 1960 to double its labor force, but Latin America will increase its labor force by 150 percent in thirty years. While this increase might be welcomed where the demand for labor is increasing, in few countries will demand grow so rapidly as supply. Although the proportions of the populations engaged in agriculture have been diminishing in most countries, proportions of the nonagricultural labor force in manufacturing have usually remained constant or declined, inflating the numbers in service occupations. Only about a quarter of the nonagricultural labor force is engaged in manufacturing in Latin America, about half that characteristic of western Europe and the United States. The difference is the result of combinations of more rapid urban growth than was ever typical of Western cities, and the slower growth of industrial demand, leaving increasing numbers in the cities unemployed or underemployed.

While migration from rural areas is usually regarded as the principal cause of the urban explosion in Latin America, most urban growth is the product of high rates of natural increase. According to United Nations estimates, of the 32 million persons added to urban areas in the first half of the 1970s (temperate countries excluded), only 11 million, or 35 percent, could be attributed to migration. In the same period, moreover, despite the great exodus from rural areas, rural populations increased by almost 7 million people. Thus, natural increase in both rural and urban areas can be expected to aggravate problems of employment in both sectors. What chances does the region have for ameliorating such problems through slower rates of growth in the future?

The parameters have been delineated by Tomas Frejka (1973), in a series of possible futures. If fertility declines in such a way that a net reproduction rate of one (i.e., replacement fertility) is achieved by the middle of the next century, then the region's 1970 population will more than double by the year 2000, will increase fivefold by the middle of the next century, and will only stabilize by about year 2100, at more than six times its current size. Even Frejka's most optimistic projection for developing countries (a fairly rapid fertility decline throughout the rest of the twentieth century and a net reproduction rate of one by the year 2000), implies that Latin America's 1970 population would be doubled early in the next century and tripled around the middle of the century. Somewhere between these extremes lies Latin America's true path. To predict it is to predict the velocity of its socioeconomic transformation and the efficiency of its programs influencing fertility. Regardless of optimism concerning either, Latin America in the years ahead faces much bigger and more-concentrated populations and problems that will require at least as much attention to "population responsive" as to "population influencing" policies and programs.

Scholarly Activities. Several regional organizations have been established in Latin America to link research and training centers in the analysis of demographic and social interaction. Programa de Investigaciones Sociales sobre Población en América Latina (PIPSAL) was established in 1973 and by 1978 had financed seventy-two research projects on the relationship between population and development. Consejo Latinoamericano de Ciencias Sociales (CLACSOS) has organized seminars on migration and human reproduction and has set up a working group for the evaluation of social-demographic statistics. While specialized graduate courses in demography and population studies are offered by universities in Mexico, Chile, Brazil, Peru, and Cuba, the major resource for formal training is the Centro Latinoamericano de Demografía (CELADE). This agency of the Economic Commission for Latin America provides the region with basic and advanced training in demography and a research fellowship program, as well as *ad hoc* courses in specific demographic subjects.

J. Mayone Stycos

See also Brazil; Caribbean region; Mexico.

BIBLIOGRAPHY

Behm, Hugo. "Socioeconomic Determinants of Mortality in Latin America." Paper presented at the World Health Organization meeting on Socioeconomic Determinants and Consequences of Mortality, Mexico City, June 1979.

Frejka, Tomas. *The Future of Population Growth: Alternative Paths to Equilibrium.* A Population Council Book. New York: Wiley, 1973.

Inter-American Development Bank. *Economic and Social Progress in Latin America: 1978 Report.* Washington, D.C., 1978.

Puffer, Ruth Rice, and Carlos V. Serrano. *Patterns of Mortality in Childhood.* Washington, D.C.: Pan American Health Organization, 1973.

Stycos, J. Mayone. *Human Fertility in Latin America: Sociological Perspectives.* Ithaca, N.Y.: Cornell University Press, 1968.

————. *Ideology, Faith, and Family Planning in Latin America: Studies in Public and Private Opinion on Fertility Control.* A Population Council Book. New York: McGraw-Hill, 1971.

United Nations, Department of International Economic and Social Affairs. *Concise Report on the World Population Situation in 1977: New Beginnings and Uncertain Ends.* Series A, Population Studies, no. 63. New York, 1979. (United Nations, 1979*a*)

————. *Demographic Yearbook, 1978.* Series R, no. 7. New York, 1979. (United Nations, 1979*b*)

————. *World Population Trends and Prospects by Country, 1950–2000: Summary Report of the 1978 Assessment.* Series R, no. 33. New York, 1979. (United Nations, 1979*c*)

————. *World Population Trends and Policies: 1979 Monitoring Report.* Volume 2: *Population Policies.* Series A, Population Studies, no. 70. New York, 1980.

Urzúa, Raúl. *El desarrollo y la población en América Latina.* Mexico City: Siglo Veintiuno, 1979.

Wilkie, James W. (editor). *Statistical Abstract of Latin America, 1978.* Los Angeles: Latin American Center, University of California, 1978.

World Bank. *World Development Report, 1979.* Washington, D.C., August 1979.

LAW

Law as it relates to population can be rather broadly defined to include legislative action, administrative rules, and binding customs of a community that influence population characteristics. "Law" is a narrower term than "policy," since it refers to controls exercised by recognized authority rather than overall plans for goals and actions, including laws, made by government. The concepts of population law and population policy may overlap in practice.

In this work, principal entries related to law are Law and fertility regulation, which includes articles on worldwide perspectives and united states, and Family law, which discusses regulation of marriage, divorce, and child custody in the United States.

For a brief survey of entries dealing with policy, see Government policy.

LAW AND FERTILITY REGULATION

1. Worldwide Perspectives   John M. Paxman
2. United States   Stephen L. Isaacs
     Eve W. Paul
     Harriet F. Pilpel

1.
WORLDWIDE PERSPECTIVES

The legal approach to fertility regulation includes more than legislation. It encompasses also legal sources such as court decisions, administrative rulings, governmental decrees, ministerial regulations, and even custom. From these are derived rules which either impinge upon or facilitate not only personal choice but also access to services that regulate fertility. Over the years, two broad categories of law have emerged as the focus of interest. First are those laws that directly affect decisions about regulating fertility. These laws specifically concern such matters as contraception, sterilization, and abortion. They establish who may do what to whom, and under what circumstances, just as they determine who can have access to what services and under what circumstances. Second are those laws that have indirect, though important, links with decisions about fertility. These range widely over such disparate subjects as age at marriage, family law, labor legislation, education policy, socioeconomic measures, and other topics. The following sections first take up the subjects of contraception, sterilization, and abortion, then turn to matters of incentives and legal age at marriage, and, finally, discuss the status of women.

Contraception. The laws that affect the availability of information and services concerned with contraception are nearly as varied as the countries in which they exist. Yet the legal constraints on contraceptives are falling away rapidly. And law and policy have been used to enhance access to services and information.

Three particularly important innovations have contributed to greater access to contraception: (1) the elimination or alteration of requirements that contraceptives be dispensed on medical prescription; (2) the requirement that they be sold exclusively in pharmacies; and (3) the incorporation of paramedical personnel into systems for delivering contraceptives, often as part of community-based social marketing schemes. In a more modest way the law has also had a role in formalizing a growing concern for the recipient of contraceptive services.

Use, availability, and distribution. The use of contraceptives as such is tightly regulated or prohibited in a diminishing number of countries. The vast majority of countries, of course, permit their use. The most extreme position is taken in Saudi Arabia, where contraceptives have been banned altogether. Several countries have recently liberalized the law and the trend continues. Spain legalized the sale of contraceptives for family planning purposes for the first time in 1978. Ireland permitted the sale and advertisement of contraceptives in 1979, although they could be imported for personal use but not for sale since 1973. But that law has been criticized because it makes access to contraception more restrictive than before because doctors must prescribe all forms of contraception.

The relaxation of these sorts of restrictions can be documented. In 1967, France completely revised its legislation and legalized contraception but required that sales of all contraceptives take place "exclusively in pharmacies." In 1974, the government permitted additionally the distribution of free contraceptives at government-authorized family planning centers. The history in Italy is similar.

In some former French colonies, particularly in sub-Saharan Africa, the influence of the restrictive French "anticontraception" law of 1920 is still apparent. In Gabon, for example, contraceptives may be prescribed only for other "therapeutic," not family planning, purposes. They may be prescribed by a commission of three physicians in exceptional cases where further pregnancy would endanger the woman's health or when the well-being of the family requires such a measure. The three-physician prescription rule also exists in Argentina and apparently was instituted for demographic reasons.

In a handful of countries the use of certain contraceptive methods is restricted or banned. The use of injectable contraceptives is prohibited in the United States; the IUD is banned in a few countries on the view that it is an abortifacient. Whether these stances are the product of sound scientific and medical decision making or of hortatory political pressure is the subject of some controversy.

The restrictions which have existed historically appear to have their roots in four interrelated factors: pronatalism, concern for "public morality," religious tenets, and consumer safety.

The role of the law in any instance is to regulate the conditions under which the various methods of contraception are distributed. For example, distribution of the condom is regulated according to two different approaches to contraception. In countries with liberal attitudes towards contraception, condoms are available through a variety of distribution channels. Regulations permit sale of condoms in many types of stores in addition to pharmacies, from vending machines, and through the mails. This is true throughout Scandinavia, in most countries of eastern Europe, in the United Kingdom, and in parts of the United States. As commercial marketing schemes are being established in the developing world, condoms are also becoming available outside the pharmacy, often in the market place and other commercial shops or from special licensees. In countries that take a restrictive view of contraception a contrasting situation prevails. In such places access to condoms is often limited by the requirement that they be sold only in pharmacies, and in a few cases only on a doctor's prescription. In theory they are available only as prophylactics against venereal disease, not as contraceptives. This is true in some French-speaking African countries.

Historically, the acquisition of oral contraceptives was subject to two major legal requirements, to a doctor's prescription and purchase from a pharmacy. Those who support these rules perceive them as part of the system for controlling dangerous drugs and poisons, which, if used indiscriminately, could otherwise threaten health. In typical circumstances only doctors are authorized to prescribe and pharmacists to sell drugs, including contraceptives, that appear on the controlled drug list. This legal situation still prevails in most countries.

The requirement of a doctor's prescription is not, however, universal. It is an essentially Western regulation based as much on the premise that doctors are readily available to the populace as on the notion that only doctors are qualified to screen patients before prescription. In countries where the ratio of doctors to population is relatively high, the requirement may have little effect on the availability of contraceptives. Where doctors are scarce, however, the requirement stifles access, a situation that has caused a reappraisal of conventional ways of dispensing the pill. Since the late 1960s, the trend toward modifying the prescription requirement for oral contraceptives has gained momentum, particularly, although not exclusively, in developing countries. Two basic approaches have been used. Either appropriately trained health and auxiliary personnel have been legally authorized to prescribe and distribute oral contraceptives as, for example, the auxiliary midwives in Thailand, or the prescription requirement for orals has been eliminated altogether, as in such countries as Bangladesh, Hong Kong, Iraq, Jamaica, Nepal, and Papua New Guinea.

Government health clinics are usually authorized to distribute, on prescription, a variety of medicaments. This authorization has been extended in some countries to cover oral contraceptives, thereby increasing the outlets at which they can be acquired. Similar arrangements have been made for distribution of contraceptives at privately operated clinics and commercial distribution points.

To complete the picture one observation is in order. Although the requirement of a doctor's prescription still predominates, there is ample evidence that it is widely ignored. In a number of countries, the pill, and other medicaments for that matter, are readily available, at least in pharmacies in the metropolitan areas, without prescription; and the authorities make little effort to control their distribution. The discrepancy between law and practice is, as always, substantial. One other point is essential. Some contraceptives can be used for reasons other than to prevent conception. The pill is indicated as a cycle regulator, the condom as a measure to prevent sexually transmitted diseases. In countries where contraception is restricted, the practice has been to avoid the rigors of law and policy by issuing these methods for noncontraceptive reasons. Once in the hands of people, they also act as contraceptives.

Legal requirements concerning intrauterine devices (IUD's) differ somewhat from those concerning the pill or other contraceptives because IUD's must be inserted by trained personnel. As a general rule, laws and regulations do not specifically regulate IUD insertion. Thus some countries treat it as part of medical practice and restrict it to doctors. France, Hungary, and Japan require that a doctor perform the insertions. In other countries in the absence of specific prohibitions, people who are not doctors have been trained to insert IUD's, apparently with safety and efficiency. For example, midwives in Pakistan inserted IUD's for more than a decade, beginning in the mid-1960s; and IUD's were the first contraceptive method introduced in China on a large scale, where they were usually inserted by either trained nurses, midwives, or "barefoot doctors." In addition, South Korea, Chile,

Sweden, the Philippines, and Thailand have specifically authorized properly trained personnel other than doctors to insert IUD's. Many other countries permit nonphysicians to insert IUD's without involving the law, the sole requirement being that the nonphysician work under a doctor's supervision.

Manufacturing. Laws controlling the manufacture of contraceptives are usually part of a larger set of laws that affect the manufacture of all pharmaceutical products. Their principal aim is to ensure quality control, safety, and effectiveness.

Import and export. Import of contraceptives may be prohibited or regulated for reasons ranging from local opposition to contraception to protection of local contraceptive-manufacturing industry, from a need to conserve foreign exchange to a desire to regulate the quality of incoming products.

Most countries will not authorize the importation of contraceptives that do not meet local standards, if such exist. Many countries, mostly in the developing world, lack the facilities to test such products and hence must rely on foreign agencies for that. Some countries forbid the importation of drugs that have not been tested and approved for use in the country of origin. Jamaica is one country which takes this tack. Similarly, exporting countries are beginning to prohibit the sales abroad of drugs (including contraceptives) that are not approved for use locally. But here some tension exists. Some countries permit the import and use of contraceptives which are not approved in one country of manufacture but can be gotten from another in which that multinational pharmaceutical enterprise has manufacturing facilities.

Information, education, and advertisement. Ever since the late nineteenth century, when the subject of contraception was discussed in earnest, there has been opposition to giving the public access to information on the subject. At that time a number of countries, including Britain and the United States (the infamous Comstock laws), banned publication and dissemination of such information because contraception was thought to promote immorality or to offend public decency. France followed the pattern in the 1920s and other civil law countries, notably Spain and Italy, prohibited the flow of information to the public. As a result the propagandistic work of such family planning pioneers as Annie Besant, Marie Stopes, and Margaret Sanger was continually in jeopardy. Since then laws and policies ranging from drug regulations to the criminal law have hampered efforts to provide individuals with accurate, up-to-date information. Not until 1971 did the Italian Supreme Court declare unconstitutional a provision in the penal code that prohibited the flow of family planning information to the public. The ultimate dismissal of a charge against the editors of an influential Madrid newspaper prompted a change in the Spanish law in 1978. France changed its law in 1967 yet the 1920 anticontraception law of France, which prohibited the dissemination of information on contraception, continues to influence the laws of a number of French-speaking African countries, such as Chad, where to disseminate "contraceptive or antinatalist propaganda" in public is still a criminal offense, potentially punishable by imprisonment. The Argentine decree of 1974 also bars public "dissemination of information" on birth control. The rationales for the Chadian and Argentine laws are based less on concern for the moral conduct of adults than on the pronatalistic designs of government policy. The restrictive point of view, however, clearly is waning. Today more and more countries are encouraging the flow of information about the regulation of fertility.

One way to ensure that young people are aware of the consequences of their sexuality is to introduce instruction into the educational system. Many countries do not, as a matter of public policy, take a position on this subject. Some do. [*See* EDUCATION, *articles on* POPULATION EDUCATION *and* SEX EDUCATION.] Sweden was the first country to introduce sex education into its school curricula and to make it (in 1956) a compulsory subject. A similar legal arrangement in Denmark, dating from 1970, was declared a valid exercise of public authority by the European Court of Human Rights in 1976. Compulsory sex education also exists in Czechoslovakia, West Germany, East Germany, and Iceland.

In the Philippines the Revised Population Act of 1972 made contraception a national policy. As a result, schools were ordered to cooperate in disseminating fertility-related information to students. The law in Luxembourg, enacted in 1978, states that "sexual information and education" will be given at all levels and that it is "complementary to the sex education given in the family." In France, instruction on contraception and ethical matters relating to sexuality is provided outside school time in "meetings" of special groups, which convene at the request of the students and with parental permission. The decision whether to convene "meetings," however, is left in the hands of individual schools. By and large in the United States in schools where sex education is offered parental permission is also sought. But many school districts do not permit such instruction and a controversy continues.

In Indonesia efforts to educate students on population and reproduction take the less controversial form of "family life education," with population education, an attempt to deal with demographic phenomena, predominating. Latin American countries, with their predominantly Roman Catholic populations, differ over whether to permit sex education *per se* or instruction about contraception or whether to promote *pro forma* education on the biological aspects of reproductive health without mention of contraception. Most make no attempt to establish courses of sex education, and instruction on reproductive health is often minimal.

Law and policies on advertising practices also affect the availability of information and may affect public access to information in at least three ways. First, drug regulations in many countries permit direct advertisement of contraceptives solely to the medical and pharmaceutical professions in professional journals. Advertisement of prescription contraceptives is commonly restricted to physicians and only advertisement of nonprescription contraceptives is allowed to the general public. On the other hand, the drug regulations often require in the interest of consumer protection that information be provided about the risks to health that accompany use of various contraceptives.

Second, access to information on specific methods of family planning may be blocked by authorities who control the advertising media. Public advertisement of specific brands of contraceptives is rejected altogether in some countries, although advertisements informing the public where family planning services can be obtained are permitted.

Third, rules controlling the display of contraceptives, particularly condoms, often require that they be hidden from public view, thus precluding self-advertisement.

Sterilization. Relatively few countries make sterilization specifically unlawful in their criminal code. Exceptions are Somalia, Spain, Portugal, and Argentina. Restrictive laws are clearly on the decline. In Italy the section of the penal code that prohibited sterilization was repealed in 1978, though some questions linger as to the legality of sterilization there.

Although most criminal statutes specifically say very little about voluntary sterilization, an initial question arises as to whether various general provisions of the criminal law could be applied in a way that would make the procedure illegal. The preoccupation is that sterilization may be considered a form of intentional infliction of "grievous bodily harm," "assault," or "mayhem," as expressed in English-based common law systems, or of *coups et blessures volontaires* (intentional wounds and injuries), as expressed in civil law systems that follow the French model. Such apprehensions have a chilling effect on attempts to offer sterilization services.

The French penal code punishes any act that results in the "mutilation, amputation, and privation of the use of a limb . . . or other permanent injury." The prevailing legal view is that sterilization for contraceptive purpose, or for any nontherapeutic reason, such as for family planning, is a mutilation, hence it is illegal even when the consent of the person sterilized is obtained. Similar views prevail in former French and Belgian colonies.

Sterilization for purely therapeutic health-linked reasons is allowed in France, but the conditions are narrow and extreme. This view may change now that the Council of Europe has recommended that sterilization services be made available as part of family planning programs.

Some countries have adopted the view that this type of legislation cannot be applied to voluntary sterilization. The Philippine law imposes penalties "upon any person who shall intentionally mutilate another by depriving him, either totally or partially, of some organ essential for reproduction." But in a 1973 opinion the Secretary of Justice stated that since several methods of sterilization do not involve removal of the organs of reproduction of both sexes, as may be true in castration, they should not be regarded as "mutilation" within the contemplation of the law. Similar interpretations have been developed in other countries, such as Mexico.

Confusion over the legal status of voluntary sterilization persists wherever laws on assault and severe bodily injury, rather than those that apply to medical care, are thought to be applicable. It is important that the tension between the two be resolved. This has been done in some situations. In many countries with English common law heritage, voluntary sterilization is explicitly considered "a surgical operation," which if done in "good faith" for the intended "benefit" of the patient is not subject to criminal penalties. In Brazil, Chile, Peru, and Turkey, the regulations and practice distinguish between sterilizations undertaken for medical reasons and those undertaken for purely family planning purposes. The medical rationales must predominate; family planning by itself is not acceptable.

Legal uncertainties have been resolved in some countries, such as Singapore and New Zealand, by enacting a new statute, which clarifies the legal position of sterilization. This tends to reemphasize the doubts as to the application of the general criminal law.

On the whole, there is a trend toward liberalizing the laws affecting the availability of voluntary sterilization. According to a recent United Nations Fund for Population Activities (UNFPA) survey, twenty countries have either laws or regulations that specifically govern voluntary sterilization: most were enacted since 1970.

Where laws specifically authorize voluntary sterilization, they generally prescribe certain preconditions or constraints. Typical legal requirements that affect access to voluntary sterilization services include the following: (1) the establishment of specific medical indications for sterilization, particularly physical defects or diseases (Czechoslovakia, Turkey, Venezuela); (2) fixing a minimum age at which sterilization can or cannot be performed or below which special justification must exist before the person may undergo sterilization (Denmark, Iceland, Norway, Sweden, United States); (3) requiring consent, not only of the individual but also that of a spouse or a person "who possesses marital status" although not legally married (Japan), of parents or guardians in the case of a minor, of a third party if the individual is unable to consent legally, or of someone else where parental consent appears not to ensure protection of a minor's interests (New Zealand, Norway, Singapore, South Africa). Also included are (4) making a minimum number of living children a prerequisite to sterilization, in some instances combined with age as a minimum formula (Panama, Czechoslovakia, India); (5) setting out screening procedures for applications, ranging from an official board to the opinion of a single physician and most often linked to the medical criteria spoken of above (Denmark, Finland, Sweden, Croatia); (6) defining which facilities may offer safe services (Denmark, Czechoslovakia, Singapore); and (7) establishing a waiting period between the request for voluntary sterilization and the actual operation (New York City).

Abortion. The use of criminal law for imposing sanctions against the practice of abortion dates from the early part of the nineteenth century when the values of Christian ecclesiastical law were reflected in modern criminal legislation, as in Spain, France, and the United Kingdom. The tenets of Islam forbid abortion only after the quickening of the child, but laws in predominantly Muslim countries are patterned on essentially Western models. No provisions existed against abortion in the traditional Chinese and Japanese legal systems. In Japan, however, abortion was made a "crime" when the Meiji government patterned an abortion law on the French Napoleonic Code. Few laws have involved such controversy yet have been so widely ignored as the abortion laws.

The legal requirements for abortion are of two different kinds: those that establish the grounds on which a pregnancy may be medically interrupted and those that establish formal procedural requirements for gaining access to abortion services. The first kind of requirements run the following range, although the laws of a given country may make abortion available for any combination of these reasons. These include (1) risk to the life of the woman; (2) risk to the woman's health, either physical, mental, or both; (3) risk of some future physical or mental impairment of a child if born; (4) pregnancy by incest, rape, including statutory rape, or other forms of criminal intercourse; (5) the effect of childbirth upon the health and welfare of the woman and her existing children and family; (6) jeopardy to the social position of the woman or her family; (7) failure of a routinely employed contraceptive means; (8) on request, usually during the first trimester, later for other reasons. The second kind of requirement affects such disparate matters as what approval procedures are required, who may perform an abortion, and where abortions may be performed.

Legal rationales. All countries place restrictions of one kind or another on abortion practice. Few prohibit it in all circumstances and for all women. Invariably, exceptions to the general prohibition of abortion are made, even if in narrowly circumscribed circumstances. For example, the Philippine law on abortion appears to make it a criminal offense without exception. General principles of criminal law would permit, however, the termination of pregnancy where it is necessary to save the life of the mother. Many countries, predominantly in Africa and Latin America, permit abortion only when the life of the mother is threatened, the narrowest of the criteria.

Countries that follow either the British or French legal traditions tend to have essentially restrictive abortion statutes. Some of these statutes fail to allow abortion for any reason, though judicial exceptions are sometimes made. For example, the Offenses Against the Person Act (1861) on which the laws of some British Commonwealth countries have been modeled, flatly prohibited "unlawful" abortion. The harshness of the act was softened, however, by the judicial decision in *R.* v. *Bourne* (1938), in which a prominent gynecologist was prosecuted for performing an abortion for a 14-year-old victim of multiple rape. The judge stated that where the doctor was of the opinion that "the probable consequences of the pregnancy will make the woman a physical or mental wreck," the jury could find that the doctor had "lawfully" interrupted the pregnancy. Bourne was acquitted. The case formed the foundation upon which rested the generally accepted legality of therapeutic abortion in the United Kingdom (until an abortion statute was passed in 1967) and hence in several former British colonies.

Many statutes permit intervention where the woman's health is threatened. Few make any attempt to define what is meant by "health," though the statutes in force in Zimbabwe and South Korea specify that the word applies only to physical health. Determining when a woman's "health" is endangered by pregnancy is left under most legislation to the judgment of individual doctors. Because of this, "health" can be considered from the broadest possible perspective, thus encompassing threats to the woman's mental as well as physical health.

Many laws permit abortion where substantial risk exists that the child, if born, would suffer from severe physical or mental abnormalities. The more recently enacted statutes extend the scope of the traditional eugenic indications, covering the hereditary transmission of men-

tal disease, mental retardation, and other severe maladies and defects, to include any damage acquired during intrauterine life, such as the effects of rubella or damage caused by the use of certain drugs during early pregnancy. The 1967 law in Turkey is one of the more explicit. Under it, doctors are able to consider whether there is a substantial risk either of fetal deformity or danger to succeeding generations, in the case of hereditary disease.

No fewer than thirty-five countries, predominantly in Europe, Latin America, and Scandinavia, have laws that permit abortion where the pregnancy results from rape, incest, or other illegal intercourse. The rape justification, at least, is founded on a predominantly moral view that women who have been raped should not be compelled to bear a child conceived under such circumstances. Frequently legislation requires, however, that before an abortion can be carried out on rape grounds, the rape must be verified or criminal proceedings against the assailant must be initiated. These often constitute additional procedural impediments.

Pregnancy because of incest is usually an adolescent predicament. While incest is a criminal offense in most countries, not all countries permit the termination of a pregnancy resulting from an incestuous relationship. While New Zealand, for example, specifies incest as a ground for abortion in its law, many countries simply permit abortion whenever the pregnancy results from any "form of sexual misconduct" that is prohibited by law. In Israel the law permits interruption of pregnancies arising from extramarital, but not necessarily premarital, sexual relations.

Consideration of age, marital status, social environment, and economic circumstances—factors that have a bearing on the decision to terminate pregnancy—becomes a legal certainty only when legislation permits them to be weighed in reaching the decision. An increasing number of countries are enacting such laws.

For example, the 1973 rules on abortion in Hungary made the procedure widely available for reasons that may be categorized as social. Under the 1978 law in Norway, abortion is available on request during the first twelve weeks if there is no serious medical reason against it. During the next six weeks, however, the pregnancy may only be terminated for specified medical or socioeconomic reasons. After the eighteenth week of pregnancy, termination is not allowed unless there are "particularly important reasons" for doing so. In no case will pregnancy be terminated if there is reason to believe that the fetus is viable. Similar provisions are in force in other Scandinavian countries and designation of a time frame beyond which termination will not be carried out is a feature of many laws.

In some countries such as the United Kingdom, social indications by themselves are not enough to be regarded as a basis for terminating a pregnancy. They must be linked to the health of the woman. Nevertheless, social or economic factors, including the woman's age, marital status, and family situation, may be taken into account in reaching the decision. This formula has been followed in India, Zambia, and to a lesser extent in Hong Kong. Age is specifically cited as a factor to be considered in the Zambian law.

Since 1970 at least ten countries have enacted laws that permit abortion "on request" during the early stages of pregnancy. ("On request" is perhaps a misnomer because access to abortion is hardly ever available simply by asking for it. Invariably other criteria must also be met, such as the concurrence of a doctor or, as in France, the existence of a "situation of distress.") After the early stages, other criteria apply. Denmark, France, Slovenia (in Yugoslavia), China, Italy, and the United States have laws and policies that permit "on request" termination of pregnancy, although in several of these countries such abortions must be carried out within a specific period of gestation (often the first ten to twelve weeks).

Japan was the first country to modernize its law. It did so in 1948. Since 1967, abortion laws in some forty countries have been revamped. In all but two of these the grounds for abortion have been liberalized. At present nearly two-thirds of the world's population lives in countries where laws permit abortions on a wide variety of grounds. In five out of the six most populous countries of the world, abortion is widely available, at least by law: China, India, the United States, the Soviet Union, and Japan. The trend toward liberalization is clear, although since 1980 or so a campaign has begun to reverse this phenomenon.

Incentives and Disincentives. Incentive and disincentive measures to regulate fertility have typically taken three forms: incentives aimed at lowering fertility rates, disincentives aimed at lowering fertility rates, and incentives aimed at increasing fertility rates. Experience with the first two is found predominantly in Asia. Europe is the seat of attempts to push fertility rates higher. Few comprehensive incentive or disincentive schemes, however, have been made a matter of national policy. Fewer still are supported by law.

Incentives and disincentives to reduce fertility rates. Cash payments to those who accept family planning have a long, somewhat erratic, and at the same time controversial, history in Asia. They have usually been associated with drives to increase the acceptance of the permanent or long-lasting methods of contraception (sterilization or IUD). The experience in India dates from 1956 when payments were first made to men who were sterilized.

Inducements were a matter of spasmodic government policy for more than a 20-year period. In Sri Lanka, cash payments were made beginning in 1979 to acceptors of sterilization, who are also granted work leave with pay in order to undergo and recuperate from the operation. After two years of experience the size of the payments is being reduced.

In Taiwan, the use of "education bonds" has been tested on a small scale. There, couples with zero to two children receive an annual deposit to a savings account for each year they have no more than two children. After ten to fourteen years the parents are able to withdraw the funds, which earn interest, to use for the cost of secondary education for their children. If the couple has a third child, the sum is reduced by 50 percent. At the birth of a fourth child the account is canceled and the funds revert to the bank.

In at least nine provinces in China, "one-child certificates" are used to reinforce the government's recently established drive to promote single-child families. These certificates entitle parents in the cities to a fixed monthly stipend until the child is 14, plus preferred treatment in housing; they entitle the child to preference in selection of schools and on job applications. In rural areas, one-child families receive additional work points plus the same grain rations, housing lots, and land plots for private cultivation as two-child couples. Additional incentives are being tested in other provinces.

In the Philippines, the 1974 Child Labor Law required the Department of Labor to develop bonus schemes as an incentive to promote family planning among Philippine workers. South Korea gives housing priority to families where one parent has been sterilized.

The use of social or economic disincentives to curb fertility rates is not widespread. Singapore is often cited as the classic example of a comprehensive disincentive scheme based on a purely demographic rationale. It has the broadest and most striking experience in the use of economic measures to "persuade couples to limit the size of their families." These include denial of maternity leave for the delivery of the third child and subsequent ones; progressively increased delivery fees at maternity hospitals as the number of children increases; denial of income tax relief after the third child; withdrawal of priority ranking for large families seeking public housing; special priorities in choice of primary schools for families with fewer than three children; and special incentives to encourage sterilization (maternity fees are waived if the woman is sterilized and children whose parents are sterilized have priority in school selection). In practice, the harshest of the sanctions in Singapore are frequently not applied.

Some of the features of the Singapore approach have

been adapted for use in other countries. The Philippines has similar rules on tax relief and maternity leave. Indonesia has limited the number of dependents for which a tax deduction can be claimed. China has made similar provisions in the areas of housing and education.

Incentives to increase fertility rates. Some industrialized countries have begun to consider ways of influencing reproductive behavior so as to increase fertility. France, the Soviet Union, and a number of eastern European nations have instituted economic measures that are based in part on demographic motives. The most important tool has been the family or child allowance, a periodic payment to families with children.

The family allowance scheme in the Soviet Union is thought to be of little significance to fertility. On the other hand, Hungary, Romania, and Bulgaria have in the past few years sharply increased the benefits available to the first few children in an attempt to increase the birth rates and encourage larger families. In Hungary incentives include reemployment guarantees and paid "postmaternity" leave.

Of the industrialized countries only the United States lacks a general family or child-allowance scheme. Few of the others use such payments for the specific purpose of stimulating fertility. France is an exception. Rather, they are used as socioeconomic measures designed to alleviate financial hardships and to ensure that children are properly cared for. As fertility in the industrialized countries falls below replacement level, however, a resurgence in interest in these schemes as a mode of stimulating fertility may be anticipated.

Legal Age at Marriage. The connection between age at marriage and fertility should be largely self-evident. Laws establishing a minimum age at marriage are nearly universal. Two distinctions are commonly found. Ages are usually set at which one can marry with or without parental consent. Often there are also different ages for men and women. Ages may differ among various ethnic and religious groups within a single country. Sometimes religious or customary laws prevail rather than legislation. Europe has the highest legal and actual ages at marriage and is the only area where countries have the same legal ages irrespective of sex. In Asia legal ages tend to be low. In the Middle East and North Africa some countries lack a minimum legal age at marriage, choosing to adhere to Muslim law, which allows girls to marry at menarche (age 12 or 13); others have moderately high legal ages. In Africa legal age at marriage is often high, reflecting the tendency to adopt European legal standards, yet actual age at marriage is early. Latin America, on the whole, has the lowest legal ages at marriage in the world. Yet the age is still higher than the ages at which many young women become sexually active and bear children.

Since 1960, fifty-four countries have altered their laws on the minimum age at marriage. Some of these are part of revisions of the civil codes, and the actual ages have not been changed. Others have raised the minimum ages. The latter appears to be the predominant trend in the developing world. A few countries, principally those in Europe where the age of majority had shifted downward, have lowered the ages. Of those that have raised the age, there is every indication that the actual age at marriage was rising well before the legislation was reformed. In these circumstances the law has merely reflected trends over time rather than created dynamic change. In Tunisia, eight years before the law was passed in 1964 establishing the minimum at 17, the mean age at marriage for women was 19.5. As of 1975 it had risen to 23.3. Malaysia and Sri Lanka also experienced increases in the actual age at marriage long before the law was changed. Only in India, which in 1978 raised the minimum ages to 18 and 21, and in Indonesia, which in 1974 set the ages at 16 for women, 19 for men, may the law have preceded practice. Both countries are interested in encouraging delayed marriage for demographic reasons. It seems clear nevertheless that the mere act of raising the age of marriage by law is insufficient to change behavior without complementary change in educational and employment opportunities.

Law, Fertility, and the Status of Women. The Declaration of Elimination of Discrimination Against Women, adopted unanimously by the United Nations General Assembly in 1967, incorporates in a single instrument the fundamental principles upon which elimination of discrimination based on sex in political activities, education, employment, marriage, and family, penal, and civil law is founded. This declaration and a number of other international instruments derive their strength from the concept that human rights and fundamental freedoms apply to all individuals without distinction based on sex or marital status.

Two types of legislation influence women's ability to regulate their fertility. The first, which has a direct influence, includes regulations concerning the distribution of contraceptives and information about them and policies affecting voluntary sterilization and abortion. These regulations and policies have been discussed above.

The second type is less direct and concerns those areas of law affecting the woman's position in the family and within the society. In this category are laws on marriage and divorce, property rights, education, employment and labor practices, and even political rights. The interdependence of the status of women and the right to plan one's family and the influence both have on fertility have been increasingly recognized by policy makers, and the law is being used in some countries to reflect this shift in thinking.

There is a trend toward legislative reform to establish

legal equality between men and women. In addition to constitutional amendments (Mexico and Yugoslavia), the greatest number of reforms have been in legislation related to employment, to the family, and to the availability of services to regulate fertility.

The largest number of recent reforms in family law have dealt with age at marriage, the concept of equal rights and responsibilities within marriage, and the rights of women upon dissolution of a marriage. Property and inheritance laws have also been reformed in a number of countries, although overcoming traditional land tenure systems has been slow and halting.

Reforms in employment legislation have been largely in two categories: (1) those guaranteeing equal pay and job opportunity for men and women and (2) those aimed at facilitating the combination of work and motherhood or parenthood. These changes have been hard-won. The courts, which are often the last resort of women seeking redress for discrimination in employment, have nevertheless handled increasing numbers of cases in recent years, implying a growing determination to overcome discriminatory practices.

Maternity protection has been recognized as a necessity for working mothers and increasingly as an appropriate cost to be shared by society and business. The number of countries in which maternity leave for working women is compulsory is growing, and only a few have no maternity protection at all. Legislation and policies for provision of child-care facilities are less advanced, despite their importance. Among eastern European countries there has been emphasis on special rights and protective measures (beyond maternity protection) for employed women.

Rural women are in need of special attention. Literacy is a particular problem, and ignorance concerning women's rights is widespread. Efforts to educate both men and women are being undertaken. Rural women, in the main, are outside the protection of the laws, as employment and laws and policies discriminating against women reflect to a certain extent the economic and power structures of society as well as the assumptions about the expected roles and abilities of each sex. So long as the economic system confines women to a domestic role while men remain the breadwinners, legislative reforms may be only cosmetic.

John M. Paxman

See ABORTION; AGE AT MARRIAGE; CONTRACEPTIVE USE; ETHICS; FAMILY PLANNING PROGRAMS; STATUS OF WOMEN.

BIBLIOGRAPHY

Columbia Human Rights Law Review editors. *Law and the Status of Women: An International Symposium.* New York: United Nations, 1977.

Cook, Rebecca J., and Bernard M. Dickens. "Abortion Laws in Commonwealth Countries." In *International Digest of Health Legislation* 30(3):395–502, 1979.

Dixon, Ruth B. "Women's Rights and Fertility." *Reports on Population/Family Planning,* no. 17, whole issue, January 1975.

Isaacs, Stephen L. *Population Law and Policy: Source Materials and Issues.* New York: Human Sciences Press, 1981.

Lee, Luke T. "Law and Family Planning." *Studies in Family Planning* 2(4):81–98, April 1971.

Paxman, John M. (editor). *Law and Planned Parenthood.* London: International Planned Parenthood Federation, 1980.

Paxman, John M., and Ruth Jane Zuckerman. "Adolescent Reproductive Health Care and Education: A Survey of Legal and Policy Alternatives." *International Digest of Health Legislation,* in press (1982).

Piepmeier, Katherine Blakeslee. "Changing the Status of Women through Law." In *Law and Planned Parenthood,* edited by John M. Paxman, pp. 91–106. London: International Planned Parenthood Federation, 1980.

Stepán, Jan, and Edmund H. Kellogg. *The World's Laws on Voluntary Sterilization for Family Planning Purposes.* Law and Population Monograph Series, no. 8. Medford, Mass.: Fletcher School of Law and Diplomacy, Tufts University, 1973. Reprinted in *California Western International Law Journal* 5(1):72–120, 1974.

———. *The World's Laws on Contraceptives.* Law and Population Monograph Series, no. 17. Medford, Mass.: Fletcher School of Law and Diplomacy, Tufts University, 1974. Reprinted in *American Journal of Comparative Law* 22(4):615–651, Fall 1974.

Stepán, Jan, Edmund H. Kellogg, and Phyllis T. Piotrow. "Legal Trends and Issues in Voluntary Sterilization." *Population Reports,* series E, no. 6, whole issue, April 1981.

Tietze, Christopher. *Induced Abortion: 1979.* 3d ed. New York: Population Council, 1979.

United Nations Fund for Population Activities. *Survey of Contraceptive Laws.* Country Profiles. New York, 1976.

———. *Survey of Laws on Fertility Control.* Country Profiles. Part 1: *Voluntary Sterilization.* Part 2: *Termination of Pregnancy.* New York, 1979.

2.
UNITED STATES

The United States has a history of conservative attitudes and restrictive laws designed to regulate fertility. By the mid-nineteenth century most states had passed laws making abortion, except to save the life of the woman, a criminal offense; and in 1873 the U.S. Congress passed the so-called Comstock laws, which prohibited the importation, transportation in interstate commerce, and mailing of contraceptives and anything having to do with abortion. Not until the 1960s and 1970s with the development by the United States Supreme Court of the constitutional right of privacy in matters of sex, marriage, and the family and the passage by the United States Congress of major family planning legislation was regulation of one's own fertility recognized as a constitutional right; not until then were services related thereto provided or paid for by the federal government.

Laws that affect fertility, like all U.S. laws, derive from a number of sources. The two most important are legislative and judicial decisions; a third, crucial in some areas, consists of regulations and enforcement mechanisms of the executive departments of government. Legislation may be passed by the United States Congress, by state legislatures, and by local councils; for example, Congress enacted the Family Planning Services and Population Research Act in 1970, and the Akron, Ohio, Municipal Council in 1978 passed an ordinance restricting the availability of abortion. In the United States, courts have the responsibility of passing upon the constitutionality of legislation. The U.S. Supreme Court, as the highest court in the nation, has made several constitutional decisions that affect the right to, and availability of, services regulating fertility. In some areas, the executive is the key rule-making body; the federal Department of Health and Human Services (DHHS), formerly the Department of Health, Education, and Welfare (DHEW), establishes guidelines for federally funded sterilizations and abortions and, through the Food and Drug Administration, regulates the distribution of contraceptives. Private organizations may also be sources of law regulating fertility in a broad sense; for example, a state medical association may determine what class of health personnel can distribute contraceptives and a local private hospital can decide under what conditions, if any, it will provide abortions.

The laws in the United States that relate to fertility can be classified in three topical categories: contraception, abortion, and sterilization. These topics are discussed in the following sections. Additionally, since the rights of minors to services under each of these categories pose special problems, these are considered in a separate section.

Contraception. In 1873 Congress passed an "Act for the Suppression of Trade in, and Circulation of, Obscene Literature and Articles of Immoral Use," known forever after as the "Comstock law" after its chief architect, Anthony Comstock. The act prohibited the importation and interstate transport and mailing of any "obscene, lewd, or lascivious book, pamphlet, picture, paper, print, or other publication of an indecent character, or any article or thing designed or intended for the prevention of conception or procuring of abortion." A number of states passed "little Comstock" acts shortly thereafter, laws that were enforced with patriotic vigor by Anthony Comstock himself, who had been named an officer of the Post Office Department, and by state and federal governments with the active assistance of one or another Society for the Suppression of Vice.

Against this background of restrictive legislation, which stayed on the books until repealed in 1971, there developed the American birth control movement. It was associated in its early days with reformist trends and later became allied with the medical profession and the movement for women's rights in the United States. The birth control movement challenged restrictive federal and state laws both in the legislatures and in the courts.

An early victory for the birth control movement in the courts in 1936 enabled physicians to import contraceptives, thus introducing a major exception to the federal Comstock Act. In 1965, after more than twenty years of attempts to develop a test case that the Supreme Court would decide on its merits, the Court did decide a challenge to a Connecticut statute.

In *Griswold* v. *Connecticut* the Court found that the Connecticut law forbidding the use of contraceptives even by married couples in their home violated a constitutional right of privacy. The Court emphasized, in particular, the importance of marital privacy. The privacy concept was expanded seven years later in *Eisenstadt* v. *Baird,* a case in which William Baird, a family planning activist, had been arrested for passing out contraceptive foam to an unmarried woman after a talk on contraception at Boston University. In striking down a Massachusetts law prohibiting the distribution of contraceptives except to a married person, the Supreme Court stated: "If the right of privacy means anything, it is the right of the *individual,* married or single, to be free from unwarranted governmental intrusion into matters so fundamentally affecting a person as the decision whether to bear or beget a child."

A third case concerning contraception, *Carey* v. *Population Services International,* was decided by the Supreme Court in 1977. Striking down a New York law that, among other things, made it a crime for anyone other than a licensed pharmacist to distribute contraceptives to persons over 16 and prohibited entirely their distribution to persons under 16, the Court said, "The Constitution protects individual decisions in matters of childbearing from unjustified intrusion by the State. Restrictions on the distribution of contraceptives clearly burden the freedom to make such decisions."

The *Griswold* case preceded and the *Eisenstadt* and *Carey* cases followed the passage by Congress of the Family Planning Services and Population Research Act in 1970, Title X of the Public Health Services Act. Title X has been the principal source of money for family planning services in the United States since its passage, having been funded since the mid-1970s at levels averaging approximately $150 million a year with roughly $100 million earmarked for services and the remainder for research. One of the stated purposes of the act is "to assist in making comprehensive voluntary family planning services readily available to all persons desiring such services."

Although Title X is the major family planning statute, it is not the only federal legislation under which family planning services are provided. Under Title XIX of the Social Security Act (Medicaid), the federal government provides funds to states to reimburse certified providers for medical services rendered to indigent recipients. Family planning is a mandatory service that states must make available to all eligible individuals of childbearing age, including sexually active minors.

Prior to October 1981, family planning services were also provided under other sections of the Social Security Act. Title IV-A of the Social Security Act (Aid to Families with Dependent Children, or AFDC) required states to provide family planning services to AFDC recipients, including sexually active minors. When the Social Security legislation was overhauled in 1975, a new Title XX (Social Services) incorporated many of the provisions of Title IV-A, including the requirement that family planning be made available to welfare recipients, the maintenance of 90 percent of the total expenditure as a federal matching grant, and the levying of a 1 percent penalty on states that fail to provide family planning services.

Title V of the Social Security Act (Maternal and Child Health and Crippled Children's Services) required that not less than 6 percent of the appropriations for maternal and child health under Title V be allocated for family planning services. In 1981, these programs were made part of maternal-child health and social services block grants to the states.

Additionally, a number of federal programs, such as the Indian Health Services Act, the Migrant Health and Community Health Centers Act, and the Comprehensive Employment and Training Act, offer family planning as part of a comprehensive benefits package.

To summarize, following the Supreme Court decisions in the *Griswold, Eisenstadt,* and *Carey* cases, coupled with a public policy supportive of birth control as expressed by the Family Planning Services and Population Research Act and other federal legislation, there appear to be few legal barriers to the distribution of contraceptives to adults in the United States. Currently, such distribution to adults is permitted in all states; a few require that the distribution be in pharmacies or through organized family planning programs. The major remaining legal issues today concern the distribution of contraceptives to minors.

Abortion. Most laws regulating abortion in the United States prior to 1973 were products of the second half of the nineteenth century. In 1800 not one state had enacted a statute on the subject of abortion, and abortion, at least prior to "quickening" (the first perception of fetal movement), was considered legal. By 1900 virtually every state had adopted a law making abortion a criminal offense and sharply restricting its practice. Many of these statutes were enacted as part of the movement to restrict the practice of medicine to licensed physicians. On the eve of the U.S. Supreme Court's landmark decision in *Roe* v. *Wade* and *Doe* v. *Bolton* (January 1973), most states still had statutes prohibiting abortions without exception or with the single exception of saving the life of the woman. Fourteen states had recently passed legislation based on the American Law Institute's Model Penal Code, which permitted abortions where the pregnancy threatened the woman's life, where it involved a substantial risk that its continuance would impair the physical or mental health of the woman, where the child would be born physically or mentally defective, and where the pregnancy resulted from rape or incest. Four states (New York, Washington, Alaska, and Hawaii) had removed nearly all the restrictions under which abortions could be obtained. The New York law, for example, permitted abortion by a physician during the first twenty-four weeks of pregnancy and thereafter to save the life of the woman.

In 1973, the U.S. Supreme Court struck down as unconstitutional a Texas law making abortion a crime except when necessary to save the life of the woman: the *Roe* v. *Wade* decision set forth guidelines about state intervention in the abortion process. In the words of the Supreme Court,

For the stage of pregnancy prior to approximately the end of the first trimester, the abortion decision and its effectuation must be left to the medical judgment of the pregnant woman's attending physician.

For the stage subsequent to approximately the end of the first trimester, the State, in promoting its interest in the health of the mother, may, if it chooses, regulate the abortion procedure in ways that are reasonably related to maternal health.

For the stage subsequent to viability, the State, in promoting its interest in the potentiality of human life, may, if it chooses, regulate, and even proscribe, abortion except where it is necessary, in appropriate medical judgment, for the preservation of the life or health of the mother.

A companion case, *Doe* v. *Bolton,* found a more liberal Georgia statute, patterned on the American Law Institute's Model Penal Code, also to be unconstitutional insofar as it required that abortions be performed in accredited hospitals and that they be approved by a hospital committee and two additional physicians.

The *Roe* decision was immediately beset by challenges. For example, Rhode Island enacted a law declaring that life begins at the moment of conception and that such a life is a "person" for purposes of the Fourteenth Amendment. This law was held unconstitutional. Other challenges followed. They concerned matters such as constitutional amendments, Medicaid, fetal protection, and the conscience of institutions. With the growth of the right-to-life movement, abortion rights have become increasingly threatened.

Constitutional amendment. An initial reaction of some members of Congress to the *Roe* decision was to propose an amendment to the Constitution that would overturn the Supreme Court's ruling. The proposed amendments generally took one of two forms, either a "human life" amendment, which would give a constitutionally guaranteed right to life to a person from the moment of conception or fertilization, or a "state's rights" amendment, which would return the regulation of abortion to the individual states, the situation that existed before *Roe* v. *Wade.* None of the amendments proposed in Congress ever commanded the needed two-thirds majority of Congress. Failing to win congressional approval, supporters of a constitutional amendment tried the other road open to them, a constitutional convention. Thus far, nineteen of the thirty-four states required to force Congress to call a convention have passed resolutions asking Congress to call a convention to pass a "human life" amendment. There has never been a convention called to amend the Constitution; although the views of scholars differ, all of them are at best guesses, since none of the questions that might arise in connection with a convention has ever been decided. Many think that a constitutional convention could not be restricted to considering the abortion issue alone but might, if it so decided, consider such other matters as, for example, the one man–one vote principle, freedom of the press, and other guarantees of individual freedom to be found in the first ten amendments to the Constitution (the Bill of Rights). In 1981 a Congressional subcommittee considered another type of constitutional amendment, one which gave concurrent jurisdiction over abortion to both the federal government and the states. Whichever had the most restrictive legislation would prevail.

Another attempt to restrict the scope of the 1973 Supreme Court opinions took the form of a proposed "human life" statute that would declare a fetus a "person" from the time of conception. Such legislation, which requires a simple majority of Congress for passage, was considered in 1981, by a congressional subcommittee. It was attacked as unconstitutional by many conservatives as well as liberals.

Medicaid and other restrictions. After *Roe* v. *Wade,* many states enacted legislation that restricted Medicaid funding to those abortions necessary to save the life of the woman or to those considered "medically necessary." Meanwhile, on the federal level, in 1976 Congress passed the first of a series of "Hyde amendments," riders to the HEW and Labor departments' appropriation bills. The 1976 Hyde amendment prohibited the use of federal funds for abortion "except where the life of the mother would be endangered if the fetus were carried to term." Congress passed in 1977, and repassed in 1978, a somewhat less restrictive version of the Hyde amendment permitting federal funding of abortions in cases of threat to the life of the woman, promptly reported rape or incest, and "severe and long-lasting physical damage" to the woman, certified by two physicians. The last two conditions were dropped from the most recent Hyde amendments, which returned to the restrictive provision whereby Medicaid funds could be used for abortion only when the woman's life is in danger.

The Supreme Court faced the issue of Medicaid abortions in four cases. The first two (*Beal* v. *Doe* and *Maher* v. *Roe*), decided in 1977, determined that neither the Medicaid statute nor the Constitution required states to pay for *elective* abortions. The third (*Harris* v. *McRae*), decided in 1980, held that the Hyde amendment itself, which prohibited funding of even medically necessary abortions, was constitutional. (The question of withholding funding where the pregnancy threatens the woman's life was not involved.) The fourth case held that state restrictions on abortion funding were constitutional.

With the Hyde amendments having tightened the conditions for federal reimbursement of abortion and the Supreme Court's rulings that neither states nor the federal government are required to pay for even medically necessary abortions, governmental entities in the United States have severely restricted the financing of abortion. However, New York and Michigan, among others, have continued to fund abortions. Some of the state restrictions have been challenged in court as violations of state constitutional provisions. Courts in several states including California and Massachusetts have held restrictive laws to be violations of state constitutional provisions of due process or equal protection of the laws.

In addition to restrictions on Medicaid, legislation has been passed at both federal and local levels restricting other sources of funding abortions. For example, Congress has forbidden the use of federal funds for abortions of Peace Corps volunteers and military personnel and their dependents and for abortion as a method of family planning in both the foreign aid program and the domestic family planning program. Moreover, federal legislation prohibits Legal Services lawyers from litigating some cases concerned with abortion, and it forbids the U.S. Civil Rights Commission to conduct studies on abortion.

Viability, standard of care, and fetal protection. Two of the most intractable legal, political, and ethical questions are "When does a human life begin?" and "What standard of care must be used on a fetus that emerges 'alive'?" For example, must intensive care be given a fetus that appears to be alive? Can a physician be tried criminally for not using extraordinary measures to save such a fetus?

The Supreme Court has distinguished between the status of a fetus before and after viability. In *Roe* v. *Wade* the Court used the phrases "potentially able to live outside the mother's womb, albeit with artificial aid" and "presumably capable of meaningful life outside the mother's womb" to define viability. Since, by definition, a fetus before it is viable is not capable of meaningful life outside the woman's womb, there may be no constitutional requirement to use heroic measures to try to save its life. After viability, there may be such a duty and a physician might be subject to prosecution for failing to take the necessary lifesaving measures.

But who determines the point of viability? In 1976, the U.S. Supreme Court, in *Danforth* v. *Planned Parenthood of Central Missouri,* ruled that the point at which viability is reached may "vary with each pregnancy, and the determination of whether a particular fetus is viable is, and must be, a matter for the judgment of the responsible attending physician." A 1979 case, *Colautti* v. *Franklin,* reaffirmed the importance of the physician's judgment in determining viability. It now appears that a physician cannot be convicted of a crime for having failed to take extraordinary measures to save the life of a nonviable fetus and that his or her good faith determination on viability will be accepted.

Spousal consent. In the *Danforth* case, the Supreme Court held that requirements of spousal consent to abortion were unconstitutional violations of a woman's right of privacy. However, if a woman has an abortion over her husband's objection, he may be able to obtain a divorce on the ground of "irreconcilable differences" in the states where that is a ground for divorce.

Institutional conscience clauses. Another issue is whether a hospital or other institution can refuse to provide abortions if abortion violates the moral principles or conscience of the institution. This issue has been considered separately for public and private hospitals. In 1977, the Supreme Court found that a public hospital was not constitutionally required to provide nontherapeutic abortions. However, there may be a constitutional mandate for a public hospital to provide "medically necessary" or, at the very least, life-saving abortions, particularly if it is the only facility in the area.

Even if public hospitals are found to have a duty to provide medically necessary abortions, a second issue arises: whether private hospitals that receive government assistance become, in effect, an arm of the state and therefore must provide abortions. Since the Fourteenth Amendment applies only to governmental action, a purely private hospital may be within its rights to refuse to provide any abortions. But if a hospital is so linked to

the state (e.g., by receiving sufficient federal funds or tax benefits or otherwise) that it becomes "clothed" in state action, it may become, for these purposes, an arm of the government to which the constitutional mandate applies. The 1973 Church amendment (named after Senator Frank Church) tried to exempt hospitals that received federal funds from having to provide abortions and sterilization. It is questionable, however, whether an act of Congress could relieve an institution considered "governmental" of its duty to obey the Constitution. Sectarian religious institutions may pose a special case.

Omnibus antiabortion legislation. A number of states (such as Illinois and Louisiana) and localities (the most publicized is Akron, Ohio) have passed omnibus antiabortion legislation that contains a number of restrictive provisions such as parental consent or notification requirements for minors, licensing requirements for facilities, reporting requirements for physicians, and extremely detailed "informed-consent" requirements for the women. The Akron ordinance, for example, imposed a twenty-four hour waiting period and a requirement that the woman be informed that the "unborn child is a human life from the moment of conception" and that "abortion is a major surgical procedure that can result in serious complications, including hemorrhage, perforated uterus, infection, miscarriage." It appears that a pattern is being established whereby each situation will be analyzed separately, and judges will determine whether the restrictions infringe on a woman's right to obtain an abortion without undue government interference. Most of these restrictions have been declared unconstitutional by federal and state courts.

Sterilization. Although the issue has never reached the Supreme Court, the right to choose sterilization, as an important means of fertility control, is presumably protected within the constitutional right of privacy.

Voluntary sterilization. Unlike the use of other methods of family planning, sterilization is considered to be irreversible and can carry within it the potential for abuse. In 1978, the Department of Health, Education, and Welfare issued regulations for federally funded sterilizations designed to eliminate coercion without curtailing access to the procedure. The regulations established standards of "informed consent" to assure voluntariness including, with two minor exceptions, a thirty-day waiting period between the giving of consent and the date of the procedure. The regulations also prohibit federal funding of the sterilization of people under 21, of institutionalized persons, of the mentally incompetent, and of women whose consent is obtained while they are in labor or undergoing abortions.

The federal regulations apply to sterilizations only where federal funding is involved, for example, under

Title XIX (Medicaid) and Title XX of the Social Security Act, Title X of the Public Health Services Act, and other programs now administered by the Department of Health and Human Services. New York City and the state of California have issued their own guidelines, similar in content to the HHS regulations, which regulate all sterilizations carried out within their jurisdictions.

Sterilization of the mentally retarded and the young. "Eugenic" sterilization of the mentally retarded—supported in the beginning of the twentieth century by a combination of Mendelian genetics and social Darwinism—has had a long tradition in the United States. Under the rationale of improving the race by eliminating undesirable traits thought to be inheritable, many states passed laws permitting the sterilization of the retarded, the insane, the feebleminded, the epileptic, and the criminal recidivist upon the application of a parent, guardian, or director of a mental institution. Many of the laws were struck down by lower courts as unconstitutional in the early part of the century.

In the 1927 case of *Buck* v. *Bell,* the U.S. Supreme Court held that a statute under which an institutionalized, allegedly feebleminded woman could be sterilized upon the order of the head of the state mental institution did not violate the due process clause of the Fourteenth Amendment. Justice Oliver Wendell Holmes tersely remarked, "Three generations of imbeciles are enough." In its only other decision in this area, in *Skinner* v. *Oklahoma,* the Court struck down an Oklahoma sterilization statute on very narrow grounds and declared that the right to procreate is a "fundamental" constitutional one. Were the issue to arise in the Supreme Court today, however, state compulsory sterilization statutes might well be held to violate the constitutional right of privacy.

The issues raised by sterilization of the mentally retarded (and the young) are among the most delicate in the field of fertility. For example, since "informed consent" is a necessary prerequisite to all medical treatment, who, if anyone, has the right to consent to the sterilization of a minor or a mentally retarded person? Does sterilization of the mentally retarded based on third-party consent violate the retarded person's right of privacy? What procedural safeguards should be established to protect the rights of minors and the mentally retarded?

HHS regulations prohibit the use of federal funds to sterilize people who have been declared incompetent by a court (unless they have been declared competent for purposes that include the ability to consent to sterilization), people who have been institutionalized, and people under 21 years of age. A physician performing a sterilization must certify that the patient appeared to be mentally competent.

Where no federal funds are involved, the situation varies from state to state. In many states, courts have held that in the absence of a specific enabling act, no one—not even a court—can authorize the sterilization of a person who does not have the capacity to give informed consent. Some states have enacted legislation specifying the conditions under which mentally retarded people may be sterilized and upon whose order. The grounds for sterilization generally fall into two categories: transmission of inheritable defects and lack of capacity to raise children. Often the statutes will require that the sterilization be in the "best interests" of the person or the society. Approvals by these state or institutional officials, or even parents, are increasingly seen as insufficient to protect the rights of the mentally retarded, and other consent mechanisms and procedural safeguards are being developed. One mechanism is the requirement of court approval before a person can be sterilized. Another mechanism is approval by an impartial review committee. Such a committee could function instead of a court or, preferably, in addition to it. The composition of a committee is, of course, crucial to its effectiveness, and it has been suggested that members be selected so that the committee will be competent to deal with the medical, legal, social, and ethical issues involved in sterilization. It seems that at least one person from the same ethnic group as the patient should be included as a committee member. The suggestion has also been made that in every case a paid patient advocate be appointed to represent the person and to ensure that his or her best interests are served.

In any case, the person against whom sterilization proceedings are being brought is considered to be entitled to certain basic procedural rights, such as adequate notice, the right to counsel, and the rights to call witnesses, to present evidence in his or her own behalf, to cross-examine witnesses, and to appeal an adverse decision.

Where no statute expressly covers the situation, courts have been asked to authorize sterilizations based on the application of a third party. Although decisions have been divided, the prevailing view is that courts cannot authorize such sterilizations in the absence of a specific legislative grant of power to do so. However, where a judge does authorize a sterilization in the absence of a statutory grant, he or she cannot be successfully sued at a later time by the person sterilized, although the hospital and physician may be. Statutory provisions are being developed to resolve the uncertainties in existing law.

Rights of Minors. Under Anglo-American common law, a minor was presumed not to have the judgment to know what his or her medical needs were and therefore could not consent to treatment. Parental consent was required, and a physician who provided treatment in the absence of parental consent might be liable for damages for assault and battery. Minors were considered akin to property of their parents in many cases, and parental control over their children was almost limitless. In recent years, the Supreme Court has accorded many, although not all, constitutional rights to minors.

Right to consent to medical treatment. With respect to medical treatment, the strict provisions of common law have always been subject to some exceptions permitting minors to consent to their own medical care. These exceptions have been enacted as statutes in some states and effected by court decisions in others. They are (1) emergency care, (2) emancipation (e.g., minors who are married, who have served in the military, or who live apart from parents and/or are self-supporting), and (3) maturity (e.g., minors who are mature enough to understand the nature and risks of a procedure and to reach an informed decision about whether to undergo it and whether the procedure is for their benefit). Many states have enacted statutes specifically dealing with medical care for minors, permitting them to consent to all kinds of medical care when they reach a stated age or specifying the kinds of care (e.g., for venereal diseases and fertility control) to which minors can consent. Additionally, under the doctrine of neglect, courts can order medical care for minors who need it.

Right to abortion. There are two major questions regarding the right of a minor to have an abortion. The first concerns parental consent, that is, whether a state can require the consent of one or both parents before an abortion is done. The second concerns parental involvement at a level less than consent, that is, parental notification or consultation.

In the aftermath of *Roe* v. *Wade,* a number of states passed laws requiring the consent of one or both parents before a minor could have an abortion. After considerable litigation on this issue in state and federal courts, the U.S. Supreme Court found in the 1976 *Danforth* decision that the right of privacy, which includes the right to terminate an unwanted pregnancy, applies to minors as well as adults and held that "the State does not have the constitutional authority to give a third party an absolute, and possibly arbitrary, veto over the decision of the physician and his patient to terminate the patient's pregnancy." Thus, the Court struck down the provision that required parental consent.

In 1979, the Supreme Court, in *Bellotti* v. *Baird II,* held that whether a minor can consent for an abortion depends on the maturity of the minor. The Court also said that if a state decides to require parental consent for abortion for a minor, it must provide an alternative procedure whereby the minor can show either (1) that she is mature enough to make her abortion decision, in consultation with her physician, independently of her parents' wishes or (2) that even if she is not able to make this

decision independently, the desired abortion would be in her best interests. If the minor is able to demonstrate either of these conditions to the satisfaction of a court or administrative agency, it must authorize the abortion. The Supreme Court specifically struck down a provision of a Massachusetts law requiring that parents be notified prior to a judicial appeal, stating that "every minor must have the opportunity—if she so desires—to go directly to a court without first consulting or notifying her parents."

Although the *Bellotti* decision did not conclusively settle the issue of whether parents must be notified or consulted, it does indicate that any absolute requirement of parental notification or consultation as well as an absolute requirement of parental consent is unconstitutional. A majority of the justices appeared to support this position in the 1981 case of *H.L.* v. *Matheson,* in which the court upheld the constitutionality of a parental notification provision for unmarried minors who were not emancipated, who had not demonstrated that they could be considered mature, and who had not asserted any special reason why their parents should not be involved.

Right to contraception. In 1977 the Supreme Court held unconstitutional a New York law that prohibited the distribution of nonprescription contraceptives to minors under 16 years of age (*Carey* v. *Population Services International*). Justice William J. Brennan, speaking for himself and three other members of the Court, observed that the law impinged upon a minor's right of privacy and that the state had not offered convincing reasons why a significant state interest would be served by restricting minors' access to contraception.

Thus, it is clear that minors do have a right of access to nonprescription contraceptives. With regard to prescription contraceptives, the issues have not yet been fully resolved because the right to access was not adjudicated in the *Carey* case: the state of New York had conceded that physicians could prescribe contraceptives for minors of any age in New York. It is doubtful that a state could require parental consent or notification in every case before birth control pills or other prescription contraceptives are dispensed. An argument that the distribution of pills to minors by a state-funded clinic in Michigan violated the constitutional rights of parents was recently found to be without merit by a federal court of appeals; the Supreme Court declined review.

Right to voluntary sterilization. The legal right of minors to sterilization is rarely litigated since few adolescents request sterilization. Generally, the issue arises in the context of a person requesting that a child, often a retarded child, be sterilized. Although the logical extension of a number of judicial decisions would be to place voluntary sterilization within the scope of the privacy rights of minors, the permanence of the operation, coupled with the potential for abuse, gives the state some additional interests not present in the abortion and contraception situations. Whether these state interests would be considered significant has not been determined. Under current federal guidelines, U.S. government funds cannot be used to pay for the sterilization of a person under 21 years of age. Even where federal funding is not involved, the right of minors to consent to sterilization is unclear; a number of states have minimum-age requirements for sterilization or specifically exclude sterilization from those medical procedures to which a minor can consent.

Conclusions. A person's control of his or her own fertility was recognized as an aspect of the right of privacy protected by the U.S. Constitution in the 1960s and 1970s. This view was followed by the passage of major federal legislation that provided government funding of family planning services across the nation, services that were used by more than four million women in 1977. Thus, although the United States does not have a formal population policy, it may be inferred from the federal judicial decisions and the legislation that the country's intention is to reduce or eliminate unwanted fertility and that the courts will protect an individual's right to decide whether and when to have children. At the same time, although polls indicate that a majority of the people support abortion rights, there is reluctance to pay for abortion as part of any government-supported program of medical care. Additionally, the right of minors to obtain confidential reproductive health services faces continuing challenges.

Stephen L. Isaacs
Eve W. Paul
Harriet F. Pilpel

See also ABORTION, *article on* UNITED STATES; BIRTH CONTROL MOVEMENT; FAMILY PLANNING PROGRAMS, *article on* UNITED STATES.

BIBLIOGRAPHY

Alan Guttmacher Institute. *Family Planning, Contraception, Voluntary Sterilization, and Abortion: An Analysis of Laws and Policies in the United States, Each State and Jurisdiction.* Prepared for the U.S. Department of Health, Education, and Welfare. Washington, D.C.: U.S. Government Printing Office, 1978.
Beal v. *Doe,* 432 U.S. 438 (1977).
Bellotti v. *Baird II,* 443 U.S. 622 (1979).
Buck v. *Bell,* 274 U.S. 200 (1927).
Carey v. *Population Services International,* 431 U.S. 678 (1977).
Colautti v. *Franklin,* 439 U.S. 379 (1979).
Danforth v. *Planned Parenthood of Central Missouri,* 428 U.S. 52 (1976).
Djerassi, Carl. *The Politics of Contraception.* New York: Norton, 1979.
Doe v. *Bolton,* 410 U.S. 179 (1973).
Eisenstadt v. *Baird,* 405 U.S. 438 (1972).
Griswold v. *Connecticut,* 381 U.S. 479 (1965).
Isaacs, Stephen L. *Population Law and Policy: Source Materials and Issues.* New York: Human Sciences Press, 1981.
Maher v. *Roe,* 432 U.S. 464 (1977).
Mohr, James C. *Abortion in America: The Origins and Evolution of National Policy, 1800–1900.* London and New York: Oxford University Press, 1978.
Paul, Eve W., and Harriet F. Pilpel. "Teenagers and Pregnancy: The Law in 1979." *Family Planning Perspectives* 11(5): 297–302, September/October 1979.
Planned Parenthood/World Population: Washington Memo. Issued biweekly by the Alan Guttmacher Institute, New York.
Roe v. *Wade,* 410 U.S. 113 (1973).
Skinner v. *Oklahoma,* 316 U.S. 535 (1942).

LIBRARIES

See ASSOCIATION FOR POPULATION/FAMILY PLANNING LIBRARIES AND INFORMATION CENTERS—INTERNATIONAL.

LIFE EXPECTANCY

See ACTUARIAL METHODS; LIFE TABLES; MORBIDITY AND LONGEVITY.

LIFE TABLES

The life table is a powerful tool for analyzing the force of mortality in a population. A hypothetical group, usually 1,000 or 100,000, is subject to age-specific rates of mortality through its life span, and the table is terminated when all of the original group have died. Useful for determining life expectancy and survival probabilities, the life table is not influenced by the accidental age structures of the populations under analysis; hence it provides standardized comparisons of mortality experience. Life tables can be constructed for countries, groups of countries, or particular areas, as well as for groups selected by sex, race, occupation, or other specified characteristics, thus giving a comparative mortality picture. The basic method involved is easily transferred to other contexts, to study risks of events such as marriage, divorce, or entry into the labor force.

In the construction of life tables, it is assumed that there is no change in mortality rates over time, that is, that the given schedule of risks remains constant. Historically of course such changes do take place; an individual is not likely to be exposed at higher ages to the age-specific risks that prevailed in an earlier period. Thus life tables refer to the experience of a synthetic or hypothetical cohort. "Generational life tables" can be constructed using the age-specific death rates that indeed prevail as the group passes through the various ages. However, these are of limited utility because full information is not available until the extinction of the group, so work on contemporary populations cannot be done; further, even for historical populations the requisite data are of uneven quality and were not collected before the 1800s. Thus, the hypothetical "period life table" is used instead to express the mortality conditions prevailing at a specific time.

The Basic Life Table. The construction of life tables has as its basis a set of mortality probabilities, shown as the $_nq_x$ column in Table 1. These are the proportions $_nq_x$ who die between the two birthdays involved, that is, the proportion at the starting age who will die in the interval. A hypothetical cohort or "radix," usually set at 1,000 or 100,000 persons, starts in the l_x column at birth, that is, at exact age zero. Through all age intervals, l_x represents the number still alive at exactly age x. The loss in each interval is calculated by multiplying the mortality probability for the interval by the number who enter it. This gives the number who die during the interval, recorded as $_nd_x$. This number is subtracted from those alive at the

beginning of the interval, to obtain the number in the l_x column who reach the next birthday, and the process is repeated.

The column marked $_nL_x$ represents person-years lived in an interval of n years by those who started the interval. Based on the assumption that deaths are uniformly distributed throughout the interval, the number alive at the midpoint is simply multiplied by the number of years in the interval, so that

$$_nL_x = n\left(\frac{l_x + l_{x+n}}{2}\right).$$

However, because deaths are not distributed evenly at the very young and old ages, where the mortality curve is not linear, more refined methods are used to estimate the precise number of person-years lived within those subintervals.

The value of T_x on any row represents the person-years lived by the population from that age forward, that is, in that interval and all subsequent ones, and is obtained simply by adding $_nL_x$ values from that row down through the rest of the table.

The $_nL_x$ column is of special interest in demography because it can represent a population all alive at the

TABLE 1. *Abridged life table, female, United States, 1974*

Age interval	Proportion dying	Of 100,000 born alive		Stationary population		Average remaining lifetime
	Proportion of persons alive at beginning of age interval dying during interval					Average number of years of life remaining at beginning of age interval
Period of life between two exact ages stated in years		Number living at beginning of age interval	Number dying during age interval	In the age interval	In this and all subsequent age intervals	
(1)	(2)	(3)	(4)	(5)	(6)	(7)
x to $x + n$	$_nq_x$	l_x	$_nd_x$	$_nL_x$	T_x	$\overset{\circ}{e}_x$
0–1	.0146	100,000	1,465	98,694	7,581,958	75.8
1–5	.0026	98,535	255	393,540	7,483,264	75.9
5–10	.0015	98,280	149	490,997	7,089,724	72.1
10–15	.0014	98,131	138	490,345	6,598,727	67.2
15–20	.0028	97,993	275	489,325	6,108,382	62.3
20–25	.0034	97,718	333	487,772	5,619,057	57.5
25–30	.0039	97,385	383	485,999	5,131,285	52.7
30–35	.0052	97,002	503	483,831	4,645,286	47.9
35–40	.0077	96,499	744	480,762	4,161,455	43.1
40–45	.0124	95,755	1,190	475,992	3,680,693	38.4
45–50	.0190	94,565	1,798	468,594	3,204,701	33.9
50–55	.0278	92,767	2,581	457,748	2,736,107	29.5
55–60	.0415	90,186	3,742	442,066	2,278,359	25.3
60–65	.0617	86,444	5,330	419,622	1,836,293	21.2
65–70	.0877	81,114	7,111	388,798	1,416,671	17.5
70–75	.1438	74,003	10,639	344,843	1,027,873	13.9
75–80	.2285	63,364	14,477	281,990	683,030	10.8
80–85	.3381	48,887	16,529	203,325	401,040	8.2
85 and over	1.0000	32,358	32,358	197,715	197,715	6.1

SOURCE: United States, 1978.

same time, as well as the total person-years lived by a cohort from birth to extinction. If the life table rates of mortality never changed, and a cohort the size of the radix were born each year, the $_nL_x$ would represent the population pyramid, that is, size of the population by age groups, and T_x the size in this and all subsequent age groups. The population would have zero growth, since the number dying each year (the total of the $_nd_x$ column) equals the radix (the number born each year). This is termed a "stationary" population.

The additional life expectancy at any age x is obtained by dividing the total person-years yet to be lived by the number of persons alive at that age, that is, T_x/l_x. The $\mathring{e}_x$ column shows the results of such calculations, and its first entry is the life expectancy at birth, the most commonly used figure from the life table.

The accompanying Table 1 is an "abridged" life table, in that it uses intervals larger than one year of age. If accurate mortality data for single years of age exist, a "complete" life table can be constructed, which differs only by using the more refined intervals. Usually, an abridged life table is adequate and eliminates cumbersome detail. It should be noted, however, that even an abridged life table almost always includes a separate row for the first year of life, because infant mortality differs markedly from that of the next few years and is itself an important index of mortality conditions in a population.

The shrinkage of the birth cohort tends to follow a typical pattern, as in Figure 1. The first year of life is especially hazardous, but the death rate quickly drops and the population then suffers little further diminution until after age 40, when the rates begin to rise. Thereafter the number of survivors falls more and more steeply.

Most life tables group all deaths as a single cause of loss, but "multiple-decrement" tables can also be calculated, for example, by showing separate columns for the major causes of death. Similarly, a table can contain two columns, to show the diminution of an original group of never-married persons by either marriage or death. Life tables have been used to study the continuation rates of participants in family planning programs and various medical treatments, as well as the useful life of industrial products.

Cause-deleted tables. There are many refinements of the life table method. Tables can, for example, be constructed with mortality rates adjusted downward to eliminate particular causes of death. This affords a measure of the relative importance of a given cause of death in a population, according to the increase in average life expectancy and survival probabilities that would occur if that cause were eliminated. The gains in life expectancy, even when major illnesses are removed from the life table, are generally modest; for example, if all cancers were eliminated from the 1969–1971 mortality rates of American white males, the gain would be only 2.31 years in expectation of life at birth. The leading cause of death among people in that category was heart disease; eliminating all diseases of the heart would add only 6.14 years to the average length of life. These gains are limited because persons "saved" from the specified cause then simply live exposed to risk of death from all other causes, which are substantial.

In cause-deleted tables an assumption is made that the different causes of death are independent, so that the elimination of one cause of death does not influence the occurrence of any other. In fact, age-specific rates of death from pulmonary edema would probably decline if the burden of other complications of heart failure were eliminated. In practice, however, a correction is not made, as its proper size is speculative. It is wise then to keep in mind that the cause-deleted life table is a useful comparative device to estimate the relative impact of diseases on current mortality patterns, but that the estimates of gains in life expectancy involve some conjecture. Moreover, to adjust a set of q_x values to eliminate a particular cause of death, accurate data by cause are needed. Such data are not terribly reliable even in the most developed countries and may be grossly unreliable elsewhere. Thus only large differences and major patterns should be trusted in cause-deleted analysis or in other cause-of-death work.

Model life tables. An examination of the structure of many empirical life tables has permitted the development of model life tables. These are drawn up to show the typical mortality picture across a range of overall life expectancies and different age patterns. They are useful in the estimation of mortality rates and life expectancies especially when data are unavailable or of doubtful qual-

FIGURE 1. *Survival curve* (l_x) *of a cohort*

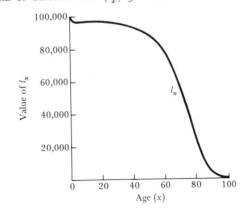

ity. Although some guesswork is necessarily involved in the choice of which model table best represents the level and age pattern of mortality in the particular population, the error involved in the choice may be a good deal less than the error encountered by using the empirical data directly.

The construction of a set of model life tables requires analysis of a substantial set of empirical life tables with reliable data from populations experiencing a range of conditions. The first major set, based on 158 sex-specific actual tables, was published by the United Nations Population Division in 1955 and became influential in work in the demography of less-developed countries.

In 1966, Ansley J. Coale and Paul Demeny published a large series of model life tables based on more than three hundred actual life tables from different populations and different time periods. These are assembled in four regional groups, North, South, East, and West, reflecting four major age patterns of mortality that appeared in the empirical tables. The North tables correspond fundamentally to Scandinavian countries, the South tables to southern European experience, and the East model to central European data. Closer to the average pattern of the entire group is the set of life tables designated "West," which reflects a large body of mortality experience from countries including the United States and Canada, Australia, New Zealand, and Japan as well as some in western Europe.

Within the regions the model tables are arranged by female life expectancy at birth from 20 to 77.5 years, in two-and-one-half year increments; corresponding male life tables are also calculated. Calculations of stable populations are provided as well, showing the age distributions and various rates that would occur given the life table mortality schedules and varying rates of natural increase.

A more recent effort, by William Brass (1975), does not present a compilation of many model tables, but rather uses a logit system to transform a standard table based on two parameters. As additional knowledge has accumulated about actual mortality patterns, it has become clear that the available model tables will require revision to encompass patterns containing especially high mortality at young and old ages and among females (United Nations, 1972).

Other Applications. The essential life table method applies to a wide range of topics and to much survey work. Applications have been published for Bangladesh for intervals from birth to resumption of menses and from conception to fetal death or live birth (Chen et al., 1974). For Korea the life table has been applied to the interval from intrauterine device (IUD) acceptance to

the next birth (Kim, Ross, and Worth, 1972) and in other work from live birth to resumption of menstruation for lactating versus nonlactating women (Kang, Hong, and Cho, 1973). Irving Sivin (1974) applied the life table method to intervals from contraceptive acceptance to the next birth, for data from numerous developing countries. From properly executed surveys, life tables can be used to measure infant and child mortality rates, marriage and dissolution of marriage rates, and duration of breastfeeding. They are increasingly being used to measure birth intervals. Where contraceptive histories or histories of abortion are recorded, these may also permit life table treatment.

David P. Smith (1980) has set forth technical procedures for several of these applications, pointing out that what life tables do for all these analyses is to show event rates at each duration of exposure, for example, the proportion of infants surviving from birth to age 1 month or 1 year or the proportion of women marrying by age 15, 20, or 25. Other types of rates for these events exist and are as widely used as life table rates, such as the proportion of children who are still living for women in a particular age group or the proportion ever married among women 15–19, 20–24, or 25–29. Though easier to calculate than life table rates, these rates give much less information and are often not so precise. Between two populations they may differ simply because the rates happen to be sensitive to age distribution differences for the populations being studied. In the example of marriage rates, if in one population most of the women aged 15–19 are close to age 15 and in the other population most are close to age 20, and if women tend to marry in their late teens in both populations, then the proportions ever married can be expected to be quite different in the two situations.

Using age-at-marriage information, the life table (Figure 2) is able to show that marriage patterns have been changing and that these changes have been relatively steady over quite a number of years. For younger age groups, the proportions married at each age are consistently lower.

As Smith emphasizes, life tables are not necessarily suitable for all types of events. An age-specific fertility rate, for example, provides a more compact summary of fertility behavior than a life table. The same is likely to be true of the mean number of children ever born or the mean number of living children. While in such instances life table rates may be possible, they will be retrospective rather than current, and they may give more detail than required. As a general rule, life tables will be appropriate when the chance of an event occurring changes sharply at different durations of exposure, when the durations are

FIGURE 2. *Life table and actual proportions ever married, by age, 1974 Sri Lanka fertility survey*

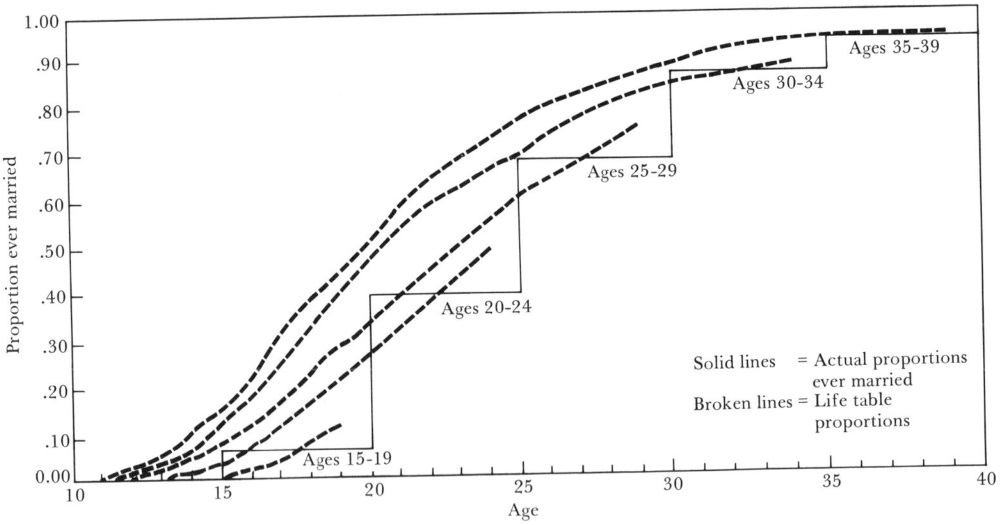

SOURCE: Smith, 1980, p. 6.

measurable, and when the events themselves are simple and unambiguous.

"Multi-state" Approaches. A fundamental new departure bearing on life table applications is the result of work by Andrei Rogers and associates (1975), who have brought many demographic analyses under a single approach. In this approach, individuals are permitted to move freely within a matrix, among several states or conditions. Transitions can occur from any state to any other state and in either direction. A ready example is the geographic one, where movement can literally be among all "states," but statistically speaking, movement can be as readily from employment to unemployment or from marriage to nonmarriage. The highly sophisticated mathematical equipment already developed in the matrix field greatly expands the potential for analysis of these events.

Many classic demographic problems, including much life table work, are special applications of this broader approach. In these instances, movement may not be totally free. In tables of working life one can move from employment to death but not the other way. In tables of married life one can move from the currently married state to the divorced one but not to the single, and so on. Matrix mathematics adapt readily to these simplifications, but more important, they adapt readily to complex conditions, letting the analyst dispose of restrictive assumptions that were formerly necessary to simplify the calculations. For example, it is no longer necessary to assume in constructing tables of working life that mortality rates by age are the same for those working and those not working, or that no one enters the labor force after a certain age. Technical problems in life table manipulations are also handled more efficiently. Thus the new methods make traditional analyses easier, permit more realistic assumptions, enlarge the scope of what can be investigated, and yield insights not previously attainable.

John A. Ross

For applications of life table methods, see FAMILY PLANNING RESEARCH; INDIRECT ESTIMATION OF FERTILITY AND MORTALITY.

BIBLIOGRAPHY

Brass, William. *Methods for Estimating Fertility and Mortality from Limited and Defective Data.* Chapel Hill, N.C.: Laboratories for Population Statistics, 1975.

Chen, Lincoln C., Shamsa Ahmed, Melita Gesche, and W. Henry Mosley. "A Prospective Study of Birth Interval Dynamics in Rural Bangladesh." *Population Studies* 28(2):277–297, July 1974.

Coale, Ansley J., and Paul Demeny. *Regional Model Life Tables and Stable Populations.* Princeton, N.J.: Princeton University Press, 1966.

Goldman, Noreen. "Far Eastern Patterns of Mortality." *Population Studies* 34(1):5–19, March 1980.

Kang, Kil Won, Jae Woong Hong, and Kyoung Sik Cho. [*A Study on the Interrelationships between Lactation and Postpartum Amenorrhea.*] Seoul: Korean Institute for Family Planning, October 1973. In Korean with tables and summary in English.

Keyfitz, Nathan. "Multistate Demography and Its Data: A Comment." *Environment and Planning A* 12(5):615–622, 1980.

Kim, Taek Il, John A. Ross, and George C. Worth. *The Korean National Family Planning Program: Population Control and Fertility Decline.* New York: Population Council, 1972.

Rogers, Andrei. *Introduction to Multiregional Mathematical Demography.* New York: Wiley, 1975.

Rogers, Andrei (editor). "Essays in Multistate Mathematical Demography." *Environment and Planning A* 12(5), whole issue, May 1980. Reprinted by the International Institute for Applied Systems Analysis, Laxenburg, Austria, 1980.

Sivin, Irving. *Contraception and Fertility Change in the International Postpartum Program.* New York: Population Council, 1974.

Smith, David P. *Life Table Analysis.* Technical Bulletin No. 6. London: World Fertility Survey and International Statistical Institute, April 1980.

United Nations, Department of Social Affairs. *Age and Sex Patterns of Mortality: Model Life-tables for Under-developed Countries.* Series A, Population Studies, no. 22. New York, December 1955.

United Nations, Economic and Social Council, Population Commission. *Report of the Ad Hoc Committee of Experts on Methods of Revising United Nations Model Life Tables.* New York, August 1972.

United States, National Center for Health Statistics. *Vital Statistics of the United States, 1974.* Volume 2: *Mortality.* Hyattsville, Md., 1978.

LITERATURE
See PUBLICATIONS.

LONGEVITY
See MORBIDITY AND LONGEVITY.

M

MACHINE-READABLE DATA FILES

Machine-readable data files (MRDF) have become an important resource for demographers. Every central statistics service or other major statistics-producing office uses computers to store and tabulate census, vital statistics, and survey data. Many of these offices now make available to the public machine-readable summary tabulations, usually more extensive than printed versions and, in some cases, disclosure-free samples for public use. Academic researchers throughout the world are routinely converting survey responses, data obtained from printed reports, parish registers, and microfilmed records to machine-readable form. In some instances these too are being made publicly available. For both primary and secondary analysis, machine-readable data files have, to a large extent, replaced the printed volume as a source of data for demographic research. Secondary analysis of data files produced for other purposes is rapidly becoming a common *modus operandi* for demographers, and even files thought to have been thoroughly exploited by the original investigators have in the hands—or on the computers—of secondary analysts yielded new and important findings.

Inventory of MRDF. Partly because the number of machine-readable data files available for secondary analysis has increased rapidly, it is sometimes difficult for individual researchers to locate the specific files appropriate to their needs. As a result, large and expensive data files are underutilized and researchers may abandon potentially fruitful projects because they believe the necessary data to be unavailable. To eliminate this problem, files are increasingly being transferred to social science data archives for distribution, and government agencies are replacing the informal distribution of data with the development of public data products, comprehensive codebooks, and user training. With the publication of rules for cataloging machine-readable data files and recommended standards for citations to them, it is now possible to include these materials in standard bibliographies.

The inventory of publicly available MRDF has come to include many files of interest to demographers. These range from summary tabulations of national census data from such countries as the United States, Canada, the United Kingdom, Norway, and Denmark, to public-use samples of census records from the monthly Current Population Surveys (U.S.) and the quarterly General Household Surveys (U.K.) Even more numerous are surveys and public opinion polls dealing with fertility, abortion, marriage, divorce, migration, living arrangements, retirement, and the employment of women. The imaginative researcher can use other people's data to create time series, to do cross-national or cross-cultural analysis, compare attitudes with behavior, and test innumerable hypotheses using a variety of subpopulations (Smith and Rowe, 1979). By their very nature MRDF are usually flexible enough to be appropriate for use in many subject areas.

Generally speaking, most MRDF contain either macrodata or microdata. The macrodata files are those that contain aggregate or summary tabulations. These are usually arranged (or sorted) by geographic area, as small as a city block or as large as a country, or by time period such as day, month, or year. Microdata files contain individual records for persons, families, and/or households. If there is only one record type, the file is termed "rectangular": if there are two or more, it is "hierarchical." Other types of complex file structures are being designed but are usually used with data-base management systems (DBMS), making them less portable. Microdata files provide greater flexibility than macrodata files because they allow researchers to create their own summary tabulations and to select their own subsets of the population.

Data Bases in the United States. Not surprisingly, the major producers and distributors of machine-readable data are in the United States, which has both more computers available to researchers and more interest in quantitative research. This domestic market did not exist as recently as ten years ago and such a market does not yet exist in other parts of the world, but there are some data producers and distributors in Canada, in western Europe, and in Latin America.

The largest body of publicly available machine-readable data in the world is produced by the U.S. Bureau of the Census. Its primary products derive from the 1970 and 1980 decennial censuses. Other major census data products include the Current Population Survey and the Annual Housing Survey. A guide to these is the *Directory of Data Files* issued by the U.S. Bureau of the Census.

The National Center for Health Statistics produces MRDF based on the National Survey of Family Growth, the National Natality and Mortality Followback Surveys, and the Health Interview and the Health Examination Surveys.

Both of the two major American social science data archives have holdings that relate to aspects of the study of population. The Inter-University Consortium for Political and Social Research (ICPSR), located at the University of Michigan, is the primary distributor of a number of files containing historical demographic material; it hosts the National Archives of Computerized Data on Aging. ICPSR publishes an annual *Guide to Resources and Services,* which fully describes its current holdings.

The Roper Center at the University of Connecticut at Storrs is the largest archive of sample-survey data in the world. Its data collection consists primarily of opinion polls and includes over a thousand files, which include data on fertility, marriage, divorce, and related subjects. Other nonprofit centers at both universities and research institutes maintain large collections of academic and government-produced data and will provide file abstracts, tape copies, and analytic reports on a cost-recovery basis. Similar services are also available from commercial data services.

Other Data Sources. The pattern of data distribution in Canada is very similar to that in the United States. Statistics Canada is the major source of government-produced data files. They distribute both User Summary Tapes and Public Use Samples from their censuses and also supply data for the Canadian Socio-Economic Information Management System (CANSIM), the national time series data base, which is updated regularly and made available to users via both batch and time-sharing systems.

In western Europe some files are available directly from government agencies or research institutes, but a growing number of files are being deposited with national data archives already established in eight countries. In the United Kingdom, this national facility is located at the University of Essex and is known as the SSRC (Social Science Research Council) Survey Archive. The Dansk Data Arkiv is located at the University of Odense in Denmark, and the Swedish Data Archive is located at the Institute of Political Science at the University of Göteborg. The oldest of the Scandinavian archives is the Norwegian Social Science Data Services located at Bergen University. The Federal Republic of Germany (West Germany) has several data archives of which the largest and most active is the Zentralarchiv für Empirische Socialforschung at the University of Cologne. In Belgium, the Archives Belges en Sciences Sociales (BASS) is located at Louvain-la-Neuve, and in the Netherlands the Steinmetz Archives are a department of the Social Science Information and Documentation Center of the Royal Netherlands Academy of Arts and Sciences in Amsterdam. The major Italian social science data archive is the Archivi e Programmi per le Scienze Sociale in Milan.

A special data facility for Latin American demographic data is the Centro Latinoamericano de Demografía in Santiago, Chile. Its data bank holds 1960 and 1970 census microdata and files on such topics as international and internal migration, fertility and abortion, and household surveys from most Latin American countries.

Since more and more information has come to be "published," or produced, in machine-readable form, and since demographers now place more of their existing data into this form, the journal *Population Index,* a primary source of bibliographic citations to demographic information, has added a special section covering publicly available machine-readable data products.

Judith S. Rowe

Information concerning the availability of World Fertility Survey record tapes can be found in WORLD FERTILITY SURVEY.

BIBLIOGRAPHY

Directory of Data Files. Issued and updated quarterly by the U.S. Bureau of the Census, Washington, D.C.

Dodd, Sue A. "Titles: The Emerging Priority in Bringing Bibliographic Control to Social Science Machine-readable Data Files (MDRF)." *IASSIST Newsletter* 1(4):11–18, Fall 1977.

———. "Bibliographic Reference for Numeric Social Science Data Files: Suggested Guidelines." *Journal of the American Society for Information Science* 30(2):77–82, March 1979.

Gorman, Michael, and Paul W. Winkler (editors). *Anglo-American Cataloguing Rules.* 2d ed. Chicago and Ottawa: American Library Association and Canadian Library Association, 1978.

Guide to Resources and Services. Issued annually by the Inter-University Consortium for Political and Social Research (ICPSR) at the University of Michigan, Ann Arbor. Describes current ICPSR holdings including those related to population study.

Population Index. Issued quarterly since 1935 by the Population Association of America in Princeton, New Jersey. Includes bibliographic citations and information on machine-readable data resources.

Rowe, Judith S. " 'Population Index' to Cite Publicly Available Machine-readable Data Files." *Population Index* 45(4):567–575, October 1979.

Smith, Kent W., and Judith S. Rowe. "Using Secondary Analysis for Quasi-experimental Research." *U.S. Social Science Information* 18(3):451–472, 1979.

MALNUTRITION

See REPRODUCTION, *article on* MALNUTRITION AND FAMINE.

MALTHUSIAN THEORY

See POPULATION THEORY.

MANPOWER

See LABOR FORCE.

MARRIAGE

The term "marriage" generally means the legal union of persons of opposite sex. Civil, religious, and other ways of establishing the legality of the union differ according to the laws and customs of countries. The proportion of the female population that is married at specific ages and over the span of reproductive years has been an important determinant of fertility rates. Age at first marriage is of interest to demographers as the age at which childbearing usually begins. International variation in that age and effects on fertility are discussed in AGE AT MAR-

RIAGE. Marriage and divorce as related to the size and composition of families are discussed in HOUSEHOLD AND FAMILY DEMOGRAPHY, and the demographic determinants and consequences of marriage in the United States are dealt with in MARRIAGE AND DIVORCE. Legal aspects of marriage in the United States are covered in FAMILY LAW. For methods for calculating marriage rates and the use of such rates, see NUPTIALITY INDEXES.

MARRIAGE AND DIVORCE

The distribution of the population by family status and marital status is an important aspect of a society, affecting its capacity for economic production, its reproductive potential, and its level of consumption. Each of the major demographic processes (fertility, mortality, migration, and nuptiality) takes place within a familial context, and various features of that context affect the probability of a demographic event, its timing, and its character. Demographic processes are causally linked with other familial processes. Fertility, for example, is associated with the participation of women in the labor force, and both are closely linked with the economic well-being of families.

This article reviews eight topics concerned with marriage and divorce as demographic processes occurring in the United States: (1) age at first marriage, (2) age at marriage and fertility, (3) premarital pregnancy, (4) marital disruption, aggregate trend, (5) marital disruption, differentials, (6) remarriage, (7) marital disruption and fertility, and (8) families headed by women.

Age at First Marriage. It is essential to distinguish two separate issues. The first concerns the determinants or antecedent conditions of the age of individuals at marriage and the factors that predispose people to marry very young. The second is the aggregate question of what determines the distribution of age at first marriage among societies, why this distribution varies, and what is associated with changes in the distribution within a single society.

Studies of individual variation within the United States have yielded relatively little valuable insight into the process by which age at first marriage is determined, although several generalizations are well documented (Carter and Glick, 1975). Men marry at older ages than women in the United States (and in most other societies). In the United States at the turn of the century, the average difference in age between spouses was about four years. By the mid-1970s, this differential had been reduced by nearly one half. At the present time, nonwhites in the United States tend to marry somewhat later than do whites, although earlier in this century this differential was just the reverse. People living in rural areas and in the southern states tend to marry earlier than do those living in urban areas and particularly in the northeastern states. In a number of early studies, an older age at marriage was associated with higher social class, although other studies have not consistently found this relationship. Roman Catholics tend to marry at older ages than do Protestants, and Jews tend to marry at somewhat older ages than do Catholics. The best-documented differential in age at first marriage is that of education. For both men and women, the more education they receive, the later they marry. Premarital pregnancy is clearly associated with early marriage.

In the United States in the early 1960s, ages at first marriage were as low as in any developed area in the world. In the years since, such ages have risen rapidly. The magnitude of this change can be seen by looking at the rise in the proportions of people never married as shown in Table 1. A number of hypotheses have been offered to explain the downward trend in marriage rates.

1. The marriage squeeze—the deteriorated position of women in the marriage market—has resulted in a rising marriage age for women, but less change for men.
2. In periods of economic uncertainty and high unemployment, people are less willing and able to marry.
3. Improved contraception and the availability of safe, legal abortion has reduced the incidence of marriage "forced" by premarital pregnancy.
4. Educational attainment has risen greatly and may account for some rise in age at marriage.
5. The position of young women in the labor market may have improved, reducing their economic incentives for marriage.
6. The messages of the women's movement or changing conditions experienced by women may have resulted in change in ideology, in which the need to marry, and marry as early as possible, is questioned by a larger proportion of women. This also could be a consequence of increased education.
7. Young couples are increasingly living together without formal marriage. Hence, the rising age at marriage reflects the failure of our legal forms and statistical concepts to keep pace with social reality.

TABLE 1. *Proportion of the population never married, by age*

Age	Women		Men	
	1977	1960	1977	1960
18	84.8%	75.6%	97.5%	94.6%
20	63.3	46.0	82.6	75.8
22	45.6	25.6	64.5	51.5
25	23.1	13.1	35.9	27.9

SOURCE: United States, 1976.

Marriage markets and the marriage squeeze. Because marriage links two individuals, each with a particular age and set of characteristics, it presents unusual problems for formal demographic theory. Societies establish sets of rules or norms with respect to who may marry whom. Typically, these rules specify age restrictions and other constraints.

Demographers have coined the phrase "marriage squeeze" to describe an instability that arises when there is a sexual imbalance in the number of marriageable persons. Such squeezes have frequently occurred in countries suffering severe war losses, with a shortage in the number of men of marriageable age. A dramatic example occurred in the Soviet Union following World War II.

An abrupt change in fertility generates a subsequent marriage squeeze. Such a change occurred in the United States as a result of the baby boom following World War II. In 1947, there were nearly 1 million more babies born in the United States than there were in 1945. In the mid-1960s the large cohort of females born in 1947 would normally have sought spouses from cohorts of slightly older males born in 1945 and earlier, but there were too few such men.

There are several possible outcomes to this kind of marriage squeeze. A larger proportion of women may remain permanently single. Women may marry later than they otherwise would; the marriage squeeze is then prolonged because in subsequent years a larger number of older women are competing with those just reaching the normal age at first marriage. Women may choose younger men for husbands or older, previously married men. This would have secondary consequences on the marriage chances and characteristics of those who are in the "used" spouse market, that is, women who are divorced or widowed. Alternatively, women may marry men who in a previous period would never have married at all. Thus, the cohort proportion of men who ever marry might increase.

Undoubtedly, the marriage squeeze has affected marriage patterns in several of these ways. Since 1970, however, the proportion of men who are not married by a given age has also increased substantially. This aspect of the rising age at marriage is not consistent with a marriage squeeze as an explanation.

Economic uncertainty. Marriage rates are known to respond to changing economic conditions. Especially important is the economic position of young people, particularly men. The past twenty years has unquestionably been a period of high unemployment for young men (under age 25). During 1958–1975, the average monthly unemployment rate for men 20–24 years of age was 7.8 percent. The position of men aged 18 and 19 was even worse.

Easterlin (1973) proposes a more complex argument concerning the economic conditions facing young people. Young people assess the economic conditions they face in marriage in relation to those that they knew while growing up. If this assessment is relatively favorable they will marry at younger ages; if it is unfavorable they will defer marriage.

Contraception and abortion. A rising age at first marriage is temporally associated with the greater availability of more effective means of contraception and increased accessibility of abortion. Most legal abortions are performed on unmarried women and seem to be associated across states and time with lower rates of first births (legitimate and illegitimate) among young women. Consequently, increased availability of safe, legal abortion might result in a decrease in the rate of first marriages if those forced by premarital pregnancies declined.

Educational attainment. Much of the increase in age at first marriage can be accounted for in terms of women staying in school longer and consequently being less available to the marriage market. During the 1960s the education-specific proportions married by specific ages changed very little. What has changed is simply that the proportion of the population having less than a high school education has correspondingly declined. College-educated women marry at older ages than high school-educated women and high school dropouts, a fact that accounts for a large fraction of the upward shift in age at first marriage. But the causal relation between education and late marriage is unclear. Prolonged schooling may be the result rather than the cause of deferred marriage. There does not appear to be a reasonable way of identifying and separating reciprocal effects.

The position of young women in the labor market. The willingness of young women to work after marrying, with or without children, may encourage males to decide that they can "afford" to get married (Davis, 1972). Samuel H. Preston and Alan T. Richards (1975) disagree with this explanation. They report that a higher proportion of women aged 22–24 had been married in metropolitan areas where the industrial structure provided fewer opportunities for female employment and also in areas where median female earnings were lower. These results persisted after controlling for the sex ratio of persons of marrying ages, the religious composition of the metropolitan area, and a variety of other population characteristics. This suggests that when employment opportunities for young women are abundant, marriage will tend to be delayed.

Changing ideology. There may have been a change in thinking regarding the need for marriage, or at least the urgent need to marry as early as possible. The women's movement conveys the message that women can be self-sufficient and happy without the dependent relationship of a traditional marriage. This view is clearly supported by, or supports, the improved capacity of women for economic independence. No studies have succeeded in separately identifying and measuring this change as an influence on age at first marriage.

Living together without marriage. The proportion of unmarried couples living together has increased in recent years. Not all, and perhaps not even most, of these couples involve young, never-married individuals. Whether the increase in this practice is sufficiently large to explain a large share of the rise in age at marriage has not yet been demonstrated. Official data may have underestimated the number of such couples in the past and thus may overestimate the recent trend. Underreporting could have occurred either by the complete omission of the individual or by misreporting the marital status, sex, or relationship of one of the members. Data may still underestimate the situation, but if the stigma attached to such relationships decreases, there may be less underreporting.

Age at Marriage and Fertility. Changing ages at marriage and the proportions of the population who marry directly affect fertility rates, both by cohort and by period. Approximately one-fifth of the decline in U.S. period fertility between 1971 and 1975 can be attributed to changes in marital status. Four-fifths is the result of declining marital fertility. Within a cohort, women who marry when very young are more likely to have second or third or more children than women marrying when they are older. For young women the spacing between births may also be closer. [*See* AGE AT MARRIAGE.]

Premarital Pregnancy. What proportion of all marriages in the United States involves a premarital pregnancy? This is an easier question to ask than to answer. Two methods have been developed by which to infer the occurrence of a premarital pregnancy. In a retrospective birth history, women or couples are asked for their histories of marriage and giving birth; a premarital pregnancy is inferred from the occurrence of a birth at some period less than eight or nine months after marriage. Record-matching studies produce data of better quality. In one study, the birth history and marriage history were collected independently of the record match. A significant fraction of women classified as premaritally pregnant from the record match adjusted the date of marriage as given in the interview to make the first birth seem to have occurred at least nine months after the marriage (Pratt, 1965).

The younger the bride, the higher the probability that her marriage involved a premarital pregnancy. Many marriages involving premaritally pregnant young women can be regarded as forced by the pregnancy. Some of these marriages might have occurred anyway, perhaps a few just as soon and others to the same spouse at a later age. Undoubtedly, some such marriages would never have occurred in the absence of pregnancy. While there is no evidence that either premaritally pregnant brides or their husbands have significantly lower socioeconomic origins than have other brides, premarital pregnancy does appear to be associated with higher levels of educational discrepancy between husband and wife.

The rate of premarital pregnancy depends on the sexual practice of teenagers and young adults prior to marriage, the rate and effectiveness of use of contraception, the availability of abortion, the degree to which unmarried women who become pregnant marry, rather than have an illegitimate child, and the pattern of age at first marriage. No clear assessment has been made of the separate or combined impacts of the "sexual revolution," the "contraceptive revolution," and the rise in the age at first marriage. The analytic difficulties are great. For example, a rise in marriage age may cause a higher rate of premarital pregnancy than previously, simply because of greater exposure to risk. On the other hand, a declining rate of premarital pregnancy resulting from increased availability of abortion may delay the marriage of many women.

According to census data on the length of the interval from first marriage to first birth, the rate of premarital pregnancy doubled from about 12 percent of all first marriages in the 1940s to 25 percent in the 1960s, and there was a small decline in the early 1970s. To infer that there has been little recent change may be misleading. In the recent period, marriages were declining in part because of an upward shift in the age at first marriages (and perhaps a decline in the cohort proportions ever marrying). If there were no change from year to year in the number of premarital pregnancies resulting in marriages, the *proportion* of the marriage cohort that was pregnant premaritally would increase.

Marital Disruption, Aggregate Trend. The trend in marital disruption has been sharply upward in the United States in recent years. During the 1920s, an average of about 175,000 divorces was granted in the United States per year, and in the 1930s about 200,000 annually. With the divorce boom following World War II, the number jumped to nearly 500,000 in 1945. The 1950s was a period of relative stability, with approximately 370,000 divorces per year. There were approximately 400,000 in 1960, more than 700,000 in 1970, and more than 1 million each year since 1975. The crude divorce rate, which indicates the number of divorces per 1,000 total population, increased from 2 in 1970 to 5 in 1975. Divorces in relation to the total number of existing marriages (the population exposed to the risk of divorce) increased from 8 to 20 percent.

A number of difficulties hamper an analytically useful assessment of the trend in marital disruption. The U.S. statistical system provides information on the number of divorces (including annulments) each year. Marital disruption, however, is probably better indexed by separations. Separations are not routinely counted by the statistical system, and indeed are much more difficult events to identify and to date precisely. In a period of increase in marital disruption, rates of separation may be increasing more rapidly than rates of divorce. A countervailing factor is the simplification of the legal divorce process, which should reduce the interval between separation and divorce and might even increase the probability of divorce following separation.

Marital disruption is more likely to occur early in marriage. This has been true for as long as records have been kept. Consequently, the number of separations or divorces occurring in a particular year and the rate at which separation and divorce occur is heavily dependent on the distribution of marriages by duration. In a period when many marriages are in their first five years, one would expect a higher rate of marital disruption. When there is a relatively low proportion of such marriages, the rate would tend to be lower. In a period when baby-boom cohorts grow up and marry, there is upward pressure on the divorce rate because an increasing share of the population is in the early years of marriage.

In the United States, the composition of the population has been changing in other ways that should affect the rate of marital disruption. The rapid increase in higher education and the recent rise in age at marriage are especially significant. Persons with high levels of education and older ages at marriage have a lower rate of marital disruption than those with less education. As the population composition shifts, other things being equal, the expected rate of divorce and marital disruption should decrease. The recent rise in divorce is all the more significant in light of this shift in composition.

Probably the most appropriate way of measuring the trend in marital disruption is to compare the histories of successive marriage cohorts. The varying size of cohorts does not confound comparisons. The period of exposure to risk is known, even when age at marriage is changing, and it is possible to focus on the length of the marriage.

The proportions of first-marriage cohorts divorcing within five years of marriage are plotted in Figure 1. It portrays a high level and rapid increase in rate of divorce and also shows that the increase was not so recent or abrupt as suggested in discussions based on numbers of divorces or divorce rates. The upward trend has been present at least since marriages of 1950–1954 and has been approximately linear since then. The abruptness of the increase in the trend in numbers of divorces arose from the coming of age of the large baby-boom cohorts.

FIGURE 1. *Proportions of first marriages ending in divorce within five years, United States first-marriage cohort*

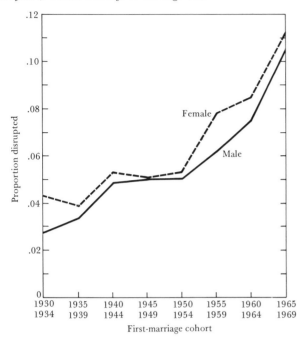

SOURCE: Sweet, 1977, p. 381; reprinted by permission.

Marital Disruption, Differentials. The stability of marriage depends on a series of background characteristics of the individual spouses, their achieved characteristics at the time of marriage (age, education, pregnancy), and the experience of marriage itself, particularly in the early years. A few of the well-documented differentials in marital dissolution are reviewed here.

Age. Persons who marry at young ages have higher risks of marital dissolution than those who marry at older ages. This is true for men and for women, blacks and whites, independently of all other factors studied. The gradient of risk declines very sharply from the mid-teens to the early twenties.

Education. More education is associated with less likelihood of marital dissolution. The education differential is, to a great extent, the result of the association between lower age at first marriage and lower educational levels.

In an analysis of 1950 census data, Paul C. Glick (1957) observed that the marriages of persons who began but did not complete a given level of education—persons with one to three years of high school or one to three years of college—tended to have higher than expected rates of dissolution.

Premarital pregnancy. Premarital pregnancy is associated with higher risks of marital dissolution. Premarital birth, however, can be distinguished from a premarital pregnancy that results in a birth after marriage. Women who had a premarital birth have a higher risk of marital dissolution than those who did not, but among women whose first birth was after marriage there is only a small difference according to whether the pregnancy was premarital (Bumpass and Sweet, 1972). Because women experiencing premarital pregnancy are also women who marry young, it is difficult to differentiate the effects of age at marriage from those of premarital pregnancy and premarital birth.

Religion. Religious differentials in marital instability have been documented for specialized samples (Landis, 1949; Burchinal and Chancellor, 1963; Christensen and Barber, 1967). These studies tend to find that Roman Catholics have a lower rate of marital disruption than do non-Catholics, which is consistent with what might be expected from Roman Catholic doctrine. Larry Bumpass and James A. Sweet (1972) report that somewhat higher than average rates of marital dissolution are found for Fundamentalists and Baptists, and that lower than average rates are found among Jews and Lutherans. In their national sample, rates for Roman Catholics are very similar to rates for Protestants other than the Fundamentalists and Baptist groups. This suggests that current differentials in marital dissolution among the major religious groups are not so large as might be expected from doctrinal and cultural differences.

Previous marriage. There is some evidence that the rate of dissolution of second and subsequent marriages may be higher than that for first marriages (Carter and Glick, 1976). This is a difficult problem to investigate: it is unclear how to achieve adequate statistical controls. For example, persons entering remarriages tend to be older than those entering first marriages. Their older age at marriage should make them more likely to achieve marital stability, yet they were younger on average at first marriage, and this might have an effect in reducing rates of stability. Bumpass and Sweet (1972) have shown that women whose first marriage is to a previously married husband have rates of marital dissolution more than twice as high as those when both spouses are marrying for the first time.

Stability of parental marriage. Women who at age 14 lived with both parents or with only one parent because of the death of the other parent have substantially lower rates of marital dissolution than those whose parental marriage was otherwise disrupted (Bumpass and Sweet, 1972). Much of the difference in marital stability by parental marital status can be attributed to differences in various social characteristics of the spouses at the time of marriage (Pope and Mueller, 1977).

Geographic location. Persons of farm origin have a slightly lower rate of marital disruption of first marriage than those of nonfarm origin. White women growing up in the Deep South have a lower rate of marital disruption than those growing up in other areas. Men and women, black and white, living in the Northeast have considerably lower-than-average rates of marital dissolution, while persons living in the western states tend to have higher rates.

These regional differences may be the product of variation in divorce law; the Northeast has had more restrictive laws than the West. Regions also vary in religious composition; the Northeast has a disproportionately high number of Roman Catholics.

Remarriage. The phenomenon of remarriage has received considerably less attention than that of marital dissolution. Marital dissolution is frequently regarded as some sort of social pathology, whereas remarriage following marital dissolution seems to be thought of as putting a person back in a normal state after a spell of social disease. Data on remarriage are less adequate than are data on marital dissolution. Census data permit one to identify persons with a remarriage, but information about when it occurred and their characteristics at that time are not available. Vital statistics data from the marriage-registration system specify the order of marriages, but they provide little information on characteristics or the timing of disruptions.

Most people who experience marital disruption, at least prior to an advanced age, eventually remarry. An application of a life table technique to national fertility data found that by the ninth year after the dissolution of marriage, 83 percent of women had remarried, 52 percent within three years after dissolution (Thornton, 1975). Other data show that of men (of all ages) whose first marriages had terminated by age 40, more than 75 percent had remarried. Men whose first marriage had been terminated fifteen or more years had a cumulative remarriage rate of nearly 90 percent (Sweet, 1973).

Men who experience marital dissolution are more likely to remarry than are women. The higher the income of a man, the higher the probability that he remarries. Blacks have a considerably lower rate of remarriage than do whites. Among women, those with children have lower rates of remarriage than those without children, and those with several children have lower rates than those with only one or two children.

The older the age at dissolution of the first marriage, the lower the rate of remarriage. Persons whose first marriages terminate by widowhood have lower crude rates of remarriage than those whose marriages terminate by separation or divorce. This lower rate is a result largely of the fact that widowhood occurs later than does separation and divorce. When age at dissolution is controlled, the differential is reversed. The rate of remarriage, however, is more closely related to age for women than it is for men.

For both men and women, there appears to be a higher rate of remarriage, other things being equal, for persons whose first marriage began at an early age than for persons whose first marriage began at a later age. This pattern may reflect the fact that persons who married young have known no other adult life than that in a married state and may find it more difficult to adapt to being single.

On theological grounds, Roman Catholics might be expected to have significantly lower rates of remarriage following marital dissolution than do non-Catholics. This differential has been found to be extremely small, although it is in the expected direction.

Rates of remarriage have been increasing through time. In the very near past, there may have been a decline in the rates of remarriage, but the evidence is not strong.

Marital Disruption and Fertility. The degree to which marital disruption produces a deficit in fertility depends on (1) the conditional probability that a woman experiencing marital disruption prior to the end of her reproductive years remarries, (2) the degree to which women have illegitimate births between divorcing and remarrying, and (3) the interval between marriages. Women experiencing marital disruption while young have a rather high propensity to remarry, and persons who remarry tend to do so rather promptly. To the degree that these probabilities and the timing of these events change through time or differ from one group to another, the fertility deficit tends to be larger or smaller.

The size of the fertility deficit associated with marital disruption depends on the degree to which women had completed their normal childbearing prior to separation from their spouse and also on the degree to which entering a second or later marriage initiates a new childbearing cycle. Couples entering a second marriage may desire to have a second family quite apart from the previous family of each spouse. A contrary pattern may prevail for other couples. Having experienced an unsuccessful first marriage, they may be wary that their second marriage may end and therefore avoid having children. A constraint on those seeking children in a second marriage is that lost exposure during the ages of high fecundity may be irretrievable at older ages as fecundity declines.

In an analysis of census data, Sweet (1974) has shown that a fertility deficit for women who were no longer in intact first marriages persisted after controlling all compositional factors for which data existed in the census. This differential was considerably smaller in 1970 than it was a decade earlier. Childlessness accounted for a substantial share of the association between marital disruption and lower fertility. Divorced women, whether remarried or not, had substantially lower fertility than those who remained in first marriages. However, women who separated and had not divorced appeared to have higher fertility than women whose first marriage remained intact. More recent cohorts of women whose marriages were disrupted had higher proportions of women with children and more children per mother. Remarriage is selective, although not highly so, of women with no children or few of them.

National fertility data were used to show that the cumulative fertility differential existing at the time of divorce is not found at the time of separation (Thornton, 1975). The fertility deficit at divorce results from lower fertility between separation and divorce. This is consistent with findings that attributed most of the fertility deficit of remarried women to "lost exposure", that is, the shorter number of years spent in a married state (Cohen and Sweet, 1974).

Families Headed by Women. In recent years, the proportion of families headed by women has risen. Among blacks, the rise has been especially marked. In the early 1960s, slightly over 20 percent of black families were headed by women, while by 1975 more than 33 percent were headed by women.

Many reports associated females as heads of families with marital disruption by divorce, separation, or desertion. A secondary source of females as heads was thought to be the bearing of illegitimate children by unmarried women. The process of becoming a female head of family is, however, far more complex, involving a whole chain of demographic events. One path to the position is a single woman bearing an illegitimate child and living separately from other family members. Another path begins with a woman marrying and bearing at least one child. Her marriage must terminate while at least one of her children is living in the household, and the child must continue to live with the mother. The mother must establish her own household rather than move in with relatives or someone else, and the mother must not remarry.

There are still other paths to becoming a female head of family. Most instances of women becoming widowed do not produce a family headed by a woman because no dependent children are present in the household. The widow without young children may establish a one-person household, which is by definition not a family. She may move into the household of an adult child or other relative and might be regarded as the "head" in a census enumeration. She may establish a household with another elderly person.

Heather L. Ross and Isabel V. Sawhill (1975) allocate the increase in number of families headed by females with children to the factors delineated in Table 2.

Summary. Much progress has been made in understanding the demography of the family. As recently as 1970, the work in the area consisted primarily of summary reports of tabulations from the decennial census and reports of simple analyses of data from unrepresentative local samples. In the subsequent decade, ten major trends in research emerged and appear to be continuing.

1. Focus has shifted from description of differences in the prevalence of various family statuses toward a greater concern for the underlying processes.

2. The academic and intellectual orientation of persons doing this work has shifted from persons trained largely as demographers or as sociologists to persons trained in both demography and sociology. In addition, economists are increasingly concerned with household and family processes.

3. A variety of policy issues pertaining to the goals and unintended consequences of alternative welfare and income-maintenance programs have focused increased attention on the demography of the family.

4. The data available for analysis of family processes have expanded considerably. The expanded content of decennial census data and the accumulation of information from the Current Population Survey and its special marital history supplements (sample surveys conducted by the U.S. Bureau of the Census) have led to improved research. Other improvements in data include the availability for public use of microdata from the decennial censuses and a number of longitudinal studies.

5. The introduction of the human life cycle as an organizing principle of research has led to important work on relationships among the phenomena in different areas of life.

6. Important progress has been made in separating complex processes, such as that of becoming a female head of family, into their component parts. These conceptual clarifications have led to further research and a better understanding of family processes.

7. In some areas, however, the limits of available data have virtually been reached. Specially conducted large-scale sample survey efforts will be necessary if a more

TABLE 2. *Components of increase in the number of families headed by females between 1960 and 1970*

Components of increase	White	Nonwhite
Population growth	25%	16%
Increased marital disruption	23	15
Increased illegitimacy	9	21
Increased likelihood that a divorcing mother will have dependent children	20	24
Increased propensity to head household	10	8
Interaction—those factors not uniquely allocable	13	17
Total	100	100

SOURCE: Ross and Sawhill, 1975; reprinted by permission.

thorough knowledge is to be gained of causes of marital disruption, for example, or their relationships with fertility.

8. Significant improvements have been made in the formal demography of marriage. However, because demographers usually consider only one sex at a time, the creation of formal demographic models of marriage systems continues to be very difficult.

9. Considerable effort has been directed toward understanding trends and differences among societies. Nevertheless, scholars have only the very haziest understanding of the decline and subsequent rise in age at first marriage in the Western world after World War II. Similarly the pattern of rapidly rising marital disruption rates across cohorts is only very poorly understood. To improve understanding of these social trends, further work is needed in the comparative study of family patterns and trends among developed societies in the West.

10. Much emphasis has been placed on the consequences of various family transitions and experiences on the position of women in American society. This is an area where the substantive issues addressed approach the limits of available data. Some further progress may be made with existing types of data in dealing with these questions. More definitive answers, however, will await the availability of data collected specifically for this purpose. In part, the problem rests on the lack of large and long-continued longitudinal studies or of large-sample retrospective studies collecting detailed life histories covering a number of different areas of life.

James A. Sweet

For a detailed discussion of family law in the United States, see FAMILY LAW. *See also* FERTILITY TRENDS; HOUSEHOLD AND FAMILY DEMOGRAPHY.

BIBLIOGRAPHY

Bumpass, Larry L., and James A. Sweet. "Differentials in Marital Instability, 1970." *American Sociological Review* 37(6):754–766, December 1972.

Burchinall, Lee G., and Loren E. Chancellor. "Survival Rates among Religiously Homogamous and Interreligious Marriages." *Social Forces* 41(4):353–362, May 1963.

Carter, Hugh, and Paul C. Glick. *Marriage and Divorce: A Social and Economic Study.* Rev. ed. Cambridge, Mass.: Harvard University Press, 1976.

Christensen, Harold T., and Kenneth E. Barber. "Interfaith versus Intrafaith Marriage in Indiana." *Journal of Marriage and the Family* 29(3):461–469, August 1967.

Coale, Ansley J. "Age Patterns of Marriage." *Population Studies* 25(2):193–214, July 1971.

Cohen, Sarah Betsy, and James A. Sweet. "The Impact of Marital Disruption and Remarriage on Fertility." *Journal of Marriage and the Family* 36(1):87–96, February 1974.

Davis, Kingsley. "The American Family in Relation to Demographic Change." In *Demographic and Social Aspects of Population Growth,* edited by Charles F. Westoff and Robert Parke, Jr., pp. 239–265. Washington, D.C.: U.S. Government Printing Office, 1972.

Duncan, G. J., and J. N. Morgan (editors). *Five Thousand American Families: Patterns of Economic Progress.* 4 vols. Ann Arbor: Institute for Social Research, University of Michigan, 1976.

Easterlin, Richard A. "Relative Economic Status and the American Fertility Swing." In *Family Economic Behavior: Problems and Prospects,* edited by Eleanor B. Sheldon, pp. 170–223. Philadelphia: Lippincott, 1973.

Glick, Paul C. *American Families.* New York: Wiley, 1957.

Landis, Judson T. "Marriages of Mixed and Non-mixed Religious Faith." *American Sociological Review* 14(3):401–407, June 1949.

Levine, Daniel B., and Charles B. Nam. "The Current Population Survey: Methods, Content, and Sociological Uses." *American Sociological Review* 27(4):585–590, August 1962.

Pope, Hallowell, and Charles W. Mueller. "The Intergenerational Transmission of Marital Instability: Comparisons by Race and Sex." *Journal of Social Issues* 32(1):49–66, Winter 1976.

Pratt, W. F. "A Study of Marriages Involving Premarital Pregnancies." Doctoral dissertation, University of Michigan, Ann Arbor, 1965.

Preston, Samuel H., and Alan T. Richards. "The Influence of Women's Work Opportunities on Marriage Rates." *Demography* 12(2):209–222, May 1975.

Ross, Heather L., and Isabel V. Sawhill. *Time of Transition: The Growth of Families Headed by Women.* Washington, D.C.: Urban Institute, 1975.

Sweet, James A. "Differentials in Remarriage Probabilities." Working Paper No. 29. Madison: Center for Demographic Ecology, University of Wisconsin, 1973.

———. "Marital Disruption and Fertility: Some Evidence from U.S. Census Data." Working Paper No. 13. Madison: Center for Demographic Ecology, University of Wisconsin, 1974.

———. "Demography and the Family." *Annual Review of Sociology,* vol. 3, pp. 363–405, 1977.

Thornton, A. D. "Marital Instability and Fertility." Doctoral dissertation, University of Michigan, Ann Arbor, 1975.

United States, Bureau of the Census. *Marital Status and Living Arrangements, March 1975.* Current Population Reports, series P-20, no. 287. Washington, D.C.: U.S. Government Printing Office, 1976.

Westoff, Charles F., and Robert Parke, Jr. (editors). *Demographic and Social Aspects of Population Growth,* U.S. Commission on Population Growth and the American Future, Research Reports, vol. 1. Washington, D.C.: U.S. Government Printing Office, 1972.

MARXIST THEORY

See ETHICS; POPULATION THEORY.

MATHEMATICAL DEMOGRAPHY

The origins and problems of mathematical demography are close to those of demography itself; mathematical questions are implicit in the early texts. John Graunt (1662) did not merely present the numbers of christenings and burials; he asked questions, some of which we can see in retrospect imply mathematical relations. He drew up a (partly hypothetical) life table, and suggested calculations of survivorship. Johan DeWit (1671) and other seventeenth-century actuaries applied survivorship rates to calculate the value of annuities. The notion of a stationary population was also understood. Leonard Euler's stable population theory was a major generalization; its ingredients were the life table and an arbitrary rate of increase (Euler, 1760). The work of these men was incipient mathematical demography, and the seventeenth and eighteenth centuries were the protoperiod, or eoperiod, of the field.

The middle or classical period was foreshadowed by Wilhelm Lexis (1875) and other students in the latter half of the nineteenth century, and it flowered in the work of Alfred J. Lotka (1939). Lotka devised and solved the renewal equation, in which the number of births in one generation is related to the number in the preceding generation, a relation from which the rate of increase is calculable rather than arbitrary. The renewal equation applies to nonstable populations as well as to stable populations, and this one equation is rich enough not only to have occupied most of Lotka's forty-year career but to find applications ranging from Geiger counters to replacement of industrial equipment in fields as varied as atomic physics and evolutionary genetics.

Lotka raised many of the questions that make up the core of our subject and provided the tools for answering them. He studied kinship and orphanhood (1931b), extinction of families (1931a), effect of age distribution on population increase in the United States (1936), the logistic curve (1939), and competition among animal species (1932).

The contemporary period has reached beyond Lotka in several directions. It has gone further with cohorts as well as with time periods; it has tackled the two-sex problem (although that seems to be beyond any simple solution); and it has developed microdemography, applied especially to reproduction and contraception, using stochastic processes and simulation.

Mathematical demography has not been pure of social preoccupations; each period has raised its own questions, and its attempt to answer them, not always successful in the immediate context, has left a residue of contributions to method and theory. The life table was elaborated for annuities sales by governments of the rising commercial states of England and Holland, and later provided the actuarial basis of the insurance business. [See ACTUARIAL METHODS; LIFE TABLES.] Age became important in calculations of future population in the late nineteenth century when the fall of the birth rate brought destabilization and the official use of overall ratios gave gross overestimates for long-term forecasts. The sudden increase of marriages and births in the 1940s forced attention to cohorts as Pascal K. Whelpton (1946) exhibited the seeming paradox that if the 1940 cross-section birth pattern continued, American women would on the average bear more than one first child.

Boundaries. No sharp boundary can be drawn around mathematical demography. The use of mathematical symbols and formulas is hardly decisive; using such symbols is merely a way of saying more simply and unambiguously what can be said in words. Richard A. Easterlin, for example, uses words to describe how a small cohort tends to have relatively high incomes at the ages of marriage and childbearing and how it is thus encouraged to have more children than its parents, who may have been a large cohort (Easterlin, 1966). This idea is directly translatable into a mathematical equation, whose solution shows cycles of two generations in length. Ansley J. Coale and Paul Demeny describe methods for filling gaps in data using prose (United Nations, 1967); they and others have also put the same material in symbols. The journal *Theoretical Population Biology* may be identified as mathematical, but Samuel Karlin, its founder, insists that theory can well be prose rather than symbols, and he has searched for contributions containing new theory in words.

Mathematical demography leans heavily on the kind of numerical analysis that is used in engineering, physics, actuarial science, and genetics. Beginning with the numerical solution to Lotka's integral equation, this side goes on through interpolation and graduation of all kinds. The overlap with statistics is especially great. Demographic data are often obtained by probability samples, and so the entire theory for estimation from samples, including the estimation of sampling errors, is enmeshed. [See SAMPLING METHODS.] Demographers have become accustomed to the fact that a sample can provide more accuracy than a so-called complete survey or census. The earlier total dependence, starting with Graunt, on data collected for some other purpose than demographic analysis, has now been reduced through use of special-purpose sample surveys that provide data for much more flexible analysis.

New means of statistical inference are now available and are likely to find use in demography. These include log-linear models for finding what main effects and what interactions are significant in cross-tabulations (Bishop, Feinberg, and Holland, 1975). The analysis is of the logarithms of the frequencies in a cross-tabulation (or of the logarithms plus 1/2 to handle zeros) and is carried out in a way similar to analysis of variance.

Estimates of population using more than one stage or method of enumeration, called "capture-recapture" by those dealing with animal censuses, have been proposed for human populations. However, their usefulness has been questioned by William Brass (1971a), who shows that in practice they pick up a disappointingly small part of the omissions for human populations.

Some demographic analyses of mortality (e.g., "Does smoking cause lung cancer?") are similar to methods of epidemiology, and epidemiologists have also worked on fecundability. Scholars who deal with the complex of problems that is the subject of this review are attached to a corresponding variety of disciplines. Aside from those who are primarily demographers, major work at the heart of the field is done by economists, biostatisticians, statisticians, biologists, and sociologists. It is no strain to think of sociologist Harrison C. White's vacancy chains (1970) as an aspect of population. Instead of following the transitions of an individual through states, White considers a state of vacancy and notes the succession of individuals who pass through it. His work has been applied to jobs, houses, and even taxicabs.

Methods and Substance. Much of mathematical demography is concerned with methods. In life tables we have a series of improvements from Edmund Halley (1693) over four centuries. Measuring segregation is by no means straightforward; definitions of social status, and measurement of movement between statuses, have generated an extensive literature. On how to estimate fecundability we have improvements from Raymond Pearl (1925) onward. For filling the gaps when registrations are incomplete or lacking altogether, we have the work of Jean Bourgeois-Pichat (1958); Coale's generalization of stable population theory to allow for falling mortality (a condition designated quasi stability); and ways of estimating infant mortality rates through reports by mothers on their own children. [See INDIRECT ESTIMATION OF FERTILITY AND MORTALITY.] Some of this activity, including the revival of Euler's stable population theory, was a response to rapid population growth in developing countries.

For those in a hurry to find usable answers, methodology seems secondary to substantive work. Yet sound conclusions depend on good methods, and method is rarely entirely separable from substance, since serious papers in the literature contribute to both. Lotka (1936) used his intrinsic rate to find the real tendency of the rate of increase that crude rates were hiding in the United States of the 1930s. When John C. Barrett and John Marshall (1969) set out to find the probability of conceiving on different days of the month (crucial for some methods of birth control) they not only had to work out practical procedures, using the known relation with body temperature to judge when ovulation had occurred, but they had to devise and apply a likelihood model for estimation of the probabilities.

Curve fitting and model tables. For more than a century, students of mortality have been trying to find a curve that would describe the age-incidence of death. It is no disparagement of these efforts to say that none has been completely satisfactory. Efforts have been so persistent because twenty age-specific rates, if five-year intervals are used, are not an economical mode of description. The two, three, or four parameters of a mathematical curve would be far more compact as description, and would provide more consistency in prediction. Clearly, we should have only as many parameters as there are separate "facts" in the age structure of mortality.

Attempts to find how many separate facts or dimensions exist have been made using factor analysis, and it seems that most real death schedules can be described by a very few factors. However, since some centuries of effort have found no family of mathematical curves that fits the whole range of age-specific rates from age 0 to 90, workers have turned to model or reference tables. The first set of these to come into common use was prepared by V. G. Valaoras for the United Nations in 1955 and was a single series indexed on expectation of life. The model life tables of Coale and Demeny (1966) include four families, each again indexed on expectation of life. Published together with a series of detailed stable populations, these have found wide application, especially in conjunction with stable population theory to estimate rates of birth, death, and natural increase for populations about which one has as little information as a single census age distribution.

The success of model mortality tables has encouraged the calculation of model nuptiality tables and model fertility tables. [See NUPTIALITY INDEXES.] Age at marriage, treated by Coale and D. R. McNeil (1972), supposes a normally distributed entry into marriageability, together with three exponentially distributed delays (to meeting future spouse, to engagement, and to marriage), which not only appeals to common sense as a convincing behavioral model but also turns out to fit closely the observed age distribution of marriage. Marital age-specific fertility has been tabulated by Coale (1971). More generally, fertility data are given by age in six or seven categories, from under 15, 15–19, 20–24, and so on (all with age measured at last birthday) to age 50 and over. A set based on a three-parameter model including marriage and marital fertility has been published by Coale and T. James Trussell (1974); earlier fittings were proposed by various scholars.

Curve fitting to population time series engaged the ingenuity of many scholars over a century or more. Some early work assumed fixed rates of increase, which meant a geometric trajectory, but Pierre-François Verhulst in 1838 saw that positing a ceiling is a better reading of Malthus and accords with common sense. He made the rate of increase proportional to the difference between the population already attained and the ceiling, and so found the logistic, long after made famous by Pearl and Lowell J. Reed (1920).

Early workers paid little attention to efficient fitting of whatever curves they might use. Pearl and Reed selected three "typical" points on a chart for their logistic, which provide three simple equations for the constants. Selected points have also been used for fitting the Makeham double exponential curve to life table functions. The fitting of fertility curves has usually been by moments, also not very efficient. With the advent of computers, much better methods became feasible.

Transitions. Central to what may be called the finite mathematics of population is the notion of states among which transitions take place at specified rates or probabilities. A general matrix of such transitions may describe migration; the states are n places of residence, and, since the person can move from any one to any other, or stay, all n^2 cells of the transition matrix can have non-zero values. If the states are ages, and if the person can move only to the next age group or die, we have a discrete form of the pure death table, that is, of the life table. If the states are ages and if a "move" to age zero corresponds to the person having a child, then we have a formal linear model of population projection. If the states are types of schools and grades, then there are other restrictions on what transitions are possible, and the result is a model of the educational system. The several occupations can be similarly recognized, perhaps by age, to provide a model for the labor force. Mobility, both geographic and social, has been extensively treated by multiple regression methods and by successively more complex probabilistic methods as a series of transitions between occupations as states. The states also have been defined as sickness and death, with or without recognition of the several ailments and causes of death.

The advantage of expressing the transitions in the form of a matrix, and premultiplying an initial vector by the matrix, rather than doing the equivalent arithmetic according to common sense, is that some very powerful theorems apply without further proof. Thus, if every state is reachable from every other (which makes the matrix irreducible) and if is reachable in the same number of moves (in which case the matrix is primitive as well), then successive application of the matrix will ultimately lead to a fixed ratio of numbers in the several states. That is, the process is ergodic; it forgets its past.

Lotka (1922) suggested the equivalent result for a continuous set of states.

Forecasting. Demographers, like meteorologists but unlike botanists or physicists, are asked to predict the future. Physicists predict within the relatively closed space of experiments thoroughly protected against outside contingencies. Economists predict in the real world but over periods of a year or two at most. Demographers are expected to predict over long periods of time, and they are unprotected against the ingression of the natural world.

Since population changes are caused by and in turn cause social and economic changes, it would seem easier to predict all of these together, but that is rarely done, and most estimates of future population are made from demographic elements alone. To put it more accurately, the estimates incorporate the demographer's intuition of extrademographic trends in the assumptions he selects for his projections. [*See* PROJECTIONS.]

Such estimates have the character of extrapolation, and until the 1930s, most discussion of the future was in terms of curves tracing the total population size, of which the logistic referred to above was the most popular. Much improvement came by separate estimates of mortality, fertility, and migration. Survivors and births are calculated for each of the cohorts alive at the beginning of each period. Although extrapolation is unavoidable, it seems better to carry it out on the separate components of population change than on the total population. Formally, extrapolation consists in finding a function of the quantity being extrapolated whose constancy in the past encourages a belief in constancy in the future. If death rates are extrapolated separately for various ages, they will progressively diverge with time, and the curve of mortality with age will lose all resemblance to what we know it to be. Since well-fitting mathematical functions with two or three parameters are not to be had, Brass (1971b, 1974) has devised a relational method for expressing change over time or between spaces. Starting with a standard life table, he expresses subsequent tables as functions of this, using two parameters for each subsequent table. The trend in these parameters is noted and their future values estimated; from these future values it is easy to construct the corresponding life tables.

Essentially the same procedure with a Gompertz (double exponential) transformation can be used for births and for marriages. Procedures of time series analysis of very general character have been developed by George E. P. Box and Gwilym M. Jenkins (1976). Ronald Demos Lee (1974) has analyzed problems of forecasting and possible improvements offered by time series analysis.

Deterministic and stochastic models. Demography started with the life table, a series of probabilities, yet in its demographic application the life table is deterministic; in a population of 10 million at a particular age in which the chance of dying is 0.01, exactly 100,000 deaths are calculated to occur. In the real world, on the other hand, random variation is universal, and all processes are stochastic processes. Demographers usually neglect stochastic theory when they deal with large populations, where random variation is relatively small. Moreover, forced to use imperfect data, they must devote their energies to coping with errors of enumeration and other biases. The problems with which they are concerned often involve expected values only, and in a linear random process the expected value is provided by a deterministic model. Stochastic models are needed where the population is small, or the variance and other moments are sought. They are also needed to provide expected values where the process is nonlinear, but in that case neither deterministic nor stochastic equations are solvable.

If variances and other moments of interest, and individual births and deaths, can be assumed to occur independently at random, then the standard cohort-survival method of projection, expressed in the form known as the "Leslie matrix," can be generalized beyond mean values. Unfortunately for application, this method underestimates variance wherever individual events are positively related. The number of deaths year by year attributed to automobile accidents, for example, is affected by changing underlying causes, as well as by multiple deaths caused by one accident. Epidemics do not strike individuals independently. The structure of interdependencies in births as well as deaths is a complex matter, but one assertion can be made with confidence: the dependencies on the whole tend to be positive, and so the variance is greater than that calculated on the assumption of independence.

The two main circumstances in which stochastic models are needed are where the population is small and where variance and other moments directly influence the phenomenon under investigation. Both apply in microdemography. For example, the fraction of men for whom cross-cousin marriage is possible depends on random variation in number of sons and daughters in families, and relatively little on the expected number of children.

In other instances, large populations are subjected to complex rules, and the mathematics even for expected values becomes intractable. Because solving for expected values requires resort to simulation, a large number of simulation programs are now in use. Procedures have been developed for matching the probabilities of a microsimulation model to a variety of cross-sectional and longitudinal surveys.

Microdemography. The major contributions so far to the new field of microdemography deal with questions of conception and birth (Sheps and Menken, 1973). By

1874, a neat equation had been found for the probability of extinction of a male line in which the probability of one son, two sons, and so on is the same and known in all generations (Galton and Watson, 1874). Various stopping rules used by parents can determine the distribution of family sizes. For example, if all parents have the same chance of producing a boy on a given birth, then their decision to stop at the appearance of the first boy, say, can have no effect on the sex ratio of births. But if some are more likely than others to produce a boy, then the rule that consists in stopping with the first boy will increase the proportion of *girls* among the births. [*See* SEX SELECTION.]

Comparison. Demographic study of the past depends heavily on comparisons, but to make these comparisons properly is not always simple. To find, for example, whether baseball players are healthier than residents of old people's homes requires standardization for age. This part of demography can be assimilated to the index number problem of economics (Kitagawa, 1964). Some, at least, of the use of life tables is to compare mortality among populations, and this can give decidedly different results from standardization, and so can Lotka's intrinsic death rate.

Explanation. The Cartesian method is to break down a phenomenon under study into simple constituent elements and then from these elements to reconstruct the phenomenon. Such a method has a frequent use in demography. Given the age distribution of a census, one compares it with the stable model based on the current life table and rate of increase. The departure of the observed age distribution from the model age distribution constructed on the basis of these last is attributed to recent trends in deaths and the rate of increase; still unexplained features are traced to wars, baby booms, and other known historical irregularities in mortality, fertility, or migration.

Features of the current foreign-born population can similarly be explained by the migration history of the country, its educational distribution by the history of school attendance, and its fraction of orphans by past mortality. Predicting the future may be too severe a test of demographic methods and theories, and predicting (i.e., explaining) a just-past census distribution may be a sufficient challenge.

Instead of explaining the census in terms of preceding births, Coale and Melvin Zelnik (1963) used the relations to ascertain what the births were. On the principle that a cohort is more completely enumerated at some of the censuses through which it passes than it is at others, they caught each cohort in the white population of the United States at the census at which it seemed to be most completely enumerated, and from its count they then estimated the births from which it originated, using a procedure that made allowance for changing rates of birth. Other kinds of redundancy in demographic data may be similarly exploited.

Questions of causation, for example, that births have a larger effect on age distribution than do deaths, that promotion in an organization is more influenced by its rate of increase than by mortality, and how much the birth rate is reduced by deferment of marriage, are also answerable in terms of demographic models, or alternatively, by the use of cross-sectional or longitudinal regression (Keyfitz, 1975).

Populations Other Than Human. In accord with the Greek root of the word, demography describes human populations. But it is self-evident that mammalian populations, subject as they are to the same elementary processes of birth, death, and migrations as humans, can be analyzed by the same mathematics. For many purposes the study of biological populations in general illuminates our understanding of human populations.

Populations of capital goods share some features with populations of people, and can be analyzed by the same means. Required reserve stocks of B-21 bomber engines in the Pacific area of World War II were calculated by a life table to find, for example, what fraction of a cohort of engines would break down after one month's service, two months' service, and so on. Similarly, each batch of light bulbs, transistors, or automobiles has its own life table.

Reliability engineering deals with the breakdowns of equipment consisting of many parts, where failure of any one part may cause the whole to fail. But the demographic study of mortality by cause (Spiegelman, 1968; Preston, Keyfitz, and Schoen, 1972) deals also with this situation, since people die through failure of heart, lungs, kidneys, or other vital parts. The hypothesis of independence of survival of the parts is less satisfactory for a biological organism than for a machine. The multiple-decrement life table, to which much of reliability engineering is devoted, is strictly more applicable in that field than in demography, where it originated.

A group of women fitted with intrauterine devices (IUD's) at a particular time are subject to the decrement of dropping the contraceptive, as well as to accidental pregnancy, and different designs of IUD's are subject to different life tables. At another level, life tables can be applied to populations of institutions (banks, factories, stores, or social clubs) once the probability of bankruptcy or other form of demise of these is known by duration.

Multiple Populations. Interaction of species has been developed with sophisticated mathematics. Alfred Sauvy (1952–1954) without presenting the mathematics shows how a predator and a prey species will generate population waves. It is in the interest of the predator species for the prey to have some refuge where it is not subject to capture, since if the predator can capture its members too

easily, he will cause it to become extinct, and its extinction will be followed by his own. One would think that a third species, also a prey to the same predator, would make things easier for the original prey, but this is not so; a second prey species increases the chance that the first will become extinct.

Equations similar to those applicable to species apply to the sexes of a human population. These equations suppose dominance of one sex, for example that all births are dependent on the number of females. Marriage is dealt with by the same methods.

Acceptance of dominance avoids the essential difficulty of the two-sex problem, on which there is a large literature. Any linear model that takes account of both parents runs into difficulties when the sex ratio departs substantially from unity; if births depend on the mean number of men and women, then if one sex drops to zero the births are reduced only by half where they should drop to zero. Yet nonlinear models seem impossible to handle mathematically. Aside from technical difficulties, the number of offspring depends on behavior that is not embraced by any mathematics using presently available data. Number of offspring of any species, including the human species, usually depends more on the number of females than on the number of males, but how much more is determined by how active the males are.

Spatial Aspects. The spatial aspects of population include parts of location theory, central place theory, diffusion, urbanization, and much that falls under ecology and geography. A summary from the viewpoint of a demographer was provided by Otis Dudley Duncan (1957), and subsequently by Jean-Noël Biraben and Françoise Duhoureau (1974). Related subtopics of interest are city size and migration, centers of population and of institutions, and geographic potential. William Alonso (1964) has provided an account of the economics of location, summarizing the long tradition of work in that field.

Nathan Keyfitz

BIBLIOGRAPHY

The literature of mathematical demography is scattered through biological, statistical, biostatistical, economic, sociological, mathematical, and demographic journals. The main journals concerned with population are *Population Studies, Demography, Theoretical Population Biology,* the French *Population* and the Italian *Genus.* Related articles can be found in the *Journal of the American Statistical Association, Biometrics, Biometrika, Social Biology,* and the *Quarterly Journal of Biology.* A number of textbooks have summarized the existing materials. In increasing order of detail, and at different mathematical levels, are Pressat (1961), Spiegelman (1968), Keyfitz (1977), and Shryock, Siegel, and others (1971). Smith and Keyfitz (1977) is a collection of the classic papers of mathematical demography.

Alonso, William. *Location and Land Use: Toward a General Theory of Land Rent.* Cambridge, Mass.: Harvard University Press, 1964.

Barrett, John C., and John Marshall. "The Risk of Conception on Different Days of the Menstrual Cycle." *Population Studies* 23(3):445–461, November 1969.

Biraben, Jean-Noël, and Françoise Duhoureau. "La mesure de la population dans l'espace." *Population* 29(1):113–137, 1974.

Bishop, Yvonne, M. M., Stephen E. Feinberg, and Paul W. Holland. *Discrete Multivariate Analysis: Theory and Practice.* Cambridge, Mass.: MIT Press, 1975.

Bourgeois-Pichat, Jean. "Utilisation de la notion de population stable pour mesurer la mortalité et la fecondité des populations des pays sous-developpés." *Bulletin de l'Institut International de Statistique* 36(2):94–121, 1958.

Box, George E. P., and Gwilym M. Jenkins. *Time Series Analysis: Forecasting and Control.* Rev. ed. San Francisco: Holden-Day, 1976.

Brass, William. "A Critique of Methods for Estimating Population Growth in Countries with Limited Data." *Bulletin of the International Statistical Institute,* 44(bk.l):397–412, 1971. (Brass, 1971*a*)

———. "On the Scale of Mortality." In *Biological Aspects of Demography,* edited by William Brass, pp. 69–110. London: Taylor & Francis, 1971. (Brass, 1971*b*)

———. "Perspectives in Population Prediction: Illustrated by the Statistics of England and Wales." *Journal of the Royal Statistical Society,* series A, 137(pt. 4):532–570, 1974. Discussion follows on pages 571–583.

Coale, Ansley J. "Estimates of Various Demographic Measures through the Quasi-stable Age Distribution." In *Emerging Techniques in Population Research,* pp. 175–193. New York: Milbank Memorial Fund, 1963.

———. "Age Patterns of Marriage." *Population Studies* 25(2):193–214, July 1971.

———. *The Growth and Structure of Human Populations: A Mathematical Investigation.* Princeton, N.J.: Princeton University Press, 1972.

Coale, Ansley J., and Paul Demeny. *Regional Model Life Tables and Stable Populations.* Princeton, N.J.: Princeton University Press, 1966.

Coale, Ansley J., and D. R. McNeil. "Distribution by Age of the Frequency of First Marriage in a Female Cohort." *Journal of the American Statistical Association* 67(340):743–749, December 1972.

Coale, Ansley J., and T. James Trussell. "Model Fertility Schedules: Variations in the Age Structure of Childbearing in Human Populations." *Population Index* 40(2):185–258, April 1974.

Coale, Ansley J., and Melvin Zelnik. *New Estimates of Fertility and Population in the United States: A Study of Annual White Births from 1855 to 1960 and of Completeness of Enumeration in the Censuses from 1880 to 1960.* Princeton, N.J.: Princeton University Press, 1963.

DeWit, Johan. *Waardye van Lyf-renten naer Proportie van Losrenten.* The Hague, 1671.

Duncan, Otis Dudley. "The Measurement of Population Distribution." *Population Studies* 11(1):27–45, July 1957.

Easterlin, Richard A. "On the Relation of Economic Factors to Recent and Projected Fertility Changes." *Demography* 3(1):131–153, 1966.

Euler, Leonard "A General Investigation into the Mortality and Multiplication of the Human Species" (1760). Translated by Nathan Keyfitz and Beatrice Keyfitz. *Theoretical Population Biology* 1(2):307–314, August 1970.

Galton, Francis, and H. W. Watson. "On the Probability of Extinction of Families." *Journal of the Anthropological Institute,* 6:138–144, 1874.

Goodman, Leo A. "On the Age-Sex Composition of the Population That Would Result from Given Fertility and Mortality Conditions." *Demography* 4(2):423–441, 1967.

Graunt, John. *Natural and Political Observations Mentioned in a Following Index, and Made upon the Bills of Mortality: With Reference to the Government, Religion, Trade, Growth, Ayre, Diseases, and Several Changes of the Said City [London]* (1662). Reprint. New York: Arno Press, 1975.

Halley, Edmund. "An Estimate of the Degrees of the Mortality of Mankind: Drawn from Curious Tables of the Births and Funerals at the City of Breslaw; With an Attempt to Ascertain the Price of Annuities on Lives." *Philosophical Transactions of the Royal Society of London* 17(196):596–610, 1693.

———. "Some Further Considerations on the Breslaw Bills of Mortality." *Philosophical Transactions of the Royal Society of London* 17(198):654–656, 1693.

Keyfitz, Nathan. "How Do We Know the Facts of Demography?" *Population and Development Review* 1(2):267–288, 1975.

———. *Applied Mathematical Demography.* New York: Wiley, 1977.

———. *Introduction to the Mathematics of Population, with Revisions.* Reading, Mass.: Addison-Wesley, 1977.

Kitagawa, Evelyn M. "Standardizing Comparisons in Population Research." *Demography* 1(1):296–315, 1964.

Lee, Ronald Demos. "Forecasting Births in Post-transition Populations: Stochastic Renewal with Serially Correlated Fertility." *Journal of the American Statistical Association* 69(347):607–617, September 1974.

Leslie, P. H. "On the Use of Matrices in Certain Population Mathematics." *Biometrika* 33(3):183–212, 1945.

———. "On the Distribution in Time of the Births in Successive Generations." *Journal of the Royal Statistical Society* 111(1):44–53, 1948.

———. "Some Further Notes on the Use of Matrices in Population Mathematics." *Biometrika* 35:213–245, 1948.

Lexis, Wilhelm. *Einleitung in die Theorie der Bevölkerungsstatistik.* Strassburg: Trübner, 1875.

Lotka, Alfred J. "The Stability of the Normal Age Distribution." *Proceedings of the National Academy of Sciences* 8:339–345, 1922.

———. "The Extinction of Families." *Journal of the Washington Academy of Sciences* 21:377–453, 1931. (Lotka, 1931*a*)

———. "Orphanhood in Relation to Demographic Factors: A Study in Population Analysis." *Metron* 9(2):37–109, August 1931. (Lotka, 1931*b*)

———. "The Growth of Mixed Populations: Two Species Competing for a Common Food Supply." *Journal of the Washington Academy of Sciences* 21:461–469, 1932.

————. "The Geographic Distribution of Intrinsic Natural Increase in the United States, and an Examination of the Relation between Several Measures of Net Reproductivity." *Journal of the American Statistical Association* 31(194):273–294, 1936.

————. *Théorie analytique des associations biologiques.* Part 2: *Analyse démographique avec application particulière à l'espece humaine.* Actualités Scientifiques et Industrielles, no. 780. Paris: Hermann, 1939.

Pearl, Raymond. *The Biology of Population Growth* (1925). Reprint. New York: Arno Press, 1976.

Pearl, Raymond, and Lowell J. Reed. "On the Rate of Growth of the Population of the United States since 1790 and Its Mathematical Representation." *Proceedings of the National Academy of Science* 6(6):275–288, 15 June 1920.

Pollard, J. H. *Mathematical Models for the Growth of Human Population.* New York and London: Cambridge University Press, 1973.

Potter, Robert G. "Births Averted by Contraception: An Approach through Renewal Theory." *Theoretical Population Biology* 1(3):251–272, November 1970.

Pressat, Roland. *L'analyse démographique: Méthodes, résultats, applications.* Paris: Presses Universitaires de France, 1961.

Preston, Samuel H. "Effect of Mortality Change on Stable Population Parameters." *Demography* 11(1):119–130, February 1974.

Preston, Samuel H., Nathan Keyfitz, and Robert Schoen. *Causes of Death: Life Tables for National Populations.* New York: Seminar Press, 1972.

Rogers, Andrei. *Introduction to Multiregional Mathematical Demography.* New York: Wiley, 1975.

Ryder, Norman B., and Charles F. Westoff. *Reproduction in the United States, 1965.* Princeton, N.J.: Princeton University Press, 1971.

Sauvy, Alfred. *Théorie générale de la population.* 2 vols. Volume 1: *Economie et population.* Volume 2: *Biologie sociale.* Paris: Presses Universitaires de France, 1952–1954.

Sheps, Mindel C., and Jane Menken. *Mathematical Models of Conception and Birth.* Chicago: University of Chicago Press, 1973.

Shryock, Henry S., Jr., Jacob S. Siegel, et al. *The Methods and Materials of Demography.* 2 vols. Prepared for the U.S. Bureau of the Census. Washington, D.C.: U.S. Government Printing Office, 1971 (3d rev. printing, 1975).

Smith, David P., and Nathan Keyfitz (editors). *Mathematical Demography: Selected Readings.* Berlin and New York: Springer, 1977.

Spiegelman, Mortimer. *Introduction to Demography.* Rev. ed. Cambridge, Mass.: Harvard University Press, 1968.

United Nations, Department of Economic and Social Affairs. *Methods of Estimating Basic Demographic Measures from Incomplete Data.* Prepared by Ansley J. Coale and Paul Demeny. Series A, Population Studies, no. 42. New York, 1967.

Whelpton, Pascal K. "Reproduction Rates Adjusted for Age, Parity, Fecundity, and Marriage." *Journal of the American Statistical Association* 41(236):501–516, December 1946.

White, Harrison C. *Chains of Opportunity: System Models of Mobility in Organizations.* Cambridge: Mass.: Harvard University Press, 1970.

MEXICO

Located in the southern part of the North American continent, Mexico is bordered by the United States to the north, the Gulf of Mexico and the Caribbean Sea to the east, Guatemala and Belize to the southeast, and the Pacific Ocean to the south and west.

With a land area of about 2 million square kilometers (772,200 square miles), Mexico is thirteenth among nations in geographic size. Within the American continents, however, it is intermediate among countries as extensive as the United States, Brazil, and Canada, and the very small Central American and Caribbean countries. The topography of Mexico is irregular; there are large, elevated plateaus and coastal plains in the north, and there are a great variety of climates. In population size, Mexico is eleventh among nations, with 70 million inhabitants in 1980. Its demographic density is 35 inhabitants per square kilometer (91 per square mile). Although its population is still growing rapidly, in the late 1970s the annual growth rate dropped below 3 percent. As a result of economic development, Mexico is a middle-income or semi-industrialized country. Both income and degree of industrialization are expected to rise substantially in the immediate future because of increasing exploitation of abundant supplies of oil and gas.

Economic and Social Development. The emergence of the Mexican nation has been marked by a series of breaks in historical continuity. The first great rupture corresponded to the period of conquest and colonization of the territory by the Spanish, and the subsequent transformation of the economic, political, sociocultural, and demographic orders. The sixteenth century was a period of precipitous decline of the native population; the several millions of indigenous inhabitants in the territory at the beginning of the century (estimates go up to 25 million) were reduced to scarcely 1 million by the end of the century. The colonial period from the seventeenth century into the nineteenth was one of organization, continuity, and a consolidation of diverse peoples that was as much racial as cultural. The new society that took shape included two unequal worlds, that of the "republic of the Spaniards" and that of the "republic of the Indians." The first of these worlds consolidated the colonial system to serve the interests of metropolitan Europe.

Mexico gained political independence from Spain in 1821. Beginning in the last third of the nineteenth century, new links were created with the industrialized world and the international economic and political community. The modernization of the economy proceeded at an accelerated pace.

The evolution of the population corresponded to that of colonial economic and social life in general; in the nineteenth century the demographic pattern was characteristic of agrarian, preindustrial societies. There were long periods of relative stability when the population slowly grew. A high fertility rate corresponded to an almost-as-high mortality rate. From the last third of the nineteenth century, following a decline in the mortality rate, the population steadily increased. From the middle of the nineteenth century to 1910 the population doubled from about 7.5 million to about 15 million.

This process was violently interrupted by the Mexican Revolution of 1910. The active military phase was followed by a period of reforms and new political institutions, which extended approximately to 1940. Subsequently, the country entered a stage of development that promoted industrialization and modernization through a policy known as "import substitution." The ensuing growth of the economy has been sustained. The gross national product doubled in almost every succeeding decade; conditions favored the formation of capital and the incorporation of a relatively abundant and cheap labor force into the modern sectors of the economy.

In spite of economic and social difficulties, especially in the most recent years, the general stability of Mexican society and its institutions has been maintained. The state is consolidated with a pluralistic character in its distribution of power. Mexico today has a mixed economy combining governmental and private sectors. The economic growth sustained during these years has resulted in definitive economic transformations. Mexico is no longer a predominantly rural and agrarian country, although rural characteristics persist. Despite a continued growth of the rural population in absolute terms, it was expected that in 1980 only a third of those employed would be in the agricultural sector, compared with almost two-thirds in 1940.

The aggregate figures conceal, nevertheless, the persistence of forces of disequilibrium in terms of income, education, and labor skills. Income distribution has remained extremely unequal, with 10 percent of the population receiving about 40 percent of the total income in the 1960s and 1970s, and the relative position of

the low-income groups has deteriorated in the course of economic transformation. The social security system, initiated in 1943, covered more than 40 percent of the total population in 1979. Medical and other assistance programs covered additional segments of the population and continue to expand. While the average daily supply of calories and proteins per inhabitant is close to or above the international minimum standards, there are nutritional deficiencies in the low-income strata, especially among infants.

Illiteracy in both the school-age and adult populations was about 25 percent in 1970, and is estimated about 15 percent in 1980, although the national educational system has continued to expand. Primary education (six years), the only instruction that is free and obligatory, was attended by only 90 percent of the children. In 1970, those who had never received schooling constituted 35 percent of the total population, but only 25 percent of the economically active. It must be said, however, that another 30 percent of the economically active had less than three years of formal instruction.

Large segments of the population have been on the margins of economic development and national growth. Unemployment and underemployment in all sectors of the economy affect a high proportion of the working-age population, above all in the rural sector. Much of the indigenous population, which is about 7 million and equivalent to 10 percent of the total population, is included in this marginal group.

This economic and social disequilibrium has altered the perception of the process of development from one centered on increasing the country's economic production to a broader concept that incorporates matters of social and political concern.

Population Characteristics. After 1970 there was a change in long-term trends, and the pace of population growth dropped off to below 3 percent per year by the end of the decade (see Table 1). This change caused a downward revision of population projections to slightly more than 100 million people by the year 2000.

In a demographic situation as dynamic as that of Mex-

TABLE 1. *Mexico, demographic indicators, 1940–1980*

Year	Population (in thousands)	Growth (natural increase)	Births (crude rate per 1,000)	Mortality (crude rate per 1,000)	Life expectancy at birth (years)	Population under 15 years	Population in localities with 15,000 or more inhbts.[d]	Population in agriculture/ cattle raising
1940	19,654	2.1%	44.4	23.3	41.4[c]	41.2%	20.0%	65.4%
1950	25,791	2.9	45.6	16.1	49.7[c]	41.8	28.0	58.3
1960	34,923	3.4	46.0	11.5	58.9[c]	44.4	36.6	54.1
1970	48,225	3.4	44.2	10.1	63.0[a]	46.2	44.9	40.9
1980	69,902[a]	2.7–2.6[a,b]	34–33[b]	8–7[a,b]	64.1[a]	44.8[a]	52.0	—

Sources of data: National census and vital statistics. [a]Mexico, 1979. [b]International Program of Laboratories for Population Statistics, 1980. [c]Benítez and Cabrera, 1967. [d]Unikel et al., 1976.

ico, absolute numbers have risen with startling rapidity. Thus, between 1930 and 1970 the number of families almost tripled, from 3.3 to 9.1 million. In 1970, 40 percent of the families had six or more members. Similarly, the number of women of childbearing age (15–49 years) increased between 1940 and 1970 from less than 5 million to 10.7 million. The economically active population has also increased rapidly, from 6 million in 1940 to 13 million in the beginning of 1970. In the latter year one-fifth of the labor force were women. A labor force of approximately 20 million is estimated for 1980.

Age and sex structure. The demographic dynamics have produced an extremely young population. In 1940, 41.2 percent of the population was under 15. In 1970, 46.2 percent was under 15 and 3.7 percent was 65 and over. The change in the dependency ratio of children and the aged to those of working age illustrates the age structure of the population and the growth Mexico is experiencing. In 1940 the ratio was only 79 dependents per 100 productive members of society but it increased to almost 100 by 1970. More recently it is decreasing.

The sex structure of the population has not changed greatly. The sex ratio of men to women showed a slight increase between 1930 and 1970, tending toward a value of 100. In the age group between 20 and 35 years there appeared to be a disequilibrium between the sexes with the census enumerating up to 5 percent fewer males than females.

Fertility. Fertility in Mexico up to the early 1970s changed only slightly. The crude birth rate, as derived from the vital statistics, showed great stability between 1940 and 1970, fluctuating around 45 births per 1,000 inhabitants. An adjusted series of crude rates of reproduction indicates a slight tendency toward increased fertility in that same period. The fertility pattern by age shows minor variations; fertility rates of young women, 15 to 24 years, tended to decrease, while those of older women, over 30 years, increased slightly. The mean age at first union remained at 24 years for men and 21 years for women.

In the 1970s fertility patterns began to change. The crude birth rate dropped below 40 births per 1,000 inhabitants. The gross reproduction rate went well under 3. Age-specific reductions in fertility have now been generalized to all cohorts of women of reproductive age, and the trend of fertility decline seems to be well established.

Mortality. The mortality rate, on the other hand, has been declining since or even before the 1920s, although more slowly in recent years. Between 1940 and 1970 life expectancy at birth increased more than 20 years. By the early 1970s it was 61 years for men and 65 years for women. Life expectancy in 1979 was estimated to exceed 64 years average for both sexes.

More and better health services and improved standards of living still can make important reductions in the mortality rate. Infant mortality was high as the eighties began—on the order of 50 deaths per 1,000 live births according to vital statistics, or of 60 according to survey data. Deaths of those under 5 years of age represented a third or more of all deaths. Among the principal causes

FIGURE 1. *Population structure of Mexico, 1940 and 1970 censuses*

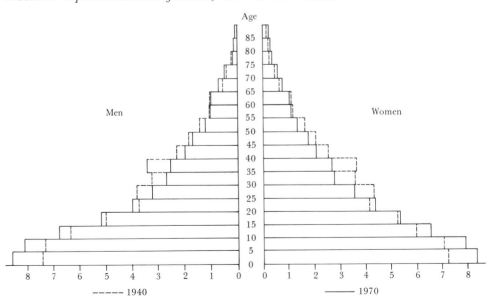

Source of data: National census data.

of death were infectious and parasitic diseases, although mortality rates and causes differed greatly depending on region and social class.

Migration. The volume of migrants has greatly increased with the growth of the population. Internally, migration has centered on the Valley of Mexico and the industrial zones. Much of this movement constitutes transfers from the country to the cities, which accelerates urban growth. The Valley of Mexico, including Mexico City, has about 14 million inhabitants, and one-fifth of the entire population of the country. Together with Mexico City the cities of Guadalajara and Monterrey have accommodated the majority of the migrants.

Despite this process of concentration in urban centers, the distribution of the population in small villages has persisted. In 1970 almost 30 percent of the population lived in more than 90,000 villages with less than 1,000 inhabitants each. The size and dynamics of rural-urban migration have relegated to second place the study of the movement of the population over the countryside, although it is estimated to be quite large.

The migration of Mexicans to the United States is an important factor in the relations between the two countries. Since the Mexican labor force was discovered by agricultural and other sectors of the U.S. economy in the last decades of the nineteenth century, movement north has been part of a Mexican migratory tradition. It was interrupted only during the Great Depression and the years that followed. After 1964 when the temporary contracts for Mexican laborers, known as the program of "braceros," were ended, this movement continued without documentation, although undocumented migration is not a new phenomenon.

This migration is clearly temporary; the majority of those who leave Mexico return after a relatively short stay in the United States, generally less than a year. While annual flow involves several hundred thousand persons, the net increment to Mexican stock in the United States, documented or undocumented, is much less. Studies of the period of the 1970s estimate this net flow from less than a hundred thousand persons up to two or three times that figure.

Data Sources. The National Information System was developed for the purpose of structuring a statistical base in the social, political, geographic, and economic fields. Censuses and the registration of vital events are part of this system.

The first population census in Mexico was held in 1895 and the second in 1900. Censuses have been conducted each decade thereafter. The census of 1980 was the country's tenth. Civil registry of vital events has been obligatory since 1929. Mexico's vital statistics that refer to live births and deaths are considered acceptable in coverage and quality.

Censuses and vital statistics were until some years ago the only sources of data. After the 1960s, a series of surveys provided deeper knowledge of the current situation and of demographic dynamics, as well as of the relationship among factors—economic, social, and other—associated with demographic processes. Surveys have been conducted on migration and occupational mobility, on fertility, use of contraceptive methods, mortality, and on income and expenditures of households. There is also a continuous quarterly survey on occupation.

Policy and Action. Mexican thought up to the middle of the present century viewed population growth as essential to occupying, integrating, and industrializing the nation. The population law of 1947 encouraged matrimony and fertility. Economic growth was sustained at rates that exceeded population growth and reinforced the idea that it was not necessary to oppose demographic trends nor desirable deliberately to influence demographic behavior. Until the middle of the 1960s, state, church, and schools were joined in a consensus in regard to the desirability or acceptability of population growth.

Nevertheless, the demographic changes and the recognition that the nation was immersed in economic and social problems resulted in a radical transformation of population policy. The demographic policy in force from 1974 gives due weight to population growth and the needs of those already born. The new population law was oriented toward regulating the demographic phenomenon, with the purpose of achieving just participation in and equitable distribution of the benefits of economic and social development.

Consideration of demographics within the framework of the overall process of national development characterizes the new population policy. The National Population Council was created with responsibility for demographic planning. It attempts to modify reproductive behavior with absolute respect for human liberty, endeavoring to enhance the well-being of the family and the individual. It seeks equitable integration of women in economic, social, and cultural activities. It supports improvements in living conditions to reduce mortality and morbidity. It promotes family planning through education, communication, and the health and social security systems that provide information and services; it influences the pace of population growth and geographic distribution by means of a full range of actions in economic, social, and cultural spheres.

The geographic distribution of people is the subject of the 1976 general law of human settlements. Regional demographic policy is oriented as much toward balancing the natural growth of the population in the different regions of the country as toward changing the concentrated nature of migration. Migration policy seeks to modify the intensity and direction of population flows, being mindful of the promotion of regional development and the distribution of the population according to the location of natural resources.

Mexico proposes to bring its growth rate down to 2.5 percent by 1982. Over the long range, it hopes to reduce growth—to 1.8 percent in 1988 and to around 1 percent by the year 2000, so as to avoid disequilibrium in the age structure. Programs and activities have been designed in the areas of family planning, communication and information, and sex education in order to attain this goal. A balance of rural and urban users of health and family planning services is desired.

Family planning activities are carried out by the health institutions and by some private organizations, which incorporate family planning with other services generally in the field of maternal and child health.

Public institutions provide more than 90 percent of family planning services. By the end of 1978 there were 1.8 million users of contraceptives in the system—1.3 million in the urban programs and close to 500,000 in the rural programs—which is equivalent to about 20 percent of the women of fertile age who are living in a union. It is estimated that another 20 percent of women practice contraception through commercial channels and the private health system.

The communication and information program has among its objectives (1) to inform the people about population growth and distribution and the relations between population and development; (2) to acquaint the people with government policies in these matters; (3) to promote the participation of the people in the demographic programs; and (4) to assist in enhancing the well-being of the population. The sex education program is directed toward increasing awareness of the significance of sexual life for individual, family, and social development. The general objective is to modify sexual and reproductive behavior by means of education.

The distributions of population and migration currents are influenced by various programs, including those for stimulating territorial decentralization of the federal public administration, those for regional integration of urban services, and those for the establishment of concentrated rural services. The program of Public Investments for Rural Development is oriented toward communities of between 300 and 3,000 inhabitants. Communities are selected on the basis of their potential for production as a means of stemming demographic dispersion.

Scholarly Activities. In the governmental sector, the National Population Council is responsible according to the law for the promotion and coordination of research for the purposes of formulating and implementing demographic policy. Evaluation of operations is carried out by the institutions that provide information and services. In research, the National Population Council is supple-

mented by the demographic research program of the National Council of Science and Technology.

Within the academic sphere, several institutions work in the area of demography. The Centro de Estudios Económicos y Demográficos of El Colegio de México is well known for its basic and interdisciplinary research, for the publication of research findings (including the journal *Demografía y economía*), and for its postgraduate programs leading to a master's degree in demography or urban development. Other institutions active in population research are the Instituto de Investigaciones Sociales of the Universidad Nacional Autónoma de México and the Centro de Investigaciones Sociales y Económicas of the Universidad de Guadalajara, and El Colegio de Michoacán, among others. The economics department of the Universidad Autónoma de Nuevo León offers a program leading to a B.A. (*licenciatura*) in demography and social statistics. In 1973 the Mexican Population Association was founded with the objectives of promoting the exchange of information, collaboration in the formulation of policies, sponsorship of studies, and the training of professionals in this discipline.

Demographic reality and the factors that determine it are an area of investigation that has become well consolidated as compared to its state in the 1960s. The fields covered range from data evaluation and the making of population estimations and projections to the study of the relations between population and development; they include studies of each of the demographic variables. In recent years Mexican scholars have reviewed the demographic research done in Mexico (Alba, 1979; Mexico, 1978; Lerner, 1967).

Demographic trends have played in the past and will play in the near future an important role in shaping development patterns in Mexico. There is general awareness that social and economic transformations are also needed, to interact constructively with the demographic transition. Present policy objectives are to respond positively to the current population dynamics and to reduce future demographic pressures on the social and economic apparatus. The institutional mechanisms needed to monitor demographic changes are in operation and population policy is well established as an integral part of national planning.

Francisco Alba

See also LATIN AMERICA.

BIBLIOGRAPHY

Alba, Francisco. *La población de México: Evolución y dilemas.* Mexico City: El Colegio de México, 1977.
———. "El estudio de la población de México." In *Ciencias sociales en México: Desarrollo y perspectivas,* pp. 89–105. Mexico City: El Colegio de México, 1979.

Benítez Z., Raúl, and Gustavo Cabrera Acevedo. *Tablas abreviadas de mortalidad de la población de México, 1930, 1940, 1950, 1960.* Mexico City: El Colegio de México, 1967.

Centro de Estudios Económicos y Demográficos, El Colegio de México. *Dinámica de la población de México.* Mexico City, 1970.

Coale, Ansley J. "Population Growth and Economic Development: The Case of Mexico." *Foreign Affairs* 56(2):415–429, January 1978.

Demografía y economía. Issued quarterly since 1967 by the Centro de Estudios Económicos y Demográficos, El Colegio de México, Mexico City.

International Program of Laboratories for Population Statistics. *The 1979 Mexico National Fertility and Mortality Survey: A Summary of Results.* Summary Series, no. 2. Chapel Hill, N.C., December 1980.

Lerner, Susana. "La investigación y la planeación demográficas en México." *Demografía y economía* 1(1):9–17, 1967.

Mexico, Consejo Nacional de Ciencia y Tecnología. *Investigación demográfica en México.* Mexico City, 1978.

Mexico, Consejo Nacional de Población. *México demográfico: Breviario 1979.* Circular de Morelia No. 8. Mexico City, 1979.

Unikel, Luis, et al. *El desarrollo urbano en México: Diagnóstico y implicaciónes futuras.* Mexico City: El Colegio de México, 1976.

Urquidi, Víctor L. "Perfil general: Economía y población." In *El perfil de México en 1980,* vol. 1, pp. 1–13. Mexico City: Siglo Veintiuno, 1970.

MIDDLE EAST

See NORTH AFRICA AND SOUTHWEST ASIA.

MIGRATION

Migration is geographic mobility that involves a change of usual residence between defined political or statistical areas, or between residence areas of different types. In general usage the term has been restricted to relatively permanent changes. The two broad classifications are international migration, referring to movement across national boundaries, and internal migration, referring to movement within the boundaries of a given nation. Most of the articles on this topic are thus located under the headings INTERNAL MIGRATION and INTERNATIONAL MIGRATION. The movement of refugees within the context of international migration is treated in a separate entry, REFUGEES. The several articles under the heading INTERNAL MIGRATION discuss theoretical formulation of causes of migrations, empirical studies of determinants and effects of current trends in developing countries, and migration within the United States. The effects of migration are also discussed in FERTILITY AND MIGRATION; URBANI-

ZATION; and LABOR FORCE. Government policies related to migration are described in DISTRIBUTION, article on DISTRIBUTION POLICY; in IMMIGRATION POLICY; and in POPULATION POLICY. Short term or cyclic mobility is discussed in CIRCULATION. Country and regional articles also contain information on migratory movements. Sources of data and methods for measuring migration are covered in MIGRATION MEASUREMENT, and related material can be found in URBANIZATION, article on MEASUREMENT, and in DISTRIBUTION, article on DISTRIBUTION, CONCENTRATION, AND DISPERSION.

MIGRATION MEASUREMENT

Migration is measured by counting either the number of people who make relatively permanent changes of residence between clearly defined geographic units, or by counting the number of such changes. A distinction is usually made according to the geographic units involved; internal migration takes place within the boundaries of one country, and international migration crosses national boundaries. Gross migration is the total movement into or out of an area. The difference between these is net migration. It is conventional to refer to internal migration in terms of "in-migration" or "out-migration" and international migration as "immigration" or "emigration."

Sources of Data. Data for measuring migration can be collected by recording the move at the time it occurs, by maintaining a continuing register of individuals within a country or other geographic unit, or by asking about past moves, previous residence, or place of birth.

The first method, direct recording, is used most frequently to collect data on international migration. Where frontiers are controlled, counts can be made of people crossing borders. Applications for passports, visas, and work permits also provide data on migration but they are less useful sources because the moves indicated may not occur. Records in the form of sea and air transport manifests are additional sources.

Data based on frontier control suffer from serious deficiencies in completeness and international comparability. Political boundaries change over time, many international migrants enter and leave a country at border points where there is no control, and information given at the point of entry as to length of stay and purpose are usually statements of intent, which may or may not correspond to actual movements. Governments vary considerably in the kinds of information obtained, how it is classified and how it is reported. Thus, two migrants entering two different countries, and each providing identical information, might be classified and reported in very different ways. In addition, there may be serious logistical problems in gathering frontier statistics; the numbers of migrants are sometimes very small in comparison to the large numbers of tourists, business travelers, and other visitors.

In an effort to improve comparability, the United Nations recommends that national governments categorize the information on total arrivals and departures as follows. An intended duration of stay of more than one year classifies a migrant as permanent. Temporary migrants differ from visitors in that they intend to work for a period of one year or less and receive pay from sources within the country they enter. Residents who remain abroad for a period of one year or less without such work and payment are in another category, as are refugees, displaced persons, and transferred populations. Tabulations by these categories aid in the interpretation of migrant statistics for any year and in making comparisons from country to country.

Continuous population registers record movement in and out of a country as well as internal moves. In spite of its advantages as a source of data, this system is not likely to be used in most countries because of the expense of setting up and maintaining current registration of each individual and each change of residence. The few countries that now have such a system include Belgium, Czechoslovakia, West Germany, the Scandinavian countries, the Netherlands, Israel, Taiwan, and Japan. Special registrations of aliens, like the annual registration required in the United States, provide some data on international migration.

Census data are the major source of information on internal migration in most countries. On the basis of answers to direct questions on place of birth, place of last residence, duration of residence in the place of enumeration, or place of residence on a specific date before the census, the population in an area may be classified as migrant and nonmigrant. Information obtained this way does not include migrants who entered and died between censuses, nor does it count all the moves that might have been made by individuals.

In many countries, periodic sample surveys provide data on migration that permit analysis of current trends. Useful information collected by surveys on characteristics of migrants, reasons for migration, and number and kinds of changes of residence supplement the information from censuses.

Estimation of Migration. Estimates of net migration can be made by comparing a population at two points in time, determining what change would be expected on the basis of natural increase, and attributing the residual change to migration. The vital statistics method for estimation uses census counts at two points in time with statistics of births and deaths to calculate net migration by the equation

$$\text{Net } M = (P_1 - P_0) - (B - D),$$

where P_1 is the population at the later census, P_0 is the population at the earlier census, B is the total of births, and D is the total of deaths in the period between the censuses.

A second approach estimates net migration for the period between two censuses by survivorship probabilities [see LIFE TABLES]. A set of life table survival rates is applied to the population at the first census in order to derive an estimate of the number of persons expected to be living at the time of the second census. The difference between the expected population and the enumerated population is the estimate of net migration. An alternative method applies reverse survival rates to the population in the second census in order to account for intercensal deaths of migrants. A third procedure averages the net migration estimates derived from the forward and reverse survival rates to allow for the assumption that both deaths and migration were evenly distributed over the intercensal period. Similar procedures for estimation use census survival rates that are computed from census age distributions. These indirect methods, however, can give estimates of only the net change attributed to migration, not immigration and emigration, and they cannot distinguish between internal and international migration.

An important advance in the methodology of migration measurement and forecasting has come from analyses of historical data on interregional population distribution. Model multiregional life tables that incorporate probabilities of migration have been developed from these distributions and these permit estimation of migrant flows in and out of specific regions instead of only net migration.

Migration Rates. Migration rates are designed to relate numbers of migrants to the size of population of the regions or countries of origin or destination. The basic rates are

$$\text{In-migration or immigration rate: } \frac{I}{P}K$$

$$\text{Out-migration or emigration rate: } \frac{O}{P}K$$

$$\text{Net migration rate: } \frac{I - O}{P}K$$

where I is the number of migrants into a region or a country, O is the number of migrants out of a region or a country, P is an appropriate measure of the population in the region or country of destination or origin, and K is a constant, most commonly 1,000. It may be noted that the concept of a rate as involving a population "at risk" does not strictly apply in the case of in-migration, immigration, or net migration. Nevertheless, the measures may be of use for substantive analysis.

Variations of these basic migration rates are sometimes useful for particular purposes. For example, rates specific for age, sex, or other characteristics may be employed where the requisite data are available. Rates to describe particular streams between two specified places of origin and destination, to compare differentials, or for other specialized analyses also have been devised, and are detailed in the basic sources cited below.

Because each move involves both an area of origin and an area of destination, and because the determination of the appropriate base population (population-at-risk of migration) can vary according to the specific purposes of the analysis and the data available, there are special problems associated with the construction of migration rates. The selection of a time period is another major complicating factor in defining rates and comparing data. For these reasons, limited use has been made of migration rates in the analysis of migration or national population growth, and no one set of rates has become standard.

Migration statistics are used primarily to study demographic trends and their economic and social relationships. The measures are most useful when they are specific for age, sex, marital status, family size, and economic status—variables that can have important effects on the labor market of sending and receiving areas and on the demand for schools, housing, transportation, food, health facilities, and social services. Many countries now have information available on internal and international migration, and compilations of international statistics have appeared in the United Nations *Demographic Yearbook.*

Regina McNamara

BIBLIOGRAPHY

Haenszel, William. "Concept, Measurement, and Data in Migration Analysis." *Demography* 4(1):253–261, 1967.

Rogers, Andrei. "Estimating Interregional Population and Migration Operators from Interregional Population Distribution." *Demography* 4(2):515–531, 1967.

————. *Introduction to Multiregional Mathematical Demography.* New York: Wiley, 1975.

Shryock, Henry S., Jr., Jacob S. Siegel, et al. *The Methods and Materials of Demography.* 2 vols. Prepared for the U.S. Bureau of the Census. Washington, D.C.: U.S. Government Printing Office, 1971 (3d rev. printing, 1975).

United Nations, Department of Economic and Social Affairs. *Methods of Measuring Internal Migration.* Series A, Population Studies, no. 47. New York, 1970.

MOBILITY
See MIGRATION.

MODELS
See INTERNAL MIGRATION, *article on* MODELS; LIFE TABLES; POPULATION MODELS; REPRODUCTION, *article on* MODELS.

MOMENTUM

Momentum in population growth is a property whereby populations change their growth rates in a relatively smooth fashion. It occurs because growth rates are generated by the interaction of fertility and mortality patterns with the age structure, and the latter cannot be modified quickly. A positive and a negative population growth momentum can be distinguished, although usually the positive momentum is implied. The essential factor in positive momentum is an age structure heavily weighted with youth, reflecting past high fertility, so that large proportions of women of childbearing age are built into the population for many years to come. Positive population growth momentum is apparent in periods when, despite a fertility decline to the replacement level, or even below that level, the population continues to increase. That is, even if the average woman produces only two children, the large numbers of women of childbearing age will still guarantee an aggregate number of births large enough to produce a positive growth rate. Only after the youthful age structure has worked itself out over about three generations (seventy-five to one hundred years) will growth entirely cease.

Conversely, after an extended period of below-replacement-level fertility, resulting in small cohorts of actual and potential parents, a negative population growth momentum will have been generated and the respective population may experience a period of population decline even if fertility rises to or above the replacement level.

Growth momentum is also in part a consequence of the interaction of the age structure with the respective age patterns of mortality. A population with large cohorts in the childbearing ages is likely to have relatively small cohorts in high mortality age groups, that is, at the lowest or at the highest ages or at both. Therefore, the crude death rate will be relatively low, reinforcing the positive population growth momentum. Conversely, a population with small childbearing cohorts will be likely to have large cohorts in the high-mortality age groups; consequently a high crude death rate results, reinforcing a negative growth momentum.

Nathan Keyfitz (1971) developed simple formulas for calculating the ultimate stationary population size when replacement-level fertility is attained at specified points in time. Tomas Frejka (1973) illustrated and discussed alternative future population growth possibilities for developed and developing countries, taking into account the momentum factor.

Tomas Frejka

See Projections.

BIBLIOGRAPHY

Frejka, Tomas. "The Prospects for a Stationary World Population." *Scientific American* 228(3):15–23, March 1973.
Keyfitz, Nathan. "On the Momentum of Population Growth." *Demography* 8(1):71–90, February 1971.

MORBIDITY

Morbidity is the extent of illness (disease), injury, or disability in a defined population. Particularly in circumstances of low mortality, such as exist now in the industrialized nations, morbidity data give a fuller description of the physical well-being of a population than do mortality data. Mortality data do not reflect the level of nonfatal illnesses or impairments, or of mental illness. They are also insufficient measures of some ultimately fatal diseases of long duration, such as many cancers, which place a high burden of restricted activity, anxiety, and medical costs on their victims and on society.

Sources of Data. Despite their value, morbidity data are difficult to obtain. Reporting is required under the International Health Regulations adopted by the Twenty-second World Assembly in 1969, as amended by assemblies in 1973 and 1981, for three diseases: plague, cholera, and yellow fever. (Smallpox was removed as a reportable disease in 1981.) About forty diseases are reportable by law to health authorities in all states in the United States. However, compliance tends to be low except in cases of more serious and rare infectious diseases. In the United States, some states require reporting for epidemics of any kind, and increasingly, for occupation-related diseases. Despite low compliance, the existing data are used to make projections about morbidity. Other routine morbidity statistics are available from such sources as hospital records, records of private physicians, insurance programs and industrial health plans, and the like.

Special studies have been undertaken in many countries to provide national morbidity information. In the United States, the ongoing National Health Interview

Survey and the National Health Examination Survey have been undertaken for this purpose. The former defines morbidity as "a departure from a state of physical or mental well-being, resulting from disease or injury, of which the affected individual is aware" (United States, 1975, p. 2). Following the concept, morbidity is assessed by asking interview respondents about specific chronic and acute health conditions that result in restriction of usual activities, bed disability, work loss, seeking of medical advice, or taking of medicines. The measurement relies on recognition by the respondent (a parent, guardian, or other responsible person if the potential respondent is a child or is incompetent to reply) that something is wrong with his or her health. The Health Examination Survey uses physical examinations, clinical and laboratory tests, and related other measurements, as well as interviews, to assess morbidity status.

Using a method similar to the surveys conducted in the United States, a major international study was undertaken by the World Health Organization in seven countries to analyze health care. Among other things, it measured "morbidity factors," including social dysfunction, bed days, restricted activity days, and sick days, as well as "perceived morbidity factors," including reported illness, its severity, its chronicity, and its urgency (Anderson et al., 1976).

Morbidity data are also obtained from surveys of a population for a specific disease or disability or to determine the health status of a particular population group, such as schoolchildren. Physical screening programs are one method for obtaining such data.

In most developing countries, morbidity statistics are very incomplete, and mortality statistics serve as a proxy for those on morbidity. In both developing and developed countries, three factors must be considered when morbidity data are analyzed and compared over time. (1) Estimates of disease incidence may rise artificially as diagnostic procedures and reporting practices improve. (2) Increased accessibility to medical care, such as that which has occurred under the national health program in Britain and the Medicare program in the United States, may promote more diagnoses, more care, and increased reporting of disease conditions. (3) Overall morbidity rates from chronic diseases may increase as the population ages, despite the overall improvement of age-specific health status as evidenced by lowered mortality.

Morbidity data for most countries are published by their respective ministries of health. The World Health Organization publishes the *World Health Statistics Quarterly,* which provides information on notifications of infectious diseases, and the *World Health Statistics Annual.* The Centers for Disease Control of the U.S. Department of Health and Human Services publish *MMWR,* the *Mor-*

bidity and Mortality Weekly Report. The Department of Health and Human Services also publishes an annual, *Health: United States.*

Morbidity Rates. Incidence and prevalence rates are the major measures used to express the quantity of a particular condition in a population. "Incidence" refers to the number of cases of disease, injury, or disability having their onset during a prescribed period of time in relation to the unit of population in which they occur; it refers specifically to new cases. The incidence rate is commonly measured per 1,000 population at risk, although some other constant (K) can be used; the usual time period is one year. The following equation may be used:

$$\text{Incidence rate} = \frac{\begin{array}{c}\text{Number of persons developing a}\\ \text{specific disease, injury,}\\ \text{or disabling condition during a}\\ \text{given time period}\end{array}}{\text{Total population at risk}} \times K.$$

For rare diseases, the constant used may be 100,000, while for common ones, a smaller constant may be used, generally 1,000 and less often 100.

By contrast, the prevalence rate expresses the number of cases of disease, injury, or disability present at a particular time and in relation to the unit of population in which they occur. It may refer to chronic cases as well as new cases. The prevalence rate therefore describes the health status of the population with respect to a particular condition. The following equation may be used:

$$\text{Prevalence rate} = \frac{\begin{array}{c}\text{Number of persons with a specific}\\ \text{disease, injury, or}\\ \text{disabling condition}\end{array}}{\text{Total population at risk}} \times K.$$

As in the incidence rate, the constant K is typically 1,000, but other constants may be used. Expressed in another way, prevalence equals incidence multiplied by average case duration.

Numerous other measures and explanatory devices have been developed to provide more detailed information about morbidity. The case rate, a type of incidence rate, is the number of reported cases of a specific illness (disease) per 100,000 population in a given year. Related to this is the mortality rate known as the case fatality rate, which is the proportion of persons contracting a disease who die of that disease.

Study and Use of Data. Demographers, epidemiologists, and public health administrators and planners are the main professional groups concerned with the measurement of morbidity. Demographers undertake such measurement from the point of view of assessing particular characteristics of a population. Epidemiologists study the nature, cause, and control, as well as the determinants, of the frequency and distribution of disease, in-

jury, and disability in a population. Public health administrators and planners organize community efforts to protect and improve the health of the population. People representing many other sectors of society, including business, labor, and the military, use morbidity data in their planning efforts. The relation of illness to productivity is increasingly being considered in national planning and in development assistance. For example, attempts have been made to measure the burden on the capacity of the work force of chronic illness such as alcoholism, or of endemic illness such as malaria.

Jeanne Betsock Stillman

Related entries are MORBIDITY AND LONGEVITY *and* PUBLIC HEALTH.

BIBLIOGRAPHY

Anderson, D. O., et al. "Morbidity Factors." In *Health Care: An International Study,* edited by Robert Kohn and Kerr L. White, pp. 58–100. London: Oxford University Press, 1976.

Cole, Philip. "Morbidity in the United States." In *Mortality and Morbidity in the United States,* edited by Carl L. Erhardt and Joyce E. Berlin, pp. 65–104. Cambridge, Mass.: Harvard University Press, 1974.

MacMahan, Brian, and Thomas F. Pugh. *Epidemiology: Principles and Methods.* Boston: Little, Brown, 1970.

MMWR, Morbidity and Mortality Weekly Report. Issued weekly by the U.S. Department of Health and Human Services, Public Health Service, Centers for Disease Control, Atlanta.

United States, Department of Health and Human Services. *Health: United States, 1979.* Washington, D.C.: U.S. Government Printing Office, 1980.

United States, National Center for Health Statistics. *Health Statistics Today and Tomorrow: A Report of the Committee to Evaluate the National Center for Health Statistics.* Documents and Committee Reports, series 4, no. 15. Rockville, Md., 1973.

———. *Health Interview Survey Procedure, 1957–1974.* Vital and Health Statistics, series 1, no. 11. Rockville, Md., 1975.

World Health Organization. *International Health Regulations, 1969: Adopted by the Twenty-second World Health Assembly in 1969 and Amended by the Twenty-sixth World Health Assembly in 1973.* 2d annotated ed. Geneva, 1974.

World Health Statistics Annual. Issued annually by the World Health Organization, Geneva. In English and French.

World Health Statistics Quarterly. Formerly titled *World Health Statistics Report.* Issued quarterly by the World Health Organization, Geneva. In English and French.

MORBIDITY AND LONGEVITY

Many degrees of ill health lie between well-being and the near moribund state. The descent may be slow and insidious toward a condition of morbidity, in which the affected person may feel unwell or an observer may recognize signs and symptoms of disease, which may eventually lead to the final state, death. We can readily record the number of deaths, and we are also able to record, with less precision, the numbers of persons known to be suffering from various ailments. When we do so, however, we are looking very often at only the tip of the iceberg, much of which lies submerged, beyond observation (Benjamin, 1964).

An understanding of the relationship of morbidity and mortality is clearly important if substantial progress is to be made in reducing mortality.

Morbidity and Mortality. Because of the difficulties and uncertainties inherent in the measurement of morbidity, attempts to study the relationship of morbidity and mortality for national populations have been rare. A recent study in France (Damiani, 1977) has used first medical consultations to measure morbidity (by cause) and related the findings to mortality. Investigations of the mortality of persons subject to specific risk factors, on the other hand, have been carried out in various countries since the turn of the century. The term "risk factor" is used to describe the history or presence of a specific disease in a person, the continued exposure to a hazardous occupation or habit, the presence of an abnormal finding on physical examination, or an abnormal result in a medical test. The survival and mortality statistics of lives subject to these risk factors are usually obtained from follow-up studies.

Follow-up studies of persons with specific impairments are also undertaken at hospitals and clinics all over the world, among members of voluntary health insurance schemes and participants in multiphase screening, among military and institutionalized persons, and among government employees and employees of large companies. Numerous examples can be found, for example, in Singer and Levinson (1976).

The hospital, clinic, life insurance, military, and employer studies just mentioned usually follow cohorts of persons suffering from specific medical conditions. They throw light on the mortality of selected lives with such impairments, but they provide only limited information about the onset of the condition and its prevalence in the community. Further information is required if we are to understand more fully the major factors associated with aging. Prospective studies, following whole communities or large random samples from the population into the future, provide more information, but they tend to be considerably more expensive and they have therefore rarely been undertaken.

The Framingham study (Kannel, Gordon, et al., 1968–1978) is perhaps the best-known investigation of this type. Beginning in 1950 it surveyed the health of the people of Framingham, a town situated approximately 22 miles (35 kilometers) west of Boston, which in 1950

had a population of 28,086. The purpose of the study was to determine the incidence of and risk factors associated with heart disease. A stratified sample comprising about half of the adult population participated in the study, which has involved a series of biennial physical examinations since 1950.

Although this study is the best known, and has provided the longest follow-up for which results have been published in detail, others can be found in various countries. In Australia, for example, the Busselton longitudinal study of health factors in a rural community in western Australia is perhaps the most important long-term prospective study of a whole community. The 3,500 subjects comprised 90 percent of the adult population. The initial survey took place in 1966, and a second survey followed in 1969.

Perhaps the most ambitious investigation undertaken by an organization relying on its own resources is the Cancer Prevention Study of the American Cancer Society. More than one million subjects (440,550 men and 562,671 women) were enrolled, largely by the efforts of some 70,000 volunteers who normally collect funds for the society. Subjects were traced annually from 1959 and asked to fill out questionnaires every second year. Copies of death certificates were obtained for all reported deaths, and the doctor was asked for information on the type of malignant neoplasm involved whenever cancer was mentioned on the certificate.

Nutrition and Mortality. About the time of the great Depression in the 1930s, the accepted belief was that diets that promoted growth and development were the most likely to increase the life span. The discovery of C. M. McCay and his co-workers in 1929 that dietary restriction, sufficiently stringent to retard growth, could extend the life span of experimental animals was almost directly contradictory (McCay, Dilley, and Crowell, 1929). When the experimental animals were subjected to pathological examination, it was found that growth retardation resulting from dietary restriction also resulted in a significant delay in the development of diseases of the lungs and kidneys and tumors of all kinds. Rats that became obese suffered an increased incidence of all age-associated disease. Many years later Morris H. Ross (1961) confirmed McCay's results.

If, as these studies suggest, the effect of dietary restriction upon life span depends upon retardation of growth, then the findings have limited clinical application, since far less severe dietary restrictions in human infants and children have serious deleterious effects upon the development of the central nervous system and resistance to disease. This obstacle altered the approach to the study of extending life span to the question of whether delay of dietary restriction until after the attainment of maturity might also be effective. Although the effects of dietary restriction after maturity have been systematically studied only recently, it is now generally agreed that restriction of food intake in adult life increases the life span of animals over that of animals permitted unlimited access to food.

Although it may not yet be possible to prescribe for humans a diet that might extend their life span, it is possible to examine some of the ways in which nutritional practices reduce the life spans of individuals to well below the maximum attainable.

Malnutrition and infection. Undernutrition appears to affect morbidity and mortality in a cyclical self-perpetuating way through increased susceptibility to infection. The situation is complicated by the fact that generally the environments where malnutrition is common are also the environments (characterized by overcrowding and lack of sanitation) that facilitate the spread of infectious disease.

The process whereby infection can precipitate malnutrition is relatively clear-cut. With even minor infections the rate of protein breakdown is increased and at the same time, appetite is decreased. As food intake diminishes, protein and other nutrient deficiencies are accelerated. The basal metabolic rate rises because of the infection, and energy requirements may increase to double the normal amount; the increased demand for glucose may result in the depletion of glucose stores in muscle fat. Carbohydrate and fat metabolism are also affected.

Because those protein and fat reserves that provide amino acids and energy during the course of an infection are low at such a time, the outcome of any infection tends to be more serious for a malnourished individual whose reserves will be depleted even under normal conditions. This may partly explain why the common childhood infections, such as measles, are rarely permanently disabling for a well-nourished child, but may be fatal to a child suffering from marasmus or kwashiorkor.

Vitamin levels also are affected by infection. So is iron metabolism; an iron deficiency can result in a reduced life span of blood cells. In addition, infections interfere with the metabolism of electrolytes such as calcium and phosphorus; and diarrhea results in loss of chloride and potassium, often fatal in the case of cholera.

To complete the cyclic relationship, it is necessary to examine the role of malnutrition in increasing susceptibility to infection. The immune response accounts for most of the resistance to infections in humans, and malnutrition seriously affects immunity and therefore resistance to infection. Immunity, however, is difficult to quantify, as the ability to resist disease is a very complex process involving both humoral immunity and cell-mediated immunity and the cooperation of both of these with several other complex systems.

There is evidence that in children suffering from kwashiorkor, both cell-mediated and humoral immunity are impaired, whereas in children with marasmus, both kinds of immunity appear to be relatively normal. It is also known that deficiencies of specific vitamins (particularly vitamins A, B, and C) can seriously impair immunity. It is clear therefore that malnutrition (or at least some forms of it) can increase the susceptibility of an individual to infection.

Overnutrition. Another important, though less obvious, aspect of malnutrition is overnutrition (and nutritional imbalance) in well-fed communities. This condition is believed by many to be a cause of a number of diseases common in the Western world, such as arteriosclerosis, diabetes, and some forms of cancer. Because such a large proportion of deaths in affluent countries fall into these categories, it is necessary to examine the relationship between them and nutrition.

Arteriosclerosis involves the deposit of cholesterol within artery walls, resulting in the arteries becoming less flexible and the lumina (passageways) gradually becoming smaller, eventually leading to interruption of the blood supply to different organs such as the cardiac muscle, which could lead to a heart attack. There is little doubt that disordered nutrition plays a most important role. Evidence for the role of nutrition is largely derived from investigations of the coronary arteries. When these provide an inadequate oxygen supply to the heart muscle, ischemic heart disease (IHD) results. This disease is the single most common cause of death of middle-aged men in many Western countries; it kills twice as many as all malignant neoplasms (the second commonest cause of death).

Some studies have tried to link IHD with various dietary practices. Jollife and Archer (1959), for example, concluded that the intake of saturated fat was the most important factor accounting for the differences in IHD death rates between countries. Yudkin (1964) suggested a closer association between sugar consumption and IHD mortality. The International Classification of Diseases (ICD) coding of cardiovascular diseases prior to 1950, however, makes the isolation of deaths resulting from IHD in earlier years extremely difficult.

Diabetes is another of the diseases common in the Western world. It can be characterized by abnormally high levels of sugar in the blood and urine and relative or absolute deficiency of insulin. There appears to be little doubt that obesity is a risk factor for the appearance of diabetes in middle age.

Recent epidemiological studies in aboriginal societies have revealed a tenfold increase in the rate of diabetes as dietary practices have changed from a primitive to a more refined, Western-type diet. Strong arguments have been made for increased intake of sucrose, or refined starch, as a contributor to the increase (Cleave, 1974; Cohen, Teitelbaum, and Saliternik, 1972; West, 1974). Some authors disagree. H. C. Trowell (1975) suggested that the very low crude-fiber content of diet in the non-Western world helps cause the disease. Risk factors for diabetes, such as obesity, excessive intake of calories, or qualitative dietary changes, are difficult to evaluate since two or more variables frequently change simultaneously. High rates of diabetes, however, have not been reported in any society in which obesity is rare (West, 1974).

Obesity is a risk factor for other diseases as well. The Framingham study (Kannel, Gordon, et al., 1968–1978) for example, has shown an accelerating increase in both heart disease and stroke with increasing degrees of overweight (Gordon and Kannel, 1973). Weight that is 50 percent above "ideal" increases the risk of these disorders among men by 100 percent and among women by an even greater percentage.

We noted previously that experimental animals that became obese suffered increased incidence of tumors. Animals subject to severe dietary restriction, on the other hand, experienced a lower incidence. It is believed that these results also apply to humans, although care must be exercised, because excessive dietary restriction can impair the immune system, rather than maintain it.

Apart from the effects of total calorie consumption, there is the question of the possible carcinogenic effects of ingesting certain nutrients or food additives. Currently there is considerable interest centered on neoplastic disease of the colon and its possible relationship to the amount of either crude fiber or fat or meat in the diet. Epidemiological studies have implicated some nineteen different specific foods as possibly being related to the development of gastric cancer (Haenszel, 1967).

There is some evidence connecting polyunsaturated fatty acids, particularly after heating (e.g., when used as cooking oil) and cancer. Nitrosamines, in widespread use for coloring and curing various fish and meat products, are potent carcinogens, capable of inducing cancer in many different parts of the body.

Clearly, nutrition is an important factor affecting mortality, and our understanding of the relationship needs further development.

Environmental Factors. Disease can be considered to be "a maladjustment of a living thing to the environment in which it dwells." The aspects of the environment that may place human health in jeopardy may be described as (1) physical-chemical, or inorganic; and (2) biological, or organic. The physical aspects comprise a very wide range from heat, humidity, and wind, to trace elements in the soil and hence in food and water.

As far as weather and climate are concerned, it is possible to predict only that extremes of heat and cold (i.e., excessive thermal stresses) are definitely harmful, that moderately hot conditions increase susceptibility to intestinal diseases, and that moderately cold conditions increase susceptibility to respiratory complaints. The mortality rate from coronary disease in middle and high latitudes is invariably highest in the colder months of January and February and lowest in the warmest months of July and August. Masako Sakamoto-Momiyama (1977), however, has made an extensive historical study of the effects of climate and geography on morbidity and mortality and has discovered a gradual but definite tendency in many developed countries over the past hundred years to advance from a seasonal variation in which deaths are concentrated in summer and winter to a nonseasonal pattern.

An inverse relationship between mortality from heart diseases and hardness of local drinking water has been found in many countries. That is, the harder the water, the less likelihood of that form of mortality. The relationship seems paradoxical to many, because one of the main elements in hard water is calcium, which is implicated in the hardening of the arteries. Measurements in Great Britain indicate that on average, the death rate falls by about 50 per 100,000 for each increase in calcium of 25 parts per million.

Small amounts of some metals and trace elements (e.g., chromium, cobalt, copper, iron, iodine, manganese, molybdenum, vanadium, and zinc) are essential to life. But other metals and trace elements are potentially toxic at quite low levels of strength, and all are very toxic at higher levels. Some are cumulative poisons in that several sublethal doses can add up to lethal levels. Because metals and trace elements do not disintegrate with time and because some can be concentrated at relatively high levels by various organisms that compose the food of humans and many animals, such substances are being closely watched. Mercury is doubtless the biggest problem. It is used in large quantities and can be converted in the environment to the highly toxic methyl forms. Lead is also a big problem. Studies of lead concentrations in ice samples show that worldwide atmospheric lead levels have increased four hundred times from 800 B.C. to the present.

Thousands of synthetic organic chemicals are in common use. Many, including some of the most highly toxic, break down rapidly in the environment. Others, including some with very low acute toxicity, pose serious chronic hazards, for they are persistent, move from the environment into organisms, and concentrate in food chains (e.g., chlorinated hydrocarbons and polychlorinated biphenyls). Dioxin contaminants found in certain herbicides are very toxic and highly teratogenic. Other chemical contaminants, known to be carcinogens, include polynuclear aromatic hydrocarbons found in soot, smoke, tars, and cigarette smoke.

A potential carcinogenic hazard recently discovered is the large number of organic contaminants in drinking water. It has been suggested that the major source of these contaminants is chlorine, which is used to purify the water but which reacts with both natural humic chemicals present in the water and waste effluents to produce possible hazardous chemicals.

The products of combustion include carbon monoxide, nitrogen oxides, sulphur oxides, and particulates, with ozone photochemical oxidants as secondary products. All are recognized as toxic pollutants, and regulatory standards have been set in a number of countries.

Other toxic substances in common use include asbestos (particularly the blue variety) and nitrites and nitrates (both introduced into the water supply from chemical plants and fertilizers). Cancer of the liver has recently been noted to be associated with the manufacture of polyvinyl chloride (PVC), which is widely used.

Radiation hazards arise from both ionizing and nonionizing radiation. Nonionizing radiation, such as that emitted from microwave ovens, radar, and radio, produces its effects primarily through the heating of tissue; high intensities produce burns, sterility, and other damage. Background ionizing radiation is encountered from cosmic radiation and naturally occurring radioisotopes. To these sources of ionizing radiation scientists have added X rays, artificial isotopes, and effluents from nuclear power plants. The problem of the magnitude of the human health hazard posed by the fission products of nuclear reactors is extremely complex and controversial. Even the physicists and nuclear engineers cannot agree.

From time immemorial, humans have been the victim of water-borne infection, either by the cholera vibrio, enteric organisms such as the dysentery and salmonella bacilli, and numerous protozoa or by worm infection through intermediate hosts such as fish, snails, and crustacea. This threat to life and health was accepted as inevitable until the development of microbiology in the second quarter of the nineteenth century. The essential role of water in the transmission of malaria, yellow fever, dengue fever, schistosomiasis (bilharzia), and onchocerciasis (river blindness) needs little elaboration.

Most of these diseases are now concentrated in the developing regions of the world, where they still cause millions of deaths and untold misery. Effective measures for controlling the diseases are available, but the administrative problems and costs are enormous. Despite the fact that in the developed world infectious diseases have been largely controlled, they are still potentially very important problems for these countries, because of the unprecedented growth of rapid international air travel. For diseases such as influenza, air travel is capable of making the whole world a single epidemiological unit.

Personal Behavior. The main factors affecting mortality that fall under the heading of personal behavior are smoking, alcohol consumption, and exercise. Experimentation with drugs has become common among adolescents and young adults, but reliable statistics on the resulting risk of addiction and premature death do not seem to be available.

Smoking has long been associated with ill health, and some governments in the past made drastic attempts to discourage the habit. King James I of England is quoted as saying in 1604 that smoking was "barbarous, beastly, hateful to the nose, a vile and stinking custom, harmful to the brain and dangerous to the lungs." Tobacco smoking in Japan was forbidden by the state in 1603, and, when that did not stop the habit, it was further decreed in 1612 that anyone caught even selling tobacco would have all his property confiscated. The sultan of Turkey introduced the death penalty for smoking in 1633, and about the same time the penalty in Russia was a beating and banishment to Siberia. Decapitation was the penalty for selling tobacco in China in 1638. In seventeenth-century Catholic Europe, to smoke in church was to risk excommunication. Smoking in public was prohibited in Germany until 1848 (Singer and Levinson, 1976). None of these severe measures had much effect. As the extensive literature linking smoking to mortality continues to grow, some governments have taken small steps to discourage the habit (tobacco taxes, warnings on cigarette packets, antismoking advertisements). Education of the population in the probable harmful effects of smoking may well produce results where past threats of penalties did not. Heated discussion as to whether smoking actually causes lung cancer continues. Few would deny the association.

The literature on the relationship between alcoholism and mortality does not appear to be as extensive, although quite a few detailed studies are available. (See, for example, Singer and Levinson, 1976.) Alcoholism, however, must be regarded as one of the major problems of the time. In the United States, for example, there are an estimated 9 million alcoholics (about 7 percent of the adult population); in France, alcoholism is said to be the third most important cause of death. In the United States, male employees of the Du Pont Company known to be alcoholics experienced mortality 3.8 times the normal rate; the mortality figures for suspected and recovered alcoholics were 3.15 and 3.0 respectively (Singer and Levinson, 1976, p. 33). The latter figure would seem to indicate that certain disease processes, initiated by alcohol, may not be reversible, or that some employees in that category were not fully recovered. The heaviest extra mortality associated with alcohol use appears to fall in the three main categories: diseases of the digestive system, motor vehicle accidents, and other accidents and homicide (Davies, 1965).

Biological Theories of Aging. The process of aging is complex and multifaceted, and the theories that have been proposed in attempted explanation vary considerably. Most gerontologists would agree with the view that there exists within us an identifiable "clock of aging," a genetically determined program that dictates that we will age and die and the rate at which this will occur. The following is the evidence for this view:

1. Each (mammalian) species has a specific life span and rate of aging, for example, just as humans begin to show signs of aging long before attaining the average life span of seventy years, rats show comparable signs well before their average life span of three years.
2. Life span is related to parents' life span; the children of long-lived parents tend to enjoy long life also.
3. The life spans of identical twins, originating from a single set of genes, tend to be the same; but this is not true for nonidentical twins, originating from two separate sets of genes.
4. Normal cells in tissue culture were found by Leonard Hayflick (1968) to undergo a finite number of doublings, the "Hayflick limit."
5. There is a strict timetable for cell death during the development of mammalian embryos (e.g., of the tissue between webbed fingers and toes) and during the metamorphosis of insects.

In recent years, the field of immunology has become very important in the study of aging. This is partly the result of realizing that nonaccidental death is by and large a consequence of the body's inability to defend itself successfully against attack by hostile agents, either extrinsic (such as bacteria and viruses) or intrinsic (such as cancer and autoimmune disease).

The majority of the body's somatic cells (those other than the sex cells) are continually dying and being replaced. During the process of replacement, an exact duplicate of the information-storing deoxyribonucleic acid (DNA) in the parent cell chromosomes must be provided for each daughter cell. One particular enzyme, or catalyst, DNA-polymerase, is primarily responsible for the accuracy of the DNA duplication and the repair of damaged DNA. The parent cell DNA is used as a pattern.

For a species to survive over any length of time, it is essential that it include an adequate proportion of mutants to ensure its ability to adjust to changes in the environment. In other words, errors, or mutations, must be possible in the duplication process. However, an error in the DNA that controls the key enzyme DNA-polymerase will result in further errors, which will make subsequent DNA duplications even more inaccurate. Eventually enough key enzymes will be affected to impair the functioning of the cell. This "error catastrophe" will occur after a variable number of cell generations (in human fibroblasts, about fifty cell generations—the Hayflick limit). The more inaccurate and error-prone the initial DNA-polymerase, the sooner some type of error catastrophe will arise, and the shorter will be the life span of the species.

In 1957, Frank Macfarlane Burnet proposed a system of immune surveillance involving specialized blood cells (T-cells), which seek out and destroy any cells that they can recognize as alien. Such alien cells may be parasites, but more commonly they are cells of the body rendered recognizably alien by a virus, by the attachment of antigens from microorganisms, or, and most importantly, by genetic abnormalities of the somatic cells.

It is now commonly believed that in the normal young person, numerous, mutated, somatic cells with the potential of forming tumors develop, but they are eliminated by the body's system of immunity. Immunity declines with age, however, as does the ability to distinguish accurately between true body cells and alien cells. The remaining protective cells then attack not only foreign and mutated cells but also normal cells, resulting in a variety of autoimmune disorders such as arthritis, rheumatism, and pernicious anemia.

Many other theories of aging have also been proposed, and it is clear that biologists, immunologists, geneticists, and endocrinologists will have important roles to play if understanding of aging and mortality is to be advanced.

Biological Age. Among human beings all the same age, wide differences in individual performances exist, and statements such as "X looks younger than his age" and "Y performs better than people his age" are frequently heard. The concept of biological age (as opposed to chronological age) is therefore intuitively appealing.

Most attempts to predict biological age use multiple-regression models. J. D. Tobin (1977) has suggested the use of four clinically important physiologic variables: forced expiratory volume in 1.0 seconds, standard creatinine clearance, systolic blood pressure, and oral glucose tolerance. Each of these variables not only is influenced by age, but in addition is associated with a disease: chronic obstructive pulmonary disease, renal failure, hypertension, and diabetes, respectively.

Biological age is hardly a new concept for actuaries, who have been preparing rates for impaired lives for decades. The approach now being adopted by physiologists is basically the same as that followed by many underwriting manuals. It is important to note that professionals in the two quite distinct disciplines have adopted the same basic approach in their separate attempts to come to grips with aging and mortality.

Summary. All the factors affecting mortality and longevity so far described are relevant both to advanced industrialized societies and to less-developed countries. The emphasis, however, is different.

Undernutrition and infectious diseases, for example, are important causes of death in developing regions. Deaths from these causes can be substantially diminished by reducing undernutrition and improving public health, which makes the problem an economic, political, and social one. Undernutrition among disadvantaged groups in the industrialized nations is still evident, however, and deaths from infectious diseases are not negligible. The unprecedented growth of rapid international air travel means that more people than ever are coming into contact with infections originating in distant lands. For diseases such as influenza, air travel is capable of making the world a single epidemiological unit.

Contamination of the environment by industrial pollutants has been cause for concern for some years in most industrialized countries. As developing regions rush to embrace industrial technology, the adverse effects on health, and mortality from the associated environmental pollution will become evident.

Inhabitants of the more wealthy industrialized nations can expect to live about seventy years, and for them advances in the biological understanding of the aging process are very relevant. A large proportion of those living in the developing regions of the world can also be expected to die of degenerative diseases, and developments in the study of biological aging are important to them as well.

John H. Pollard

See also Epidemiologic transition; Mortality; Public health.

BIBLIOGRAPHY

Acsádi, George T., and János Nemeskéri. *History of Human Life Span and Mortality.* Translated by K. Balás. Budapest: Akadémiai Kiadó, 1970.

Benjamin, Bernard. "Demographic and Actuarial Aspects of Ageing." *Journal of the Institute of Actuaries* 90:211–238, 1964.

Benjamin, Bernard, and John H. Pollard. *Analysis of Mortality and Other Actuarial Statistics.* London: Heinemann, 1980.

Burnet, Frank Macfarlane. *Intrinsic Mutagenesis: A Genetic Approach to Ageing.* New York: Wiley, 1974.

Cleave, T. L. *The Saccharine Disease: Conditions Caused by the Taking of Refined Carbohydrates, Such as Sugar and White Flour.* Bristol, England: Wright, 1974.

Cohen, A. M., A. Teitelbaum, and R. Saliternik. "Genetics and Diet as Factors in Development of Diabetes Mellitus." *Metabolism* 21(3):235–240, March 1972.

Cox, P. R., and W. F. Scott. "International Studies in Generation Mortality." *Journal of the Institute of Actuaries* 104(pt. 3):297–333, 1977. See especially A. D. Wilkie's comments on pages 328–329.

Damiani, Paul. "Mesure de la morbidité: Liaison avec la mortalité." *International Statistical Review* 45(1):39–50, April 1977.

Davies, Karl M. "The Influence of Alcohol on Mortality." *Proceedings of the Home Office Life Underwriters Association* 46:159–178, 1965.

Gordon, Tavia, and William B. Kannel. "The Effects of Overweight on Cardiovascular Disease." *Geriatrics* 28(8):80–88, August 1973.

Haenszel, William. "Epidemiology of Gastric Cancer." In *Neoplasms of the Stomach*, edited by Gordon McNeer and George T. Pack, pp. 3–28. Philadelphia: J. B. Lippincott, 1967.

Haenszel, William, John W. Berg, Mitsuo Segi, Minoro Kurihara, and Frances Locke. "Large-bowel Cancer in Hawaiian Japanese." *Journal of the National Cancer Institute* 51(6):1765–1779, December 1973.

Hammond, E. Cuyler. "Smoking in Relation to Mortality and Morbidity: Findings in First Thirty-four Months of Follow-up in a Prospective Study Started in 1959." *Journal of the National Cancer Institute* 32:1161–1188, 1964.

Hayflick, Leonard. "Human Cells and Aging." *Scientific American* 218(3):32–37, March 1968.

International Union for the Scientific Study of Population. *Population Science in the Service of Mankind: Conference on Science in the Service of Life, Vienna, 1979.* Liège, Belgium, 1979. In English and French.

Jolliffe, Norman, and Morton Archer. "Statistical Associations between International Coronary Heart Disease Death Rates and Certain Environmental Factors." *Journal of Chronic Diseases* 9(6):636–652, June 1959.

Kannel, William B., Tavia Gordon, et al. *The Framingham Study: An Epidemiological Investigation of Cardiovascular Disease.* 33 vols. Washington, D.C.: U.S. Government Printing Office, 1968–1978.

Lilienfeld, Abraham M., Morton L. Levin, and Irving I. Kessler. *Cancer in the United States.* Cambridge, Mass.: Harvard University Press, 1972.

McCay, C. M., W. E. Dilley, and M. F. Crowell. "Growth Rates of Brook Trout Reared upon Purified Rations, upon Dry Skim Milk Diets, and upon Feed Combinations of Cereal Grains." *Journal of Nutrition* 1(3):233–246, January 1929.

Moriyama, Iwao M., Dean E. Krueger, and Jeremiah Stamler. *Cardiovascular Diseases in the United States.* Cambridge, Mass.: Harvard University Press, 1971.

Pollard, A. H. "The Interaction between Morbidity and Mortality." *Journal of the Institute of Actuaries* 107(pt. 3, 436): 233–302, September 1980.

Pollard, John H. "Factors Affecting Mortality and the Length of Life." In *Population Science in the Service of Mankind: Conference on Science in the Service of Life, Vienna, 1979*, pp. 53–79. Liège, Belgium: International Union for the Scientific Study of Population, 1979. With a summary in French on page 80.

Ross, Morris H. "Length of Life and Nutrition in the Rat." *Journal of Nutrition* 75(2):197–210, October 1961.

Sakamoto-Momiyama, Masako. *Seasonality in Human Mortality: A Medico-geographical Study.* Tokyo: University of Tokyo Press, 1977.

Singer, Richard B., and Louis Levinson (editors). *Medical Risks: Patterns of Mortality and Survival; A Reference Volume.* Lexington, Mass.: Lexington Books, 1976.

Tobin, J. D. "Physiological Indices of Aging." In *Proceedings of the Vichy Conference.* Paris: Institut de la Vie, 1977.

Trowell, H. C. "Dietary-fiber Hypothesis of the Etiology of Diabetes Mellitus." *Diabetes* 24(8):762–765, August 1975.

West, Kelly M. "Diabetes in American Indians and Other Native Populations of the New World." *Diabetes* 23(1):841–855, October 1974.

Wilkie, A. D. Comment on "International Studies in Generation Mortality" by P. R. Cox and W. F. Scott. *Journal of the Institute of Actuaries* 104(pt. 3):328–329.

Yudkin, John. "Dietary Fat and Dietary Sugar in Relation to Ischaemic Heart-disease and Diabetes." *Lancet,* no. 7349, pp. 4–5, 4 July 1964.

MORTALITY

Mortality, with fertility and migration, determines the size of human populations, their composition by age and sex, their racial and ethnic characters, and their potential for future growth. Because demographers are interested in changes in mortality rates over time and in variations in rates among groups, directly and indirectly related articles are found throughout this work. The two articles that comprise the following entry, MORTALITY TRENDS, present long-term mortality trends. Elsewhere, EPIDEMIOLOGIC TRANSITION discusses changes over the years in causes of death. MORBIDITY AND LONGEVITY focuses on personal and environmental influences on the aging process and risks of mortality. Policies and programs to reduce mortality are described in PUBLIC HEALTH. The special risks in the first years of life are discussed in INFANT AND CHILD MORTALITY. LIFE TABLES shows how both age-specific and sex-specific mortality rates are used to estimate life expectancy. Methods for approximating rates where death registration is not adequate are given in INDIRECT ESTIMATION OF FERTILITY AND MORTALITY. Mortality as a component of growth is also briefly discussed in WORLD POPULATION.

MORTALITY TRENDS

1. HISTORICAL TRENDS   Regina McNamara
2. POST–WORLD WAR II TRENDS   George J. Stolnitz

1.
HISTORICAL TRENDS

Skeletal remains studied by paleodemographers give evidence that the average man and woman in prehistoric times lived about 18 to 25 years. By the Neolithic period, the beginnings of agriculture, and consequently more stable food supplies, probably increased the average life span, although there is speculation that settlement of people in communities may have had the opposite effect. Parasitic and communicable diseases could have increased, and mortality rates may have risen.

For the Egyptians, according to evidence based on study of mummies, life expectancy at birth was just over 22 years. The Greeks and early Romans lived, on the average, 25 to 30 years, and the late Romans lived 35 years. Because these estimates come from burial inscriptions, which are likely to underrepresent deaths of women and children and pertain to the upper classes, these figures are crude approximations that probably reflect the lowest levels of mortality in their time.

From fragmentary documentation limited to a few European countries, such as parish registers from the Middle Ages, records of the British aristocracy from 1330, and some registration of vital statistics in France in the sixteenth century, slight gains in life expectancy are indicated by the end of the seventeenth century. Nevertheless, few survived to age 40 even in relatively good times. In certain periods, conditions seem to have allowed for a relative decline in the death rate and an increase in the population, but in other periods the devastation and spread of disease caused by warfare, poor harvests, severe winters, and the plague created widespread misery and death. The plague is said to have killed one-fourth of the population of Europe, about 25 million people, in 1348–1350. Crowding of people in preindustrial European cities apparently caused mortality from infectious diseases that was at least as high as that in the previous era, but the known evidence is not sufficiently reliable for comparisons in time and across regions.

Records from about 1700 for the Scandinavian countries, France, England, and Wales are considerably more complete, and they show that the early years of the eighteenth century brought the onset of the first known consistent and extensive decline in mortality rates. The reasons for that decline and for its variation from region to region are not universally agreed upon, but the trend is unmistakable. One viewpoint is that the downward trend was produced by abatement of the great plagues and crop failures, not by improvements in normal years. The last major plague was in France in 1720, when Marseilles and other cities in the south lost from one-third to three-fourths of their populations, although the disease was virtually extinct in other parts of western Europe by that time. The precise reasons for the disappearance of severe epidemics of plague are not known. Either humans, rats, or both might have developed a natural immunity, and indoor rats were apparently displaced by outdoor rats, which were poor hosts for disease-carrying fleas.

Western European countries were not rid of famine until after the great potato famine in Ireland in the 1840s but overall food production is thought to have been increased by crop rotation from the late 1600s, better fertilizers and implements, and the introduction of corn and potatoes from the New World. When transportation of crops improved, surplus food in one area could be shipped to deficit areas, and supplies became more stable over larger regions. Nevertheless, the significant reduction of mortality rates among the aristocracy in the eighteenth century, a group presumed to have always had an adequate supply of food, suggests that there were additional causes of the overall mortality declines and population growth. Male British peers born from 1780 to 1829 could expect to live 48 years, as compared with 33 years for those born between 1680 and 1729.

The relative contribution of medical science versus social and economic development to mortality decline is the subject of debate among demographic historians. The growth of hospitals, dispensaries, and midwifery services; additions to knowledge of physiology and anatomy; and the introduction of smallpox inoculation and vaccination were contemporary with substantial mortality declines. Inoculation and vaccination may have reduced deaths from smallpox in England from about a quarter of the total deaths in 1700 to an insignificant number in 1900. The death rate from scarlet fever was probably lowered because of the modification of the balance between the virulence of the infective organism and the resistance of the host. Improved living conditions, especially improvements in nutrition, are thought by some writers to have made a much more important contribution to mortality decline than medical advances, but the extent to which such benefits were enjoyed by the general population in the eighteenth and early nineteenth centuries is arguable. Socioeconomic differentials in mortality were such that the general population born around 1850 in England had an average life span equal to that achieved by the aristocracy born a century earlier.

The importance of better housing, public sanitation, and water supplies for the control of infectious diseases was well recognized by the second half of the nineteenth century; these are accepted as a major cause of the consistent decline in mortality. Gains in life expectancy averaged about 9 years in northern European countries between 1840 and 1900. Sand filters for the water of the Thames River were introduced into the London water system in 1828, and the method spread quickly across Europe. The water closet was introduced in 1778, although it was probably not in general use before 1830. The introduction of cotton undergarments to replace rarely washed woolen clothing and widely diffused changes in attitudes toward personal hygiene, as indicated by amounts of soap used, are thought to have made substantial contributions to the decline of mortality in England and Wales in the early nineteenth century by reducing diseases of the intestinal tract and those transmitted by body lice. Additional sources of mortality decline were the beginning of antiseptic practices in surgery in the 1860s and the acceptance of the germ theory of disease.

Reduction of deaths from infectious diseases of all kinds accounts for the major part of the rapid decline in the mortality rate that produced a life expectancy of about 50 years by 1900 in northern Europe, North America, and Oceania and further gains of around 20 years in the next half century. In those countries of Europe that had a comparatively late onset of mortality decline, the pace was more rapid. Life expectancy did not exceed 35 years in Italy in the 1870s, and a steady fall in the mortality rate did not start until 1875; but the drop in crude death rates from 30 per 1,000 population to around 15 that had taken 150 years in France and 125 years in England was accomplished in about 55 years. The Soviet Union gained 26 years in life expectancy from 1927 to 1962. Similar progress in Greece raised the average life span 20 years between the 1920s and 1950s.

By the mid-1950s, deaths from infective and parasitic diseases in most of the developed regions were at a low level and were no longer significantly influencing the general mortality trend. Infant mortality declines were substantial between the late 1930s and early 1950s, and rates are well below 20 per 1,000 live births in most developed countries. Declines in overall mortality rates have leveled off since the 1950s, with life expectancies in developed countries currently ranging from about 65 to a little over 75. Further gains will most likely depend on the reduction of socioeconomic and sex differentials in mortality rates and on medical breakthroughs in the treatment of diseases affecting older age groups, primarily cardiovascular diseases and cancer.

Some small gains in life expectancy are recorded for a few developing nations for the first quarter of this century, but for most the onset of the accelerated decline in mortality rates dates from the mid-1940s, immediately after World War II, and later. The causes are generally held to be the improved techniques for controlling infectious disease, especially penicillin and the use of DDT against malaria; general social and economic improvements affecting education, housing, sanitation, and nutrition; and expansion and improvement of medical facilities and services. The role of international organizations in applying Western medical technology to at least some areas of developing countries is cited as a major contribution to mortality decline.

When the relative weight of each of these factors is argued, Sri Lanka is the country most often discussed. Sri Lanka's death rate dropped slowly and steadily from 31.0 in 1905 to 21.5 in 1945. It fell to 14.0 in 1947 and continued downward to 9.0 in 1975. The changes are thought to correlate closely with slow improvements in hygiene and medical care up to 1946 and with an intensified malaria control campaign after 1946. But the sudden drop is also attributed to social and economic factors benefiting the population after World War II and to an increased demand for medical services.

The patterns of decline from high to low mortality levels have been summarized by Abdel R. Omran (1971) as an "epidemiologic transition" with three stages. The "age of pestilence and famines" is characterized by high and fluctuating mortality rates with expectation of life at birth varying between 20 and 40 years. Most of the already-developed countries were in this stage from prehistoric times to the eighteenth century and most developing countries emerged from this stage in the early or mid-twentieth century. In the second age, that of "receding pandemics" more people survive the fewer epidemics, the rate of decline accelerates, and life expectancy at birth increases to about 50 years. In the final stage, the "age of degenerative and man-made diseases," the mortality rate continues to decline and approaches stability at a relatively low level, life expectancy reaches 70 years, and fertility rather than mortality is the crucial factor in population growth.

Regina McNamara

See also EPIDEMIOLOGIC TRANSITION; HISTORICAL DEMOGRAPHY; PALEODEMOGRAPHY; PUBLIC HEALTH.

BIBLIOGRAPHY

Kitagawa, Evelyn M. "On Mortality." *Demography* 14(4):381–389, November 1977.
McKeown, Thomas, and R. G. Brown. "Medical Evidence Related to English Population Changes in the Eighteenth Century." In *Population in History: Essays in Historical Demography,* edited by David V. Glass and D. E. C. Eversley, pp. 285–307. London: Edward Arnold, 1965. Chicago: Aldine, 1965.
Omran, Abdel R. "The Epidemiologic Transition: A Theory of the Epidemiology of Population Change." *Milbank Memorial Fund Quarterly* 49(4, pt. 1):509–538, October 1971.
Preston, Samuel H. "Mortality Trends." *Annual Review of Sociology* 3:163–178, 1977.
United Nations, Department of Economic and Social Affairs. *The Determinants and Consequences of Population Trends.* Rev. ed. Volume 1: *New Summary of Findings on Interaction of Demographic, Economic, and Social Factors.* Series A, Population Studies, no. 50. New York, 1973.

2.
POST–WORLD WAR II TRENDS

The decades since the end of World War II have been witness to massive transformations in mortality conditions and prospects throughout the globe. In more-developed regions (MDR's), including all of the world's nations having the lowest mortality rates during modern times, longevity trends that have endured for a century or more are about to end. In less-developed regions (LDR's), containing three-fourths of the world's population and all of its countries with the highest mortality rates, probably no development of the postwar era has operated on a broader demographic scale or had more pervasive human and social consequences than the revolutionary upsurges in longevity that have taken place almost everywhere.

"More-developed" as used here consists of continental Europe including the Soviet Union, Canada and the United States in North America, Japan and Israel in Asia, and Australia and New Zealand in Oceania. All other areas, that is, all Africa and Latin America, plus all Asia and Oceania except the countries just mentioned, are included under the term "less-developed."

The following three sections deal in succession with some global patterns and then with MDR's and LDR's in greater depth. MDR-LDR contrasts of special interest will be emphasized often, as will the major differences to be expected between recent trends and prospective trends in both regional groupings.

The accompanying data in Tables 1 and 2, while selective, can serve to introduce the themes to be highlighted. It should be kept in mind that the indicated values are all subject to error, with the margins of possible inaccuracy for LDR's being especially wide. The low and high values in the array of national measures for MDR's can be assumed to be closely accurate, but most of those at the low end of the LDR list and some at the high end cannot. For this reason, only quartile measures are shown for LDR's, although the biases from estimation errors are still probably such as to raise the LDR third quartile values relative to the MDR minima. The estimates for the early 1950s and late 1970s, if treated as approxima-

TABLE 1. *Estimated or projected values of expectation of life at birth, by sex, for world and major regional groupings, 1950–1955, 1975–1980, and 1995–2000*

| | Expectation of life at birth | | | | | | | | |
| | 1950–1955 | | | 1975–1980 | | | 1995–2000 | | |
Region	Total	Male	Female	Total	Male	Female	Total	Male	Female
World	47.2	46.0	48.4	57.4	56.0	58.9	64.4	62.8	66.1
MDR's	65.2	63.0	67.4	71.9	68.3	75.5	73.6	70.1	77.3
National values									
Low	57.8	56.0	58.5	69.2	65.0	70.7	71.4	67.1	73.4
High	72.6	70.9	74.5	76.1	74.7	79.3	76.8	73.9	80.0
LDR's	42.5	41.6	43.5	55.1	54.0	56.2	63.0	61.7	64.4
National values									
1st quartile	33.5	32.0	35.0	47.3	44.4	49.0	56.0	54.4	57.6
3rd quartile	51.4	49.1	53.1	63.5	61.7	65.0	69.7	67.6	71.4
Africa	37.4	36.0	38.9	48.7	47.2	50.3	57.9	56.2	59.6
Latin America	52.0	49.9	54.1	63.4	61.1	65.8	69.7	67.5	71.9
North America	69.0	66.3	72.0	73.2	69.2	77.0	74.3	70.1	78.2
East Asia	47.5	46.0	49.0	64.7	62.8	66.7	70.6	68.3	73.0
South Asia	39.4	39.3	39.4	51.8	51.6	52.1	61.0	60.4	61.6
Europe	65.4	63.2	67.7	71.9	68.9	75.0	74.2	71.2	77.4
Oceania	60.8	59.0	62.6	65.7	63.7	67.8	69.8	67.6	72.0
Soviet Union	61.7	60.0	63.5	69.6	65.0	74.3	71.4	67.1	76.0

Source of data: United Nations, 1980.

TABLE 2. *Estimated or projected values of crude death rates, for world and major regional groupings, 1950–1955, 1975–1980, and 1995–2000*

| | Crude death rate | | |
	1950–1955	1975–1980	1995–2000
World	18.5	11.5	8.8
MDR's	10.1	9.4	10.1
National values			
High	13.9	13.0	12.6
Low	6.9	6.4	5.8
LDR's	22.6	12.2	8.4
National values			
1st quartile	17.2	8.3	6.6
3rd quartile	30.9	19.0	11.7
Africa	27.1	17.1	10.6
Latin America	14.5	8.4	6.0
North America	9.4	9.0	9.8
East Asia	19.2	8.6	7.8
South Asia	24.8	14.1	8.8
Europe	10.9	10.6	10.7
Oceania	12.4	9.0	8.5
Soviet Union	9.2	8.9	10.0

Source of data: United Nations, 1980.

tions, are not likely to distort seriously the majority of levels and trends in question, although the data for Africa, whether estimated or projected, should be regarded as rough orders of magnitude at best. The end-of-century projections, of course, are subject to the usual pitfalls confronting long-term speculations.

Global Aggregates. With allowance for these statistical precautions, it appears probable that average length of life globally has risen by about a decade, from something like the indicated 45-plus years to 55-plus years, over the past quarter-century. Almost certainly, the actual increase being estimated was a multiple—surely double if not triple or more—of any longer-run rate of global change in history (see Stolnitz, 1955; United Nations, 1973). (Past periods of recovery from major catastrophies are not being compared at this point.) Europe's black death, the great floods and famines that have recurred throughout history in the Orient, and World War II, to name a few examples, each involved changes of an episodic rather than long-term nature and regional rather than global populations, or both.

As a result of the accompanying drop in the death rate, from under 20 per 1,000 to about 12 per 1,000, today's 1.8 percent or so rate of world population growth is about 0.75 percentage points higher than it would have been in the absence of the drop. Stated another way, the drop accounts for something like 40 percent of the world's current growth rate.

A second major conclusion, one directly seen from Table 1, is that the global measurements represent but poorly those of their underlying MDR and LDR components. The level of life expectancy in more-developed nations was some 50 percent higher in the early 1950s than in the less-developed nations, 65 years compared to 40 or so years, and is still roughly 30 percent higher, or 70-plus compared to about 55 years. Similarly for trends, the contrast between the two broad development groupings is strong, with the indicated rise in LDR figures almost double the change in MDR figures for the past quarter-century.

The resulting considerable convergence between mean longevities in the two sets of regions is historic. It is probably the first such instance since the nations in the more developed regions began their long-run climb to higher longevities between one hundred and two hundred years ago. The recent reduction of the "development gap" between MDR's and LDR's with respect to length of life undoubtedly ranks with the foremost instances of international convergence in any major social or economic sphere of behavior.

The projections of life expectancy in Table 1 imply that all of these main MDR-LDR comparative patterns will endure for the rest of this century. The projected differences in levels by 1995–2000 remain very large, ten years or more; the pace of the trend upward is anticipated to be far greater on average among LDR populations; and convergence is expected to continue.

Associated with these anticipated patterns, or helping to explain them, are numerous underlying expectations, some rather obvious and others relatively obscure. It is clear, for example, that the enormous advantage of the developed regions in regard to mortality is related to such factors as far higher average incomes (amounting to a current average differential of 10 to 1 or more); higher levels of education; more-advanced technology in all or practically all areas of application; far superior communication and transportation systems; much older political systems and much greater political stability as a very general rule; and long-established, more efficient civil services in the areas of medicine, public health, and sanitation. In each of these instances, the MDR advantages hold not only on average but for each nation with respect to practically all national areas in LDR's.

It is far from surprising, therefore, that the gap in the mortality figures between individual more-developed and less-developed nations continues to be so large, despite the convergent tendencies just noted between their averages. The Table 1 estimates for 1975–1980 suggest that the lowest level of life expectancy (combined sexes) for any national population in MDR's is still substantially higher than all but the topmost national levels

among LDR's. But in addition, the data suggest a good deal more about underlying causes and patterns, as can best be seen by discussing each group of populations on its own.

More-developed Regions. Although differences in social, economic, and political structures among individual MDR's have been enormous historically, and often remain major today, their impact on national mortality differentials has become progressively muted over the past quarter-century. As shown in Table 1, the low-high spread of national life expectancies for combined sexes fell from 15 years in the early 1950s to only about 6 years in 1975–1980, a 60 percent drop. Similar magnitudes of change can be seen to have held for each sex. Whatever may have been the causal mechanisms making for substantial intercountry differentials in the early 1950s, either the nature of the causal factors or their relative impacts have changed radically.

This is not the place to attempt a quantitative explanation of causes or their relative importance, but it can be plausibly argued that converging standards of health care technologies, rather than traditional socioeconomic explanations, have been the key factors. In particular, explanations centering on income differences are almost surely not the main answer, as can be seen from regression types of analysis. Also and probably much more indicatively, there is the fact that differences between male and female life expectancy within most MDR nations have come to exceed most differences (for either sex) between nations. It would be difficult or impossible to explain the 7-plus year differential shown in Table 1 for 1975–1980 (or the essentially unbroken rise in male-female differentials among all MDR populations since as far back as 1920) by an approach placing main emphasis on income, education, occupation, or similar variables. Rather, combinations of biological and cultural variables, along with aspects of life style largely unrelated to socioeconomic status, seem to be the predominant causal elements.

It is true, as frequently documented, that appreciable mortality differentials among socioeconomic subgroups within more-developed regions are commonplace. But it is also true that such differentials are large only in comparison with low rates of mortality and can be substantially narrowed by appropriate governmental policies for public health and medicine.

In any event, it is clear that only limited gains can be expected from further increases in per capita income, consumption, or similar indicators of standard of living in MDR's. While increasing proportions of total output allocated to health-related services (rather than increasing total output as such) can play a worthwhile role, it may well be that such changes in life style as improved body care through exercise, voluntary (as opposed to economically imposed) dietary discipline, reduced smoking, and lower alcoholic consumption will accomplish as much or more. Such agents of change are essentially independent of income levels, and indeed may well be negated, rather than abetted, by rising standards of living.

Probably more important by far is the fact that future upward trends in MDR life expectancies are coming to depend, almost by necessity, upon what happens to death rates beyond midlife. This stems from the little noted but central fact that the primary sources of previous long-run gains in MDR longevity—control of communicable diseases and especially declines in mortality from infancy to midlife—are close to becoming exhausted. Today, neither of these (largely overlapping) causal processes can significantly lengthen life. Communicable diseases in recent years have come to account for less than 5 percent of deaths from all causes; even if they were totally eliminated, the resulting rise in expectation of life at birth would be only fractional (see, for example, United Nations, 1975). Similarly, if female deaths under age 50 fell to zero in each more-developed nation, total length of life would only rise by some 3 to 4 years, depending on the population, or well below the average increases shown in Table 1 since the early 1950s. For males, the corresponding increases would be somewhat larger, 5 to 6 years, but would still be below increases since about 1940. For either sex, such ceiling effects, however obviously welcome in terms of the individuals concerned, would be minor proportions of the 20 to 30 year gains registered by most MDR populations since 1900.

Of special interest in this connection (though not documented in Table 2) is that infant mortality rates fell by more than 50 percent between 1950 and 1970 in the large majority of MDR populations. Upward fluctuations apart, the maximum possible future declines nearly everywhere in MDR's will therefore have to be less—indeed, much less as a rule—than the declines recorded within a relatively short recent period.

Past history shows that mortality gains beyond age 50 or 60, while often not insubstantial by some standards, have contributed only marginally to total length of life, despite the enormous medical, social, and economic advances that have taken place over the past century. (Depending on the area and period, MDR life tables often show appreciable percentage changes over time in upper-age expectations of life, but even these can be seen to have only limited impacts on total length of life. In recent years, for example, a rise by as much as 10 percent in average length of life beyond age 60 in MDR populations would tend to raise their expectation of life at birth by only about 2 percent.)

There is no historical basis for supposing that anything like the long-run increases in longevity found throughout the MDR's can be approximated again unless and until changes of a radical or even revolutionary kind take place in the technologies available for dealing both with the chief killers in old age—heart disease, cancer, and stroke—and with the ravages of aging in general.

It is no accident, therefore, that the 1995–2000 values shown in Table 1 for MDR's imply so little change in life expectancy over the last decades of this century. Simply interpreted, the projections assume no retrogressions of consequence, further declines in mortality rates at younger ages within the limited confines of downward change still possible, and moderate rather than spectacular mortality gains at older ages.

The resulting historic changeover of longevity prospects will not, of course, evolve simultaneously among the more than one billion inhabitants of the more developed regions. The relative homogeneity of their current situations is such, however, that similar changeovers should become quickly and increasingly evident in all national populations within these regions.

Should such changeovers occur as expected, they would have two demographic effects worth noting. One is on age distribution. In the past, declines in mortality rates by age have had only limited impact on relative numbers by age and have tended, if anything, to reduce somewhat the average age of population rather than raise it. (For empirical illustrations, see Stolnitz, 1956*b*.) These initially surprising tendencies are readily explained. Although declining death rates from birth onward obviously increase the numbers reaching later ages, say above 50 or 60 years, they also lead to rising numbers at all younger ages, particularly below age 15. On average, such declines in the past have tended to offset each other and also have tended to shift the average age either erratically or somewhat downward. However, with today's age-specific death rates until mid-life so close to zero, their future declines are increasingly likely to become outweighed by the age-composition effects of declines at the upper ages.

In brief, future mortality trends in all or nearly all the world's more-industrialized societies are increasingly likely to have "aging" effects on their populations. Such effects could be expected even if mortality declines in the older ages turned out to be no more than moderate, and they would become spectacularly evident if the declines were outstandingly large.

Either way, it would be the first time in MDR history, or indeed recorded demographic history anywhere, that downward trends in mortality have added appreciably to, rather than been offset by (or neutrally associated with), the "aging" effects caused by declining fertility.

The second demographic impact, if the expected mortality trends emerge, concerns their probable effects on crude death rates in the MDR's and thereby on their crude rates of natural increase. As a very general rule in the past, declining death rates by age have been sufficiently pronounced to dominate the effects of changing age composition on the overall death rate (whether such change arose from the mortality shifts themselves, migration, or most especially, fertility change). Accordingly, when age-specific death rates fell in an MDR population, it could be confidently expected that the crude death rate would also fall.

Today and in the future, however, age-composition effects may well predominate over mortality changes proper. This shift has apparently been true in Europe since the 1960s and could readily appear in almost all MDR's if their recent demographic patterns continue. Should that happen, the "aging" tendencies now found in nearly all MDR populations as a result of falling fertility could be expected to push their death rates up by more than mortality declines can pull them down.

Accordingly, barring unprecedented downtrends in upper-age mortality (and perhaps even then, given the "aging" impacts of such trends), future MDR death rates appear more likely to rise than to fall, hence to reduce growth rates rather than raise them, in the decades ahead. This could well occur in the face of continued or steady increases in life expectancy, a prospect that, if fulfilled, would again mark a first in known demographic history.

This possibility is obviously expected according to the projections in Tables 1 and 2, which show the overall MDR crude death rate to be increasing between the late 1970s and 1990s even while life expectancy increases in each more-developed region.

The emerging prospects of greatly slackened or newly structured mortality downtrends in the MDR's, along with their newly emerging demographic consequences, are also bound to have profound impacts on nondemographic patterns—consumption and savings; entry to and participation in the labor force and retirement patterns; social security and pensions; voting behavior; fiscal policy; income distribution; and, among many others, trends in population settlement.

Less-developed Regions. Within a decade in numerous instances and no more than two decades in most, many of the world's low-income nations have passed through successions of longevity stages that today's highest-income nations with the lowest mortality rates needed generations or even half-centuries to reach and leave behind. It is safe to say that nothing in history would have prepared a pre–World War II or even a 1950 observer for the mortality trends that soon emerged—whether in terms of their size and speed; number of na-

tions involved; diverse ecological, geographic, political, and historic contexts; numbers of people affected; or the mortality levels reached in relation to continued poverty and economic backwardness.

As of 1950, practically every population in Latin America and Asia lived under mortality conditions that in western and northern Europe, for example, had been abandoned for nearly a century or more. In nearly all of Africa, life expectancies must have been at levels far below those of Europe in still earlier periods. By 1975, if not earlier, nearly all of Latin America, much of Asia (including, apparently, China), all of northern Africa, and possibly a few parts of sub-Saharan Africa had reached longevity levels that the industrialized regions as a group did not attain before 1900 and some MDR nations did not reach until the 1920s or 1930s. An interesting, though extreme, indication of some of the initial LDC trends is that every less-developed country with reasonably reliable vital registration records as of the early to mid-1950s—perhaps a dozen in all—was experiencing mortality declines that rivaled or exceeded the maximum rates of change ever recorded previously for the world's nations with lowest mortality rates (see Stolnitz, 1956a).

It is true that the general comparative picture as between the recent LDR mortality transitions and the earlier ones of MDR populations would be much more varied and less dramatic if the facts could be more fully known. Accurate vital records exist for only a small minority of the world's less-developed areas, including probably less than 10 percent of their population even today, while the trends suggested by various indirect methods of estimation are only adequately or semi-adequately reliable at best. Nevertheless, unless the best estimates available are wildly off the mark, it appears probable that the recent LDR downtrends have been far more rapid than those prevailing among MDR populations when they began to move from their own premodern longevity patterns to an average level of some 55 years, the approximate LDR average today (see Stolnitz, 1955). The average annual longevity gain of about one-half year suggested by Table 1 for LDR's as a whole since the early 1950s suggests a pace appreciably beyond most maximum rates of transition on record in the MDR nations.

These comparisons, if approximately valid, are the more noteworthy, and the more surprising, for many reasons. For one, the suggested LDR gains have occurred among populations that have typically been much poorer and more economically disadvantaged than were their MDR predecessors when experiencing similar gains. Much of sub-Saharan Africa plus the large populations of South Asia, in particular, are still at real per capita income levels that are far below those attained in the relevant nineteenth-century or early twentieth-century periods by all of today's MDR's. Nearly all populations in LDR's over the past quarter-century have had to contend with a far more disadvantaged agrarian base, less industrialization experience, less-developed transportation networks, and more backward public administration systems than have prevailed in most MDR's for the better part of a century at least (see Stolnitz, 1975; United Nations, 1979).

It seems reasonable to conclude, therefore, that innovations in public health, mass medical care, and sanitation have been the primary or even predominant causes of the recent LDR trends. If so, political will—both national and international—must have been the essential engine of change. The changes in mortality rates in dozens of LDC's were too sudden and large, too closely linked in time and space with the inception of governmentally sponsored health programs, and too simultaneous among nations (or subnational areas) of widely differing historic backgrounds, for general social change or overall economic development to have been the strategic determinants. Numerous well-documented cases record that mortality rates in a less-developed area began to fall, continued to decline, or, at the least, failed to reverse direction in the face of adverse short-run economic fluctuations or even negative longer-run movements. Conversely, practically no well-documented case records that lower mortality rates have been nullified, or need have been nullified, because of economic setbacks as such. Perhaps above all, no instance exists in which economic setbacks as such have led to a sustained reversal of an earlier downtrend of mortality rates. To appreciate fully the strength of these facts, one need only consider the innumerable agrarian and other economic reverses that have troubled Third World areas throughout the postwar decades.

For example, the food-shortage crises during the 1970s in Bangladesh, Ethiopia, and the Sahel, while clearly severe, resulted in dramatically increased deaths mainly because of political reasons. Political genocide in Bangladesh, indifference or worse in Ethiopia, and international sloth in coping with a readily manageable shortfall in the Sahel's food supply were the essential culprits. Bangladesh especially and the Sahelian areas in large part appear to have regained or improved upon their precrisis mortality rates. The situation in Ethiopia is obscure but has been made irrelevant for present interpretive purposes by political disorders. Indochina, of course, is a case study in genocidal processes, far removed from conventional considerations of death control or economic development.

None of this is to deny that economic and social factors are significant and could be crucial. Food intake, if insufficient over a prolonged period, must obviously lead to fatal consequences at some point. So must social disorganization affecting the delivery of essential health services, however sophisticated these may be. The continued great gaps in mortality rates between MDR's and LDR's are clearly attributable in major ways to differences in standards of living (per capita income, consumption, education, and housing among others) and perhaps equally to the higher outlays for expensive health care that only wealthier nations can afford. Much the same must be true, though in different contexts, of the gaps in mortality rates between higher-income and lower-income LDR's, as illustrated in Table 1 by the figures for Latin America and Africa.

This much recognized, the foregoing interpretation of key causes of the postwar trends nevertheless appears valid because of two empirical generalizations. The first is that development stages and living standards apparently act as permissive, rather than as precise or decisive, determinants of actual and prospective mortality rates. At least, that seems to be true over a very broad range of possibilities. So long as income or consumption levels in nations with high mortality rates have not deteriorated to the point of frequent mass physical breakdowns, their governments today can realistically be assumed to have the potential to exercise substantial controls over rates of disease and death. This assumption is particularly true with respect to infectious and communicable causes of death, mankind's main killers throughout history. Egypt and India between World Wars I and II and in the early postwar period are two prominent instances among many; in each, life expectancy rose appreciably despite declines in food consumption from per capita levels that were already miserably low.

More generally, a drop today in average calorie or protein intake has very different implications for the mortality rate in a typical less-developed economy than it did in earlier periods. Much depends upon whether or not local water supplies have been chemically treated or villages have health systems that prevent malaria. Probably of leading importance, also, have been postwar advances in technical capacities (whether achieved by domestic or international agencies) to deliver emergency health services and food relief at times of crisis. (For opposing arguments to main causes of the LDR postwar experience, see Schultz, 1976; for a generally supporting argument, see Preston, 1975.)

A second generalization, related to the first, is that the health care resources needed to achieve rapid and substantial reductions in initially high mortality rates have declined immensely. Amounts and types of health care needed to raise life expectancy from 40 to 45 years, or from 45 to 50 years, have become far more accessible to the world's poorest nations with the highest mortality rates than they were in the first half of this century. Increases in per capita incomes (or changes in income distribution or both) needed to achieve either such five-year gains have thereby been enormously reduced compared to earlier periods.

With peace, domestic political stability, and only modest amounts of international cooperation, Third World nations everywhere or nearly everywhere could soon be expected to reach a minimum plateau of 50–55 years as their assured levels of life expectancy. Possibly limited parts of Africa and a few rainforest areas such as the Amazon, where climatic obstacles to health might be overriding, could prove to be the main exceptions to this prediction.

The situation is likely to change beyond a longevity plateau of some 55–60 years. Once the combination of main communicable and noncommunicable causes of death begins to tilt significantly towards the latter category, the combination of conditions for achieving large new gains in longevity also must shift. That was true for most MDR populations between about 1900 and the end of the interwar period, when the new health technologies prerequisite for achieving further large gains were either yet to be discovered or entailed increasing amounts of health care resources, more-individualized methods of medical treatment, and more-complicated public health and sanitation delivery systems. Should this history be essentially repeated in the LDR's, it can be expected that the going will be slower for the many LDC populations that have reached or gone beyond 55–60-year level of life expectancy. Such slowdowns have, in fact, become prevalent during the past decade or two, indicating that further considerable gains in longevity will be increasingly dependent upon rates and patterns of overall development.

Even so, one should not underestimate either the potentials of existing health care technologies or the enormously enhanced potentials now available for diffusing knowledge of new advances in such technologies, whether from MDR or LDR sources. Analogous earlier influences go far to explain the phenomenal longevity gains found in Japan, eastern Europe, and most of southern Europe since the late pre-World War II or early postwar periods, when these populations were reaching or exceeding 55–60-year life expectancies. The more recent situation in Sri Lanka, where longevity has reached nearly 65 years despite persistently lagging economic development, should alert us also to the potentials of income-distribution policies, when these are added to public health policies under certain circumstances. In Latin America, under very different policies and despite frequent economic setbacks, a substantial number of popu-

lations also appear to have reached the 65-year level. The United States, a much wealthier nation and one that was economically more developed than any of these LDR's by the early part of this century, first reached the same level about 1940.

The foregoing interpretations point to an important corollary. The probable end of phenomenal rates of gain in LDR longevity since about 1965–1970 does not in itself signal the onset of long-run reversals, at least not from economic or other nonpolitical causes. Despite frequent alarms to the contrary, there is no instance on record of such reversals. And, to repeat, there are very few instances indeed of even short-run setbacks in longevity for economic reasons.

Conclusions. The following list of propositions concerning the less-developed regions sums up, and goes somewhat beyond, the previous discussion. We disregard for this purpose questions of domestic or international political instability, assume that development performance among LDR populations will not depart markedly from average postwar levels, and presuppose that national policies and market forces affecting the distribution of income or consumption will operate much as they do at present.

1. Reductions in mortality rates and associated gains in longevity should continue to take place everywhere or almost everywhere among LDR populations; they should be moderate or substantial in many instances, and could well be spectacular in a few, during the rest of the century.

2. The relative importance of communicable and noncommunicable causes of death in the LDRs will tilt sharply toward the latter, despite occasional public health setbacks such as some post-1970 increases in malaria.

3. Downtrends of mortality rates in many less-developed areas have probably been more rapid in the first half of the 1950–1980 period than in the second, and they might well be slower still during the remaining decades of this century. Presumably, the causes of death most yielding to health care programs have often lost importance relative to less-yielding causes as longevity has risen. Presumably, too, the areas most favorable ecologically to successful health programs have been the first to achieve major gains, and the gains in less favorably situated areas might well be lower. Unfortunately for interpretation, the main empirical instances for assessing this point are in regions such as sub-Saharan Africa and Brazil's Amazon basin, where highly unfavorable political or ecological conditions and extremely sparse or unreliable information combine to obscure the causal picture.

4. Traditional or historic links between low consumption of food and high mortality rates have become enormously loosened in the postwar era, to an extent that continues to defy the predictions of many agriculturists, other food-related researchers, and many or most public health experts. Simply, the world's poor and poorest populations are found able to live longer, even if miserably, than has been thought possible by the scientific community. "Subsistence," a standard concept in the social sciences and the biological literature, has turned out to be unexpectedly elastic as a basis for predicting probable or even possible relationships between food and mortality.

5. The main testing grounds for many of the foregoing judgments and expectations are likely to be the forty-odd nations identified by the Food and Agriculture Organization of the United Nations (FAO) as "most severely affected" by continued lags in food production. Located primarily in sub-Saharan Africa and South Asia, and containing upward of 1 billion inhabitants, these areas come closest to stretching deficiencies in food intake toward breakdown or other calamity. Subject to severely deprived living conditions at best, the areas tend also to be among the most vulnerable anywhere to adverse agrarian fluctuations and the additional human costs to be expected whenever economic or other special setbacks are present (see FAO, 1979, chap. 1; 1980, pp. v, 1-11-1-19).

6. Except possibly for areas where international migration is a major component of total population change, the expected demographic "mix" in the LDR's of appreciable future declines in mortality rates, relatively young age distributions, and medium to high fertility should result in their attaining lower crude death rates on average by the end of the century than will be found among MDR populations. The postwar appearance (probably for the first time in modern era) of dozens of such comparisons between LDR and MDR populations is a forerunner of patterns that should become typical in the near future. To cite but one example among many, life expectancy and the crude death rate about 1960 were both lower in Taiwan than in France, by about 10 percent and no less than 40 percent respectively. The projections in Tables 1 and 2 suggest that such patterns will be the rule, rather than the exception, in the late 1990s.

7. Changing age distributions in the LDR's over the rest of this century should, as a rule, reinforce the effects of declining mortality rates on crude death rates, rather than offset such effects, unlike the expected MDR pattern. Because of declining fertility in many LDR's, the relative size of the population under 5, an age interval of especially high death rates, should fall and the population proportions at most of the ages of low mortality should rise.

8. Expected mortality declines in the LDR's between now and the year 2000 should be of a kind that lowers average age, or leaves it essentially unchanged, again unlike the MDRs. Contrary effects, or those of MDR type, on age from declining mortality rates should not begin to appear until well into the next century.

9. For the above reasons, the substantial projected declines in LDR death rates cited in Table 2 do not appear unreasonable. The overall LDR death rate decline, if it occurred, would contribute something like another one half percentage point to the overall LDR population growth rate over the next two decades, in addition to the full percentage point drop contributed during the previous three decades. It is an interesting commentary on today's LDR growth potentials that the total of 1.5 points so estimated for 1950–2000 exceeds the maximum rates of natural increase found among northern and western European populations since the start of their own rapid expansions of population in the nineteenth century (see Thompson, 1953).

10. Such numerical effects of mortality trends on the rate of natural increase (or on the rate of total population growth) should not be confused with causal effects. It is at least plausible that sustained and spreading downtrends in mortality in many less-developed areas could act powerfully to direct fertility aspirations away from traditional patterns and toward lower fertility norms, thereby reducing birth and growth rates. This possibility remains to be demonstrated but could, if it proved to be operative, become a potent agent for change not only of fertility, but of social modernization more generally.

George J. Stolnitz

See also MORBIDITY AND LONGEVITY; PUBLIC HEALTH.

BIBLIOGRAPHY

Food and Agriculture Organization of the United Nations. *Agriculture: Toward 2000.* Rome, July 1979.

———. *The State of Food and Agriculture, 1979.* Rome, 1980.

Preston, Samuel H. "The Changing Relation between Mortality and Level of Economic Development." *Population Studies* 29(2):231–248, July 1975.

Schultz, T. Paul. "Interrelationships between Mortality and Fertility." In *Population and Development: The Search for Selective Interventions,* edited by Ronald G. Ridker, pp. 284–289. Baltimore: Johns Hopkins University Press, 1976.

Stolnitz, George J. "A Century of International Mortality Trends." *Population Studies* 9(1):24–55, July 1955.

———. "Comparison between Some Recent Mortality Trends in Underdeveloped Areas and Historical Trends in the West." In *Trends and Differentials in Mortality,* pp. 26–34. New York: Milbank Memorial Fund, 1956. (Stolnitz, 1956*a*)

———. "Mortality Declines and Age Distribution." *Milbank Memorial Fund Quarterly* 34(2):178–215, April 1956. (Stolnitz, 1956*b*)

———. "International Mortality Trends: Some Main Facts

and Implications." In *The Population Debate: Dimensions and Perspectives; Papers of the World Population Conference, Bucharest, 1974,* vol. 1. New York: United Nations, 1975.

Thompson, Warren S. *Population Problems.* 4th ed. New York: McGraw-Hill, 1953.

United Nations, Department of Economic and Social Affairs. *The Determinants and Consequences of Population Trends.* Rev. ed. Volume 1: *New Summary and Findings on Interaction of Demographic, Economic, and Social Factors.* Series A, Population Studies, no. 50. New York, 1973.

United Nations, Department of International Economic and Social Affairs. *Concise Report on the World Population Situation in 1977: New Beginnings and Uncertain Ends.* Series A, Population Studies, no. 63. New York, 1979.

———. *Selected World Demographic Indicators by Country, 1950–2000: Demographic Estimates and Projections as Assessed in 1978.* Series R, no. 38. New York, 1980.

United Nations, Economic Commission for Europe. *Economic Survey of Europe in 1974.* Part 2: *Post-war Demographic Trends in Europe and the Outlook until the Year 2000.* Geneva, 1975.

N

NATALITY
See FERTILITY.

NEAR EAST
See NORTH AFRICA AND SOUTHWEST ASIA.

NEW ZEALAND
See OCEANIA.

NIGERIA

Located on the west coast of Africa, Nigeria is the largest country in population size on the continent, and the tenth largest in the world. The official population estimate for 1980 was about 85 million, although some estimates place the figure lower, at about 77 million. Population growth is rapid; the official figure is 2.5 percent per year, but this is likely an underestimate.

Nigeria extends over an area of about 923,768 square kilometers (356,667 square miles), entirely north of the equator, from the Atlantic Ocean in the south to the Sahara in the north. It is bounded by the republics of Benin and Niger on the west and north and by the republics of Chad and Cameroon on the east. The nationwide average of population density is about 85 persons per square kilometer. However, population density varies considera-

bly from region to region, ranging from extremely high concentrations in some eastern and southwestern states and in areas around Kano, Katsina, Sokoto, and Jos in the northern region to as low as 24 persons per square kilometer in other areas. Large tracts of land in the northern states are virtually uninhabited.

Four physical regions can be distinguished. A sparsely populated and little-developed area of dense swamp and mangrove forest 10 to 60 miles wide is situated along the Atlantic coastline. Bordering this area is a 50–100-mile-wide belt of tropical rain forest and oil palm bush. Then open woodland and grass savannah extend north about 300 miles and meet the southern edge of the Sahara.

This diversity of terrain, coupled with favorable soil conditions and abundant rainfall, allows for a variety of agricultural produce. The area near the rain forest is suitable for cocoa, palm products, and rubber. Groundnuts, cotton, and cattle are raised on the northern savannah areas. The size of the country and its varieties of climate and soil give Nigeria the potential to become a leading agricultural nation.

The geographical location and topographical features of Nigeria also make fishing a viable industry. Along the Atlantic coast commercial fishing firms are supplying seafood for domestic and export markets, while the numerous rivers forming the Benue and Niger watershed provide fish mainly for local consumption.

Nigeria's major natural resources are petroleum deposits in the midwestern and eastern states, tin in the hilly central area of the country, and hydroelectric power that has been harnessed by the large Kainji Dam on the Niger River, providing the major source of electricity. A member of the Organization of Petroleum Exporting Countries, Nigeria is now mining its high-quality petroleum deposits and changing the agrarian base of its national economy. Its push for industrialization and the size of its internal market have lured substantial foreign investment.

The population of Nigeria is composed of more than 200 different cultural groups. They can be broadly classified into five categories: the Muslim Sudanic cultures in the northern savannah area; the nomadic pastoralists in the same area; the forest and independent coastal village communities in the southeast; the former forest kingdoms of the southwest; and the many small groups in the central and eastern parts of the country. The three dominant ethnic groups in the country, which comprise nearly 60 percent of the population, are the Hausa-Fulani, mainly in the northern savannah area, the Yoruba in the southwestern states, and the Igbo in the eastern states. The other large groups are the Tiv, Nupe, Ibibio, Efik, Ijaw, Edo, and Kanuri.

Religion is to a large extent regionalized. The northern states are predominantly Muslim, while the south has a large percentage of Christians. A substantial number of Yoruba in the south are also Muslim. About half of all Nigerians are Muslim, between 32 and 40 percent are Christian, and the remainder adhere to a variety of traditional religious practices.

Population Characteristics. The information available for measuring the size and growth patterns of Nigeria's population is of uncertain quality. Results of censuses taken in 1952/53, 1962, 1963, and 1973 are all open to question on various grounds. The Rural Demographic Sample Survey, 1965–1966, gives nationwide figures for most demographic indexes for that period. Many other surveys have been done subsequently on local and subnational levels, giving more recent indications of demographic patterns and trends. However, they are limited for providing national indexes. Vital registration, limited to a few selected urban areas, is very uneven. In 1979 a vital registration decree was promulgated that made the registration of births and deaths compulsory. However, as of 1981 the program had not yet been implemented. The most recent census, in 1973, was not accepted and was declared null and void.

Consequently, the results of the 1963 census are still officially used as the baseline for current national and state estimates. The total population figure from the 1963 census was about 56 million. The validity of this figure has been queried by a number of Nigerian demographers because of alleged massive overcounts. At present, the official population estimate for Nigeria for 1980 is about 85 million. If adjustments are made for the alleged overenumeration, the 1963 figure is estimated to be about 48 million and the 1980 figure to be about 77 million. These two sets of figures inevitably cause confusion; the Nigerian government uses the larger estimate as the official figure for planning while many international agencies use the smaller.

In recent pronouncements, the government is considering undertaking a census in the next few years. The past history of census taking, voiding the 1962 and 1973 results, has made this a controversial issue. However, the use of 1963 as the baseline for planning in the 1980s and 1990s can no longer be justified.

The official growth rate for the country used for planning purposes is 2.5 percent per year. It is generally acknowledged that this is an underestimate. Evidence from other African societies at similar stages of economic development, and from numerous direct and indirect estimates of fertility and mortality for Nigeria, indicates that the growth rate for Nigeria is higher, possibly between 2.8 and 4.0 percent per year. The United Nations has recently used a 3.2 percent annual rate of natural increase for 1975–1980 as a median variant estimate in projecting Nigeria's population (United Nations, 1979, table 1-A, p. 16).

Estimates of the crude birth rate in the 1970s ranged from about 50 to 60 births per 1,000 population. Some evidence suggests that the national birth rate may be rising, possibly reflecting improvements in health care and nutrition. More important influences however may be the fundamental changes taking place in reproductive behavior as a result of forces of modernization such as "western" education, urbanization, and employment in the modern sector. Prolonged abstention from intercourse after the birth of a child has traditionally been the major control on fertility. Abstention can last up to two to three years and is reinforced by the traditional mores of society. When these mores change as the society modernizes, the abstention period is shortened, and unless other means of birth control are used, the fertility rate may increase.

Several researchers have attempted to document and to analyze the changing fertility pattern in Nigeria. A number of studies done throughout Nigeria have shown a positive association between "western" education, for example, and fertility (Olusanya, 1975; Trevor, 1975; Morgan with Ohadike, 1975). Ron Lesthaeghe, Hilary Page, and Olukunle Adegbola (1981) have examined some of the effects of women's education, age of marriage, and the use of contraception on fertility of a sample of Lagos women. They found that as women become more educated they marry somewhat later, thus reducing fertility during the teenage years and the early twenties. They also found that with the decline in traditional forms of child-spacing (e.g., breastfeeding and post partum abstention) fertility increases particularly during the middle and late twenties. However, fertility after thirty years of age may decrease owing to lower desired family size and increased contraceptive use and effectiveness. It should be noted that it is difficult to know whether the increased fertility due to the abandonment of traditional child-spacing methods will be fully compensated for by the adoption of modern contraceptive methods. Thus, there may be an increase in fertility levels until the adoption of family planning becomes more widespread.

The persistent trend of high levels of fertility has also been studied in the southwestern and eastern areas of Nigeria. These studies indicate that the rural agricultural populations do not as yet see any reason to limit family size. In fact, the traditional reinforcements for a large family persist: availability of child labor, social security of parents, and family prestige (Caldwell, 1977, chaps. 3, 8, 10).

Comprehensive mortality data in Nigeria are scarce. The Rural Demographic Survey, 1965–1966, yielded a crude death rate for the country of 26.9. Estimates for the 1970s suggest a decline, possibly approaching 20 deaths per 1,000 population.

The infant mortality rate obtained from the Rural Demographic Survey, 1965–1966, was 178 per 1,000 population. It is very likely that this rate declined in the 1970s. However, regional variations may be significant; in some areas the rates may be much higher, while in urban areas the rates may be quite low.

Life expectancy at birth, estimated from the Rural Demographic Survey, 1965–1966, was 37.2 years for males and 36.7 years for females. The United Nations has estimated life expectancy at birth for the 1975–1980 period to be 45.9 years for males and 49.2 years for females.

In order to get more accurate, up-to-date figures on fertility and mortality, a national demographic sample survey was initiated by the National Population Bureau in July 1980. In 1981, using the same sample frame as a base, the bureau conducted the Nigerian Fertility Survey with technical assistance from the World Fertility Survey, funded by the Nigerian government and the United Nations Fund for Population Activities (UNFPA). These surveys will provide more recent and, it is hoped, more reliable data for the computation of rates and trends on a national basis.

The age-sex structure of Nigeria's population, based on the 1963 census, shows that 43 percent (43.8 percent for males and 42.1 percent for females) are under 15 years of age. The working population, from 15 to 64 years, makes up about 55 percent (53.8 percent for males and 56.1 percent for females), and the aged population, 65 years and older, accounts for about 2 percent. These proportions will undoubtedly change because of continuing high fertility and the supposed decline in infant mor-

tality, thus increasing the proportion in the under-15 age group and increasing the dependency rate. Such changes will have major ramifications for provision of education, social services, health, and ultimately employment as the expanding youth population enters the labor market.

Migration. Migration data represent the single largest demographic data gap for Nigeria. The only national data come from the Rural Demographic Survey, 1965–1966, which found a rural to urban migration movement. More recent evidence suggests that this rural exodus has increased. This situation only compounds the problems of employment, housing, and amenities in urban areas. Lagos, the federal capital and largest city, is the destination of many migrants from Nigeria and from neighboring countries. Recent data from the Lagos State Interim Regional Plan, 1980–2000, indicate that Lagos is growing at a rate of 9 percent a year. The plan projects a population size for the metropolitan area for 1980 at about 4.5 million. In the year 2000, the population will likely be close to 13 million. As the plan states, this is a minimum estimate, as it takes into account the planned transfer of the federal capital to Abuja in the central part of the country.

Data from the 1963 census showed that almost 20 percent of the population lived in cities or towns of 20,000 or more. This percentage has undoubtedly increased. Other cities that are rapidly growing because of immigration are Kano, Kaduna, Port Harcourt, and Ibadan. With the establishment in 1975 of nineteen states and the naming of new capitals for them, the stream of migrants to these capital cities has also presumably increased.

The recent report of the UNFPA Mission of Needs Assessment for Population Assistance (1981) recommended a study of internal migration in Nigeria, in addition to looking at patterns of immigration from neighboring countries.

Planning for Projected Growth. In its guidelines for the Fourth National Development Plan, 1981–1985, the Nigerian government recognized the consequences of high rates of population growth: reduction in the standard of living and per capita income; intensification of shortages of housing, water, education, and health services; increases in the burden on the economically active population; and investment in consumption and social services rather than in productive activities. The government concluded, however, that, because of expectations of a growing economy, these consequences "do not yet give cause for alarm."

When the population of Nigeria is projected at different rates of growth to the year 1999 based on the official 1963 census figure of 56 million versus the reduced estimate for 1963 of 48 million, then this conclusion of the Nigerian government may be disputed. (See Table 1.) In the year 1999, if the growth rate remains constant at 3

TABLE 1. *Projections of Nigeria's population based on assumed rates of growth (in millions)*

Year	Higher series[1]			Lower series[2]			Index: 1963 = 100		
	2%	2.5%	3%	2%	2.5%	3%	2%	2.5%	3%
1963	56	56	56	48	48	48	100	100	100
1969	63	65	67	54	55	57	113	116	120
1974	70	73	78	60	62	66	124	130	139
1979	77	82	90	66	69	77	137	146	161
1984	85	91	104	73	77	89	151	163	186
1989	94	102	121	80	87	103	167	183	216
1994	103	115	140	89	97	119	184	204	250
1999	114	128	162	98	109	138	203	229	290

[1]Accepting the 1963 census population of 56 million.
[2]Assuming a November 1963 population of 48 million. See Olusanya, 1969.
SOURCE: Olusanya, 1975, p. 273; reprinted by permission.

percent per year until then, which is very likely, the population of Nigeria will be around 162 million. If the reduced population estimate is used, the population will be 138 million, only 24 million fewer. In either case, planning for education, health, and agriculture and rural development, all given priority by the new civilian government, will be seriously affected.

Education. Universal primary education (UPE), inaugurated in the 1976/77 school year, yielded a grade 1 enrollment of almost 3 million, 31 percent greater than expected. The increased costs for building classrooms and for teachers' salaries have been identified as major problems in the implementation of UPE. These problems will naturally be carried over to each level of education as the school cohorts advance. Projections of primary school enrollment for 1984/85 are close to 14 million children, a doubling in ten years. As the "blueprint" for the national policy on education states, "the problem facing the whole federation is what to do now with 2.1 million primary school leavers in June 1982." Even if 40 percent go on to secondary schools, 1.3 million school leavers are out on the job market, with high expectations of finding urban-based employment with their school leaving certificates. Problems that the Implementation Committee for the National Policy in Education (1978) addressed include (1) lack of a system for gathering, processing, and disseminating data, including demographic information, among the different levels of government concerned with education; (2) the lowering of education standards; and (3) the need for closer linkages between the National Manpower Board and the Federal Ministry of Education to determine the number of pupils who would need education in particular disciplines to meet national needs and to revise school curricula appropriately.

Health. The guidelines for the Fourth National Development Plan, 1981–1985, recognize that health services are inadequate relative to the demand from the rapidly growing population. Even with gains made in training of medical and paramedical personnel in Nigeria, and an extensive construction program of health facilities in rural areas, the coverage of the present population is insufficient, and services are limited because of lack of drugs and equipment. The Basic Health Services Scheme (BHSS), a national program to provide preventive care and referral services, has been established for a more even distribution of health services, particularly in rural areas, using paraprofessional personnel. A part of this scheme includes family health, of which maternal and child health and family planning services are a major component. The United Nations Fund for Population Activities is supporting the family health component within the BHSS. Additional assistance is being given to the scheme from other international agencies, including the World Health Organization, UNICEF, and the World Bank. The effect of the scheme on fertility will not be known for some time, as it has just begun implementation.

Agriculture and rural development. Agriculture employs about 70 percent of the total labor force. The guidelines for the Fourth National Development Plan outline the problems of the sector, namely, provision of adequate extension services, agricultural inputs (fertilizers, seed, etc.), storage facilities, credit, market information, physical infrastructure, manpower, and land tenure. However, even if the ambitious government effort under its Green Revolution Program to deal with these problems is implemented successfully and social amenities are provided in the rural areas, it is very doubtful that rural-urban migration will be stemmed unless new work opportunities are created in rural areas and unless educational priorities are established.

Policy and Action. As of 1981 Nigeria does not have a comprehensive population policy that is directed toward clearly defined demographic objectives. Policies and development strategies such as programs to reduce mortality or to introduce family planning are seen primarily as means to improve the general welfare. However, such programs taken as a whole do show the government's growing recognition of the importance of population factors in the country's development.

The third and fourth development plans as well as the new federal constitution have increasingly emphasized population-related policies and programs. In the Fourth National Development Plan period, 1981–1985, the government will more actively support family planning activities within the framework of maternal and child health programs. Information and education activities for family planning for married couples will also receive more government attention. As a way to increase women's participation in development, and cognizant of the demographic implications, the government proposes to promote social and economic activities for women of childbearing age. There is also particular concern about the possibility of a rampant increase in illegal abortions. A bill to legalize abortion was introduced in the National Assembly in 1981. Although the bill was defeated, it is expected that the abortion issue will be addressed again in the next few years. Research and training activities will also be emphasized during 1981–1985 to increase the understanding of the relationship between socioeconomic development and demographic trends.

As a further indication of its concern in the population area, in June 1981 the government submitted a request for assistance to the Governing Council of the United Nations Fund for Population Activities. The program included a request for assistance in basic data collection (e.g., demographic surveys, a census, and vital registration), the establishment of population units in the planning ministries at the federal and state levels, the establishment of a national family planning training program and contraceptive distribution system, curriculum development in population education, and the promotion of demographic research and training at the university level. This request provides the framework for government action and international assistance in the population area for the 1980s.

The institutional base for population activities is provided under the federal constitution. A National Population Commission has been established under the president and vice president to undertake periodic enumerations (e.g., sample surveys, censuses); to establish and maintain the machinery for continuous and universal vital registration; to advise the president; and to publish and provide population information to facilitate economic and development planning. The commission is composed of a chairman and one representative from each state.

The secretariat of the commission is the former National Population Bureau, which collects, compiles, and processes population statistics at the federal level. It is the source for all ministries for obtaining data for planning. State offices of the commission channel population statistics to the central headquarters.

The National Planning Office of the Federal Ministry of National Planning has a population unit that deals with population planning particularly in the formulation of the Fourth National Development Plan. It also works closely with an advisory body called the National Population Council, which until the establishment of the National Population Commission helped to formulate population policy. The council continues to advise the government on family planning.

Family Planning. The first family planning clinics in Nigeria were opened in Lagos in 1957 and in Ibadan in 1959. The Family Planning Council of Nigeria, now the Planned Parenthood Federation of Nigeria (PPFN), an affiliate of the International Planned Parenthood Federation (IPPF), was formed in 1964. The federation has 106 clinics in fourteen states, mainly in urban areas. The federal government gives a small annual allocation to the PPFN.

A number of programs in family planning and maternal and child health have been sponsored through universities. The Department of Obstetrics and Gynaecology of the University of Ibadan developed a clinic program of family planning services including sterilization and menstrual regulation, and has assisted in setting up a community-based distribution program for family planning in several hundred villages north of Ibadan. A detailed multiround KAP survey of women attending a family planning clinic in a rural hospital was done by the University of Ife, which also conducted a national KAP survey in the early 1970s. The Institute of Child Health, University of Lagos, has supported family health projects including family planning in various cities around the federation. The Cross River State Ministry of Health has supported a program of maternal and child health and family planning in two of its local government areas. The Niger and Sokoto state governments have also included family planning in their health delivery systems, although this is not well developed, and the Basic Health Service Scheme has family planning as a part of its family health service. The major donors for population and family planning related activities are the UNFPA, the Population Council, IPPF, USAID, the Pathfinder Fund, and the Ford Foundation.

Scholarly Activities. Demographic teaching and research have advanced significantly in five of the fourteen Nigerian universities. The universities of Ibadan, Ife, and Lagos, and to a lesser extent Ahmadu Bello University and the University of Nigeria at Nsukka, are the main centers. Ife has established a department of demography and social statistics that offers a bachelor's degree in demography, and graduate programs in demography are available at Ibadan, Ife, and Lagos, although none is yet fully developed.

Besides the work done in academic institutions, population research is undertaken by the Federal Office of Statistics, the National Population Bureau, the National Manpower Board, and the Nigerian Institute for Social and Economic Research. Not surprisingly, the directory of demographers issued by the Economic Commission for Africa (ECA) shows that Nigeria has the largest number of demographers and population specialists on the continent. In a bibliographic review of population literature from 1960 to 1974, more than five hundred references to works by Nigerian authors were compiled.

Scholarly output seems likely to continue at an equally impressive rate. In April 1980 the Population Association of Nigeria, composed of about fifty members from the academic and government communities, held its first meeting. Annual conferences and publication of a journal are to be part of its ongoing activities.

John A. McWilliam

See SUB-SAHARAN AFRICA.

BIBLIOGRAPHY

Caldwell, John C. (editor). *The Persistence of High Fertility: Population Prospects in the Third World.* Canberra: Australian National University, Department of Demography, 1977.

Caldwell, John C. (editor), and Nelson O. Addo, Samuel K. Gaisie, Adenola A. Igun, and P. O. Olusanya. *Population Growth and Socioeconomic Change in West Africa.* A Population Council Book. New York and London: Columbia University Press, 1975. Chapters 9–15, by various authors, are devoted to Nigeria.

Goddard, A. D., M. J. Mortimore, and D. W. Norman. "Some Social and Economic Implications of Population Growth in Rural Hausaland." In *Population Growth and Socioeconomic Change in West Africa,* edited by John C. Caldwell, pp. 321–336. New York and London: Columbia University Press, 1975.

Lagos State, Ministry of Economic Planning and Land Matters. *Lagos State Interim Regional Plan, 1980–2000.* Lagos, 14 January 1980.

Lesthaeghe, Ron, Hilary J. Page, and Olukunle Adegbola. "Child-spacing and Fertility in Lagos." In *Child-spacing in Tropical Africa: Traditions and Change,* edited by Hilary J. Page and Ron Lesthaeghe. New York and London: Academic Press, 1981.

Lucas, David, and John A. McWilliam. *A Survey of Nigerian Population Literature.* Monograph No. 4. Lagos: Human Resources Research Unit, University of Lagos, 1976.

Lucas, David, and Gabisu Williams. *Nigeria.* Country Profiles. New York: Population Council, February 1973.

McWilliam, John A., and Chukwudum Uche. *Nigeria: Selected Studies; Social Science Research for Population and Family Planning Policies and Programme.* Research for Action, no. 1. London: International Planned Parenthood Federation, May 1976.

Morgan, Robert W., with P. O. Ohadike. "Fertility Levels and Fertility Change." In *Population Growth and Socioeconomic Change in West Africa,* edited by John C. Caldwell, pp. 187–235. New York and London: Columbia University Press, 1975.

Nigeria, Federal Ministry of National Planning. *Guidelines for the Fourth National Development Plan, 1981–85.* Lagos, 1980.

Nigeria, Implementation Committee for the National Policy on Education. *Blueprint, 1978–1979.* Lagos, October 1978.

Olusanya, P. O. *Socio-economic Aspects of Rural-Urban Migration in Western Nigeria.* Ibadan: Nigerian Institute for Social and Economic Research, 1969.

————. "Population Growth and Its Components: The Nature and Direction of Population." In *Population Growth and Socioeconomic Change in West Africa,* edited by John C. Caldwell, pp. 254–274. New York and London: Columbia University Press, 1975.

Trevor, Jean. "Family Change in Sokoto: A Traditional Moslem Fulani/Hausa City." In *Population Growth and Socioeconomic Change in West Africa,* edited by John C. Caldwell, pp. 236–253. New York and London: Columbia University Press, 1975.

Udo, Reuben K. "Migration and Urbanization in Nigeria." In *Population Growth and Socioeconomic Change in West Africa,* edited by John C. Caldwell, pp. 298–307. New York and London: Columbia University Press, 1975.

United Nations, Department of International Economic and Social Affairs. *World Population Trends and Prospects by Country, 1950–2000: Summary Report of the 1978 Assessment.* Series R, no. 33. New York, 1979.

United Nations Fund for Population Activities. *Nigeria: Report of Mission of Needs Assessment for Population Assistance.* New York, 1981.

NORTH AFRICA AND SOUTHWEST ASIA

1.
REGIONAL SURVEY

North Africa and Southwest Asia are bounded by natural features: in the north the Mediterranean Sea, the Black Sea, the Caucasus Mountains, and the Iranian plateau; in the east the Indian Ocean; in the south the East African highlands and the Sahara; in the west the Atlantic Ocean. Part of the area is known as the Middle East.

Within the region, twenty-three political units can be identified, twenty-one of which are members of the United Nations (Western Sahara and the Gaza strip of Palestine are not). The Palestine Liberation Organization (PLO) became in 1979 a fourteenth member of the United Nations Economic Commission for Western Asia (ECWA). In the absence of statistical data the PLO is not included in this article as a statistical unit.

The area has an ideological unity, having become Muslim within a few decades of the Hegira (A.D. 622) and having remained so ever since. The religious, cultural, political, and economic explosion of the seventh century is the last of three monotheistic movements of this area, after Judaism and Christianity. The population of the area, more than 200 million by 1980, is a minor although central part of the Islamic populations of the world. Religious uniformity is paralleled by an ethnic and linguistic unity, for nineteen of the twenty-three units are predominantly Arabic (the exceptions are Cyprus, Israel, Sudan, and Turkey).

The demography of each country is almost the same throughout the region: early marriage of females, high proportions of the population marrying, no illegitimacy, high marital fertility, high remarriage rates of males, with simultaneous or consecutive polygamy taking up the remaining females. The mortality rate began to decline in the 1950s, giving rise to unprecedented population growth. This decline has still some way to go and will result in further increases in the rate of population growth unless canceled by declines in fertility, which are unlikely. Large increases in numbers are unavoidable for a long time to come, even if growth rates begin to decline. One United Nations projection for the area suggests that the 197 million population in 1977 will reach 366 million by the year 2000.

Sociologically, the most outstanding feature seems to be the orientation of women to family and household. Female literacy, educational attainment, labor force participation, and activity in public life are among the lowest in the world.

Demographic problems and population policies can only be understood with insights into the central cultural features of Islam. The primary emphasis of Islamic societies is on unity of religious and temporal power residing in a strong, central, decision-making institution. The mosque and the state are largely inseparable. Political power is translated through family power, religion, and tribal allegiance.

Location and Description. Most of the countries of North Africa and Southwest Asia have a colonial past.

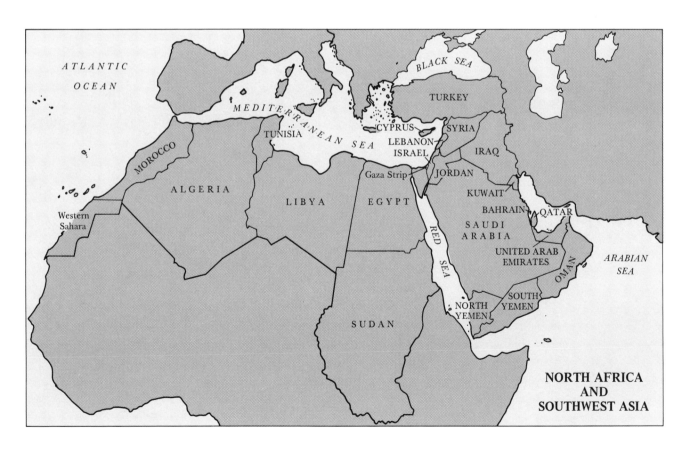

Western Sahara, freed by Spain, was still (in 1981) in the throes of a postcolonial struggle between Algeria and Morocco. The three countries of the Maghreb (Morocco, Algeria, Tunisia) were parts of the French Empire; northern Morocco and a few southern enclaves were ruled by Spain, and Tangier had its own international governance. Libya was under Italy; Egypt, Sudan, Cyprus, Palestine, Iraq, and South Yemen were under Great Britain in different relationships; Syria and Lebanon were under France. Kuwait, Bahrain, Qatar, the seven components of the United Arab Emirates (UAE), and Oman had looser forms of association with Great Britain, while independent Saudi Arabia and North Yemen refused most foreign contacts. Turkey's sovereignty, under the Ottoman sultans, was limited through the "capitulations" that gave foreigners privileged positions outside Turkish law.

In 1981, thirty-six years after the end of World War II, Arab policy was still dominated by the conflict between Palestinian Arabs and Israelis. The human losses in this conflict, however dramatic in media presentation and however tragic individually, were quite insignificant demographically and did not compare with those in the war of liberation in Algeria (1 million), the north-south fighting in Sudan (750,000) and the fraternal war in the Yemens (250,000). The estimates of these losses are very approximate and make for uncertainty in the demographic data.

By and large, the tradition of the area is agricultural and pastoral, which influences many other aspects of life, including reproduction and direction of individual destiny. Local tradition goes back to the earliest cradles of what is now European civilization: the Nile valley under the pharaohs, and the sequence of Sumerian, Babylonian, Assyrian, and other states in the Tigris and Euphrates valleys. Libya (ancient Cyrene), Tunisia (Carthage), Algeria (Caesarea, modern Cherchell), and Morocco (Volubilis) acted as granaries for republican and imperial Rome.

Population Characteristics. The twenty-three units of the region are very uneven in area and population (see Table 1. Two (Turkey with 46 million and Egypt with

TABLE 1. *Population size, growth, and density, North Africa and Southwest Asia*

	Population estimates (millions), 1981	Annual growth, 1975–78	Area in sq km, 1978	Population per sq km, 1978	Population per sq km of arable land, 1981
North Africa and Southwest Asia	216	2.8%	13,067,000	15	
North Africa	*114*	*2.8*	*8,525,000*	*12*	*95*
Algeria	19.3	3.3	2,381,741	8	44
Egypt	43.5	2.1	1,001,449	40	1,533
Libya	3.1	4.2	1,759,540	2	33
Morocco	21.8	3.1	446,550	2	107
Sudan	19.6	3.4	2,505,813	7	62
Tunisia	6.6	2.7	163,610	37	87
Western Sahara	0.2	8.9	266,000	1	—
Southwest Asia	*102*	*2.9*	*4,542,000*	*21*	*2,480*
Bahrain	0.4	10.5	622	555	5,460
Cyprus	0.6	−0.1	9,251	67	2,940
Iraq	13.6	3.5	434,924	28	2,410
Israel	3.9	2.2	20,770	178	4,170
Jordan	3.3	3.4	97,740	31	1,180
Kuwait	1.4	6.1	17,818	67	17,270
Lebanon	3.2	2.5	10,400	290	—
Oman	0.9	3.1	212,457	4	2,970
Palestine (Gaza strip)	0.4	3.6	378	941	—
Qatar	0.2	5.7	11,000	18	16,590
Saudi Arabia	10.4	3.1	2,149,690	4	7,370
Syria	9.3	3.2	185,180	44	1,070
Turkey	46.2	2.3	780,576	55	1,330
United Arab Emirates	1.0	8.4	83,600	7	15,590
Yemen, North	5.8	2.3	195,000	29	420
Yemen, South	2.0	3.1	332,968	6	500

Source of data: Estimates compiled by the author from various sources with numerous adjustments.

43 million) account for more than 40 percent of the total. The smallest five—the Gaza strip, Bahrain, United Arab Emirates, Western Sahara, and Qatar—add up to little more than 2 million. The large number of migrants and the tendency for some countries to prefer a *de facto* population count and others a *de jure* count are likely to produce double counting and omissions.

Density and growth. The more than approximately 200 million people in the area's 13 million square kilometers (5 million square miles) are equivalent to about 5 percent of the world population in 10 percent of the world's area. This is 15 persons per square kilometer (38 per square mile), half the world's average population density.

Such an average conceals great variation among countries (see Table 1). The lowest densities are in Western Sahara, Libya, Saudi Arabia, Morocco, Oman, South Yemen, United Arab Emirates, and Sudan. The highest densities are in the Gaza strip, Bahrain, Lebanon, Israel, and North Yemen. Variations within countries are even greater than between countries. For example, when only

the habitable area of Egypt is considered, then the average density increases from 40 to well over 1,000.

The reported population sizes in Table 1 are not of even reliability. In fact, data problems in this area are so severe that in many instances widely different figures are equally plausible. When a variety of reported alternatives was available, the one chosen was most consistent with other estimates and most plausible.

Two of the countries have annual rates of growth markedly higher than the others (Western Sahara with 8.9 percent and Kuwait with 6.1 percent). Such high rates result from immigration: for combat in Western Sahara and for economic pursuits in Kuwait. Foreign immigration is more marked here than elsewhere because of the small receiving populations and because the process began earlier in Kuwait than in other parts of the Arabic part of the Persian Gulf. The explosive changes taking place in this area since the mid-1970s will not show in data until the next round of censuses and estimates.

TABLE 2. *Dependency ratio, proportion under 15, labor force, and female participation, North Africa and Southwest Asia*

	Dependency ratio,[1] 1975	Percentage of population under 15, 1979	Economically active population as percentage of total population, 1975	Percentage of females in total active population 1975
North Africa and Southwest Asia		43%		
North Africa		*44*		
Algeria	106.7	48	23%	—
Egypt	82.8	41	31	14%
Libya	111.2	46	25	—
Morocco	95.7	47	29	—
Sudan	95.0	44	—	—
Tunisia	95.3	43	—	—
Western Sahara	79.7	41	—	—
Southwest Asia		*42*		
Bahrain	95.3	44	27	6
Cyprus	56.2	25	—	—
Iraq	105.4	47	25	4
Israel	68.4	33	—	—
Jordan	111.9	52	23	6
Kuwait	84.8	46	31	12
Lebanon	86.9	40	27	18
Oman	94.9	45	—	—
Palestine (Gaza strip)	124.1	48	—	—
Qatar	88.7	45	47	2
Saudi Arabia	90.1	45	21	2
Syria	115.7	49	25	21
Turkey	80.5	39	41	38
United Arab Emirates	43.3	34	53	3
Yemen, North	102.0	45	25	12
Yemen, South	84.8	46	27	19

[1]Population under 15 years and over 64 years divided by the population aged 15–64 (times 100).
Source of data: Estimates compiled by the author from various sources with numerous adjustments.

Age and sex composition. Most of the populations in North Africa and Southwest Asia are young. Their age pyramids are typically wide-bottomed, because in most countries more than 40 percent are young people under 15. In several countries, proportions under age 15 approach 50 percent, and exceed it in Jordan. With the basic shape of the age pyramids determined by the high proportions of the population at young ages, the rest of the pyramids are also similar in most countries. The exceptions to these general features are of three kinds: Cyprus and Israel because of much lower fertility; to a lesser extent Egypt and Turkey because of somewhat lower fertility; and the United Arab Emirates because of the number of immigrants of working age received by a small population. Western Sahara and Lebanon are borderline cases for probably entirely different reasons: the Christians and some Muslims of Lebanon control their fertility, while Western Sahara harbors volunteer fighters from

other societies. The latter are presumably young adults like the immigrants to the United Arab Emirates.

Unusual ratios of males to every 100 females are reported from the United Arab Emirates (225), Qatar (150), Kuwait (121), and Bahrain (112), all no doubt the result of male labor immigrating to countries with small populations. Such high proportions of males are not representative of the indigenous societies. The two Yemens report very low sex ratios (South, 91; North, 98). These are consistent with war losses, selective for males, and the large numbers of migrant Yemenis who have traditionally roamed Arab lands in all recorded times.

The dependency ratio of children and the aged to every 100 people of working age is close to 100, or even higher (as in Algeria, Libya, Iraq, Jordan, Gaza, Syria, North Yemen; see Table 2). The seven countries with low proportions of population under 15 show dependency ratios nearer to 80 or below (Cyprus and Israel, Egypt

TABLE 3. *Fertility and nuptiality, North Africa and Southwest Asia, 1970–1975*[1]

	Crude marriage rates per 1,000 population	Crude divorce rates per 1,000 population	Crude birth rates per 1,000 population		General fertility rates per 1,000 women aged 15–49
			1970–75	1981	
North Africa and Southwest Asia			43.1	40.6	
North Africa			*43.3*	*43*	
Algeria	4.7	0.5	48.8	46	225.2
Egypt, 1977	9.9	2.0	37.7	41	189.3
Libya	6.9	1.8	45.0	47	311.9
Morocco	—	—	46.8	43	215.7
Sudan	—	—	47.8	46	324.3
Tunisia	8.4	1.1	40.0	33	163.7
Western Sahara	5.1	2.2	20.9	—	75.4
Southwest Asia			*42.8*	*38*	
Bahrain	—	—	45.0	37	224.0
Cyprus	8.8	0.3	22.2	21	71.1
Iraq	10.6	0.6	48.1	47	219.8
Israel, 1977	8.1	1.0	26.1	25	112.7
Jordan	7.3	1.3	47.6	46	179.4
Kuwait, 1976	5.0	1.5	43.3	41	207.7
Lebanon	6.1	0.5	39.8	34	184.3
Oman	—	—	50.0	49	—
Palestine (Gaza strip), 1966	6.5	1.3	44.3	51	—
Qatar	—	—	50.0	44	—
Saudi Arabia	—	—	49.5	49	220.8
Syria	9.2	0.5	45.4	42	213.7
Turkey, 1967	—	0.3	39.0	32	163.9
United Arab Emirates	—	—	50.0	37	196.6
Yemen, North	—	—	49.6	48	220.7
Yemen, South	—	—	49.6	48	220.7

[1]Annual rates for one of the years falling within the period 1970–1975, unless otherwise indicated in the table.
Source of data: Estimates compiled by the author from various sources with numerous adjustments.

and Turkey, United Arab Emirates, Western Sahara, and Lebanon).

Fertility Trends. With the exceptions of Cyprus and Israel, and to a lesser extent Egypt, Lebanon, Tunisia, and Turkey, the countries of North Africa and Southwest Asia have high fertility. The birth rates per 1,000 population and fertility rates per 1,000 females aged 15–49 are shown in Table 3. Birth rates of 50 reported for Oman and Qatar draw attention; it is seldom that such high rates are reliably reported for large human populations. The United Arab Emirates' 50 refers to natives only, whereas the rather low general fertility rate of 197 is based on natives and immigrants. For the five countries for which data are available for over a quarter of a century, the crude birth rates are shown in Figure 1. Rapid declines appear for the two countries with low fertility at the outset. Algeria shows erratic increases in fertility over the reporting period, although these may only be improvements in the reporting system.

High fertility is tied to high proportions of the population marrying early. Age at marriage has risen recently in several countries for which data are available, but both fertility and proportions marrying early are still relatively high. Only in Tunisia is the proportion of the pop-

ulation married at young ages already low [*see* AGE AT MARRIAGE]. For thirteen countries for which data are available the median percentage of married females aged 15–19 is 32. If data were available for the other ten countries, the median would be higher. Women in societies above the median produce seven children on average, those below, six. Around the median proportion married there is great variation in fertility, but at the extremes, low proportions of population marrying young mean low fertility, and high proportions marrying young mean high fertility.

The declines in proportions marrying young are more definite than the declines in the number of children. There may be a degree of "catching up" with missed fertility by females marrying at later ages. Such a reaction does not negate the fertility importance of late marriage. Even if women affected were to catch up completely and produce the same number of children after marrying late as when marrying early, there would still be a decline in the rate of growth as the same eventual fertility would be spread over a longer period.

Mortality Trends. The twenty-three countries are less uniform with regard to mortality than fertility. Some are close to the lowest mortality rate that can be achieved

FIGURE 1. *Live births per 1,000 population in Algeria, Egypt, Tunisia, Cyprus, and Israel, 1950–1972*

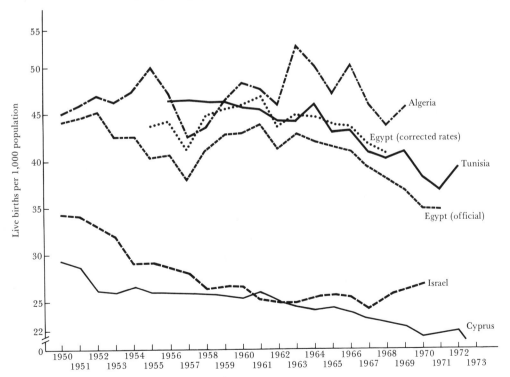

Source of data: United Nations, 1977*b*, pp. 49, 173.

without further medical breakthroughs (e.g., Kuwait). Others have mortality rates still so high that the age pattern can be only dimly discerned (e.g., North Yemen).

Much of Table 4 depends on models rather than on real data. Thus, for example, identical male life expectancies are found for Libya and Morocco. Jordan is the only country in Table 4 with female life expectancy at birth lower than that for males; there, life expectancy for both sexes had risen by 1981 to 56 years. All other countries with relevant data show the female life expectancy at birth longer than that of males by 2.2 years to 5.1 years.

Life expectancies at birth below 50 years have been suggested for Sudan, Oman, Saudi Arabia, and both Yemens. Reported life expectancies at birth above 60 years come from Bahrain, Kuwait, and Lebanon. Cyprus and Israel report life expectancies above 70 years.

In 1981, twelve countries had infant mortality rates in excess of 100 per 1,000 live births. Cyprus and Israel reported rates below 25.

Trends in International Migration. Migration was not a marked phenomenon in North Africa and Southwest Asia until the Palestine wars and until the oil era. Historically, Levantines had always moved around in the Middle East and North Africa. Greeks, Armenians, and Syrians performed important commercial functions as far south as Khartoum. Lebanese ranged as far west as Liberia and the Ivory Coast. Yemenites appeared as petty traders and skilled craftsmen all over the Arabian peninsula and beyond, and Egyptians worked as educators and administrators in various territories. Cyprus, like Malta and other island populations, traditionally sent much of its demographic surplus abroad. Neither commercially nor anthropologically, however, were these groups important in numerical terms, although at their peak they involved larger numbers than the migrations

TABLE 4. *Mortality, North Africa and Southwest Asia, 1970–1975[1] and 1981*

	Crude death rates per 1,000 population		Infant mortality rates per 1,000 births		Life expectancy at birth, 1970–75		Both sexes, 1981
	1970–75	1981	1970–75	1981	Male	Female	
North Africa and Southwest Asia		13					
North Africa		*13*		*117*			*54*
Algeria	15.4	14	86.3	127	52.9	55.0	56
Egypt, 1978	10.5	11	101.3	90	51.6	53.8	55
Libya	14.8	13	—	130	51.4	54.4	55
Morocco	15.7	14	149.0	133	51.4	54.5	55
Sudan	20.2	18	93.6	141	43.0	45.0	46
Tunisia	12.6	8	125.0	123	54.0	56.0	57
Western Sahara	4.5	—	5.3	—	—	—	—
Southwest Asia		*12*		*110*			*58*
Bahrain	7.0	8	63.0	78	← 65.3 →		62
Cyprus	9.8	8	27.2	16	70.0	72.9	73
Iraq	14.6	13	85.8	92	51.2	54.3	55
Israel, 1977	6.9	7	17.8	16	71.3	74.9	74
Jordan	14.7	13	89.0	97	52.6	52.0	56
Kuwait, 1976	4.8	5	39.1	39	66.4	71.5	70
Lebanon	9.5	8	65.0(45)	45	61.4	65.1	65
Oman	19.0	19	138.0	142	← 46.0 →		47
Palestine (Gaza strip), 1966	8.1	14	—	118	—	—	53
Qatar	20.0	14	—	138	← 55.0 →		55
Saudi Arabia	20.2	18	—	118	44.2	46.5	48
Syria	13.6	9	112.5	81	54.5	58.7	62
Turkey, 1967	11.7	10	153.0	125	← 53.7 →		61
United Arab Emirates	19.0	9	138.0	65	—	—	60
Yemen, North	26.3	25	210.0	160	37.6	38.7	40
Yemen, South	23.1	21	180.7(170)	170	40.6	42.4	44

[1]Annual rates for one of the years falling within the period 1970–1975, unless otherwise stated in the body of the table. Plausible rates from reasonably reliable sources when very different from rates accepted for this table are shown in parentheses.
Source of data: Estimates compiled by the author from various sources with numerous adjustments.

that led to the creation and growth of the state of Israel.

In the nineteenth and early twentieth centuries numerically important groups of settlers went from France to Morocco, Algeria, and Tunisia, and from Italy to Libya. Later these groups shrank as a result of political changes, the rise of xenophobic feelings, the achievement of independence, and the loss of privileged positions held by foreigners.

Palestinian refugees arrived by the hundreds of thousands in Jordan, Syria, Lebanon, and the Gaza strip as a result of the Israeli wars during the quarter of a century following the abandonment of the British mandate in Palestine. Many went to perform important economic and educational functions in these and other Arab countries. Most remained in refugee camps and have stayed for more than a demographic generation, displaying high fertility and remarkably low mortality rates.

Waves of Palestinian immigrants into the oil-producing countries were dwarfed by waves of immigrant laborers from other Arab countries and from the Indian subcontinent. In Saudi Arabia in the 1970s critical segments of the labor force came from as far afield as South Korea. Some data on immigrants are available for the early 1970s (in numbers and as proportions of the receiving population): Bahrain (40,000, 18 percent), Kuwait (391,000, 53 percent), Libya (225,000, 10 percent), Oman (6,000, 34 percent of the labor force), Saudi Arabia (400,000, 33 percent of the labor force). The sending countries were Egypt (220,000), Jordan (200,000), Lebanon (80,000), Syria (90,000), Tunisia (50,000), the two Yemens (225,000). Rough estimates in the press for the late 1970s suggest an increase from 1 million in the early 1970s to 2.5 million by the late 1970s. Some analysts think that the 2.5 million had already been reached by 1970. The extreme material disparities among the Arab countries of the region stimulated this migration and also attracted non-Arab immigrants from Pakistan, India, and Bangladesh (e.g., 50,000 Pakistanis in the United Arab Emirates and 30,000 in Kuwait). By the late 1970s only 40 percent of the inhabitants of Kuwait were indigenous, and only 25 percent in the United Arab Emirates and Qatar. These migrations were further facilitated by the ease with which immigrants could transfer their earnings back to their countries of origin.

For twelve countries estimates are available for both average annual population growth and natural increase. Assuming that the difference between the two is the result of net migration, we can classify the twelve countries (without parentheses) as follows:

• *Countries of net immigration:* Western Sahara, Iraq, Israel, Kuwait, Lebanon, Saudi Arabia, Turkey, North Yemen, (Libya), (Bahrain), (Qatar), (United Arab Emirates)

• *Countries of net emigration:* Algeria, Egypt, Cyprus, Syria, (Jordan), (Oman), (Gaza strip), (Morocco), (South Yemen)

This division is confirmed by other information on migratory movements for all except Lebanon and Turkey. The countries within parentheses possibly belong to the given group, but the necessary data are not published. Sudan and Tunisia probably have zero net migration.

Legislation on naturalization in most of the twenty-three countries (with the obvious exception of Israel) is rather rigid. Because of this, the distinction between *de jure* populations and *de facto* populations acquires importance both in the receiving and in the dispatching countries. Foreign inhabitants of a country can for generations remain *de jure* citizens of another. Some countries will report their "legal" population within their national boundaries and without. Others will omit citizens living abroad. National practices and definitions are not consistent with each other and result in double counts and omissions.

Age at Marriage, Divorce, and Polygamy. The effectiveness of age-at-marriage legislation is limited in circumstances where the age is uncertain. Moreover the practical significance of the legal minimum age at marriage does not go much beyond mere formality. Strict interpretation of the Koran tends to follow biological indicators, such as "soon after the onset of menstruation," which could mean an age as young as eight. Five or more years of difference between the sexes at age of marriage, common in these countries, is twice the usual difference in Western countries. However, declining proportions of young brides imply higher ages at marriage and a narrowing of the age differentials between sexes.

The relatively late age of males at marriage increases the demographic need for polygamy. The Koran allows four wives at any time. A fifth can be taken only if one of the four is divorced first. This arrangement is legally quite simple, but it can have discouraging financial implications.

The actual incidence of polygamy is unknown, mainly because of reluctance by authorities to report on the subject. There is little doubt that polygamy is declining in most countries of the region.

Polygamy varies according to social class. There is less polygamy among urban dwellers than among villagers and less among the latter than among the desert dwellers, or bedouin. Polygamy is of importance to the highest social classes for reasons of prestige and to secure male progeny and to the lowest social classes to ensure farm and domestic labor. Because of the required bride price, its profitability is a delicate calculation in the latter situation.

For the bedouin of the Negev desert it has been shown that the fertility of wives in polygamous unions tends to be lower than that of wives in monogamous unions. The societal impact of polygamy with regard to fertility is also downward because it keeps out of the marriage market those young men who cannot afford marriage.

In Tunisia polygamy has been abolished for all new marriage contracts. In most other countries its impact is slight. Often, as in Morocco, polygamy takes the form of consecutive monogamy, in the form of frequent divorces and quick remarriages, rather than the traditional simultaneous polygamy.

Rural-Urban Distribution and Nomads. City size is a misleading indicator of urbanization in several of the twenty-three countries. The large villages of cotton growers in the Sudan Gezira with 20,000 and more people are slow in acquiring the essential features of urban life. Some analysts would question whether even some large cities such as Sana, the capital of North Yemen, have urban characteristics. Excluding "metropolitan" Bahrain, Kuwait, and Qatar, in the other countries more than half of the population is still rural. Nevertheless, it can be said that while the proportion of city dwellers is still low in most of the twenty-three countries, the process of urbanization is under way.

The region takes in the most rural of rural areas in every meaning of the word, but at the same time it contains some of the world's most metropolitan cities: Cairo, Alexandria, Istanbul, and Casablanca, not to mention smaller ones that are historically important and well known such as Baghdad and Jerusalem.

The region is characterized by very uneven distribution of population, with large areas almost uninhabited. However, desert dwellers exist in significant numbers. While subject to a long process of settlement, and with fertility rates generally somewhat lower than those of villagers, they still count in the millions. Sudan alone has probably more than one million nomads, but much nomadism appears nowadays in diluted forms of seminomadism or straightforward transhumance. Regular seasonal movements take place for purposes of cultivation or animal husbandry, but a permanent base exists with fixed buildings where wives live. In Iraq and Jordan most nomads are settled, the numbers involved over the last century reaching the hundreds of thousands.

Depending upon definitions, in the early 1980s up to 1 million nomads could be found in Saudi Arabia: around 500,000 each in Algeria, Libya, and Oman: up to 100,000 each in Jordan and Iraq: and small numbers in Western Sahara, Morocco, Egypt (both in the western

desert and in the Sinai peninsula), and South Yemen. The few thousands in Kuwait were settled in the early 1970s. Only traces were left in Syria and Israel. While difficulties of enumeration and definition are great, it may be said that there are 3 million nomads in North Africa and Southwest Asia, or 1.5 percent of the total population.

Economic and Social Stratification. The division of the labor force into primary, secondary, and tertiary industries is a relatively available indicator. Several of the twenty-three countries appear to be skipping secondary industries and are moving from primary directly to tertiary, in part because few opportunities are available in the secondary industries.

In Table 2 the percentage of the economically active population is shown. The United Arab Emirates have more than half of its population, and Qatar has almost half, in the labor force. These high proportions are due to the heavy immigration of workers for the purposes of oil production and the other employment it finances. In Kuwait, the economically active proportion declined to 31 percent of the total population as the immigration process there started earliest and gradually brought along women and children, who did not participate in the labor force. In all the other countries except Egypt (31 percent) and Turkey (41 percent), less than 30 percent of the populations are economically active. Relatively low fertility and relatively high urbanization and industrialization account for the rates in Egypt and Turkey. Table 2 shows also the female proportion of the labor force. One-fifth of the labor forces of Syria, South Yemen, and Lebanon consists of females; and Turkey is at a high 38 percent.

Literacy, Education, and Language. Progress is being made in the education of females, although less than in that of males. The Yemens, Saudi Arabia, Morocco, and Sudan have low percentages of females of school age actually in school (8, 24, 27, and 20 percent respectively), but others have close to 50 percent or well above it.

The twenty-three countries have one large advantage over many other nonindustrialized regions: the Arabic language. Because it has an established printed form and is widespread, it is an available tool for education and all other activities in the developmental processes.

The region contains a myriad of linguistic minorities, some of pre-Arabic antiquity, and some exist in every country. There are also sizable ethnic minorities. In 1956, 61 percent of Sudanese spoke languages other than Arabic. In Algeria and Morocco from a fifth to a third of the populations speak Berber languages. The Kurds of Iraq speak an Indo-European language. Other groups are less important in size; examples are the Circassian founders of Amman, who use the Cyrillic alphabet, and the Armenian and Assyrian refugees from Turkey in Syria with their own alphabets.

Statements and Actions on Population Matters. Of the twenty-three territories, twenty-one expressed views on the population problem in response to a 1979 United Nations survey. Six said the fertility of their populations was too low, four that it was too high. In the two years between 1974 and 1976, those changing their position did so in the direction of "too low" (Bahrain and Saudi Arabia). These and other perceptions carried over only partly into policy, that is, the appropriateness and effectiveness of government action was accepted by only some governments. Seven thought that they should influence mortality rates downward. Ten thought that fertility should be affected (six up, four down). Five out of twenty-one thought they could influence spatial distribution of population, but fifteen thought that the rural-urban migration should be decelerated. Jordan would even reverse it. Nine considered that emigration was important and could be higher; twelve saw immigration as significant and, if anything, too low.

Two of the governments believed that although fertility rates were too high, government intervention would be inappropriate (Bahrain and Jordan). Lower aggregate fertility was desirable in these two instances for reasons of individual health and welfare, rather than to bestow macroeconomic benefits on the society as a whole. Iraq felt that government intervention to maintain fertility at current satisfactory levels was justified.

Four of the countries undertook to help establish family planning policies and programs in the 1960s: Egypt, Tunisia, Turkey, and Morocco. Tunisia has also incorporated induced abortion into its program and is the only country with reported legal abortions (rising from 742 in 1967 to 12,427 in 1974). There is a marked decline in Egypt's fertility, some in Tunisia's, and none in Morocco's, while the Turkish decline seems to have preceded the policy. Studies of the Egyptian and Tunisian declines report as causes either the government policy or the general development process. [*For a discussion of government policy in the region, see* FAMILY PLANNING PROGRAMS, *article on* DEVELOPING COUNTRIES.]

Demography as a Scholarly Activity. Demography as a scholarly pursuit has begun at national universities and national research institutes. No national learned journals have as yet existed long enough to be called permanent, but prominent analytic efforts are found in Egypt, Turkey, Tunisia, Algeria, and Morocco.

The Population and Statistics divisions of the Economic Commission for Africa, and the more recently created Economic Commission for Western Asia, play important roles in the collection and dissemination of data and population studies. Another United Nations crea-

tion, the Cairo Demographic Centre, has contributed to demographic analysis and compilation of demographic data. The Association of Maghrebian Demographers, in existence since about 1970, opened its ranks to non-Maghrebian Arab demographers about 1975. An African Association of Population Studies, serving the whole of Africa, was created in 1978; its learned journal *Jimlar mutane* was in its third year in 1980. Demographers and social statisticians from the twenty-three countries appear in increasing numbers at international scientific conferences.

Only two countries (Egypt and Turkey) have institutes of population research; another thirteen rely on population work done in institutes of general research; and six have population interests looked after in their planning institutions. In eight countries, planners are assisted by permanently designated bodies; in eleven, planners are themselves responsible for formulating population policy, and in two (Bahrain and Qatar) there is no central planning organization.

Karol J. Krótki

BIBLIOGRAPHY

Clarke, J. I., and W. B. Fisher (editors). *Populations of the Middle East and North Africa: A Geographical Approach.* New York: Africana Publishing Corporation, 1972. London: University of London Press, 1972.
France, Institut National d'Études Démographiques. "Le Maghreb." Special number of *Population,* vol. 26, March 1971.
Henry, Alice, and Phyllis T. Piotrow. "Age at Marriage and Fertility." *Population Reports,* series M, no. 4, November 1979.
Jimlar mutane. Issued biannually since 1978 by the African Association of Population Studies, Nairobi.
United Nations, Cairo Demographic Centre. *Demographic Measures and Population Growth in Arab Countries.* Research Monograph Series, no. 1. Cairo, 1970.
———. *Fertility Trends and Differentials in Arab Countries.* Research Monograph Series, no. 2. Cairo, 1971.
United Nations, Department of Economic and Social Affairs. *Demographic Yearbook, 1976.* Series R, no. 4. New York, 1977. In English and French. (United Nations, 1977a)
———. *Levels and Trends of Fertility throughout the World, 1950–1970.* Series A, Population Studies, no. 59. New York, 1977. (United Nations, 1977b)
———. *Demographic Yearbook, 1977.* Series R, no. 6. New York, 1978. In English and French.
United Nations, Department of International Economic and Social Affairs. *Demographic Yearbook, 1978.* Series R, no. 7. New York, 1979. In English and French.
———. *World Population Trends and Policies: 1977 Monitoring Report.* 2 vols. Volume 1: *Population Trends.* Volume 2: *Population Policies.* Series A, Population Studies, no. 62 and no. 62-add. 1. New York, 1979.
United Nations, Economic Commission for Western Asia. *De-*

mographic and Related Socio-economic Data Sheets for Countries of the Economic Commission for Western Asia. No. 2. Beirut, January 1978. Some thirty unnumbered pages and a foldout sheet.

———. *The Population Situation in the ECWA Region.* Beirut, 1980. At the time of writing, reports of twelve countries are available (Oman and PLO are missing). Judging from the numbering of tables, reports for all fourteen members of ECWA are intended for eventual inclusion in a joint compendium.

2.

ISRAEL

A relatively new country, Israel is small yet heterogenous and complex. Changes in the composition of the population have been integral features of the evolution of Israeli society. One of the dominant themes in the sociopolitical conflicts in Israel has been the relative size and growth of Jewish and Arab populations and related issues of immigration and fertility. The open-door immigration policy formulated when Israel was established in 1948 has been one of the clearest expressions of Zionism. This policy, along with sociopolitical and economic processes, resulted in a mass migration to Israel in the three years subsequent to statehood, at a rate unprecedented in modern demographic history. Mass migration has been, and continues to be, the dominant factor shaping Israeli society.

Despite substantial efforts devoted to security problems and to the social and economic absorption of over 1.5 million immigrants in the three decades after 1948, Israel has experienced an exceptionally rapid growth in economic investment, national product, and expenditure—both total and per capita. Moreover, immigrants to Israel with high levels of mortality and fertility have undergone in the span of two decades extremely rapid transitions in both vital processes. Issues associated with the continuity of Israel as a viable state in the Arab Middle East, the changing Arab-Jewish and Arab-Israeli conflicts, and the dynamics of Israel's socioethnic and socioeconomic structure are to a large extent consequences of population patterns and policies. In turn, population patterns of the 1950s, have implications for political conflict and social changes in Israeli society through the twenty-first century.

Israel represents an intensified microcosm, speeded up, of population issues and responses around the world. Among these are the most active immigration policy in modern history, rapid mortality and fertility transitions, social layers of differential fertility, planned population distribution, and extreme demographic differences vis-à-vis hostile neighbors. Other issues and responses are a demographic future depending on individual couples in Israel as well as on international politics, regional population trends affecting security prospects, reproductive practices subject to religious and national proscriptions, and efforts at policy considerations that fall short of policy goals.

Location and Description. Israel's total area is 20,770 square kilometers (8,019 square miles), according to the 4 June 1967 borders but including the whole of Jerusalem. The country is bounded on the north by Lebanon, on the east by Syria and Jordan, on the southwest by the United Arab Republic, and on the west by the Mediterranean Sea and Gaza. The southernmost boundary is at the Gulf of Aqaba.

Centuries of overcultivation and overgrazing have depleted the natural vegetation of the region. The hills, coastal sand dunes, and the Negev are mostly covered with scrub. Much of the country north of Beersheba, however, is under intensive cultivation or reforestation, and efforts are under way to make the Negev arable. Agriculture accounts for only about 5 percent of national income. More than 30 percent of national income is derived from industry and construction, with an additional 18 percent from the service sector.

During ancient times the area occupied by present-day Israeli and Jordanian territories changed boundaries frequently. The succession of rulers from 1400 B.C. to the sixteenth century included the Canaanites, Hebrews, Assyrians, Babylonians, Persians, Selevcids, Maccabees, Romans, Arabs, Mamelukes, and Ottoman Turks. Ottoman rule, which began in 1516, lasted for some four hundred years; during the latter part of the period, in 1880, modern Jewish resettlement began. In 1920, the British, who had conquered the area during World War I, acquired Palestine and Transjordan (now the Hashemite Kingdom of Jordan) as mandates of the League of Nations. British rule lasted for nearly thirty years until 1948, when the new Jewish state of Israel was founded. Following the Six Day War of 1967, an expanded territory, administered and controlled by Israel, contained more than 1 million Arabs.

Population. At the end of 1979 the population of Israel numbered 3.8 million, of whom 3.2 million, or 84 percent, were Jews and 618,000 were non-Jews (mostly Arabs). The Jewish population was made up predominantly of immigrants who arrived during the twentieth century and their Israeli-born descendants. In 1979, 25 percent of the Jewish population was of European birth, 20 percent was born in Asian or African countries, and 54 percent was native born. Of the native born, 31 percent was of European origin, 47 percent of African or Asian origin, and 22 percent was third generation. The non-Jewish population is divided into three mainly religious subpopulations—Muslims (78 percent), Christians (14 percent), and Druze (8 percent).

In 1980 there were nearly one million households in Israel. An average of four persons dwells in a Jewish household (excluding one-person households). Among the non-Jewish, average household size is more than six persons. These differentials reflect differential fertility patterns of the two groups.

The average number of children born to a Jewish family is less than three. Families of African or Asian origin have 3.1 children on the average, those of European origin have 2.7. The average number of children born to non-Jewish families is about six, varying according to religion, rural or urban residence, occupation, education, and other socioeconomic characteristics. For instance, the number of children born to Muslim, Druze, and Christian women is about 7, 7, and 3, respectively.

Marriage is almost universal among Jews and non-Jews in Israel. In 1978–1979, the median age at first marriage was 25 years for Jewish men and 22 for Jewish women. These averages have been declining over time for Jewish men. Among non-Jews, the median age at marriage in 1978–1979 was 23.6 years for men and 19.5 years for women.

The proportion of women of reproductive ages (15–49)

varies substantially by ethnoreligious origins. In 1978 the pattern was as shown in Table 1.

Growth patterns. Population size increased in the three decades after the establishment of the state of Israel, from 800,000 in 1948 to 3.8 million in 1979; the Jewish population increased from 650,000 to 3.2 million in 1979 and the non-Jewish population from 150,000 to about 618,000. The demographic sources of these growth patterns, summarized in Table 2, differ sharply.

TABLE 1. *Proportion of women of reproductive age in Israel, 1978*

Population group	Percentage of women aged 15–49 of all women by origin
Jews, by origin	*47.3*
Israel	44.5
Europe-America	37.8
Africa	71.8
Asia	61.1
Non-Jews, by religion	*43.0*
Muslim	41.6
Christian	51.2

Source of data: Estimated from official government figures.

TABLE 2. *Selected demographic data, Israel, 1979*

Characteristic	Israel	Jewish population	Non-Jewish population
Population size (thousands)	3,836	3,218	618
Average household size	3.7	3.4	6.5
Average household size (excluding one-person households)	4.3	4.0	7.1
Percentage urban	86.7	90.3	67.8
Median age at marriage:			
Men	n.a.	25.0	23.6
Women	n.a.	22.1	19.5
Birth rate (per 1,000 per year)	24.7	22.0	39.2
Death rate (per 1,000 per year)	6.9	7.2	4.9
Natural increase (per 1,000)	17.8	14.8	34.3
Infant mortality (per 1,000 births)	16.0	12.8	25.4
Total fertility rate	3.2	2.8	5.9
Expectation of life at birth:			
Men	71.5	71.9	69.1
Women	75.0	75.6	72.0
Average age	29.0	30.5	20.8
Percentage in age group 0–14	33.3	30.4	48.1
Percentage employed in agriculture	6.2	5.4	10.4
Percentage in age group 15–19 enrolled in secondary school	48.0	53.1	29.0

n.a. = not available.
Source of data: Official government figures.

In 1979 birth rates were 22 per 1,000 population among Jews and 39.2 per 1,000 among non-Jews. The Jewish birth rate has been declining since the early 1950s as a consequence of a considerable fertility decline among Asian and African Jewish couples and changes in the age structure of the population. Although Muslim fertility remains high, fertility levels were beginning to fall in the 1970s. The fertility patterns of Jewish immigrant groups of various ethnic origins have been converging.

Expectation of life was about 74 years among Jews in 1979, an increase from about 68 years in 1950. Migrants from European countries and the Israeli-born (irrespective of ethnic origin) have enjoyed relatively high life expectancy. However, mortality changes among African and Asian immigrants were revolutionary. These immigrants had a low life expectancy before immigration—between 30 and 40 years depending on country of origin. Following immigration, life expectancy increased almost immediately to 60–65 years. This implies an increase averaging 12–17 years per calendar year and is probably a world record. Estimated infant mortality rates for immigrants from Yemen and North Africa were 370 and 270 per 1,000 births, while rates immediately after immigration were about 35 per 1,000.

These mortality reductions reflect the concerted efforts on the part of the Israeli government to provide health and medical care. In turn, these changes have had profound effects on related population patterns in Israel.

Among Arabs, expectation of life was about 71 years in 1979, an increase from about 50 years in 1950. Infant mortality among non-Jews, however, was still twice as high as among Jews. Crude death rates were higher among Jews—7.2 per 1,000 compared with 4.9 among non-Jews, a reflection of the very young age structure of the non-Jewish population.

It follows from these differential patterns that natural increase has been dissimilar among the Jewish and non-Jewish communities in Israel. Among Jews it was about 15 per 1,000 in 1979, and the prospects for the future were for further declines, as the African and Asian section of the Jewish population proceeded in its transition toward low fertility and small family size. Natural increase among non-Jews was about 35 per 1,000 in 1979. It declined in the 1970s as a result of fertility reductions. However, natural increase among non-Jews was more than twice as high as among Jews. The possibility that such differential patterns will continue, even if at a declining rate, might, in the absence of considerable Jewish immigration, have social and political implications. It represents a potential source of strain and tension.

Immigration patterns. The most important source of growth of the Jewish population since the modern resettlement of Israel has been immigration. In the half-century before the establishment of the state, more than 500,000 Jewish immigrants arrived in Palestine. Between 1948 and 1978 more than 1.5 million immigrants arrived; in the first three and a half years (1948–1951) almost 700,000 immigrants arrived—a period referred to as "mass immigration." The average rate of immigration has varied significantly over the years; during 1948–1949, the rate exceeded 20 percent per year but it was less than 1 percent per year during 1966–1968.

Immigration to Israel has also varied in its ethnic composition. Up to 1950 the majority of immigrants came from European countries; between 1951–1957 and 1960–1968, most immigrants were of African or Asian origin. Indeed, the shift of immigrants from European to Asian or African origin, and since 1970 back to European (particularly Russian), has had major implications for the evolving ethnic mosaic in Israel. Most important, the ethnic divisions have been interrelated with socioeconomic variation based on origins. The majority of immigrants since 1969 have been from European and American countries since the Jewish communities in Asian and African countries have been depleted of population.

Differentials in growth. During 1948–1951, the Jewish population grew at an annual rate of 24 percent, with immigration responsible for nearly nine-tenths of the increase. Between 1952 and 1964, the annual growth rate of the Jewish population was 3.5 percent, of which about half was accounted for by immigration. Since 1964 the growth rate has been declining. In contrast, the growth rate of the non-Jewish population, which has always been predominantly the result of its high rate of natural increase, remained at nearly 4 percent per year up to the mid-1970s. Since then, the non-Jewish growth rate has declined. But because the volume of Jewish immigration has tended to decline over time, the non-Jewish population has in fact been increasing more rapidly than the Jewish population since the late 1950s.

Age structure. Differentials in demographic patterns between Jewish and non-Jewish sectors are reflected in the age structure of these two communities. The age structure of the Jewish population is younger than that of western European populations, but much older than that of the non-Jewish population in Israel. The percentages in the 0–14, 15–64, and 65-and-over age groups in 1978 among Jews were 30, 60, and 9, respectively; among non-Jews they were 50, 46, and 4. One implication of the very young age distribution of the non-Jewish sector of the population is that even if fertility declines considerably in the coming years, birth rates, and therefore population growth, will decline only slightly.

Since it can safely be predicted that fertility levels of the African and Asian section of the Jewish population in Israel will continue to decline, future growth of the Jewish population will depend upon the volume of immigration even more strongly than in the past. Projections of the Jewish and the non-Jewish populations have shown that the fraction of non-Jews is almost bound to increase within the next thirty years; this population issue causes some concern among Jews in Israel.

Rural-urban distribution. The changing patterns of geographic distribution of the Israeli Jewish population can be divided into two main periods. The first extends from the foundation of the state in 1948 to 1952—the period of mass immigration and rapid population increase. Immigration and settlement were regulated and organized by government policies. In this period, deserted Arab villages and towns were settled by new Jewish immigrants; when these areas were populated, immigrants were directed to new villages far from the central areas of Israel and to newly created towns. As a result of these government policies, population distribution shifted within the country. The proportion in the northern, central, and southern areas (the former two were heavily populated by Arabs) increased while that in regions of the major cities—Jerusalem, Tel Aviv, and Haifa—decreased.

Population distribution in the second period—after 1952—was affected by three major factors. First, since the newly settled immigrant populations were relatively young and predominantly of oriental origin, they had a high potential for rapid natural increase. Second, the contribution of immigration following mass immigration provided additional potential settlers for these newer developing areas. Both these factors could be expected to strengthen shifts in population distribution toward the less-settled areas of the country. However, a third factor—internal migration—was operating as a counterbalance. Internal migration streams were stronger from the newly developed and more sparsely settled areas toward central areas that were more densely populated and more developed. This countervailing tendency was contrary to declared government policy, which offered economic incentives to residents settling in new towns. Hence, although Israel's policy was effective in terms of initial settlement, it was ineffective in terms of internal migration.

Nevertheless, the combined effects of settlement and differential natural increase were more powerful, and population did indeed shift toward development towns. A reflection of that shift was the growth in the southern region from 3.8 percent of the total population in 1952 to nearly 13 percent in 1975.

Literacy and education. Israel's compulsory educational system covered eight years of tuition-free schooling until 1969, when it was increased to nine years. Nevertheless, among Jews 53 percent of the adult population (aged 14 or over) had attained at least nine years of schooling, according to data relating to 1970; and, in 1970, only 9 percent of the Jewish adult population, consisting mainly

of older immigrants of African or Asian origin, were still illiterate. Among the non-Jewish adult population, only 15 percent had had at least nine years of schooling, whereas some 36 percent were still illiterate (in 1961, 9 and 50 percent, respectively). The percentages of those attaining at least nine years of schooling can be expected to increase in the coming years in both communities, as more of the younger generations reach adulthood. In 1978, about 20 percent of the Jewish population had more than twelve years of education compared to less than 6 percent of the non-Jewish population. The proportion with higher education is increasing among the young. In 1978, for Jews more than one-fourth of the European-born have more than twelve years of education compared to less than 9 percent of the Asian- or African-born; almost 40 percent of Israelis of European origin had higher education compared to less than 10 percent of Israelis of Asian or African origin.

Population Growth and Socioeconomic Development. Since 1955 national income in Israel has quadrupled in real terms, but, as noted earlier, population has been growing substantially too. Nevertheless, even allowing for population growth, national income per capita more than doubled between 1955 and 1970. This increase can be seen in the different economic sectors and in private as well as public expenditures. For instance, in the early 1950s Israel had to rely heavily on importation for its agricultural supplies. Not only has the total value of the net product in agriculture increased considerably (in real terms), but the per capita product has quadrupled since the 1950s. It should also be noted that although total agricultural production has increased substantially, the labor force actually engaged in agriculture has declined both as a fraction of the total labor force and also in absolute terms. This was possible through the increasing application of modern technology to agriculture.

Whereas the growth rate of agricultural production has slowed in recent years, that of manufacturing continued its fast growth. Consequently, during the 1960s, the relative contribution of agriculture to the national income declined while that of manufacturing increased.

Public expenditures on education and on public health have increased considerably since the 1950s, in total and per capita values. In fact, expenditures on education have increased fourfold, reflecting both the achievement of universal elementary education and an extension of the educational system to higher levels.

Expenditures on public health per capita have more than doubled since the 1950s. In 1948 there were 66 hospitals, 7 of which were government-operated; in 1966 there were 158 hospitals, 34 of them government-operated.

The size of the labor force has naturally increased with

population growth, but not so rapidly. The decline in the general rate of participation of the population in the labor force has been the result of two factors. The extension and growth of the educational system has meant that increasing numbers of young persons receive full-time education; it has also raised the age of entry into the labor force. In addition, the population of Israel is aging, which means that even with constant rates of age-specific participation in the labor force, the general percentage of the population participating is bound to decline. Future trends are very difficult, if not impossible, to predict with accuracy. They depend to a great extent on the volume and origin of future immigration.

Policies and Actions. The focus of population concern in Israel and, before the foundation of the state, in Palestine, has always been political. During and even before the British rule of Palestine, the Jewish community and its leaders aimed at increasing the size of the Jewish population, in absolute and relative terms. Therefore, as a matter of policy, the Jewish community invested a great deal of effort in maximizing the volume of Jewish immigration. Until the establishment of the state of Israel, Jewish immigration was controlled by the British government, which at times restricted its volume. Only very limited migration was permitted into the country during World War II, for example, and the restrictions were only slightly relaxed afterward. Conflicting political ambitions of the Jewish and Arab communities in the country, restrictions imposed on Jewish immigration by the British, and news of the fate of European Jewry were three important elements in the concern of the Jewish community over the low and declining Jewish birth rates before the foundation of the state of Israel. Unlike immigration activities, however, the concern over the birth rate during that period did not bring about any significant consequences.

Population policies. Israel's independence meant that the volume of immigration was then controlled by the Israeli government, depending only on the capacity of Israel to absorb more immigrants and on the willingness and ability of Jewish people in other countries to emigrate to Israel. One of the first laws passed by the Knesset was the Law of Return, according to which every Jewish person, irrespective of origin, was entitled to immigrate to Israel and to settle there with the aid and assistance of the state. Israel's immigration policies enabled and encouraged hundreds of thousands of Jewish people from many countries to immigrate to Israel during the period 1948–1951, and subsequently.

Population committee. The volume of immigration started to decline after 1952, both because of economic difficulties and because the number of potential immigrants in the diaspora had declined. At that time, pressures for action toward the establishment of a pronatal policy in Israel were intensified. These pressures came from various sources; but especially the right-wing political parties and, even more so, the religious parties, which always had considerable political power in Israel's government and administrative machinery. Consequently, Prime Minister David Ben-Gurion appointed a Population Committee in April 1962.

The committee was asked to inquire into and to advise the government on two main concerns: the differential fertility between the Jewish and the Arab populations and the problem of the economically deprived families, whose numbers increased as a result of the immigration waves of the 1950s. The second problem was not entirely socioeconomic. Significantly, a substantial portion of these families were immigrants of African or Asian origin.

The Population Committee's report, submitted to Prime Minister Levi Eshkol in April 1966, recommended that a special body be established within the governmental framework to deal with the problem of low Jewish natality and to promote the welfare of large families. For example, it suggested that working conditions for married women be arranged to permit them to have larger families and that loans be made available to "growing" families to finance larger apartments.

Induced abortion was unlawful in Israel until 1977, except for the purpose of "preserving the woman's health." In practice, however, the law was not enforced after 1952 and violators were prosecuted only in special circumstances, for example, if the abortion resulted in the death of the woman. In 1977, a more liberalized abortion law was passed permitting abortion in an approved medical institution for a variety of reasons, including whether the additional birth would cause social or economic hardship. The abortion request needed approval by a committee consisting of two medical practitioners and a social worker. In late 1979 this socioeconomic clause was removed from the legislation and a more limited and restrictive abortion law remained. It is not clear what the effects of the legal changes have been or will be on abortion patterns. According to data collected in 1975, 28 percent of married Jewish women below age 55 had had at least one induced abortion. Among women married for twenty years, 36 percent had had at least one abortion. For native-born Israeli women the percentage was even higher—48—while among Asian- or African-born Jewish women the percentage was 28.

Family planning. There are no public family planning services in Israel, but contraceptives are available through private channels. A sample survey in 1975 of Jewish married women below age 55 revealed that only 30 percent used the pill or an intrauterine device (IUD) and an additional 17 percent used mechanical contraceptives. One-third of Jewish women reported using only natural methods such as withdrawal or rhythm. This is one of the reasons behind the relatively high levels of induced abortions. The proportion of women using contraceptives—and more efficient ones—has increased among the young and among the native-born. Among Jewish women married in the period 1965–1974, 58 percent of those planning their families used the pill or the IUD; among those married in the period 1955–1964 the proportion was 44 percent, among those married in the period 1945–1954 it was 28 percent.

Population programs. The government decided in April 1967 to establish a Demographic Center as an administrative unit in the prime minister's office. Apparently the government intended the center to initiate actions recommended by the Population Committee. The stated aim of the center was "to act systematically in carrying out a population policy intended to increase fertility by creating a more favorable pronatal atmosphere." An increase in Israel's birth rate was declared "crucial for the whole future of the Jewish people."

Activities of the center to date have been in three areas: research, publicity, and experimentation. Research has been initiated on Israeli attitudes toward having a third and fourth child. The center has promoted large families through various public channels such as radio and television. It has also initiated a small-scale program through which couples intending to have another child may, under certain conditions, apply for a low-interest loan for the purpose of acquiring a larger apartment.

The committee's report and recommendations have been evaluated critically on a variety of demographic and socioeconomic grounds (Friedlander and Goldscheider, 1979).

In 1980, a series of revised population recommendations, consistent with the earlier pronatalist orientations of the committee's report, were prepared by the Demographic Center. The emphasis was on the need for increased fertility among selected segments of the Jewish population.

Dov Friedlander
Calvin Goldscheider

BIBLIOGRAPHY

Bachi, Roberto. *The Population of Israel.* Jerusalem: Scientific Translations International, 1977.
Friedlander, Dov, Zvi Eisenbach, and Calvin Goldscheider. "Modernization Patterns and Fertility Change: The Arab Populations of Israel and the Israel-administered Territories." *Population Studies* 33(2):239–254, July 1979.
Friedlander, Dov, and Calvin Goldscheider. "Immigration, Social Change and Cohort Fertility in Israel." *Population Studies* 32(2):299–317, July 1978.
———. *The Population of Israel.* New York: Columbia University Press, 1979.
Friedlander, Dov, and Eitan Sabatello. *Israel.* Country Profiles. New York: Population Council, February 1972.

NORTH AMERICA

In geographic terms North America consists of Canada, the United States, the islands of Greenland, Bermuda, Saint Pierre and Miquelon, and the region often called "Central" or "Middle" America that includes Mexico and the mainland and offshore islands south to the isthmus of Panama. [*The demography of the region south of the United States is discussed in* LATIN AMERICA *and* CARIBBEAN REGION. *See also* CANADA; MEXICO; UNITED STATES.]

Greenland, the world's largest island, lies for the most part within the Arctic Circle. More than 80 percent of its approximately 2,180,800 square kilometers (842,000 square miles) is covered by ice. The territory was first colonized around A.D. 980 by the Norseman Eric the Red, but the Norse colony, whose population rose to a peak of 10,000 in the twelfth century, eventually succumbed to disease and official neglect. Recolonized in the eighteenth century by Danish settlers, Greenland is now part of the kingdom of Denmark and has had home rule since 1979. Its population in the late 1970s was estimated at 50,000, almost all of whom live along the western coast. Bermuda, a British crown colony off the eastern coast of the United States, has a larger population of about 62,000 on 52 square kilometers (20 square miles) of coral rocks, islets, and islands. Saint Pierre and Miquelon, a group of nine small islands off the eastern Canadian coast, is an overseas department of France. A population of about 6,000 inhabits a total area of approximately 241 square kilometers (93 square miles).

Regina McNamara

BIBLIOGRAPHY

Bermuda, Census Office. *Report of the Population Census, 1970.* Hamilton: Bermuda Government, 1973.
Denmark, Danmarks Statistik. *Folke- og boligtaellingen: Grønland, 26 oktober 1976* (Population and Housing Census: Greenland, 26 October 1976). Copenhagen, 1978.
France, Institut National de la Statistique et des Etudes Economiques. *Recensement de la population du territoire de Saint-Pierre et Miquelon, 1974.* Paris, 1974.
Hudson, F. S. *North America.* London: Macdonald & Evans, 1974.

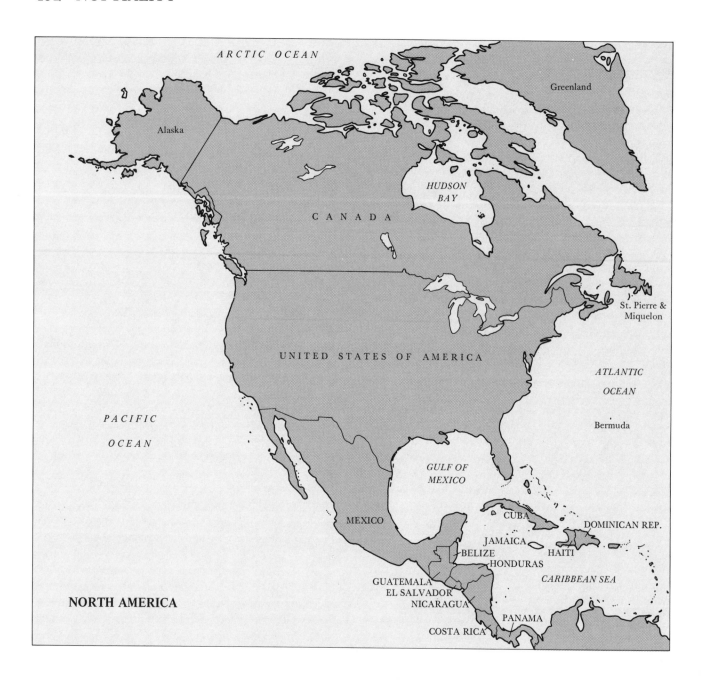

NORTH AMERICA

NUPTIALITY

See MARRIAGE.

NUPTIALITY INDEXES

The index of nuptiality most commonly used is the crude marriage rate, calculated by dividing the total number of marriages in a year among residents of an area by the total population of that area. A refinement of this measure is the general marriage rate, which takes into account variations among areas in the size of the population of marriagable age by restricting the denominator to the population age 15 and older. Further refinements allow for differences in marital status and sex composition as well as age composition. These are, however, based primarily on vital statistics, and such information is often lacking or inadequate. This article describes some of the indexes of nuptiality that can be calculated readily from marital-status information in census and surveys and illustrates their use by presenting nuptiality measures derived from recent census data for thirty-five Asian and Pacific countries.

Sources of Information. When a population is accurately classified across marital-status categories, separately by sex and for each age group, useful information is provided on each of the major aspects of nuptiality. Percentages of population who are single at the youngest ages indicate the tempo of recent nuptiality, whereas percentages still unmarried at older ages indicate the prevalence of lifelong nonmarriage. There are, of course, the usual problems inherent in cross-sectional information of any kind. One cannot discern the patterns of the past from current marital statuses alone, nor can one know from percentages single among younger cohorts what their future nuptiality experience will be or their ultimate level of nonmarriage. Properly defined, however, the "single" or "never-married" percentages by age do index the prevalence and pace of one of the most important of personal and social transitions.

Historical changes in the process of first marriage can be seen from comparisons of marriage-status distributions across points in time—thence derives the analytic significance of the time series of marriage-status data that exist for many societies. The use of cross-sectional information on the current marital statuses of the ever-married is more problematic. A person's life history can include a variety of changes among the "currently married," "widowed," "divorced," and "separated" statuses, yet the status most recently attained and recorded is all that is given in most censuses. Nevertheless, these aspects of nuptiality also can be examined with marital-status data.

All the indexes discussed below are applicable to cross-sectional information on marital status; indeed, in many instances they were devised because direct information on marriage events or retrospective marriage histories were not available. Other nuptiality indexes are infrequently calculated from complete marriage histories or from registration data on marriage events. Marriage histories are rare, though they are collected more commonly now than in the past, and marriage registration continues to be incomplete in many countries. Indexes can also be based on vital statistics and census data in combination, but these too are exceptional.

Current Marital Status. We can study trends and differentials in nuptiality by looking directly at the percentages of population single in each age group and at their patterns across space and time; but it is often convenient to examine one or more summary indexes of nuptiality derived from the detailed data. We can illustrate some of the alternatives with the aid of the long time series of Japanese census data (see Table 1). Except for 1945, census cross-sections are available quinquennially for Japan from 1920 to 1975. These cross-sectional data also indicate the experience of certain real cohorts born between 1900 and 1930. (The first cohort described married around 1920 and the last cohort around 1950.)

These percentages of women single by age group provide some useful detail on what has occurred with Japanese marriage patterns. In each age group there is a general tendency for the percentages single to rise in the first half of the century and to stabilize by the 1960s. In the age group 15–19, the percentage single was at its highest (near 100) in 1955 and rose no further, whereas the upward trends at ages 20–24 and older continued until at least 1960. Because marriage is nearly universal among females in Japan, the percentages single for the oldest age groups change but little.

Singulate mean age at marriage. To fill the need for a summary measure of the timing of first marriage from data of this kind, John Hajnal (1953) proposed a measure he called the singulate mean age at marriage (SMAM) based upon one cross-sectional schedule of percentages single by age group. The singulate mean is computationally very straightforward, but stringent assumptions are required: that there be no differentials by

TABLE 1. *Percentages single among Japanese females by age group and mean ages at marriage, 1920–1975*

Age group	1920	1925	1930	1935	1940	1945ᵃ	1950	1955	1960	1965	1970	1975
15–19	82.3	85.9	89.3	92.5	95.6	(96.1)	96.6	98.3	98.6	98.6	97.9	98.6
20–24	31.4	29.6	37.7	44.9	53.5	(54.4)	55.3	66.5	68.3	68.1	71.7	69.3
25–29	9.2	7.8	8.5	11.1	13.5	(14.4)	15.2	20.6	21.6	18.9	18.1	20.9
30–34	4.1	3.5	3.7	4.0	5.3	(5.5)	5.7	7.9	9.4	9.0	7.2	7.7
35–39	2.7	2.3	2.4	2.4	2.9	(3.0)	3.0	3.9	5.5	6.8	5.8	5.3
40–44	2.1	1.9	1.8	1.8	2.0	(2.0)	2.0	2.3	3.2	3.7	5.3	5.0
45–49	1.9	1.8	1.6	1.5	1.6	(1.6)	1.5	1.7	2.1	3.0	4.0	4.9

Diagonal cohort values (Hajnal's one-census SMAM's for cohorts): 21.1^b, 21.9, 22.5, 23.0, 23.3, 23.6, 24.3

	1920	1925	1930	1935	1940	1945ᵃ	1950	1955	1960	1965	1970	1975
Period SMAM's
One-census (Hajnal)	21.1	21.1	21.8	22.5	23.3	(23.4)	23.6	24.6	24.9	24.7	24.5	24.3
Two-census (Agarwala)		21.3	22.0	22.8	23.4	23.4	23.6	24.8	24.5	24.2	24.5	24.4

ᵃHypothetical data obtained by averaging percentage single in 1940 and 1950 at each age. ᵇDiagonals represent Hajnal's (one-census) SMAM's for cohorts. S_{50} is assumed to be equal to $_5S_{45}$.
Source of data: Official census reports.
SOURCE: Smith, 1978.

marital status for mortality and migration and, especially, that the nuptiality pattern not have changed recently. When these assumptions are met, the cross-sectional percentages can be taken to represent the experience of a hypothetical cohort.

For any cross-section (or hypothetical cohort) of 100 persons

$$\text{SMAM} = \frac{\left(\sum_{x=0}^{50} S_x\right) - \left(50 S_{50}\right)}{100 - S_{50}}$$

or

$$\frac{1500 + \left(\sum_{x=15}^{50} S_x\right) - \left(50 S_{50}\right)}{100 - S_{50}},$$

where S_x is the percentage single at age x. SMAM is equivalent to the mean number of years spent in the single (never-married) state by those in the hypothetical cohort who marry by age 50. In actual situations five-year data are often used requiring multiplication by 5 to recognize that the hypothetical cohort lives for 5 years under each percentage. The percentage single at age 50 (usually the average of $_5S_{45}$ and $_5S_{50}$), but sometimes, as in the calculation below, simply as $_5S_{45}$) is subtracted from 100 to give the percentage ever marrying in the denominator. The subtraction of $50 S_{50}$ from the numerator removes the never-marrying from consideration. If data are not available below some lower age limit (e.g., age 15 in the second formula above), it is assumed that no marriages occurred earlier. Taking Japan in 1925 to illustrate the calculation, we have

$$\text{SMAM} = \frac{\begin{array}{c} 1500 + 5\Sigma \, (85.9 + 29.6 + 7.8 + \\ 3.5 + 2.3 + 1.9 + 1.8) - (50) \times (1.8) \end{array}}{100 - 1.8}$$
$$= 21.1$$

for a hypothetical cohort of 100. The calculation of the SMAM for genuine cohort data (the diagonals in Table 1) is similar. For the cohort of females aged 15–19 in 1925, for example, we have an SMAM of 21.9 years obtained as follows:

$$\text{SMAM} = \frac{\begin{array}{c} 1500 + 5\Sigma \, (85.9 + 37.7 + 11.1 + \\ 5.3 + 3.0 + 2.0 + 1.7) - (50) \times (1.7) \end{array}}{100 - 1.7}$$
$$= 21.9.$$

The assumption of unchanged nuptiality is an especially serious drawback to the use of the index, since in many instances the researcher needs a measure with which to assess changes believed to be taking place. When the index is calculated in the presence of changing

nuptiality—say, steadily rising ages at first marriage—the singulate mean represents the average experience of an indeterminant period preceding the census. In these circumstances singulate means calculated from two consecutive censuses in fact are estimates for two partially overlapping periods of time.

One solution to this problem is provided by S. N. Agarwala's method (1962) of obtaining "decade synthetic" percentages single. Ratios of percentages single in successive age groups in two censuses (i.e., for cohorts) are used. These permit the percentage marrying between, say, ages 20–24 and 25–29 to come from actual experience, since those 20–24 at the first census are the same women who are 25–29 at the second census. Thus the ratio of the two percentages single gives the proportion who married between the two ages. Such ratios are then applied sequentially to the entire movement of a hypothetical cohort, to produce the percentage who would be left single at each age. The SMAM is then calculated from these figures in the usual manner, and it reflects the nuptiality behavior of the population during the intercensal period.

The Japanese data allow the computation of Agarwala's means for the quinquennia 1920–1925 through 1970–1975. Table 2 is an illustrative calculation for the 1920–1925 quinquennium (year Z to $Z + 5$) based on the percentages single (S_x's) in Table 1. Percentages single under age 15 are presumed equal to one hundred. For some data the ratios in column 2 will exceed unity because of faulty data or selective mortality or migration.

Agarwala's mean ages at marriage calculated from Japan's quinquennial censuses appear in Table 1, as do one-census (Hajnal) singulate means, and finally, singulate means calculated for genuine cohorts (diagonals). The relationship between Hajnal's and Agarwala's period means depends largely on the trend in nuptiality. From the first quinquennium shown through 1950–1955, the two-census singulate mean is always higher than or

TABLE 2. *Illustrative calculation of "quinquennia synthetic" percentages single*

(1) Age group (x to $x+5$)	*(2)* $_5S_X^{Z+5}/_5S_{X-5}^{Z}$	*(3)* "Quinquennia synthetic" percentages single
10–14	1.000	100.0
15–19	.859 (.859/1.000)	85.9 (.859 × 100.0)
20–24	.360 (.296/ .823)	30.9 (.360 × 85.9)
25–29	.248 (.078/ .314)	7.7 (.248 × 30.9)
30–34	.380 (.035/ .092)	2.9 (.380 × 7.7)
35–39	.561 (.023/ .041)	1.6 (.561 × 2.9)
40–44	.704 (.019/ .027)	1.2 (.704 × 1.6)
45–49	.857 (.018/ .021)	1.0 (.857 × 1.2)
		SMAM = 21.3

SOURCE: Smith, 1978.

equal to the surrounding one-census means since each one-census estimate reflects to a degree the earlier marriage patterns of the past. Since the upward trend ended after 1960, the relationship between Hajnal's and Agarwala's singulate means is less systematic.

Coale's three-parameter model. Ansley J. Coale's observation that, with appropriate rescaling, diverse schedules of first marriage frequencies by age have an essentially common form (Coale, 1971) introduces another approach to summarizing our age schedules of the percentage single. Coale's empirically derived standard curve of first marriage frequencies by age describes marriages in Sweden in the period 1865–1869. Underlying those marriage frequencies is a schedule of marriage risks by age, which applies to those who will ever marry. This schedule of marriage risks is fitted very closely by a double exponential form. Schedules for other populations can be fitted by the curve

$$r(a) = (.174/k)e^{-4.411e^{-(.309/k)(a-a_0)}}$$

where $r(a)$ is the risk of marriage at age a, a_0 is the age after which marriage begins, and k indexes the tempo at which marriage occurs, relative to the tempo in the Swedish comparison population. When k is less than 1.0, the proportion of the population ever married rises more rapidly with age than in the comparison population, and when k exceeds 1.0 it occurs less rapidly. Another parameter, C, the proportion ultimately ever-married, adjusts the $r(a)$ to allow for those in the population who will never marry. The model evolved mainly out of work with European data, but application of Coale's model to Asian and Pacific census data suggests a high degree of conformity to the basic pattern. It should be noted that the same assumptions are made here as with Hajnal's SMAM. In particular, both methods are best suited to application with cohort data, though cross-section applications are common.

Thus we have alternative one-parameter (SMAM) and two-parameter (a_0 and k) approaches to summarizing the patterns of behavior which generate the number of first marriages by age. Estimates of these nuptiality parameters for females in Asian and Pacific countries are shown in Table 3. Comparisons across countries can be made easily with these data. For example, in relation to the other countries of South Asia, Sri Lankan females begin to marry much later and first marriages are still occurring at older ages (both a_0 and k are high). The result is a substantially higher SMAM.

Other indexes of nuptiality. Thus far we have looked only at summary indexes of the schedule of percentages single (or ever-married). Using information on the *currently* married (regardless of past marital history) and considering absolute numbers as well as percentages,

Coale and his colleagues developed another set of nuptiality indexes well known to most demographers. The "index of marriage pattern" (Coale, 1969) is defined as follows:

$$I_m = \frac{\sum_i m_i F_i}{\sum_i w_i F_i},$$

where w_i and m_i are numbers of women and currently married women, respectively, in age groups i (15–19 through 45–49), and where the F_i are a schedule of extremely high marital fertility rates that serves as a standard set of weights. I_m has a theoretical range from zero (no one currently married in the 15–50 age range) to unity (everyone in that age range currently married).

The index of marriage pattern is one of a family of indexes designed to measure marital and illegitimate fertility levels as well as marriage patterns. When illegitimate fertility can be discounted the following very useful relationship exists:

$$\frac{\sum_i m_i f_i}{\sum_i w_i F_i} = \frac{\sum_i m_i F_i}{\sum_i w_i F_i} \times \frac{\sum_i m_i f_i}{\sum_i m_i F_i}$$

or $I_f = I_m \times I_g$, where I_g is an index of marital fertility level and I_f is an index of overall fertility level (the f_i are a schedule of marital fertility rates). The indexes conveniently separate the "marital structure" and "marital fertility" components of overall fertility. (See Coale, 1969, for a slightly more complex decomposition appropriate when illegitimate fertility cannot be discounted.)

Since I_m can reflect in some measure the age composition of women between ages 15 and 50, a somewhat better index of nuptiality is given by Coale's age-standardized version of I_m (Coale, 1969):

$$I_m^* = \frac{\sum_i (m_i/w_i) F_i}{\sum_i F_i}.$$

This index, incidentally, can be calculated even when *percentages* currently married are the only data available.

The idea underlying Coale's index of marriage pattern can easily be extended further. For example, Terence H. Hull and Rinigsih Saladi (1977) break down the complement of I_m into several components with analogous definitions, including indexes of proportions single (I_s), divorced (I_d), widowed (I_w), and separated (I_p). Ad-

TABLE 3. *Selected nuptiality indexes for countries of Asia and the Pacific at recent census dates, females only*

Geographic area and country	Year	Indexes of first marriage				Single (I_s)	Total (I_{em})	Div/Sep $(I_d + I_p)$	Widowed (I_w)	Currently married (I_m)	Not currently married (incl. single) (I_u)
		SMAM	a_0	k	C						
ASIA											
South Asia											
Bangladesh	1974	15.9	11.5	.388	.996	.049	.951	.015	.046	.890	.110
India	1971	17.1	10.0	.624	.996	.091	.908	.006	.035	.868	.132
Nepal	1971	16.8	10.0	.596	.992	.085	.915	.003	.030	.882	.118
Pakistan	1972	19.2	12.5	.592	.991	.177	.823	.004	.020	.800	.201
Sri Lanka	1971	24.1	13.5	.933	.936	.388	.612	.006	.018	.588	.412
Southeast Asia											
Brunei	1971	19.5	12.0	.658	.950	.356	.644	—a	.021	.623	.376
Burma[b]	1953	19.3	10.5	.772	.920	.231	.767	.024	.052	.691	.307
Indonesia	1971	19.0	12.0	.615	.990	.157	.843	.046	.058	.739	.261
Kampuchea[c]	1962	21.3	14.5	.595	.978	n.a.	n.a.	n.a.	n.a.	.742d	n.a.
Philippines	1975	23.2	13.5	.850	.939	.398	.601	.004	.013	.584	.416
Sabah	1970	20.2	11.5	.763	.970	.230	.770	.011	.027	.731	.269
Sarawak	1970	21.1	12.5	.755	.965	.274	.726	.023	.025	.678	.322
Singapore	1970	24.4	16.0	.737	.965	.432	.568	.006	.014	.547	.453
Thailand	1970	21.9	12.9	.790	.970	.303	.698	.031	.020	.646	.354
Western Malaysia	1970	22.2	12.6	.588	.986	.323	.677	.009	.029	.640	.360
East Asia											
Hong Kong	1971	23.8	18.5	.466	.962	.460	.540	.003	.005	.532	.468
Japan	1975	24.3	18.0	.564	.952	.331	.669	.014	.008	.647	.353
Macao	1970	25.6	16.5	.803	.948	.533	.467	.001	.020	.445	.554
Ryukyu Islands	1965	25.5	16.5	.793	.978	.403	.597	.042	.022	.534	.466
South Korea	1975	23.7	18.5	.453	.998	.370	.630	.007	.020	.602	.398
Taiwan	1975	23.3	16.5	.598	.992	.380	.620	.006	.008	.606	.394
PACIFIC											
Polynesia											
American Samoa	1974	23.3	14.6	.761	.971	.381	.619	.021	.011	.587	.413
Cook Islands	1976	24.4	15.6	.777	.929	.458	.542	.010	.010	.522	.478
Fiji	1966	21.1	14.4	.593	.968	.282	.718	.008	.015	.694	.306
French Polynesia	1962	25.6	13.6	1.053	.744	.568	.436	.011	.012	.408	.592
Niue	1971	24.8	14.8	.878	.901	.441	.560	.011	.005	.543	.457
Tonga	1966	24.0	14.3	.849	.934	.399	.601	.010	.010	.581	.419
Tuvalu	1973	20.9	12.8	.708	.963	.261	.739	.079	.028	.632	.368
Western Samoa	1971	22.0	15.3	.588	.973	.329	.671	.055	.014	.603	.397
Melanesia											
New Caledonia	1976	22.5	14.5	.703	.881	.373	.627	.018	.013	.596	.404
Solomon Islands	1970	22.3	13.2	.801	.959	.314	.686	.008	.031	.647	.353
Vanuatu	1967	21.0	14.3	.591	.975	.257	.743	.006	.032	.706	.294
Wallis and Futuna	1969	25.4	10.2	1.341	.931	.449	.551	.082	.053	.417	.583
Micronesia											
Guam	1960	20.5	15.5	.442	.916	.245	.755	.010	.010	.735	.265
Trust territories	1973	21.8	12.9	.784	.969	.337	.664	.035	.016	.612	.388

n.a. = not available.   aDivorced and separated women are included in the figure for widowed (I_w).   bUrban only.   cExcludes Phnom Penh.   dI_m^* computed from percentage currently married by age.
Source of data: Official census reports.
SOURCE: Smith, 1978.

ditionally an index of the proportion ever married, or I_{em} can be used (Smith, 1978). This expanded set of indexes can be diagrammed as shown in Figure 1.

Either I_s or I_{em} can serve as an index of the first marriage process. Hull and Saladi note that the indexes of proportions widowed, divorced, and separated combine into an index of "marital disruption," whereas the inclu-

sion of I_s leads to an index of the proportion unmarried (I_u):

$$I_u = (I_w + I_d + I_p) + I_s.$$

I_m and I_u are complements, as are I_{em} and I_s. Further disaggregation along other dimensions is limited only by the availability of data.

FIGURE 2. *Expanded set of indexes of marriage patterns*

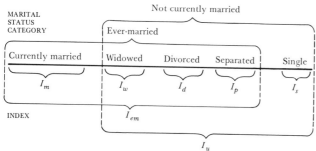

SOURCE: Smith, 1978.

Marital-status data have been collected in Asian and Pacific censuses since the beginning of census taking in the region. Notable series of some length, all beginning early in the twentieth century or even before, exist for Sri Lanka, India, Burma, Taiwan, the Philippines, and Japan. Nearly all countries of Asia and the Pacific now produce national distributions of population by age, sex, and marital status, and these tables are usually shown separately for administrative subareas. With few exceptions, Asian and Pacific countries have adhered to a common *de facto* definition of current marital status. This fact is of extreme analytic importance in a part of the word in which societies and marriage institutions vary a great deal. On balance, Asian and Pacific censuses offer a more than adequate statistical basis for comparative studies of changing nuptiality.

Nuptiality indexes are shown for thirty-five Asian and Pacific countries in Table 3. The range of Coale's original index of marriage pattern is from nearly 0.890 in Bangladesh to less than half that level in Macao and a few Pacific countries. The sources of differences between countries can be seen readily.

Relationships among Nuptiality Indicators. Pearson correlation coefficients measuring the degree of association among national indexes of female nuptiality are given in Table 4. Correlations among Asian countries and among Pacific countries are shown separately. In general, strong positive correlations prevail among measures of female marriage timing. Among both Asian and Pacific countries the two timing indexes shown, SMAM and the percentage single at age 20–24, have more than 90 percent of their variation in common. Similarly, both these timing measures are negatively correlated with Coale's index of the impact of nuptiality on fertility (I_m).

Late marriage, as indexed by variables 1 and 2 in Table 4, is negatively associated with the percentage ever marrying, the C parameter. That is, a relatively high degree of nonmarriage tends to occur in the countries where marriage is latest. This is true in both Asia and the Pacific but especially in the Pacific.

Since the mean age at marriage in the Swedish standard population used by Coale is 11.37, measured from a_0, the age when marriage begins (Trussell, 1976), the SMAM, a_0, and k parameters are linked for any other population by the relationship: $\text{SMAM} = a_0 + 11.37(k)$. For a given SMAM, an increase in one component implies a reduction in the other. This relationship sug-

TABLE 4. *Zero-order correlations among indexes of female nuptiality in countries of Asia and the Pacific*[1]

Index	(1)	(2)	(3)	(4)	(5)	(6)
(1) Percentage single 20–24		.965	−.077	.713	−.693	−.883
(2) SMAM	.965		−.254	.837	.581	−.935
(3) a_0	.887	.834		−.742	−.002	.423
(4) k	.228	.365	−.163		.401	−.888
(5) C	−.316	.300	.038	.552		−.606
(6) I_m	−.934	−.930	−.740	−.400	−.400	
Pacific						
(7) Means	46.2	22.8	14.0	.776	.930	.590
(8) Standard deviations	13.5	1.8	1.4	.221	.006	.097
Asia						
(9) Means	41.8	21.5	13.8	.668	.972	.664
(10) Standard deviations	22.4	3.0	2.8	.143	.002	.123

[1]Correlations for Pacific countries ($N = 14$) are shown in the upper triangle formed by figures in rows and columns (2)–(6); correlations for Asian countries ($N = 20$) are shown in the lower triangle. Correlations are not weighted for population size.
Source of data: National data in Table 3.
SOURCE: Smith, 1978.

gests why the a_0 and k components of the SMAM are found to be negatively correlated in both Asia and the Pacific.

SMAM is closely associated with the level of k in the Pacific ($r = .837$) but only weakly (and negatively) associated with the level of a_0 ($r = -.254$). In contrast, SMAM is most closely correlated with a_0 in Asia ($r = .834$). Different sources of variation in marriage timing prevail in Asia and the Pacific. These results also suggest that the fertility implications of nuptiality differences within each of the regions stem from different aspects of nuptiality: in Asia, mainly from variations in the onset of marriage; and in the Pacific, mainly from differences in the tempo of first marriage (for example, in the prevalence of late unions). A similar conclusion is suggested by the degrees of dispersion on these variables. Asian nations are much more diverse than are Pacific countries with respect to all the variables except the k parameter.

Patterns of Geographic Variation. The overall Asia-Pacific distinction is not especially important with respect to differences in the timing of nuptiality. Most variation in SMAM, for example, is among countries within these regions rather than between regions. In studies of Asian nations, distinguishing South Asia, Southeast Asia, and East Asia is important, whereas in studies of Pacific nations distinguishing Polynesia, Melanesia, and Micronesia is not useful. The Asian interzonal variations in SMAM are due largely to differences in a_0 whereas the less systematic variations among zones in the Pacific reflect a_0 and k more equally.

The female marriage pattern in South Asia appears to be relatively homogeneous, with both early onset and a rapid tempo of entrance to marriage. (Sri Lanka is an interesting exception with its very slow tempo.) Female marriage in East Asia is also fairly homogeneous, especially with respect to SMAM. However, these similar SMAM's are achieved by rather different combinations of a_0 and k, and k is the major cause of variation.

Southeast Asian female marriage patterns are diverse, as is Southeast Asia itself. The Islamic countries of the region have both low a_0's and low k's in a pattern very much like that of countries of South Asia. At the other extreme, the Philippines and Thailand, in addition to Singapore, begin to approach the East Asian level on SMAM. The Philippines and Thailand have been noted as traditional societies with late marriage, whereas Singapore is largely East Asian (Chinese) in its cultural composition.

Peter C. Smith

See also AGE AT MARRIAGE; HOUSEHOLD AND FAMILY DEMOGRAPHY; MARRIAGE AND DIVORCE.

BIBLIOGRAPHY

Agarwala, S. N. *Age at Marriage in India*. Allahabad, India: Kitab Mahal, 1962.

Coale, Ansley J. "The Decline of Fertility in Europe from the French Revolution to World War II." In *Fertility and Family Planning: A World View*, edited by S. J. Behrman et al., pp. 3–24. Ann Arbor: University of Michigan Press, 1969.

————. "Age Patterns of Marriage." *Population Studies* 25(2):193–214, July 1971.

Hajnal, John. "Age at Marriage and Proportions Marrying." *Population Studies* 7(2):111–136, November 1953.

Henry, Alice, and Phyllis T. Piotrow. "Age at Marriage and Fertility." *Population Reports*, series M, no. 4, whole issue, November 1979.

Hull, Terence H., and Rinigsih Saladi. "The Application of Hutterite Fertility-weighted Indexes to Studies of Changing Marriage Patterns." Population Institute Working Paper No. 13. Jogjakarta, Indonesia: Gadjah Mada University, 1977.

Smith, Peter C. "Indexes of Nuptiality: Asia and the Pacific." *Asian and Pacific Census Forum* 5(2):1–3, 6, November 1978.

Trussell, T. James. "A Refined Estimator of Measures of Location of the Age at First Marriage." *Demography* 13(2):225–233, May 1976.

OCEANIA

Oceania consists of Australia, New Zealand, and the tropical islands of the Pacific (see Table 1). Its land and water area covers 10 percent of the earth's surface, yet the land area bears a population of fewer than 22.5 million. Like North America, Oceania has experienced heavy migration (over 60 percent of the population is of European descent), and its population has undergone a similar demographic transition. The non-Europeans, who form the minority in Australia and New Zealand and the majority in the Pacific islands, have high or declining rates of mortality, with transitions similar to those in much of the Third World. Thus, in this one region are seen the two sets of global population problems: Australia and New Zealand have low growth and aging populations; but the Pacific, recovering from the declines that followed eighteenth- and nineteenth-century European contact, has very high growth and young populations.

Australia. The continent of Australia is sparsely populated (crude density is 1.88 per square kilometer, 4.87 per square mile) but highly urbanized. In 1976, 70 percent of the population lived in cities of 100,000 persons or more, with primary cities in most states. Differentials in density are extreme: vast empty expanses stretch over nearly all of the continent, but cities dot the southeastern seaboard and the far southwest. Australia is industrialized, although primary products still account for about 53 percent of its export income. Immigration has been promoted as a means of achieving population growth while

natural increase has been modest, and has followed trends generally similar to those in other countries whose populations are of European origin (98 percent in Australia), predominantly Protestant (59 percent; Catholics account for 27 percent), and highly literate.

Location and description. Australia, in the southwestern part of the Pacific region adjacent to Asia, has been inhabited by indigenous Aborigines for more than 30,000 years. European colonization began in 1788, and in 1901 six British colonies federated as the Commonwealth of Australia. Its land area (7,682,300 square kilometers; 2,966,136 square miles) makes it the fifth largest country in the world, but deserts and uninhabitable regions predominate outside the temperate south and east. In the interior and the tropical north, extensive pastoralism, mining, and the export of raw materials to chronically unstable markets have proved to be the only means of development. Increasing self-sufficiency in oil and the expansion of manufacturing have been accompanied by concern over foreign control and the capital-intensive nature of many industries.

Population characteristics. Frequent head counts ("musters") preceded the first census taken in the colony of New South Wales in 1828. All the colonies periodically conducted their own censuses until they joined the first decennial British Empire censuses in 1881, 1891, and 1901. Since 1911 the Australian Commonwealth government has taken the censuses (1921, 1933, 1947, 1954, 1961, and thereafter quinquennially). Executed on a *de facto* basis, these have always been highly reliable. Consti-

499

TABLE 1. *Baseline demographic data, Oceania region*

Country or territory (Fully independent italicized)	Population mid-1979 (thousands)	Annual growth rate (percent)	Crude birth rate	Crude death rate	TFR	Infant mortality rate	Life expectation at birth (years)	Basis of vital rates[1]
American Samoa	31.4	1.5%	34	4	5.4	20	67	R
Australia	14,615.9[2]	1.2	15	7	1.9	11	73	R
Cook Islands	18.5	−0.7	27	9	4.5	33	61	R
Fiji	619.0	1.8	27	7	4.0	46	62	R
French Polynesia[3]	144.6	2.2	36	8	5.6	68	61	R
Guam	100.0	0.6	26	4	3.8	22	76	R
Kiribati	57.3	1.6	35	14	4.7	87	52	E
Nauru	7.3	0.8	22	5	n.a.	n.a.	n.a.	R
New Caledonia	139.0	1.2	27	7	4.1	25	64	R[4]
New Zealand	3,148.5[2]	0.0	16	9	2.1	13	72	R
Niue[5]	3.6	−2.1	26	7	4.3	33	62	E
Norfolk Island	1.9	1.1	9	7	n.a.	n.a.	n.a.	R
Papua New Guinea	3,079.0	2.8	44	16	7.1	125	49	E
Pitcairn Island	[100]	n.a.	n.a.	n.a.	n.a.	n.a.	n.a.	n.a.
Solomon Islands	221.2	3.5	45–50	14	7.1–7.7	46	54	E
Tokelau Islands	1.6	0.0	24	7	n.a.	n.a.	n.a.	R
Kingdom of Tonga	95.8	1.7	n.a.	10	n.a.	60	58	E
Trust Territory[3]	132.5	2.3	43	11	7.0	59	61	E
Tuvalu	7.4	4.6	24	15	2.8	42	59	E
Vanuatu	114.5	4.4	45	15–19	n.a.	97–107	50–60	E[6]
Wallis and Futuna	10.2	3.2	43	11	n.a.	54	n.a.	R
Western Samoa[5]	155.0	0.8	37	8	6.7	36	62	E

[1]R = mainly computed directly from registration data; E = mainly estimated.   [2]Australia and New Zealand, 1980.   [3]Some data pre-1973.
[4]"Unknown completeness."   [5]Data 1971–1976, estimated from 1976 census.   [6]"Rough estimate."   n.a. = not available.
Sources of data: Australia, 1981; New Zealand, 1981; South Pacific Commission, 1980; United States, 1980.

tutionally, full-blooded Aborigines were excluded from the tabulations until 1971. The estimated population of Australia on 30 June 1979 was 14,418,200.

As regards vital data, figures are available in varying degrees of detail for all the colonies between 1856 and 1900. Since then the Commonwealth has gradually standardized the collection and tabulation of vital statistics. Aboriginal vital events were excluded until 1966. Net international migration statistics are available from 1860, and detailed and reliable statistics on arrivals and departures are available from 1924.

Various demographic studies have been undertaken. The Australian Bureau of Statistics' Population Survey, taken quarterly between February 1964 and February 1978, and then monthly, provides continuous information on employment. Supplementary surveys, such as those on birth expectations in 1977 and 1979, fertility surveys in Melbourne and in New South Wales, and a national survey of social mobility have also been conducted.

In comparison with that of other industrialized countries Australia's population is "young," although an incipient aging trend is evident. Thus in 1976 the dependency ratio (population under 15 and over 65 per 100 persons aged 15–64) was 56 compared with 63 in 1961 during the "baby boom." The dependency burden was chiefly on account of the young population and would

have been greater had immigration of adults not been at such a high level.

The age structure has been strongly affected by fertility. Between 1954 and 1976, the total population grew by 55 percent, the age group 15–64 by 56 percent, and the number of women in the reproductive ages by 58 percent. However, the age group of women at the most fecund ages (20–29) grew by 78 percent, reflecting the high fertility years after World War II.

Australia's labor force was estimated at 6,646,800 in December 1979. Among persons aged 15 years and over, it included 80 percent of the men and 45 percent of the women (42 percent among married women). Women comprised 37 percent of the labor force, but had an unemployment rate of 8 percent compared with 5 percent among men and 5 percent among married women, and 16 percent and 22 percent for both sexes aged 15 to 19.

In the nineteenth century Australian fertility levels were higher than in the British Isles, from which most settlers came. In the last quarter of the century, fertility began a relatively rapid decline as a result of changes within the family, particularly the increased burdens of child rearing resulting from new social patterns such as mass education and the reduction of child labor. The fertility decline continued into the Depression and war years. In common with other developed countries the

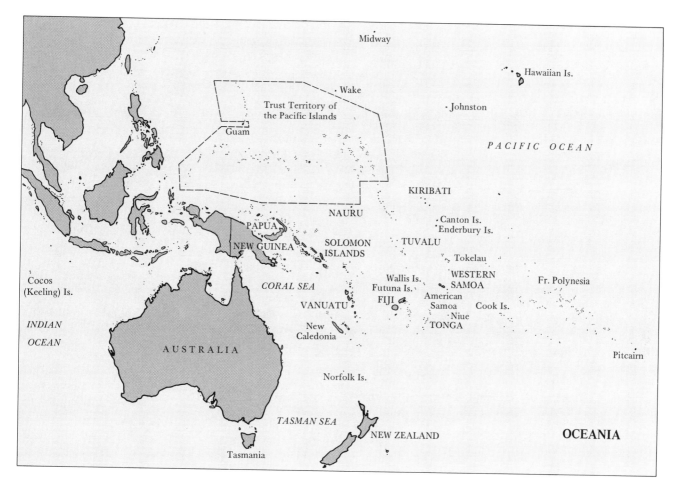

birth rate then increased after World War II, peaking around 1961. The total fertility rate, 1956–1960, was 3.4. The causes of the increase were broadly similar to those for North America, a difference being a prolongation into the early sixties. Since then, as is characteristic of other industrialized countries, fertility decreased, and by the late seventies had reached subreplacement level. The total fertility rate in 1979 was 1.94. Earlier, remarkably high levels of use of oral contraceptives aided the trend, while recently a major factor has been a change in timing and spacing of births.

The Australian mortality transition has closely paralleled that of New Zealand. It began early, in the latter half of the nineteenth century, reached levels below those in other developed countries, and continued to drop until after World War II. In the 1960s, levels stabilized. Generally, Australian levels of life expectation have been a little below those for New Zealand (in 1970–1972, 67.9 years for males and 74.6 years for females), but at present Australian levels are marginally higher.

In 1976 the Aborigines (144,381) and the Torres Strait Islanders (16,531) comprised about 1 percent of the population. These peoples had been decimated through dis-

ease in the nineteenth century but today have an accelerating rate of growth (39 percent increase from 1971–1976) and a youthful age structure (in 1971, over 40 percent under 15 years). Traditionally the Aborigines and Torres Strait Islanders occupied the whole of Australia, with densities highest in the south and east; now they live mostly in Queensland and the Northern Territory, where they accounted for 2 percent and 27 percent of the total population, respectively, in 1971. The percentage living in the urban areas almost doubled from 1961 to 1971 (from 23 percent to 44 percent).

For the non-Aborigine majority of the population, immigration has been a major source of growth, particularly since World War II. Between 1947 and 1980, 3.7 million immigrants arrived in Australia; it is estimated that 77 percent of them have settled permanently. Immigrants and their children have been responsible for half of the nation's postwar population growth. As 41 percent of the immigrants in the period 1945 to 1970 were aged 20–34, at peak childbearing age, immigration has had a multiplier effect on the number of births. The labor force was of course also greatly affected, especially because the immigrants clustered in certain industries, notably manufacturing, building, and construction. Immigrant levels of skill were similar to those of the total Australian population, but there were great variations among the groups according to place of origin.

A major effect of the postwar immigration has been to alter the ethnic composition of the Australian population. Whereas before the war most immigrants were of British extraction (chiefly from the United Kingdom, New Zealand, and Canada), since the war 55 percent have been non-British. The composition of the postwar immigration stream has changed over time, reflecting economic changes and the effect of assisted-passage schemes and migration agreements made initially with the International Refugee Organization, and then with a range of governments in Europe (also Turkey). The first groups were British and displaced persons from continental Europe, followed increasingly by other northwestern Europeans, and then by southern Europeans and growing numbers of Asians including Indochinese refugees. The British component was unrestricted until January 1975; since then only the trans-Tasman migration interchange between Australia and New Zealand has been unrestricted. This has ebbed and flowed but currently favors Australia, where New Zealanders presently constitute almost 20 percent of Australia's immigrants.

Although Australians are mobile (40 percent of the population moved internally between 1966 and 1971), few Australian-born people live outside their state or territory of birth (12 percent in 1971). Most moves occur within urban centers or between urban centers and neighboring rural districts. Although there is migration to economic boom areas and to the "sun belt" of Queensland, counterbalancing migration tendencies keep Australian internal migration in a state of dynamic equilibrium.

Policy and action. Discussion, legislation, and policy in the demographic area have centered on international migration. Generally, as in countries such as Canada, immigration has been used to "turn the economy" through the labor force. It has also been seen as a means of achieving high population growth, 1 percent annually through immigration alone. It was not until the 1970s that this thirty-year-old policy was questioned as the social costs as well as the advantages of heterogeneity became evident. In the early 1970s the government introduced restrictions, but since 1976 these have been eased and admission criteria regarding such matters as family reunion, refugee status, and occupational skills have been altered.

Scholarly activities. An early and outstanding contribution to demography was the 1904 Royal Commission inquiry into the decline of the birth rate and the mortality of infants in New South Wales.

The first department of demography ever established is located at the Australian National University in Canberra. This department has been active in research both within Australia and internationally. Demographic research is also conducted by the federal government, notably the Australian Bureau of Statistics and the Department of Immigration and Ethnic Affairs, as well as in various departments in universities throughout Australia.

Australia is one of the few countries to have instituted a National Population Inquiry. This study, directed by W. D. Borrie, investigated all aspects of Australia's population and led to a series of reports on a wide variety of demographic concerns (see Australia, 1975, 1978).

New Zealand. New Zealand has a highly urbanized but relatively low-density population of 3 million. Almost 90 percent are of European, mainly British, descent, and a further 9 percent are the indigenous Polynesian Maoris. The mortality and fertility transitions have been similar to those in other industrialized countries, varying only in detail. The relatively high growth rate, until recently, has been sustained by immigration. The Maori minority has deviated markedly from the usual transition model.

Location and description. New Zealand is long, narrow, and mountainous; it is composed of two major and many minor islands, located 1,800 kilometers southeast of Australia. The country was first settled by Maoris in the Middle Ages, then by Europeans in the nineteenth century; it became a British colony in 1840. Throughout the twentieth century it has been an independent social democracy within the British Commonwealth.

A highly productive and scientific pastoral industry is the basis of New Zealand's export economy, but it employs only 12 percent of the labor force in this way and is extremely vulnerable to international market forces. Diversification into both agriculture and manufacturing and the exploitation of energy resources other than petroleum may improve this delicate position.

Most New Zealanders are Protestants; 15 percent are Roman Catholic and 20 percent report "no religion" or refuse to answer survey questions on the topic. Education has been free and compulsory since 1877, so that literacy is universal. The country has an advanced social welfare system that has minimized socioeconomic disparities and guaranteed the population access to health care.

Population characteristics. Regular *de facto* censuses of both Maoris and Europeans have been taken since the 1850s and more or less quinquennially since 1871. Enumerations of Europeans have been reasonably reliable throughout much of the period, but for Maoris high levels of accuracy were reached only after World War II. Vital registration was introduced for Europeans in 1855 and was already both reliable and detailed by the 1880s. Separate and less-detailed vital registration for Maoris began in 1913, becoming reasonably accurate after World War II but still lacking certain details. In 1962 the two systems were fused and were equally accurate.

With no land boundaries, New Zealand is able to maintain accurate data on arrivals and departures. There have been no nationwide labor force, fertility, or other demographic surveys; employment is studied by a twice-yearly enumeration of all establishments with two or more workers. In 1972–1973 New Zealand participated in the World Health Organization cross-national perinatal mortality study.

New Zealand is sparsely populated (12 persons per square kilometer; 31 per square mile), and settlement is restricted to 25 percent of its land area. Even though there is considerable variation, densities are relatively low even in prime farming areas and cities.

New Zealand's age-structure has always been younger than in most developed countries because of its patterns of international migration and high fertility. Currently, however, a long-term aging of the population appears to be underway. Until 1936 the dependency ratio (population under 15 and over 65 per 100 people aged 15–64 years) decreased to 49. Since World War II, there has been an increase to 72 (1961), then a decrease to 63 (1976). This burden, consisting chiefly of youthful dependents, would have been higher had it not been for the continued immigration of young adults during the period, reaching 44 percent of labor-force growth in 1951–1956. Against this was the multiplier effect of young migrants upon the births and thus on dependency.

Growth of the labor force has also come from increased female participation, from 26 percent of all women aged 15 and over in 1956 to 37 percent in 1976, and notably of married women who were 32 percent of the female labor force in 1956 and 57 percent in 1976. Female participation in the labor force follows a bimodal distribution by age, with lower proportions at 25–34 years than at adjacent ages. Unemployment has long been well below 1 percent of the labor force but has recently risen to 4 percent, including those on special works schemes. The labor force is also affected by the population base. During the two decades 1956–1976, while the total population grew by 44 percent, the labor force age groups grew by 49 percent, females of reproductive ages by 52 percent, and the group aged 20–29 by 80 percent.

In common with other high-growth populations the Maori age structure has been very youthful; almost 50 percent were under 15 in 1951. Dependency burdens were extremely high, increasing to 110 in 1966 because of declines in the mortality rates. Since then they have declined rapidly, to 88 in 1976, as fertility rates have fallen.

Fertility for Europeans in New Zealand has closely paralleled that in Australia, both for trends and their determinants. In the late nineteenth century, however, the decline of the European birth rate was extremely rapid. Moreover, the postwar peak in 1961 was exceptionally high for a developed country, but today the level is just below that of replacement, which was reached later than elsewhere in the industrialized world. Unique features were heavy use of both oral and injectable contraceptives, low levels of induced abortion, and relatively high rates of adolescent fertility, particularly ex-nuptial births. Legally there is no such thing as illegitimacy in New Zealand. Spacing of low-parity births appears to be close together and increasingly so.

Maori birth rates were lower than European rates (30–39 per 1,000) in the 1850s, because of cohort effects produced by high mortality. From then on until the 1960s Maori birth rates were over 40. Since 1964, however, the Maori birth rate has declined rapidly. Today the Maori total fertility rate is 2.8, which brings the national rate slightly above replacement level.

Reliable data indicate that the mortality trends of Europeans in New Zealand have long been similar to but in advance of those in other developed countries. Good health has been attributed to the low population density, high levels of nutrition, and even to the selective effect of the migration process. Social welfare legislation (1900s) and free health care introduced in the 1930s maintained this advantage, but in life expectancy New Zealand was overtaken by Sweden in the 1940s and by some other countries in the 1960s and 1970s. In 1976 life expectancy for the European population was 69.4 years for males and 75.9 for females.

Maori mortality rates reached very high levels in the nineteenth century primarily through exposure to diseases introduced by European settlers. Life expectation gradually increased from an estimated 25 years (c. 1850) to 33 (c. 1905) to 48 years (1945). Since then it has increased rapidly, in 1976 reaching 63.4 years for males and 67.8 for females. Maori-European differentials have continued to decrease, while notable improvements have been shown at all ages, particularly at the perinatal ages, with one of the lowest perinatal rates in the world. Concern is still felt, however, over mortality at the postneonatal and early childhood ages and for Maori women at the immediate postreproductive ages.

Like Australia's, New Zealand's growth has been sustained by a high level of immigration, but unlike in Australia, in New Zealand immigrants have come overwhelmingly from the United Kingdom, as well as from Australia itself, with minor components from the Pacific, the Netherlands, North America, and elsewhere. Migration has fluctuated in response to economic trends and government intervention, resulting in heavy gains in the 1960s and net losses in the late 1970s. As noted earlier, the trans-Tasman migration stream has been the dominant factor. Running unevenly over the decades, it currently favors movement to Australia.

Together fertility and migration have produced continued population growth except in depression years, during World War II, and in the late 1970s, when subreplacement-level fertility and net migration loss have produced what appears to be a temporary reduction in population. Within this context the Maoris were a sharp exception; from mortality-induced declines in the mid-nineteenth century, the Maori population so recuperated that by the 1960s their rate of growth, 4.02 percent in 1956–1961 (entirely by natural increase), was among the highest anywhere. Since then the rate has declined.

There has always been a maldistribution of population in New Zealand. Beyond its long term and high degree of urbanization (83 percent of the total population lives in towns and cities, as do 76 percent of Maoris), there has been a steady drift north, a result of economic forces, coupled recently with retirement migration. Levels of internal migration, which appear to be below those of the United States or even Australia, may be masked by the international migration, particularly the trans-Tasman flow; in fact New Zealand might be viewed as part of a wider Australian entity centered on southeastern Ausralia.

Policy and action. New Zealand has neither a policy nor a systematic review concerning population matters; the closest approach to a review is a mid-1970s study by the Planning Council. The government intervenes in the field of immigration, while complex social and health legislation affects morbidity and mortality rates. Similarly, many acts and regulations indirectly influence internal migration. The effects of recent controversial legislation bearing on contraception, sterilization, and abortion are not yet clear.

Scholarly activities. Population research is carried out in diverse government ministries and in sociology, geography, and other departments in the universities. The University of Waikato has the country's only Population Studies Centre. The Demographic Society publishes quarterly the *New Zealand Population Review*, which com-

plements government demographic publications, particularly by the Department of Statistics.

Pacific. The third component of Oceania is the islands of the Pacific region, an intertropical zone spread through 50° longitude on either side of the International Date Line. The population of almost 5 million is widely scattered; the only significant land mass is Papua New Guinea (see Table 2).

High population growth rates and high relative densities, particularly on some atolls (e.g., Betio in Kiribati reaches 4,959 per square kilometer, 12,844 per square mile), make continued Malthusian conditions quite probable. The gross national product (GNP) is generally very low.

Location and description. The Pacific region has three cultural areas: Melanesia (with 84 percent of the region's population), Polynesia (10 percent), and Micronesia (6 percent). More than 800,000 Melanesians live outside the region (in the western half of New Guinea, in Indonesia), while almost one-third of all Polynesians live in New Zealand and another 20 percent live mainly in Hawaii (part of the United States) and Easter Island (owned by Chile). Although nonindigenous people live throughout the region, they constitute more than 50 percent of the population only in Fiji (primarily Indians) and New Caledonia (primarily French).

Formerly, the Pacific region included trust territories and colonies of the United Kingdom, the United States, New Zealand, France, and Australia; but in August 1980 there were nine nation-states (Fiji, Kiribati, Nauru, Vanuatu, Papua New Guinea, Solomon Islands, Tonga, Tuvalu, and Western Samoa), varying in population size from about 3 million in Papua New Guinea to only 7,500 in Nauru. There were also eleven territories, several of which were soon to be independent, varying in size from 100 to 144,600. French and English are official languages, and literacy levels are reasonably high outside Melanesia. Today most Micronesians and Polynesians are Christians; in Melanesia, however, indigenous cults still widely persist, while Fijian Indians are Hindus, Sikhs, and Muslims. Melanesia's mountainous terrain inhibits even modern modes of communication between

TABLE 2. *Population and area of the Pacific region*

	Population, 1979	Land, sq km	Sea, sq km	Percentage of land
Including Papua New Guinea	4,798,200	551,033	29,390,000	1.8%
Excluding Papua New Guinea	1,808,200	88,790	26,270,000	0.3%
Percentages for Papua New Guinea	62%	84%	11%	—

its isolated and diverse linguistic and cultural groups. The remainder of the land areas of the Pacific region varies from high (volcanic) islands to coral atolls. Despite its geographic spread, Polynesia is culturally and linguistically homogeneous.

Economics are marginal, levels of per capita aid are amongst the highest in the world, trade deficits are common, and often the chief occupations are government service and tourism. Remittances from migrants and the sale of postage stamps are important income supplements in some areas. Mineral exploitation has given Nauru a high, equally distributed income, but nickel production has not had a similar effect on New Caledonia. Agriculture, fishing, and hunting are generally for subsistence, particularly in Melanesia; but the Pacific region processes and exports coconuts and copra (throughout), sugar (Fiji), coffee and cocoa (Papua New Guinea), fish (America Samoa), and some other products.

"Rural" and "urban" are inappropriate terms in the Pacific context, where two nation-states are only the size of small towns. Nevertheless, the bulk of the population can be crudely classified as rural, living at the subsistence level; and there is evidence of disparities of income and life style between this sector and the "urban-based" sector. In New Caledonia and French Polynesia more than 50 percent of the population is urban. Only five urban centers exceed 30,000 population.

Population. Data on population, vital statistics, and related matters vary greatly in scope and quality. Administrative enumerations of the population gave way after 1945 to systematic and relatively reliable censuses. Special demographic surveys have been carried out on a variety of topics, notably population growth and distribution, cultural-demographic relations, and fertility.

The age structure is generally young with burgeoning cohorts reaching reproductive ages, producing an age-bulge at 15–29 years. This situation is especially true in countries where lowered fertility has constricted the number of children. Emigration of young adults distorts the age structure of some territories, reducing this bulge and so increasing the dependency ratio.

Total fertility rates were generally high (around 5 to 7 births per woman) until the 1960s. They declined first for the Fijian Indians, then in the 1970s for other Fijians and for much of Micronesia and Polynesia, to as low as 2.7 for Tuvalu. The declines have been variously attributed to general socioeconomic change, aggressive family planning programs, and changing age at marriage (Fijian Indians). Emigration may have affected the birth rate in some territories. In Melanesia the fertility rate may rise as traditional constraints weaken under social change.

Mortality rates have declined in the recent past throughout Micronesia and Polynesia and in parts of Melanesia (e.g., Fiji). Today life expectancy often exceeds 60 years, but in Papua New Guinea and elsewhere in Melanesia it may still be below 50. A cause of the variation is differential exposure to disease, particularly malaria, which is endemic throughout areas of lower altitude in Melanesia.

Populations declined following early European contact, notably through introduced diseases. Today, however, growth is generally rapid, despite declines in fertility in Micronesia and Polynesia. High growth will continue in those areas as the swollen cohorts of the 1960s reach reproductive age. The rate of growth should accelerate in Melanesia because of the high levels of fertility and declines in the mortality rate. Except for territories associated with New Zealand and the United States, growth will not be stemmed by legal emigration, but there is illegal emigration from some Pacific countries. With changing economic climates intraregional migration has generally decreased.

Policy and action. In Polynesia and Micronesia there is some recognition of the problems of population growth and of pressure on resources, particularly land. Some development plans outline policies, particularly family planning programs. In Melanesia, Fiji, concerned with rapid growth, has integrated family planning into the health services. This is true also for some Polynesian nations, for example, Tonga. Although successful in the 1960s, the Fijian program has slowed down, primarily because of declining rates of acceptance by the indigenous Fijians.

Scholarly activities. Demographic analysis is primarily undertaken by the United Nations, other international agencies, and the South Pacific Commission. Demographers have been employed, generally with external aid funds, in universities in the region, while universities outside the region (particularly in the United States, New Zealand, and Australia) are involved in Pacific research.

Ian Pool
Ruth S. J. Farmer
Sheila Macrae
Janet E. Sceats

BIBLIOGRAPHY

Australia, Bureau of Statistics. *Australian Demographic Statistics Quarterly, March 1981.* Canberra, 22 August 1981.

Australia, National Population Inquiry. *Population and Australia: A Demographic Analysis and Projection; First Report of the National Population Inquiry.* 2 vols. Canberra: Australian Government Publishing Service, 1975.

———. *Population and Australia: Recent Demographic Trends and Their Implications; Supplementary Report of the National Population Inquiry.* Canberra: Australian Government Publishing Service, 1978.

Caldwell, John C., Graham E. Harrison, and Pat Quiggin. "The Demography of Micro-states." In *The Island States of the Pacific and Indian Oceans,* edited by R. T. Shand, pp. 121–144. Canberra: Australian National University, 1980.

Lucas, David. "Population Trends in the Island States of the Pacific and Indian Oceans." In *The Island States of the Pacific and Indian Oceans,* edited by R. T. Shand, pp. 145–166. Canberra: Australian National University, 1980.

Lucas, David, and Helen Ware. "Fertility and Family Planning in the South Pacific." *Studies in Family Planning* 12(8/9):303–315, August/September 1981.

Neville, R., J. Warwick, and C. James O'Neill (editors). *The Population of New Zealand: Interdisciplinary Perspectives.* Auckland: Longman Paul, 1979.

New Zealand, Department of Statistics. *Monthly Abstract of Statistics, July 1981.* Wellington, July 1981.

New Zealand Population Review. Formerly titled *Population Review.* Issued quarterly since 1974 by the New Zealand Demographic Society, Wellington.

Pool, Ian. *The Maori Population of New Zealand, 1769–1971.* Auckland: Auckland University Press and Oxford University Press, 1977.

Rafiq, M. "Some Evidence on Recent Demographic Changes in Papua New Guinea." *Population Studies* 33(2):307–312, July 1979.

Ruzicka, Lado T., and John C. Caldwell. *The End of the Demographic Transition in Australia.* Australian Family Formation Project, Monograph No. 5. Canberra: Australian National University, 1977.

Shand, R. T. (editor). *The Island States of the Pacific and Indian Oceans: Anatomy of Development.* Development Studies Centre, Monograph No. 23. Canberra: Australian National University, 1980.

South Pacific Commission. *South Pacific Economies, 1978: Statistical Summary.* Nouméa, New Caledonia, 1980.

United States, Bureau of the Census. *World Population, 1979: Recent Demographic Estimates for the Countries and Regions of the World.* Washington, D.C.: U.S. Government Printing Office, 1980.

OPTIMUM POPULATION

See ECOLOGY; RESOURCES AND POPULATION.

ORGANIZATIONS AND AGENCIES

The principal organizations and agencies engaged in population research and action are treated in individual articles in this encyclopedia: UNITED NATIONS; UNITED NATIONS FUND FOR POPULATION ACTIVITIES; INTERNATIONAL PLANNED PARENTHOOD FEDERATION; INTERNATIONAL UNION FOR THE SCIENTIFIC STUDY OF POPULATION; POPULATION ASSOCIATION OF AMERICA; and ASSOCIATION FOR POPULATION/FAMILY PLANNING LIBRARIES AND INFORMATION CENTERS—INTERNATIONAL. Much of the work of the U.S. Bureau of the Census is discussed in DATA COLLECTION, article on UNITED STATES CENSUS; the large international donor agencies are surveyed in INTERNATIONAL POPULATION ASSISTANCE; and the historical development of various organizations related to family planning is reviewed in BIRTH CONTROL MOVEMENT. The work of the United Nations Statistical Office, which publishes the *Demographic Yearbook,* is explained in DATA COLLECTION, article on INTERNATIONAL SYSTEMS, while academic activities are described in EDUCATION, article on TEACHING DEMOGRAPHY. Numerous publishers of population literature are mentioned in PUBLICATIONS, articles on SERIALS AND REFERENCE WORKS and BIBLIOGRAPHIC RESOURCES. Closely related to these articles is DIRECTORIES, which reviews published listings relevant to the field of population. In addition to the articles cited here, individual country and regional articles should be consulted, as should the index for names of other national and international organizations and agencies.

PQ

PACIFIC ISLANDS
See OCEANIA.

PAKISTAN

A predominantly Muslim country, Pakistan came into existence in 1947 as a result of the political partition of the Indian subcontinent after independence from British rule. It had two wings, East and West Pakistan, until 1971, when East Pakistan became an independent country known as Bangladesh. The data presented here refer to areas that now constitute Pakistan and that formerly comprised West Pakistan.

Description. Pakistan ranks as the ninth largest country in the world in population size. The mid-1979 population was estimated at 84.1 million (Hobbs, 1980). With a persistently high birth rate, around 43–44 per 1,000 population, and a moderate death rate, around 14–15 per 1,000, the country has the very high rate of annual growth of 2.8–3.0 percent. Because of the high birth rate, Pakistan has a young population, with 43 percent below age 15.

Pakistan is a largely agricultural country with about 74 percent of its population living in rural areas and about 57 percent of its civilian labor force employed in agricultural occupations. Cotton, cotton yarn, cotton cloth, rice, and carpets remain the major export items

and are important sources of foreign exchange. However, home remittances by Pakistanis employed overseas, particularly in Middle Eastern oil-exporting countries, have registered a sharp increase in the last few years. At $1,100 million in 1977–1978 they dominated foreign exchange earnings and were projected to increase by $50 million annually during 1977–1983 (Pakistan, 1978, p. 55). This phenomenon has important implications for income distribution and has had a positive impact on visible consumption by the families receiving remittances. The desire to seek employment overseas has been greatly strengthened in recent years, and emigration of persons with certain skills (e.g., carpenters and masons) has led to shortages of such persons in Pakistan.

The gross national product (GNP) per capita was estimated to be US$270 in 1979, which, although higher than some more-populated countries such as India and Bangladesh, is well below the average for the developing world. It is expected that the proportion of the labor force engaged in agriculture will decline gradually. In order to meet the food requirements of a rapidly growing population the government is trying to augment production by increasing cultivable land, improving irrigation systems with' large-scale efforts toward control of waterlogging and salinity, and introducing multiple cropping. Despite an apparently adequate per capita calorie supply, the Micro-Nutrient Survey of 1976–1977 found that 57 percent of children under 5 showed low weight in relation to their age. Also, many preschool children and lactating and pregnant women were found to be anemic.

507

Population Characteristics. Decennial censuses and sample surveys are the two main sources of demographic data in Pakistan. Although a system of vital registration has existed since before the Pakistani state came into existence, data yielded by this system have not provided reliable estimates. Major sources of demographic data, along with a listing of the commonly used demographic variables on which data are available, are shown in Table 1. There have been problems associated with the reliability and validity of most of the data sources listed. Underenumeration in the census and misreporting of age in the census and surveys are two of the problems often mentioned in demographic writings.

The 1951 census of population enumerated 33.7 million people as inhabitants of Pakistan. By the 1972 census the population had almost doubled to 62.5 million (see Table 2). The U.S. Census Bureau estimated that there was a net underenumeration of 16 percent in the 1961 census and of 6.3 percent in the 1972 census. The intercensal estimates of annual growth rate between 1961–1972 range from 2.7 to 3.2 percent. Most demographers and planners who have analysed population growth data for Pakistan agree that the estimate of 3.2 percent is too high and that the rate of population growth during the decade of the 1980s was 2.8–2.9 percent.

Pakistan has four provinces: Punjab, Sind, North West Frontier Province (NWFP), and Baluchistan, in order of population size. Punjab, with about 26 percent of the country's total land area (307,374 square miles; 796,097 square kilometers) has 58 percent of the total population while Baluchistan with 44 percent of the land area has only 4 percent of the population. Punjab in 1972 had the very high density of 471 persons per square mile, compared with only 18 for Baluchistan. The densities for Sind and NWFP were 257 and 292 per square mile (un-

TABLE 1. *Availability of demographic data (x = data available), various sources, Pakistan, 1961–1976*

Data sources[1]	Age	Sex	Marital status	Children ever born	Children still living	Household listing/ composition	Births last year	Deaths last year	Urban-rural breakdown	Provincial breakdown	Pregnancy history	Where available
1951 census	x	x	x						x	x		Published
1961 census (total population)	x	x	x						x	x		Published
1972 census (total population)	x	x	x			with CO x			x	x		Published
PGE 1962–65 (est. total population)	x	x	x				x	x				Published
PGS 1968,[1] 69,[1] 71 (est. total population)	x	x	x	x[2]	x[2]		x	x	x			Published
PGS latest 1976[3] (est. total population)	x	x	x	x	x	with CSO x	x	x	x	x		CSO
NIS 1968 (ever-married women sample)	women 10–49	some husbands interviewed	ever-married only	x	x		x		x		x	Tapes available
PFS 1975 (ever-married women sample)	x[4]	x[4]	x[4]	x	x	x	x		x		x	Tapes at WFS, London
HED survey, 1973 (est. total population)	x	x	x	x	x	x			x	x		Published
LFS 1974–75 (est. total population)	x	x	x						x	x		Published
Registration	x	x	x			x						No published data available
Other[5]												

[1] Abbreviations for surveys and agencies are as follows: CO = Census Organization; CSO = Central Statistical Office; PGE = Population Growth Experiment; PGS = Population Growth Survey; NIS = National Impact Survey; PFS = Pakistan Fertility Survey; HED = Housing, Economic, and Demographic Survey; and LFS = Labor Force Survey.
[2] Only for 1971; unpublished data.
[3] PGS data have been collected for 1976–1978. The report for 1977 is forthcoming.
[4] Data on these characteristics available for all members of sampled households.
[5] Two surveys—one on migration and another on "Population and Development?"—are currently under way and would yield national-level data on fertility and mortality.

TABLE 2. *Estimates and projections of population and growth rates, Pakistan, various years*

Data sources	Unadjusted population (thousands)	Adjusted for undercount in various censuses[1] (midyear est.)	Annual growth rate (percent)	
			Unadjusted totals	Adjusted totals[1]
1951 census	33,740[a]	40,382	1.8[a]	2.4–2.5
1961 census	42,880[a]	51,719	2.4[a]	2.6–2.7
1972 census	62,462[b]	69,326	3.2[c]	2.7
1979 (est.)		84,075		2.8[d]

Sources of data. [1]Hobbs, 1980, tables 1 and 3.   [a]Afzal, 1974, p. 2.   [b]Official government figures.
[c]Calculated by the author.   [d]Projected growth rate from 1975–1979.

adjusted figures). The country as a whole had a density of 211 persons per square mile (81.5 per square kilometer) in 1972 compared with 139 in 1961. This represents an intercensal increase of 52 percent between 1961 and 1972.

The total number of households in the country was enumerated at 7.2 million in the 1960 Housing Census and had risen to 10.9 million by the time of the 1973 Housing, Economic, and Demographic Survey (HED survey). In 1973, the average number of rooms per housing unit was two, and 63 percent of all houses were *kutcha* (unbaked bricks and mud). Only 1 percent of the houses in rural areas were *pucca* (baked bricks and cement) compared with 32 percent of such houses in urban areas.

Of the 64.9 million persons enumerated in 1972, 47.9 million, or 74 percent, were living in rural areas while the remaining 16.9 million, or 26 percent, were urban, an increase from 18 percent in 1951 and 22 percent in 1961. The intercensal increase in urban population was 60 percent during 1951–1961 and 75 percent during 1961–1972; the corresponding increases for rural areas were 20 and 44 percent. These figures indicate considerable rural-urban migration. In 1972 Karachi and Lahore were the two major cities, with populations of 3.5 million and 2.1 million, respectively. The populations of four other cities, Lyallpur (recently renamed Faisalabad), Hyderabad, Rawalpindi, and Multan had exceeded 500,000 and were likely to reach the one million mark by 1981. There is an indication, however, that the pace of urbanization declined over the period 1961–1972 compared to the previous intercensal period, 1951–1961. The ratio of urban to rural growth declined from 3:1 in the earlier period to 1:1.7 in the latter period. Various other indexes show that the pace of urbanization was higher in the earlier than in the later period (Afzal and Abbasi, 1979). A similar pattern was found for each of the four provinces.

Socioeconomic Characteristics. The proportion who were literate among those aged 10 and over was 13 percent in 1951, 18 percent in 1961, and 22 percent in 1972;

thus, only about one-fourth of the current population of Pakistan is literate. The proportion of males who were literate is distinctly higher than that of females. Two-and-a-half times more males than females were literate in 1972 (30 percent and 12 percent). Differences between the urban and rural areas are also marked, particularly in respect to females. According to the 1974–1975 Labor Force Survey, only 5 percent of rural females were literate compared to 33 percent of urban females; the corresponding figures for rural and urban males were 29 percent and 60 percent. Of all those literate, about two-thirds had attained less than ten grades of education, while 6.5 percent in urban and 1.3 percent in rural areas had a B.A. or higher degree.

Of all males aged 10 and over, 78 percent were in the civilian labor force in 1973 (HED survey) compared with 81 percent in 1961 and 79 percent in 1951. Corresponding rates for females were notably lower—only 9 percent in the labor force in 1973 and 1961 compared with a mere 3 percent in 1951. Censuses in Pakistan, however, seem to have grossly underestimated female work outside the home. Data from two national surveys, the National Impact Survey (NIS) and the Pakistan Fertility Survey (PFS) provided rates at least twice as high as those from the censuses and labor force surveys. Of currently married women, 19 percent in the NIS and 18 percent in the PFS reported that they were working at the time of the survey. Both the nature of the questions and the responses given by male members of the family lead to considerable underenumeration of females engaged in paid employment in censuses and labor force surveys (Shah and Shah, 1980).

Rates of unemployment for both males and females have been reported to be about 2 to 3 percent of the civilian labor force, which is unexpectedly low. It is generally agreed in Pakistan that unemployment rates when measured in terms of persons actively looking for work are too low because of widespread underemployment and disguised unemployment.

A large proportion of employed males (57 percent) and females (67 percent) were engaged in agricultural occupations in 1973. This is somewhat lower than the 1961 level when 60 percent of males and 73 percent of females were so engaged. Only 9 percent of the labor force was engaged in professional, administrative, and clerical work in 1973. It is interesting that relatively more employed females were engaged in professional occupations in both 1961 and 1973 than employed males. Professional women are predominantly teachers and medical workers such as doctors and nurses, occupations that are regarded as honorable for women.

Age, Sex, and Marital Status. Almost half of the population of Pakistan is in age groups usually termed as dependent on those of working age, that is, less than 15 and over 59. Thus, about 34 million of the 69.7 million were classified as dependents in 1972, giving a dependency ratio of 95 economic dependents per 100 productive members of society. This ratio (calculated as the number of persons less than 15 and over 59 divided by the number of persons aged 15–59) may, however, overestimate actual dependency, since many of those below age 15 and over age 59 are in the labor force as part-time or full-time workers. The proportion of persons in dependent age groups has remained roughly the same since 1961 because of the continuing high birth rate and only moderate increases in life expectancy.

The number of males in Pakistan's population has been higher than the number of females as a result both of higher female mortality and of greater underenumeration of females. The sex ratios (males per 100 females) were 117, 116, and 113 in the censuses of 1951, 1961, and 1972. Of all women a steady 44–45 percent were in the childbearing ages (15–49) in the same censuses. Thus, there were a total of 12.7 million (or 14.6 million according to adjusted figures) women of reproductive age in 1972.

Marriage has great importance in Pakistani society. Sex and procreation are expected to take place only within marriage; furthermore, religion requires every Muslim male and female to marry. The legal age for marriage is 16 for females and 18 for males. Recognizing methodological and data-quality differences in various studies, it is reasonable to assume that women in Pakistan marry at around 16–18 years of age on the average. More than 90 percent of women aged 25–34 were reported to be married in 1951, 1961, and 1973. Such high proportions in the peak reproductive ages have serious implications for fertility. Pakistani planners have projected that the mean age at marriage for females during the Fifth Five-year Plan period (1978–1983) will rise to 20 years, but this projection is optimistic given other sociocultural conditions in the country.

Mortality. Demographers generally agree that in the early 1960s life expectancy at birth was about 47.5 years

for males and 45 years for females, based on the mortality estimates rendered by the 1962–1965 Population Growth Estimation (PGE) data. After making certain adjustments and using smoothing techniques, the U.S. Census Bureau suggested an upward revision of the 1962–1965 life tables and calculated life expectancy at birth to be 49.3 years for males and 46.7 years for females. The bureau also estimated a slight increase in life expectancy for males and females by year 1971, reaching 50.2 years for males and 47.1 years for females. The higher life expectancy for males is consistent with the lower crude death rate (CDR) for males shown by the PGE data. Crude death rates for males and females were calculated to be 17 and 20 respectively. While there are slightly fewer female deaths among infants compared to male deaths (135 and 137 respectively), age-specific death rates in broad age categories over the age range 1–44 were consistently higher for females than for males.

Indirect estimates suggest that the CDR was around 30 per 1,000 population in 1950. After 1950 there was a sharp decline in the CDR and the rate was estimated to be 19 per 1,000 population in 1960 on the basis of PGE data. The U.S. Census Bureau calculated the 1961 CDR to be higher than the PGE estimate, at about 22 per 1,000. Estimates of the 1979 crude death rate range from 14 (Pakistan, 1978) to 16 (Hobbs, 1980). There is again considerable variation in estimates of the infant mortality rate (IMR). The Planning Commission believes the IMR to be as low as 105 per 1,000 live births (as shown by the 1971 PGS data) while the U.S. Census Bureau estimated the rate to be 142 in 1971. Other writers using data from the Pakistan Fertility Survey of 1975 (World Fertility Survey) estimated the infant mortality rate at about 129 per 1,000 live births (Kabir, 1978).

Fertility. The estimates of the crude birth rate (CBR) in the country range from 41 to around 45. In its initial plan the Planning Commission (1978) estimated the CBR to be 43.6 in 1977–1978. This figure has been revised down to 41 for July 1980 in the revised plan issued in February 1981 (Pakistan, 1981). The U.S. Census Bureau has estimated it at around 44–45. Estimates of the total fertility rate also vary in different data sources but generally fluctuate between 6 and 7 children per woman. Fertility of married women in the country has been estimated to be between 7.9 and 10.2 children per married woman according to various sources. The latter figure is generally regarded as an overestimate and most writers agree on a marital total fertility rate (MTFR) of about 8–9. The 1975 PFS provided a MTFR of 8 children per woman; this MTFR yields a gross reproduction rate of 3.9 daughters per woman.

Surprisingly, the number of children ever born per currently married woman was 4.4 in urban and 4.1 in rural areas in the 1975 PFS survey. The higher fertility of urban women was also found in the 1968–1969 NIS, which showed urban and rural women to have had 4.3 and 4.0 children ever born, respectively. The ideal family size declined somewhat between 1968–1969 and 1975—from 4.2 to 3.9 in urban and 4.5 to 4.3 in rural areas. The small decline in ideal family size was, however, not matched by action (use of contraceptives) aimed at reducing fertility, as is clear from the next section.

Policy and Action. The high rate of population growth has been an expressed concern of the government since 1965 when a national family planning program was started. Through the program the government planned to reduce the CBR from 50 to 40 in five years. The main contraceptive method made available was the intrauterine device (IUD), although sterilization and conventional methods were also available. The basic strategy of the program was to use paramedical personnel trained to insert IUD's and establish motivational campaigns. The core of the program consisted of the local midwife (*dai*) who had been, and continues to be, the attendant for most births in the country. About 20,000 midwives were hired during the first few years of the program. The program strategy was reformulated in 1971 after authorities realized that it had not achieved the desired results. An attempt was made to institute a Continuous Motivation System (CMS) through the use of male-female teams, who were supposed to cover a designated area with supplies and continuously influence motivation.

Data from the 1968 NIS showed that 12.1 percent of eligible women had ever used a contraceptive method and 5.5 percent were currently using one at the time of survey. In the 1975 PFS, rates of use had apparently declined somewhat to 10.5 percent and 5.2 percent. Performance in urban areas was better than in rural areas and the rate of use rose in urban areas between 1968 and 1975. In rural areas, however, not only had rates of use declined but the average age of current users was higher in the latter survey—35.2 in 1975 compared with 31.2 in 1968.

Some of the reasons for the low use of contraceptives by Pakistani women can be found in religious attitudes and beliefs, fear of side effects, and objections by husbands or other relatives. Of all nonusers, 43 percent said that they did not intend to use contraception in the future according to the 1975 PFS. Half of those who did not intend future use cited religious reasons; another one-sixth said that they would not use contraception for fear of side effects. Thus, despite a continuous government program featuring a variety of delivery systems to make contraceptives available and to promote their use, levels of use in the country remained low and the general sociocultural environment did not seem to provide en-

couraging grounds for expecting rapid gains in the near future.

Reduction in the population growth rate is one of the main objectives of the government's Fifth Five-year Plan (1978–1983). This revised plan covering the period 1980–1983 projects a decline in the crude birth rate from 41.0 to 37.5 per 1,000 over the plan period, and proposes to reduce the population growth rate from 2.9 percent to 2.7 percent (Pakistan, 1981). The Population Division hopes to achieve these objectives by launching a multisectoral approach in which development planning and population welfare planning may be integrated. This decline is expected partly because of the positive intentions toward contraception expressed by 57 percent of those who had never used it in 1975; the validity of this expectation remains to be seen. In addition to the national government program, voluntary efforts, such as that by the Family Planning Association of Pakistan, have been made for many years. Abortion is illegal but certain medical (and paramedical) personnel and midwives are known to make it available.

Scholarly Activities. None of the universities in Pakistan has an independent department to teach population. Some sociology departments offer courses in population that are required for the master's degree in sociology. The Social Science Research Center at the University of Punjab, Lahore, offers a one-year program providing a diploma in demography. One of the basic research centers where population investigations are conducted is the Pakistan Institute of Development Economics in Islamabad, which has two distinct sections dealing with population research. Research is also conducted by the population section of the Planning Commission and the research directorates within the government's population-planning program. Population-related research has been published in journals such as the *Pakistan Development Review, Pakistan Journal of Family Planning,* and *Manpower Review.* Publications of the Family Planning Association of Pakistan and the Pakistan Sociological Association also provide population-related research materials.

Nasra M. Shah

See also ASIA; BANGLADESH; INDIA.

BIBLIOGRAPHY

Afzal, Mohammad. *The Population of Pakistan.* Islamabad: Pakistan Institute of Development Economics, 1974.
Afzal, Mohammad, and Nasreen Abbasi. "Urbanization and Internal Migration in Pakistan, 1951–1973." Draft report. Islamabad: Pakistan Institute of Development Economics, 1979.
Hobbs, Frank B. *Pakistan.* Country Demographic Profile pre-

pared for the U.S. Bureau of the Census. Washington, D.C.: U.S. Government Printing Office, March 1980.

Kabir, Mohammad. "Infant and Child Mortality Levels in Pakistan." *Genus* 34(3/4):143–152, 1978.

Manpower Review. Issued quarterly since 1975 by the Manpower Division, Islamabad.

Pakistan, Ministry of Planning and Development, Population Division. *Fifth Five-year Plan: Population Welfare Planning Plan, 1980–83.* Islamabad, 1981.

Pakistan, Planning Commission. *The Fifth Five-year Plan, 1978–83.* Karachi: Printing Corporation of Pakistan Press, 1978.

Pakistan Journal of Family Planning. Discontinued. Issued quarterly from 1967 to 1969 by the National Research Institute of Fertility Control, Karachi.

Shah, Nasra M., and Makhdoom A. Shah. "Trends and Structure of Female Labour Force Participation in Rural and Urban Pakistan." In *Women in Contemporary India and South Asia,* edited by Alfred de Souza, pp. 95–123. New Delhi: Indian Social Institute, 1980.

PALEODEMOGRAPHY

As a branch of historical demography, paleodemography is a heterogeneous but well-defined field of study with a substantial and growing amount of data and literature. It can be distinguished by its specific sources and methodology, rather than by any particular period or historic era studied. It is not restricted to the study of prehistoric populations. In practice, where historical demographic research comes to an end for lack of conventional sources, such as population statistics relevant to past periods, parish registers, genealogies, or tax records, there begins the domain of paleodemography, which uses any other sources as well as a variety of methods and analytic approaches in order to generate information for the history of population.

Thus, paleodemography can be defined as the study of past populations (generally medieval or earlier), using specific methodology for the analysis of sources other than written historical records. These include anthropological materials (skeletal remains) and archaeological materials and observations. Other sources include toponymic material (place names), paleogeographical information (climatic conditions), and paleopathological and ethnohistoric findings as well as ethnographic or cultural anthropological data relevant to recent populations, which can be interpreted from a historical demographic viewpoint.

Development of the Field. The first paleodemographic studies were carried out by investigators into antiquity who used archaeological materials. From the Roman era,

many epitaphs (tombstone inscriptions) have withstood the vicissitudes of centuries and survived to the present day, preserving records of the sex of the deceased persons and their age at death. In 1886, Karl Julius Beloch began to exploit this unique source material, the Corpus Inscriptionum Latinarum, by constructing indexes of the probable length of life in given periods from 1,831 Roman epitaphs found in three Italian regions. A long series of researchers followed his example, among others A. G. Harkness in 1896, who extended the research to age at marriage, which was often recorded in Italy if the inscription was set up by the surviving spouse.

Demographers also recognized the importance of these epitaphs for historical demography. In 1937, Walter F. Willcox wrote a methodological note on the research concerning the length of life in the early Roman Empire. The next year, V. G. Valaoras published a study on the expectation of life in ancient Greece. In 1960, John Durand dealt with the problem of mortality estimates from Roman tombstones in general. About the same time, Louis Henry and George Acsádi offered critical comments, respectively, on R. Etienne's and János Szilágyi's works. Recent studies of epitaphs, such as those written by M. Hombert and C. Préaux, A. R. Burn, J. C. Russell, H. Nordberg, K. Hopkins, and K. K. Éry have been more cautious and more judicious than the pioneering works in their handling of the observations.

Skeletal evidence may be a much more reliable source of paleodemography than a collection of sporadic epitaphs. Karl Pearson, the distinguished English scholar of statistics and biometrics, was the first to analyze burial series in order to gain information about ancient mortality. In an important step in 1902, he examined whether his material, a series of Egyptian mummies from the Roman era, fulfilled the requirements of a true sample, that is, whether it belonged to a specific population and whether each member of the population had an equal chance of being mummified. In the course of his analysis he made allowances for the inevitable shortcomings of the sample.

Since Pearson obtained the description of the Egyptian series from the archaeologist W. Spiegelberg, he did not face the other cardinal problem arising in connection with anthropological materials, which concerns accuracy in determining the age and sex of skeletal remains. In fact, it was only in the 1920s and 1930s when, starting with T. W. Todd's activity, the mortality analysis of skeletal series gained momentum. Todd studied the changes in the pubic bone that are caused by age, a topic he later extended with the collaboration of D. W. Lyon and J. D'Errico to age changes in other bones. When studying the skeletal remains of Pecos Pueblo in 1930, E. A. Hooton already found it quite natural that those who are privileged to examine skeletal finds at excavations have to attempt estimations of population size and trends. In 1936, the anthropologist L. Franz and the demographer-statistician Wilhelm Winkler published a study of the early Bronze Age mortality in Lower Austria. The next year, Henri V. Vallois dealt with distribution of deaths by age among Paleolithic and Mesolithic men. In 1939, Franz Weidenreich analyzed the duration of life of fossil man in China. Following these works, paleodemographic aspects were adopted in historical anthropology and in archaeological research, as witnessed by the publications of W. W. Howells, R. Riquet, P. R. Giot, F. Ivaniček, K. Gerhardt, M. Fusté, K. Bröste and J. B. Jörgensen, A. X. Cunha, A. V. Kidder, N. G. Gejvall, D. Ferembach, L. Schott, and others.

In the process of this research, paleodemography emerged. As early as 1927, J. Matiegka outlined an idea for a "prehistoric demography," but without much success for want of adequate anthropological material. Around 1950, however, the existence of paleodemography could not be overlooked. Demographers, such as Louis I. Dublin, Alfred J. Lotka, and Mortimer Spiegelman, although with some healthy skepticism, as well as anthropologists (e.g., Ilse Schwidetzky and M. F. Ashley-Montague), summarized earlier paleodemographic findings in their books.

The development of paleodemography, of course, resulted mainly from those efforts that were focused exclusively upon its complex field. Such research was conducted, for example, by J. Lawrence Angel, who, from 1947 onward, published many papers on paleodemographic topics, including health, environmental, and paleopathological aspects, and raised the issue of studying fertility on a skeletal basis. The anthropologist János Nemeskéri and the demographer George Acsádi recognized the interdisciplinary character of the field and were considered the founders of the "Budapest school," an informal cooperation between anthropologists, demographers, archaeologists, pathologists, and other experts. Through wide interdisciplinary collaboration, the Budapest school revised the methods of determining age and sex, raised the methodological standards, broadened the horizon of paleodemographic research, insisted upon demographic requirements in opening up necropolises, and effected complete excavations.

Ideas and efforts similar to those represented by the Budapest school characterize the works of most researchers concerned with paleodemography during the last two decades. Analyses of newly discovered skeletal series or reassessment of earlier studies greatly enriched the literature on paleodemography, among others those published by M. S. Senyürek, M. R. Sauter, L. Bartucz, B. Skerlj, M. S. Goldstein, V. Shaefer, H. Grimm, O. Necrasov, S. T. Genovés, G. Kurth, F. E. Johnston, C. E. Snow, Q. Milanesi, P. D. Stewart, J.-N. Biraben, K. McKinley, R. L. Blakely, A. E. Mann, J. P. Bocket, A. Kralovánszky, L. Klepinger, and C. M. Mobley. Paleodemography received full recognition from archaeologists in 1960, through the publication of two paleodemographic chapters written by Howells and Vallois in *The Application of Quantitative Methods in Archaeology* (Heizer and Cook, 1960).

The number of monographs devoted exclusively to the topic of paleodemography proliferated in the 1970s. Several scholars made an attempt to outline the field of paleodemography and summarize its findings or offered critical reviews; among them were Angel (1969), Don R. Brothwell (1971), Milan Stloukal, Don E. Dumond, Kazumasha Kobayashi, William Peterson, Nancy Howell, Claude Masset, and others. The first book that dealt with both methodology and analysis of paleodemographic material, mostly from the viewpoint of history of longevity and mortality, was published in 1970 by Acsádi and Nemeskéri. Their work was followed by further volumes. In 1976 A. C. Swedlund and G. J. Armelagos wrote on "demographic anthropology," and R. H. Ward and K. M. Weiss edited a collection of studies on the demographic evolution of human population. In 1978 D. H. Uberlaker published a study of human skeletal remains, and in 1981 Fekri A. Hassan made a detailed review of paleodemography from an archaeological perspective.

As the large and growing body of relevant publications bears witness, "skeletal demography" should be considered the mainstream of recent paleodemographic research. The important role of skeletal materials in paleodemography is understandable in view of the quantity of demographic information that can be obtained from them. Human remains provide an opportunity to determine sex and age at death—and hence, length of life—of the deceased persons. There is even a possibility of finding some clues as to the number of children ever born to a woman. On this basis, if the series and their analysis comply with the methodological requirements, inferences can be made in respect to parameters of mortality and longevity and, to a limited extent, to health conditions and reproduction.

There are, of course, other ways to estimate the size of an ancient or prehistoric population or its density in a given area. For example, between 1949 and 1959, Nougier and Peyroni fulfilled Matiegka's plan for a prehistoric demography by using archaeological and population geographic approaches to estimate population size and density in prehistoric France. Similar works relevant to American prehistory have been based on pottery evidence, and paleogeographic and ethnohistoric approaches have been used in reconstructing the peopling of early Africa.

Cultural anthropology, on the other hand, uses an ecological approach. Although the interest of anthropology in population dynamics and density under various ecological conditions dates as far back as the 1890s, this kind of research became more relevant to paleodemography beginning in the mid-1940s with studies of the cultural and natural areas of the tribal groups of North America; the relationships between population, food supply, and building in pre-Columbian Mexico; the ecology of Central Asian pastoralism; Maya settlement patterns; and the consequences of food production. Studies of population problems involving Pleistocene man, on the size of Pleistocene hunting communities, and on Stone Age economics were mostly based on experience gained from research concerning more recent groups of hunters and gatherers.

Paleodemography is also supported by two fields of study. One consists of demographic observations (relevant mostly to survival and reproduction) made in connection with contemporary nonindustrial societies. Ethnographic observations or ecological findings with demographic implications can be used in paleodemography as analogies or as assumptions for certain calculations. Indeed, in the investigation of skeletal series, it is indispensable to take into account all relevant historic conditions that can be inferred from the archaeological and other findings as well as contemporary analogies offered by demographic, anthropological, ethnographic, ecological, and epidemiological research. The second field provides findings in the study of behavior or ecology of primates that can be used in paleodemographic research as comparative materials. For example, similarities in survivorship have been found between Australopithecines and Indian Knoll skeletal series.

Analysis of Epitaph Series. From the standpoint of mortality, the problems that emerge in the course of an analysis of epitaph series are numerous and serious. In many instances, probably because of ignorance of age, only the name and perhaps the relationship of the deceased to the commemorator were inscribed. Even when the age was given, it was probably recorded incorrectly since the ancient Romans were not much concerned with the accurate reckoning of age. As is usual in many developing countries today where the exact knowledge of age is not important, the Romans, who used the decimal system, also had a great preference for certain digits and tended to round off their ages to figures ending with zero or five. The consequence of the widespread ignorance of the exact ages and of this "zero-five" preference is a sharp heaping of deaths at ages with 0 or 5 as terminal digits, as shown in Figure 1.

FIGURE 1. *Distribution of deaths by age at death based on Italian epitaphs from the Roman era*

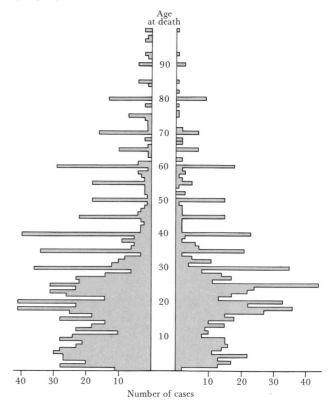

Source of data: Beloch, 1886.

Many procedures are available for handling the problem raised by age heaping, but Figure 1 reveals another shortcoming of the epitaph series that is not easily manageable. Most inscriptions were made for urban dwellers during the first three centuries A.D. Although it was not only well-to-do families that erected tombstones for their deceased members, and tradesmen, artisans, and often liberated (manumitted) or nonliberated slaves also were commemorated by epitaphs, the custom was not generally observed among any group, so that the epitaph samples are not representative of any population or subpopulation. In other words, the frequency of certain ages in an epitaph series is determined by mortality on the one hand and by social customs and circumstances relevant to setting up tombstones (for example, the availability and capability of commemorators) on the other. Without the knowledge of these selective customs and circumstances, the epitaph series cannot provide reliable data on mortality.

The sex and age distribution of persons commemorated by epitaphs from three Italian regions shown in Figure 1 (the same series of inscriptions analyzed by Beloch) vividly illustrates not only the very considerable age heaping but also the extent of the bias caused by the nondemographic factors mentioned earlier. It is clear that females were less frequently commemorated by epitaphs than males. Six out of every ten epitaphs commemorated males while only four were for females, which corresponds to a sex ratio of about 67 females per 100 male deaths.

Such a sex ratio in a population of deceased persons is, of course, improbable unless an exodus or decimation of females took place, which, again, would be unlikely in these regions. A strange sex ratio is indeed quite general in epitaph materials.

Another improbable feature of Figure 1 is the distribution of deaths by age, which shows no affinity to any type of age-at-death distribution that has been observed statistically for populations with high mortality rates either in contemporary developing countries or in developed countries in the past. It seems that, in the Roman era, epitaphs were made only in exceptional cases for infants and, also, rarely for one-year-old or two-year-old children. At the same time, older children and young adults are overrepresented in the epitaph series at the expense of older persons. These peculiarities of the epitaph material are strikingly manifested in Figure 2 where the male and female epitaph distributions (adjusted for age heaping)

are compared with the appropriate model life table distributions, namely with the proportions of male and female deaths of a stationary population at mortality level 4 of Coale and Demeny's South model life table. The mortality level selected for comparison corresponds with expectations of life of 27.0 years for males and 27.5 years for females, which are near to the values that can be computed from Roman era series.

Although the criticism of direct inferences from epitaph series on mortality, without considering the selectiveness of the samples, is legitimate, it does not mean that further exploitation of the Roman era inscriptions from a paleodemographic viewpoint would be unwarranted. Hitherto, the epitaph material yielded valuable information on the probable social differentiation of mortality and gave some hints as to regional and urban-rural differences and variations of age at marriage (the median age at marriage of the Roman females of the "respectable classes" can be estimated at about 15 years) and marital duration. Some inferences can even be drawn about certain aspects of sex-specific and age-specific mortality. It can be accepted, for example, that the Roman era distributions in Figure 2 clearly indicate a minimum of the proportion of deaths at young ages. The Roman era minimum occurred in the same age group (10–15 years) for

FIGURE 2. *Comparison of proportion of deaths from epitaph and skeletal series of the Roman era*

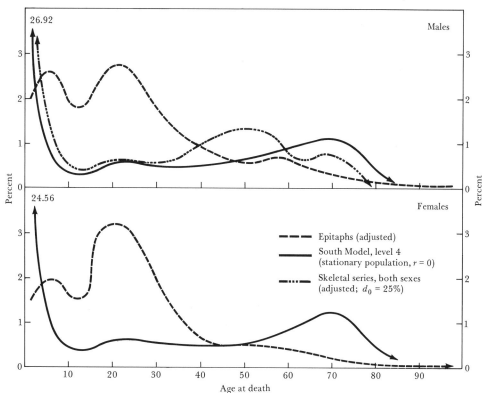

Source of data: Acsádi and Nemeskéri, 1970, pp. 296–297.

both sexes and coincides with the minimum of the model distribution. In each instance, the minimum is followed by a distinct mode concurring with an increased juvenile mortality around age 20, which is also marked on the model distributions, though less conspicuously. Very probably there were also differences between the sexes in the age-specific mortality. This is suggested by the fact that the female mode corresponding with juvenile mortality rises steeply after age 15 (the assumed median age at marriage) and is more pronounced than that of the male, perhaps partly because of early and high maternal mortality. There is also a possibility that child mortality might have been higher than that permissible at level 4 of the South model, and it is not inconceivable that the old-age mode of the distribution of deaths might have fallen at a somewhat younger age (around 55–60 years) than that around 70 years as indicated by the model.

Analysis of Skeletal Series. A direct way to check the reliability of information gained from epitaph series is to compare them with information obtained from skeletal series. Figure 2 also presents the distribution of deaths by age (both sexes together compared with the male distributions) based on the skeletal remains of 120 persons from the completely excavated necropolis at Keszthely-Dobogó (in the former Pannonia province), which dates back to approximately A.D. 340–410. This small skeletal series gives evidence that the pattern of age-specific mortality in the Roman era could not differ from more recent patterns so radically as the epitaph series imply.

It should be noted that the distribution of the Keszthely-Dobogó series is in Figure 2 adjusted for accidental age heaping and for infant mortality. The distribution of the adjusted skeletal series shows affinity with the model distribution; in fact, between ages 10 and 25 the two curves almost coincide, and at most other ages, they run parallel. Curiously, however, the Keszthely-Dobogó series seems to confirm three mortality features of the Roman era that may be inferred from the epitaphs: (1) higher child mortality, (2) earlier normal ages at death than those shown in level 4 of the South model, and (3) longer life expectancy of males than of females (at age 20 males could expect a further 31.3 years of life while females could expect only 25.1 years). Further research may prove whether such peculiarities really existed.

If the skeletal series are at least approximately representative samples of deaths, which they often are not, and even if the internal inconsistencies of the series are detected and adjusted, in the absence of data on the composition of the living population, life tables can be computed only from the distribution of deaths by sex and age, under the assumption of stationary conditions of the population. Indeed, it may practically be taken for granted that stationary conditions prevailed for the bet-

ter part of the last million years of population history, considering that the average annual growth rate preceding the Neolithic period has been estimated at below 0.003 percent. But it might have been even lower in the early Paleolithic era, and even during the Neolithic "demographic revolution" in the Middle East it was probably between 0.08 and 0.12 percent. Evidently, the factor of population growth, at least preceding the Neolithic period, was in most cases negligible. It was close to negligible in later historical periods, too. Therefore, if the period of burials was long enough (i.e., embraced many generations), the population was closed, and the difference in size between the population that started use of the graveyard and the population that abandoned it was not too great, stationary conditions may be assumed.

In this instance, the researcher does not calculate a "periodic" life table, that is, a life table of a hypothetical cohort based on periodic mortality rates, but constructs instead a life table of the succeeding generations, following the demographic paradigm of relating the observed events (deaths) to the events (births) that necessarily precede them. On this basis, the researcher may estimate what proportion of those who were born died during a given year of life and what proportion survived. With the help of these data, every parameter of a life table can be computed. Indeed, under stationary conditions, the three different approaches to the construction of a life table—periodic tables, cohort tables, and paleodemographic tables (Halley-type tables)—give the same results.

The researcher, however, is not necessarily restricted to the assumption of a stationary population. If there is any reason to presume that the population studied was subject to natural increase or decrease or that a hypothesis concerning population growth should be introduced, then the $d(a)$ distribution of deaths by age can easily be transformed to a derivative $d'(a)$ distribution that corresponds to a given rate of population growth by using the formula

$$d'(a) = d(a)e^{ra},$$

where r equals the assumed rate of annual growth, a denotes the age, and e is the basis of the natural logarithm. In the case of a low rate of supposed natural increase, the adjustment for population growth makes relatively little difference. Taking as an example the distribution of a small Copper Age skeletal series (in Alsónémedi, Hungary) and supposing that the annual rate of population growth was as high as 0.1 percent ($r = 0.001$), the life expectancy at age 20 would increase only by one-tenth of a year, from 25.66 years computed with the assumption of stationary conditions to 25.75 years.

If the total number of persons (D) buried in a graveyard, the expectation of life at birth ($\mathring{e}_0$), and the length

(t) of the burial period (i.e., the period during which the cemetery was used) are known, the size of the population can be estimated by using the formula

$$P = k + D\mathring{e}_0/t,$$

where k is a correction factor, which for medieval graveyards takes a value approximately 10 percent or less of that of the fraction in the formula. If, in addition, the chronology of the burials is known, estimates can also be made for population trends. By using certain assumptions, derived perhaps from the demography of contemporary peoples having the same economic and sociocultural characteristics as those whose remains are investigated, further estimates can be made relevant to reproduction, family size, and population composition; and, in fact, the researcher may aim at the "reconstruction" of a once-living population.

One technical problem concerning the reliability of paleodemographic findings based on skeletal series arises from the accuracy of the methods of determining age and sex. It is relatively simple to identify sex on the basis of the pelvis, or, in its absence, identification can be based on many other bones that have recognizable sexual characteristics. From skeletal remains, however, only the individual's biologic age can be estimated, which, though closely correlated, does not necessarily coincide with the chronological age. In addition, the stages of different skeletal age determinants do not correspond to a single year of age but to shorter or longer life periods. They also may show variability by race or in time.

During the last decades, in recognition of the importance of age and sex determination for paleodemographic research, a new field of extensive activity has unfolded. In addition to the standard literature of forensic medicine, which is also concerned with the same problem, scores of works have offered a critical review of age determination and its effect on paleodemographic research. This work has set higher standards for estimating sex and age and has improved the accuracy of the methods. It is noteworthy that this field of paleodemography is closely related to paleopathology and that many scholars conduct research in both of these interlocking areas.

Some Findings of Paleodemography. Paleodemography must satisfy our interest in the dramatic story of the evolution of mankind, aid in understanding the present, and facilitate prediction of the future. Among the more important questions, as mentioned before, are how the human life span has evolved, how the shape and level of mortality curves have changed over time, and how differentials related to the changing natural and socioeconomic environment have developed. One must also bear in mind the problem of future evolution.

Figure 3, which shows some paleodemographic mor-

tality curves along with those from model life tables, gives some hints as to where the search for possible answers should be directed. The model life tables in Figure 3 were selected from the United Nations' series, specifically those of level 0 for both sexes (UN0B) and level 20 for females (UN20F), and from the regional tables by Coale and Demeny, including selected levels from 1 to 24 for females in the South model (marked S1F to S24F; the distribution of deaths was taken at $r = 0$). The three paleodemographic series (based on Acsádi and Nemeskéri, 1970) are (1) the "Archanthropus" type, a combination of the *Sinanthropus pekinensis* and Solo man series featuring a mortality level so high that it is improbable, (2) the "Maghreb" type, constructed on the basis of the Taforalt and Afalou series, which date back to the epipaleolithic times in the Maghreb, and (3) the "medieval" type based on several tenth- to twelfth-century Hungarian series.

Model life tables, representing the wisdom gained through observations relevant to the modern demographic transition, cannot answer the question whether the length of human life has been extended and, thus, whether it is expandable in the future; instead they suggest that the "normal age" (i.e., the old-age mode of the distribution of deaths) increased from 60–70 to over 80 and the mode became more and more pronounced. The models that represent high mortality, however, do not necessarily reflect a primeval mortality type. Indeed, many paleodemographic series indicate that in earlier times the normal age at death might have rested at younger ages and might have moved historically across a very wide range, perhaps between age 25 and age 65, although the existence of a small modal group around 60–75 years can also be demonstrated in many series. It may also be inferred from the paleodemographic evidence, keeping in mind the findings relevant to primates or australopithecines, that during human evolution not only have the chances of reaching an older age improved but the length of life itself has expanded. It is also probable that the present situation of females living longer than males is a relatively recent historical development. In earlier times, all evidence indicates that young adult females had considerably shorter life expectancy than males.

The question of particular interest is whether the presumption of a generally high or very high pretransitional (or prehistoric) fertility level on the basis of the assumed generally high mortality is justified, or whether one must reckon with more than one demographic transition. Carlo M. Cipolla, indeed, has stressed that demographic changes were incident to both the industrial revolution of the nineteenth century and the agricultural revolution of the Neolithic period. Edward S. Deevey distinguished three main upturns in population history, the earliest

FIGURE 3. *Life table parameters; paleodemographic series compared with models*

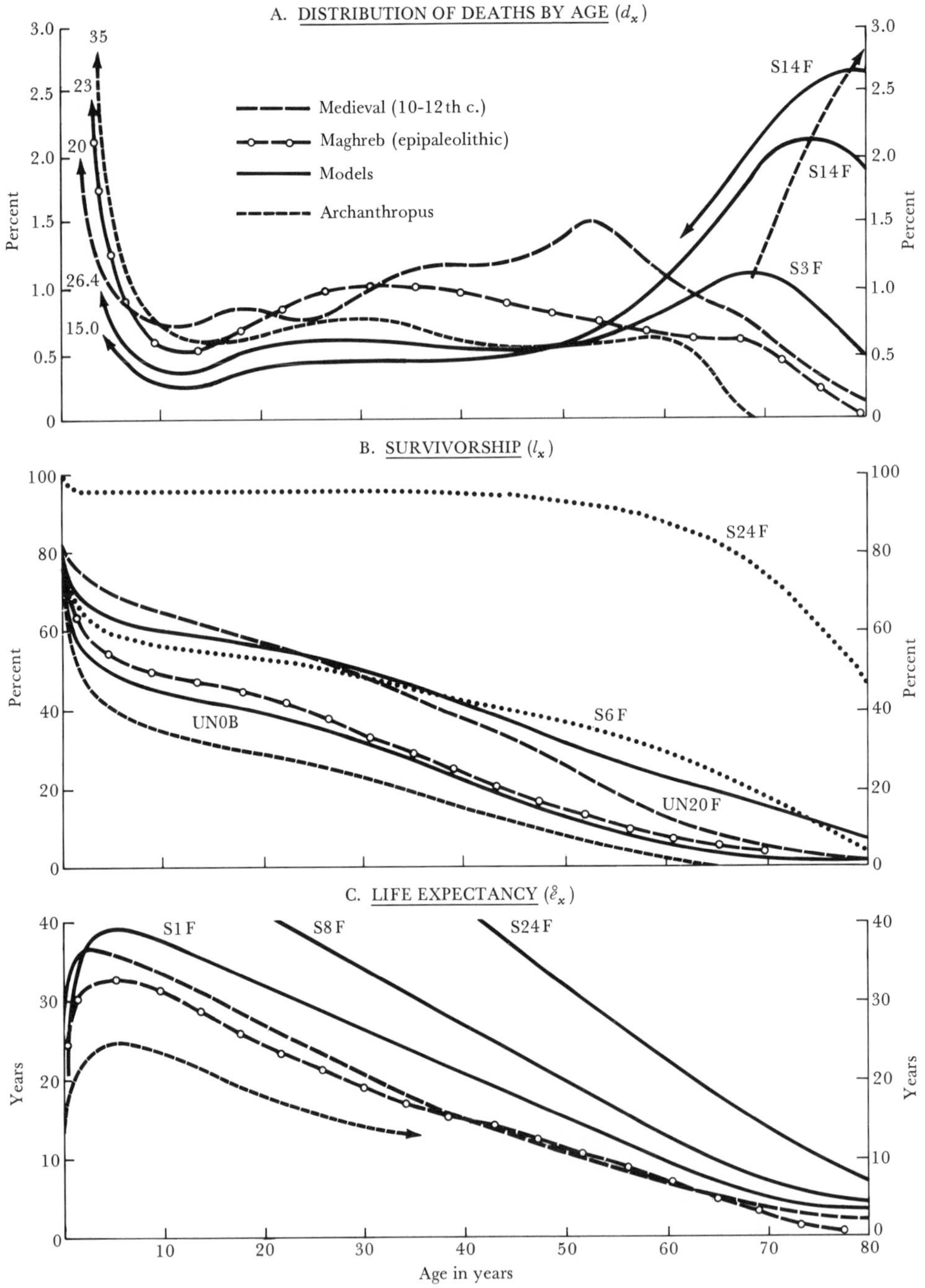
A. DISTRIBUTION OF DEATHS BY AGE (d_x)
Medieval (10-12th c.)
Maghreb (epipaleolithic)
Models
Archanthropus
Percent
35
23
20
26.4
15.0
S14F
S14F
S3F
B. SURVIVORSHIP (l_x)
S24F
S6F
UN0B
UN20F
C. LIFE EXPECTANCY ($\mathring{e}_x$)
S1F
S8F
S24F
Years
Age in years

about 100,000 years ago. Paleodemographic studies finally established it as probable that there were more than one, two, or even three transitions. The theory of multiple demographic transitions is based on separate studies that have pointed to regional differentiation of mortality as well as to temporal changes that indicate several transitions in different places at different times. These transitions did not necessarily follow the patterns of the modern transition; the changes might have been very slow or relatively rapid and they might also have had population consequences either of little importance or so far-reaching as the hypothesized sudden replacement of Neanderthal man by the anatomically modern *Homo sapiens*. The transitions should not always have been initiated by changes in mortality, since mortality was not generally so high as to exclude transitions caused by fertility changes.

George T. Acsádi

See also HISTORICAL DEMOGRAPHY.

BIBLIOGRAPHY

Acsádi, George T., and János Nemeskéri. *History of Human Life Span and Mortality.* Translated by K. Balás. Budapest: Akadémiai Kiadó, 1970.

Angel, J. Lawrence. "The Bases of Paleodemography." *American Journal of Physical Anthropology* 30(3):427–437, May 1969.

Beloch, Karl Julius. *Die Bevölkerung der griechisch-römischen Welt.* Leipzig, 1886.

Brothwell, Don R. "Palaeodemography." In *Biological Aspects of Demography,* edited by William Brass, pp. 111–130. London: Taylor-Francis, 1971.

Cipolla, Carlo M. *The Economic History of World Population.* Baltimore: Penguin Books, 1962.

Deevey, Edward S., Jr. "The Human Population." *Scientific American* 203:195–204, 1960.

Hassan, Fekri A. *Demographic Archaeology.* New York: Academic Press, 1981.

Heizer, Robert F., and Sherburne F. Cook (editors). *The Application of Quantitative Methods in Archaeology.* Viking Fund Publications in Anthropology, no. 28. Chicago: Quadrangle Books, 1960.

Jarcho, Saul (editor). *Human Paleopathology.* New Haven, Conn.: Yale University Press, 1966.

Swedlund, A. C., and G. J. Armelagos. *Demographic Anthropology.* Dubuque, Iowa: W. C. Brown, 1976.

Uberlaker, D. H. *Human Skeletal Remains.* Chicago: Aldine, 1978.

Ward, R. H., and K. M. Weiss (editors). *The Demographic Evolution of Human Populations.* New York and London: Academic Press, 1976.

PLANNED PARENTHOOD

See BIRTH CONTROL MOVEMENT; INTERNATIONAL PLANNED PARENTHOOD FEDERATION.

POLICY

See DISTRIBUTION, *article on* DISTRIBUTION POLICY; GOVERNMENT POLICY; IMMIGRATION POLICY; POPULATION POLICY.

POPULATION, WORLD

See WORLD POPULATION.

POPULATION AGING

See AGING POPULATION.

POPULATION AND DEVELOPMENT

Interactions between socioeconomic development and population are the subject of the present article. Closely related is FERTILITY AND DEVELOPMENT, *in which can be found a discussion of the macro- and microconsequences of fertility for development, and on the macro- and microdeterminants of fertility as affected by development.*

This brief account discusses some of the complexities of interactions between population and socioeconomic development, looking both at population as a whole and at the constituent demographic processes. It does not endeavor to summarize the large literature on these relationships that has appeared over the last 25 years or to review the various analytical approaches that different researchers have taken. A short guide to further reading on population and development follows this essay.

That fertility and mortality fall in the course of socioeconomic development is a well-established empirical fact. Studies of this phenomenon in the historical experience of the industrialized countries led to the notion of demographic transition which, despite the many reservations that have been expressed about its value as theory, remains perhaps the central organizing principle of the population field. [*See* DEMOGRAPHIC TRANSITION THEORY.] Beyond this gross empirical generalization, however, the relationships between population processes and development are not simply characterized. Clearcut, uncontradicted interpretations of research findings in the area are comparatively rare; ensuing contention on policy implications is common.

Population Growth and Development. Demographic transition theory typically supposes either that fertility decline is a lagged response to a mortality decline, the latter presumably induced by economic growth or associated public health measures, or that both mortality and fertility respond (not necessarily together) to changes brought about by social and economic development. In both instances, particularly the first, there is an underlying assumption that population and its constituent demographic processes form a system with some kind of homeostatic quality. A high-mortality, high-fertility, low-growth rate "equilibrium" is disrupted, but the system can eventually establish a new equilibrium at low levels of mortality and fertility. A traditional society suddenly finds that it has to deal with a variety of new threats and opportunities—new technologies, much larger surviving birth cohorts, and a rapidly changing external economic and political environment. In the demographic sphere, the society has to regain control over its growth of numbers. Controls previously used, typically to support rather than to restrain high reproductive levels, may have become embedded in a broad sociocultural framework and not be readily available for revamping in response to the need for a new demographic regime. Individuals and families, however, can be expected to perceive how adjustments in their own demographic behavior can serve their interests and eventually to act accordingly, even when normative pressures oppose them. This is the kernel of "classical" demographic transition theory: that external changes, such as an exogenous mortality decline, present a challenge to family welfare, and families respond by adopting a demographic strategy (variously emphasizing out-migration and adjustments in marital and birth control) to try to maintain their position in the society and economy. When migration options are limited, the familiar birth rate transition is predicted.

The major inadequacy of this conceptualization of how population processes are affected by development is that it takes for granted a similarity of interest between individuals or couples on the one hand and society on the other.

Both fertility and migration are decided on by individuals and couples, not by societies. Usually, it is possible with some investigation to see why a particular rate of childbearing makes sense for an individual or family, or indeed why in some instances childbearing at rates even above the limit set by biological factors would be rational. While individuals are not perfect in reacting to changing conditions, the assumption that they can detect and act on their best interests in demographic as in other matters is not a bad one. At the family or individual level, a sufficient change in surrounding conditions will be reflected, although not without some blur, in altered demographic behavior.

Aggregating the demographic actions taken by members of a society, however, does not necessarily give an overall pattern that also makes sense for the society. Witness the familiar but nevertheless astonishing phenomenon of a resource-starved country such as Bangladesh doubling its population in a generation, with little prospect of slowing this growth in the near future.

In a very gross sense, societies can be said to organize themselves (deliberately or not) to support a particular pattern of childbearing and particular patterns of migration appropriate to the resources, technologies, and mortality risks they face. But confronted with large or rapid changes in resources, technologies, and mortality risks, the evident advantages to society in shifting to a new demographic regime (for example, a regime of low fertility) often do not translate into perceptions of similar advantage accruing to individuals who adopt the new pattern. There is in fact no particular reason why such a

translation should be expected in the contemporary world, where rapid and pervasive political and technological change is the dominant reality. Only in an arbitrary accounting sense can demographic processes be separated out from this ferment and be given the appearance of forming an autonomous system.

In summary, we have the following picture: at the society-wide level, a social and economic system that supports a particular pattern of fertility and patterns of population redistribution; at the individual level, families or their individual members seeking out and acting on their own interests, with demographic behavior at least in its voluntary aspect being an instrument of those interests; and a transitional problem of the two levels being uncoupled. The variation among development styles and strategies, in terms of their demographic impact, essentially comes down to whether, and if so how, this coupling of private and public interests is restored.

The main route for recoupling individual and social demographic interests, rarely taken with any deliberate population policy intent, is through actions that "internalize" the costs of demographic behavior within small social units in the society. Decentralization of economic accounting is a powerful means to effect this internalization, although the historical record shows numerous combinations of different legal, fiscal, and administrative constraints also being applied.

Internalization at the level of the local community is one such option. Creation of the production brigade and production team as the organizational basis for rural development in modern China is an obvious instance of this level of internalization. In many European countries in their preindustrial and early industrializing stages, small community groups played somewhat analogous roles in bringing social pressure to bear on demographic behavior, especially marriage.

In the modern world it has been more common to push the accounting unit right down to the nuclear family, requiring parents themselves to bear the costs they incur and in particular the costs of their fertility behavior. A large share of the fertility reduction associated with urban life and an industrial economy is plausibly a consequence of internalization of the costs of children within families, occurring independently of any explicit population policy. The process follows from a rapid increase in direct child costs that parents come to see as necessary, an increasing difficulty in dispersing those costs over kin and community groups, and higher costs of missed employment opportunities for the mother. The pronatalist incentives adopted in present-day eastern Europe are efforts to subsidize child costs to prevent fertility from falling far below replacement levels.

The emphasis above has been on the demographic

impact of socioeconomic change. There are also relationships in the opposite direction: effects of population growth on development. Many such links have been posited, some favoring, others impeding population growth. On the one hand, population growth is held to stimulate technological and institutional innovation, in particular by inducing a decline in the ratio of wages to rents. In western Europe, for example, changes as varied as the breakdown of feudalism, the expansion of trade, and the formalization of contracts and property rights have been traced by some economic historians to population pressure. On the other hand, few economists would dispute that contemporary population growth rates of 2–3 percent per year (much higher than the rates prevailing during the industrialization of Europe or Japan) are on balance a serious burden to the development effort in poor countries. Most of the economic advantages attributed to population growth can fairly readily be attained by other means. It does not of course follow that a growth rate reduction will necessarily speed development; much would depend on how the reduction is achieved. Different means of reducing population growth could have positive, neutral, or negative impacts on economic growth. As instances of a negative effect, one need only mention an increased death rate or emigration of a technical and managerial elite, both of which would lessen population growth but at a high cost to society. Similarly, certain kinds of measures to reduce fertility might have adverse effects on the incentive structure of the economy. The difficult problem for public policy in this area is to find measures influencing population growth that yield benefits clearly outweighing their costs.

Mortality and Development. Mortality decline has been the most dramatic demographic feature of the post–World War II world. Life expectancy in the developing countries has risen from about 35 years in 1930 to some 55 years in 1980. Contributing to the mortality decline have been three main factors: transference of medical knowledge from the developed countries, expansion of public health facilities, and improved economic conditions among the population. The relative significance of these factors, a matter of considerable contention among researchers, has been largely resolved in an important empirical study by Samuel H. Preston (1976).

Preston shows first that there is a reasonably tight but nonlinear relationship between life expectancy and per capita income among countries at a given time, and second that this relationship has shifted systematically over time (see Figure 1). The relationship is comparatively steep at low-income levels, flattening out at higher levels. The major shifts over time have been twofold: (1) a decline in the per capita income level (in real terms) at which this flattening takes place—that is, in the income

FIGURE 1. *Scatter plot of relations between life expectancy at birth and per capita national income for nations in the 1900s, 1930s, and 1960s*

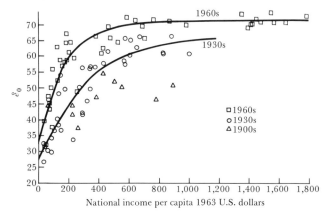

National income per capita 1963 U.S. dollars

SOURCE: Preston, 1976, p. 67; reprinted by permission.

level above which further income increases can be expected to make only slight contributions to improve mortality; and (2) an overall upward movement of the life expectancy-income relationship—a country with a given real per capita income today is likely to have a considerably higher life expectancy than a country reaching that same income level some decades earlier would have had.

The shifts in the relationship can be traced to specific changes in major causes of death. At low-income levels, declines in death rates from infectious, respiratory, and cardiovascular diseases, resulting from medical and public health interventions, have been pronounced. In contrast, death rates from diarrheal diseases (associated with malnutrition and generally unfavorable living conditions) have not changed much among low-income populations in recent decades.

Preston's cross-sectional analysis indicates that less than one-fifth of the overall mortality improvement in the world in recent decades is attributable to rising per capita incomes. The long-held popular view that mortality has become increasingly dissociated from economic levels because of diffusion of medical and public health knowledge is to quite a large extent borne out. At the lowest per capita incomes, the effect of development on mortality remains clearly strong—particularly when development is given a distributional dimension in addition to concern with economic growth. Even here, however, further public health interventions can be envisaged that would favorably affect contemporary mortality patterns without substantial income growth. Programs aimed at overcoming malnutrition through education in food values or aimed at promotion of breastfeeding and the cheap and readily diffused oral rehydration therapy combating diarrheal diseases are likely to raise higher the mortality–per capita income curve of Figure 1.

High mortality has various adverse effects on the economic development process apart from its immediate impact on welfare. There is the obvious waste of human resources, often embodying substantial investments in education and skills. High mortality may also militate against the kind of planning orientation needed to induce high rates of saving and investment, and it is typically associated with heavy morbidity, with consequently impaired labor productivity. Mortality risks are often highly skewed by socioeconomic class, however, so that these effects are not felt uniformly throughout the population. The objective of reducing the mortality rate, while universally supported, does not necessarily translate into program activities benefiting the groups where the risks are highest.

Migration and Development. Economic development is closely identified with the process of urban industrialization, movement of labor from a low-productivity agricultural sector to a high-productivity and largely city-based industrial sector. The association of industries and cities is not immutable; it is governed by locational and scale economies that conceivably could be much altered by new transport and communication technologies and by emerging disamenities of very large cities. To a limited extent, it is also governed by public policy. For the present and the foreseeable future, however, urbanization can be seen as an inevitable accompaniment of economic development. [*See* INTERNAL MIGRATION; *article on* DETERMINANTS; URBANIZATION, *article on* DEVELOPING COUNTRIES.]

Certain regularities in the way patterns of migration change in the course of development are observable, and some writers have sought to characterize these as a "mobility transition" paralleling the transition in birth and death rates. The limited circular migration of preindustrial society changes during development to a phase of massive population movement, particularly rural-urban migration but also migration to frontier areas (pioneer settlement) and often to foreign job markets. In the later stages of industrialization the countryside has in effect been emptied out; migration to cities and the frontier slackens, but an intensive and ever-increasing circulation of people within urban areas continues.

Individual variation among countries in patterns of urban hierarchy, in resource endowments, and in styles of development vitiate any general theory based on such observations. At a more modest level, however, a comparatively successful (that is, empirically supported) economic theory of rural-urban migration now exists, centered on the work of Michael P. Todaro and others (e.g., Todaro, 1976). In essence, rural-urban migration flows can be substantially explained as individual responses to perceived differences between present real income and expected real income at the place of destination. Expected income, roughly speaking, equals the urban wage multiplied by the probability of the migrant obtaining an urban job. Individuals seek to maximize their expected gains from migration. A paradoxical implication, empirically borne out, is that efforts to accelerate the creation of urban jobs may sometimes *raise* urban employment through their stimulation of rural-urban migration.

A particular feature of contemporary large cities in developing countries that complicates any simple two-sector depiction of migration and development relationships is the emergence of a large "informal" sector in the urban economy. This sector, once disparaged and deplored (for example, by analogy with city slums in developed countries) is now more often seen as a dynamic economic force, active not only in commerce and services but also in manufacturing.

Projections of urban and rural population growth under plausible assumptions about natural increase and economic expansion indicate clearly that most developing countries are not imminently facing an absolute decline of rural population. For example, in a country presently 20 percent urban (such as India), with a rate of natural increase of 2 percent per year and an urban population growing at a fairly typical rate of 5 percent per year, it would take twenty-three years for the rural population to begin to decline. At a natural increase rate of 3 percent it would take fifty-five years. Since agricultural development, including changes induced by the high-yielding crop varieties of the Green Revolution, is likely to be at best only moderately labor-absorbing over the next decades, already-serious problems of rural employment will become even more critical. Rural development strategies directed at relieving these problems may well generate new mobility patterns in the population, for example, short-term rural-to-rural labor migration and greatly increased rural-urban commuting.

On a world scale, disparities among countries in levels and rates of economic development and in per capita resource endowments generate significant international migration. For an increasing number of countries (among them, Bangladesh, Colombia, Egypt, Pakistan, and Turkey), remittances from migrants working abroad are a major source of investment capital for economic development. The returning migrants are thought to be an innovative force in their society. For resource-rich migrant-receiving countries, access to both skilled and unskilled foreign labor can overcome critical domestic labor shortages that would otherwise impede economic growth. Most of this international labor migration is temporary rather than permanent. Its continuation is dependent on the receiving countries' economic conditions and policies, making it a vulnerable component of a development strategy for the sending country. [*See* INTERNATIONAL MIGRATION.]

Fertility and Development. Certain components or concomitants of development, such as urbanization, freer access to education, and greater participation of women in the labor force outside the household, are widely believed to have a significant impact in depressing fertility. (Studies that explore these relationships in most instances do not greatly clarify the precise mechanisms involved and are less than conclusive on the question of causality, which is critical for drawing policy implications.) The complexities that research in this area must confront can best be seen by a brief overview of the range of development effects.

To a large extent, effects of development on fertility work through alterations in the setting within which fertility decisions (and related decisions that incidentally affect fertility) are taken. Three routes of impact might be distinguished: (1) through alterations in the array of economic benefits and costs associated with marriage and fertility; (2) through shifts in the organizational context of marital and fertility decision making that affect social and administrative pressures on individuals or couples; and (3) through changes in internalized values concerning marriage and fertility instilled by education, socialization and acculturation. In practice, the divisions are inevitably somewhat arbitrary.

Economic benefits and costs. Fertility, like other kinds of behavior subject to individual choice, tends to respond to changes in expected net economic benefits attaching to it. The increasing monetization of exchange relations that comes with economic development gives greater salience to this calculus. (Of course, no careful or even conscious calculation of benefits and costs need be assumed.) The economic shifts that take place are mostly in the direction of reducing the net benefits of high fertility. The time entailed in child raising may be seen as more costly—for the poor, competing with opportunities to increase their earnings; for the better off, competing with newfound forms of consumption. Where education is a possibility, its cost is often onerous. This cost, together with other direct costs of children and the physical demands of their upbringing, is more likely to be borne fully by parents rather than shared among kin. Furthermore, the uncertainties generated by rapid social change make any economic returns expected from children less assured. For example, parental control over children's marriage, often a means to an economic end, may be lost. Despite this, the new social environment may yet leave many parents in poor countries with few alternatives to children as a

source of economic security, however unsure the intergenerational contract. Improvements in health conditions presumably also affect the economics of fertility, altering individual planning horizons and parental expectation of death or debility both for themselves and for their children. The net impact here is probably a downward pressure on births. Finally, government-supported family planning programs may lower the direct economic cost of birth control.

Social and administrative pressures. Social pressures from kin or community in preindustrial societies are easily overstated, reflecting an exaggerated notion of the existing degree of conformity of behavior. In influencing fertility, they are probably not strongly felt on the direct question of family size (except perhaps regarding childlessness and very small families), but rather on several related issues—age at marriage; approval or disapproval of particular practices of birth control and child raising (such as extended breastfeeding); and restrictions on sex roles, divorce, and remarriage. (An exception may be West Africa, which seems strongly pronatalist about family size.) With development there is typically a weakening of the social groups whose interests generate these pressures. Individuals and families thus face fewer sanctions in instances where self-interest (whether leading to large or small families) diverges from social prescription. New pressures now come to bear directly on fertility, however, as the programs embodying government anxiety about population growth move beyond simple distribution of contraceptive services. Exhortation to limit fertility may be ineffectual, but attempts to characterize large family size as antisocial or to mobilize local administrative resources to meet preset family planning targets bring into play potentially more powerful forces.

Internalized values. The values and attitudes that supposedly set a firm base of consumer sovereignty for decisions affecting fertility are themselves in flux as the certitudes of traditional society, such as they were, diminish. One important set of changes seen by many observers in the empirical record is in attitudes toward spouse and children. The increasing economic autonomy of the nuclear family, where this occurs, has its emotional counterpart. Conjugal ties are strengthened as more-distant ties weaken, with far-reaching consequences; and the balance of rights and obligations between parents and children shifts in favor of children. (In much of Europe and Asia, however, there is increasing evidence that a considerable degree of nuclear family autonomy existed before the onset of economic development.) A different sort of attitudinal change is seen in the expanding domain of decision making itself. The range of matters thought to call for individual or parental deliberation rather than a simple following of custom or belief is widened, with contraception and fertility decisions prominent among those newly emphasized.

Impact on fertility. What can be said about the net impact on fertility of these various kinds of changes in setting? In general, very little. More of them are likely to be antinatalist than pronatalist in their effect, but the balance cannot safely be judged in a particular instance without many more details of the situation than are usually at hand. In part the problem lies in the very different constellations of forces that bear on fertility at different economic levels within any society. For example, widening economic opportunities for richer families and deteriorating conditions of life for the poor may each increase the burden of children that their respective parents feel. An opposite, upward pressure on fertility among the higher-income groups may result from acceptance of the "modern" practice of early weaning, while at the lowest income levels the prevailing high infant mortality rates are linked both biologically and socially to high fertility. Another factor militating against prediction of the course of fertility as development proceeds might follow from the increasingly deliberate control that parents exercise over fertility. Plausibly, the socially enmeshed valuations of the various components of the reproductive process in preindustrial society are less volatile than the private valuations that have tended to supplant them.

Further Reading. A valuable bibliographic essay on population and development, not to be quickly outdated, was prepared by Cassen (1976). Cassen sets out the main findings of and controversies among researchers and provides a judicious critical commentary on them. Not critical, but virtually encyclopedic in scope, is the revised edition of the United Nations study of the determinants and consequences of population trends (United Nations, 1973), a new version of a work that when it first appeared (1953) stood nearly alone in the field. Collections of review essays that aspire to cover most of the subject and also have bibliographic value are U.S. National Academy of Sciences (1971) and Tabah (1975); Hawthorn (1978) and Hauser (1979) are more idiosyncratic than these but address certain new research directions. The quarterly journal *Population and Development Review* endeavors cumulatively to span the field in a style that avoids disciplinary jargon and unnecessary technicalities.

A large-scale effort to assess the accomplishments and needs of population and development research from the standpoint of policy value was mounted by the International Review Group of Social Science Research on Population and Development, an *ad hoc* body of population experts established in 1976. A particular feature of the Group's Final Report (Miró and Potter, 1980) and the twelve lengthy, separately issued appendixes to it, is the emphasis given to variation of population and development issues and research findings across major world regions.

Most recent investigations of population and development interrelations have been cast as applied economics, drawing especially on the assumptions and analytical techniques of microeconomics. Ridker (1976) gives an array of such studies; Easterlin (1980) is a more eclectic collection. A broader economic approach is taken in the monograph by Simon (1977), whose conclusions, however, are controversial. Studies not proceeding from an economic orientation are comparatively few; Goldscheider (1971) is a significant example. In the case of migration, a structural approach that complements the economic theory mentioned earlier is set out in Piore (1979).

The historical record of demographic change and development is the empirical base against which knowledge of subject can be measured. Important historical studies of aspects of population and development include Clark (1977), Glass and Revelle (1972), Kuznets (1979), McKeown (1976), Preston (1976), and Tilly (1978).

Geoffrey McNicoll

See also FERTILITY DETERMINANTS, *article on* SOCIOLOGICAL AND ECONOMIC THEORIES, *in which can be found a discussion of how the disciplines of sociology and economics construct frameworks for understanding the determinants of fertility. Also related are* FERTILITY AND MIGRATION; FERTILITY DECLINE, *article on* THEORIES; RESOURCES AND POPULATION.

BIBLIOGRAPHY

Cassen, Robert H. "Population and Development: A Survey." *World Development* 4(10/11):785–830, October/November 1976.

Clark, Colin. *Population Growth and Land Use.* 2d ed. London: Macmillan, 1977.

Easterlin, Richard A. (editor). *Population and Economic Change in Developing Countries.* Chicago: University of Chicago Press, 1980.

Glass, David V., and Roger Revelle (editors). *Population and Social Change.* London: Edward Arnold, 1972.

Goldscheider, Calvin. *Population, Modernization and Social Structure.* Boston: Little, Brown, 1971.

Hauser, Philip M. (editor). *World Population and Development: Challenges and Prospects.* Syracuse, N.Y.: Syracuse University Press, 1979.

Hawthorn, Geoffrey (editor). *Population and Development.* London: Frank Cass, 1978.

Kuznets, Simon. *Growth, Population and Income Distribution.* New York: Norton, 1979.

McKeown, Thomas. *The Modern Rise of Population.* New York: Academic Press, 1976.

Miró, Carmen A., and Joseph E. Potter. *Population Policy: Research Priorities in the Developing World.* London: Frances Pinter, 1980.

Piore, Michael J. *Birds of Passage: Migrant Labor and Industrial Societies.* Cambridge: Cambridge University Press, 1979.

Population and Development Review. Issued quarterly since 1975 by the Population Council, New York.

Preston, Samuel H. *Mortality Patterns in National Populations: With Special Reference to Recorded Causes of Death.* New York: Academic Press, 1976.

Ridker, Ronald G. (editor). *Population and Development: The Search for Selective Interventions.* Baltimore: Johns Hopkins University Press, 1976.

Simon, Julian. *The Economics of Population Growth.* Princeton, N.J.: Princeton University Press, 1977.

Tabah, Léon (editor). *Population Growth and Economic Development in the Third World.* 2 vols. Dolhain, Belgium: Ordina Editions, 1975.

Tilly, Charles (editor). *Historical Studies of Changing Fertility.* Princeton, N.J.: Princeton University Press, 1978.

Todaro, Michael P. *Internal Migration in Developing Countries: A Review of Theory, Evidence, Methodology, and Research Priorities.* Geneva: International Labour Organisation, 1976.

United Nations, Department of Economic and Social Affairs. *The Determinants and Consequences of Population Trends.* Rev. ed. Volume 1: *New Summary of Findings on Interaction of Demographic, Economic, and Social Factors.* Series A, Population Studies, no. 50. New York, 1973.

United States, National Academy of Sciences, Study Committee of the Office of the Foreign Secretary. *Rapid Population Growth: Consequences and Policy Implications.* 2 vols. Baltimore: Johns Hopkins Press, 1971.

POPULATION ASSISTANCE

See INTERNATIONAL POPULATION ASSISTANCE.

POPULATION ASSOCIATION OF AMERICA

The Population Association of America (PAA) is a scientific and professional society of individuals and organizations interested in the determinants and consequences of population trends. Established in 1931, it had in 1980 approximately 2,700 members, primarily in the United States. Members, most of whom are found in academic institutions or in government employ, are active in general demography, family planning, and population policy. Interests of the members range from the production of demographic statistics including population estimates and projection to analysis of the interrelationships between population and social and economic trends and conditions.

The PAA's purposes, as set forth in its certificate of incorporation, are "to promote the improvement, advancement, and progress of the human race by means of research with respect to problems connected with human population, in both its quantitative and qualitative aspects, and the dissemination and publication of the results of such research." The association's annual scientific meeting serves as a forum for the presentation of professional research papers on a wide variety of population-related subjects. Publications include the quarterly *Demography,* the professional journal for American demographers, and a quarterly newsletter, *PAA Affairs.* In 1935, the association initiated a bibliographic journal, which is now the quarterly *Population Index,* published jointly by the association and the Office of Population Research, Princeton University.

The PAA is governed by a board of directors, which consists of twelve elected directors (four elected each year for three-year terms), the officers of the association (president, president-elect, first vice-president, second vice-president, and secretary-treasurer), and the immediate past president. The board meets at the association's annual meeting and on at least one other occasion each year; the functions of the board are performed between meetings by an executive committee consisting of the officers of the association. The association's offices are in Washington, D.C.

Much of the association's work on behalf of the profession is done through its standing committees. These include the Public Affairs Committee, which seeks to increase understanding among members of Congress and within the executive branch of the federal government of the role of demographic factors in public programs and policies, and to ensure support for population research. The Committee on Population Statistics reviews statistical activities at federal and state levels relative to the scope and timeliness of data being collected and provisions for their release and dissemination. PAA maintains liaison with the American Association for the Advancement of Science and is a member of the Federal Statistical Users' Conference. It was instrumental in founding the Committee of Professional Associations on Federal Statistics and is represented on the Technical Advisory Committee of the U.S. Bureau of the Census. Other committees, whose purposes are suggested by their names, are the Committee on State and Local Demography and the Committee on Exchanges with China.

PAA maintains an open membership policy with several classes of membership. It remained a relatively small organization until the postwar years when scientific, official, and popular attention to the field brought about a significant expansion of the organization both in terms of its size and disciplinary backgrounds of its members.

John Frederick Kantner

BIBLIOGRAPHY

Notestein, Frank W. "Reminiscences: The Role of Foundations, the Population Association of America, Princeton University, and the United Nations in Fostering American Interest in Population Problems." *Milbank Memorial Fund Quarterly* 49(4, pt. 2): 67–85, October 1971.
Population Association of America. *1980 Directory of Members: Population Association of America.* Washington, D.C., 1981.

POPULATION COMPOSITION

See COMPOSITION.

POPULATION EDUCATION

See EDUCATION, *article on* POPULATION EDUCATION.

POPULATION GROWTH

See FERTILITY AND POPULATION GROWTH; MOMENTUM; PROJECTIONS; WORLD POPULATION.

POPULATION MODELS

The application of models is not new in the field of population: regression analysis, structural equations and econometric models, dynamic feedback, linear programming and gaming methods, macrosimulation and microsimulation, Markov chains, stable population, and analytical methods have all been used. With the critical importance assumed by population problems, the variety of such models and their policy applications have grown rapidly.

Global and regional models have been used to project population growth and its components, as well as natural resources, over the next thirty years or more, so as to anticipate emerging problems and identify limiting factors. In planning economic development, many countries have used macromodels to study the impact of population size, distribution, and composition on economic growth, standards of living, school-age population, labor force, and productivity. Linear programming models have been developed for setting targets and allocating resources within family planning programs. Microsimulation has been used to study the interplay of demographic variables with family planning programs. Operations research techniques have been applied to increase the efficiency of clinics, and gaming models have been used to train family planning program managers. A host of analytical models have contributed to a better understanding of the demographic impact of contraception and family planning programs, the effects of different mixes of contraceptive methods and continuation rates, and the interactions between demographic variables and contraceptive practice. Thus, a wide range of problems has been studied using suitable models.

Classification, Scope, and Applicability. In general, models used in population topics can be classified under four main headings. (1) Structural equations describe the relationships among a set of interacting variables, along with some exogenous factors. They require estimates of parameters involved and permit projection of the variables into the future. (2) Macromodels are deterministic and not subject to random fluctuations. They also involve estimation of parameters independently of the model, and they forecast variables for future time periods on the basis of different assumptions. (3) Microsimulation techniques differ from macrosimulation because the events for each "individual" are simulated stochastically by using a probability mechanism. While this calls for a greater input of information in terms of probability distributions, the output provides a measure of random fluctuations in the estimates. (4) Analytical models are a kind of residual category, consisting mostly of mathematical models used in formal demography.

The scope and applicability of a model are dictated by its inputs and outputs. The inputs may be policy alternatives (or action strategies), values of the parameters, current values of the exogenous variables, and prior values of the endogenous variables. The outputs may include the current and projected values of the endogenous variables and, in any policy analysis, should typically reflect measures of effectiveness of the policy.

Models may differ significantly in their scope, as regards space, time, and comprehensiveness. The actual "geographic coverage," such as a particular country or locality, and the potential coverage, reflecting transferability to other areas, have to be considered. The "time span" of the model should reflect both the actual and potential time range of application. The "systems scale" relates to whether the model applies to a country, a region, or a clinic and whether the problem narrowly concerns family planning or broader aspects of the demographic-socioeconomic system.

The potential objectives of models vary widely. Examples include an examination of factors limiting the growth of the world ecosystem; the relations between population growth and economic development; the interaction of social, demographic, and biological factors affecting human reproduction; the interplay of strictly demographic factors; the optimum allocation of resources to family planning programs; and the efficient operation of family planning clinics. The methods used are equally varied. These range from regression, path analysis, economic models, and dynamic and linear programming, to analytical models, simulation, and games. The scale of the studies also shows a large range, from the world ecosystem, the demographic-economic system of a country, or women of reproductive age in a community, to the detailed operations of a single clinic.

Actual use of the models in policy formulation and decision making has been uneven so far. The Club of Rome instituted widely publicized global studies of the "limits to growth" of the ecosystem (Meadows et al., 1972). The model of the Indian demographic-economic system formulated by Ansley J. Coale and Edgar M. Hoover (1958) had perhaps some impact on India's Second Five-year Plan. The TEMPO demographic-socioeconomic model has been tried for various countries, including the Philippines, Puerto Rico, Bangladesh, and Taiwan, to compare strategies of family planning for the reduction of unwanted births, with some applications of planning (TEMPO, 1970). Models have been used to compare the relative efficiency of family planning programs among the states of India (Jain, 1971). A linear programming model was used in Honduras to assess the feasibility of reducing the birth rate with a ceiling on the resources committed to the program (Lawrence, Mundigo, and Revelle, 1972). The use of a simulation model in Atlanta by family planning program managers increased their awareness of the importance of continued use of contraceptives and the use of more effective contraceptive methods to reduce unwanted pregnancies (Urban, 1972).

Analytical and simulation models used in research have also indirectly influenced the choice of family planning strategies. For instance, simulation by FERMOD, a computer model of family building based on expected values, and other models has drawn attention to the importance of using extremely effective contraception if the individual woman is to avoid unwanted pregnancies over a long period, since contraceptive effect rises exponentially with the effectiveness of the method used. By contrast, even ineffective methods of contraception, when practiced widely, appear to reduce the prevailing crude birth rate. Microsimulation of fertility and family planning may well provide a means for carrying out, in the computer, "controlled experiments" of various strategies of family planning and forecasts of the likely effects of measures that go beyond family planning.

Policy Uses of Models. Population models have been used to resolve policy issues at three levels.

1. At the level of socioeconomic or development policy, population issues are viewed as significant decision variables, used to aid broader socioeconomic and development objectives, such as economic growth and improvement in quality of life. In such models population parameters are typically treated as policy variables.

2. At the level of population policy and planning, models are still strategic in character but are narrower in their policy objectives. Population parameters are taken as the goals, and family planning and other program inputs (resource allocations, program strategies, tactics, and design) are the principal decision variables.

3. At the level of organization and administration of family planning programs, the concern is for such matters as tactics of programs, efficiency of service-delivery systems, and management and operation of clinics. Both decision and policy variables relate to family planning programs.

The comparative examination of empirical models reveals their inadequacies in providing a single comprehensive policy model to aid in solving population problems. While many of the attempts at model building yield serendipitous findings of policy import, they are mostly addressed to scientific issues that typically are not of immediate policy relevance. As may be expected from the divergence of research and policy objectives, a model for either purpose cannot be readily used for the other.

Features to Be Considered. Policy models have to be developed systematically by formulating their specifications in terms of their intended purposes. There are a few essential requirements for such models.

Time span, lead time, and impact time. The time horizon of the policy or decisions is a basic consideration in the choice of the model. The variables, structure, and interactions that are modeled should be relevant to whether the policy issue is short-term or long-term and should span the lead time necessary to implement the policy or to have the desired impact on the system. For instance, implementing a large-scale family planning program may take two to three years while it may take much longer for it to have an impact on fertility.

Range of multiple factors. The process of development is too complex to be dealt with in terms of a single and sovereign factor. While the multiplicity of factors that affect development may be readily conceded, the authority to make decisions may be broad or narrow. The objectives of policy may likewise be comprehensive or limited. A government's planning commission may be concerned with the whole spectrum of economic development and social change, but its ministry of health may formulate and implement plans only regarding health and family planning matters. The model has to be tailored to the range of policy objectives, whether it be the interplay of demographic variables only or the broader demographic-socioeconomic nexus.

Causality. Unlike scientific research, in policy models causality is of importance only insofar as it provides alternative courses of action, alternative instruments of policy, or suggests priorities. In modeling for policy, the nature of the relationship between every pair of input variables has to be understood. Are the two factors "independent" in the model? If they are, can they be manipulated separately? Improvement in the public health system by control of infectious and contagious diseases has operated more or less independently of any major social change whereas reduction in infant mortality is more closely tied with the level of living and education of the parents. Dramatic reductions in the general mortality level have been secured in many regions of the world in the last twenty years because of public health measures even in the absence of significant socioeconomic development. Perhaps we cannot expect similar reductions in infant mortality without any change in the level of living. This has implications when either factor is an objective of policy.

Differentiation and inequality. Variability, differentiation, inequality of distribution, and heterogeneity in human communities are sometimes used as instruments of growth and development; sometimes their control is the objective of policy. In either circumstance, the model should include such elements since they provide policy instruments or have impact on policy objectives.

Biological, social, and economic growth or change models emphasize variability and differentiation as contributory to development of complex organization. Cyclic theories of growth anticipate a broadening of differentials during growth with a narrowing of differentials as the system tends to a stable climax. The historic trends in fertility differentials in the West have been explained by similar hypotheses. In these models inequality is regarded as a necessary concomitant to growth.

Aggregation and disaggregation. The purpose of a policy model is to analyze the consequences of different paths of action for the objectives and not to explain individual behavior. Groups of individuals may well serve as the unit of analysis so long as the policy consequences can be forecast. Such a model is certainly no substitute for an analysis on the individual level, for we may not be able to infer the attitudes or behavior of individuals from it.

The aggregate model need not be a statistical collection of individual level models. Certain facets of individual behavior may cancel out in the aggregate while other factors such as heterogeneity and differentiation may appear.

Disaggregation of the policy model is necessary to the extent that the policy or its consequences may be differentiated for various segments of the population. Such disaggregation is usually secured by separating the rural from the urban sector, by identifying socioeconomic classes, and so forth. Classical demography disaggregates by age groups since reproductive potentials change with age and the process of building the family is cyclical.

Uncertainty. There are many uncertainties associated with a policy model. There are uncertainties about external or exogeneous variables in the environment; about the relationships and structure of the model; about the data used for estimation of parameters. Uncertainty is permissible to the extent that it does not alter the policy outcome of the model.

The cultural and political environment are strongly limiting on the national decision maker. For this reason, there cannot be universal policy models applicable to all countries; at best, there can only be regional models. Even these have to be adapted to suit the particular country and context.

Sensitivity and robustness. A model is sensitive to a particular factor if small alterations in it are likely to result in amplified effects on the objectives. By contrast, the model is robust with respect to information inputs if large variations in them do not affect policy conclusions significantly. The perfect model, while able to identify those policy instruments to which the objectives are sensitive, should be robust with regard to data errors. For instance, if fertility reduction is the objective, the model should be able to identify which are the most sensitive factors: increase in age at marriage, decrease in the proportion married, decrease in marital fertility, and so forth. Allocation of resources among family planning, female education, and encouragement of females to participate in the labor force will depend to a large extent on the relative sensitivity of these factors as revealed by the model.

Policy models for developing countries have to be robust with regard to the parameters and information inputs since such countries rarely have reliable statistical systems. Most of them do conduct population censuses periodically, though the quality of response is often limited by the level of education and modernization of the people. For this reason, policy models which require detailed or precise data may carry too high a degree of uncertainty to be useful.

A policy model should be evaluated in terms of its ability to choose the "best" policy among the available alternatives. Such an evaluation should, therefore, be done not only on the basis of statistical predictability from past period data, but also in terms of considerations just mentioned, such as time span, lead and impact times, range of multiple factors involved, causality, heterogeneity and differentiation within the population, aggregation and disaggregation, degree of uncertainty, and the sensitivity and robustness of the model.

Types of Models. To adapt a model for policy uses, its relative strengths and weaknesses for any specific application have to be assessed. The four types of models mentioned earlier differ considerably in these respects.

Models using structural equations. Models using simultaneous structural equations have been developed for Costa Rica, the Philippines, Taiwan, and other countries. Such models use, for short-term forecast, cross-sectional data for a wide range of interacting causal factors, with reciprocal or chained links, since the basic structure may not remain unchanged in the long run. These models can be disaggregated as needed, subject to data availability, and the unit of analysis is flexible depending on the type of questions raised.

Macromodels. Deterministic or macromodels have generally been used for studying long-run, limiting, and stable conditions. The model may be strictly demographic or demographic-socioeconomic, and it is usually at the national or world level. Dynamic interplay of various factors is accounted for. Since the perspective is both long-term and aggregative, the variables are usually limited to a few gross indicators; if they are "exogenous" (not determined by the interactions within the system) their values over time are also required. With such a long-run perspective, no measure of random variation is needed, nor are disaggregated or detailed output factors.

An illustration of a macromodel with dynamic feedback chains is the study of the "limits to growth" concept by Donella H. Meadows and colleagues (1972). This model was formulated to forecast limiting factors to world growth in the long run. The basic indicators included natural resources, food per capita, population, industrial output per capita, pollution, and birth and death rates. The dynamic growth relationships were specified numerically in terms of several difference equations. A major finding was that to achieve ecological equilibrium, it is necessary to curb both economic and population growth. Population growth was found to be more sensitive to number of children desired than to the effectiveness of birth control. The results received widespread attention, but they have been criticized extensively on methodological grounds.

Microsimulation models. Experiments with stochastic microsimulation (the Monte Carlo method) indicate that it can be fruitfully employed for forecasting short-run outputs from various inputs specified in terms of joint probability distributions. Disaggregation is possible to a limited extent, and stochastic uncertainties can be estimated. Multiple inputs can be used, but the needed data inputs unfortunately grow geometrically with the number of variables. Causal relationships are reflected in the joint probability distributions. This method is not well suited for long-run modeling because of the detailed inputs and outputs, unforeseeable changes in probability distributions over time (or the dubious assumption of their constancy), and the diminishing importance of "random errors" over the long run.

Analytical models. Analytical models are a residual group containing a variety of methods. These are usually formulated to examine stable or limiting conditions over the long run. The variables are often limited to a few that are closely interlinked, and they are sometimes made to conform to theoretical formulations. The "stable population" is a widely known example of this group (United Nations, 1968).

K. Sivaswamy Srikantan

For further discussion of applications of models, see FERTILITY AND DEVELOPMENT; INDIRECT ESTIMATION OF FERTILITY AND MORTALITY; INTERNAL MIGRATION, article on MODELS; RESOURCES AND POPULATION. *For discussion of theories that underlie the development of models, see* FERTILITY DECLINE; POPULATION THEORY. *See also* POPULATION POLICY.

BIBLIOGRAPHY

Coale, Ansley J., and Edgar M. Hoover. *Population Growth and Economic Development in Low Income Countries: A Case Study of India's Prospects.* Princeton, N.J.: Princeton University Press, 1958.

Jain, Sagar C. *Comparative Study of Effective and Non-effective Family Planning Programs in India: Report of the Feasibility Study Design.* Chapel Hill, N.C.: Carolina Population Center, 1971.

Kruskal, William H., and Judith M. Tanur (editors). *International Encyclopedia of Statistics.* 2 vols. New York: Free Press, 1978. Includes numerous articles relevant to population models; see under "demography," "models," and "population" in the index.

Lawrence, Charles E., Axel I. Mundigo, and Charles S. Revelle. "A Mathematical Model for Resource Allocation in Population Problems." *Demography* 9(3):465–483, 1972.

Meadows, Donella H., Dennis L. Meadows, Jørgen Randers, and William W. Behrens, III. *The Limits to Growth: A Report for the Club of Rome's Project on the Predicament of Mankind.* A Potomac Associates Book. New York: Universe Books, 1972.

Potter, Robert G., and James M. Sakoda. "A Computer Model of Family Building Based on Expected Values." *Demography* 3(2):450–461, 1966.

Srikantan, K. Sivaswamy, and Alfred Blumstein. "Policy Applications of Population Models: A Comparative Review." *Socio-economic Planning Sciences* 11(1):1–11, 1977.

TEMPO, General Electric's Center for Advanced Studies. *Description of the Economic-Demographic Model.* Prepared for U.S. Agency for International Development. Santa Barbara, Calif., 1970.

United Nations, Department of Economic and Social Affairs. *The Concept of a Stable Population: Application to the Study of Populations of Countries with Incomplete Demographic Statistics.* Series A, Population Studies, no. 39. New York, 1968.

Urban, G. L. "A Model for the Management of Family Planning Systems." Working Paper No. 613. Cambridge, Mass.: Sloan School of Management, Massachusetts Institute of Technology, 1972.

POPULATION POLICY

1. Overview   J. Mayone Stycos
2. United States   Michael S. Teitelbaum

1.
OVERVIEW

Rates of birth, death, migration, and population growth have concerned governments from the earliest times, but the concept of a population policy specifically designed to change demographic behavior is of relatively recent origin. While the objectives of population policies in contemporary developing nations tend to reflect concern for excessively rapid population growth, any historical lessons must be derived from European experience, where concern for declining population rates have dominated policies.

European experience, while of interest for developing countries, should not be taken as a standard. In most instances such policies as do exist have lacked clear goals, strong convictions, and consistent programs. Moreover, by the time most European countries began to think seriously about altering declining growth rates, a century or two of slow but profound social and demographic change had passed. Most European countries were, therefore, reacting to the late stages of the demographic transition and, in introducing policies to raise or sustain fertility, were trying to turn back the clock. There are several reasons why many developing countries today are in a much better position to introduce successful policies to slow population growth, or even to sustain it at high levels.

First, most developing countries are at an early stage of the demographic transition—mortality rates are falling, but fertility is still high. At the same time, the most powerful processes of modernization—urbanization, industrialization, and education—are also in their early stages. This may be an ideal moment for introducing policies designed to affect rates of growth, for such policies can be directed at accelerating or retarding a recent or imminent trend. From this advantageous moment, policies aimed at effecting declines in fertility rates will be swimming with the tide if social and economic modernization is taking place. On the other hand, policies designed to sustain high birth rates will not yet be swimming against a very powerful tide.

A second advantage developing countries have today is that they may profit from the extraordinary store of knowledge on population accumulated in the past two or three decades, far more than was available to developed countries when they initiated their attempts to alter population trends three or four decades ago. Since 1950 the

Population Index has been classifying about 4,500 items per year, or well over 100,000 books and articles on population in the last twenty-five years.

Further, although the demographic data available in the developing countries have been less than satisfactory, their collection and analysis have been improving rapidly in recent years. Whereas seventy-three countries failed to conduct a national census in the ten-year period 1945–1954, only thirty failed to do so in the period 1965–1974. Vital statistics data have also improved greatly, especially since the widespread introduction of sample surveys. Annual natality and mortality data are now available for about three-quarters of the African, two-thirds of the Asian, and one-half of the South American populations. The availability of computers and the development of analytic techniques to assist in the elaboration and interpretation of deficient data have provided scientific tools for assisting in the development of population policy that scarcely existed two or three decades ago.

The number of technically trained personnel also increased dramatically throughout the 1960s. For example, the Centro Latinoamericano de Demografía (CELADE) in Santiago, Chile, and the International Institute for Population Studies, Bombay, initiated training activities in 1957; the Cairo Demographic Centre did so in 1963 and the Accra, Ghana, and Yaoundé, Cameroon, institutes in 1972. By 1972, the three older centers had awarded 776 first-grade and 191 second-grade diplomas.

A third advantage possessed by the developing countries today is the concept or spirit of development, the conviction that the state can and should use national policies to improve individual well-being. Although rates of economic growth in developing countries since World War II have been slower than many had hoped, real progress has been achieved in the recent past, and much of the credit has been given to development planning.

If planning for development is a new concept, serious planning for population growth is even newer. Population variables traditionally tended to be exempted from the planning process; they were taken as parameters or givens rather than as targets for planned intervention.

In the 1960s, however, the international community increasingly stressed the need to take demographic variables into consideration and to make them subject to deliberate interventions by the state. As early as 1962, the United Nations General Assembly recognized the close interrelation of economic development and population growth and advised member states "in formulating . . . economic and social policies . . . to take into account the latest relevant facts on the interrelationship of population growth and economic and social development" (United Nations, 1963).

In 1966 the General Assembly recommended "further

study of the implications of the growth, structure, and geographical distribution of population for economic and social development, [including] programmes carried out at all levels of government activity" (United Nations, 1967). When, on Human Rights Day in 1966, twelve heads of state announced that "the population problem must be recognized as a principal element in long-range national planning," they in effect signaled that population variables were in line for intervention just like other economic and social variables. In 1970 the United Nations Economic and Social Council approved this concept when it announced that the World Population Conference would be devoted to "consideration of basic demographic problems, their relationship with economic and social development, and population policies and action programs needed to promote human welfare and development." Soon after, a policy unit was added to the United Nations Population Division. By the mid-1970s even representatives of regions traditionally hostile to the notion of demographic planning were advocating population policies. Thus, a report of the Economic Commission for Latin America (ECLA) speaks of the "unquestionable . . . need for a consistent body of policies oriented by a general strategy of development, and destined to attack from its roots the problems of population growth neither planned nor desired, and of concentration of wealth and spread of poverty" (United Nations, ECLA, 1975*b*, p. 648).

At the national level, probably more governments today recognize the existence of population problems than at any previous point in history. In response to a United Nations questionnaire prior to the 1974 World Population Conference, 25 of 89 developing countries reported that they considered their rates of population growth to be excessive. A considerably larger number were concerned about excessive growth in their metropolitan areas. In a review of 70 development plans, B. Maxwell Stamper (1973) found that problems of population growth or age structure were mentioned in 27 plans: 19 mentioned population growth as a deterrent to economic growth, 18 mentioned it in connection with problems of unemployment, and 16 with respect to its impact on educational requirements. Dorothy L. Nortman and Ellen Hofstatter (1980) show that of 132 developing countries, 35 had an official policy to reduce the population growth rate in 1979. The combined population of these countries comprised over three quarters of the developing world. Another 31 countries were supporting family planning programs without explicit demographic objectives. Thus, at the official level there is a growing consensus among nations that demographic problems are important enough to merit policies to deal with them.

Defining Population Policy. What constitutes a policy, and what are the ingredients of a good one? "Policy" may be defined as a statement of important goals, accompanied by a specified set of means to achieve them. A well-elaborated set of means constitutes a program. Good policy embodies a theory linking ends and means in such a way that human behavior is influenced. From a technical point of view, the clearer the statement of the ends and the better the theory linking the means with the ends, the better the policy. The ends need to be clear enough to be translatable into program targets, and the means adopted need to be able to achieve the specified targets. Thus policy must be based on scientific input—on testable propositions about causes and effects—but it also requires value judgments. The administrator or political leader chooses between alternative courses of action not only in terms of their impact on the goal, but also in terms of their legitimacy, cost, potential popularity, and effects on other goals, among other things.

It is consistent with this view to exclude from population policy those governmental actions that influence demographic trends without intending to. As a minimum, policy makers must be aware of these events or actions and their relation to population variables. If they are seeking to sustain the national birthrate and are unaware that the Health Ministry's antivenereal disease program is helping to raise fertility, they can hardly include the health program as part of their population policy, regardless of how much it affects the goal they are trying to achieve. The more sophisticated the policy, the greater the range of variables, demographic and nondemographic, that will be controlled or at least taken into account. Unlike a theory, a policy is not a guide to understanding the world but to controlling it. The mere identification of actions that influence population does not make them part of policy.

Knowledge and Policy. On the other hand, if theory without policy is for academics, policy without theory is only for gamblers. Does the policy maker today have enough theory available? The impressive recent increases in demographic knowledge, techniques, and technical manpower have already been described. But a complicating factor is that many developing countries now want to integrate population policies with broader development policies. Both at the level of ends and at the level of means, they want solutions for population problems more tightly embedded in the broader strategies of development. At the same time, recent advances in demographic analysis have made it apparent that demographic behavior is subject to more complex causation than was previously realized. That the policy makers and the theorists are tending in the same direction (i.e., viewing population in a broader, more complex framework) may be intellectually pleasing, but it is small comfort to the population planner who wants to get on with the job. Therefore heavier investments in policy research are very much needed. They are possible now because the data base has improved so markedly; they are timely because governments increasingly are recognizing the need for complex population policies. Demographic knowledge over the past two decades has directly concerned population policies. In fact, the policies section of *Population Index* constituted only 3.2 percent of all citations in 1975. This is only slightly higher than the 1960 figure of 2.9 and lower than the 1965 figure of 3.7 percent. In addition to quantity, there is the question of the quality of the research. A summary of the research pattern in Latin America would probably describe the situation in many countries in other regions as well: "Throughout the 1960s, social research institutes and centres tended to limit themselves to demography in the strictest sense, for the most part leaving the study of the relationship between population and development and of policy design to social doctrinists, whose main source of inspiration was the ideological controversy concerning the nature of the social order and the role of Latin American countries in the world system" (United Nations, ECLA, 1975a, p. 657).

The Commitment to Population Policy. In general, despite the wide publicity given to population policies, governments do not have a very profound commitment to this area. Bernard Berelson has summarized the situation in the developed countries as follows: "Population is a concern of most of these countries . . . but at the same time it does not rank very high on the agenda of national problems. It is more given than problematic, more to be adjusted to than changed. Moreover, it seems unlikely that population problems will gain enough priority in these countries over the next years to produce a fully consistent policy position based exclusively or largely on demographic considerations" (1974, p. 786).

In the developing countries, the degree of commitment to population policies should be reflected in national development plans. In his review of seventy such plans, Stamper found that "most countries used very little demographic data in their plans. . . . Most countries did not plan for the consequences of short-term population growth . . . most plans focused on current needs and shortages without looking at projected future needs, and they often did not view the demographic components of these shortages as partial causes" (1973, pp. 4–5).

Even the World Plan of Action adopted at Bucharest in 1974 seems to reflect ambivalence about population policy. Continual insistence that such policies are a sovereign *right* only highlights the absence of references to the responsibility of countries to formulate policies. Moreover, whenever this right to formulate policy is men-

tioned, it is hedged with qualifications about "outside interference" and about consistency with "basic human rights and national goals and values."

Without doubt, the suddenness with which population has emerged as an important variable, the prominence it has achieved, and its advocacy as a subject for policy by developed countries have caused suspicion in the international community. Whatever the cause, the signs of ambivalence are clear and can affect the degree of commitment to population policies.

There are other signs that commitment may not be deep. In 1974 the U.S. National Academy of Sciences held a series of regional conferences on population policies in the developing nations. In summarizing the results, the Academy noted that "none of the countries represented has any significant political parties actively pressing for the adoption of policies explicitly intended to affect demographic behavior" (1974, p. 101). A recent paper on population by the Economic Commission for Latin America (United Nations, ECLA, 1975a, p. 676) noted that "State action has often taken place without there being any real consensus." The absence of consensus and political commitment and the suspicions revolving around international tensions have contributed to the low priority often given to population policies, even in some of the countries that adopt them.

The most important nonpolitical step toward increasing commitment would be to demonstrate to national leaders that population variables are critical in the development process, that their course can be altered without distorting other aspects of development, and that a well-elaborated policy is a necessary step. Such demonstration will require that greater resources be allocated to research on policy.

Most international population assistance currently goes to family planning programs and to biomedical research. Of the $186 million distributed for population in 1972, only around $17 million could be categorized as demographic, and within that category only a minimal amount had policy application. There has since been little change in these proportions. [*See* INTERNATIONAL POPULATION ASSISTANCE.]

Research alone will not be enough; nor should governments use the absence of research as an excuse to delay experimentation in this area. In fact, a willingness to experiment with different patterns of programming in combination with carefully defined research and evaluation will produce the most useful results. The complexities of the development process and the intricate ways in which demographic factors influence and are influenced by other elements in the development process call for greater experimentation in the programming area—but experimentation that is systematically monitored, measured, and evaluated. A combination of stepped-up basic and applied research on policies and more vigorous efforts to communicate the results of such research to policy makers should not only intensify their commitment, but increase their ability to control demographic growth and its consequences.

Indeed, for most nations today, a population policy is more of a necessity than a luxury, for, as well put by Alva Myrdal, "A nation without a conscious (population and family) policy leaves to chance and mischance an area of social reality of the utmost importance, which in consequence will be exposed to the untransmitted impact of policies arising in other areas."

J. Mayone Stycos

See also DISTRIBUTION, *article on* DISTRIBUTION POLICY; LAW AND FERTILITY REGULATION.

BIBLIOGRAPHY

Berelson, Bernard. "Summary." In *Population Policy in Developed Countries,* edited by Bernard Berelson, pp. 771–789. New York: McGraw-Hill, 1974.

Nortman, Dorothy L., and Ellen Hofstatter. *Population and Family Planning Programs: A Compendium of Data through 1978.* 10th ed. New York: Population Council, 1980.

Pearson, Lester B. (editor). *Partners in Development: Report of the Commission on International Development.* New York: Praeger, 1969.

Stamper, B. Maxwell. "Population Policy in Development Planning: A Study of Seventy Less Developed Countries." *Reports on Population/Family Planning,* no. 13, whole issue, May 1973.

United Nations, Department of Economic and Social Affairs. *The Population Debate: Dimensions and Perspectives; Papers of the World Population Conference, Bucharest, 1974.* 2 vols. Series A, Population Studies, no. 57 and no. 57–add. 1. New York, 1975. In English, French, and Spanish.

United Nations, Economic Commission for Latin America. "Population and Modernization in Latin America." In *The Population Debate: Dimensions and Perspectives,* vol. 1, pp. 656–676. New York: United Nations, 1975. (United Nations, ECLA, 1975*a*)

————. "Tendencias demográficas, desarrollo y distribución del ingreso en América Latina." In *The Population Debate: Dimensions and Perspectives,* vol. 1, pp. 648–655. New York: United Nations, 1975. (United Nations, ECLA, 1975*b*)

United Nations, General Assembly. "Population Growth and Economic Development." Resolution 1838 (XVII), 18 December 1962. In *Resolutions Adopted by the General Assembly during Its Seventeenth Session, 18 September–20 December 1962.* New York, 1963.

————. "Population Growth and Economic Development." Resolution 2211 (XXI), 17 December 1966. In *Resolutions Adopted by the General Assembly during Its Twenty-first Session, 20 September–20 December 1966.* New York, 1967.

United States, National Academy of Sciences. *In Search of Population Policy: Views from the Developing World.* Washington, D.C., 1974.

2.

UNITED STATES

Like most developed countries, the United States has never elaborated an explicit policy regarding population growth and distribution. It does, however, have a set of policies and programs that cumulatively amount to a policy on population and that can be analyzed as such.

At the beginning of the 1980s the United States was experiencing record low levels of fertility and mortality rates, high levels of net immigration, and, in comparison with other developed countries, quite high rates of natural increase and population growth. Fertility levels as measured by the general fertility rate have been fluctuating in recent years in the range of 65–70 births per 1,000 women aged 15–44. The total fertility rate has been fluctuating around 1.8 children per woman. The crude birth rate is on the order of 15–16 births per 1,000 population, rising slightly as a result of the increasing number of women of reproductive age.

The mortality rate, too, is at record lows. Indeed, declines in the mortality rate have been more rapid than anticipated in the population projections of the U.S. Bureau of the Census, necessitating revisions of the life table estimates for future projections. The infant mortality rate is on the order of 12–13 per 1,000 live births; expectation of life approximates 70 years for males and 77 years for females, and the crude death rate is between 8 and 9 per 1,000.

The U.S. population is heavily affected by both internal and international migration. The population is a highly mobile one, with one in six households changing residence each year. In recent years internal migration has generally tended to flow away from the industrial northeast and north central states and toward the southwest and southeast. People have also tended to migrate toward nonmetropolitan areas.

At the same time, the United States receives a larger number of international migrants and refugees for permanent residence than does any other country. In 1980, the number of legal immigrants and refugees was on the order of 800,000. In addition, an unknown but evidently large number of persons enter the United States illegally. (Given the clandestine nature of this flow, no accurate data are available.) The number of emigrants from the United States has been systematically underestimated: it is probably at least 100,000 per year—nearly three times the figure employed in Census Bureau estimates and projections. Overall, there are likely to be as many as 1 million net immigrants to the United States each year. These immigrants also have effects on internal distribution of population within the United States, since they are apparently heavily concentrated in only a few states and regions, especially New York, California, Texas, Illinois, and Florida.

Natural increase in the United States in the early 1980s is on the order of 0.7 percent per year, which is quite high by the standards of most other industrialized countries. For example, the percentage of natural increase in France is 0.4, in West Germany −0.2, in the United Kingdom 0.1, in the Netherlands 0.4, in Poland 1.0, in Italy 0.2, and in the Soviet Union 0.8. If plausible levels of total net immigration are added to the U.S. levels of natural increase, then total annual population growth within the United States is probably 1.0 percent or greater as of 1980.

Given this demographic setting, U.S. population policy has been characterized by three broad perspectives.

1. In principle all persons are guaranteed access to family planning services and abortion, both through legislative mandate and judicial requirement. In fact such access applies only to methods of family planning; there is a continuing controversy over government support for abortion.

2. Massive investment in reduction of the mortality rate is made through expenditures in the areas of medical services and preventive health. There is considerable domestic debate as to the advisability of current policies regarding health care, but the magnitude of the investment cannot be doubted.

3. Policy with regard to immigration and refugees is apparently incoherent. The United States has a long tradition of openness to immigration, but in the past decade the country has proved to be politically and administratively incapable of enforcing its own laws regarding such flows. The issue is a controversial and emotional one in domestic politics. [See IMMIGRATION POLICY.]

There have been various attempts at high governmental levels to examine and integrate policies related to population policy and to improve their impact and coherence. The first attempt was the Commission on Population Growth and the American Future, established by President Richard M. Nixon in 1970, chaired by John D. Rockefeller III, and directed by Charles F. Westoff. The most recent attempt was the establishment by the House of Representatives of the Select Committee on Population, chaired by Congressman James H. Scheuer and directed by Michael S. Teitelbaum.

The Commission on Population Growth and the American Future was established in 1970 and reported in 1972. At the time of its work, the U.S. fertility rate was declining but still above replacement level, and natural increase was in excess of 1 percent per year. Along with the environmental movement burgeoning in the 1970s went a general concern about the "population bomb" and a relatively simplistic linking of the deterioration of the environment to population growth. Under these circumstances, the commission concentrated heavily upon the implications of population growth for the United States with a high level of sophistication. It concluded that "no benefits—economic, environmental, governmental, or social—would result from population growth continued beyond that which our past growth implied and that, therefore, eventual population stabilization was desirable" (Westoff, 1974, p. 731).

The commission made specific recommendations in a broad array of areas, including contraception, sterilization, abortion, teenage pregnancy, sex education, child care, adoption, equal rights for women, immigration, illegal aliens, national distribution and migration policies, racial minorities and the poor, population statistics and research, and the handling of population data within the federal government. Perhaps one of the most far-reaching proposals of the commission, and one that has not as yet been acted upon, was the creation of an Office of Population Growth and Distribution within the Executive Office of the President and the immediate addition of personnel with demographic expertise to the staffs of the Council of Economic Advisors, the Domestic Council, the Council on Environmental Quality, and the Office of Science and Technology. In these respects, as in many others, the commission was farsighted, as it perceived the importance of population change for a broad array of U.S. policy concerns and recognized that the U.S. government was ill equipped to anticipate and plan for coming demographic change. Unfortunately, the situation as perceived by the commission in 1970 was little improved by 1980.

While the commission was established by act of Congress and included four members of Congress among its twenty-four members, it was less the creature of Congress than of the executive branch. Its report was submitted to both President Nixon and Congress. Nixon's response was much delayed and largely negative; he was particularly critical of the commission's endorsement of abortion reform and provision of contraceptives for teenagers. Few of the recommendations of the commission were incorporated into Congressional legislation.

In a sense the successor of the commission was the Select Committee on Population, established in 1977 by the U.S. House of Representatives. The Select Committee was a creature entirely of the House, consisting of sixteen members and chaired by Congressman James H. Scheuer of New York. Its mandate was broad, authorizing it "to conduct a full and complete investigation and study of the causes of changing population conditions and their consequences for the United States and the world; national, regional, and global population characteristics relative to the demands on limited resources and the ability of nations to feed, clothe, house, educate, employ, and govern their citizens and otherwise afford them an improved standard of living; various approaches to population planning . . . which would be most effective in coping with unplanned population change; and the means by which the U.S. Government can most effectively cooperate with and assist nations and international agencies in addressing successfully, in a noncoercive manner, various national, regional, and global population-related issues" (House Resolution 70, September 28, 1977).

Like the commission, the Select Committee defined its mandate to include a broad array of public policies that affected or were affected by population change. By the time of the Select Committee's work in 1978, U.S. fertility had dropped well below replacement level, and the alarm about rapid population growth in the United States had abated. Hence the committee concentrated more heavily upon the impact of U.S. population change on a wide variety of public policies than upon the implications of population growth *per se*. The committee published a 130-page report devoted solely to domestic consequences of United States population change (U.S. Congress, 1978a), ranging across an array of subjects including the consequences for investment, natural resources, and per capita gross national product (GNP); the implications of the changing age composition for education, child care, labor force, the elderly population, and government budgets; and the geographic redistribution of the U.S. population in all of its ramifications. The committee's conclusions about the capacity of the U.S. government to deal with dramatic changes in the size, composition, and location of the U.S. population were very similar to those of the commission, namely, that the federal government was ill-equipped indeed, and that there should be a major effort to improve its capacity to anticipate and deal with such changes.

Another difference of emphasis between the commission and the committee also reflects changes in demographic circumstances between 1970 and 1978. Over this period, natural increase in the United States had declined sharply and total net immigration to the United States had increased greatly. Also, as noted, the flow of illegal or undocumented migrants to the United States apparently had accelerated. The commission had considered that at the time of its writing, early in this period, there were approximately 1 million or more illegal immigrants in the United States, which it considered to be a "serious situation." It recommended that Congress immediately "pass legislation that will impose civil and criminal sanctions on employers of illegal border crossers or aliens in an immigration status in which employment is not authorized. To implement this policy, the Commission recommends provision of increased and strength-

ened resources consistent with an effective enforcement program in appropriate agencies" (U.S. Commission on Population Growth and the American Future, 1972, p. 116). With regard to legal immigration, the commission recommended that "immigration levels not be increased and that immigration policy be reviewed periodically to reflect demographic conditions and considerations" (p. 117). Given the date of the commission's report and in view of subsequent developments, its assessment of the immigration issue may fairly be considered prescient.

The Select Committee, established at the end of the period, dealt in greater depth with the issues revolving around legal and illegal immigration to the United States. Its separate report on the subject made sixteen specific recommendations, including serious enforcement of existing U.S. immigration law, rapid expansion and improvement of data collection and research on the dimensions and impacts of immigration to the United States, and a comprehensive review of the Immigration and Nationality Act of 1965 to make the existing law more enforceable, equitable, and flexible. While the committee did not specifically endorse employer sanctions as recommended by the commission, it was generally in support of these and demurred from making a specific recommendation only because enforcement of existing law fell squarely within the purview of another House committee, namely the House Committee on the Judiciary. Overall, the Select Committee laid much greater emphasis on the importance of immigration, both legal and illegal, to the United States than did the Commission on Population Growth, if for no other reason than that the volume and demographic significance of immigration had increased dramatically during the eight years that stretched between these two enterprises. Legal admissions of immigrants and refugees rose from 373,000 in 1970 to over 600,000 in 1978. In addition, the committee reported that consensus of estimates of the numbers of illegal aliens in the United States in the mid-1970s was 4 to 6 million, as distinct from the commission's 1970 estimate of approximately 1 million. Finally, the levels of domestic fertility and natural increase declined substantially over the same period, thereby increasing the demographic significance of even a constant level of immigration.

Both the commission and the committee were strong supporters of federal programs for family planning. The commission's report was prepared during the very early years of the federal program, and strongly supported its expansion. The committee was able to review eight years of experience with this program, and reported that "the Federally-supported family planning program has been very effective in enrolling low-income women and helping them to reduce their unwanted fertility" (U.S. Congress, 1978b, p. 2). It also reported, however, that as recently as 1976 approximately 2 million adolescents and about 1.5 million low-income women remained unserved by this program, and it therefore recommended that "Congress should expand substantially funding for family planning services under Title X of the Public Health Services Act" (p. 11). More important, members of the committee in their individual capacities as members of Congress worked actively in the legislative process to support such an expansion; with the support of many other members of Congress, they successfully brought about important increases in funds authorized for this key program.

One development in part stimulated by the Select Committee bears special mention, and it is one that would have been strongly supported by the commission as well. The Office of Management and Budget decided to examine in its annual budget message the long-term consequences for federal programs of demographic change. In a concise but comprehensive essay appearing in the budget for fiscal year 1980, this office reported a broad range of impacts of demographic change and sought to project into the future well beyond its normal five-year time span as to the implications of such changes for the federal budget. As demonstrated by this essay, the interest in demographic change may be increasing within the executive branch.

In summary, the United States at present, like most developed countries, has no coherent set of explicit policies on population. However, all major factors of population change are addressed by various, usually unrelated, policies and programs that vary also in effectiveness. The level of knowledge within the U.S. government about the policy implications of population change is quite low, but there are encouraging signs of interest in both the legislative and executive branches.

Michael S. Teitelbaum

See also FAMILY LAW; IMMIGRATION POLICY; LAW AND FERTILITY REGULATION, *article on* UNITED STATES.

BIBLIOGRAPHY

Teitelbaum, Michael S. "Right versus Right: Immigration and Refugee Policy in the United States." *Foreign Affairs* 59(1):21–59, Fall 1980.
United States, Commission on Population Growth and the American Future. *Population and the American Future.* Washington, D.C.: U.S. Government Printing Office, 1972. New York: New American Library (Signet), 1972.
——. *Research Reports.* 7 vols. Washington, D.C.: U.S. Government Printing Office, 1972.
United States, Congress, House of Representatives, Select Committee on Population. *Domestic Consequences of United States Population Change.* Washington, D.C.: U.S. Government Printing Office, 1978. (U.S. Congress, 1978a)
——. *Fertility and Contraception in the United States.* Washington, D.C.: U.S. Government Printing Office, 1978. (U.S. Congress, 1978b)
United States, Office of Management and Budget. "Population Change and Long-range Effects on the Budget." In *The Budget of the United States Government, 1980,* pp. 52–57. Washington, D.C.: U.S. Government Printing Office, 1979.
Westoff, Charles F. "United States." In *Population Policy in Developed Countries,* edited by Bernard Berelson, pp. 731–759. New York: McGraw-Hill, 1974.

POPULATION REGISTERS

See DATA COLLECTION, *article on* NATIONAL SYSTEMS.

POPULATION THEORY

The number of people in a city, a nation, or the world—what determines that number and how it in turn affects power and welfare—has been a persistent theme of social science, whose topicality shows no sign of diminishing in the last decades of the twentieth century. Philosophers, counselors to princes, theologians, and legislators have elaborated population doctrines and promoted policies based on them, or else they have promoted policies and created doctrines to buttress them. Views of population are linked to views of the state and of society as a whole, as well as to the objective facts of population technology and social organization at the time of their enunciation.

Antiquity. As early as the time of Confucius in the sixth century B.C., Chinese writers saw that when the population was too small the land was idle and taxes were not paid; when it was too large hardship ensued. A primitive notion of "optimum" size is implicit in their thought. A land empire, in which periods of local prosperity alternated with famines, floods, and epidemics, could usefully shift people from overpopulated to underpopulated regions. Voluntary movements were seen as being in the right direction but sometimes too small and hence to be reinforced by administered transfers. Rapid growth took place twice in Chinese history—after A.D. 1000 and in the eighteenth century, with the introduction, respectively, of fastgrowing crops from Southeast Asia and of maize, potatoes, and peanuts from America. In both instances, scholars were conscious that expanded food supplies brought about the increase of population.

Greek thought on population developed in city-states with constitutional rule by the minority who were citizens. According to Plato, a population must be sufficient to defend itself against its neighbors, and the optimum size thus depends partly on the strength of these neighbors; but no city should exceed its capacity to provide materially for its citizens (*Laws,* V, 637). Effective rule and civil order depend on whether the citizens know one another, which sets another limit to size. In his discussion Plato used the arbitrary figure of 5,040 landholders, a number sufficient for the various specialties the state requires. This total is divisible by 59 numbers and so would facilitate the allocation of tasks and the division of property. When more or fewer children were needed to attain the ideal, the change in fertility could be realized by appropriate honors or negative sanctions; fostering immigration or dispatching citizens to the colonies were also acceptable policies for influencing the total. Aristotle was especially concerned that the city not be too large; he advocated abortion, rejecting infanticide except as a eugenic measure (*Politics,* I, 1; VII, 4).

With their tightly administered land empire and ceaseless wars on their borders, the Romans needed men even more than China or India. Any excess of men could go forth as an army and conquer the lands that would sustain them. Roman writers condemned celibacy and advocated monogamous marriage as the type that would produce the most offspring. Vice leads not only to individual ruin but to collective depopulation (Cicero, *De republica,* IV, 5). The literary emphasis on virtue and on Rome's need for men did not prevent small families, especially in the upper and middle classes, or an increasing dependence on hired barbarians.

Christian Thought. Christian thought developed in the declining Roman Empire, but encouraging population growth to meet the secular needs of the empire formed very little part of it (Noonan, 1965). To the Church Fathers, virginity was the ideal; only for those too weak to abstain from temptations of the flesh was marriage recommended. In the fourth century Augustine reacted against the pessimistic heresies of Gnosticism and Manicheism, which condemned marriage and procreation as producing material human bodies in which the Light would be imprisoned. He sought a justification for marriage, and found it above all in procreation. His doctrine of the marital goods (offspring, fidelity, symbolic stability) dominated Christian thought for a thousand years, during which marriage remained the second-best state. "I am aware," Augustine wrote, "of some that murmur 'What if all men should abstain from sexual relations, whence will the human race subsist?' I answer, so much more speedily would the City of God be fulfilled and the end of the world hastened."

The contrast to the prior Hebrew teaching is striking. The early Christian theologian did not refer to the injunction of Genesis to increase and multiply, nor did he speak of spreading Christianity by having children. In

the thirteenth century the less austere Thomas Aquinas reintroduced the Aristotelian concept of nature; just as it is the nature of the eye to see, so it is the nature of the genitalia to procreate—the very word tells that. It is right and pleasurable to do what is according to nature.

In 1930, the papal encyclical Casti Connubii synthesized a variety of themes from many historical epochs. Pius XI condemned contraception on the grounds of the need to propagate the human race and to bear children for the Church of Christ, as well as on Augustine's three goods of marriage. He recalled Aristotle and Aquinas in arguing that "no reason can make congruent with nature what is intrinsically against nature." He used nineteenth-century theology to condemn the biblical sin of Onan. Following the lead of the Lambeth Conference, which in 1930 opened the door to contraception in the Anglican church, most Protestant groups have found little difficulty in reversing their previous stand against birth control. But Roman Catholic doctrine up to 1980 has yielded only the theologically confusing concession of the rhythm method, sanctioned by Pius XII in 1950 after much debate within the church, which seemingly shifted its concern from the intention of contraception to the method.

The Cycle of Population and Empire. The Arab historian Ibn Khaldun, who lived before the eighteenth century invented the idea of progress, saw history as the rise, prospering, and fall of states and civilizations (Mahdi, 1957). According to his fourteenth-century account, when a tribe becomes numerous under an aggressive chief, it enters on a career of conquest, builds or captures a capital city, and adapts its tribal religion in order to strengthen loyalty to the chief. The tribal chief's successors make themselves absolute rulers of an expanding state, build palaces and temples, and sponsor the arts and the sciences. Rule comes to depend less on the respect for a senior kinsman and more on a tightly organized bureaucracy and army. The city expands with the expansion of the hinterland supplying its food.

Later generations of rulers, attracted to luxury, lose their martial virtues. The original population declines; foreign mercenaries are hired for the army and foreign officials for the administration. These can only be paid by high taxes, levied on both the artisans and the surrounding peasantry. The absorption of the rulers in luxury, the decline of the native population, and the spread of intrigue in the bureaucracy and army lead to the loss of the provinces on whose food and other raw materials the state depends. Having broken the original bonds of kinship and perverted religion to the service of the state, the rulers are helpless when the artificial military and civil structure dissolves. In the last phase the provinces have fallen away, commerce is undercut by taxes and insecurity, and the birth rate declines further. If it is not conquered by a newly rising population, the state burns out like a lamp wick when the oil is exhausted.

In Europe from the sixteenth through the eighteenth century, states competed ceaselessly for military, political, and economic power. Absolute rulers had an interest in maximizing their territories' populations, from which both armies and manual workers could be recruited. The monarch's wealth was seen as a function of the total value produced by his kingdom less whatever was paid in wages. Since the wage per worker would always diminish as the number of workers increased, people were an unqualified asset to their masters. A king could no more have too many subjects than a modern farmer can have too many cattle. "One should never fear there being too many subjects or too many citizens," wrote Jean Bodin, "seeing that there is no wealth nor strength but in men" (*La république*, book V, chap. 2). The goods they produced could be exported for gold or silver, and so people were money. For Frederick the Great it was a certain axiom that "the number of the people makes the wealth of states" (Strangeland, [1904] 1966, p. 131). For Johann Süssmilch, a chaplain in Frederick's army, the interests of the sovereign coincided with the divine order, and both would be furthered by more Germans. With minor exceptions, other French, Italian, and Spanish mercantilists unanimously favored population growth. Giovanni Botero offered advice on how larger populations might be attained: agricultural and especially industrial prduction should be encouraged; the export of raw materials should be forbidden and that of manufactured goods fostered. The English writers were more qualified in their encouragement of population growth; William Petty, as a prime example, both accepted the thesis that men create wealth and feared the poverty and social turmoil consequent on too great numbers.

Political Arithmetic and the Physiocrats. The numerical study of population starting in the seventeenth century, rather than earlier speculations, marked the beginning of demography. When John Graunt worked up bills of mortality (1662), he observed many constant features of deaths and births. Estimating that the ratio of deaths to births was 14 to 13 in London, as against 52 to 63 in the countryside, he calculated the immigration from the countryside needed to maintain and increase London's population. The statistics were poor, but Graunt made what reasoned adjustments he could and did not hesitate to draw conclusions. The concept of a cohort that is diminished by death as it goes through successive ages was clear to him, though his estimates of its diminution were too high. (The life table implied in his calculations has an expectation of life at birth of about 17.5 years, as against the 27.5 years of Edmund Halley's table for Breslau. The

European urban average of the time was probably between these two figures.) Graunt calculated age distributions from the life table, although he did not quite understand the notion of a stable as against a stationary age distribution, apparently first stated precisely by Leonard Euler in 1760.

Petty's new science of "Political Arithmetick" based on empirical work by Graunt among others, raised exciting perspectives in the Royal Society of London. Toward the end of the seventeenth century, Gregory King assembled enough data to produce a realistic estimate of England's population: 5.5 million. Such work as that of Graunt, Petty, Halley, and King, who made good use of the crude data at hand, when combined with later theorizing on population, convinced legislators of the need for censuses and vital statistics.

By the eighteenth century the mercantilists' emphasis on numbers was tempered by the recognition of the relation between numbers and poverty. Richard Cantillon, standing between the mercantilists and the physiocrats, saw that an overcrowded state could acquire some relief by exporting manufactured goods and importing food, a frequent mercantilist theme. Cantillon's masterpiece, *Essai sur la nature du commerce en général* (1755), made land or nature the source of all wealth. Population is created by the means of subsistence, which depend not only on nature and such institutions as property rights in land but also on the decisions that princes and landowners make. If those who control the land want horses for hunting and war, the human population will be smaller than if they prefer domestic retainers. That French landowners preferred Dutch cloth reduced France's population and increased Holland's. The prince's way of living sets the style for smaller landholders. Cantillon does not moralize, but by implication he tells the rulers by what personal sacrifices they could increase population. That in China bearers carry travelers on litter-chairs, he says, explains why compared with Europe the human population is larger, the horse population smaller.

François Quesnay, in opposition to the mercantilists, held that men must not be encouraged to multiply beyond the point of comfort. Inadequate opportunity to work generates laziness, misery, and other social costs. Quesnay, a physician, was interested in social reforms that would heal the body politic; his way to a healthy society was to increase capital, especially in agriculture, in order to make labor more productive and so bring more men into existence. Government should not interfere with nature or with markets but provide an institutional framework within which the sum of men's natural individual acts will serve the common interest. Rules governing property and marriage are essential to avoid irresponsible procreation, but generally physiocrats (the world means "rule by nature") wanted as little regulation as possible.

Less concerned than the mercantilists with foreign trade, the physiocrats emphasized the circulation of wealth within the state. The way in which the costs of one class become the income of another was formalized in a *tableau économique* that analyzed the gross product, so that physiocracy anticipated the macroeconomics of the twentieth century as well as the liberalism of the nineteenth. In showing how the growth of agriculture underlay economic advance, it even anticipated one twentieth-century school of economic development. Labor produced only enough for its own subsistence and for population replacement; all surplus was attributable to land. We shall see how Karl Marx reversed this theory with his better-known imputation of all surplus value to labor.

The Enlightenment and Malthus. Some mercantilists feared a growth of population beyond the subsistence level already in sight, but most expressed confidence that any number of new subjects could produce their own subsistence. The latter view was incorporated in the very different framework of the eighteenth century's new theory of progress and human perfectibility. Among others, the Marquis de Condorcet, William Godwin, and Daniel Malthus held that the numbers of men determine available resources, rather than vice versa. In the era that they saw dawning, such past coercive institutions as property and the family, and the punishment of criminals would disappear, their objectives to be realized through the individual consciences of perfected men. No growth of population in an adequately organized society could conflict with progress, in Godwin's view, for the new City of Man (like Augustine's City of God) would harmonize all social classes and the whole of society with its material base. "There is in human society a principle whereby population is constantly maintained at the level of the means of subsistence," for "the goods of the world are a common fund from which all men can satisfy their needs" (Godwin, [1793] 1946, pp. 466, 520).

These views, which he heard first from his father, Daniel, stimulated Thomas Robert Malthus to seek a more realistic analysis of how population relates to resources. By his famous "principle of population," the number of people, if unchecked, grows in geometric progression, while the resources on which they depend at best increase arithmetically. Moreover, the capacity of men to multiply, and through their multiplying to make themselves miserable, would be accentuated by the very changes in institutions designed to attain an earthly paradise. Malthus's persistence in opposing this thesis to the optimism of the *philosophes* established him as the central figure of population doctrine. For his immediate predecessors—

David Hume, Adam Smith, and Quesnay—population growth was primarily a sequel to an increase in production; demand for labor (as for shoes) produces the supply in a self-regulating system. Malthus opposed to this natural harmony the conflict between population and its means of subsistence.

To ascertain the power of population one had to look at a territory where good land was plentiful. America showed a doubling of population in less than twenty-five years. In countries settled longer the pace of growth was much slower, and most of Malthus's writing and research concerned the nature of the checks by which the rate of growth is held down. He found that in Europe late marriages made for small families. This moral restraint, incorporated in custom and in individual responsibility, he termed a "preventive" check. Also included under preventive checks were vices such as homosexuality, adultery, birth control, and abortion, and these Malthus certainly did not recommend. When preventive checks were inadequate, such "positive" checks as wars and epidemics would supplement them. The ultimate positive check, standing behind all the others, was famine, but this did not often come into operation.

Malthus was part moralist, part scholar. His system was inductive and deductive as it developed in different writings; and he incorporated both biological and social causes. His thoughts have been translated into graphical and mathematical models, using in particular his view that resources determine numbers of people, as the physiocrats had thought, and not vice versa, as most mercantilists held. This view can be traced through numerous predecessors, even with resemblances in the phrasing. Malthus's "Population does invariably increase when the means of subsistence increase" ([1798] 1960, p. 52) recalls Cantillon's "Men increase like mice in a barn if they have access to unlimited subsistence" ([1755] 1952, p. 47). And one can go back through the Comte de Mirabeau and others, ultimately to the succinct "When goods increase, they are increased that eat them" of Ecclesiastes 5:11.

It was for Malthus to derive from this proposition an entire philosophy of history and a theory of society, as well as an inexhaustible source of policy recommendations. All poor laws and personal charity must be so arranged that those receiving doles do not respond by increasing the number of their offspring. For those individuals and nations failing to exercise the preventive check of moral restraint, through chaste postponement of marriage until prospective parents could care for their children, the more severe positive checks of war, pestilence, and famine would become operative. Avoidance of these must be the central aim of policy.

Malthus's intentions were liberal and humane. He

advocated the conversion of hunting estates that could be used for agricultural production, the more efficient use of land already occupied, and the development of industry. While education of the masses was feared by Godwin, Malthus favored universal literacy. He promoted medical assistance for the poor and a wider democracy, all in terms consistent with the mature version of his population theory. From the second edition of the *Essay* on, Malthus stressed that progress was possible, that "on the whole the power of civilization is greater than the power of population" (1960, p. 593). By the organization of property, individuals can be encouraged to discipline themselves to adapt without pain, indeed with personal gain, to forces that ineluctably control society as a whole. The population dilemma can be resolved by an ethic of individual responsibility, and the standard of living can accordingly rise. This was Malthus's answer to the French Revolution.

Malthus remains one of the most controversial figures in social thought. Regarded as a reactionary by those who dreamed of an earthly paradise, he in fact helped develop the economic theories that propelled the revolutionary social changes of the nineteenth century. The traditionally pious accused him of blasphemy for urging men to take responsibility for the size of their families; had not the Creator himself enjoined all to be fruitful and multiply? Had not the sixteenth century reformer Martin Luther declared that any man hesitating to start a family because he lacked property or a job showed a want of faith? One of the most vigorous attacks came from P. J. Proudhon, who held that early marriage is the surest guarantee of good morals. To defer love in the name of moral restraint would restrict marriage to superannuated spinsters and aging satyrs. Like other socialists, Proudhon argued that the imprudence of the working classes was not the cause of their misery but a consequence; with the institution of a society based on justice, people would not want more children than could be provided for (Vialatoux, 1959).

That Malthus's ideas were simple has not saved him from misinterpretation, much of it based on the first edition of the *Essay,* a hastily written pamphlet, and disregarding his carefully researched later editions and other works. Writers pointed to the absurdity of geometric increase, as though Malthus was so dull as to think that population actually does grow geometrically. He was regarded as being against population rather than against misery. In France "malthusien" denoted a narrow, pessimistic view of resources, with a consequent acceptance of parsimony. In England and elsewhere, "Malthusian" or "neo-Malthusian" came to designate a proponent of contraception. In fact, Malthus explicitly disavowed birth control.

Contraception goes back to the beginning of human history, with references to it in the Kahun Papyrus, the Bible, the writings of Charaka (an Indian physician of the first century B.C.), Herodotus, al-Razi (A.D. 900), and other Islamic scholars. Nearly all known human cultures have had sufficient knowledge of the facts of human reproduction to be able to use at least coitus interruptus, and most have had other devices as well. Among moderns, contraception appeared in the writings of Condorcet, and especially Francis Place, who was followed by Richard Carlile, Charles Bradlaugh, and Annie Besant. These did not share the puritanical view that hunger and sex were the stick and carrot without which people would be slothful, and they found in contraception the full answer to the problem Malthus had posed.

Marx and Other Socialist Writers. Karl Marx was generally well disposed toward the classical economists, of whose school he was a wayward member. But he repeatedly attacked not only Malthus's doctrines but also his motives and personality. According to Marx, Malthus had propagated a "vile and infamous doctrine, this repulsive blasphemy against man and nature." No general law of population could be valid for all societies; each had its own law. The irreducible opposition between population and welfare, far from being universal, was in Marx's view the special predicament of capitalism, with its impoverishment of the proletariat. The reproduction of the working class made new workers cheap and so permitted the bourgeoisie to extract surplus value from their work. But to ask the proletariat to be more responsible was futile, for the very degradation inherent in capitalism ruled out an appeal to their highest natures. The transformation of capitalism to socialism would eliminate the Malthusian dilemma. As on the other points, Marx started with the classical premises and reached a conclusion very different from that of classical harmony.

The history of capitalist society, as he viewed it, is divided between a period of original accumulation of wealth and one of maturity and imperialism. In the period of original accumulation all the conclusions of Adam Smith and David Ricardo are valid, with only a change of terms and some simplification. Marx divided capital into constant, C (for example, buildings and machinery), and variable, V (including consumer goods such as food bought with workers' wages). Constant capital is so called because it is merely reproduced without a quantitative change in the product: all surplus is earned on labor. The capitalist tries to use all the labor he can employ, for thus he makes the largest profit. If it costs six hours per day to produce labor (the amount of time the average worker required to feed, clothe, and house himself and his family at a subsistence level) and if the goods he produces sell for the equivalent of twelve hours' time, then the capitalist's surplus value is six hours multiplied by the number of workers he employed. The rapid increase of population in early capitalism was due to the demand for labor, just as Adam Smith had said.

For the second or "imperialist" period, however, Marx diverged sharply from the classical economists. The wage rate is V/P, variable capital divided by population, as before. But now as technical progress and competition force capitalists to substitute machines for men, the "reserve army" of the unemployed grows continually. Workers respond by lowering their birth rate as less labor is demanded, and Marx pictured a struggle around the ratio V/P, with the capitalists trying to shift the resources they control from V to C, and the workers seeking to counter this effort by reducing P. Unfortunately for the system as a whole, the birth rate cannot fall fast enough to prevent capitalism from producing the surplus workers that are its gravediggers.

That labor-saving methods of production make an increasing fraction of the population redundant has been a popular fear before and since Marx. Today the identification of surplus population with unemployment is found in underdeveloped countries, while the countries with the largest stock of capital have more often encountered a labor shortage.

The world at large sees Malthus and Marx as "the two great antagonists, battling eternally" (Sauvy, 1963, p. 13). But the very vehemence of Marx's attack stemmed from the lack of a substantive rebuttal, as his *Critique of the Gotha Program* pointed out: "If [Malthus's] theory of population is correct, then I can*not* abolish this [iron law of wages] even if I abolish wage-labor a hundred times, because this law is not only paramount over the system of wage-labor but also over every social system" (Marx and Engels, 1959, p. 124). Marx and Malthus agreed that the condition of the proletariat was miserable and that its misery should be alleviated. For Malthus the solution was to increase individual responsibility, for Marx to attain a collective condition called socialism; but in the analytically superior part of their work, both concentrated on posing the problem.

Marx and Malthus agreed profoundly on the material base of social existence. At Marx's graveside Friedrich Engels summed up his collaborator's contribution: "Marx discovered the law of evolution in human history: the simple fact previously hidden under ideological growths, that human beings must first of all eat, drink, shelter and clothe themselves before they can turn their attention to politics, science, art and religion." Malthus made the same point with equal clarity in his own summing up, published four years before his death: "Elevated as man is above all other animals by his intellectual faculties, it is not to be supposed that the physical laws to which he is subjected should be essentially different from those which are observed to prevail in other parts of animated nature" (Malthus, 1830).

That the workingman can avoid increasing misery, both collectively and individually, by restricting his family, that mothers should in effect become a trade union and declare a childbearing strike, was a theme of Leftist social reform in the writings of John Stuart Mill, Eduard Bernstein, and others. But Marxists insisted that advanced capitalism could always undercut the working man with more efficient equipment; in the race between voluntary reduction of the work force and substitution of labor-saving devices, the latter would necessarily win. Relief must be sought in revolution rather than in contraception.

Marx bequeathed his opposition to Malthus to succeeding Marxist thinkers. Vladimir I. Lenin in particular stressed that evolving technique would undercut the law of diminishing returns. Much of Joseph Stalin's argument has the tone of the mercantilists: the growth of population facilitates economic advance. The population problem of the developing countries has now become a topic of public discussion in the Soviet Union. In the dominant view, industrialization is the solution in those countries, just as it was in the Soviet Union, where the growth of cities, the development of culture, and the involvement of women in public activity cut the birth rate by more than half. And if high growth rates continue in developing countries, the infinite power of science and technology can overcome any shortage of food and materials that may arise. Billions and billions of people will be required to master the earth and the solar system. Birth control propaganda is unnecessary on the one hand and useless on the other, since people will not heed it before their societies are industrialized.

But less orthodox Soviet writers, less confident that even socialist industry will solve the population problem, encourage family planning before the advent of industry. Merely achieving the maximum number of inhabitants is hardly a worthy goal for humanity, and as a goal of individual countries it recalls the feudal rulers who boasted of the number of their subjects. A policy choice must be made between doubling the prosperity of a fixed number of people every twenty years and doubling the population instead, leaving the standard of living unchanged. Better than a choice between the two investment policies would be a combination of the best of both. While reiterating the obvious truth that birth control is no substitute for industrialization, Soviet writers are now coming to concede that more resources will be available for investment if dependency ratios of children and the aged to workers can be reduced.

Density and the Division of Labor. Emile Durkheim marked society's change from a small, undifferentiated clan or tribe to the complexity of the early twentieth century, noting that interdependence of groups increases with the greater specialization of sectors of society. The complex society, he concluded, comes with population growth. As a tribe increases in volume and density, individuals and groups compete more and more intensely; only by specialization can they find shelter from competition. "In the same city the different professions can coexist without having to harm each other, for they pursue different objectives. The soldier seeks military glory, the priest moral authority, the statesman power, the industrialist wealth . . .; each can thus reach his goal without preventing the others from reaching theirs" (Durkheim, [1902] 1960, p. 249). For Durkheim, population growth, through the "moral density" that arises from it, is responsible for the advance from a simple, segmented society to a complex, organic one.

Among peasant populations, one that is small and stationary is more likely to stay with slash-and-burn agriculture, which under many circumstances of low density produces more with less labor. Higher density forces a shorter fallow period and ultimately annual crops, even though these mean more work. A "gradual adaptation to harder and more regular work is likely to raise the efficiency of labor in both agricultural and nonagricultural activities; the increasing density of population opens up opportunities for a more intricate division of labor," says Ester Boserup (1965, p. 75). Note how this paraphrases Durkheim's thesis.

The Biological Perspective. Corresponding to Malthus's preventive check is the observation of ecologists and ethologists that fertility in many species of birds and animals depends on density. It is known that beyond a certain point mortality is dependent on density through the ultimate check of starvation. But starvation is not very often seen in nature and, even combined with predators, disease, harsh weather, and other disasters, does not seem to exercise the continuous control that would explain the relative constancy of numbers in most species of higher animals. Rather the constancy is explained by a territorial mechanism of reproductive control, to accord with long-term food supplies. Among some species of birds, at the beginning of the breeding season each male lays claim to an area of suitable size and keeps out other males; all of the available ground is thus parceled out as individual territories. The often furious competition for an adequate piece of ground takes the place of direct competition for food. This territoriality is a special situation; some species compete merely for membership in a hunting group in which only so many are accepted. Those without territory, or left out of the hunting group, have no opportunity to reproduce. The pecking order among birds has the same function; those low on the scale are a reserve that can fill in for casualties among the established members or be dropped, as circumstances require.

By such territorial and analogous mechanisms, population is maintained comfortably below the ceiling imposed by resources. The analogy to Malthus's preventive check comes as close as is conceivable for species lacking human foresight. Man has indeed the possibility of foresight, yet he offends more than most species in overgrazing, overfishing, and generally overexploiting his habitat.

Population and the Gifts of Nature. The classical school of economics developed from Malthus the law of diminishing returns, and indeed increments of any one factor of production eventually generate lessening amounts of income. The doctrine was given mature expression by John Stuart Mill: "The niggardliness of nature, not the injustice of society, is the cause of the penalty attached to overpopulation. An unjust distribution of wealth does not even aggravate the evil, but, at most, causes it to be somewhat earlier felt. It is vain to say that all mouths which the increase of mankind calls into existence bring with them hands. The new mouths require as much food as the old ones, and the hands do not produce as much" (1848). The operation of the law may be long postponed if there is vacant land to which people may move and, subsequently, if technical improvements are developed; but over the longer run its course is seen as inexorable. The law is applied to an increase in the land under cultivation through the presumed fact that rational men would start to till the most fertile and accessible portions first, so that any new lands added to the nation's agriculture would be less and less productive. As population grows in any country closed to trade, poorer lands will necessarily be brought into use, and any excess over the return to labor on marginal land will be taken as rent by landowners in the natural operation of the market. Population growth beyond a certain point would provide landlords with an increasing proportion of the national product. The model requires an agricultural community of fixed land and techniques with a growing population.

But quite different conditions apply in industry, where the factors of production are extensible and the division of labor advantageous. True, industry depends on a supply of raw materials, but the limits of these are more distant than the coming shortage of agricultural land. If in some sectors of the economy returns increase with added effort while they diminish in others, then there will be a certain size of population at which overall production per head will be at a maximum. It is useful to consider production a function of population whenever the economy is relatively static while population grows—the situation of some countries today.

In the 1920s England and some other advanced countries seemed to have passed their optimum of production and arrived at the point of rapidly diminishing returns.

The best coal deposits were being exhausted, cotton was attacked by the boll weevil, and for these and other commodities prices could only rise in response to increasing scarcity, with a resultant fall in the standard of living. Population control was an important part of the answer. Such concerns are now widely expressed.

The Environment. Contemporary ecologists are interested in optimum population in a given situation, but they sharply reject the theory of gradually diminishing returns and continuous changes held by classical economists. Their writings constitute a radical attack on the modern system of production and consumption. At best, the kinds of damage not now entered in private or national accounting schemes must be deducted from the calculation of national product and income. At worst, the word "production" itself is seen as an ironic misnomer for such a process as depleting supplies of invaluable crude oil (which ought to be saved for lubrication) by destroying it in an inefficient way of moving people from place to place and by creating unbreathable air that may well be raising mortality rates. If the population of Malthus's time was pushing against a food ceiling, that of today seems to be pushing against a ceiling of space, air, water, and mineral resources.

The problem for us is whether such complaints really have a bearing on population. Parking space is short not because there are too many people in the country, or even too many automobiles, but because people want to live in large cities, or because they all want to go to the same place at the same time. The air is polluted because either automobiles are badly designed or some other solution to the transport problem should replace them. The present system of production would quickly direct itself along lines that preserve the environment and enable it to take care of far more people if manufacturers were charged for the damage their products cause. They receive income for their goods and should pay for their bads, as Kenneth E. Boulding says (1966, p. 9). He proposes to rescue national-income accounting by distinguishing "that part of the Gross National Product which is derived from exhaustible and that which is derived from reproducible resources, as well as that part of consumption which represents effluvia and that which represents input into the productive system again."

At least up to now, technology has year by year enabled more people to live better. Most economists believe that future technology can remedy the defects that present technology is bringing about—that we can continue, for instance, to secure the larger crops that fertilizers provide and escape the accompanying water pollution. As any mineral approaches exhaustion, price changes will ensue and so force the substitution of other minerals or nonmineral products. The productive system is flexible

enough to cope with the disturbances in the environment that it creates. The process is not entirely automatic, however, and ecologists deserve credit for having brought such matters to public attention and for having agitated for reforms at some immediate danger points.

On their side, ecologists stress how tenuous and potentially unstable are relations between man and habitat and how ignorant science is of the operation of atmospheric, oceanic, and other systems, especially of their disequilibria and discontinuities. We use DDT to eradicate malaria and to save crops from insects; both uses have the effect of building population on DDT. What happens to the population when DDT-resistant strains of insects develop and when contamination of the environment by DDT rises to intolerable levels? If such dangers are real, then the present world population of about 4 billion may be much above the long-term carrying capacity of the planet. This especially affects the underdeveloped world, which lives so close to the hunger margin; but developed countries have little basis for complacency. Smog is not proportional to the number of automobiles in an area but in a given local configuration of the landscape suddenly comes into existence at a certain point in the increase of automobile density. Moreover, any simplification of ecological systems (as from intensive agriculture, which reduces the number of species present, or from the so-called green revolution, which reduces the number of subspecies or strains) aggravates their instability, exposing population to sudden adverse changes.

Ecologists have contributed a justified apprehension of instability in the systems on which our lives depend, and they have shown how much mankind is gambling on the further process of science. This negative contribution is important. We now badly need the positive contribution of further facts and a model that will take simultaneous account of population numbers, technology, human behavior, and the environment, and that will allow for instabilities and disequilibria in the many variables.

Nathan Keyfitz

For related articles dealing with theory in the field of population, see FERTILITY AND DEVELOPMENT; FERTILITY DECLINE, *article on* THEORIES; FERTILITY DETERMINANTS, *article on* SOCIOLOGICAL AND ECONOMIC THEORIES; INTERNAL MIGRATION, *article on* MODELS. *See also* BIRTH CONTROL MOVEMENT; DEMOGRAPHIC TRANSITION THEORY; EPIDEMIOLOGIC TRANSITION, *article on* UNITED STATES.

BIBLIOGRAPHY

Bodin, Jean. *The Six Bookes of a Commonweale* (1606; English translation of *Six livres de la république,* 1576). Edited by Kenneth D. McRae. Cambridge, Mass.: Harvard University Press, 1962.

Boserup, Ester. *The Conditions of Agricultural Growth: The Economics of Agrarian Change under Population Pressure.* Chicago: Aldine, 1965.

Botero, Giovanni. *The Reason of State* (1589). Translated and edited by P. J. Waley and D. P. Waley. New Haven, Conn.: Yale University Press, 1956.

Boulding, Kenneth E. "The Economics of the Coming Spaceship Earth." In *Environmental Quality in a Growing Economy,* edited by Henry Jarrett, pp. 3–14. Baltimore and London: Johns Hopkins University Press, 1966.

Cantillon, Richard. *Essai sur la nature de commerce en général* (1755). Reprint. Paris: Institut National d'Etudes Démographiques, 1952.

Davis, Kingsley. "The Theory of Change and Response in Modern Demographic History." *Population Index* 29(4):345–366, October 1963.

Durkheim, Emile. *De la division du travail social* (1902). Paris: Presses Universitaires de France, 1960.

Godwin, William. *An Enquiry Concerning Political Justice and Its Influence on Morals and Happiness* (1793). 3 vols. Edited by F. E. Priestley. Toronto: University of Toronto Press, 1946.

Graunt, John. *Natural and Political Observations Mentioned in a Following Index, and Made upon the Bills of Mortality: With Reference to the Government, Religion, Trade, Growth, Ayre, Diseases, and Several Changes of the Said City [London]* (1662). Reprint. New York: Arno Press, 1975.

Hutchinson, E. P. *The Population Debate: The Development of Conflicting Theories up to 1900.* Boston: Houghton Mifflin, 1967.

Mahdi, Muhsin. *Ibn Khaldūn's Philosophy of History: A Study in the Philosophic Foundation of the Science of Culture.* Chicago: University of Chicago Press, 1964. London: Allen & Unwin, 1957.

Malthus, Thomas Robert. *On Population* (1798). Edited by Gertrude Himmelfarb. New York: Modern Library, 1960.

———. "A Summary View of the Principle of Population" (1830). Reprinted in *On Population: Three Essays,* by Thomas Robert Malthus, Julian Huxley, and Frederick Osborn. New York: New American Library (Mentor), 1964.

Marx, Karl, and Friedrich Engels. *Basic Writings on Politics and Philosophy.* Edited by Lewis S. Feuer. Garden City, N.Y.: Doubleday, 1959.

Mill, John Stuart. *Principles of Political Economy* (1848). 2 vols. Edited by J. M. Robson. Toronto: University of Toronto Press, 1965.

Noonan, John T., Jr. *Contraception: A History of Its Treatment by the Catholic Theologians and Canonists.* Cambridge, Mass.: Belknap Press, Harvard University Press, 1965. New York: New American Library, 1967.

Petersen, William. *The Politics of Population.* Garden City, N.Y.: Doubleday, 1965.

———. *Malthus.* Cambridge, Mass.: Harvard University Press, 1979.

Petty, William. *Political Arithmetick* (c. 1676). Reprinted in *The Economic Writings of Sir William Petty,* edited by Charles H. Hull, vol. 1, pp. 233–313. New York: Kelley, 1963. First written c. 1676; first published surreptitiously in 1683 as *England's Guide to Industry.* The first authorized edition was published posthumously in 1690 by Petty's son.

Pius XI. Casti Connubii. *Acta apostolicae sedis,* vol. 22, 1930, pp. 539–592. Translated as "On Christian Marriage" in *Catholic Mind* 29:21–64, 1931.

Quesnay, François. "Hommes." *Revue d'histoire des doctrines économiques* 1:14ff, 1908.

Spengler, Joseph J. *French Predecessors of Malthus: A Study in Eighteenth-century Wage and Population Theory.* Durham, N.C.: Duke University Press, 1942.

Strangeland, Charles Emil. *Pre-Malthusian Doctrines of Population: A Study in the History of Economic Theory* (1904). Reprint. New York: Kelley, 1966.

Sauvy, Alfred. *Malthus et les deux Marx: La problème de la faim et de la guerre dans le monde.* Paris: Denoel, 1963.

———. "Population Theories." In *International Encyclopedia of the Social Sciences,* edited by David L. Sills, vol. 12, pp. 349–358. New York: Macmillan and Free Press, 1968.

Vialatoux, Joseph. *Le peuplement humain.* 2 vols. Paris: Editions Ouvrières, 1959.

PREGNANCY TERMINATION

See ABORTION.

PROJECTIONS

Population projections are calculations of future demographic quantities and trends obtained by using accumulated substantive knowledge and applying the most recent methodology. The desire to predict the future of populations has been an important stimulus to the evolution of demographic methods, which in turn has been the principal prerequisite to refining population projections. Population projections are among the basic ingredients for social and economic planning. They illustrate possible trends in human resources, indicate the needs of a population, and provide a basis for judging whether attempts should be made to alter demographic trends. Many countries have national projections prepared by a government office, usually by the principal statistical institution. The Population Division of the United Nations produces a comprehensive set of national, regional, and global estimates and projections, revised every five years. The current edition, *World Population Trends and Prospects by Country, 1950–2000; Summary Report of the 1978 Assessment* (1979), includes projections for 210 countries.

Population projections are as old as demography. In 1696, Gregory King tried his hand at projecting the population of England and Wales for six hundred years—up to A.D. 2300. Had his projection materialized, the population would have numbered about 8 million in 1975 instead of its actual 49 million inhabitants. Given the state of the art in his time, King was no doubt at a comparative disadvantage; yet even today, after centuries of advance in demographic methods and accumulation of knowledge, population projections serve only as illustrations of more or less likely futures. This lack of precision does not imply that demographers have nothing to say about future population trends. On the contrary, a number of features of future population growth are put forward with reasonable assurance. In many ways, population projections are more reliable than numerous other types of calculation about the future.

Even though King's projection failed to materialize, he cannot be criticized for his threefold approach to the problem. (1) He assembled the best data currently available, but unfortunately that best was no more than an estimate of the total population. (2) He evaluated past growth trends and wound up with a remarkably good estimate: that it had taken the population 435 years to double to its 1696 size. (3) On the basis of this estimate he made a guess that the next population doubling would take six hundred years.

At present, when preparing and computing population projections demographers proceed along similar lines.

In most situations we know more about the population in question than its total size. We usually have information about such characteristics as its age and sex composition, health and mortality patterns, fertility behavior, marital patterns, geographical distribution and mobility, occupation, income and wealth distribution, and educational levels. Of course, the available data differ in quality from one country to another, for example, the data for Sweden are better than those for Sri Lanka, which in turn are better than data for Senegal.

Today, not only do we have knowledge about past trends in the total population size of a country but we can also make comparisons between countries. Furthermore, data are usually available on the historical changes of various population characteristics. Moreover, as the science of demography develops, it provides a continuously improving understanding of the forces that underlie population change.

The ability to formulate assumptions about future trends depends to some extent on the quality of base data. There is, however, hardly a guarantee that a projection, particularly into a far distant future, will not be off the mark as much as was King's. The point is that prediction is not the only function of population projections. Another reason for constructing them is to provide a range of alternative future trends, possibly to illustrate the growth consequences of differing assumptions. Thus, for instance, a major part of the analysis in the report of the Commission on Population Growth and the American Future (United States, 1972) was based on two alternative projections, assuming that Americans would con-

tinue to have either three-child or two-child families. Starting from 209 million in 1972, in one hundred years the two-child family would result in a population of about 350 million persons, whereas the three-child family would produce nearly a billion.

Even with all its detailed information (seven large volumes of papers) about many structural and qualitative features of the population and with good knowledge of past trends, the commission decided to present alternative projections rather than only one projection in the style of King. Furthermore, projecting a mere one hundred years into the future, the range between the alternatives in 2070, 650 million, was three times larger than the initial 1970 U.S. population. The calculations showed that with the two-child family, the population would be 70 percent larger in one hundred years but with a three-child family it would grow fivefold. Since the basic assumptions used in computing these projections are known, they can be discussed.

Following the great Depression, and particularly in the post–World War II period, U.S. fertility deviated from its gradual decline and produced the baby boom of the 1950s, in which families with three or four children were commonplace. By the time the commission's projections were computed in 1972, average fertility of the U.S. population had declined abruptly. In 1957 the total fertility rate had been 3.8 births per 1,000 women of reproductive age, but by 1972 it had fallen to 2.0; that is, an imaginary woman passing through her childbearing years would have borne almost four children had she conformed to fertility patterns of 1957, but only two children had she followed 1972 fertility patterns. Between 1972 and 1976, fertility continued to decline to an all time low in 1976; in that year the total fertility rate was slightly less than 1.8.

This cursory look at U.S. fertility trends, together with our understanding of what caused these trends and similar trends in other countries enables us to make at least four comments about the commission's projections.

1. In view of childbearing patterns of the recent past, future population growth trends are more likely to approximate the numbers associated with the two-child family assumption, that is, a U.S. population of about 350 million in the 2070s rather than those associated with the three-child family assumption.

2. If the 1972–1976 fertility levels were to persist over time, the United States would have a population smaller than 350 million in the 2070s.

3. One should not rule out a possible reversal of fertility trends, namely a possible new baby boom. If such a fertility increase were to occur soon and if it lasted for as long as the previous baby boom, the U.S. population in 2070 would be larger than the 350 million.

4. As the relatively large generation born in the 1950s passes through the prime childbearing years, if it were to have children at present rates, that is, 10 percent to 20 percent below the two-child average, the U.S. population would still grow at a rate of about 0.5 percent per year for at least twenty years. Given the growth momentum created by the post–World War II baby boom, it was unlikely that the U.S. population would stop increasing for some years to come. The total fertility rate would have had to decline to 1.2 and remain there throughout the 1970s and 1980s in order to bring about immediate zero population growth [see MOMENTUM].

Mortality trends and migratory movements shape population growth trends in interaction with fertility behavior. Modern population projections are carried out using the so-called component method: one takes the base population divided into age and sex groups and then projects each group by applying assumed mortality, migration, and fertility patterns.

For countries such as the United States that have achieved low mortality rates and where almost all children survive into adulthood, it is relatively simple to establish assumptions about future mortality trends. U.S. mortality rates, for instance, declined significantly in the late nineteenth century and throughout the first half of the twentieth century. Since the late 1950s further decline has been limited. Average life expectancy at birth for white males increased from about 48 years at the beginning of the century to almost 68 years by 1960 and remained at that level until the mid-1970s; for white females the increase in life expectancy was even larger, from 51 years in 1900 to 74 years by 1960 and to 77 years in 1976. Not surprisingly, the U.S. Bureau of the Census in its 1975 population projections assumed only minor declines in the mortality rate in the future.

Immigration and emigration are subject to many economic and social factors, but because U.S. legislation contains specific stipulations, the Census Bureau has assumed 400,000 annual legal immigrants with a reasonable degree of confidence. The actual annual number of immigrants is higher as a result of clandestine immigration, but it is not known by how much. Estimates of the total number of illegal immigrants in the United States in the mid-1970s went as high as 12 million persons. Although the actual figure was almost certainly lower, there was undoubtedly substantial illegal immigration which, if continued, will considerably influence future U.S. population growth. Also, the annual number of permanent emigrants from the United States is unknown, but in the mid-1970s it was significantly smaller than the number of immigrants.

Having assembled basic demographic knowledge on the current state and past trends of the U.S. population,

we can maintain that the U.S. population in 2070 is likely to be around 350 million inhabitants. It should be added that this projection is based on the following assumptions: average fertility behavior oscillating around the two-child family, a slight improvement in health and thus in mortality conditions, and an average net flow of 400,000 immigrants per year. How close this projection comes to the actual U.S. population in 2070 depends on the extent to which these assumptions prove true.

It has become standard procedure to review periodically population projections. Between 1947 and 1975 the U.S. Bureau of the Census published twelve sets of projections, usually with three or four different combinations of assumptions to accommodate ranges of future possibilities (see United States, 1975, table L). Nevertheless, the demographic situation was changing so rapidly that occasionally a few years after the projections had been computed the actual population was no longer within the projected range. According to the 1947 projections, the 1950 U.S. population was projected to be between 145 and 148 million, but in reality it was 152 million; and according to the 1971 projections, the 1975 population was projected to be between 216 and 218 million but it was actually 213 million.

These population projections were rapidly rendered obsolete as a result of unexpected trends in fertility. In the late 1940s fertility increased more than had been assumed, and in the early 1970s fertility continued to decline instead of leveling off as expected.

Population projections not involving fertility assumptions, that is, projections concerned only with specific population segments that are already born before the projection, can be relatively more reliable than "complete" population projections. It is, for example, a relatively simple task for the Census Bureau to project the population of voting age over the next fifteen years or so, because the persons being projected are alive at the time of computation.

Thus it was determined that there were going to be 150 million U.S. inhabitants of voting age as of November 1976. This number had to be adjusted because it included people who were not eligible to vote, such as aliens and inmates of prisons, mental hospitals, and other institutions. Similarly, a rather high degree of accuracy can be achieved in projecting the school-age population at different levels of schooling, entrants to the labor force, the population of retirement age, and any other specific age-sex groups, provided the base population of the projection has already been born at the time of computation. Thus, at least for the low-mortality nations, one can say that short-term projections of population segments alive at the time of computation should be quite accurate. However, even short-term projections of total populations, especially of the segments that are yet to be born, are much less reliable and serve less well as base data for social and economic planning purposes.

Much of what has been said about the U.S. population in general and about U.S. population projections in particular applies to other countries with low rates of mortality and fertility.

High fertility in developing countries, however, created and perpetuated an age composition with a large proportion of young people: around 40 percent of the population below age 15, about 25 percent in the prime childbearing ages of 15–29, and only about 5 percent of the total over age 60.

The recent combination of rapidly declining mortality rates and relatively high fertility rates has brought about rates of population growth of unprecedented levels. In practically all developing countries in the early 1970s the rate of natural increase was above 2 percent per year, often around 3 percent or even higher. The doubling time for a population growing around 3 percent per year is 23 years, at 2 percent per year 35 years and, for comparison, at 0.5 percent per year 140 years.

The significance of a young age-structure becomes even more evident when it is realized that as a consequence of declining mortality rates, an increasing number of children will survive to adulthood and presumably form families, that is, marry and have children of their own. In this way a young age-structure alone provides a significant reservoir of future population growth. Thus, population growth generates a momentum that takes several generations to work itself out [*see* MOMENTUM].

China is the largest among the developing countries and is also one of the countries for which very few demographic data are available. Experts differ about the relia-

bility of the published data; even the statistical authorities in the central government seem to have some doubts about their accuracy. This may, in fact, be one of the reasons why the Chinese have been reluctant to publish detailed population data. Foreign experts have tried to estimate the size of China's population, its age-sex structure, and the levels of fertility and mortality, and to reconstruct China's recent demographic history. Their estimates have often varied considerably in the past, but in recent years the appearance of official figures has narrowed the range considerably. According to the latest figures from Beijing, China's population totaled almost 983 million by the end of 1980 and the natural increase rate had fallen below 11 per 1,000. No vital rates were made public for 1980, but in 1979, the birth rate was reported as 17.90 and the death rate as 6.24 per 1,000. Some experts believe that the actual population total, natural increase rate, and birth and death rates are higher than the official figures indicate, but there is general agreement that birth and natural increase rates fell sharply during the 1970s as a result of the Chinese family planning effort.

The enormous diversity among countries in fertility and mortality trends and levels adds up to the global demographic picture shown in Figure 1. The picture is a simplified one. In addition to concealing heterogeneity, it also hides the probability that, as many believe and have attempted to document, the rate of natural increase of the developing countries has reached a turning point and started to decline. Since this probable decrescendo was clearly reinforced by a diminishing rate of natural increase in the developed countries, it seemed beyond doubt that the world population growth rate in the mid-1970s was falling.

FIGURE 1. *Estimated basic demographic measures, the world, developed countries, and developing countries, 1950–1975*

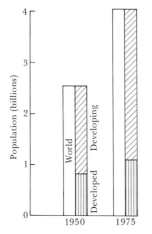
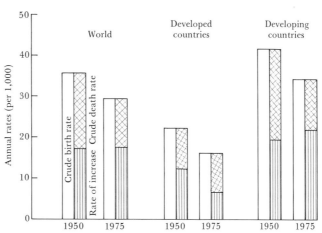

Source of data: United Nations, 1979.

Will the decline of the world's population growth rate continue or even accelerate? Or will it be reversed? How long might it take for developing countries to reach rates of growth similar to those in developed countries? What seem to be the prospects for population growth for the near and more remote future, of the world, of the developed countries, of the developing countries?

Experience shows that extrapolation from past trends does not yield reliable predictions. A better understanding of possible future population growth can be gained by outlining various hypothetical developments and discussing the chances each has to materialize.

As a starting point, let it be assumed that fertility behavior at the replacement level is adopted on a worldwide basis, namely, that the average couple bears as many children as are needed to guarantee the survival of two of them to adulthood (each adult is "replaced" by one child). If such fertility patterns were adopted in the mid-1970s and maintained thereafter, the total population of the developed countries would grow from their 1975 size of 1.1 billion to 1.3 billion in the year 2000 and 1.4 billion in 2050, a growth of 25 percent between 1975 and 2050. In the developing countries, the 1975 population of about 2.9 billion would increase to 3.6 billion in the year 2000 and 4.4 billion in the year 2050, a growth of more than 50 percent between 1975 and 2050. Even under this extremely unlikely assumption the world would still have almost 6 billion inhabitants by the year 2050.

Barring man-induced or natural catastrophes of major proportions, these calculations appear to be unrealistically low for the developing countries and consequently for the whole world. In the developing countries average fertility is about twice as high as that assumed above; in the mid-1970s fertility and mortality patterns implied four children surviving to adulthood for every two adults of childbearing age. Probably no more than about one-third of the population in the developing countries were experiencing unusually steep fertility declines, whereas changes in fertility behavior of the other two-thirds were moderate and gradual and for some of them were of no significance at all.

Evidently one has to make some less radical assumptions about fertility decline in the developing countries as a whole in order to illustrate more feasible alternatives. One possibility is to assume that 1975 fertility would be transformed to the two-child family pattern by the turn of the century. Compared with the historical experience of the developed countries in the late nineteenth and early twentieth centuries, this would still be a startlingly rapid change, and thus we label this illustration the "rapid demographic transition." If, however, fertility decline in the developing countries were to require an

amount of time comparable to that experienced by the developed countries, one could expect the developing countries to reach the two-child family level by the middle of the twenty-first century. This time frame is referred to as the "traditional demographic transition." To many this may seem a rather conservative assumption, which provides some justification for considering the calculations that result from it as on the high side.

To return to the developed countries, the projection assuming a continuing two-child family pattern is reasonable but not necessarily correct. There is no guarantee that a prolonged deviation from such a trend in either direction could not occur. In Eastern Europe and the Soviet Union, fertility oscillated around this level during the early and mid-1970s; in the remainder of Europe and in North America, however, fertility continued to decline below the replacement level and, as of late 1976, was showing no signs of a reversal. Nevertheless, even if continued fertility below replacement (say 10 percent below) were assumed for the developed countries, it would not make a significant difference in terms of future growth of the world population in the coming fifty to one hundred years. With a fertility level 10 percent below replacement, the population of the developed countries would still number 1.3 billion in the year 2000 and 1.2 billion in the year 2050, instead of 1.3 and 1.4 billion, respectively, with a continuous two-child family fertility pattern. Furthermore, the nature of world population growth is going to be determined increasingly by population growth trends in the developing countries, because these countries in 1975 held almost 75 percent of the world's population, a proportion that is bound to increase, possibly to as much as 90 percent by the second half of the twenty-first century. Thus, for the following calculations, a long-term two-child family fertility pattern in the developed countries is applicable.

It remains to be mentioned that mortality rates throughout the world are assumed to continue to decline and eventually (during the first half of the twenty-first century) to reach the low levels prevailing in Scandinavia. Such an assumption presumes that further decline in mortality rates will be limited in most of the developed countries and more or less significant but gradual in the developing countries. Should major epidemics, wars, famines, or environmental deterioration occur in the future, of course, mortality rates would not continue to decline at the speed assumed.

The data assembled in Table 1 illustrate the parameters of hypothetical future world population growth.

The first projection is labeled the "illusory demographic transition" for a good reason. It assumes worldwide fertility at the replacement level commencing in the mid-1970s and remaining at that level thereafter. It

TABLE 1. *Hypothetical trends of world population growth, 1975–2100*

Type of projection	Region	Population (billions)			
		1975	*2000*		*2100*
Illusory demographic transition					
Two-child family fertility pattern adopted universally in mid-1970s in both developed and in developing countries	Developed countries	1.1	1.3	1.4	1.4
	Developing countries	2.9	3.7	4.4	4.6
	World total	4.0	5.0	5.8	6.0
Rapid demographic transition					
Two-child family fertility pattern adopted in developed countries in mid-1970s and in developing countries by the year 2000	Developed countries	1.1	1.3	1.4	1.4
	Developing countries	2.9	4.5	6.5	6.8
	World total	4.0	5.8	7.9	8.2
Traditional demographic transition					
Two-child family fertility pattern adopted in developed countries in mid-1970s and in developing countries by the year 2040	Developed countries	1.1	1.3	1.4	1.4
	Developing countries	2.9	5.3	11.6	13.9
	World total	4.0	6.6	13.0	15.3

might be reasonable to assume this for the developed countries, but in almost no developing country could such a radical reduction of fertility occur. Available evidence, knowledge, and experience indicate that average fertility levels in the developing countries are going to be significantly higher than is assumed in this projection for at least a decade or two, and consequently the computed world population growth trends are understated. With a considerable degree of confidence one can state that the world population is going to number more than 5 billion inhabitants in the year 2000 unless an unexpected major reversal of mortality trends takes place. With a lesser degree of confidence but not without justification, one can assert that the world population is likely to reach a number higher than 6 billion inhabitants during the twenty-first century.

Evidence seems to be accumulating to support the notion that the traditional demographic transition projection can be considered an illustration of the upper limits of future world population growth. In a number of developing countries—with varying social, economic, climatic, historical, and religious conditions—for which reasonably good documentation of recent fertility trends exists, a distinctly more rapid decline of fertility has occurred than was true in the demographic transition of many of the now-developed countries. Keeping in mind the qualifications and assumptions, one can state that world population is not likely to be larger than 6.5 billion in the year 2000 and that it is not likely to reach 13 billion by the middle of the twenty-first century. On demographic grounds, however, one cannot categorically rule out the

traditional transition projection because it is conceivable that the demographic transition in the developing countries as it seems to be underway in the mid-1970s might decelerate considerably, that is, the decline in fertility rates might slow, mortality rates might increase, or both.

By this process of elimination one arrives at the rather broad conclusion that future world population growth is likely to take place between the two extremes illustrated by the illusory and the traditional demographic transitions. One might even go one step further in order to provide a more concrete picture and say that it seems plausible to assume that world population in the year 2000 will number about 6 billion inhabitants and that by the middle of the twenty-first century world population could be almost stabilized at around 8 to 11 billion (see Figure 2).

Probably more than ever before in human history, many national (and local) governments and international organizations are not merely passive observers of demographic trends but are actively involved in influencing the directions of population change. World, national, and subnational demographic trends—growth of populations, trends in rates of mortality, migration, fertility—are an expression of myriads of individual conscious and subconscious decisions. These decisions are in turn shaped by the economic and psychic activities of the families concerned to increase their own welfare as much as possible and by the social environment, including governmental policies. Policies that have an impact on demographic trends include both those that are designed to do so and many others for which such impact is a second-

FIGURE 2. *World population growth trends, 1900–2100*

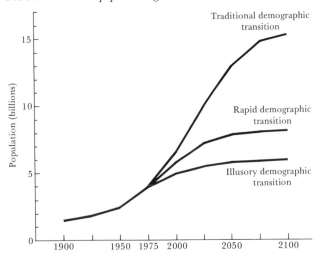

SOURCE: Adapted from Frejka, 1973.

ary consideration or an unforeseen side effect. With regard to national welfare, national governments are the centers where the current demographic properties and trends of the population are evaluated and decisions whether to modify them are taken.

According to a 1974 study by the United Nations, out of 148 governments, 85 considered their national population growth rates acceptable, 42 considered them excessive, and 21 considered their growth rates deficient. The perception of deficient population growth rates has resulted in serious population policy measures mainly in developed countries. In Bernard Berelson's words, it "appears that nations in particularly sensitive positions, as perceived locally (for example, Argentina, France, Israel), and nations with birth rates near or below replacement (for example, Bulgaria, Greece, Hungary, Japan, Poland, Romania) are not comfortable in those situations and seek remedies against 'demographic decline'" (Berelson, 1974, p. 773). In the developing countries, population policies designed to curb growth rates prevail. Thirty-three governments with 76 percent of the population of the developing countries have policies to reduce the population growth rate, and another 31 governments with an additional 16 percent of the population in the developing countries support family planning activities for other than demographic reasons.

The extent of the effect of population policies on demographic trends is difficult to assess, because numerous other components of the changing social environment simultaneously influence demographic behavior. Yet the experience of many countries has demonstrated that demographic trends are not only the result of the normal flow of events but are also modified by population poli-

cies. Policies regulating international migration, especially in tightly administered areas, tend to be the most effective policy measures; policies improving public and personal health conditions and thus lowering mortality rates tend to have a similar record; policies attempting to modify fertility behavior vary considerably in their effectiveness. According to Berelson, "Across the world it may be fair to say that developing countries have done better in lowering birth rates than the developed countries have done in increasing them; or, perhaps alternatively, that it is easier to lower birth rates by policy measures than to raise them" (1974, p. 788). However difficult it might be to assess the extent of impact, for instance of the antinatalist policies in the developing countries, nobody will dispute the proposition that fertility in almost all the countries with such policies would currently be higher than if there had not been such policies.

Future growth trends of any national population will reflect a complex interaction of numerous factors that in sum amount to the interaction between a nation's momentum of population growth—positive, stable, or negative—and its determination to modify this momentum. Consequently, since a large and increasing proportion of the world's population resides in the developing countries, the future size of the world population depends to a large degree on the extent to which fertility trends in the developing countries are modified.

Tomas Frejka

See also FERTILITY AND POPULATION GROWTH; FERTILITY DECLINE; FERTILITY DETERMINANTS.

BIBLIOGRAPHY

Berelson, Bernard. "Summary." In *Population Policy in Developed Countries,* edited by Bernard Berelson, pp. 771–789. New York: McGraw-Hill, 1974.

Frejka, Tomas. *The Future of Population Growth: Alternative Paths to Equilibrium.* New York: Wiley, 1973.

Glass, David V. "Demographic Prediction." *Proceedings of the Royal Society,* series B, 168(1011):119–139, 15 August 1967.

Grauman, John V. "Success and Failure in Population Forecasts of the 1950's: A General Appraisal." In *Proceedings of the World Population Conference, 1965,* vol. 3, pp. 10–14. New York: United Nations, 1967.

Keyfitz, Nathan. "On Future Population." *Journal of the American Statistical Association* 67(338):347–363, June 1972.

Mauldin, W. Parker. "Fertility Trends, 1950–75." *Studies in Family Planning* 7(9):242–248, September 1976.

United Nations, Department of International Economic and Social Affairs. *World Population Trends and Prospects by Country, 1950–2000: Summary Report of the 1978 Assessment.* Series R, no. 33. New York, 1979.

United States, Bureau of the Census. *Projections of the Population of the United States: 1975 to 2050.* Current Population Reports, series P-25, no. 601. Washington, D.C.: U.S. Government Printing Office, October 1975.

United States, Commission on Population Growth and the American Future. *Population and the American Future.* Washington, D.C.: U.S. Government Printing Office, 1972. New York: New American Library (Signet), 1972.

————. *Research Reports.* 7 vols. Washington, D.C.: U.S. Government Printing Office, 1972.

Westoff, Charles F. "The Predictability of Fertility in Developed Countries." In *Prospects of Population: Methodology and Assumptions,* pp. 206–214. New York: United Nations, Department of International Economic and Social Affairs, 1979.

PROXIMATE DETERMINANTS

See FERTILITY DETERMINANTS, *article on* PROXIMATE DETERMINANTS.

PUBLIC HEALTH

As a field of activity, public health deals with the diagnosis of problems and the advancing of policies and programs to raise the level of health of a human population. The health of a group may be viewed as the state of physical and social well-being of its members in relation to their environment, especially the extent of development of their capacities for survival and efficient maintenance over time. The goals of public health include reduction of morbidity and mortality and achievement of patterns of fertility that will most benefit the group. Efforts to facilitate use of birth control through family planning programs have health as a direct objective and may reinforce other activities to promote health. Such programs are discussed in more detail elsewhere in this work. [*See* FAMILY PLANNING PROGRAMS.]

The public health field draws on various basic sciences and disciplines and extends into the broad areas of socioeconomic and political development. In many ways, the public health field utilizes and contributes to basic concepts and methods for the study of population dynamics, and it greatly influences population phenomena.

Evolution of Public Health. The field of public health today continues several themes or lines of development that were evident in earliest times and converged especially as a result of social changes caused by the Industrial Revolution and the progress of modern science and technology. One such theme is concern for environmental determinants of human health, as expressed in ancient Greece in Hippocrates' *Airs, Waters, and Places,* seen later in nineteenth-century sanitation movements, and manifest in the twentieth century with the linking of biological, physical, and engineering knowledge in environmental health science.

Another theme has been concern with specific prevention of communicable disease, as represented by precepts in biblical writings, by medieval responses to epidemics, and by the concept of quarantine which in early modern times initiated appointment of community health councils and health officers. A parallel theme is the ancient tradition of curative medical care, which led to the establishment of medieval Arabic and European medical schools. It linked with the medieval system of church-connected hospices and later public hospitals and dispensaries for the poor. This tradition has burgeoned with the technological progress of recent times.

Still another theme links public health to social reform movements. Ever since the period of rapid urbanization in Europe, concerns for the special social problems of underprivileged groups have been closely associated with public health in reformist legislative and judicial action. A final, main theme has been concern for statistical analysis of human population dynamics, which emerged with the "political arithmetic" of the seventeenth century: the pioneering work of William Petty and John Graunt in England can be said to have fathered modern demography and public health planning; and it was concern for population policy also that led Johann Frank in Germany to the first modern formulations of integrative governmental health policies.

These different themes effectively converged in the functions of governmental health boards and departments only in the late 1800s. Since then, in countries throughout the world, commonalities have continued to develop in public health concepts, experience, and institutions. At national levels, responsibility for health leadership is usually vested in a ministry or department of health, with comparable structures at state or provincial and local levels. Along with increasing investment in health, wider scope of health interests, and transition in the nature of health problems in different countries, changes also occur in their organizational responses: more involvement with special aspects of health by other official bodies and private groups, mechanisms to strengthen general health planning, and concerns for decentralizing actual implementation of health work. At the international level, after earlier steps, the League of Nations established a Health Organization concerned with a spectrum of global health issues; it was succeeded in 1946 by the World Health Organization (WHO).

Theory of Public Health Action. Out of worldwide experience has emerged a general body of public health concepts, knowledge, and methods, applicable in different situations. In order to facilitate understanding of current progress and future steps in this field, such common features can be briefly reviewed, under the categories of policy leadership, problem analysis, intervention strategies, and program organization.

Policy leadership. A key concept of public health is that it involves responsibility for policy leadership to advance a set of functions: monitoring level of health, analyzing problems, identifying possible actions, helping concerned publics to understand health needs, mobilizing responses by whatever instrumental agencies are appropriate, directly organizing programs as may be required, coordinating related efforts, and working eventually to institutionalize changes that help maintain better health. This broad view of the leadership role is needed, even when focused on a particular segment of the population or on a particular category of health problems, in order to deal effectively with the combination of factors, and various steps, which may influence health improvement. Such leadership usually has a legal base, under governmental powers to protect the public welfare, and an executive base that combines technical, administrative, and fiscal responsibilities. Optimally, public health leaders have some political stability and also have access to legislative, regulatory, and judicial processes. One of their primary concerns, indeed, is to achieve general support and such specific policy measures as are needed.

Problem analysis. The analytic framework used by public health is that of human ecology, which views current health as a result of a complex network, or system, of interactions among different factors. Among them are aspects of the environment, possible injurious agents, and characteristics of the human population, including not only intrinsic biological features but also demographic and social characteristics such as size, density, mobility, and age and household composition. The major diagnostic disciplines in public health, epidemiology and biostatistics deal with aggregate phenomena, but they have been noteworthy among basic sciences for their capacity to draw upon insights from other disciplines, ranging from molecular biology to behavioral sciences, in building new knowledge. In this field, studies may have several aims: (1) defining an existing situation as a problem, including description, population affected, likely trends, and extent of human burden imposed; (2) clarifying various causal factors and their operation; (3) identifying practical indicators of the problem, to use in program planning; (4) guiding development of modes of intervention; and (5) analyzing changes over time, including the effects of intervention.

Intervention strategies. Inferences about causal relationships can lead to identifying possible modes of intervention, which can be categorized in various ways. One way is to separate modes of intervention at the environmental level from those at the personal level. Environmental modes include (1) physical interventions, to separate noxious agents from human contact (e.g., in water or air), (2) biological interventions (e.g., types of insect control), and (3) social interventions to modify adverse patterns or influences (e.g., as may affect mental health or addiction or strengthen the care of children). Personal-level modes include (1) physical methods (e.g., contraception against unwanted pregnancy, occupational safety devices), (2) biological interventions (e.g., immunization, nutrition, care by a midwife), and (3) behavioral protection (e.g., exercise, avoidance of risk). Obviously, different kinds of intervention may complement one another. Some may be protective at a more general level (e.g., water supply) while others may be aimed at a specific problem (e.g., child-proof medicine bottles). Possible modes of intervention can also be analyzed for technical and operational feasibility under different conditions. Furthermore, within each category, mechanisms might be classified according to "levels" of prevention. The ideal, at a primary level, is prevention of a health problem; secondary-level steps might ameliorate a health problem that already exists (e.g., medical treatment); tertiary-level steps might ease resultant longer-term disability.

Historically, initial public response to health problems has tended to concentrate on secondary measures applied to individual cases appearing "in series," with high expense and little effect on the incidence of the problems. The public health approach seeks more systematically to understand underlying dynamics, and to mobilize intervention mechanisms having broad effects that aim more to promote health and prevent illness with lower total costs, and further to establish such measures on a self-sustaining basis that will require only minimal monitoring thereafter.

Program organization. Field program activities organized to invoke various kinds of public health interventions also have certain common patterns. A basic need is for sensitive and practical indicators of the health problems which can be tools for interpretation, planning, and action. Optimally such indicators may be linked to demographic events such as births, deaths, and marriage. In its pilot stages, a health program can gain from working with private groups having the advantages of credibility, flexibility, and low profile. There is usually need also to work with other government agencies concerned with related functions. Design of field program activities requires translation of intervention strategies into operational functions, tasks and roles, utilizing expert insights from education, medicine, nursing, engineering, administration, and other fields. Whatever its functions, in principle the program must recognize appropriate existing local institutions, networks of influence, and group boundaries. Moreover, involvement of local people in planning and implementation is needed for both immediate efficiency and longer-term maintenance of the program.

The kind of organizational structure best suited to providing direction and support for field activities is a recurrent issue—whether to have a centralized administration concentrating on a particular type of problem (termed a "vertical" program because initiatives from the top of the administrative structure can be transmitted directly to subordinate levels) or to seek the integration of a new set of problem-related activities into the functions performed by a multipurpose, continuing, decentralized program (a "horizontal" model). The vertical program may offer more simplicity, thrust, and short-term efficiency, while a horizontal program may be more complex and vulnerable to breakdown but better fitted to evolution and long-run maintenance of locally based activities. Public health organizations involve other special problems of staff development and incentives, supervisory networks, logistical flows, and management information systems. For example, needs for adaptability in such programs may clash with traditional fiscal systems. Furthermore, a feature of successful major programs has often been the presence of a semi-independent institution able to provide support through research and evaluation, training, pilot studies, and general advocacy. Effective program development also requires careful consideration of priorities for action among different geographic areas and within population subgroups, according to access and need. There are usually critical considerations of program timing, including gradual phasing in of efforts to allow for learning how to be effective, to be efficient, and to expand program coverage.

Areas of Action. Public health policy and program activities can be grouped in different ways by problem type. A number of broad and important problem categories are listed below. This list might of course be expanded and be subject to different priorities in particular areas. Under each category, selected observations aim to illustrate some of the general features of public health previously noted, and to indicate the current range of problems, approaches, and further challenges in this field.

Nutrition. The quantity and quality of food consumption directly influence most fundamentally the survival, physical and mental development, and productivity of a human group. Poor nutrition also raises susceptibility to the respiratory and intestinal groups of disease, which are main killers in poorer populations. It is estimated that malnutrition due to basically inadequate intake of proteins and carbohydrates is linked to about half the deaths under age 5 in less-developed countries. Governmental

policies and programs seeking to achieve adequate and continuing supplies of staple foods for all must of course deal with a complex system including many aspects of agriculture, trade, transportation, pricing, and means for assuring access by poor and vulnerable groups. Public health professionals have a crucial role in this general system, in assessing and monitoring the basic problems, considering alternative approaches, and meeting special needs. A direct approach through supplemental feeding programs is appropriate in times of famine, in certain institutional settings, and perhaps as an incentive along with other services. However, such programs have many problems and may be counterproductive if they divert from building long-term self-sufficiency of food supply.

Public health efforts have also dealt with more specific nutritional deficiency problems. For example, beriberi in Asia declined with improvement of diet and use of synthetic thiamine. Pellagra was a main cause of death, disability, and mental disease in the southern United States; it disappeared with diet changes and with the enrichment of bread with niacin. Iodine deficiency in some areas of the world has caused serious problems of thyroid disease, mental deficiency, and death; analysis of this problem and its resolution through routine iodization of salt illustrates the ideal "transitional" role of public health programs. In the poorest countries, problems of blindness from vitamin A deficiency and debility from iron-deficient anemia are currently receiving special attention. On the other hand, especially among people with incomes just above poverty level, problems of obesity may become serious.

Water and wastes. Water-related diseases include a group of infections that may be directly water-borne (such as cholera, typhoid, and other bacterial, viral, and parasitic infections) and that can be reduced by purifying drinking water, and another group of intestinal and skin infections whose spread can be reduced by improving general hygiene through increasing the quantity of water easily available. Public health action leading to introduction of safe and convenient water systems in Western countries caused rapid decline of these problems. In developing countries today, water problems and nutrition are perhaps most crucial factors for health, but many major cities and rural areas still have inadequate community water supply and sewage services. The population estimated to have not even "minimum access" to adequate water and waste systems ranges from about 70 percent in Asia and in sub-Saharan Africa to about 40 percent in Latin America.

Programs dealing with this problem, however, may involve relatively high costs; total pending needs for community water and sanitation facilities worldwide have been estimated to require some $200 billion. Also, there are special organizational problems. Matters of design and construction may involve separate government departments; new local bodies often must be formed to deal with continuing financial and maintenance needs; and rural areas especially require accompanying education and sanitation programs. Another problem noted in current analyses relates to motivation. In Western countries such improvements were often strongly supported by health arguments. In developing countries today the official ministries vested with responsibility for health tend to focus instead on curative care facilities. The arguments for upgrading drinking water supplies tend to be based on a rather diffuse set of objectives, such as more general health protection for the poor, greater public convenience, and meeting other urban needs for water. These compete poorly with arguments for public investment in other projects more amenable to claims of immediate economic return. Noteworthy also are the implications of water and waste systems for population change. Extensions of water supply may have important influence on rates and patterns of urban growth. The adequacy of methods used to forecast population trends will influence the design and ultimately the efficiency of building such systems.

Vector-borne diseases. Among the diseases transmitted among humans through other living vectors, malaria has perhaps been most dramatic in its historical impacts and recent developments. During the 1950s, the estimated number of cases worldwide was still at least 300 million, with about three million deaths annually. Useful new knowledge by then included sensitive measures of malaria occurrence, drug therapy, and methods for interrupting mosquito transmission by domiciliary spraying with residual insecticide. After pilot experience with such methods for control purposes, WHO and other international agencies assisted the development of ambitious national campaigns to eradicate the disease from endemic areas. These programs involved preparatory and attack phases, spraying DDT to interrupt transmission and to minimize the numbers of people still infectious. Such efforts were administered by special, centralized organizations and were generally very effective. In India during a decade malaria declined by a thousandfold, from about one hundred million cases to one hundred thousand annually.

The next goal was to switch, during consolidation and maintenance phases, to continuing and careful surveillance to detect and treat any new cases, only spraying again rarely if an outbreak should occur. It was hoped to economize by changing to a decentralized system and integrating malaria surveillance with delivery of other basic health services. However, such local systems were still poorly developed and subject to other diversions, leaving wide gaps in coverage. Recurrence of serious disease outbreaks then led to on-again, off-again efforts at control, development of insecticide-resistant mosquitoes and drug-resistant malaria parasites, and major subsequent resurgences of the disease. These have had high human and economic costs; after virtual elimination of the disease from large areas, worldwide incidence is reported to have risen again by 1980 to a level of over 150 million cases and 1.5 million deaths. Efforts now aim at reestablishing systems to apply more effective insecticides and treatment methods and to strengthen other local steps to interrupt the vector and disease cycle.

Other infectious diseases. Other diseases communicated through air, food, and contact with infected people still pose great challenges. Tuberculosis was a major killer in Western countries during the process of industrialization, and although now specific treatment is available it still poses serious threats in poor countries. On another scale, the kind of influenza virus pandemic that in 1918 killed about twenty million people in the world, including some half million in the United States, could occur again. For a number of serious problems of infectious disease more basic research is still essential. Effective immunization methods have been developed against diphtheria, tetanus, pertussis, poliomyelitis, yellow fever, and measles. Despite this achievement, in the poorer countries less than 10 percent of some one hundred million children born each year are receiving the available kinds of immunizations. In West Africa alone measles still kills about one-half million children annually. Currently, WHO is assisting an Expanded Programme on Immunization to help national governments produce such vaccines and develop the necessary extended service systems.

Noteworthy especially for its historical significance and practical lessons is the recently successful worldwide campaign to eradicate smallpox. Against this ancient scourge, the technical solution of vaccination began to be widely applied in the nineteenth century. More recently an improved stable vaccine was developed, and heavy investments were made in national vaccination programs. Yet in many rural areas of the world, smallpox still was causing some two million deaths yearly by 1967, when the global eradication program began. This effort benefited from effective institutional research and training support services. It especially demonstrated the value of close cooperation between governments and WHO in fiscal aspects, in use of some seven hundred professionals from around the world to assist directly in field operations, and in developing local capacities for such work. The crucial organizational principle, however, was to shift away from the kind of weak program model that focuses on getting reports that certain services presumed to be useful (in this case, immunizations) are being performed in each area, by field staff who are assigned numerical targets for such achievement. The new model focused its attention not on routine immunization activity but instead on the most crucial and relevant indicator—occurrence of the actual smallpox cases. The newer program involved two prongs: one was an aggressive and imaginative system to detect every appearance of cases of the disease; the other ensured that for each such case a package of defined actions was carefully performed (for this program, these included education, isolation, and vaccination of contacts). This revision in basic program design led, essentially within a decade, to eradication of smallpox.

Maternal and child health. The crucial event of human reproduction will continue to be a main focus of attention in public health. Maternity and early childhood involve high potentials for serious damage and also for long-term benefits and present opportunities for feasible and effective programs of intervention. For example, for all the births occurring in a population under very adverse conditions, deaths may occur to as many as 3 percent of the mothers and within a year to 30 percent or more of the infants; whereas a combination of practical health measures can reduce such losses to less than 0.03 percent and 3.0 percent, respectively. General nutrition and sanitation can be improved with education and assistance in the home setting. Infant survival and child health are improved by better diet for the mother and by simple precautions at delivery, with access to medical care for complications. Other effective measures include encouraging close nurturance and prolonged breastfeeding of the infant, care with further diet, early immunizations, access to simple treatment for dehydration and infections, guidance in how to prevent accidents, fostering continuity of support and stimulation, and helping to avoid the mother's becoming pregnant again too quickly or having more children than the family can care for well. At school age, there are further needs and opportunities to reinforce preventive health behaviors. This set of basic concerns for maternal and child health can be taken to constitute the core of "primary health care."

Public health programs working efficiently on these matters in poor areas have had certain notable features of design and organization: concentration first on such simple and important preventive actions as can be extended effectively to the whole population being served rather than seeking to provide "comprehensive" service to a few; active participation of community members in various ways; involvement of indigenous birth attendants and medical practitioners; maintaining direct helping relationships with households and women's groups; and extensive use of closely supervised auxiliary field staff. Such programs may use special mechanisms to as-

sure detection and recording of all births in an area, since these are the critical events for planning and operational purposes (e.g., for initiating services, assessing infant mortality, and guiding family planning work). Other key indicators include measures of survival and weight gain. In a poor, high-fertility area, maternal and child health program needs can be heavy, involving up to 30 percent of the total population (perhaps 20 percent of whom are children aged 0–5 and 10 percent of whom are mothers). In transitional and richer areas, maternal and child health programs deal with problems of less magnitude but still with basic elements similar to those just described (e.g., need for improved diet, better delivery conditions, and early immunizations), especially among the underprivileged, with additional problems relating to such factors as family fragmentation and urbanization.

Alcohol. Misuse of alcohol has become a serious and apparently increasing health problem worldwide. Per capita alcohol consumption has been rising in developed and in many less-developed countries. In the United States alone, with an estimated ten million problem drinkers, alcohol misuse is identified as a cause in more than 10 percent of all deaths each year (linked with deaths from cirrhosis, violence and accidents, cancer, and effects on pregnancy); and total costs are held to exceed $42 billion annually. In response to such problems, government and private groups have advanced diverse policy and program steps ranging from limiting the advertising and availability of alcohol to treatment for alcoholism. Internationally, a WHO Project on Prevention of Alcohol-related Problems is seeking to help organize knowledge, experience, and mutual assistance toward effective prevention. A U.S. Surgeon General's report for 1979, in proposing elements of a national preventive program, recognized the view of alcoholism as a group phenomenon, whereby the overall degree of access and of social approval influences the level of per capita consumption and the extent of abuse. It favored further policies to influence pricing, advertising, and outlets. Also, concerned groups are emphasizing newer approaches to early education which encourage peer pressures against alcohol abuse.

Smoking. A WHO group has estimated that, of any "single action," control of cigarette smoking could most improve health and prolong human life. In the United States, smoking is linked to more than three hundred thousand deaths each year and to chronic diseases in more than 10 million people. Surveys show heavy tobacco consumption also in Europe, Asia, and Latin America, with less in Africa. Similar patterns occur worldwide: higher use by "blue-collar" males and rising trends among women and youth. In response, a WHO Expert Committee on Smoking Control has proposed preventive program strategies. World tobacco production rose greatly in the last decade, and the Food and Agricultural Organization (FAO) of the United Nations has become concerned with related tax and trade issues and possible replacement crops. With the development of national antismoking programs in Europe and the United States, some declines in male usage are now occurring. Initially, such programs have tended to concentrate on public information to encourage people to stop smoking; important newer steps aim at mobilizing peer support among school children for not starting to smoke.

Toxic agents. Proliferation of toxic chemical agents by industrial processes, especially in recent decades, has created major threats to human health that are only beginning to receive systematic study and response. In the United States more than thirteen thousand toxic substances are known to be in commercial use and more are added every year; more than two thousand are suspected carcinogens. Many of these not only contaminate work places and commercial products but also invade the general environment. Toxic effects known to occur range from impairments of physical development to cancer and degenerative disease. Poorer countries already have severe problems with some toxic agents (e.g., insecticides) and such problems will increase. The complexity and sensitivity of this area is reflected in the wide variety of agencies in the United States that are now engaged in research in and management of problems posed by toxic agents. The range of public health interventions that may be required is indicated in the U.S. Surgeon General's 1979 report, *Healthy People,* which outlines proposals for further action in the areas of training, public education, medical service, technical improvements, legislative and regulatory steps, and related economic measures.

Cardiovascular disease. Along with modernization came a marked rise in incidence of cardiovascular disease, and it remains the main cause of death in Western countries. Recently, however, there has been some decline; since 1968 in the United States, deaths from heart disease have fallen by more than 20 percent and from stroke by more than 30 percent. Programs for prevention have encouraged the public to avoid known multiple risk factors by moderating diet, stopping smoking, exercising, managing stress, and detecting and treating hypertension. Hypertension is an especially important component which, for example, afflicts about 15 percent of the United States population, especially women and blacks. Experience is now showing that public health efforts can effectively attack this problem. In the United States, the proportion of people who have become aware of and are controlling hypertension has doubled in recent years. Urban community programs have been able to raise the level of detection and treat-

ment to more than 70 percent of those in need, by systematic approaches through institutions and work places and by tracking and follow-up. Community programs in Europe have also included steps to reduce the fat content of local foods, and to form "hypertensive clubs" for afflicted people to help each other.

Cancer. Efforts to control cancer, the second leading cause of death in the United States, have tended so far to encourage early detection and treatment of cancers of the breast, cervix, prostate, bowel, and bladder. Program activities have included professional and public education, screening, and referral services. Notable especially has been the general acceptance and effectiveness of the "Pap test" for early cervical cancer. Reviews of such efforts, however, still note a patchwork nature and strong tendencies to finance curative facilities but not relatively inexpensive preventive work. Moreover, it is clear that major prevention of certain types of cancer should be achieved ultimately through reducing exposures to smoking, toxic compounds, and alcohol and overexposures to sun and radiation. An International Agency for Research on Cancer now aims especially to advance prevention work.

Violence. The category of violent injury, including accidents, suicides, and homicides, causes seriously high losses in both poorer and richer countries. Even with declines in overall mortality, this category has tended to account for a relatively constant proportion (6 to 7 percent) of all deaths in different countries. Causal patterns vary between different subgroups of population. In Western countries, violent injuries have become the leading cause of death for people between 1 and 44 years of age; and since they especially afflict the young they cause major loss of productive years of life. In the United States, about 150,000 violent deaths occur annually, including some 51,000 from motor vehicle accidents and 30,000 from firearms, and about one half of fatal accidents involve alcohol use. For public health action a primary need is gaining public and professional concern for the preventability of such problems. Effective preventive measures against accidents aim at critical safety factors with specific steps relating to education, engineering, law enforcement, and economic incentives. Current efforts, for example, deal with accident-oriented training for vulnerable groups (e.g., to prevent falls among the aged), extending the use of smoke detectors, improving motor vehicle safety restraints, controlling drunken driving, strengthening laws against hand guns, and adjusting automobile and industrial rates to reward safer design and performance.

Mental health. The occurrence of serious psychosis is a problem worldwide. Some of such mental disease, due to certain types of infection and malnutrition, is now being prevented in richer countries. For other kinds of serious psychosis, modern drug treatment can ease symptoms, but prevention still awaits further research. With industrialization and change in family systems, Western countries experienced heavy demand for public facilities to care for long-term mental illness. This institutional load is declining, with rise in systems for outpatient care.

More demanding of public health attention now are problems of psychological and social dysfunction among groups being affected by stressful shifts in population patterns. Rapid economic change and urbanization are increasing family disruption and social vulnerability. The growing numbers of the elderly, many of them alone and relatively poor, may be subject increasingly to psychogeriatric disorders. Meanwhile, large numbers from "baby-boom" cohorts have entered early adulthood subject to social and economic frustration that may be reflected in delinquency, drug and alcohol addiction, and violence. Increases in teenage and out-of-wedlock births and in marital disruption have raised the numbers of single-parent poor families, resulting in increasing numbers of children living in poverty and in broken homes. Such conditions predict a rise in special kinds of mental health problems.

The responses of public health programs in the United States in recent years have included more use of locally based mental health centers. These still tend to deal largely with individual crisis problems, while community prevention efforts at a deeper level, including steps to help avoid early pregnancies, have been generally weak. National concerns for strengthening mental health efforts have involved debates on basic issues of welfare and employment policies. More specific program recommendations have recently focused on preventing and controlling stress, through helping to build new sources of social support to individuals through family, neighborhood, and other groups, and through educational efforts to equip children better to cope with stressful situations. Much still remains to be done.

Genetics. The genetic composition of human populations, with its many health and demographic implications, is known still to be changing in different ways. Mutations occur naturally and have been shown to rise with toxic exposures. Forces of natural selection involve the potent mechanisms of mortality differentials and now of fertility differentials. Clusterings of gene types in endogamous groups change with social mobility and migration. Knowledge of genetic mechanisms at the cellular level has progressed, especially regarding the occurrence of specific disorders resulting from single-gene defects and chromosomal abnormalities. Over a thousand of these are so far identified, which in the United States are estimated now to cause about one-tenth of childhood

deaths. For this type of problem, public health approaches are developing at several levels: prenatal screening to allow informed preventive action; diagnosis during pregnancy and the availability of abortion; routine testing of newborns to detect metabolic defects and prescribe ameliorative regimes; possible later therapies; and establishment of confidential genetic register systems for future information of persons at high risk. Such efforts receive increasing attention with respect to technical, educational, organizational, economic, and ethical aspects. Less well understood yet are the genetic components in many common chronic diseases, which apparently arise from interactions between hereditary factors and environmental influences.

The concept of eugenics proposes that a human population might establish conditions that would influence favorably its own biological evolution. To this end, pioneers such as Frederick Osborn have noted that the main need is for societies to provide equality of individual opportunity, to assure access to birth control, and to cherish diversity. There is great caution especially about inadequate knowledge of the roles, or the possible implications, of genetic contributions to positive human attributes such as intelligence and altruism. Tragically, however, others have linked genetic notions to destructive racism, rendering the subject very sensitive. Careful scientific and ethical expression of the eugenic concept has evolved at least in the areas of family planning and genetic disease control. Newer developments in molecular biology and in technology, such as artificial insemination and sperm banks, will raise levels of public interest and debate about this subject. To deal with the general issue will ultimately require a much stronger knowledge base and ethical framework than are now evident and will call for major concern by the field of public health.

Clinical medicine. The concept of public health includes the work of clinical practitioners providing direct medical services to individuals. Such curative medical services can reduce distress and damage when illness occurs and can be a channel for certain primary measures to prevent illness and promote health. Also, the availability of personal medical care is valued as a symbol of higher living standards and of governmental concern. Overall levels of health in human groups have been influenced in important ways by certain types of medical services—for example, the widespread availability of antibiotics and improved obstetrical care. It has been difficult, however, to relate causally the levels of health in different areas to such simple indicators as numerical ratios of doctors or hospital beds to people.

The pattern of clinical medical services in the United States and Western Europe has tended strongly toward centralized hospitals for intensive care of acute episodic illness of people nearby, combined with the availability of individual, largely urban, practitioners. In Eastern Europe, more central planning has led to better geographical distribution of medical facilities and, through polyclinic services, to better amalgamation of curative and preventive medical activities. More recently, countries such as China and Tanzania have developed innovative systems using auxiliary and lay persons to assure continuing local availability of simple curative and preventive medical services on a wide scale. Whereas modern Western patterns of medical care have tended to view people as dependent upon the professional system (for example, as implied in the use of such terms as "provider," "delivery," "patient," and "client,"), the newer patterns aim toward shifting to local people more responsibility in developing health activities.

The high costs of medical care have become especially burdensome. Advances in medical science have multiplied the expense of training, technology, and facilities, while rises in economic level, public awareness, and political pressures have greatly increased demands for such services. Effects of these increases include greater amounts of direct governmental support, extension of health insurance systems, greater attention to needs for operational efficiency, and rising concerns for encouraging more financing from local sources. A hope is sometimes expressed in the United States that more strengthening of preventive health services will help to reduce the rising expenditures for personal medical care. This hope is paradoxically wrong. The costs of personal medical care for people who die at younger ages tend to be lower, on the average, than the medical costs incurred during the final years before death of older people. Among the elderly, demands for newer medical technology (such as replacement of arthritic joints) can be expected to rise. Public health work indeed can continue to achieve huge net social and economic benefits, through preventing disability and premature death. Such total gains in production, which rely upon a high level of public health, then can indeed provide a basis for a rise in consumption of specific medical services that can ease the end-phase of life.

Moye Wicks Freymann

See also Epidemiologic transition; Morbidity; Morbidity and longevity.

BIBLIOGRAPHY

Bryant, John. *Health and the Developing World.* Ithaca, N.Y.: Cornell University Press, 1969.
Bulletin of the World Health Organization. Issued bimonthly in Geneva since 1947. In English and French with a separate edition in Russian.
Hobson, William (editor). *The Theory and Practice of Public Health.* 5th ed. Oxford, New York, and Toronto: Oxford University Press, 1979.
Rosen, George. *A History of Public Health.* New York: MD Publications, 1958.
United States, Office of the Surgeon General. *Healthy People: The Surgeon General's Report on Health Promotion and Disease Prevention.* Washington, D.C.: U.S. Government Printing Office, 1979.
WHO Chronicle. Issued bimonthly since 1947 by the World Health Organization, Geneva. In Arabic, English, French, Russian, and Spanish.
World Health Forum. Issued quarterly since 1980 by the World Health Organization, Geneva. In Arabic, Chinese, English, French, Russian, and Spanish.
World Health Organization. *World Health Organization Publications: Catalogue, 1947–1977.* Geneva, 1977. A supplement was issued in 1978.
———. *The Work of WHO, 1978–1979: Biennial Report of the Director General to the World Health Assembly and to the United Nations.* Geneva, 1980.

PUBLICATIONS

1. SERIALS AND REFERENCE WORKS   Richard Hankinson
2. BIBLIOGRAPHIC RESOURCES   Susan Kingsley Pasquariella

1.
SERIALS AND REFERENCE WORKS

This article is concerned with the literature of demography and population studies, not with the subjects covered by that literature. It deals with the books, monographs, serial publications, working papers, bibliographies, thesauri, and catalogs used by those working in the population field. This analysis of the literature of population intends primarily to provide an introduction to the wide variety of serial publications on human population topics. Its secondary emphasis is on the publications intended to assist those wishing to use the available literature, such as bibliographies, thesauri, catalogs, and other information materials and guides.

Journals. Many journals are devoted exclusively to population topics, and an even larger number of journals publish occasional articles on population topics. Population journals range from the highly technical to the popular, and from concern with worldwide demographic issues to a focus on the demographic problems of a subnational area or ethnic group. They are published on more or less regular schedules, which can vary from once a week to once a year, although some journals appear more irregularly.

Core journals. It is generally agreed that fewer than half a dozen population journals qualify as core journals. However, although consensus is likely that the English-language journals *Demography* and *Population Studies* and the French-language *Population* would be included, considerable variations could be expected in the selection of other titles. In an attempt to provide some objectivity to the selection process, two different approaches were used to try to identify the core journals. First, a representative international group of demographers was selected by taking a random sample of forty members of the International Union for the Scientific Study of Population (IUSSP) together with the fifteen current officers of the Union. A search was then conducted of the *Social Sciences Citation Index* data base for all journal articles by these fifty-five people for the years 1977–1979. The references provided for these articles were analyzed, and the journals cited in those references were noted. The results are shown in Table 1. Second, a similar citation analysis was undertaken for all articles published in three of the leading population journals, *Demography, Population Studies,* and *Population,* for the year 1979. The references provided for each of the articles published were examined in the same way. The results are shown in Table 2. The results of these two small-scale analyses indicate that there is a small core of primary population journals and that most references are made to articles that are published in those

few core journals. The evidence also suggests that population specialists tend to refer to articles published in the more influential journals of other disciplines (such as economics or sociology), rather than in other journals devoted primarily to population topics.

The oldest of the core journals is *Population Index,* which began publication in 1935. Following the multiplication of population journals after World War II, *Population Index* has concentrated more on the service it provides through its annotated bibliography, and less on publishing original articles. Two of the primary journals began publication in the mid-1940s. The French-language journal *Population* began publication in 1946, at the Institut National des Etudes Démographiques, the French government-supported demographic research institute in Paris. In 1947, the Population Investigation Committee in England started to publish *Population Studies.* Both journals continue to be of primary importance and are among the most frequently cited journals in the field. In 1964, these core journals were joined by the Population Association of America's *Demography,* which, on the basis of the preliminary evidence presented here, has become the most frequently cited journal in the discipline. The Population Council's *Studies in Family Planning* began publication in 1963 and, although primarily concerned with family planning, has had a significant impact on the field of population as a whole, possibly because of the emphasis given to maximizing the journal's distribution and making it available in several languages. *Family Plan-*

TABLE 1. *Journals cited six or more times by fifteen IUSSP officers and a random sample of forty IUSSP members, 1977–1979*

Journal cited	15 IUSSP officers	40 IUSSP members	Total
Demography	14	30	44
American Sociological Review	7	26	33
Population Studies	25	7	32
Family Planning Perspectives	4	20	24
Population	11	7	18
Social Forces	5	11	16
Social Biology	4	12	16
Studies in Family Planning	8	4	12
Journal of Regional Science	8	1	9
Review of Economics and Statistics	7	2	9
American Journal of Sociology	3	6	9
Milbank Memorial Fund Quarterly/ Health and Society	4	4	8
Population and Development Review	5	2	7
Sociological Methods and Research	0	7	7
Population Index	2	4	6
American Journal of Public Health	4	2	6

TABLE 2. *Journals containing articles cited more than twelve times by authors in* Demography, Population Studies, *and* Population *during 1979*

Journal cited	Demography	Population Studies	Population	Totals
Demography	(49)	36	3	(88)39*
Population Studies	31	(76)	4	(111)35*
Studies in Family Planning	5	17	9	31
Population Index	10	14	3	27
American Sociological Review	23	2	0	25
American Journal of Sociology	25	0	0	25
Journal of Political Economy	15	8	0	23
Population	3	13	(74)	(90)16*
Journal of the American Statistical Association	11	5	0	16
Science	7	8	0	15
Rural Sociology	13	1	0	14
Social Forces	9	5	0	14
Theoretical Population Biology	4	8	0	12

*Excludes citations for the journal concerned (inclusive figures are provided in parentheses).

ning Perspectives, published by the Alan Guttmacher Institute, also probably owes some of its impact to its widespread distribution. In 1975, the Population Council began publication of *Population and Development Review,* which by 1979 was beginning to be cited more frequently. The subject areas covered by these seven journals overlap to a considerable degree, but analysis of contents reveals some distinguishing features. The feature articles in *Population Index* in recent years are either methodological or bibliographic essays. *Demography* and *Population Studies* cover very much the same subject area, with perhaps slightly more emphasis on methodological articles and articles on the United States in *Demography*. *Population,* on the other hand, acts as the vehicle of the French-speaking school of demography, reflecting some of the features, such as a concern with declining fertility in Europe, that distinguish that school from the English-speaking demographers as a whole. *Population* also can be distinguished from the two primary English-language journals in that it tends to include, in addition to items of interest primarily to demographers, items of general social interest such as articles on suicide in the prison population, judicial statistics, housing, education, and social security. The titles of *Studies in Family Planning* and *Family Planning Perspectives* indicate their subject emphasis, as does that of *Population and Development Review,* which is concerned primarily with the relations between demographic factors and Third World development, with particular emphasis on implications for public policy.

Regional and national population journals. This category of journals also includes those whose primary focus is on population topics, although most articles published are concerned with a specific region, country, or language group. These journals may be of importance to the geographical area that they serve, but the evidence of the brief citation analyses presented in Tables 1 and 2 indicates that their influence is confined to those areas. Nevertheless, they do occasionally publish original or translated articles by authors from outside that area and on topics related to other areas. Table 3 lists some of the population journals that can be included in this category.

Subdisciplinary population journals. A third category of journals deals with a specific aspect of population studies. A prolific field for journals of this kind is family planning. Among the most influential journals in this area are *Studies in Family Planning* and *Family Planning Perspectives,* which fall into the category of core population journals because of the frequency with which they are cited. Also to be noted are *Advances in Planned Parenthood,* focusing on family planning programs as a whole; *Contraception,* focusing on the methodology of contraception; *Contraceptive Delivery Systems,* focusing on research on contraceptive delivery systems; and the *Journal of Biosocial Science,* which includes coverage of a wide range of family planning topics. *Population Reports,* previously published by George Washington University and now published by the Population Information Program at Johns Hopkins University, provides technical information on many aspects of contraception, family planning, and abortion, and can be considered a journal in this category. There are also several journals that are primarily concerned with family planning in specific countries. They include (*Egyptian Population and Family Planning Review*), France (*Contraception, fertilité, sexualité*), Great Britain (*British Journal of Fam-*

TABLE 3. *Regional and national population journals*

Region or country	Title	Language of publication	Summaries in other languages
Africa	*Jimlar mutane*	English & French	None
Austria	*Demographische Informationen*	German	None
Bangladesh	*Rural Demography*	English	None
Belgium (Flemish-speaking)	*Bevolking en Gezin*	Dutch	English
Belgium (French-speaking)	*Population et famille*	French	English
Brazil	*Boletim demográfico*	Portuguese	Some English
Canada	*Canadian Studies in Population*	English & French	English & French
Canada (Quebec)	*Cahiers québécois de démographie*	French	None
China	*Renkou yanjiu*	Chinese	None
Czechoslovakia	*Demografie*	Czech	English & Russian
Czechoslovakia	*Demosta*	English, Esperanto, French, Russian, & Spanish	None
Czechoslovakia	*Populační zprávy*	Czech	English (published separately)
Egypt	*Dirasāt sukānīyah*	Arabic & English	Arabic & English
Egypt	*Population Sciences*	English	None
Hungary	*Demográfia*	Hungarian	English & Russian
India	*Demography India*	English	None
India	*Population Review*	English	None
Indonesia	*Majalah demografi Indonesia*	Indonesian & English	Indonesian & English
Indonesia	*Warta demografi*	Indonesian	None
Italy	*Genus*	Italian, English, & French	Italian, English, & French
Japan	*Jinko mondai kenkyu*	Japanese	English
Japan	*Jinkogaku kenkyu*	Japanese	English
Morocco	*As-soukan*	French	None
New Zealand	*New Zealand Population Review*	English	None
New Zealand	*Quarterly Population Bulletin*	English	None
Poland	*Studia demograficzne*	Polish	English & Russian
Portugal	*Revista do Centro de Estudos Demográficos*	Portuguese	English & French
United Kingdom	*Population Trends*	English	None
West Germany	*Zeitschrift für Bevölkerungs-wissenschaft*	German & English	German, French, & English
Yugoslovia	*Stanovništvo*	Serbo-Croatian	English, French, or Russian

ily Planning), India (*Health and Population: Perspectives and Issues* and *Journal of Family Welfare*), New Zealand (*Journal of Family Planning*), and South Korea (*Journal of Family Planning Studies*). Family planning journals intended more as newsletters than as vehicles for the publication of original research studies are also published in many countries and by many international organizations.

Several other subfields of demography have journals devoted to them. In historical demography, apart from the bilingual annual *Bibliographie internationale de la démographie historique*, in French and English, there are the French-language journal *DH: Bulletin d'information*, the English-language *Local Population Studies*, and the Italian-language *Bollettino di demografia storica*. The migration field includes the journals *International Migration*, published in English, French, and Spanish by the Intergovernmental Committee for European Migration in Geneva; *International Migration Review*, published by the

Center for Migration Studies on Staten Island, New York; *Studi emigrazione,* published in Italian and French by the Centro Studi Emigrazione in Rome; and *Hommes et migrations,* published in Paris. *Population and Environment: Behavioral and Social Issues,* originally called the *Journal of Population,* published by the American Psychological Association, started publication in New York in 1978 and is concerned with behavioral, social, and environmental aspects of population. The journal *Theoretical Population Biology* emphasizes methodological studies that are more concerned with population biology than human demography but contains sufficient articles of relevance to be also listed here.

Popular journals. A fourth category consists of journals whose primary object is communication of new information in a popular way, rather than publication of technical or original research. Despite their avowedly popular approach, there is some merit in listing them here because they sometimes include substantive articles as well as information and are not only widely distributed but are also cited by those working in this area. Journals falling into this category include the International Planned Parenthood Federation's *People,* published in London; *International Family Planning Perspectives,* published by the Alan Guttmacher Institute in New York; and the Population Reference Bureau's *Population Bulletin* and *Intercom,* published in Washington, D.C. The journal *American Demographics,* first issued in 1979, also falls into this category, as its stated intention is to popularize demography and bring its findings to the public, particularly the business world, in a usable form. The East-West Center's *Asian and Pacific Census Forum* provides information on censuses in Asia.

United Nations. A fifth category includes the population journals published under the auspices of the United Nations, including the Population Division's *Population Bulletin of the United Nations,* the *Population Bulletin of the United Nations Economic Commission for Western Asia,* the Centro Latinoamericano de Demografía's *Notas de población,* and the United Nations Fund for Population Activities' *Populi.* These journals, which are halfway between in-house journals and regular refereed population journals, exist primarily to disseminate information rather than to publish new and innovative research findings, although they do include some original articles on population topics.

Journals in other fields. A significant percentage of articles of immediate demographic relevance is published in journals whose primary focus is not on demography. As Tables 1 and 2 show, authors submit articles to journals in other disciplines, including medicine, geography, family studies, statistics, history, biology, economics, development studies, and sociology. In order to provide some further indication as to which of the journals might be of the most interest to demographers, an analysis was made of the number of articles from them cited in *Population Index* over the three-year period 1977–1979. This analysis shows that there were more than a hundred journals averaging more than two articles of direct demographic relevance per year. Of these, forty-five journals published more than four relevant items a year (see Table 4).

Bibliographies. Given the increasing number of articles published in so many journals and in such a variety of languages, bibliographies of the field are indispensable. Researchers will require the bibliographies of demography and population studies that appear in serial and nonserial form; they will also depend on bibliographies published in other fields.

Population serial bibliographies. For many years the demographic community was served by one serial bibliographical journal solely devoted to the literature of demography, *Population Index.* Edited and published since 1935 at the Office of Population Research in Princeton, New Jersey, it is an official publication of the Population Association of America. It is received by every member of that association and by members of the IUSSP as a benefit of membership. Published in English, it attempts to cover all the relevant literature in the Western and Slavic languages, and items in other languages where possible. Each quarterly issue contains about 900 citations, more than 90 percent of which are annotated and classified under twenty broad subject headings and some seventy subheadings. Its coverage includes not only books, monographs, journal articles, working papers, and theses published on population and demography but also items culled from intensive, regular searches of the literature of disciplines associated with demography, including economics, sociology, statistics, geography, and medicine. In addition to the bibliographical section, each issue also contains a selection of articles of current interest, many of which take the form of bibliographic essays, and a selection of statistical tables.

Population Index also publishes some issues devoted to specific subjects, such as its periodic listing of government serial publications containing vital or migration statistics. An annual cumulative author and geographical index is provided as part of the normal subscription and cumulative indexes covering longer periods of time are published as needed (Princeton University, 1971). *Population Index* is currently being computerized and, as of January 1982, is a contributing data base to the POPLINE system now available at the U.S. National Library of Medicine.

In 1978, *Population Index* was joined by the *Review of Population Reviews,* an abstract journal published by the Committee for International Cooperation in National

TABLE 4. *Journals occasionally publishing demographic articles,*[1] *1977–1979*

Averaging 4–5 per year	Averaging 6–7 per year	Averaging 8–9 per year	Averaging 10+ per year
Annales: Economies, sociétés, civilisations (Paris)	*Annals of Human Biology* (London)	*Biuletyn Instytut Gospodarstwa Spolecznego* (Warsaw)	*American Journal of Public Health* (Washington, D.C.)
Annals of the American Academy of Political and Social Science (Philadelphia)	*British Medical Journal* (London)	*Ekistics* (Athens)	*Environment and Planning A* (London)
Economic Development and Cultural Change (Chicago)	*Cahiers ORSTROM: Série sciences humaines* (Paris)	*Journal of Interdisciplinary History* (Cambridge, Mass.)	*Journal of Family History* (Minneapolis)
Economie et statistique (Paris)	*Demografía y economía* (Mexico City)	*Revista brasileira de estatística* (Rio de Janeiro)	*Journal of Marriage and the Family* (Minneapolis)
Geographical Review (New York)	*Human Biology* (Detroit)	*Soviet Geography* (Washington, D.C.)	*Social Biology* (Madison, Wis.)
Historical Methods (Washington, D.C.)	*Journal of Development Studies* (London)	*Vestnik statistiki* (Moscow)	*Wiadomości statystyczne* (Warsaw)
International Labour Review (Geneva)	*Pakistan Development Review* (Islamabad)	*Wirtschaft und Statistik* (Mainz)	
Public Health Reports (Hyattsville, Md.)	*Philippine Economic Journal* (Manila)		
Raumforschung und Raumordnung (Cologne)	*Review of Public Data Use* (Arlington, Va.)		
Regional Studies (Elmsford, N.Y., & Oxford)	*Rural Sociology* (Knoxville, Tenn.)		
Review of Regional Studies (Birmingham, Ala.)	*Science* (Washington, D.C.)		
Revista cubana de administración de salud (Havana)	*Social Forces* (Chapel Hill, N.C.)		
Revista de statistica (Bucharest)	*Social Science and Medicine* (Elmsford, N.Y., & Oxford)		
Statistisk tidskrift (Stockholm)	*Statistika* (Sofia)		
Statisztikai szemle (Budapest)	*World Health Statistics Quarterly* (Geneva)		
Tijdschrift voor economische en sociale geografie (Amsterdam)			
Transactions of the Institute of British Geographers (London)			
Total = 17	Total = 15	Total = 7	Total = 6

[1] This table includes all articles selected for citation in *Population Index* over a three-year period. It is therefore indicative only of and dependent on the judgment of the editors of *Population Index* as to whether an article is of demographic relevance or not. It does not intend to indicate the quality of the articles included. Further information on the journals listed here can be found either in standard reference works, such as *Ulrich's International Periodicals Directory,* or in the annual cumulative index to *Population Index.*

Research in Demography (CICRED) in Paris with assistance from the United Nations Fund for Population Activities (UNFPA). The *Review,* formerly part of the *CICRED Bulletin,* is published quarterly in English, French, and Spanish editions. With the cooperation of the editors of some eighty journals in the field of population and related disciplines, the *Review of Population Reviews* is able to list the contents of recent and forthcoming issues of those journals, together with appropriate abstracts. This cooperation enables the *Review* to cut to a minimum the gap between publication and citation, but it means that the items covered are restricted to those published in cooperating population journals.

In addition to these two journals covering global literature, the *European Demographic Information Bulletin* has been published since 1970 by the European Centre for Population Studies in the Hague. This publication, using the same subject classification and style as *Population Index,* differs both in its regional emphasis and in its use of French and German as well as English as working languages. The late 1970s brought a substantial increase in the development of such regional publications. The most developed is *DOCPAL resumenes sobre población en América Latina.* This is a computer-generated, annotated bibliographic journal using Spanish as a working language currently published twice a year. It is concerned with the population literature from and about Latin America. First issued in June 1977, it is one part of a much wider initiative to improve the flow of population information within the region by making known and available published and unpublished reports, articles, and other documentation about the population of Latin America and the Caribbean. Consequently, it differs in some respects from *Population Index:* the annotations are in Spanish (although an English translation of the title is always provided) and are longer and designed to replace as far as possible the need of many users to see the original document. A backup documentation service is also provided, and a much higher proportion of unpublished documents is included.

In 1978 the first issue of an African regional equivalent to the Latin American *DOCPAL resumenes* was published. Entitled *PIDSA Abstracts,* this journal uses English and French as its working languages and is published by the United Nations Regional Institute for Population Studies (RIPS) at the University of Ghana in Legon, a suburb of Accra. This service complements another African initiative with its origins in France. Entitled *Démographie africaine: Bulletin de liaison,* this journal includes information on persons working on African demography, missions, ongoing census and research projects, conferences, training programs, and recent literature. Over the past few years, responsibility for this publication has been transferred to the United Nations Institut de Formation et de Recherche Démographiques (IFORD) in Yaoundé, Cameroon, for the French-language version, and to the United Nations Regional Institute for Population Studies for an English-language version published under the title *African Demography.*

In contrast, no regional journal of population abstracts is currently published for Asia, although there have been some useful attempts to provide this kind of service at the national level, for example the annual *Demography and Development Digest* published by the Demographic Research Centre at the University of Lucknow in India. Most other national population bibliographies are prepared and updated on an *ad hoc* basis and are discussed later in this article. The only near-equivalent is *ADOPT: Asian and Worldwide Documents on Population Topics,* published monthly by the Clearing House and Information Section of the Division of Population and Social Affairs of the United Nations Economic and Social Commission for Asia and the Pacific (ESCAP) in Bangkok. With English as a working language, this publication provides citations and annotations to some of the relevant English-language literature, together with a partial backup documentation service. The Regional Office for South-East Asia of the World Health Organization in New Delhi has published a periodical entitled *Bibliography on Human Reproduction, Family Planning and Population Dynamics: Annotated Articles and Unpublished Work in the South-East Asia Region.* This periodical was followed in 1977 by the publication of *Document on Human Reproduction, Family Planning and Population Dynamics,* a serial appearing irregularly.

In addition to the above regionally oriented population abstract journals, some other bibliographies concerned with specific aspects of population are also published periodically. A publication entitled *Population et développement: Bibliographie sélective,* published by the Centre Démographique ONU Roumanie (CEDOR) in Bucharest, provides annotated citations in French of the literature concerned with the relations between demographic and socioeconomic development, with primary emphasis on developing countries. The annual *Bibliographie internationale de la démographie historique,* a joint venture of the International Committee of Historical Sciences, the Société de Démographie Historique in Paris, and the IUSSP, attempts to cover the worldwide literature in historical demography. It includes short annotations for some citations, using English and French as working languages, and geographical, chronological, and author indexes. An annual bibliography entitled *Population and the Population Explosion* has been published by the Whitston Publishing Company, in Troy, New York, since 1970. It is not annotated and is confined primarily to North American English-language materials. In the family planning field, the first number of the abstracting journal *Family Planning Résumé* appeared in 1977 out of the Community and Family Study Center at the University of Chicago. The International Planned Parenthood Federation in London is also providing a current awareness service with its quarterly publication *IPPF Co-operative Information Service,* which lists relevant new acquisitions by contributing libraries but which does not provide abstracts. The Planned Parenthood Federation of America's *Current Literature in Family Planning,* which does include annotations, also provides a useful awareness tool for the family planning field.

Information on bibliographic serial publications can

be found in the standard reference works and in the list of sources published annually as part of *Population Index*.

Nonserial population bibliographies. Although most are not yet serial publications, population bibliographies have been compiled and published in several countries and, in many cases, are being updated periodically. Table 5 provides some information on countries that have published such official national bibliographies. Of course, many other relevant bibliographies are being published by many different organizations, but this section is confined to comprehensive national bibliographies prepared in or by the authorities of the country concerned.

This table was compiled from a review of citations

included under section Q, "Bibliographies, Directories, and Other Information Services," of *Population Index*. All but one of the bibliographies were compiled and produced within the countries named, either by a government organization or by a prominent university. Thus the many bibliographies that have been produced in developed countries on developing country populations are excluded. The table indicates that although some countries, notably Argentina, Austria, Czechoslovakia, Egypt, Italy, the Netherlands, South Korea, the Soviet Union, and West Germany, are served by comprehensive population bibliographies, many countries are not adequately covered. The need felt by some scholars working in certain European countries for

TABLE 5. *Countries for which official population bibliographies were published during 1968–1979*

Country	Sponsoring agency	Date(s) of publication	Years covered
Algeria	Secrétariat d'Etat du Plan	1969; 1972	Up to 1972
Argentina	Centro de Estudios de Población	1978	Up to 1977
Austria	Universität, Wien, Institut für Geographie	1980	1945–1978
Bangladesh	Bangladesh Institute of Development Studies	1976; 1978	n.a.
Canada	Dominion Bureau of Statistics	1966	1900–1966
Czechoslovakia	Výzkumný Ustav Sociálině Ekonomických Informací	Annually, 1968–	1968–1979
Egypt	Population and Family Planning Board	1979	Up to 1976*
Guatemala	Universidad del Valle de Guatemala	1978	1960–1976*
Indonesia	Gadjah Mada University	1974	1930–1972
Italy	Università di Roma	1966; 1973	1930–1972*
Madagascar	ORSTOM (Paris)	1975	Up to 1973*
Netherlands	Netherlands Interuniversity Demographic Institute and Netherlands Demographic Society	Annually, 1970–	1970–1979
New Zealand	University of Otago	1972	1838–1970*
Nigeria	University of Lagos	1976	1960–1974*
Pakistan	Pakistan Institute of Development Economics	1977	1950–1976
Papua New Guinea	Institute of Applied Social and Economic Research	1978	n.a.
Philippines	University of the Philippines	1974	n.a.*
South Korea	Korean Institute for Family Planning	1974; 1977; 1978; 1979; 1981	Up to 1980
Soviet Union	University of Moscow	1971; 1977	1965–1975
West Germany	Bundesinstitut für Bevölkerungsforschung	1979	1966–1975*

n.a. = not available.　　*With annotations.

national population bibliographies has resulted in the initiation of an international project to develop information of this kind. Under the guidance of the IUSSP Working Group on National Bibliographies, annotated population bibliographies are being developed for as many of the smaller language groups in Europe as possible. These bibliographies, which are being published in English or French, will cover the period since 1945 and will conform to the *Population Index* subject classification. By the end of 1980, substantial progress had been made toward the completion of bibliographies for Belgium, Czechoslovakia, the Netherlands, Norway, West Germany, and Sweden. In addition, plans were under way for several additional countries to participate in the project, including Austria, East Germany, Hungary, Italy, Poland, Romania, Switzerland, and Yugoslavia. December 1981 was the target date for completion of this international project, which should substantially advance international knowledge on what has been published in the demographic field.

Serial bibliographies in other fields. Scholars wishing to keep abreast of the new literature published in demography and population will frequently find it necessary to use the bibliographical serial publications and other services which, although primarily designed to cover other disciplines, include some items of relevance to demographers. Several of these bibliographies are also available for searches by computer, which increases their availability and their usefulness to the researcher. For obvious reasons, different scholars will find different bibliographical publications more or less relevant to their needs, depending on their own subjects and areas of concern. However, in an attempt to provide an overview of the relevance of such secondary sources to demographers as a whole, Table 6 has been compiled, based again on the experience of the editors of *Population Index*.

This table concerns citations included in *Population Index* for which the original sources were the bibliographical serial publications indicated. The table shows that there are at least twenty bibliographical serial publications that include an average of ten or more original citations of interest to demographers each year. The fact that such a significant percentage of relevant demographic publications is found in the information publications of disciplines other than demography indicates that publications aspiring to provide comprehensive coverage of the demographically relevant literature cannot rely on monitoring the population literature alone. A continual, time-consuming review of the literature and information services of other disciplines is required if adequate coverage of the relevant population literature is desired.

Published Catalogs. The published catalog provides one of the most comprehensive sources of information on publications in the population field. There are four published catalogs that are of major importance. The first to be published was the cumulative *Population Index* (Prince-

TABLE 6. *Nondemographic bibliographical serial publications including items of demographic relevance*

10–29 items per year	30–49 items per year	50+ items per year
Bibliography of Reproduction	*American Statistics Index*	*Biological Abstracts*
Bulletin analytique de documentation politique, economique et sociale contemporaine	*Dissertation Abstracts International, A: Humanities and Social Sciences*	*Current Contents: Social and Behavioral Sciences*
Bulletin signaletique: Section 521, *Sociologie, ethnologie*	*Excerpta Medica:* Section 17, *Public Health, Social Medicine and Hygiene*	*Geo Abstracts D: Social and Historical Geography*
Current Geographical Publications	*Public Affairs Information Service: Bulletin*	*Index Medicus* (150 per year)
Excerpta Medica: Section 22, *Human Genetics*	*Sociological Abstracts*	
Geo Abstracts C: Economic Geography		
International African Bibliography		
Journal of Economic Literature		
National Library of Medicine Current Catalog		
Psychological Abstracts		
Public Affairs Information Service: Foreign Language Index		

Source of data: Population Index, 1977–1979.

ton University, 1971), which contains all the citations published in the journal over the period 1935–1968. It is published in nine volumes: four volumes in which the citations are presented in alphabetical order and five volumes in which they are presented by geographical region or area. Approximately 75,000 citations are included. Work is currently under way to prepare a supplementary cumulative index by subject, author, and geographic region or area for the period 1969–1977, as a product of plans to computerize all citations from 1969 onward.

In 1976, the *Catalogs of the Bureau of the Census Library* were published (U.S. Bureau of the Census, 1976). In twenty volumes, this catalog contains approximately 323,000 citations reproduced from the catalog cards of the Bureau of the Census Library. The main catalog, in dictionary style, covers the general collection, the U.S. census collection, and the foreign and international collection. Separate catalogs contain the entries for the computer science micrographics collection and the state and local government collection. The first supplement to this catalog was published, in five volumes, in 1979.

The *Catalogue of the Population Council Library* (Population Council, 1979) is a photographic reproduction of the catalog cards of the library, which was established in 1952. Approximately 10,000 books, pamphlets, documents, theses, and unpublished materials are included. The first two volumes are organized by author, title, and added entry; the third volume is arranged by subject.

The fourth major catalog is the *CPC Microcatalog* (Carolina Population Center, 1978), a computer-produced catalog on microfiche of the library holdings of the Carolina Population Center at Chapel Hill, North Carolina, covering the social science aspects of population and family planning. Unlike indexes in book form, the 40,000 entries it contains can be searched in several different ways, including searches with terms drawn from the Carolina Population Center's *Population/Family Planning Thesaurus* (Lucas and Osburn, 1978), and by a keyword-in-context index. It is updated on an annual basis and is now available on-line through DIALOG Information Services, Inc., in Palo Alto, California. Unlike the three catalogs noted above, the *CPC Microcatalog* can be consulted only by using a microfiche reader.

Although not strictly speaking a catalog, one final reference tool of a similar nature deserves to be included here. It is *The International Population Census Bibliography: Revision and Update, 1945–1977* (Goyer, 1980). Originally published in six volumes and a supplement by the University of Texas in Austin starting in 1965, this comprehensive guide to the world's national population censuses has been extensively updated and revised.

Dictionaries and Thesauri. Several dictionaries and thesauri have been developed to cope with the terminol-

ogy of demography and with the additions and changes to the working vocabulary used by demographers. The basic source of definitions in the area remains the *Multilingual Demographic Dictionary,* published in English, French, and Spanish by the United Nations in 1958 and issued in subsequent editions in about fifteen languages, including Czech, Finnish, German, Italian, Brazilian Portuguese, Russian, Serbo-Croatian, and Swedish.

The need for a revision of this basic reference work soon became apparent as the traditional areas of demographic study such as fertility and migration expanded; new areas, such as historical demography and mathematical demography, developed, and rapid changes occurred in related fields, such as genetics, computer processing, survey design, family planning, and morbidity. In 1969, a special committee was set up by the IUSSP with the task of preparing a new dictionary (Siegel and Baum, 1977). This project was developed with the cooperation of the United Nations Population Division and with funding from the U.S. Agency for International Development (USAID). By mid-1974, the sections of the dictionary relating to fertility, family planning, and nuptiality had been approved in provisional form and were published by the IUSSP (Grebenik and Hill, 1974). The French-language version was published in 1981, but by September 1981 no other language versions were yet available (Henry, 1981). Editions of the dictionary were originally planned for publication in English and Spanish as well as French with a Russian version to be published subsequently.

Since publication of the *Multilingual Demographic Dictionary* in 1958, some attempts have been made by others to fill the growing need for publications of this kind. In 1974, the Carolina Population Center published *A Glossary of Selected Demographic Terms* (Chanlett, 1974), which presents terms in English, French, and Spanish, with emphasis on the terminology of dual-record population-measurement systems. Definitions of selected terms are also provided. In 1978, a *Glossary of Population and Housing* (Logie, 1978) was published, providing equivalent terms in English, French, Italian, Dutch, German, and Swedish. Although much of this glossary is concerned with housing, it contains sections on demography, migration, statistics, individuals, populations, age groups, households, and family. In 1979, a French-language *Dictionnaire de démographie* (Pressat, 1979) was published, which presents a selected number of demographic terms in alphabetical order, together with definitions and explanations of the technical terms used in demography. A system of cross-references to other relevant terms is also included.

In the related field of thesauri, several relevant publications became available in the 1970s, particularly in the field of family planning. The first of these was the *Fertility*

Modification Thesaurus (Speert and Wishik, 1973) compiled at the International Institute for the Study of Human Reproduction at Columbia University. It is an elaboration of the U.S. National Library of Medicine's Medical Subject Headings (MeSH) in the area of development and evaluation of family planning programs. This was followed by the Carolina Population Center's *Population/Family Planning Thesaurus* (Lucas and Osburn, 1978), first published in 1975 and revised in 1978. This thesaurus explains demographic terms, provides information on their interrelationships, and includes a guide to the use of the thesaurus in both manual and computerized information retrieval systems. The terms listed are mapped to the Medical Subject Headings (MeSH) and to the *Fertility Modification Thesaurus* mentioned previously. The subject scope of this thesaurus is the social science aspects of population and family planning, and so it is somewhat broader in scope than the *Fertility Modification Thesaurus.* Indonesian-language and Spanish-language editions of the *Population/Family Planning Thesaurus* have also been published. A third family planning thesaurus, the *Population/Fertility Control Thesaurus* (Kolbe and Bergman, 1976) has been produced by the Population Information Program, now located at Johns Hopkins University. This thesaurus is based on the biomedical literature collected and stored in the POPLINE computerized data base, which is provided and maintained by Columbia University Center for Population and Family Health Library/ Information Program and Johns Hopkins Population Information Program and includes citations and abstracts in the subjects of contraceptive technology, population law and policy, and family planning programs. The terms used are also mapped to the Medical Subject Headings (MeSH), to the *Fertility Modification Thesaurus,* and (although in scope only) to the *Population/Family Planning Thesaurus.*

Of course, each of these three broadly similar thesauri serves a useful purpose for the organization that compiled it, but the choice presented to the new user seeking the thesaurus most appropriate for a particular need will be simplified if the number of thesauri is reduced. In 1981, a thesaurus that combined, updated, and replaced the *Fertility Modification Thesaurus* of Columbia University and the Population Information Program's *Population/ Fertility Control Thesaurus* was published. This *POPLINE Thesaurus* has been created for use in indexing and retrieving documents in the POPLINE data base. It also included a first input of demographic terms provided by *Population Index,* to be used in searching the data base of *Population Index* citations which were planned for inclusion in POPLINE in January 1982. A related publication that, although not a thesaurus, is also designed to assist in the organization of printed and written materials in the field of family planning, should be mentioned: the Inter-

national Planned Parenthood Federation's *Population and Family Planning Classification* (Forget, 1975) provides a classification scheme that is now in use in organizations around the world both within and separate from the IPPF. It is primarily designed to fulfill both the needs of a library and filing system and the requirements of an information retrieval system.

In addition to the three existing thesauri focusing on various aspects of family planning, a first attempt has been made to prepare a thesaurus for population studies as a whole. Under CICRED's auspices the *Population Multilingual Thesaurus* (Viet, 1979) was published in 1979. English, French, and Spanish editions are available. This thesaurus, which is the product of a collaborative effort by many individuals and groups working in the three languages, is designed as a tool to assist in the processing of population information. Each language volume consists of three substantive parts: first, the listing of the themes or subjects selected in a descriptor group display (which is preceded by a short list of the main subject category fields); second, an alphabetical listing of all the words forming the descriptors, presented in the form of a KWOC (Key Word Out of Context) index; and third, a hierarchical index. The usefulness of this thesaurus will depend on the mechanisms that are developed to refine, improve, and update it on a regular basis, as a continuously evolving concept and not a static one, and this will be the responsibility of a working group set up under the auspices of the United Nations POPIN network. Its publication represents an important first step toward providing the controlled vocabulary that is needed both for the storage and retrieval of population information in computerized form and for the exchange of population information between cooperating institutions. In the same way that the vocabulary used in the *Population Multilingual Thesaurus* is compatible with that used in the Organisation for Economic Co-operation and Development's *Macrothesaurus* (Viet, 1978), it would be a significant step forward if a similar compatibility could be achieved between this thesaurus and the *POPLINE Thesaurus,* and efforts to achieve this are under way.

Other Serial Publications. Apart from journals, there is a universe of serial publications. They vary in availability from those that are hard to obtain to those that are very widely distributed.

Working papers. Many institutions engaged in demographic research publish series of working papers. These series may include preliminary studies circulated for comment before subsequent revision and final publication as well as studies published in their final versions. Examples are the several series published in connection with the World Fertility Survey, and the series published by the International Institute for Applied Systems Analysis, the International Planned Parenthood Federation, the IUSSP, and the Population Council. Working paper series in population are published by many universities, including the Australian National University, Chulalongkorn University, Columbia University, East-West Center, Gadjah Mada University, Harvard University, University of Lucknow, Universidad de la Habana, Université Catholique de Louvain, University of Alberta, University of Chicago, University of Copenhagen, University of Durham, University of Ghana, University of Leeds, University of Michigan, University of North Carolina, University of Texas, University of Wisconsin, and Yale, to name but a selection of the better known. Although the majority are issued by academic institutions, many are also published by intergovernmental, governmental, and private institutions whose staffs undertake research and who wish to make that work more widely available.

Statistical series. The primary characteristics of statistical series are that they are issued by national statistical offices and that they consist primarily of analyses of demographic statistics. These publications can present analyses of the statistics gathered on a regular basis or analyses of specific censuses or surveys. National governments publishing such series include those of Australia, Austria, Canada, France, Finland, India, Indonesia, Israel, Japan, Kenya, the Netherlands, New Zealand, the Philippines, Portugal, Sweden, the United Kingdom, the United States, and Zambia. Several state and provincial governments in the United States and Canada also issue such series of analyses of subnational-level data.

Estimates and projections. Serial publications presenting official estimates and projections are also issued primarily by national statistical offices. Compilations of estimates and projections based on official data are also published at the regional or global levels by several intergovernmental agencies.

Information publications. Some serial publications have as a primary objective the distribution of population-related information to the widest possible audience. In contrast to the working paper, which is primarily concerned with distributing new research to a limited audience, the information publication can be concerned with information that is not necessarily new but that, in the opinion of the publishers, warrants wider distribution. Publications in this category include translations of selected studies, to make them available in one of the more widely spoken international languages, and some of the publications of private American organizations such as the Population Council or the Population Reference Bureau. The series of *Population Reports* issued by the Population Information Program at Johns Hopkins University is a good example of such publications.

Annual Publications. Somewhere between the journal, published on a more or less defined schedule, and books which appear once, although they might subsequently be reprinted or revised for second or further editions, there exists a type of population literature that is neither book nor journal: it consists of publications, primarily in book form, that are published on a regular, annual basis. For many years, the French-language *Annales de démographic historique,* published by the Société de Démographic Historique in Paris, has appeared as an annual publication, representing the most influential publication devoted solely to historical demographic topics. Finnish population research has also been summarized in an annual publication in English entitled *Yearbook of Population Research in Finland,* published by the Väestöntutkimuslaitos, as has Japanese research in the *Annual Reports of the Institute of Population Problems,* which is published in Japanese with English summaries.

The United Nations Fund for Population Activities publishes *Population Programmes and Projects,* which consists of two volumes. Volume 1, *Guide to Sources of International Population Assistance,* is issued every three years, with occasional supplements, in English, French, and Spanish. Volume 2, *Inventory of Population Projects in Developing Countries around the World,* is issued annually in English only. The UNFPA has also taken over publication of the *Annual Review of Population Law,* detailing changes in legislation relevant to population matters around the world, which was previously the responsibility of the Law and Population Programme at Tufts University. Similarly, the U.S. federal institutions concerned with population research publish two annual inventories entitled *Population Sciences: Inventory and Analysis of Federal Population Research* and *Population Sciences: Inventory of Private Agency Population Research.* Both are prepared and published by the Interagency Committee on Population Research.

In addition to these regular annual publications on population, there has been a growing trend to publish annual compilations of research in various subject areas, some of which include sections of relevance to demographers. Such titles include the *Annual Review of Sociology* and the *Annual Review of Anthropology,* both published by Annual Reviews of Palo Alto, California. The first of such publications devoted specifically to population topics appeared in 1978, entitled *Research in Population Economics: An Annual Compilation of Research,* published by Jai Press of Greenwich, Connecticut. This publication is scheduled as the first of a series of annual volumes devoted to research on the interrelations of demography and economics.

Richard Hankinson

See also DIRECTORIES; MACHINE-READABLE DATA FILES. *For additional information on serials and reference works for international data, see* DATA COLLECTION, *article on* INTERNATIONAL SYSTEMS.

BIBLIOGRAPHY

Carolina Population Center, University of North Carolina. *CPC Microcatalog.* Rev. ed. Chapel Hill, 1978. On 400 fiche.

Chanlett, Eliska (editor). *A Glossary of Selected Demographic Terms.* An Occasional Publication of the Laboratories for Population Statistics. Chapel Hill, N.C.: Carolina Population Center, 1974. In English, French, and Spanish.

Forget, Jacqueline P. *Population and Family Planning Classification.* London: International Planned Parenthood Federation, 1975.

Goyer, Doreen (compiler). *The International Population Census Bibliography: Revision and Update, 1945–1977.* New York and London: Academic Press, 1980.

Grebenik, Eugene, and Allan Hill. *International Demographic Terminology: Fertility, Family Planning, and Nuptiality.* IUSSP Papers, no. 4. Liège, Belgium: International Union for the Scientific Study of Population, 1974.

Henry, Louis (compiler). *Dictionnaire démographique multilingue: Volume français.* Liège, Belgium: Ordina Editions, 1981.

Kolbe, Helen K., and Rita F. Bergman. *Population/Fertility Control Thesaurus.* Washington, D.C.: George Washington University, Population Information Program, April 1976.

Logie, Gordon (compiler). *Glossary of Population and Housing.* International Planning Glossaries, no. 1. Amsterdam and New York: Elsevier Scientific Publishing, 1978. In Dutch, English, French, German, Italian, and Swedish.

Lucas, Caroline, and Margaret Osburn. *Population/Family Planning Thesaurus: An Alphabetical and Hierarchical Display of Terms Drawn from Population-related Literature in the Social Sciences.* 2d ed. Revised by Karen Long and Carann Turner. Chapel Hill, N.C.: Carolina Population Center, 1978. A supplement by Carann Turner was issued in 1981.

Population Council. *Catalogue of the Population Council Library.* 3 vols. Boston: G. K. Hall, 1979.

Pressat, Roland. *Dictionnaire de démographie.* Paris: Presses Universitaires de France, 1979.

Princeton University, Office of Population Research. *Population Index Bibliography, Cumulated 1935–1968 by Authors and Geographical Areas.* 9 vols. Boston: G. K. Hall, 1971. A cumulative index for 1969–1977 is in preparation.

Siegel, Jacob S., and Samuel Baum. "IUSSP International Demographic Terminology Project." In *Proceedings of the Tenth Annual Conference, Association for Population/Family Planning Libraries and Information Centers, St. Louis, Missouri, April 18–21, 1977,* edited by Rita F. Bergman and Joan P. Helde, pp. 232–244. New York: APLIC–International, December 1977.

Speert, Kathryn H., and Samuel M. Wishik. *Fertility Modification Thesaurus with Focus on Evaluation of Family Planning Programs.* New York: International Institute for the Study of Human Reproduction, Columbia University, 1973.

United Nations, Department of Economic and Social Affairs. *Multilingual Demographic Dictionary.* Series A, Population Studies, no. 29. New York, 1958.

United Nations Fund for Population Activities. *Population Programmes and Projects.* 2 vols. Volume 1: *Guide to Sources of International Population Assistance, 1980.* Volume 2: *Inventory of Population Projects in Developing Countries around the World, 1979–80.* New York, 1981. Periodically revised and reissued; volume 1 is revised triennially; volume 2 is updated annually.

United States, Bureau of the Census. *Catalogs of the Bureau of the Census Library.* 20 vols. Boston: G. K. Hall, 1976. A supplement, in five volumes, was issued in 1979.

Viet, Jean. *Macrothesaurus for Information Processing in the Field of Economic and Social Development.* Rev. ed. Paris: Organisation for Economic Co-operation and Development, 1978. Available in English, French, and Spanish editions.

2.
BIBLIOGRAPHIC RESOURCES

Computerized bibliographies and indexing or abstracting services for population literature are many and varied in their comprehensiveness, subject coverage, availability, and timeliness. The following discussion is restricted to descriptions of (1) those services dedicated solely to coverage of one or more areas of population and (2) other readily available data bases that, although not exclusively devoted to coverage of population, nevertheless provide access to substantial proportions of the literature of the field.

Population-specific Information Resources. The major information resources for population materials include *ADOPT, DOCPAL resumenes sobre población en América Latina, PIDSA Abstracts,* POPLINE, POPULATION BIBLIOGRAPHY, *Population Index, Review of Population Reviews,* and *UNFPA Project Publications: Abstracts.*

ADOPT. Published monthly since January 1975, *ADOPT: Asian and Worldwide Documents on Population Topics* is an annotated bibliography produced by the Reference Centre of the United Nations Economic and Social Commission for Asia and the Pacific (ESCAP) in Bangkok. Each issue contains bibliographic citations for published and unpublished documents—including journal articles, monographs, and technical reports—and, since November/December 1978, subject and country indexes that are cumulated annually. Each entry includes an abstract and subject descriptors.

DOCPAL. The Documentación sobre Población en América Latina system (DOCPAL) in Santiago, Chile, was created in March 1976 by the United Nations Centro Latinoamericano de Demografía (CELADE) with funding from the International Development Research Centre (IDRC) in Ottawa as a regional documentation center to assist Latin American countries in the collection, storage, processing, and retrieval of population documents about Latin America.

The computerized DOCPAL data base consists (as of April 1981) of 15,000 bibliographic citations of documents written since 1970. Types of documents covered include journal articles, conference papers, books, chapters of books, and unpublished manuscripts produced primarily in English, French, Spanish, and Portuguese. Each document record includes subject descriptors assigned with reference to the Spanish edition of the *Population Multilingual Thesaurus* (Viet, 1979) and an informative abstract. Searches of this data base are available by mail from DOCPAL, and on-line interactive searching is possible in Santiago.

In addition to maintaining and updating the DOCPAL computer system, DOCPAL also produces a biannual collection of abstracts, *DOCPAL resumenes sobre población en América Latina.* Each computer-produced issue of this periodical, first issued in June 1977, contains indexes and between 600 and 700 summaries of both published and unpublished population documents, arranged in nineteen subject categories. Entries include informative abstracts in Spanish. A cumulative index of the first four issues has been published.

DOCPAL also provides a document copying service on request.

PIDSA. The Population Information and Documentation System for Africa (PIDSA) is operated by the Regional Institute for Population Studies at the University of Ghana, Legon, under an agreement between the United Nations and the government of Ghana. Intended to capture and make available documentary information about population matters in sub-Saharan Africa, PIDSA was conceived within the framework of the proposed global Population Information Network (POPIN). Its main publication, *PIDSA Abstracts,* is a semiannual, containing citations, abstracts (in English for English-language documents and in French for French-language documents), and indexing applied according to the *Population Multilingual Thesaurus* augmented with terms specific to Africa. Volume 1, number 1, appeared in December 1978. Each issue contains some 300 entries. Subject headings include Population (General); Population Distribution; Population Size and Growth; Mortality and Morbidity; Fertility, Nuptiality, and the Family; Migration; Demographic and Economic Interrelations; Demographic and Non-economic Interrelations; Population Policy; Methods of Research and Analysis; Demographic Data (Production of); Meetings and Conferences; Official Statistical Publications; and Bibliographies. Photocopies of cited documents are available on request for a small charge. PIDSA also issues an irregular newsletter, which first appeared in June 1980.

PIDSA at present uses manual methods but plans to mechanize in a manner compatible with POPIN. It has been developed using the experience of DOCPAL, has compatible methodology, and when mechanized will be able to exchange data bases with DOCPAL. It is also developing links to other African information systems under the Pan African Documentation and Information System (PADIS) operated by the United Nations Economic Commission for Africa (Brandreth, 1981).

POPLINE. A cooperatively produced computerized bibliographic retrieval service, POPLINE is available through the U.S. National Library of Medicine's Biomedical Communications Network. It consists of more than 100,000 bibliographic citations and abstracts of the published and unpublished biomedical and social science literature in the fields of population and family planning. This system became operational in 1980. Contributors to the data base include Johns Hopkins University's Population Information Program, Columbia University's Center for Population and Family Health Library/Information Program, and Princeton University's *Population Index.*

Although POPLINE was only recently established, portions of the data base have existed as separate entities for some time. POPINFORM, that section of POPLINE contributed by Johns Hopkins and Columbia universities with the financial support of the United States Agency for International Development (USAID) has been available for computer searching commercially since 1973.

International in scope, POPLINE offers the greatest depth and breadth of subject coverage of any computerized population-oriented system. Bibliographic entries are accessible by author name, title, country of origin, date of publication, document type, and subject. Both free-text and controlled vocabulary searching are possible. Subject retrieval of citations utilizes either the Medical Subject Headings (MeSH) of the U.S. National Library of Medicine or the more specific vocabulary developed by Columbia, Johns Hopkins, and Princeton universities. Documents cited in this interdisciplinary data base include monographs, monograph chapters, conference proceedings, periodical articles, dissertations, theses, government and international agency publications, internal memoranda, and unpublished papers such as conference presentations and technical reports. The data base is updated at a rate of approximately 1,300 citations per month. Most of the citations are of materials produced since 1965, although input is not restricted to current material.

POPLINE is the only computerized population data base that contains English-language abstracts for most entries. Photocopies of most documents cited are available on request from the Population Information Program or the Center for Population and Family Health; both literature searches and copies of cited documents are provided free of charge to requesters from developing countries. The data base is available internationally for computer searching.

POPULATION BIBLIOGRAPHY. An on-line data base consisting of the bibliographic records of the Carolina Population Center Library, University of North Carolina at Chapel Hill, POPULATION BIBLIOGRAPHY became operational in February 1980. Computer access to this system is provided by DIALOG Information Services, Inc., located in Palo Alto, California. POPULATION BIBLIOGRAPHY is the first interdisciplinary data base focusing on the social and behavioral science aspects of the population field. It also includes bibliographic information on related documents in biomedical and health areas.

The file of 51,022 records (as of May 1981) dates from 1966 and is updated bi-monthly. Citations are retrievable by text-words, thesaurus-based subject headings, author name, title, publication year, and language, in addition to other bibliographic elements. Documents cited include monographs, dissertations, journals, journal articles, and conference proceedings as well as government publications and unpublished documents, reports, and papers. All of these are housed in the Carolina Population Center Library, many in special collections of reprints, area files, bibliographies, and annual reports. Features of this system include citations to the unpublished papers presented at the annual meetings of the Population Association of America, and the capability to retrieve citations by geographical focus of the cited item. Information contained is international in scope. POPULATION BIBLIOGRAPHY is available commercially to users in the United States and abroad.

Population Index. One of the oldest and most definitive bibliographies in the field of demography, *Population Index* is an official publication of the Population Association of America. It is edited and published by the Office of Population Research at Princeton University.

Produced quarterly since 1935, *Population Index* is international in scope and is arranged as a classified and annotated bibliography of monographs, journal articles, and secondary source materials relevant to all aspects of demography. It includes approximately 900 bibliographic citations per issue with brief accompanying abstracts classified under twenty broad subjects categories and approximately seventy subclassifications. Each issue also contains an article of methodological interest, a signed literature review, or a special bibliography, together with information on future professional meetings and conferences, newly published bibliographies, directories, periodical titles, and official statistical publications. Geographical and author indexes appear in each issue and are cumulated annually. Available by subscription, the index is distributed worldwide. Circulation in 1980 was approximately 4,500. In 1978 *Population Index* began computerization of the citations included in the published journal from 1969 to 1978. This data base was made available as part of the U.S. National Library of Medicine's POPLINE system during 1982.

Review of Population Reviews. The Committee for International Cooperation in National Research in Demography (CICRED), Paris, in association with the United Nations Fund for Population Activities (UNFPA), New York, publishes the *Review of Population Reviews* four times a year. Each issue of this annotated bibliography contains summaries of articles that have appeared in eighty-three periodicals published in thirty-seven countries. Cited articles are also assigned subject-heading descriptors from the *Population Multilingual Thesaurus.*

The *Review of Population Reviews* is distributed worldwide and free of charge to national demographic research centers affiliated with CICRED and to individuals or organizations interested in population matters. It is published in English, French, and Spanish.

UNFPA Project Publications: Abstracts. Published quarterly since June 1980 by the Library of the United Nations Fund for Population Activities in New York, *UNFPA Project Publications: Abstracts* covers the broad spectrum of population activities funded by the UNFPA, including family planning, censuses and population dynamics, basic data collection, formulation of population policy, population communication, education, and information. Presented in loose-leaf format, each issue includes 100 bibliographic descriptions of reports and publications of UNFPA projects indexed by project numbers, geographical areas, subject, United Nations executing agency, and author. Each issue also contains cumulative indexes. As of July 1981, 500 project publications and final reports had been included, providing information about 350 UNFPA projects.

Many citations listed in this publication are also computer-searchable in the POPLINE system.

Other Information Resources. Information resources that include significant coverage of population topics are *Biological Abstracts, Excerpta Medica, Index Medicus, Psychological Abstracts, Science Citation Index, Social Science Citation Index,* and *Sociological Abstracts.*

Biological Abstracts. Produced semimonthly in Philadelphia by the BioSciences Information Service, *Biological Abstracts* has been published since 1926. Focusing on coverage of periodical literature in the theoretical and applied life sciences, it includes citations of articles appearing in more than 8,000 periodicals published in ninety countries. Article titles are given in the original language of publication (with English translations), and most entries include signed English abstracts. Abstracts are accompanied by indexing terms assigned through the use of the BASIC (Biological Abstracts Subjects in Context) computerized indexing technique. Recent relevant monograph and periodical titles are listed in each issue.

Biological Abstracts citations, in addition to references from *Biological Abstracts/RRM,* are available for computer searching from DIALOG Information Services, Inc., as the BIOSIS PREVIEWS data base, which contains more than three million records of documents published since 1969. The data base is updated monthly. The ORBIT service of the System Development Corporation in Santa Monica, California, also provides computer access under the name BIOSIS/BIO7479/BIO6973.

Excerpta Medica. Published monthly in Amsterdam, *Excerpta Medica* provides bibliographic references and abstracts to the international literature of human medicine and related disciplines, and specializes in coverage of drug and pharmaceutical literature. Citations are organized in forty-three separately issued sections and two literature indexes. Of primary interest to population researchers are sections on public health, social medicine, hygiene, and obstetrics and gynecology. Although coverage overlaps somewhat with *Index Medicus, Excerpta Medica* is known for its inclusion of articles published in European periodicals. More than 3,500 biomedical journals are regularly scanned for input. The printed *Excerpta Medica* has been published since 1947.

Bibliographic data for 1,346,913 abstracted and indexed items (as of May 1981) published since 1974 are available also for computer searching through DIALOG Information Services, Inc. The data base is updated monthly with citations appearing in the printed *Excerpta Medica* and an additional 100,000 nonjournal citations annually. Documents covered include journal articles, books, monographs, dissertations, and conference reports.

Index Medicus. Published monthly by the U.S. National Library of Medicine, *Index Medicus* contains each year approximately 240,000 bibliographic references to articles published in more than 2,600 international biomedical periodicals. A recent addition to the coverage of this service is the inclusion of selected monographs and conference proceedings. References are arranged under the National Library of Medicine's Medical Subject Headings, a list of which is published annually as Part 2 of the January issue of *Index Medicus.* Each issue includes an author index.

Citations listed in this publication are accessible for computer searching in the MEDLINE (MEDlars on LINE) data base, containing (as of May 1981) more than 3.3 million indexed citations accessible on-line (current year and two preceding years) and off-line to 1966. The data base is updated monthly. Approximately 250,000 citations from more than 3,000 international journals and chapters or articles from selected monographs are added annually. Seventy percent of MEDLINE records are citations for English-language documents, and over 40 percent of recently added records contain author abstracts. Both *Index Medicus* and MEDLINE are available worldwide and are considered to be among the major information resources in the field of biomedicine. On-line access to MEDLINE is provided by the U.S. National Library of Medicine; DIALOG Information Services, Inc.; Bibliographic Retrieval Services, Inc.; and the State University of New York (SUNY) computer network.

Psychological Abstracts. A monthly publication of the American Psychological Association, Washington, D.C., *Psychological Abstracts* is an abstracting service covering the world's literature in psychology and related behavioral science disciplines. Publication began in 1927. Each issue contains approximately 2,000 citations and abstracts of the published literature of psychology, including regular annual coverage of more than 900 periodicals and 1,500 books, technical reports, and monographs. References are arranged in sixteen categories. The data bank of *Psychological Abstracts,* consisting of 334,021 citations (as of May 1981) to literature published since 1967, is available for computer searching through DIALOG Information Services, Inc., under the name PSYCHINFO and through the ORBIT service of the System Development Corporation under the name PSYCH ABSTRACTS. The data base is updated monthly at a rate of approximately 25,000 references annually.

Social Science Citation Index and Science Citation Index. Two monthly publications of the Institute for Scientific Information in Philadelphia are the *Social Science Citation Index* and the *Science Citation Index.* The former includes indexed citations to every item considered significant in 1,000 social sciences journals and selected social sciences articles from 2,200 additional journals in the natural, biomedical, and physical sciences. Many monographs are cited as well. This index attempts to cover every area of the social and behavioral sciences.

Science Citation Index, which focuses on coverage of the worldwide literature of science and technology, estimates its coverage at 90 percent of the world's significant scientific and technical literature. It includes citations of significant items, including journal articles, reports of meetings, letters, and editorials, from 2,600 scientific and technical periodicals.

Quarterly issues of each of these indexes include a source index, a citation index, and a Permuterm subject index. These indexes, considered to be more current than many other indexing and abstracting services in the biomedical or social sciences, are available for computer searching through DIALOG Information Services, Inc., under the names SCISEARCH and SOCIAL SCI-SEARCH. Since 1977 *Social Science Citation Index* on-line has also been available from the System Development Corporation's ORBIT service under the name SOCIAL SCIENCE CITATION INDEX. In May 1981 the index SCISEARCH contained more than three million citations of literature published since January 1974, and the index SOCIAL SCISEARCH contained more than 965,000 records of the literature published since 1972. Both data bases are updated monthly.

In addition to these two indexes, the Institute for Scientific Information provides a variety of services, including publication of *Current Contents,* which consists of the tables of contents of periodicals indexed in the citation indexes.

Sociological Abstracts. A publication of Sociological Abstracts, Inc., located in San Diego, California, *Sociological Abstracts* covers the international literature of sociology and related disciplines. It began in 1952 and is produced five times yearly, with each issue containing more than 1,000 citations and abstracts segregated into thirty general subject categories and sixty-two subclassifications. More than 1,200 journals and other serial publications are scanned annually for relevant items. Documents covered include monographs, conference papers, dissertations, and journal articles.

Sociological Abstracts, containing 104,507 citations (as of May 1981) of literature published since 1963, can be searched on-line through DIALOG Information Services, Inc. This data base is updated quarterly, and citation records include both abstracts and indexing data.

Susan Kingsley Pasquariella

BIBLIOGRAPHY

Brandreth, Michael. "The Population Information and Documentation System for Africa." Report prepared for the International Development Research Centre, Ottawa, 2 October 1981.

DIALOG Information Services, Inc. *Database Catalog.* Palo Alto, Calif., May 1981.

Population Information Activities of United Nations Regional Commissions and Agencies and Other Organizations. "Statement by the Committee for International Cooperation in National Research in Demography." Paper prepared for the Population Information Network Consultative Meeting, Geneva, 27–30 April 1981.

———. "Statement by the Economic and Social Commission for Asia and the Pacific." Paper prepared for the Population Information Network Consultative Meeting, Geneva, 27–30 April 1981.

———. "Statement by the Economic Commission for Latin America (ECLA), Latin American Demographic Center (CELADE)." Paper prepared for the Population Information Network Consultative Meeting, Geneva, 27–30 April 1981.

Shipman, Patricia E., and Carann Turner. "Tools for Reference Information: Indexing and Abstracting Services." In *Proceedings of the Eleventh Annual Conference, Association for Population/Family Planning Libraries and Information Centers— International, Atlanta, April 11–13, 1978,* edited by Rita F. Bergman and Joan P. Helde, pp. 163–185. New York: APLIC–International, December 1978.

System Development Corporation, SDC Search Service. *ORBIT Databases.* Santa Monica, Calif., May 1981.

Viet, Jean. *Population Multilingual Thesaurus.* Paris: Committee for International Cooperation in National Research in Demography, 1979. Available in English, French, and Spanish editions.

PYRAMIDS
See COMPOSITION.

QUANTITATIVE DEMOGRAPHY
See MATHEMATICAL DEMOGRAPHY.

RATES AND RATIOS

Much of the demographic literature becomes readable by the mastery of a relatively few rates and ratios. The rates fall into simple types according first to the kind of population counted in the denominator and second to the kind of events counted in the numerator. The ratios may deal with events also, but unlike rates they are not tied strictly to the number occurring within a fixed time period (usually one calendar year). This distinction is sometimes blurred in practice but remains conceptually useful.

Rates. The following five categories of rates reflect the wide range of subject matter dealt with in the population field. The simplest category, crude rates, is presented first.

Crude rates. This group of rates uses the total population as the denominator, usually the estimate as of mid-year. (The concept of the denominator is the average number of persons alive during the calendar year, that is, the person-years lived in the year, which is usually approximately set by the mid-year estimate.) Crude rates include the following:

- *Crude birth rate:* the number of live births in the year, per 1,000 population at mid-year
- *Crude death rate:* the number of deaths in the year, per 1,000 population at mid-year
- *Crude marriage rate:* the number of marriages (not persons marrying) in the year, per 1,000 population at mid-year

- *Crude divorce rate:* number of divorces (not persons divorcing) in the year, per 1,000 population at mid-year
- *Crude rate of natural increase:* difference between the crude birth and death rates

This list can be extended; the common element is that the total population is the denominator, which in many instances is the only information readily available. The result is "crude," since the population at risk of certain events, such as births, is really only females and only those of a certain age rather than everyone.

Age-specific rates. Identical to crude rates are age-specific rates but with an age restriction for both numerator and denominator. The age-specific fertility rate for women 20–24 counts only live births to women of that age at the moment of birth in the numerator and only women of that age (midyear estimate) in the denominator. Thus a *schedule* of rates is created, showing for fertility, for example, the rate established by women 15–19, 20–24, and so on through 40–44 or 45–49. For mortality, age-specific rates are calculated over the entire range of ages and separately by sex.

Restricted rates. Any rate can be calculated for a special subgroup. An age-specific fertility rate can be restricted, again in both numerator and denominator, to births to married women; this is termed the "marital age-specific fertility rate." In this instance, strictly speaking, only legitimate births should enter the numerator, but data are often poor on out-of-wedlock births, and definitional problems arise where common-law marriages are frequent. Therefore this rate is useful mainly in countries where births occur predominantly to married women. A death rate can be calculated for white males aged 40–44 living in New York State. All such restricted rates, in effect, look strictly at one subgroup at a time, counting only its members and events affecting them. In some situations, the membership criteria are subject to rapid change, for example, residence in New York or age 44; again, the procedure is to count any events occurring to individuals who fit the definition at the moment of the event and to seek a denominator that expresses the true average population at risk during the year that fits that same definition. Thus a birth to a woman who is 24 at the birth but 25 at the time of the survey interview is counted in the rate for women 20–24. (A half-year age correction may be needed in the denominator, since women who give their age as 25 in the survey and report on births during the previous twelve months were on average a half year younger during the period.)

Rates by topic. Specialized rates and measures have been developed for each substantive topic. For marriage, there are proportions currently married by age and proportions ever married. There are crude marriage and divorce rates and a remarriage rate (second or later marriages per thousand population of currently divorced and widowed persons in a particular age group). Technical measures have been developed for calculating the mean age at marriage [*see* NUPTIALITY INDEXES].

For fertility, analysis starts with the crude birth rate, then the age-specific rates, then often the marital age specific rates. The *general fertility rate* is in a sense intermediate between the crude and the age-specific rates. As the number of births per 1,000 women of childbearing age (usually taken as 15–44), it requires less information, but it still removes the possible confounding due to the presence of males, children, and old people in the denominator. It is also used as a summary rate when age-specific detail is not required.

A *total fertility rate* (TFR) is also calculated, which expresses the total number of births a women would have if she followed the current schedule of age-specific rates throughout her lifetime. One simply totals the rates at the various ages, multiplying by 5 since the woman lives under each rate for five calendar years. In many Western countries the TFR is now close to the replacement level. A closely related measure is the *gross reproduction rate* (GRR), which differs only by being the number of daughters rather than children the woman would have. Thus if the *sex ratio* at birth is 105 males per 100 females, then 100 of every 205 births are female, or 48.8 percent. Then a TFR of 2 becomes a GRR of 0.98, meaning that 1,000 women are replacing themselves in the next generation by 980 daughters, assuming no mortality.

In fact of course, there is loss due to death, and so a *net reproduction rate* (NRR) is calculated. From a generational perspective, 1,000 females born will suffer some early mortality, and not all will live through the reproductive ages to produce children according to the age-specific fertility rates. The correction is an easy one: instead of multiplying each age-specific rate by the 1,000 women, it is multiplied by the number of females surviving to the midpoint of the age group, for example, to age 17.5 for the group 15–19, again times 5 since each women spends five years in that age bracket. This is simply the $_nL_x$ column of the life table, the average number of years lived during the five-year span by females who survived to that point. In current life tables for the West more than 97 percent survive to age 17.5 and about 95 percent to age 42.5. Thus in the West the correction is small, and the NRR is quite close to the GRR. For the developing world much greater differences can occur, with the GRR being as much as half again as large as the NRR. In the United States in 1905–1910, for nonwhites the GRR was 2.24 but the NRR of 1.33 was only three-fifths as large.

The perspective behind the TFR, GRR, and NRR is how one generation produces the next. This is of course different from the *annual rates* discussed earlier because the time between generations may be short or long. Thus two populations can have the same NRR, but if children come at later ages in one, it will have a lower crude birth rate, all else being equal. In both populations, each generation replaces itself with the same number of children, but one takes longer to do it and will grow less over the next century.

Mortality analysis proceeds from the crude death rate to age-specific rates, separately for males and females, and then to other groups of interest. Both sexes are analyzed, whereas for fertility usually only females are considered. Births to fathers, that is, male age-specific fertility rates, are also of interest in the unusual situations where the necessary data are gathered. Because fathers are usually older than mothers, the male rates give a longer generational length than the female ones; consequently population projections made on the male side show slower growth than on the female side. Methods of reconciling this difficulty, called the two-sex problem, are complex and have never been developed successfully in simple form.

Sophisticated mortality analysis depends on the life table and its derivative measures. Of these the best known is life expectancy at birth, that is, the average number of years lived per person.

The *infant mortality rate* requires specific mention. It is defined as the number of deaths in the first year of life among 1,000 births. Unlike the above rates it does not use the average mid-year population of persons aged 0 to

1.0. To do so would involve serious empirical difficulties, since after birth the surviving group falls off quickly in the first few days and weeks and then less rapidly. In many countries, reliable data on this curve are not available, making the average population alive during the first year quite uncertain. Thus a *probability* of infant death is used instead: of 1,000 who *start* the first year the proportion who die before the first birthday. In practice, this figure is usually approximated by dividing the number of infant deaths in a calendar year by the number of live births in the same year, notwithstanding the fact that some deaths so included are of infants born the previous year. This and related problems of measurement of infant mortality are discussed by Henry S. Shryock, Jr., Jacob S. Siegel, et al. (1975) and by A. H. Pollard, Farhat Yusuf, and G. N. Pollard (1974).

Standardized rates are often used to improve comparisons among populations. Because a crude death rate, for example, will be higher in a population with more old people, a correction is needed to focus the comparison on the mortality risks themselves, not upon the accidents of the age distributions. This can be accomplished by *direct standardization*, wherever the age-specific mortality rates are known, by simply applying the same age distribution to every population. Multiplication of the age-specific mortality rates by this standard age distribution provides new crude rates, which can then be studied as a measure of mortality conditions alone. This method works best when the standard age distribution employed is reasonably close to the average for the populations analyzed and when there are no radical differences between the age distributions involved.

Indirect standardization, a less satisfactory technique, is used when the age-specific rates are not known and the only information on each population is its crude rate (total deaths and total population) and its age distribution. Then a single, standard set of age-specific mortality rates is applied to the various age distributions to provide modified crude rates. The changes that appear between the original crude rates and the modified ones then reflect how the age-specific rates helped produce the original crude death rates.

Intrinsic rates. More advanced demographic literature often uses an intrinsic birth rate, death rate, or increase rate. These are the rates that prevail in a stable population, where the age distribution is smooth and unchanging. Because in such a population the rates cannot reflect any accidental short-term feature of the age distribution, they are considered the "intrinsic," or "true" rates. Like the age distribution itself, they emerge from the two schedules of age-specific fertility and mortality rates. In a stable population, the intrinsic rates, like the age distribution, never change.

Ratios. Ratios differ from rates in the sense explained earlier in that, strictly speaking, a rate counts the number of events in a restricted time period, for example, one year, and would be only half that value for a half year. A ratio prevails at a particular point in time, and in this sense it is a prevalence concept rather than the incidence concept underlying a rate. Examples are the *sex ratio*, the number of males per 1,000 females and the *child-woman ratio*, that is, the ratio of children aged 0–4 to women of childbearing age. Another is the *dependency ratio*, which is conceived as the number of economic dependents per 100 productive members of society. The latter is calculated simply as the ratio at a particular point in time of very young and very old persons to those in the intermediate ages, often ages 0–14 and 65 and over divided by those 15–64. Other examples include the *abortion ratio*, which relates numbers of abortions to numbers of births or pregnancies, both in a common time period [*see* ABORTION, *article on* INDUCED ABORTION], and the *illiteracy ratio*, which relates numbers of illiterates in a population to the size of that population.

John A. Ross

Because each substantive area of demography has developed rates and ratios appropriate to its own needs, many articles in this encyclopedia include examples of their use. Sources of data for construction of these measures are described in DATA COLLECTION, *in* MIGRATION MEASUREMENT, *and, when data are not complete, in* INDIRECT ESTIMATION OF FERTILITY AND MORTALITY. *For applications, see* AGE AT MARRIAGE; HOUSEHOLD AND FAMILY DEMOGRAPHY; SMALL-AREA ANALYSIS. *For analyses of rates to determine components of demographic change, see* URBANIZATION, *article on* DEVELOPING COUNTRIES. *For construction of rates and ratios for special areas of study, see* DISTRIBUTION, *article on* DISTRIBUTION, CONCENTRATION, AND DISPERSION; LABOR FORCE; MORBIDITY; URBANIZATION, *article on* MEASUREMENT.

BIBLIOGRAPHY

Haupt, Arthur, and Thomas T. Kane. *The Population Reference Bureau's Population Handbook.* Washington, D.C.: Population References Bureau, 1978.

Palmore, James A. *Measuring Mortality: A Self-teaching Guide to Elementary Measures.* Papers of the East-West Population Institute, no. 15 . Honolulu: East-West Center, May 1971.

———. *Measuring Fertility and Natural Increase: A Self-teaching Guide to Elementary Measures.* Rev. ed. Papers of the East-West Population Institute, no. 16. Honolulu: East-West Center, 1972.

Pollard, A. H., Farhat Yusuf, and G. N. Pollard. *Demographic Techniques.* Rushcutters Bay, Australia: Pergamon Press, 1974.

Shryock, Henry S., Jr., Jacob S. Siegel, et al. *The Methods and Materials of Demography.* 2 vols. Prepared for the U.S. Bureau of the Census. Washington, D.C.: U.S. Government Printing Office, 1971 (3d rev. printing, 1975).

United Nations, Department of Economic and Social Affairs. *Multilingual Demographic Dictionary.* Series A, Population Studies, no. 29, New York, 1958.

World Fertility Survey. *Colombia Fertility Survey, 1976: A Summary of Findings.* Voorburg, Netherlands: International Statistical Institute, 1978.

REDISTRIBUTION

See DISTRIBUTION.

REFUGEES

Although refugees have existed throughout history, only in the twentieth century have they gained a significant place in international law and policy. The size, scope, and variety of the world's refugee problems have become a major challenge to diplomacy and relief work. The problem of definition contributes to the variety of estimates of how many refugees there are in the world and where they are located. This article reviews definitions, the various estimates of the number of refugees in the contemporary world, and the efforts to develop an international system of refugee rescue, relief, and resettlement.

Definitions. A "refugee" may be defined at the outset simply as a person seeking asylum in a foreign country. Asylum refers to protection granted or afforded by a state to a person in its territory. Current international law and practice recognizes that each state has the right to grant asylum; the refugee has no recognized right of asylum vis-à-vis the state. Control over entry into a country is still recognized as a sovereign power. Since international law deals with relations among states, the rights of states are not set aside by claims of individual rights.

The priority of the state is important in understanding international agreements regarding refugees. The United Nations Universal Declaration of Human Rights (Article 14) states that "Everyone has the right to seek and enjoy in other countries asylum from persecution." Originally, the draft of the article (then number 12) stated that "Everyone has the right to seek and *be granted* in other countries asylum from persecution" (our italics). Still, the adopted version (Article 14) does not make a right of asylum meaningless from an individual's point of view: although no right to be granted asylum is recognized, the article implies that once given to a person it should not be revoked by forced repatriation (refoulement) to the country from which he or she comes.

The 1951 United Nations Convention on the Status of Refugees, amended by the 1967 Protocol Relating to the Status of Refugees, gives the basic definition currently used in practice by the United Nations, governments, and various organizations in relief work. The Geneva Convention Relating to the Status of Refugees (28 July 1951) defines a refugee as "a person who as a result of events occurring before January 1, 1951, owing to well-founded fear of being persecuted for reasons of race, religion, nationality, membership in a particular social group or political opinion, is outside the country of his nationality and is unable, or owing to such fear, is unwilling to avail himself of the protection of that country; or who, not having a nationality and being outside the country of his former habitual residence as a result of such events, is unable or, owing to such fear, is unwilling to return to it." The 1967 Protocol broadens the scope of the 1951 convention definition as mentioned above by removing the time limitation.

The United Nations definition contains two elements: being outside of the country of nationality or residence and persecution or fear of persecution on the specific grounds mentioned in the convention. This leaves many gray areas. Persons displaced within their own country, no matter how tyrannous the regime, are excluded. Those fleeing a country whose policies make economic survival impossible are not defined as refugees. They are seen as economic migrants, despite suffering or death caused by government policy that impels people to flee. In short, the line between political and economic causes is not always clear. Nor is the relation between the requirement of being outside a country and the humanitarian motives that undergird concern for the plight of refugees.

How Many Refugees Are There? Estimates of the number of refugees vary widely, depending on sources. They reflect (1) different definitions used for estimation purposes (e.g., displaced persons within their own country as a result of civil war or disturbance); (2) varying bases of estimates (e.g., the sending or receiving country or an international agency); (3) different criteria for when a person ceases to be a refugee (how firmly resettled in a new country a person must be); and (4) the obviously fluid nature of the refugee phenomenon.

Two sets of refugee figures are presented in Table 1. One focuses on the area of origin and the other on the area of asylum. Both sets are taken from the World Refugee Surveys of the United States Committee for Refugees (USCR). The data on origin are from the 1980 survey and the data on asylum from the 1981 survey. The need to give origin and destination data separated by one year exemplifies the data problem. The USCR survey changed detailed reporting format from a focus on coun-

TABLE 1. *Estimated number of refugees by area of origin (1980) and area of asylum (1981)*

| Area | Origin, 1980 | Asylum, 1981 | | Total |
		Refugee	Internally displaced	
Africa	4,045,200	3,589,340	2,735,000	6,324,340
Asia	7,292,500	1,994,500	170,000	2,164,500
Latin America	1,085,300	189,600	50,000	239,600
Middle East	3,312,500	1,962,200	1,600,000	3,562,200
Europe	229,750	354,600	—	354,600
Total	15,965,250	8,090,240	4,555,000	12,645,240

Sources of data: USCR, 1980, pp. 33–34; 1981, p. 32.

try of origin to country of asylum. Detailed information necessary to reconstruct an origin/asylum matrix was not published in 1981. Further, in the 1981 survey, the editors attempted to exclude "firmly resettled" persons from estimates. The result is that the 1981 estimate of the number of refugees is 12.6 million, while the 1980 estimate, which included 3 million persons thought to be firmly resettled (e.g., in the United States), was 16 million.

In 1981, of the 12.6 million refugees, 8.1 million, or 64 percent, were persons outside their country and the remaining 4.6 million or 36 percent were the estimated number of persons displaced within their own country. The majority of the estimated refugees (slightly more than 50 percent) were located in Africa. Of the 6.3 million African refugees, 3.6 million were outside their country and 2.7 million were internally displaced. All but 10,000 of the internally displaced were estimated to be in three countries: Ethiopia (1.8 million), Zimbabwe (660,000), and Uganda (265,000). Of the 3.6 million refugees outside their country on the African continent, 2 million were from Ethiopia. Three other countries were estimated to be the origin of more than a quarter million each: Chad (396,000), Rwanda (335,000), and Zaire (277,000). The difference between the 4 million of 1980 and the 6.3 million in the 1981 estimates was due to a number of increases, most notably the new movement from Chad and increases from Ethiopia, each on the order of 400,000.

In 1981, Asia had about 2.2 million estimated refugees, 2 million of whom were outside their country. Afghanistan was the largest source (1.5 million). The most striking contrast in Table 1 is the reduction of total estimated refugees from 7.3 to 2.2 million. The 1980 estimates of USCR included estimates of 4 million internally displaced persons in Kampuchea and 1 million in Laos that were omitted in the 1981 estimates. In addition many Indochinese in the 1980 estimates of origin were residing in countries of resettlement and were considered firmly

resettled in third countries outside the region. These statistical reductions were partially offset by an increase of 800,000 Afghan refugees. The hazards of this statistical exercise are, nevertheless, starkly underscored.

The Latin American refugees are widely dispersed. Of the 189,600 estimated for 1981, the largest group was in Mexico (46,000). Honduras (33,000), Argentina (26,000), and Brazil (25,000) are other notable countries of asylum. The Central American countries are the places of asylum for 61,400 of the estimated Latin American refugees outside their country. The only country estimated to have internally displaced persons in the 1981 USCR survey was El Salvador with 50,000. The instability in Central America is clearly reflected in these estimates, which, if anything, seem to be on the low side, especially with regard to internal displacement.

In the Latin American case, we again face a large reduction in estimates from one year to the next. The difference is primarily due to the country of origin/asylum format. Many of the Latin Americans who settled outside the region, and who were reported in the 1980 estimates, were considered firmly resettled and omitted from the 1981 survey. Most notable were the 665,000 Cubans estimated to be in the United States in the 1980 figures and nearly 200,000 Argentinians in Europe. Repatriation also took place to Chile. The major new group in 1981 not included in the 1980 estimates were the 89,000 refugees from El Salvador. The fluidity of the situation and the Latin American tradition of small movements of elites is underscored by these comparisons, as is the danger of trying to reconcile origin and destination data. What is clear is the new importance of Central American developments for refugee generation.

The Middle East estimated total refugee population increased from 3.3 to 3.6 million. Of the refugees outside their country, Palestinian refugees were the bulk in both years, increasing by about 87,000 to 1,844,000 in 1981. The internally displaced in 1980 were in Lebanon (1 million), Iraq (300,000) and Cyprus (194,000). In 1981, the

REFUGEES

estimates of internal refugees increased from 1.5 to 1.6 million. However, the countries of origin changed radically. Estimated Lebanese displacements declined to 400,000; Cypriot displacements increased marginally to 200,000; Iraq disappeared from the list; Iran had an estimated 1 million displaced persons.

Europe was estimated to be the place of asylum for 355,000 in 1981, with 78,000 in France, 70,000 in West Germany, and 63,000 in England. Many of the refugees are from Eastern bloc nations, but a sizable group are from developing countries who are not firmly resettled.

Rather than getting lost in statistical detail and efforts at data reconciliation, the major outlines of Table 1 ought to be highlighted. Whether one looks at origin or asylum, almost all, 97 to 98 percent, of the estimated world refugees are in developing countries. Africa contains half of the world's refugees. The scope of the definition of refugees (inclusion of internally displaced and firmly resettled) changes estimates by millions and the fluidity of situations from one year to the next can markedly affect estimates.

Within the developing world, the poorest countries also bear a disproportionate burden. Table 2 lists the twelve countries with the highest ratio of refugees to local population and gives their GNP per capita. In all cases, more than 1 in a 100 are refugees. In Somalia, there was 1 refugee for every 3 inhabitants. Eight of the twelve countries are in Africa and eight had less than US$500 GNP per capital. In contrast, the United States resettled 677,000 refugees between 1975 and 1980 (or 1 refugee for every 329 inhabitants) and had a GNP per capita of $9,700 in 1978 (USCR, 1981, p. 34).

As dramatic as these figures are, they do not point up some of the other longer-range costs. Sarah K. Brandel

TABLE 2. *Refugees in countries of asylum, ratio of refugees to local population, and GNP per capita*

Country	Refugees, as of 1 Jan. 1981	Ratio, refugees to population	GNP per capita
Somalia	1.5 million	1:3	US$ 130
Jordan	716,400	1:5	1,050
Djibouti	42,000	1:10	450
Lebanon	229,400	1:14	1,030
Burundi	234,600	1:19	140
Cameroon	266,000	1:32	460
Sudan	490,000	1:38	320
Syria	209,400	1:41	930
Swaziland	10,000	1:60	590
Pakistan	1.4 million	1:62	230
Zaire	400,000	1:73	210
Angola	73,000	1:92	300

Source of data: USCR, 1981, p. 41.

(1980) reports that on the Horn of Africa, for example, the precarious ecological balance between livestock, grazing land, and people always threatened by drought has been virtually destroyed by refugee movements along the border between Somalia and Ethiopia. Tension between refugee and local populations (e.g., in Thailand, Hong Kong, or even Miami in the United States) and the asylum country's own security (e.g., Lebanon and Thailand) are added to demands on resources, already strained in many developing countries, whether they be in the form of money, land, water, health, or transportation.

Some may be tempted to add refugees to a litany of problems of the developing world. The implication, of course, is that it is "their" problem. Such a view would be shortsighted both in terms of the genesis of refugee movements and their implications for the developed world. Almost sixty years ago, refugees were recognized as an international problem. They remain so from all but the most isolationist perspectives in the West and from the perspective enunciated by the Eastern bloc nations that ascribes the problems to Western imperialism and neocolonialism. The issue now is what is being done and what might be done to deal with the problem.

Organized International Aid. Coordinated international attention to refugees followed World War I. Prior to that time, the plight of refugees was seen as depending on a solution to the political problem that caused the displacement. Most efforts to aid refugees were undertaken privately and were aimed at relief rather than resettlement or reintegration.

In 1920, bilateral negotiations were undertaken by European countries to transfer populations. "Refugee" was not an officially recognized status, and many persons, primarily Russians, found themselves in the quandary of being unwanted in the places they lived, unwilling to return to their country, and unable to travel for lack of internationally recognized documents. With the end of open immigration, it became clear that refugees were an international problem, caused by international relations, and not a problem easily solved by overseas migration to the New World.

In 1921, a meeting of private relief agencies petitioned the League of Nations to appoint a commissioner for refugees to secure repatriation of Russian refugees and to provide for their assistance. The League appointed Fridtjof Nansen as high commissioner for Russian refugees in Europe. Nansen had experience in prisoner exchange carried out under League auspices. His mandate was to define refugees' legal status, to coordinate relief efforts, and to bring about the repatriation of Russian refugees or see to their resettlement elsewhere or their employment in countries of temporary asylum. In 1923, Greek and Bulgarian refugees were added to his mandate.

The major innovation of this effort was the Nansen passport, which provided an internationally (though not universally) recognized document that permitted travel and provided a kind of recognition of refugee status. During this interwar period, the range of persons of interest to the high commissioner increased. In addition, a high commissioner for refugees coming from Germany was appointed in 1933. The two offices were joined in 1938 as High Commissioner for Refugees under the Protection of the League of Nations, with a five-year mandate, subsequently extended to 1946.

Meanwhile, in 1938, at the Evian-les-Bains conference called by U.S. President Franklin D. Roosevelt, an Inter-governmental Committee on Refugees (IGCR) was developed to help with resettlement of refugees from Germany and Austria. In 1943, at the Bermuda Conference, the mandate was extended to Spanish refugees and other refugees resulting from World War II. In 1943, the United Nations Relief and Rehabilitation Administration (UNRRA) was established to prepare for prisoner exchange and return of exiles.

In July 1947, the International Refugee Organization (IRO) was created as a nonpermanent, specialized agency of the United Nations with a three-year mandate to supplement the IGCR and UNRRA. The IRO's subsequent demise was due to U.S. opposition to the forcible repatriation insisted on by some communist states. U.S. support for IRO was ended by the much-criticized condition of the U.S. Congress that U.S. contributions not be used for international refugee organizations (the IRO being the object of the prohibition) whose membership did not take part in free movement, that is, who did not permit exit or demanded forced repatriation. In 1952, Belgium and the United States sponsored the Brussels Resolution, which led to the Inter-governmental Committee for European Migration (ICEM) to transport Europeans whose living conditions were inadequate to countries willing to receive them.

Shortly before the scheduled demise of the IRO (1 July 1950), the United Nations General Assembly passed a resolution creating a United Nations High Commissioner for Refugees (UNHCR) to take over the legal protection of refugees and displaced persons from the IRO as of 1 January 1951. The office of the high commissioner was also given the mandate to seek permanent solutions to refugee problems through repatriation and resettlement and to provide for emergency assistance and maintenance of refugee populations. Over the ensuing years, the main work of the UNHCR has been monitoring the mil-

lions of refugees worldwide, assisting in their aid and relief through contracts with voluntary agencies and with national governments, in providing protection for refugees by negotiating with governments of asylum countries to permit relief aid, and in seeking permanent solutions through voluntary repatriation or resettlement.

Concurrently, the UNHCR is the major international organization in this field. It is supplemented by the United Nations Relief and Works Agency for Palestinian Refugees in the Near East (UNRWA). Relief and transportation for resettlement are carried out through the network of international and national voluntary agencies and through the ICEM, with its long and specialized experience in transportation.

The UNHCR was envisaged as primarily affording temporary protection and as coordinating relief and resettlement efforts. The agency is not an operational one, in the sense of actually carrying out relief, transport, and other services. Rather, it uses its "good offices," moral persuasion, and position as a politically neutral body focusing on humanitarian concerns. It negotiates with sending governments, countries of asylum, international relief organizations, voluntary agencies, and others to relieve suffering and to resettle refugees in their original country or elsewhere.

Most of the actual care and resettlement of refugees is done by international and national voluntary organizations and by the governments in countries of asylum, although the long-standing nature of some refugee situations, for example, in Africa, has led to the UNHCR's involvement in some relief and resettlement work. The size and variety of refugee movements has in fact strained UNHCR resources.

There is a growing conviction that refugee movements will be a permanent fact of international life. This reflects the growing number of nations, the realities of building a state, and the effects of mass communication on awareness of population dislocations. As a result, major questions are being raised concerning the adequacy of international definitions and machinery, notably the UNHCR, for responding to refugee emergencies.

Charles B. Keely
Patricia E. Elwell

See also IMMIGRATION POLICY.

BIBLIOGRAPHY

Brandel, Sarah K. "Refugees: New Dimensions to an Old Problem." *ODC Communiqué* 1980/3. Washington, D.C.: Overseas Development Council, 1980.
Fragomen, Austin T., Jr. "The Refugee: A Problem of Defini-

tion." *Case Western Reserve Journal of International Law* 3(1):45–69, Winter 1970.

Holborn, Louise W. *Refugees, a Problem of Our Time: The Work of the United Nations High Commissioner for Refugees, 1951–1972.* 2 vols. Metuchen, N.J.: Scarecrow Press, 1975.

Plender, Richard. *International Migration Law.* Law and Population Series, no. 2. Leiden, Netherlands: Sijthoff, 1972.

United States, Congressional Research Service. *World Refugee Crisis: The International Community's Response.* Library of Congress report prepared at the request of Senator Edward M. Kennedy, Chairman, Committee on the Judiciary, United States Senate. Washington, D.C.: U.S. Government Printing Office, 1979.

United States Committee for Refugees. *1980 World Refugee Survey.* New York, 1980.

——. *1981 World Refugee Survey.* New York, 1981.

REGISTRATION SYSTEMS

See DATA COLLECTION, *article on* NATIONAL SYSTEMS.

REPRODUCTION

1. MODELS   Jane Menken
2. MALNUTRITION AND FAMINE   Zena A. Stein
                                Mervyn Susser

1.

MODELS

Mathematical models of the human reproductive process are used to meet a broad range of needs. Most of these models attempt to relate the proximate determinants of fertility to other overall measures of fertility such as total fertility rates, age-specific birth rates, or birth intervals. The impetus for the development of such models has come in part from the difficulty of performing meaningful experiments in real populations. Investigators have turned to models to understand which components of the reproductive process are most important in determining fertility, how they interact, and what the magnitude of the potential effects of changes in the components might be. In many circumstances, accurate data on some of the components of fertility are not available. The models may be used to determine whether or not differences in these components could affect fertility substantially. In this way, they are used as aids to decide what kinds of studies are needed and which measurements are crucial to an understanding of fertility in actual populations. The models may also provide a means for estimating either a specified fertility indicator from the components of

reproduction or a given component from knowledge of other proximate variables and fertility itself.

Most existing models employ a basic outline of a woman's reproductive life span [*see Figure 1 in* FERTILITY DETERMINANTS; *article on* PROXIMATE DETERMINANTS]. The limits of the potential reproductive years of women are determined by menarche and menopause. The limits of the actual reproductive span depend more, in most situations, upon marriage and marriage dissolution. Within marriage, the factors influencing birth intervals are the primary determinants of fertility. Reproductive models summarize the relationship between intermediate fertility variables and fertility in the form of mathematical equations.

In recent decades a number of different types of reproductive models have been developed, ranging from relatively simple to highly complex ones (Henry, 1972; Menken, 1975). One of the simplest of these models, developed primarily by John Bongaarts (1976), will be summarized here.

Let the fertility rate, expressed in births per 1,000 women, be represented by the variable *FR*. Since some women are sterile or not married, *FR* is less than the fertility rate among women who are reproducers. To find this rate, the marital fecund fertility rate (MFR), *FR* is divided by *S*, the proportion of all women who are both fecund and married:

$$MFR = FR/S. \qquad (1)$$

From renewal theory it is known that the equilibrium rate of occurrence of an event equals the inverse of the mean duration of the interval between two successive events. This finding can be applied with good approximation to the rate of childbearing among women in the mid-reproductive years when fertility rates are close to equilibrium and the intermediate fertility variables do not vary by age. If *B* represents the mean birth interval (calculated by using all births in a time interval as the sampling frame), then

$$MFR = 12,000/B, \qquad (2)$$

where *B* is expressed in months and *MFR* is calculated per 1,000 married fecund women per year. Substitution of equation (2) in equation (1) yields

$$FR = 12,000 \, S/B. \qquad (3)$$

Under the assumption that the three principal components of the birth interval are independently determined, *B* equals the sum of the mean durations of each of the subcomponents:

$$B = P + L + G, \qquad (4)$$

where P = mean duration of the postpartum amenorrhea interval (months); L = mean duration of the 1-conception interval (months); and G = full term pregnancy of 9 months duration. After substitution of equation (4), equation (3) becomes

$$FR = 12,000\, S/(P + L + G). \qquad (5)$$

This basic version of the model can be refined further by introducing the determinants of the 1-conception interval. It can be shown (Sheps and Menken, 1973; Bongaarts, 1976) that

$$L = \frac{O}{1 - A} + \frac{AI}{1 - A}, \qquad (6)$$

where A = the proportion of all conceptions that ends in a spontaneous abortion or still birth; O = mean duration of the ovulation interval (months); and I = mean duration of nonsusceptability associated with an intrauterine death (months).

The first term on the right side of this equation represents the average total time women ovulate during the 1-conception interval and the second term equals the time they are nonsusceptible. It can further be demonstrated that O equals the inverse of the population's harmonic mean fecundability F:

$$O = 1/F. \qquad (7)$$

Substitution of equation (7) in equation (6) and of (6) in (5) finally results in the complete version of this reproductive model:

$$FR = \frac{12,000\, S}{P + \dfrac{1}{(1 - A)F} + \dfrac{AI}{1 - A} + G}, \qquad (8)$$

where the denominator is simply the mean interval between live births. A very rough estimate of the total fertility rate (TFR), can be obtained by multiplying equation (8) by the number of years women are both fecund and married, the EP, or effective reproductive period:

$$TFR \approx FR \times EP. \qquad (9)$$

The following simple example of an application serves to illustrate how the above model can be used in the analysis of the effect of changes in these variables on fertility. Assume that in a hypothetical group of women the following estimates have been obtained:

S = proportion of women fecund and married   0.90
P = mean postpartum amenorrhea duration   10 months
L = mean duration of 1-conception interval   9 months

In that case, the fertility rate for these women is $12,000 \times 0.9/(10 + 9 + 9)$, or 386 births per 1,000 women per year, as estimated from equation (5). Assume further that a study of postpartum amenorrhea has demonstrated that another group of women has a mean postpartum amenorrhea interval 7 months above average, that is, 17 months. According to the model, fertility in this group of women should be 20 percent below average, or 309 births per 1,000 women per year. If women in both groups all become fecund at age 15 and reach secondary sterility at age 43, then their fecund period lasts 28 years (43 minus 15); if they marry at age 18, their effective reproductive period is 25 years. The total fertility rate will be $25 \times (386/1,000)$ or 9.6, in the first case and $25 \times (309/1,000)$, or 7.7, in the second, so that the reduction in total fertility rate is also 20 percent. It is interesting to note that a 70 percent increase in the postpartum amenorrhea interval results in only a 20 percent decrease in fertility. This finding becomes intuitively clear when one considers that changes in fertility are tied to alterations in the total birth interval. A change in a proximate determinant that affects *one component* of the birth interval by a given percentage can only produce a much lower percentage change in the entire birth interval.

The model of the reproductive process just presented is a useful descriptive and analytical tool. It highlights the importance, first, of the birth interval and its components as the determinants of fertility rates within the reproductive span and, second, of the duration of reproductive life and its influence on total fertility and therefore on crude birth rates. Because the model leads to analytic expressions for indexes such as mean birth interval lengths and fertility rates and because it includes only a limited number of factors, it is relatively easy to study the effects of changes in each of these components. However, as soon as more realism is sought, either by allowing variation among women or with age in each determinant, or by the inclusion of more factors that influence the occurrence of births in real life (e.g., differential age at marriage, widowhood, coital frequency, and contraception), the mathematics can rapidly become intractable. Researchers have turned to computer models in which results are *calculated* from specific parameter values and a set of assumptions about the action and interaction of the factors. These models have been of several types, each useful in a variety of situations.

Macrosimulation models usually generate results month by month, obtaining, for example, the number of conceptions at age 20 years 10 months by multiplying the number of women in the ovulating interval in that month by the fecundability at that age. The fertility *rate* nine months later is calculated as the number of conceptions multiplied by the proportion leading to live births $(1 - A)$ and divided by the total number of women. The number in the ovulating interval at age 20 years 11 months is equal to the number in the previous month, minus the number conceiving the previous month, plus the number of newly married, plus the number ending their periods of postpartum amenorrhea following either a live birth or fetal death. Although computer programming of such models can be tedious, the method itself is straightforward.

Microsimulation differs in that an entire reproductive history is generated for a sample of *individuals* by using random numbers to determine the occurrence and timing of each successive event for one individual at a time. For example, if a sample woman is in the first month of marriage and her fecundability is 0.20, a random number between 0 and 1 can be chosen. If the random number is greater than 0.20, she does not conceive in that month. If it is less than 0.20, a conception is recorded in her history as occurring in that month. Another random number can be generated to determine whether a live birth or an abortion is the next event. Step by step, the life of this one woman is thus determined. The fertility rate at a particular age can later be found by counting the number of histories in which a record of a birth at that age is recorded and dividing by the number of women, exactly the same procedure one would use on data from a real survey, vital statistics records, and the census.

Microsimulation models are most useful under two circumstances: either when the number of variables involved is large and their interrelationships are complex or when interest is focused upon characteristics of samples. For example, the fertility rate given in equation (8) is an expected or mean value; it could vary among samples, not because any of the intermediate fertility variables were different, but simply because of random variation. A microsimulation model could be used to draw many samples of a given size so that the values and variations in the birth rate (or any other statistic, for that matter) could be studied. Anthropologists concerned with the study of small groups have made increasing use of large-scale microsimulation models in recent years (Dyke and MacCluer, 1973; Wachter, Hammel, and Laslett, 1978).

Mathematical models of reproduction that allow for greater variation in the determinants of fertility than the simple model presented earlier are useful in many situations. Much of the pioneering work was carried out by Louis Henry (1972) and Mindel C. Sheps and her colleagues (see Sheps and Menken, 1973). These models allowed fundamental studies of the relationships between fertility determinants and birth intervals and birth rates

to be carried out. Recently, more complex models based on the advanced mathematical theory of age-dependent branching processes (Mode, 1975) have been proposed.

Through the use of models of the reproductive process, whether macrosimulation or microsimulation or mathematical in nature, investigators have been able to study the potential impact on fertility of family planning programs, of contraceptive use according to effectiveness, of postponed marriage, or availability of marriage partners, of spouse separation, and many other factors. Those mentioned thus far have modeled the entire reproductive history of a couple or a population. Models limited to specific factors, however, also have a long history. For example, models of fecundability and of the duration of the ovulation interval have been employed to demonstrate that fecundability varies among women in most populations and to consider methods of estimation and types of data that best reflected these differences (for references, see Menken, 1975). From these studies, it has been concluded that survey data are usually inadequate for measuring fecundability directly because reliable estimates of how long it took until conception occurred are virtually impossible to obtain. In addition, where contraceptive practice is the norm, women who are not users are so highly selected for subfecundity or concealed fertility control that an estimate of their conception rates cannot reflect the population level well.

A model of the period of postpartum amenorrhea has been used to document the role of breastfeeding in prolonging the period until ovulation resumes. Other models have examined the effect of contraception when initiation of its use overlaps with the period of amenorrhea. Still others have considered the impact of abortion and the extent of variation of abortion rates among women. In each instance, the model helped sharpen scholars' understanding of the type and magnitude of influence of certain fertility determinants.

Reproductive models in demography are used for multiple purposes; to describe fertility and estimate its parameters, to indicate variables for which data are essential, to predict the effects of continuation or change in these parameters, and to simulate experiments in an area where experiments on actual populations are difficult or impossible to undertake. Their various roles in fertility research all stem from a basic difference between verbal theory and a mathematical model. While verbal theories may express ideas well, they are frequently based on assumptions about variables and their relationships that are not clearly stated. From a verbal argument it is sometimes difficult to detect all implications of either continuing or attempting change in a system. Models, however, require rigorous and exact definitions of variables and their dependencies. They provide the most rigorous way to assess both the short-term and the long-term implications of any theory concerning the levels, interrelationships, and changes in fertility determinants. With constant reminders that each model is a representation of reality, an abstraction that is only as good as its approximation to reality, one can examine the full range of effects implicit in the theory of fertility it represents.

Jane Menken

See also FAMILY PLANNING PROGRAMS, *article on* EFFECTS ON FERTILITY.

BIBLIOGRAPHY

Bongaarts, John. "Intermediate Fertility Variables and Marital Fertility Rates." *Population Studies* 30(2):227–241, July 1976.

Dyke, Bennett, and Jean Walters MacCluer (editors). *Computer Simulation in Human Population Studies.* New York: Academic Press, 1973.

Henry, Louis. *On the Measurement of Human Fertility: Selected Writings.* Translated and edited by Mindel C. Sheps and Evelyne Lapierre-Adamcyk. A Population Council Book. New York: Elsevier, 1972.

Menken, Jane. "Biometric Models of Fertility." *Social Forces* 54(1):52–65, September 1975.

Mode, Charles J. "Perspectives in Stochastic Models of Human Reproduction: A Review and Analysis." *Theoretical Population Biology* 8(3):247–291, December 1975.

Sheps, Mindel C., and Jane Menken. *Mathematical Models of Conception and Birth.* Chicago: University of Chicago Press, 1973.

Wachter, Kenneth W., Eugene A. Hammel, and Peter Laslett. *Statistical Studies of Historical Social Structure.* New York: Academic Press, 1978.

2.
MALNUTRITION AND FAMINE

Nutrition affects reproduction, undernutrition in some ways and overnutrition in others. Malnutrition is common in much of the world, and will be the main concern of this article. That the relationships are complex is demonstrated by the evidence of the interaction of nutrition with both fecundity (physiological capacity to produce a live child) and fertility (actual reproductive performance). This article discusses biological, social, and behavioral aspects of fecundity and fertility in relation to nutrition. A major distinction may be made between effects of the chronic, moderate malnutrition that prevails in the poorer classes of many developing countries and the acute malnutrition resulting from famine and starvation. The focus here is on the reproductive process in females,

primarily because the literature contains relatively little information about the male response to poor nutrition.

Effects of Chronic Malnutrition

In general, the fertility of a population is determined both by its fecundity and by the inhibition of fertility. Social and behavioral factors influence both fecundity and fertility. Fecundity, for instance, has increased in developed countries over the past century with the increasingly precocious onset of the menarche and, at the same time, the probable deferment of the mean age at menopause. More obvious, if unmeasured, factors in this increase include the variable frequency of pelvic infections such as tuberculosis and the venereal diseases, which have their origin in social and economic conditions and in behavioral norms for sexuality and which are markedly influenced by hygiene, forms of treatment, and contraception. In general, however, social and behavioral factors promoting or inhibiting fertility are likely to override the factors influencing fecundity. The most important of these factors influencing fertility are (1) celibacy, which is a function of the mean age at marriage (or other forms of regular sexual union) and the prevalence of marital disruption; (2) deliberate birth control by contraception or induced abortion; and (3) breastfeeding, which can delay the return of ovulation after a woman has given birth. One or more of these factors reduce fertility to well below its potential level in all known populations. This fact complicates any analysis of the effect of nutrition on fecundity, since the confounding behavioral factors must be controlled before useful conclusions can be drawn from fertility differentials among populations. These issues are discussed at greater length by John Bongaarts (1980). [*See* FERTILITY DETERMINANTS, *article on* PROXIMATE DETERMINANTS.]

Evidence from Fertility Differentials. Analysis of fertility differentials in populations in which contraception and induced abortion are virtually absent, and which differ in nutrition or other factors under study, provides one strategy. However, the impact of the remaining behavioral factors (mating, marriage, and lactation) still makes it difficult to draw conclusions. Thus in the United States, neither the Hutterites nor the Amish practice birth control; among those who had reached the end of the childbearing years in 1950, Hutterite women had an average of 9 births (Eaton and Mayer, 1953), and Amish women had an average of 6.3 (Cross and McKusick, 1970). Since both groups enjoy more than a sufficiency of food, the general level of nutrition cannot explain the difference.

In the Middle and Far East, Bangladeshi, Kuwaiti, and Saudi Arabian women also do not practice birth control. In recent times, only the Bangladeshi women have suffered undernutrition and famine. Yet women in all three groups have an average rate of about 7 births (United Nations, 1975). General nutrition again seems to be neither the sole nor the overriding influence. In fact, in a comparison of the fertility of the Hutterites (average 9 births) and the Bangladeshi (average 6.5 births), the underlying demographic factor resides in the mean interval between births. The length of this interval can be explained in turn by the duration of breast feeding and consequent amenorrhea, which is far longer among the Bangladeshi (Bongaarts, 1980).

The maximum potential level of fecundity in a population can be estimated in terms of a reproductive model that yields a fecundity rate. This rate is defined as the average number of births women of a given population would have over their reproductive lifetimes in the absence of celibacy, contraception, induced abortion, and lactation. That is, the limits are set by age of menarche and menopause. In a group of developed countries the fecundity rate equaled 15.4 births per woman and in a group of poor, less-developed countries, 15.2 births (Bongaarts, 1978). This difference in fecundity was not statistically significant. Since in the less-developed countries food is often scarce and a large proportion of the population suffers from at least moderate degrees of chronic malnutrition, this study suggests that nutrition could have little impact on the duration of the fecund period.

Chronic Malnutrition and the Components of Fecundity. Six components of fecundity can be identified: (1) age at menarche, (2) age at menopause, (3) prevalence of permanent sterility, (4) duration of inhibition of ovulation by breastfeeding, (5) production of sperm, and of ova (in nonpregnant, nonamenorrheic women), and (6) probability of intrauterine death. A population will have relatively high fecundity if it has high values for factors 2 and 5 and low values for factors 1, 3, 4, and 6. We shall briefly review the evidence for an effect of chronic malnutrition on each of these components of fecundity and in turn, where appropriate, on fertility.

Age at menarche. Menarche occurs in the early or middle teens. In the contemporary Western world, the average age is about 13 years. In developing countries average age is typically higher—13–14 in India, 13.4 in Sri Lanka, 15.0 among the Bantu in South Africa, 15.7 in Bangladesh, and 18.8 among the Bundi in New Guinea. Although authorities disagree about the relative contributions of various biological, environmental, and socioeconomic factors to age of menarche, most believe that nutrition has a substantial impact. Various pieces of evidence, direct and indirect, support the nutritional hypothesis. In the United States it has been found that girls

well nourished in terms of a critical weight and degree of fatness reached menarche two years earlier than girls of lesser weight and fatness (Frisch, 1972). Certainly leanness combined with an unusual degree of physical training, as in ballet dancers (Frisch, Wyshak, and Vincent, 1980) and athletes (Feicht et al., 1978), is associated with delayed menarche as well as irregular cycles and secondary amenorrhea. Weight and body composition reflect nutritional intake only to a degree; exercise and energy expenditure can have powerful effects on both these indexes. In anorexia nervosa, failure to eat is accompanied by amenorrhea and a prepubertal circadian pattern in the secretion of gonadotrophin (Boyar, 1978). In a number of women, though, secondary amenorrhea precedes weight loss, and in others, menstruation does not follow when normal weight is regained. An Indian study, however, concluded that girls who received diets higher in calories and proteins had earlier menarche (Bhalla and Srivastava, 1974). Thus the improved diet and increase in body size over the past century in Western societies could explain the advance in age of menarche of about four months per decade on average, that is, about three years in this century (Tanner, 1968). Menarcheal age now seems to be stationary. As would be predicted from these changes over time, socioeconomic status and age at menarche have been found to be negatively correlated in a number of countries, although in recent times these differences have disappeared in some developed countries (Susser and Watson, 1971). Differences ranging from a few months to about two years have been found between high-income and low-income groups and between urban and rural populations (Zacharias and Wurtman, 1969).

Unlike fecundity, fertility depends far less on age at menarche than on age at marriage. For this reason, even substantial changes in age at menarche following improvements in nutrition can be expected to raise fertility by at most a small percentage.

Menopause. The median age at menopause seems to vary across societies, although the available data are limited because of flaws in methods of study. Also, the data indicate deferment of age of menopause in, for example, the United States and in England over the past fifty years (MacMahon and Worcester, 1966). No good evidence connects these variations in age at menopause with nutrition. Nor does available evidence suggest an impact of nutrition on the mean age at last birth, which might be taken as a crude index of continuing fecundity if not of age at menopause.

Prevalence of permanent sterility. The known variations in causes of female and male sterility relate predominantly to infections—venereal (both bacterial and viral), chronic tuberculosis, and a number of others. There is no evidence that nutrition plays a role.

Lactation amenorrhea. The term "lactation amenorrhea" is often used to refer to the temporary absence of menses postpartum, because it is now well established that breastfeeding is the principal determinant of the duration of this amenorrhea.

The question of interest here is whether maternal malnutrition affects amenorrhea independently of the duration and pattern of breastfeeding. Recent studies in poorly nourished rural populations in Bangladesh (Chowdhury, 1978) and Guatemala (Delgado et al., 1978) suggest that moderate malnutrition has rather small effects on duration of lactational amenorrhea. In the Guatemalan investigation, for example, women were divided into three groups on the basis of body size as a substitute for their nutritional state. The "low-nutritional-status" group had a mean weight of 43.7 kilograms and a mean period of amenorrhea of 14.8 months, the "high-nutritional-status" group had a mean weight of 55.6 kilograms and a mean period of amenorrhea of 13.2 months. Lactation, not nutrition *per se,* was the major determinant of amenorrhea. There was a fairly consistent (although statistically not significant) difference of the order of one month, however, between the amenorrhea intervals of women with high-caloric and low-caloric intake. [*See* BREASTFEEDING.]

Production of sperm and ova. Since it is virtually impossible to estimate the rate of production of gametes directly on a population basis, it is necessary to rely on indirect measures such as the rate of conception among nonpregnant, nonamenorrheic women. The mean waiting time to conception serves as a convenient, simply measured indicator of the rate of conception that is often available. A useful measure of waiting time available from vital statistics is the interval between marriage and first birth. Waiting time is more accurately measured by the number of months between the occurrence of the first postpartum menses (a good indicator of the resumption of ovulation) and the next conception. Malnutrition seems not to affect this interval.

Intrauterine mortality. Severe prenatal undernutrition reduces birth weight and also raises infant mortality at least through the first three months of life (Stein et al., 1975). Good evidence for a link between malnutrition and intrauterine mortality does not exist, however. Indeed, the Guatemalan investigation discussed earlier suggests that chronic maternal malnutrition did not add to intrauterine mortality. In this population maternal nutritional status did not affect the waiting time between first postpartum menses and the next birth. Any significant increase in intrauterine mortality, whether abortions or fetal deaths, should have lengthened the waiting time. The absence of a relationship between nutritional state and waiting time implies, therefore, that the link

between maternal nutrition and intrauterine mortality is either absent or weak. A possible explanation for this finding is suggested by animal studies and by the studies of the Dutch famine of 1944–1945. When nutrients are insufficient to meet the needs of both mother and fetus, the fetus is given priority and nutrients are mobilized from maternal tissue until the mother's reserves are severely depleted.

Effects of Famine

"Famine," according to the *Oxford English Dictionary,* is "a period of extreme and general scarcity of food." The starvation is extreme, affects the whole population, and is limited in duration. Famine is an acute episode which, if continued long enough, will result in the death of the population. People experience a sensation of gnawing hunger, day and night. There are psychological manifestations (irritability and apathy), antisocial behavior (suspiciousness, aggressiveness, finally cannibalism), illnesses (infections, famine oedema, osteomalacia) and death (which comes sooner to men than to women and to those at the extremes of life than to the middle-aged). In the newborn, the starvation of the mother during pregnancy reduces fetal growth, and results in a reduction in mean birthweight and a decrease in viability for at least the first three months of life. There is, finally, a reduction in fertility that can become absolute. Once food becomes available, recovery of the population is rapid. The Dutch famine (Stein et al., 1975) provides the best-documented evidence of the effects of famine on fecundity and fertility.

Circumstances of the Dutch Famine. If famine supervenes in a poorly nourished population, the transition from chronic malnutrition to starvation may be ill defined. Except in major wars, most famines occur in such circumstances. In the Dutch famine (or *Hongerwinter*) of 1944–1945 there was no such problem. Before the famine and certainly after, the Dutch population was not at the margin of survival either in its health and physiological state or in its values and mores. These conditions made the famine state distinct from states that preceded and followed it. At the same time, results from the Dutch famine should not be casually extrapolated to populations suffering from chronic malnutrition.

Equally likely to frustrate assessment of famine effects in the kinds of places where famine most often occurs is the absence of systematic vital statistics and other supporting data. In the Netherlands, statistics were well developed, and they were maintained throughout the famine period.

The famine was a final episode in the long wartime ordeal of the Dutch people during World War II. From

September 1944 until May 1945, the Nazi occupation authority allowed no food to be imported into the cities from rural supply areas. In that year too, an early and severe winter froze the barges in the canals, aggravating the food crisis. The general, severe, and acute deprivation of food lasted six months. In the first week of May the Allied armies crossed the Rhine, liberated the western Netherlands, and relieved the famine.

The main impact of the famine was felt in the large cities of the west. The geographic distribution of the famine enabled the "famine" cities in the west and "control" cities in the north and south to be designated.

Famine Effects on Fertility. In the famine area, a distinct fall in the number of births was evident, beginning nine months after the onset of acute starvation (which is dated from mid-October 1944). Thus, for births conceived early in the famine, during November and December 1944, there was a slight decline in numbers; for births conceived in January 1945, there was a moderate decline; for births conceived from February through April 1945, there was a marked decline. The famine was relieved 7 May 1945, and the number of conceptions must have risen almost immediately. Births following conceptions in the period as soon as the fourth to eighth week after the famine (June 1945) had restored numbers to the prefamine level and, temporarily, to an even higher level (see Figure 1).

The official rations declined to below 1,500 calories daily in September 1944, but not before November did a decrease in subsequent births reflect infertility in the co-

hort of conceptions. This asynchrony of onset of famine and infertility suggests that it took some time before couples exhausted their resources of bodily nutrients. By contrast, with relief of the famine, recovery of fertility was immediate. It seems that with the provision of nutrients, the preconditions of fertility (sexual activity and fecundity) were restored at once. In the famine cities the relationship between food rations and fertility was strong and convincing below a threshold ration of about 1,500 calories. In the northern cities, too, when caloric rations fell below this level, a decline in fertility was detectable. In the southern cities, there was no such relationship, presumably because many of them were freed from occupation at the time of the Hongerwinter and therefore had available food supplies from the surrounding countryside and the liberated armies over and above the official ration.

Infertility affected the social classes differently. The decline in fertility in classes engaged in white-collar occupations though present, was less remarkable than that in classes engaged in manual labor, in which both the decline and the postwar rebound were steeper. In the control cities, divergence between the classes was much less marked.

Mechanisms of Famine Effects. In attempting to understand the likely mechanism of infertility as a result of famine, we considered several possibilities. Following Kingsley Davis and Judith Blake (1956), we deal with the "intermediate variables" (intercourse, conception, and the maintenance of gestation) in turn.

First, with regard to intercourse, involuntary abstinence and a decline in coital frequency were likely to have played some part. Contemporary reports emphasize the lassitude of the starving Dutch population and their diminished libido. A decline in male libido has been documented also in reports of prisoner-of-war camps and under conditions of experimental starvation (Keys et al., 1950).

Second, with regard to the potential for conception, in women anovular cycles and infecundability must be considered as mechanisms, and in men, oligospermia. From the direct reports of gynecologists in practice at the time, we know that amenorrhea was extremely widespread. Indeed, famine-related amenorrhea has often been observed, for example, in Greece during World War II, and in prisoner-of-war and concentration camps (Hytten and Leitch, 1971).

Third, with regard to the maintenance of gestation, the possibility that births declined because of an excess of spontaneous abortions must be considered. The fertilized zygote may have failed to implant itself in the uterus, or once implanted, it may have failed to go to term. Human evidence of the effects of starvation on early fetal loss is

FIGURE 1. *Fertility and caloric ration, famine cities, number of births and official average daily caloric ration at estimated time of conception for period June 1944 to December 1946, inclusive*

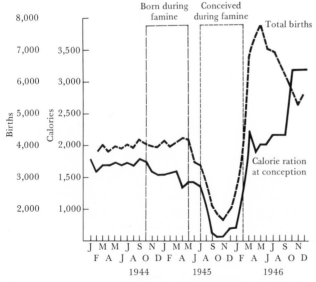

SOURCE: Stein et al., 1975; adapted by permission.

anecdotal. C. Gopalan and A. Nadamuni Naidu (1972) refer to a pregnancy wastage rate of 30 percent observed by Sundar Rao among poor Indian women, but the data presented are not of a kind that can be rigorously evaluated. Aaron E. Ifekwunigwe (1971) says of the Biafran experience in the late 1960s, "When pregnancy took place, the incidence of miscarriage was also markedly raised." V. G. Valaoras (1946) in writing of the Greek famine during World War II mentions "the numerous miscarriages and abortions observed during that time."

A similar impression of a rise in miscarriages and abortions was formed by observers in the Netherlands, but the information on abortions for the 1944–1945 period is also anecdotal. The relation of number of births to exposure to famine, however, does not support the idea that fetal loss was an important factor in the decline in fertility in the Netherlands. Fetal loss would have operated in the first two to three months of gestation, so that when the famine was lifted pregnancies already started would have survived to term, raising the fertility rates about seven to eight months later. Such a rise is not clearly evident in the data.

On the alternative hypothesis, that a decline either in intercourse or in fecundity or both was responsible for infertility caused by famine, then the recovery of fertility would not be detected before the elapse of the normal mean gestation period. The data favor the second alternative. The rise in births began about 290 to 300 days after the relief of the famine and suggest that the rise stemmed from an increase in conceptions after liberation.

To explain the differences in rates of conception between the social classes during the famine, three interpretations can be considered.

1. *Voluntary control of fertility.* The social controls (sexual taboos, age at marriage, contraception, abortion) that differentiated the fertility of the classes before and after the famine might have been altered during the famine, so that the upper classes relaxed their control of fertility or the lower classes increased their control. This reversal of the usual behavior among the classes seems an unlikely one.

2. *Variation in physiological resistance to infecundity.* At the onset of the famine, the higher social classes may have been in better health and, in particular, better nourished, than the lower classes. This advantage might have sustained relative fecundity in the upper classes in the face of the famine.

3. *Access to food.* Those who obtained more food would have been protected against the severe effects of starvation. During the famine the higher social classes with their superior resources in money, property, and influence may have obtained more food than the lower social classes. This explanation has most to commend it. The

lower classes were worse hit by the famine in many respects. Thus they suffered a disproportionate increase in deaths, and the clinical signs of malnutrition in adults as well as children were most commonly seen in the poorer sections of the cities. This third explanation of the social class difference in fertility during the famine emphasizes the influence of current nutritional state on fecundity.

One of the chief lessons learned from the well-documented Dutch famine is the great resilience of human populations exposed to the harshest environmental forces. Early in May 1945, the people were so weakened that the very survival of many was in doubt. The liberation armies were supported by emergency nutrition teams and brought plentiful supplies of food. Within one month of liberation from the Nazi occupation, many in the Netherlands were restored to the normal activities of everyday life and to the business of rebuilding their families and their shattered cities.

Conclusions

This review demonstrates that severe undernutrition to the degree of famine impairs human reproduction. The evidence that moderate chronic malnutrition affects fecundity is more equivocal but is suggestive, and these postulated effects result in a surprisingly small decrease in fertility. Among the components of fecundity examined here, the most likely to be affected by chronic malnutrition are age at menarche and the duration of lactational amenorrhea. For either component, among groups of women whose caloric intakes differ by several hundred calories per day, fertility rates can be expected to differ by no more than a few percentage points. Although the other components of fecundity cannot be assessed quantitatively for lack of evidence, their impact on fecundity and fertility is certainly less than that of age at menarche and amenorrhea. Thus even substantial improvement in the nutrition of the underdeveloped countries will at most result in a slight increase in fertility.

The effects of acute, severe malnutrition, in sharp contrast with chronic malnutrition, are marked and unequivocal. Famine reduces fertility substantially, and almost certainly reduction in fecundity, as well as in libido, is a determinant of this infertility. The precise causes of this reduction remain to be determined. The change in fecundity is most likely to be a direct result of severe malnutrition. Psychological stress and anxiety could also affect both fecundity and libido.

Zena A. Stein
Mervyn Susser

See also FERTILITY DETERMINANTS, *article on* PROXIMATE DETERMINANTS.

BIBLIOGRAPHY

Bhalla, Maya, and J. R. Srivastava. "A Prospective Study of the Age of Menarche in Kanpur Girls." *Indian Pediatrics* 11(7):487–493, July 1974.

Blix, Gunnar, Yngve Hofvander, and Bo Vahlquist (editors). *Famine: A Symposium Dealing with Nutrition and Relief Operations in Times of Disaster.* Symposia of the Swedish Nutritional Foundation, no. 9. Uppsala, Sweden: Almqvist & Wiksell, 1971.

Bongaarts, John. "A Framework for Analyzing the Proximate Determinants of Fertility." *Population and Development Review* 4(1): 105–132, March 1978.

———. "Does Malnutrition Affect Fecundity? A Summary of Evidence." *Science* 208(4444):564–569, 9 May 1980.

Boyar, R. M. "Endocrine Changes in Anorexia Nervosa." *Medical Clinics of North America* 62(2):297–303, March 1978.

Chowdhury, A. K. M. Alauddin. "Effect of Maternal Nutrition on Fertility in Rural Bangladesh." In *Nutrition and Human Reproduction,* edited by W. Henry Mosley, pp. 401–410. New York: Plenum, 1978.

Cross, Harold E., and Victor A. McKusick. "Amish Demography." *Social Biology* 17(2):83–101, June 1970.

Davis, Kingsley, and Judith Blake. "Social Structure and Fertility: An Analytic Framework." *Economic Development and Cultural Change* 4(3):211–235, April 1956.

Delgado, Hernán, Aaron Lechtig, Elena Brineman, Reynaldo Martorell, Charles Yarbrough, and Robert E. Klein. "Nutrition and Birth Interval Components: The Guatemalan Experiences." In *Nutrition and Human Reproduction,* edited by W. Henry Mosley, pp. 385–399. New York: Plenum, 1978.

Eaton, Joseph W., and Albert J. Mayer. "The Social Biology of Very High Fertility among the Hutterites: The Demography of a Unique Population." *Human Biology* 25(3):206–264, September 1953.

Feicht, C. B., T. S. Johnson, B. J. Martin, et al. "Secondary Amenorrhoea in Athletes." *Lancet* 1:1145–1146, 1978.

Frisch, Rose E. "Weight at Menarche: Similarity for Well-nourished and Undernourished Girls at Differing Ages, and Evidence for Historical Constancy." *Pediatrics* 59(3):445–450, September 1972.

Frisch, Rose E., Grace Wyshak, and Larry Vincent. "Delayed Menarche and Amenorrhea in Ballet Dancers." *New England Journal of Medicine* 202:17–19, July 1980.

Gopalan, C., and A. Nadamuni Naidu. "Nutrition and Fertility." *Lancet* 2(7786):1077–1079, 18 November 1972.

Hytten, Frank E., and Isabella Leitch. *The Physiology of Human Pregnancy.* 2d ed. Oxford, England: Blackwell, 1971. Philadelphia: Lippincott, 1971.

Ifekwunigwe, Aaron E. "Recent Field Experience in Eastern Nigeria (Biafra)." In *Famine,* edited by Gunnar Blix, Yngve Hofvander, and Bo Vahlquist, pp. 144–154. Uppsala, Sweden: Almqvist & Wiksell, 1971.

Keys, Ancel E., Josef Brožek, Austin Henschel, Olaf Mickelson, and Henry Longstreet Taylor. *The Biology of Human Starvation.* 2 vols. Minneapolis: University of Minnesota Press, 1950.

MacMahon, Brian, and Jane Worcester. *Age at Menopause: United States, 1960–62.* Vital and Health Statistics, series 11, no. 19. Rockville, Md.: U.S. National Center for Health Statistics, October 1966.

Stein, Zena, Mervyn Susser, Gerhart Saenger, and Francis Marolla. *Famine and Human Development: The Dutch Hunger Winter of 1944–1945.* New York: Oxford University Press, 1975.

Susser, Mervyn, and William Watson. *Sociology in Medicine.* 2d ed. London and New York: Oxford University Press, 1971.

Tanner, J. M. "Earlier Maturation in Man." *Scientific American* 218(1):21–27, January 1968.

United Nations, Department of Economic and Social Affairs. "Selected World Demographic Indicators by Countries, 1950–2000." Population Working Paper No. 55. New York, 28 May 1975.

Valaoras, V. G. "Some Effects of Famine on the Population of Greece." *Milbank Memorial Fund Quarterly* 24(3):215–234, July 1946.

Zacharias, Leona, and Richard J. Wurtman. "Age at Menarche: Genetic and Environmental Influences." *New England Journal of Medicine* 280:868–875, April 1969.

RESEARCH, FAMILY PLANNING
See FAMILY PLANNING RESEARCH.

RESOURCES AND POPULATION

In recent years, especially in richer industrialized societies, idle speculation has given way to urgent debate on current policies as the conviction grows that the shape of the future can and must be controlled.

Opposing Views. Two views prevail as to the future availability of natural resources, one reflecting pessimism and the other optimism.

The pessimistic view, which can be called the limits thesis, involves four propositions:

1. That there are definite limits to population and economic growth;
2. That these limits are very near;
3. That, if these limits are approached too closely, worldwide death rates will soar; and
4. That, even if these limits are further away, population and economic growth *ought* to stop.

The "definite limits" mentioned in the first of these propositions are those imposed by a finite earth, by the fact that air, water, minerals, land, and all usable energy sources consist of fixed stocks that can be exhausted or of flows that can be overloaded. The emphasized "ought" in the fourth proposition, denoting strong moral obligation, is based on three ethical assumptions: (1) that, after a certain point, already exceeded by the rich in both developed and developing countries, the quality of life may actually decline as more and more material goods are introduced; (2) that present habits of wasteful consumption are using up resources that should be conserved for future generations; and (3) that, if the rich would consume less, more would be left for the poor of the world.

As evidence that limits are near, advocates of the limits thesis point to energy and food problems; to areas of the earth beset by deforestation, erosion, and desertification; and to the fact that reserves of many minerals will not last long if consumption continues at current rates (Meadows, 1972; Brown, 1978).

The opposing, optimistic view, sometimes called the "cornucopian thesis," consists of three propositions:

1. That there are limits to growth only if science and technology cease to advance, which is unlikely;
2. That, even if scientific advances were to cease, the limits to growth would still be far away; and
3. That, in any event, economic growth is beneficial for society and *ought* to continue.

These three propositions are based on the belief that, as long as technological development continues, the earth is not really finite, because technology creates resources. Thus, the earth is yet huge relative to the demands being made upon it by people, and the possibilities for substituting more abundant resources for scarcer resources are so great that there is no reason that population and economic growth cannot continue for a very long time.

The "ought" in the third proposition stems from the belief that no society has reached the point where all its material needs are satisfied; growth is the only practical way to create a surplus that can be redistributed to the poor; and growth poses challenges for humanity, giving us a sense of purpose and encouraging greater achievements.

Proponents of the cornucopian thesis believe that history provides their best evidence. If people see behind them a relatively steady stream of progress in material welfare and no signs that technological developments are slowing down, they may reasonably ask why there is such concern about the future (Beckerman, 1974; Simon, 1981).

Clearly, the limits thesis is in the ascendancy today, and a general pessimism overshadows the more hopeful cornucopian view. But it is worth remembering that neither of these views is new. Cycles of pessimism and optimism have occurred throughout history, and will undoubtedly continue. The critical question at present is whether current pessimism is more than just a stage in

another cycle. To what extent is this most recent change of heart about the future of humanity associated with new information about constraints on resources and the environment? Has something in the physical or economic world changed to make serious shortages of material or environmental resources more imminent today than they seemed to be just ten or twenty years ago? What role does population growth play in the possibility of these potential constraints?

An Alternative View. A middle view would say that the debate between proponents of the limits thesis and the cornucopian thesis has become falsely polarized and unproductive. The relevant question is not whether to grow or not to grow but how to redirect present and future economic output in ways that will better serve humanity. Clearly, there are physical constraints to population and economic growth, but most of them are distant enough to be managed by adequate planning, good will, and international cooperation, provided that action is not delayed. For the present, the most serious problems are the political, social, and institutional barriers to getting on with the job. A slowdown in the rate of growth, particularly population growth, is important to achieve, because that would reduce the number and intensity of problems that must be resolved simultaneously; but by itself it cannot resolve these nonmaterial constraints in the near future.

This discussion is organized around a series of questions inspired by a French schoolchild's riddle: "If lilies in a pond double each day and on the thirtieth day have covered the pond, on what day is the pond half covered?" The answer is "On the twenty-ninth day." This riddle has been used to suggest that the limits to growth may be surprisingly near. But as an analogy to the world situation, its answer is not so obvious. It depends on whether the pond (the total of world resources) is expanding in size, and, if so, at what speed; whether there are limits to the expansion of the pond; how near we are to those limits; and whether the lilies (the world's population) and their demand on nutrients in the pond (per capita consumption) continue growing at constant rates until they hit the edge of the pool. In other words, the answer depends on the relative rates of growth in demand for and supply of material and environmental resources, and on whether knowledge about what is happening to supply affects the rate of growth in demand and vice versa. Hence we ask the following questions:

1. Are there signs to indicate whether in the past the world has been winning or losing the race between rising demand for material and environmental resources and increasing supplies of these resources?
2. What is likely to happen to demand in the future?

Will its rate of growth speed up, slow down, or remain the same?

3. How far and how rapidly can supply (the size of the pond) expand? Is there indeed a limit? If so, when is it likely to be reached?

Many of the projections on prospects for the future given below are drawn from a study by Ronald G. Ridker and William D. Watson (1980). The time frame chosen was 1975 to 2025, long enough to capture significant consequences of population growth but short enough to allow a degree of confidence that something useful might be said about the future.

This study projects that, barring serious disruptions in current trends and despite declining population growth rates, the world's population will reach nearly 9.4 billion in 2025, compared to 4.3 billion in 1979, and that the world's per capita gross national product (GNP) might then be as high as $2,600 (in 1971 dollars), compared to $1,000 in 1972. Given these projections, the rate of increase in consumption of nonfuel minerals and energy will decline during the period, although absolute consumption levels will be vastly greater at the end of the period. When these projections are compared with projections of potential supplies, and when the nature of the difficulties in actually obtaining these supplies is considered, it becomes clear that the problems we face in the next half century are associated less with physical exhaustion than they are with unequal distribution of resources, the security of supply lines and trade, environmental problems associated with high levels of use, and above all, with the transition problems in moving from one resource regime to another in an orderly way.

In the world as a whole there appears to be enough land and water to meet food demands during the next half century. But this land and water—plus the technology, capital, and institutions required for their efficient use—are not distributed in the same way as population. International movements of food will have to increase if per capita consumption is not to fall in regions such as South Asia where food production is already barely keeping pace with population growth.

The situation with respect to nonfuel minerals is similar. We must find substitutes for less abundant resources such as tin, tungsten, and lead and more ways to use abundant materials such as aluminum, cement, and glass. Mechanisms must be found to help countries, especially the poorer ones, cope with the disruptive shifts in terms of trade that such changes in the use of resources generally entail.

The world's energy problems are the most serious, difficult, and dangerous of all the resource problems before us. We already face balance-of-payment and security problems so far as petroleum and nuclear power are concerned. During the next fifty years these problems will be compounded by the fact that reasonably priced sources of both petroleum and natural gas will be exhausted. This does not mean that the world must learn to live without liquid and gaseous fuels, but it does mean that ways must be found to acquire these fuels from other sources. Adequate alternatives do exist. Liquids and gases can be produced from coal, shale, tar sands, and vegetation, to mention only the most likely sources. Nuclear power and solar energy (captured by using flat plate collectors, photoelectric cells, biomass, and wind, for example) can be substituted for liquids and gases in many uses. The problem is to employ these alternatives in an orderly, equitable, and safe way—safe both environmentally and strategically.

In all this, a decline in future population growth would be of considerable help, for it would provide the world with more time and resources with which to address these problems. But whatever future population growth rates may be, the world will still be faced with unsolved problems resulting from past growth. There are no simple explanations or one-dimensional solutions.

The Past: Winning or Losing? We turn now to our first question: what is the record to date in balancing population and economic growth against available supplies? To answer this question, we can look at several kinds of evidence: (1) socioeconomic indicators of levels of material well-being to tell whether the living standard for most people has been rising or falling; (2) changes in relative price levels, which reflect changes in the scarcity of resources; and (3) indications of improvement or deterioration in the quantity or quality of material or environmental resources.

The first two types of evidence are not especially pessimistic, yet neither are they definitive. By the usual measures of material well-being—per capita incomes, calories consumed, shelter and clothing, hours of leisure, protection against physical dangers and major famines, medical care, infant mortality, or life expectancy—the average person in 1982 is better off than his parents or grandparents. However, there are severe problems with the distribution of these benefits. In general the poor share in them far less than the well-off, and although average incomes have risen, the absolute numbers of persons below minimally acceptable income levels also have increased. Moreover, the poorest countries have benefited least, and the gap between developing and developed nations has widened. As for the second kind of evidence, on trends in the market prices of resources, for the United States the real costs of most raw materials declined or were generally stable from 1870 until at least 1970. Nevertheless, prices often reflect artificial forces, are available only for marketed articles (ignoring such factors as air and water quality), and may not reflect the future costs of pollution.

The third kind of evidence, on the depletion of particular resources, is of poor quality and open to divergent interpretations. Examples of deterioration can be found, but it is difficult to say whether they are omens of approaching global overload or manifestations of transitional, localized, or manageable problems. Examples of improvement can also be found, but it is nearly impossible to strike a balance between them and signs of deterioration. Clarification is needed of the nature of the confusing situation we face in several important areas.

Renewable biological resources. Data on world production of beef, mutton, wool, fish, and cereals can be used to suggest that per capita production may have peaked in recent years (Brown, 1978). But before concluding that such figures signal the beginning of a general decline or the approach of physical limits, the specifics of each situation must be considered. For example, the decline in per capita production of wool since 1960 and mutton since 1972 is related to the development of synthetic fibers and possibly also to changes in tastes that made it less profitable to raise sheep and supply mutton. Beef and cereal are products on which data are insufficient to assert that a new trend has begun, let alone a declining trend.

One can also point to the food shortages of the mid-1960s and early 1970s in Africa and Asia as evidence of net loss; but these shortages were the result not of global shortages of land or water but of regional droughts, questionable policies, and the absence of global contingency plans to cover lean periods. While droughts were slashing yields in Africa and Asia, American farmers were still being encouraged to withhold land from production; the Argentine government was discouraging production and export by holding domestic wheat prices below world levels; and the Soviet Union suddenly decided to import grain rather than cut back on demand as it had previously done after a poor harvest. Many people have advocated the development of a global reserve of food grains to see the world through such periods, but such a reserve has not been established.

On the other hand, the trends in per capita production of wood and fish definitely appear to be declining, wood since 1966 and fish since 1970. If production technologies do not change, there is reason to believe that such decline will continue as a result of overexploitation. But technologies *are* changing, in some countries dramatically. Unlike modern agriculture, fishing was still in the hunting and gathering stage a few years ago and forestry was not much further advanced. But increasingly, techniques from settled farming are being applied. The changes are more rapid in forestry than in fisheries and in developed countries than in developing countries. But all indications are that new techniques will be further developed and spread as they become increasingly profitable because of increasing prices of forestry and fish products.

In large measure, the crux of the problem is unequal distribution of productive capacity and purchasing power. Even though some parts of the world have the potential for surplus production, the poor countries simply cannot afford to buy adequate quantities of food grains in international markets when their own supplies fall short.

Petroleum. The data on world oil production per capita show a steady rise to 1974 and then a distinct leveling off and possibly a decline. If this change were the result of depletion of petroleum reserves, one could predict a steady decline in the future. But it appears, at least in part, that depletion of working oil fields in many parts of the world plus discoveries in the Middle East led to concentration of production in the hands of a small group of countries, which, for political as well as economic reasons, were able to band together to raise the price so rapidly that per capita consumption ceased growing. There is little doubt that low-cost petroleum resources will one day be exhausted. But that day probably lies well beyond the year 2000. There are indeed very serious dangers in the current world energy situation, but they stem from the fact that importing countries have become increasingly dependent on supplies from a politically unstable area of the world, not from the growing likelihood of imminent exhaustion of supplies.

Environment. Environmental quality might appear to be one area where deterioration on a global scale is indisputable. Pressure on the environment has indeed increased with economic and population growth, with different patterns in developed and developing countries.

In any country where pollution regulations are taken seriously, levels of such mass pollutants as carbon monoxide, particulates, hydrocarbons, sulfates, and suspended solids in water have been measurably reduced. In the United States, for example, the Council on Environmental Quality (1978, p. 14) reports that between 1973 and 1976 annual carbon monoxide emissions dropped from 81.3 to 69.7 tons, or by 14.3 percent, as automobile emission controls were enforced in the wake of the Clean Air Act of 1970. But the United States, like other rich countries, can afford to trade off some economic growth for environmental quality. In most developing countries, safeguarding the environment has so far generally taken second place in the struggle to raise living standards. This priority could be shortsighted; prevention is typically cheaper than abatement and cleanup after pollutants are released, and some kinds of pollution can seriously affect production capacity. But this approach is understandable, given the more immediate problems these countries face.

There are other growing environmental problems that no country is yet controlling, in part because methods of economic control are not always known. These include highly toxic trace substances with long half-lives such as arsenic, lead, certain pesticides and herbicides, and radioactive pollutants, all of which can become concentrated into lethal doses as they move through food chains. Still other problems such as the buildup of carbon dioxide in the atmosphere are not being controlled because of uncertainty about their effects. Environmental problems such as these may be our most threatening legacy from past population and economic growth. We return to them at the end of this article.

Future Demands. For our second question, we turn from the past to the future: what is likely to happen to the rate of growth of demand for resources? To answer, it is important to distinguish between rates of growth in population (the lilies in the pond) and rates of growth per capita demand for various resources (how much each lily consumes of nutrients in the pond) and between rich and poor countries. Population growth rates have fallen drastically in the West and appear to have peaked in most of Asia and Latin America. However, while these changes are leading to a declining global growth rate, they are unlikely to be sufficient to reduce the absolute size of annual additions. Even the reduced rate of the year 2000 will translate into some 97 million additional people annually according to the current United Nations "medium variant" population projections—up from an annual increment of about 73 million in the late 1970s. The United Nations medium variant projection of 1978 puts the total global population at 6.2 billion in 2000 (compared to 4.3 billion in 1979) and about 10.5 billion when births and deaths ultimately come into balance and human numbers stop increasing, somewhere about 2075 (United Nations, 1981). Thus, even though the *rate of growth* in demands for the earth's resources represented by numbers of people will ease, the sheer *size* of those numbers will still place increasing pressures on material and environmental resources for a long time to come.

Per capita demand for material goods in poor countries is likely to expand as fast as growth in their incomes permits. That is likely to be faster than growth rates in rich countries, especially since most of the developing countries are attempting to expand the share of output coming from the manufacturing sector and to mechanize agriculture. But their incomes are still so low that their demands for resources will not weigh very heavily in total world consumption for some time to come. Less-developed countries currently account for only 20 percent of the world's output of goods and services, and that percentage is not likely to rise to more than about 23 percent by the year 2000.

Of more importance in determining demand for resources is what happens in rich countries. The best conjecture is that growth in demand for material goods will slow down significantly because the rate of growth in per capita real incomes is likely to fall and because a declining fraction of income is typically spent on material goods as incomes rise. The slowdown in the rate of labor productivity, and hence income, in developed countries is already under way. It is likely to continue for a variety of reasons, including increasing investments for new forms of energy, environmental controls, additional health and safety requirements, and more of what is sometimes called on-the-job leisure—a willingness to work but only at a more relaxed pace as incomes rise. Moreover, the quantities of material goods that people demand are likely to rise at a slower rate as incomes continue to rise in developing countries.

Putting all these factors together leads to projected rates of growth in demand for resources that decline significantly over the coming decades. While many imponderables underlie any such projections, they at least take into account the two most important determinants of demand for resources: probable changes in population growth and likely changes in per capita demands for material goods.

As development continues, the developing countries' share of the world consumption of commercial energy is projected to grow from 16 percent in 1972, when these countries accounted for 71 percent of world population, to 47 percent in 2025, when they will account for about 85 percent of global numbers. The U.S. share of world consumption of energy is also projected to come more into line with its population. In 1972, with just over 5 percent of the world's population, the United States consumed 32 percent of total energy, but this share is projected to fall to 14 percent when the country's population makes up just 3 percent of the world total, as estimated for 2025.

In sum, the answer to our second question appears to be that the lilies (population) and their demands on the nutrients in the pond (resources) are unlikely to grow so rapidly in the future. The *absolute amount* of resources required will increase dramatically—world energy requirements could be five times greater in 2025 than they were in 1975, for example—but this increase is still significantly less than what was anticipated just a few years ago.

This leads to our third question: what can be said about the size of the lily pond (the resources) and the extent and speed with which it can expand?

Resource Supplies to 2025. The question of supplies of resources in the future is vastly more difficult to answer because it requires projections of new discoveries and techniques of production as well as judgments about rates of diffusion and increases in production capacity. Adequate answers are impossible without highly detailed, quantitative studies, few of which have been undertaken. The best we can do here is to discuss a related question: are resources adequate to meet the demands that are likely to be forthcoming during the next twenty-five to fifty years? If so, at least we know that we have some breathing space.

Current and prospective reserves. The notion that resources may be inadequate to meet demands in the near future frequently comes from the observation that known reserves of many resources will be exhausted in only a few decades if current rates of consumption continue. Under reasonable assumptions, currently known reserves of copper, for example, would be exhausted in 2010, reserves of nickel in 2014, and those of petroleum in 1995.

However, calculations of such "exhaustion dates" ignore three important points.

The first is that current rates of consumption are unlikely to continue; demand will probably slacken.

The second is that current reserves are only a small portion of the resource base. Current reserves are regularly augmented through new discoveries and the mining of less concentrated ores, made economically feasible by technological improvements and increases in market prices. An estimate of what is likely to be added to current reserves in a given time period—what can be called "prospective resources"—ought to be included before calculating "exhaustion dates."

The concepts of reserves, prospective reserves, and resources are illustrated in Figure 1. "Resources" (the entire box in Figure 1) include all the materials that may someday be used. No good quantitative estimates of this concept exist, since they depend on all the discoveries, technological changes, and price changes that may ever occur, factors that cannot be predicted. Estimates have been made of minerals in the earth's crust (the outer perimeter to a depth of 1 kilometer or 1 mile), but as estimates of available resources they are clearly too high; it is inconceivable that every last kilogram or pound of minerals in the earth's crust will someday be mined.

At the other extreme are "current reserves" (represented by the upper left-hand box in Figure 1), for which reasonably good estimates do exist. These are quantities of resources that are known and available for economic exploitation with current technologies and at current

FIGURE 1. *The resource base*

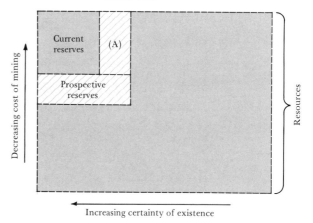

SOURCE: Ridker and Cecelski, 1979; reprinted by permission.

prices. They are similar to inventories, and since exploration and development are costly, little effort is made to find proof of new reserves if what is already known is considered adequate to meet demand for the next ten to twenty years. Even these estimates are incomplete and conservative. Frequently, private companies withhold or underreport such figures. Also, for many countries, data are incomplete. For example, there are no published data on reserves, let alone prospective reserves, of chromium for Oceania or for copper and phosphate rock in China.

When current reserves begin to be depleted, the search for additional reserves is intensified. Changes in prices and technology can also affect estimates of reserves. For example, if prices increase or costs of mining decrease, it becomes economical to mine lower-grade ores, and the quantities available for current exploitation must be reassessed. "Prospective reserves" is a concept developed to bridge the gap between current reserves and resources. It represents estimates of the quantities likely to be added to current reserves because of the discoveries and changes in prices and technologies projected to occur within a specific time period. In this instance, we limited the term only to discoveries likely to occur during the next half century (portion A of "prospective reserves" bordering the "current reserves" box in Figure 1).

The third problem with calculating "exhaustion dates" is that it says nothing about what is likely to happen when these dates draw near. Certainly the resource in question will not suddenly disappear from the market. Instead, its price will begin rising in anticipation of coming shortages, thereby stimulating mining of lower-grade ores and encouraging conservation, recycling, and the search for substitutes. In all these ways, demand is dampened and supplies are stretched, thereby smoothing the transition to use of another resource. Obviously, if the price rise is abrupt and steep, serious disruptions could occur. But consideration of particular resources suggests that except for petroleum such an event is unlikely, at least unlikely solely as a consequence of depletion of a given grade of resources.

Consider, for example, aluminum, which at 8.3 percent is the third most abundant element in the earth's crust (after oxygen at 45.2 percent and silicon at 27.2 percent). Table 1 indicates that reserves and prospective reserves would be exhausted by 2038 without a price rise, but this estimate is based only on aluminum derived from bauxite. Given today's technology, the price of bauxite (relative to other prices) would have to rise by at least 20 percent and perhaps as much as 80 percent (the latter equivalent to a 10 percent increase in the price of finished aluminum) to justify switching to other, much more abundant sources of aluminum such as clay and shale. But because of technological developments that will improve the efficiency of obtaining aluminum from these sources, this cross-over price is likely to fall significantly over time, certainly before bauxite is exhausted. Thus it is possible, with adequate planning, that sources of aluminum other than bauxite will be phased in as bauxite is depleted so that no serious economic consequences ensue.

Other examples are nickel, copper, and cobalt, all of which are listed in Table 1 as having hypothetical exhaustion dates prior to 2045. But the reserve and prospective reserve figures listed in the table include only land-based resources. Once seabed sources of these three minerals are added in, surely an appropriate step during the next twenty-five years or so, the world reserve figures of these minerals could increase enormously. Indeed, the future problem with nickel, copper, and cobalt may not be shortages but falling relative prices for land-based supplies of these minerals, which could hurt prospects for the developing countries that are major producers, for example Zaire, which produces cobalt, and Peru and Chile, important producers of copper.

The situation with respect to petroleum is not too dissimilar. The analysis underlying Table 1 suggests that *in the absence of political constraints* production could keep up with the growth in demand without a real price rise above its current level until sometime between 1995 and 2010 (depending on a variety of assumptions about income and price elasticities and the cost and availability of substitutes). This is not to say that cartel actions or production shortfalls will not increase the price before that date; but thereafter the price *must* rise in order to hold demand in line with production from a diminishing supply. The increase in the price of petroleum, however, will make it profitable to produce synthetic liquid fuels from other, far more abundant sources such as oil shale,

TABLE 1. *Dates when price must rise to avoid exhaustion of selected resources*[1]

Resources	Based on currently known reserves only (year)	Based on reserves plus prospective reserves (year)
Nonfuel minerals		
Aluminum	2025	2038
Chromium	2048	2095
Cobalt	2004	2016
Copper	2010	2041
Iron	2053	2094
Lead	2000	2016
Manganese	2061	2112
Molybdenum	2014	2480
Nickel	2014	2032
Phosphate rock	2034	2120
Potash	2104	2368
Sulfur	2010	2036
Tin	2003	2030
Titanium	2043	2151
Tungsten	2009	2037
Vanadium	2060	2180
Zinc	1993	2065
Energy		
Coal	2050	3000
Petroleum	1995	2010
Natural gas	2005	2024
Uranium	2005	2030–2070

[1]These projections are based on the "standard world case" (see Ridker and Watson, 1980) and assume that recycling rates remain unchanged and that the rate of growth in demand during the period 2015–2025 remains constant thereafter.
Source: Ridker and Cecelski, 1979, table 6; reprinted by permission.

tar, sands, coal, and possibly also vegetation (which can be used to produce alcohol). Given today's technology, it would take a 50 to 90 percent increase in the price of oil to justify the switch to liquid fuels from such sources, but by the turn of the century the necessary increase in price may be more like 10 to 20 percent. Here again, long-term exhaustion is not the worry so much as shorter-term problems of dependency on imports and longer-term problems of making an orderly transition from one source of energy to another. Such problems could prove especially difficult for poor countries that are deficient in alternative fuels such as coal. It will take substantial foresight, planning, and good will to forestall these difficulties.

Overall picture to 2025. There is, of course, a good deal of uncertainty in any sketch of resource supplies during the next half century. Estimates of reserves and of rates of additions to reserves are poor. Technological developments such as nuclear fission that could guarantee energy supplies for centuries may come along sooner or later than we think. After the near-meltdown of a nuclear reactor at Three Mile Island near Harrisburg, Pennsylvania, in the spring of 1979, and especially if such accidents are repeated, the United States, and perhaps other countries as well, may decide not to live with the risks of nuclear fission. Cartels controlling sources of supplies can be established or break up. Environmental problems could be severe.

The point of this section is a limited one: depletion of minerals and fuels and rising world prices for resources are not the central problems to be faced in the next half century. Rather, transitional problems will arise—those of adjusting to increased oil prices, transferring to new energy and mineral sources in an orderly fashion, and adjusting to changes in the global distribution of suppliers as new reserves of resources are tapped and the balance of political power shifts as a result.

While these problems are in part a legacy of the population and economic growth that has occurred so far, they will not be greatly affected by likely changes in these growth rates during the next half century. The Ridker-Watson study found that cumulative energy requirements from 1975 to 2025 would be reduced by 8 percent if the world's population were to grow to 6.7 billion rather than 9.4 billion in 2025, a decline of 29 percent, and by 16 percent if world GNP per capita were $2,600 instead of $3,900 (both in 1971 dollars) in 2025, a decline of 33 percent. Much of the reason for this difference in response is the fact that a slowdown in *population* growth rates would mean an increase in the rate of per capita economic growth, which would partially offset the decline in energy requirements due solely to changes in population, while a slowdown in *economic* growth has far smaller effects on population growth. Indeed, if there is any effect it is likely to be in poor countries, where population growth might be reduced by the fall in the standard of living, which would cause a rise in the death rate.

But the impacts on energy requirements of each of these changes taken independently are relatively small. It would require the combined impact of slowdowns in both population and economic growth rates to make a more significant difference. If, for example, both reductions were to occur simultaneously, a 25 percent savings could be achieved over the next fifty years. But even then, because of the enormous magnitudes involved, that 25 percent savings could be used up in four or five more years of population and economic growth. (Needless to say, a slowdown only in U.S. population and economic growth rates would accomplish even less; indeed, within the limits of the Ridker-Watson study, it would save little more than a year's worth of global energy consumption in 2025.) Thus a slowdown in population growth, particularly if it came along with a slowdown in economic growth, would buy a little time with which to find solu-

tions—and that could be very important—but by itself it does not constitute a solution.

Environmental Constraints and Risks. Certain environmental problems may in the end prove to be the most severe and difficult to resolve of all the problems the world faces in coming decades.

It is convenient to group these problems into three categories. The first includes those problems that can be controlled at reasonable cost with current technology, in particular such the mass pollutants of air and water as particulates, sulfates, hydrocarbons, carbon monoxide, and suspended and dissolved solids. The second category covers environmental problems that are mainly local or national in scope. Examples are conflicts over land use, includng the siting of power plants and mining operations; water shortages; nuclear reactor accidents; disposal of spent nuclear fuel; local weather modifications; and soil erosion. The third group involves problems that are more global in scope, for example, global climate changes, nuclear proliferation, and pollution of the oceans.

Problems capable of control at reasonable cost. If pollution emissions per unit of output were to remain constant in the future, environmental concentrations of the mass pollutants would soon rise to intolerable levels in many regions of the world, affecting not only comfort but also the productivity of labor, land, and fisheries. Most of these emissions can be controlled at modest cost. In the United States, for example, Ridker and Watson (1980) estimated that, without controls, the cost of pollution damages would have been the equivalent of 8.6 percent of the gross national product (GNP) in 1975. But actual damage costs in 1975 were closer to 3.2 percent of GNP because of control policies costing only about 1 percent. With the enforcement of environmental laws already passed, such as the National Environmental Policy Act of 1969 and the Clean Air Act of 1970 and its subsequent amendments, plus anticipated changes in the next two decades, pollution damage and control costs in the United States are projected to amount to 1.5 percent and 2 percent of GNP, respectively, by the year 2000. These figures allow for some slippage from strictly enforced standards when pressures on resources mount. A case in point is the Environmental Protection Agency's suspension in May 1979 of its ban on a gasoline additive that increases hydrocarbon emissions in order to allow more unleaded gasoline to be produced during the gasoline shortage. If there were no such slippages, pollution damage and control costs in the United States might be closer to 1 percent and 3 percent of GNP, respectively, in 2000.

For this category of environmental problems, pollution control policies are more important in determining what happens than are population and economic growth rates. In countries where these policies are weak, pollution problems can be expected to mount at least as fast as the growth of GNP, that is, much faster than the growth of population alone. But in countries where stringent policies are applied, these problems can be reduced to acceptable levels at costs that are relatively modest compared to the value of the total output of the economy.

Other domestic environmental problems. Other problems in the domestic environment differ from those that can be reasonably controlled in three ways.

First, either the technologies or the institutions for controlling these problems are not so well worked out. In most countries there is considerable room for improving efficiency of water use, but the institutional mechanisms for allocating water among users are seldom well developed. Methods of controlling soil erosion are well known but are difficult to apply because widely dispersed farmers have incentives to maximize short-run production and, if necessary, to compensate for erosion losses by using more fertilizer, adding marginal lands, and reducing fallow periods. Land reclamation procedures for arid regions pose special problems that are not yet solved. The probability of nuclear accidents cannot be reduced to zero any more than can that of accidents in coal mines; yet the more accidents there are, the more difficult the problems of locating nuclear installations and mines will become.

Second, many of these problems will show up in conflicts among local groups or between regional and national interests over water rights, power plant and mining sites, conversion of agricultural lands, and so on. While difficult to predict, these conflicts could at times become so severe and widespread that national economic growth is affected.

Third, until solutions are found to these problems, they are likely to mount with population and economic growth, unlike what can be expected in regard to most mass pollutants. For example, Ridker and Watson (1980) found that if the U.S. population in 2025 were 28 percent less than the 304 million projected in one of their scenarios, there would be 12.5 percent less land disturbed by mining, 25 percent fewer electric power plants, and 23 percent fewer nuclear power plants, and thus many fewer occasions to arouse local opposition to environmental threats.

Potentially severe global problems. Among global concerns regarding the environment are changes in global climate, ozone depletion, ocean pollution, and nuclear proliferation. In addition, a variety of potentially serious regional problems could have global repercussions. Among these are the loss and deterioration of soils, loss of genetic variability due to the spread of one-crop agriculture, release of long-lived radiation from uranium mill tailings, accidents with nuclear reactors and problems of storing nuclear waste, and the proliferation and buildup of toxic chemicals in food chains.

For a variety of reasons, virtually all the problems in this category are unlikely to be effectively controlled in the near future. In some instances, control is technically and institutionally difficult. Ultimately, for example, the spread of nuclear weapons depends only on the diffusion of relevant knowledge, which is almost impossible to control. Controlling the worldwide increase in nuclear power plants, which itself may be impossible, may thus only marginally delay the spread of nuclear weapons. It may be possible to control the buildup of carbon dioxide in the atmosphere from increased burning of fossil fuels but only by Herculean means. Such means would involve global agreements to capture carbon dioxide from stack gases; to reverse the trend toward deforestation, which removes the trees that absorb it; and, in the end, perhaps to reduce combustion itself.

But these difficulties are frequently compounded by insufficient knowledge to judge whether controls are needed at all and, if so, how strict they should be. Do carbon dioxide and the spread of fission reactors have to be controlled, or can we wait, hoping that less environmentally damaging alternatives such as solar energy and possibly energy from nuclear fusion will come along before these problems become acute? What level of risks are we really subjecting ourselves to when we allow more nuclear plants to be built; and how do they compare with those we accept in other areas like coal mining and with those we could face in the absence of nuclear power, such as a drop in living standards? Then, too, it is difficult to mobilize support for such actions. Even with the same facts, countries with little coal and no oil are likely to view the risks and benefits of nuclear energy quite differently from the way the United States does.

As a consequence, these environmental pressures can also be expected to increase with population and economic growth. Whether they will become so severe during the next half century as to limit such growth is an open question. They could limit it if the more pessimistic assumptions about carbon dioxide and the risks of nuclear power prove to be true, or if a number of these types of pressures act in concert to overload ecological systems. But little confidence can be placed in these, or any other, assumptions.

These are all areas of extreme uncertainty and high costs of error. The growth of such uncertainties and risks might be slowed somewhat by restricting population and economic growth. But they cannot really be reduced except by getting on with the task of developing alternatives to fossil fuel combustion and nuclear fission, finding ways to store and safeguard nuclear wastes, and improving our knowledge of ways of dealing with carbon dioxide and the biological effects of radiation.

Implications. Consideration of this array of both short-term and long-term problems should lead one to question the usefulness of espousing either the limits thesis or the cornucopian thesis on the future of man. During the next quarter to half century, the world will be faced with a series of transition problems requiring the substitution of one resource for another, in particular shifting from reliance on petroleum and natural gas to other fuels. In the process, some countries and groups within countries will be hurt while others are benefited. All the while, uncertainties and risks of the type just discussed will undoubtedly mount, quite possibly making the earth an increasingly dangerous place to live.

Population and economic growth play important roles in exacerbating these problems in those situations where other means of resolving them are not present or are not adequate. For example, in countries with strictly enforced pollution control policies, economic and population growth need not generate significantly greater quantities of pollutants; and in countries with the capacity to develop synthetic liquids and gases from other available resources, the depletion of petroleum and natural gas reserves should not be a cause for great alarm. More generally, the greater a country's scientific and institutional capacity to resolve problems, the higher the sustainable rate of growth can be without overloading the system. As a consequence, the link between population and economic growth on the one hand and resource and environmental problems on the other tends to be looser in developed countries and tighter and more inflexible in developing countries. But rapid rates of population and economic growth cause at least some problems everywhere. What can be done about them?

Should population growth be restricted? Certainly, for this step would slow the speed with which all the problems we have discussed must be solved and reduce the ultimate size of the global population that will have to be sustained, once zero population growth is reached. But even a cessation of population growth cannot resolve all these problems or keep them from mounting over time.

Should per capita economic growth be restricted? Unlike a cessation in population growth, the consequences of an economic slowdown are ambiguous. On the one hand, it would help in the same sense as a slowdown in population growth, by providing more time to find solutions. On the other, it would mean less trained manpower and less surplus output that could be diverted to seek and implement solutions.

Each new human birth entails an additional packet of resource and environmental problems. In contrast, eco-

nomic growth can be used for different ends than it is now. While it adds to the problems that need solution, it also adds to the capacity to solve problems.

Moreover, considering the legitimate aspirations of poor countries for a decent standard of living and the reluctance of the rich to redistribute wealth on any significant scale, a slowdown in economic growth is likely to lead to conflict. If nuclear power continues to spread, the results could be devastating. From this perspective, the risks of restricting economic growth may be substantially greater than the environmental and resource problems associated with its continuation.

Should greater efforts be made to conserve resources? By all means, again on the grounds that it buys time. Indeed, if taken seriously, conservation should be a wiser course in the next decade or so than a slowdown in population growth, the consequences of which will take more time to be felt. It appears, for example, that in the United States people can save considerably on energy consumption without sacrificing either personal comfort or economic growth.

In the end, all these problems must be addressed. Uncertainties about the effects of more carbon dioxide in the atmosphere can only be reduced through fundamental research into climatology and related fields. Risks associated with nuclear fission can only be contained through improved security measures and efforts to find and adopt acceptable energy alternatives. Poverty-stricken countries and groups within countries can only be helped by lifting the barriers to the flow of resources, knowledge, and technical and managerial skills into them or by shifting people out of them.

There are no simple explanations for these problems, and no simple solutions. We have no choice but to work on both the causes and the symptoms simultaneously. Understanding the true nature of limitations to the world's resources and environments is a first step in that direction.

Ronald G. Ridker
Elizabeth W. Cecelski

See also ECOLOGY; ETHICS; POPULATION THEORY.

BIBLIOGRAPHY

Barnett, Harold J., and Chandler Morse. *Scarcity and Growth: The Economics of Natural Resource Availability.* Baltimore: Johns Hopkins University Press, 1963.

Beckerman, Wilfred. *In Defense of Economic Growth.* London: Jonathan Cape, 1974.

Brown, Lester R. *The Twenty-ninth Day: Accommodating Human Needs and Numbers to the Earth's Resources.* New York: Norton, 1978.

Council on Environmental Quality. *Environmental Quality 1978:*

Ninth Annual Report. Washington, D.C.: U.S. Government Printing Office, 1978.

Meadows, Donella H., Dennis L. Meadows, Jørgen Randers, and William W. Behrens, III. *The Limits to Growth: A Report for the Club of Rome's Project on the Predicament of Mankind.* A Potomac Associates Book. New York: Universe Books, 1972.

Ridker, Ronald G., and Elizabeth W. Cecelski. "Resources, Environment, and Population: The Nature of Future Limits." *Population Bulletin* 34(3), whole issue, August 1979. Issued by the Population Reference Bureau, Washington, D.C.

Ridker, Ronald G., and William D. Watson. *To Choose a Future: Resource and Environmental Consequences of Alternative Growth Paths.* Baltimore and London: Johns Hopkins University Press, 1980.

Simon, Julian L. *The Ultimate Resource.* Princeton, N.J.: Princeton University Press, 1981.

Smith, Vincent Kerry (editor). *Scarcity and Growth Reconsidered.* Baltimore and London: Johns Hopkins University Press, 1979.

United Nations, Department of International Economic and Social Affairs. "Long-range Global Population Projections, Based on Data as Assessed in 1978." Population Working Paper No. 75. New York, August 1981.

RETURN MIGRATION

See CIRCULATION.

RURAL-URBAN MIGRATION

See INTERNAL MIGRATION.

ST

SAMPLING METHODS

Although no aspects of sample design are unique to demographic surveys, such surveys do have distinctive features that result from the basic nature of demographic data. We must recognize that collection of demographic data presents great challenges to survey specialists. Data on deaths are notoriously deficient in many places, and even the numbers of live births and years of age may, in many situations, have appreciable errors. Nevertheless, in most situations it has been feasible to obtain demographic data of useful quality. Difficulties and doubts are less than for surveys concerning such matters as income and wealth, agriculture, and attitudes. Compared to those fields, demographic sample surveys have several special characteristics and advantages that affect their design.

Special Aspects of Demographic Samples. First, the distributions of most demographic variables do not suffer from the skewness that troubles economic, agricultural, and other data. The numbers of years, of births, and of ages have narrow ranges, and many other variables are dichotomous. For such data, equal selection probabilities usually suffice, hence the complexities of unequal selection can be avoided.

Second, most demographic data are published as simple counts and as percentages for categories, although more complex analyses, such as life tables, are also needed, and multivariate analyses are increasingly being performed.

Third, any adult respondent can usually give fairly adequate demographic information about the entire household, whereas for many other kinds of data this single source would lead to prohibitive biases. Fertility and birth questions are usually addressed to women, who usually can be found at home and who have high response rates. Results of the World Fertility Surveys show only 1 to 5 percent refusals from the mostly rural and developing country populations (Verma, Scott, and O'Muircheartaigh, 1980).

Fourth, relatively stable models exist for demographic variables. They are less affected by drastic variations because of seasonal fluctuations (as in agriculture) or catastrophic changes (as in epidemics). Sudden changes in demographic trends are also exceptional. This stability permits use of data collected on arbitrary dates, and much information applies months and even years after it was collected.

Fifth, for demographic data relatively large samples are both needed and feasible, in contrast to some market research and social and psychological studies, where a few hundred cases can yield useful new information, and where larger errors can (and must) be tolerated. For rare events, such as births and deaths, large samples are needed to reduce coefficients of variation to reasonable levels. Moreover, to detect important changes in the levels of these rates high precision is needed. Even larger samples are necessary to produce useful estimates for subclasses such as age-specific rates, and especially for domains such as geographic regions. Finally, the needs for

601

data for local areas, together with feasibility of collection and with relative stability, result in the widespread use of complete censuses of population data.

Probability Sampling, Randomization, Frames. Inferences about populations are often drawn from arbitrary and informal samples. "Chunks," or fortuitous samples, form the bases of most research in history, medicine, and other fields. "Expert's choice," judgmental, and purposive selections are widely used, often without clear connections to the populations of interest. "Quota sampling" is a form of purposive selection still widely used in polling. These kinds of selections depend heavily on broad assumptions, often only implicit, regarding the distributions of the survey variables in the population. Ideal probability sampling, on the contrary, permits inferences without such assumptions by using strict randomization in all selection procedures.

Probability sampling depends on mechanical random selection and ensures that every element in the population of interest has a known, positive probability of selection. The mechanical operation of selection, indispensable for probability sampling, is achieved by using a set of numbers, selected properly from a table of random numbers, to identify the physical units that will comprise the actual sample. Careful listings and good operational procedures in the office and in the field are vital to this process. Their importance arises from the need for statistical inference through this chain of conditions: statistical inference → probability sampling → mechanical selection → listings, or "frames." The symbol → denotes "needs" or "requires."

A "frame" denotes procedures, however complex, that yield the equivalent of a listing of all elements (the units providing the information to be collected and analyzed). Elements might be dwellings, or households, or married women in the population. Full lists of these are not usually available, but their equivalents can be created through several stages of selection. For example, the selection first of districts, then of census enumeration areas (EA's), then of segments of the areas, and finally of dwellings would yield samples of women in four stages of selection. This procedure, termed "area sampling," often provides reliable frames because of the relative reliability and practicality of identifying every element of the population uniquely with dwellings and these with area segments.

The nature of available frames affects sample designs. Relevant factors include the types of sampling units at each stage, the extent of coverage, and the accuracy and completeness of lists. Other relevant factors are the amount and quality of auxiliary information which can be used for stratification of the sample, for measures of sample size, and for estimation. Imperfections in the frame and in related procedures cause some variable errors, as do biases resulting from noncoverage and nonresponse to interviewers. But often one can investigate, reduce, and limit the effects of these imperfections. Hence, whereas the ideal properties of probability sampling are not reached in practice, its distinction from judgmental samples is justified and useful. The World Fertility Survey has shown the general usefulness in most countries of area sampling, of enumeration areas, and of sampling of dwellings and households.

Element Sampling. Elements are selected individually in element sampling. This requires a good listing of individual elements to serve as the selection frame. Furthermore, it is economical only when the population is reasonably accessible for individual observation. These conditions can be obtained for recent births in hospitals, for residents of restricted areas where good population registers exist, and also for mail questionnaires or telephone interviews when there are good, complete lists.

"Simple random sampling" (SRS) is a selection of n different sample elements from a population of N elements, making each of the n selections separately and with equal probability from all the still unselected elements. It plays a basic role in sampling theory because of its simple mathematical properties, and it yields a design in which each possible combination of n different elements out of N has the same probability of being selected.

In "unrestricted random sampling" (URS) all possible combinations of n selections are allowed, including repeated selections of an element. It can be obtained by making n separate selections, each with equal probability from all N elements, with replacement after each selection. This design is even closer than SRS to classic statistical theory of independent and identical distribution (IID) of the sample, but it is not used in survey practice.

Both SRS and URS are basic examples of "equal probability selection methods" (EPSEM) for all N elements in the population. Both methods achieve an equal selection probability $f = n/N$ for all N elements. I shall note other kinds of EPSEM designs, as well as probability samples that are not EPSEM. SRS is seldom used in practice, but we may regard all other probability sample designs as modifications of it, as restrictions or controls that deliberately suppress some kinds of possible combinations in favor of more desirable ones. Stratification and clustering are the two most important modifications.

Stratification. Stratification permits only those combinations that have the desired number of selections from each stratum. In general, three motives, singly or in combinations, lead to the common use of stratification: (1) to reduce variances—either through proportionate sampling or by making a deliberately disproportionate allocation for larger sample sizes from the more variable and the less costly strata; (2) to improve the separate sample estimates for important domains or subpopulations; and (3) to utilize different field procedures or different methods in separate strata, or perhaps in separate frames of the population.

Sampling fractions, as well as methods of selection, estimation, and observation, may differ between strata. The stratum weights represent relative sizes and add to unity, $\Sigma W_h = 1$; but the basis for the weights depends on the nature of the data and of the analysis. They usually represent proportions of population sizes, and this is often represented by numbers of population elements, N_h, and then $W_h = N_h/N$.

In "stratified element sampling" all elements are individually divided (either sorted or classified) into separate strata. Then from each stratum a random sample of elements is selected independently, and separate estimates are calculated for each stratum. These separate stratum estimates are then combined from the entire sample for the population estimate. The sampling fraction in the hth stratum is designed and controlled to be $f_h = n_h/N_h$.

"Proportionate stratified random sampling of elements" is most common: from each stratum the same proportion, $n_h/N_h = n/N = f$, of elements is selected randomly and independently. This results in a sample that is a miniature representation of the population, because the proportions of the strata in the sample equal those in the population: $n_h/n = N_h/N$.

When "systematic random selection of elements" is used, every, say, third or tenth or fiftieth element in the listing is selected. If, for example, every tenth item is taken, the selection interval, F, is 10. After a start, r, selected at random from 1 to 10, the selection interval is applied. Thus elements numbered $r, r + F, r + 2F$, and so on are selected from the listing of N elements. With $N = nF$ elements on the list, n elements are selected, each with the equal probability $n/N = f = 1/F$. The EPSEM selection of the random start ensures an equal probability of selection to all elements. Theoretical difficulties exist, but this is a good and convenient method of selection in most practical situations. Often the listing contains some natural stratification, alphabetical or geographical, for example, with acceptably random order within those rough strata. In such instances one may use systematic sampling as a convenient substitute for proportionate sampling.

"Poststratification" is another method for producing the gains of proportionate sampling. This can be used when the entire group of N population elements cannot be sorted or identified into strata before SRS selection, but it is still possible to know each stratum's size. The n elements of the sample must be identified clearly as to the stratum to which each belongs. Sample stratum means,

$\bar{y}_h$, are then multiplied by their stratum weights W_h. In practice, poststratification is used in more complex selections. It serves here as an example of an important principle: that estimation methods may serve as alternatives to selections for using auxiliary information (such as stratum sizes W_h).

"Disproportionate allocation" of sample sizes is often used deliberately in two kinds of situations. First, it is used to produce domain estimates (means) with greater precision (lower variance). For example, some regions, provinces, or urban areas may be oversampled. Second, "optimal allocation" may be used to reduce the variance for the overall mean by allocating the total sample size, Σn_h, or the total cost, $\Sigma J_h n_h$, where J_h are the costs per element within strata. What should the sample sizes be to produce the minimal variance for the fixed cost, or the minimal cost for a fixed desired variance? It turns out that the n_h should be proportional to $W_h S_h / \sqrt{J_h}$, where $S_h^2 = \Sigma(y_{hi} - \bar{y}_h)^2/(N_h - 1)$ are the element variances within strata. If the weights, W_h, equal N_h/N, then for minimal variance the sampling fractions must be made proportional to $S_h / \sqrt{J_h}$, that is, $f_h = n_h/N_h \propto S_h/\sqrt{J_h}$. These formulas pertain to stratified element sampling but can be adapted to cluster sampling, which is more complex. Gains from optimal allocation occur in sampling establishments where large differences in values of S_h and J_h can be ascertained for strata. On the contrary, these can seldom be found for demographic data; for these it seldom pays to depart from the simplicity of proportionate sampling (unless for better domain estimates).

Cluster Sampling. Individual selection of elements is often too expensive because of costs of listing or field locating or both. Hence most widespread surveys use "clusters" as sampling units, where the clusters contain varying numbers of elements. Each population element must be uniquely and clearly identifiable with one of these sampling units. As compared to element samples of an equal number of elements, in cluster sampling typically (1) the cost per element is lower because of lower costs of listing and locating, (2) the element variance is higher usually because of homogeneity of elements in clusters, and (3) the costs and problems of the statistical analysis are greater. In widespread samples, the lower cost per element more than compensates for the two disadvantages. Among the different methods of selection, clustering has the greatest effects on variances, hence on designs.

In sample design, once the elements are determined by survey objectives, the choice of clusters must take account of the physical distribution of the population, of the available frames, and of survey resources. Many varieties are available, and especially relevant is the discussion for the World Fertility Surveys (Verma, Scott, and O'Muircheartaigh, 1980).

Most countries have usable frames of census enumeration areas (EA's), and a "single-stage sample of complete clusters" can be had by selecting a systematic sample of EA's with probability $f = 1/F$. For example, complete enumeration of all households in 1/1,000 of EA's yields samples of 1:1,000 of all elements (persons, women, households) who are identified in the field with dwellings in the selected EA's.

However, the EA's often average too many households, perhaps hundreds, and then we may resort to "multistage sampling," by subsampling the primary sampling units (PSU's), here the EA's. The selection formula for two stages may be $f = 1/F = 1/F_1 \times 1/F_2$; for three stages this would become $f = 1/F = 1/F_1 \times 1/F_2 \times 1/F_3$. For two stages, for example, a selection of 1:1,000 may be obtained from a sample of 1/200 of EA's, followed by subsampling within all selected EA's with 1/5. This subsampling would probably depend on fieldwork, by either creating segments (of roughly equal numbers of dwellings) or listing all households. Those segments or listings would then be subsampled with intervals of 5.

Often the PSU's (here the EA's) vary too much from their average size. The above procedure, for example, could have wild variations among PSU's in subsample size. Control of subsample size is important and can be obtained roughly with "size-stratified subsampling." For example, strata of large, medium, and small units can be sampled respectively with $1/100 \times 1/10$, or $1/200 \times 1/5$, or $1/1,000 \times 1$, with the second stage in each instance controlling the expected number of interviews.

Control of subsample size can be had by sampling with "probabilities proportional to measures of size" (PPS), when these can be approximated. The selection formula becomes $f = 1/F = \text{Mos}_\alpha/Fb \times b/\text{Mos}_\alpha$, where Mos_α are the measures of size. Here $f = 1/F$ is the desired equal probability for elements and b is the desired subsample size. The same measures of size used for selecting the PSU's must also be used for subsampling with rates b/Mos_α within the selected PSU's. Because actual sizes differ from the measures of size, the achieved sample sizes will also differ from the desired subsample size; the achieved control of the subsample size is only approximate.

In designing clustered and multistage samples three considerations seem most important.

1. The nature of PSU's and the number, a, of "primary selections" (PS) from them are most important in design, after the nature and number, n, of elements. One must consider the factors $n = a \times b$, where b is the average number of subsampled elements per PS, and greatly affects the practical aspects of fieldwork.
2. Stratification of PSU's is often useful. This leads often

to "paired selections": two selections (PS) from each of $H = a/2$ strata. Sometimes this is done conveniently with systematic selection with PPS.
3. In practice, variations in sizes of clusters and subsamples are unavoidable, and they are increased by lack of responses, especially so when dealing with subclasses. Therefore sample means become ratio means: the means $\bar{y} = y/n$ are ratios in which both y and n are random variables—for example, total births, y, divided by total women, n, in the sample for birth rates.

Inference from Sample Surveys. The theory of sample surveys deals mostly with means of large samples. From computations of variances of means one obtains standard errors and the usual confidence intervals around the mean. Standard statistical theory involves more complicated analytical statistics and inference, but it disregards the complexities of correlated observations common in survey sampling, especially in clustered samples. Briefly:

1. Descriptive statistics (e.g., estimates of means and of regression coefficients) from large, complex samples are good and "consistent" estimates, not much affected by the correlated observations. But inferential statistics—like standard errors, probability intervals, and tests of significance—are affected, especially by clustering (Kish and Frankel, 1974).
2. Design effects measure the effects of complex design on variances as judged against the standard of the usual random assumptions. For example, for a mean of a complex sample we have $\text{deft}^2 = $ computed variance/(S^2/n), where "deft" means the design effect (that is, the change in variance due to the use of a complex design rather than SRS), and S^2 is the variance for SRS. These factors have been shown to differ greatly by variables, by sample sizes, by populations, and by sample design. Disregarding the clustered design effect may cause variable, unknown, and significant underestimation of the proper confidence intervals and overestimation of "statistical significance."
3. Inferences for means of subclasses and their comparisons and for analytical statistics will tend to suffer also, though usually less than for the overall sample means. (The last four references in the bibliography give many examples of these conjectures.)

Sample surveys can be designed to obtain complex data, rich and deep in content. They can be tailored flexibly to fit a variety of needs and methods of collection. The observation procedures can be directed to obtain data that are relevant and reasonably accurate for defined aims in many situations. That small samples can be inexpensive is well appreciated and they are being used ever more extensively to supplement censuses and registration systems as well as independently to acquire more current, timely demographic information.

Leslie Kish

See also DATA COLLECTION; FAMILY PLANNING RESEARCH.

BIBLIOGRAPHY

Cochran, William G. *Sampling Techniques.* 3d ed. New York: Wiley, 1977.

Hansen, Morris H., William N. Hurwitz, and William G. Madow. *Sample Survey Methods and Theory.* 2 vols. New York: Wiley, 1953.

Kish, Leslie. *Survey Sampling.* New York: Wiley, 1965.

Kish, Leslie, and Martin R. Frankel. "Inference from Complex Samples." *Journal of the Royal Statistical Society,* series B, 36(1):1–37, 1974.

Kish, Leslie, R. M. Groves, and Karol J. Krótki. *Sampling Errors for Fertility Surveys.* World Fertility Survey, Occasional Papers, no. 17. Voorburg, Netherlands: International Statistical Institute, January 1976.

Verma, Vijay, Christopher Scott, and Colin O'Muircheartaigh. "Sample Designs and Sampling Errors for the World Fertility Survey." *Journal of the Royal Statistical Society,* series A, 143(4):431–473, 1980.

SEX EDUCATION

See EDUCATION, *article on* SEX EDUCATION.

SEX SELECTION

In the past two decades techniques to establish partial or full control over the sex of one's unborn children have received widespread attention. At least one method, separation of Y-carrying ("male") sperm by using bovine serum albumin, appears to have achieved moderate success *in vitro.* Much of the mathematics of the effects of selection has been worked out. These developments and certain implications of successful sex selection for couples and societies are considered in this article.

Techniques. A brief review of recent research suggests the variety of approaches taken. The technique most widely reported is one that associates the probability of a male or female birth with the timing of intercourse relative to ovulation. Briefly, it supposes that prolonged delays between intercourse and fertilization favor X-carrying ("female") sperm, which apparently survive slightly longer than Y-carrying sperm at the temperature of the female reproductive tract. If daughters are wanted, the time delay is achieved by having intercourse a few days prior to ovulation. (It has also been suggested that alkaline and acidic douches differentially affect the motility

of the two sperm types, but this cannot be demonstrated *in vitro.*)

Artificial insemination is required for other methods of selection, which attempt to separate either X-carrying or Y-carrying sperm prior to insemination. Electrical separation has been tried in animal studies, but with mixed results. While early successes led researchers to believe that the two sperm types have opposite surface charges, more recent reports suggest that they do not, and this avenue of research no longer seems as promising as it once appeared to be.

Other techniques include filtering, centrifugation, and sedimentation through bovine serum albumin, approaches that exploit the different motility and sizes of the two sperm types. The third technique has seemed the most promising. All select more successfully for sons than for daughters, but with present staining techniques their degree of selectivity cannot be determined closely. It has been postulated that sperm might also be killed selectively by pills or gels placed in the female reproductive tract, by a pill taken by the male, or by immunization of one or the other partner.

The methods just listed attempt to exploit extremely small differences between X-carrying and Y-carrying sperm, which may sharply limit their effectiveness. (For example, the mean difference in the radii of the two sperm types is 1 percent, and in swimming speeds perhaps 0.2 percent). Most of these methods are also likely to be injurious to the sperm type they select for, a consideration that has tended to be overlooked.

Finally, amniocentesis presently allows the sex of the developing fetus to be determined by about the fourth month of pregnancy. Less intrusive methods may appear, based for example, on the possibility of retrieving fetal cells from the cervical area. Either technique could be followed by abortion of a fetus of unwanted sex.

Quantitative Analysis. As techniques for sex selection come into use, they will permit couples to increase the probability of having sons when they wish and daughters when they wish. In actual situations, couples will think in terms of the total number of children they want, how the number should be divided between sons and daughters, and in what order they prefer children of each sex to be born. A leading question then is what strategy the couple should follow from birth to birth if their final goal is, for example, one child of each sex, or one son and two daughters, or some other combination.

Suppose that techniques were available that gave couples fixed probabilities of having a son and of having a daughter. Let the probability of having a son, P_s, be greater than 0.5, and let the probability of having a daughter, P_d, perhaps also be greater than 0.5. Computations for relatively small desired family sizes (at most two children of one sex, but with no constraint on the number of the other sex), allow a few conclusions to be made.

First, if equal numbers of sons and daughters are desired, couples should try first for the sex having the lower probability of success. If they initially fail, this strategy gives them an extra chance at the harder target. At a societal level the strategy ensures a more nearly equal sex ratio than alternative strategies but not necessarily a more nearly equal ratio among first children or last children.

Second, if unequal numbers of sons and daughters are wanted, and if $P_s = P_d$ (that is, if the techniques available for begetting a son are equally as effective as the techniques for begetting a daughter), then it is best to try first for the more-desired sex. (This leaves more opportunities to try again if the first attempt fails.) If $P_s \neq P_d$ this will only sometimes be the case. Depending on the magnitudes of P_s and P_d the strategy selected (that is, the order in which to try for sons and for daughters) will also sometimes depend on whether the couple is willing to risk having excess births to meet their target, or whether they will stop at a specified family size regardless of sex composition. Societally, the overall sex ratio and the sex ratio by birth order both depend on the choice of strategies adopted.

Third, if children of one sex are favored, and if the probability of having children of that sex is much less than the probability of having children of the other sex, the overall sex ratio among offspring might be more nearly equal in a population whose couples try for more children of the favored sex than in one whose couples try for equal numbers. This finding is contra-intuitive. To see why it is so, let $P_s = 0.5$ and $P_d = 1.0$; that is, assume that couples trying for sons can succeed only half the time and that couples trying for daughters can always succeed. Then, in a population wanting one child of each sex trying first for the harder target (sons), after the first birth, half of children will be sons and half daughters. The parents of sons then try for daughters, and succeed, while those with daughters try for sons, and succeed only half of the time. The result is an excess of daughters. Stronger preferences for sons, such as for two boys and one girl, produce a more balanced sex ratio by reducing the proportion of couples who would be trying for daughters and thus subjecting more births to chance. This situation continues to hold up to probabilities of P_s approximately 0.6 and P_d approximately 0.9 for couples wanting one child of each sex and those wanting two sons and one daughter, provided that those couples wanting one child of each sex stop after the second birth and those wanting two sons and a daughter stop at three, irrespective of the children's sex.

Stopping rules influence these outcomes. To continue the example, if P_s approximates 0.6 and P_d 0.9, and if couples wanting one child of each sex continue to produce offspring until they have *at least* one son and one daughter, completed family sizes will average 2.3 children, of whom 46 percent will be sons. Couples wanting two sons and one daughter, if they continue until reaching at least these numbers, will average 3.5 children, 59 percent of them sons. If they stop at two children and three children, respectively, the proportion of sons will be 45 percent in the first population and 54 percent in the second.

A factor that should also be taken into account is the effect on outcomes of variance in P_s and P_d. Where there is a sex preference, the effect of variance in the probabilities is to increase the proportion of the less-desired sex. At each birth, couples with probabilities above the average are more likely to have reached their target and to drop out of the reproducing population, leaving those couples with below-average probabilities.

Discussion. From an evolutionary standpoint, couples whose children are of whichever sex happens to be in the minority have a selective advantage. The chance of future descendents is necessarily greater for the minority sex than for the majority sex, since a proportion of the latter must always be left out in procreation. This fact, incidentally, can account for the near universality of balanced sex ratios in nature if the sex composition of offspring has genetic components, an observation made by R. A. Fisher in 1930.

Widespread sex selection may, however, have highly unpredictable results. An example is the question of the dominance of the firstborn. As birth rates decline, higher proportions of all children are first and second births, and among these first births are necessarily more frequent. A great deal of research confirms a marked preference for sons in many societies, and some studies indicate a particular desire that the firstborn be male. To the extent that greater conformity and greater orientation toward achievement characterize firstborn children, should first births come to dominate, and should males be a high proportion of these, the relative position of women in the family and in society might easily deteriorate.

At a societal level, the effects of unequal overall numbers of males and females have been experienced historically in some small populations, in areas of new settlement, and in expanding urban centers. Also the institution of inheritance by primogeniture has societal repercussions of the sort implied by unequal numbers, because it restricts marriage and childbearing. Neither of these examples exhibits particularly attractive features. Urban centers are noted for their mix of tension and anomie, to which the excess of single persons contributes at least to some degree. Primogeniture has traditionally been associated with powerful legal or religious sanctions and with the options, for single persons, of monastic or military careers that were not always entered into with conviction and were occasionally pernicious.

With this background, all that can be said is that a situation with very different numbers of the two sexes is unlikely to be optimal, either for society or for the individual members of the majority sex. They may or may not be favorable to the minority sex. At issue, however, is stress, not social collapse. Given strong preferences by parents for a particular sex and the technical means to pursue them, it is likely that the experiment of partial control would be officially tolerated in most countries, at least initially. Over the longer term, a sharp imbalance in the sex ratio might stimulate countermeasures, although one suspects that the disproportion between the sexes would never quite be enough to bring this about. Where marriage contracts are negotiated early in life, parents have a particular incentive to keep numbers of sons and daughters balanced. In all societies, balances would be favored by the variety of alternative strategies that may be used, the variance in preferences among couples, the likelihood that even couples with a strong preference would want at least some children of the less-favored sex, and finally, by failures whenever individual probabilities are much below 1.0.

All of the above is speculative in the sense that no techniques of sex selection are presently available to whole populations. Nonetheless, the direction of movement is toward the possibility of sex selection for larger numbers, and ethical sensitivity to the degrees of imbalance that might or might not be acceptable is certainly necessary.

David P. Smith

See also VALUE OF CHILDREN.

BIBLIOGRAPHY

For further reading on partial sex control, see Keyfitz (1977), Mason and Bennett (1977), Smith (1974), and McDonald (1973) on mathematics; David et al. (1977), Diasio and Glass (1971), Goodall and Roberts (1976), More O'Ferrall et al. (1968), and Sevinc (1968) on techniques; and Largey (1973) and the references therein on social implications of altered sex ratios.

David, G., C. Jevlin, A. Boyce, and D. Schwartz. "Motility and Percentage of Y- and YY-bearing Spermatozoa in Human Semen Samples after Passage through Bovine Serum Albumin." *Journal of Reproduction and Fertility* 50(2):377–379, July 1977.

Diasio, Robert B., and Robert H. Glass. "Effects of pH on the Migration of X and Y Sperm." *Fertility and Sterility* 22(5):303–305, May 1971.

Goodall, H., and A. M. Roberts. "Differences in Motility of Human X- and Y-bearing Spermatozoa." *Journal of Reproduction and Fertility* 48(2):433–436, November 1976.

Keyfitz, Nathan. *Applied Mathematical Demography.* New York: Wiley, 1977.

Largey, Gale. "Sex Control and Society: A Critical Assessment of Sociological Speculations." *Social Problems* 20(3):310–318, Winter 1973.

Mason, Andrew, and Neil G. Bennett. "Sex Selection with Biased Technologies and Its Effect on the Population Sex Ratio." *Demography* 14(3):285–296, August 1977.

McDonald, John. "Sex Predetermination: Demographic Effects." *Mathematical Biosciences* 17:137–146, 1973.

More O'Ferrall, G. J., T. N. Meacham, and W. E. Foreman. "Attempts to Separate Rabbit Spermatozoa by Means of Froth Flotation and the Sex Ratio of Offspring Born." *Journal of Reproduction and Fertility* 16(2):243–252, July 1968.

Sevinc, Afif. "Experiments on Sex Control by Electrophoretic Separation of Spermatozoa in the Rabbit." *Journal of Reproduction and Fertility* 16(1):7–14, June 1968.

Smith, David P. "Generating Functions for Partial Sex Control Problems." *Demography* 11(4):683–689, November 1974.

Steinbacher, Roberta. "Preselection of Sex: The Social Consequences of Choice." *The Sciences* 20(4):6–9, April 1980.

Williamson, Nancy E. "Boys or Girls? Parents' Preferences and Sex Control." *Population Bulletin* 33(1), whole issue, January 1978. Issued by the Population Reference Bureau, Washington, D.C.

SEX UNIONS
See MARRIAGE.

SMALL-AREA ANALYSIS

Communities, counties, cities, and states are increasingly interested in information on population to use for planning and to determine how accurately allocated revenues are reaching their target. This article describes the types of small-area data frequently desired and presents some typical problems and their possible solutions. Reference is chiefly to the United States, but the methods apply more generally.

Small areas encompass a wide range of sizes and geographic-administrative units such as states, counties, cities, towns, villages, neighborhoods, and even city blocks. Thus depending on the purpose a small area may be a state of 5 million persons or a population unit with fewer than 500 persons.

Uses of Data. Small-area data are used variously by governments, private industry and trade associations, scholars, and the general public. In the area of government, small-area data play an important role in locating and analyzing problems. In addition to data on each small area being useful for studying that particular area, such analysis also helps to interpret data for larger areas. This analysis is particularly important for understanding heterogeneous regions, where, for example, some areas are growing and others declining. Small-area data also figure in the formation of policy as public interest groups and others use them to develop, justify, and buttress their points of view. These data can also enlighten debate in the legislatures and courts by serving as a commonly accepted set of facts.

Small-area data play an increasing role in the implementation and management of government programs. In the United States they are used in formulas that target federal and state funding to local governments. The General Revenue Sharing program has used data on per capita income, total population, and governmental revenues to direct over $50 billion in the 1970s to more than 39,000 state and local governments in the United States (U.S. National Research Council, 1980). A striking feature of these 39,000 entities is the number of very small units: half have populations under 2,500; two-fifths, under 1,000; and nearly one-fifth, under 500. This program has stimulated the U.S. Bureau of the Census to prepare postcensal estimates of population and per capita income for these areas.

Projections of small-area populations are used for planning sewage treatment and water supply facilities, health care facilities, transportation systems, school construction or closings, and civil defense programs. Small-area data are also used in evaluating the effects of government programs and for identifying the characteristics of the populations served.

In the private sector, industry and trade associations use small-area estimates and projections in their market research for making decisions about products, promotion, and distribution and for planning future site locations. Small-area data are raw materials for much basic scholarly research on social conditions and change. In combination with other local statistics, small-area population estimates are used for constructing vital rates such as birth, death, and morbidity rates and labor-force statistics such as unemployment rates.

The public at large uses small-area data both for general information and for specific purposes. Citizens concerned about local education want data on children, differences in tax rates for different-size communities, and the racial and ethnic composition of different school districts.

In all these applications, small-area data on total population are the most basic. Many questions call for more specialized breakdowns by characteristics such as age, income, race, or ethnicity. In some instances these breakdowns may be obtained directly, but often it is more feasible first to estimate total population and then to partition the estimates for the subgroups.

Data Collection. To obtain data for a few areas it may be feasible to canvass the population directly, but this method becomes too costly when the desired number of area estimates is great. Even when a census is taken, considerations of cost and respondent burden may dictate collection of certain characteristics only on a sample basis, so that the resulting estimates have large variance. Generally census or survey statistics are used in conjunction with symptomatic data from administrative records. Symptomatic data (e.g., number of school enrollments) are useful to the extent that they are correlated with the quantity of interest (e.g., total population). In most instances, however, data are collected for purposes other than the desired small-area estimation, leading to problems of relevance, accuracy, and timeliness. Because definition and coverage of symptomatic data are set for administrative reasons, data may fail to correspond to the variables used in models for producing small-area estimates. Also, administrative data may not be subject to quality control and may contain substantial errors. Finally, the time reference of the data may not coincide with that desired.

Consideration is given here to postcensal estimates, to projections, and to population characteristics.

Postcensal estimates. After a census has been taken, estimates of total population are calculated either for the present or for a date between the present and the most recent census. They are generally derived from models in conjunction with symptomatic data. There is a choice of several methods. For this exposition we recognize three classes: (1) demographic accounting models, (2) fitted functional models, and (3) logical models. These categories are not rigid, and a particular method may utilize elements from all three.

1. *Demographic accounting models* express the postcensal population size as the sum of the population size at the latest census (base period) and the change since then. This change is stated as the excess of births over deaths plus net immigration. Methods based on this approach include the U.S. Census Bureau's component methods I and II and the so-called administrative records method (Shryock, Siegel, et al., 1975; U.S. Bureau of the Census, 1980; U.S. National Research Council, 1980). These methods estimate net natural increase from vital statistics or life tables and estimate migration on the basis of administrative data. Component methods I and II estimate migration for the noninstitutional population under age 65 on the basis of differences between observed school enrollments and those that would be expected if there

were no migration. Separate data are used to estimate changes in the institutional populations—those living in prison, college dormitories, military barracks, long-term hospitals. In some applications, changes in the population aged 65 and over are inferred from changes in enrollments in Medicare, the U.S. national health program in which nearly all of the 65-and-over population are enrolled. The administrative-records method differs from component methods I and II essentially in that it estimates net internal migration from addresses on tax returns and estimates net external migration separately, from other data sources. For estimates of population for the most local levels of government, only the administrative-records method is used by the Census Bureau (U.S. Bureau of the Census, 1980; U.S. National Research Council, 1980). Other symptomatic accounting methods, such as the composite method, use different data and models for estimating changes to different segments of the population (e.g., age-sex classes such as females over age 65). Such an approach is useful when different symptomatic data are available for different segments of the population; also, assumptions underlying a particular model may hold for some segments of the population and not for others.

2. *Fitted functional models* include regression models, such as the ratio-correlation method, the ratio-difference method, and the regression-sample method. The ratio-correlation method uses data from two preceding censuses to fit an equation that predicts changes in population from changes in symptomatic data such as vital statistics, labor-force statistics, automobile registrations, and housing construction. The name derives from the form of the dependent and independent variables: the dependent variable assumes the form of the ratio of postcensal population for the small area (e.g., a state) to the larger aggregate (e.g., the nation) divided by the analogous ratio for the censal figures; the independent variables assume similar forms. The ratio-difference method is similar to ratio-correlation but relies on differences between the small-area–large-area ratios for the postcensal and the censal periods. The regression-sample procedure modifies these approaches by estimating the regression equation anew each time postcensal estimates are made rather than using the same regression equation based on two previous censuses. This method demands current sample estimates of population for some regions (in the United States taken from the Current Population Survey) in order to fit the regression equation (Ericksen, 1974; Purcell and Kish, 1979).

3. *Logical models* include the housing-unit method, the vital-rates method, and mathematical-extrapolation methods. Here the model is assumed rather than esti-

mated (as in the regression methods). The housing-unit method estimates population change by change in the product of estimated housing units and estimated average number of occupants per unit. The vital-rates method, useful for crude but simple estimates, assumes that the ratio of the postcensal birthrate to the censal birthrate is the same for the same area (e.g., a state) and a larger area (e.g., the nation) for which an estimate of postcensal population is available. From data on the number of current births to residents of the small area an estimate of current population can be simply obtained. The method also may be used with death rather than birth statistics, and the corresponding population estimates may be averaged. Mathematical methods include linear extrapolation, geometric extrapolation, apportionment methods, component methods, and other techniques used for making population projections (Shryock, Siegel, et al., 1975).

Small-area projection. Especially important are small-area projections because counties and communities frequently have problems that require estimates of future populations. Long-term population size and geographic-distribution projections are needed, for example, for national transportation planning; shorter-term projections are useful for many communities in the 1980s to help decide school closings. There is of course an interplay of many factors in each of these illustrations: the construction of a major transportation network in a metropolitan area may affect population redistribution patterns, and local political concerns affect decisions about which schools to close. Nevertheless, projections can decrease the margin of ignorance and make their own contribution to the decision-making process.

Two techniques useful for small-area estimation involve "controlling to totals" and "averaging alternative estimates." When small-area estimates are made for parts of a larger area, it is generally recommended that the estimate of the larger-area population be obtained first and that the separate, small-area estimates be uniformly scaled (or controlled) so they sum to the larger total. The usefulness of controlling to totals arises from the typically greater accuracy (in terms of relative error) of the larger-area estimate. When particularly accurate data (e.g., special census counts) are available for some of the small areas, then the method for controlling may be modified to leave these estimates largely unchanged. After the small-area estimates have been controlled to totals, the estimates for each area provided by alternative methods may be averaged. When the estimates are of comparable accuracy, or if they are unbiased, then averaging improves their accuracy. When these conditions do not hold, it is useful to weight the estimates (U.S. National

Research Council, 1980). In recent experiments with empirical Bayes estimators, carefully chosen weighted averages of sample estimates and regression estimates were more accurate than the sample estimates alone (Fay and Herriot, 1979).

Estimation of characteristics. To estimate "characteristics" (e.g., age-sex, income, labor force, school-age population) for small-area populations it is sometimes possible to obtain the estimates directly from symptomatic data, such as school enrollment data, or Medicare registrations. Many times, however, it is necessary first to estimate the total population and then assign characteristics to the estimated population by using synthetic, regression, and other techniques. To use the synthetic method, one starts with estimates of the desired parameter for subgroups of a large area, such as national mortality rates by age, and then assumes that the parameters for these subgroups are the same for all subareas. Thus, if $x_1, x_2, \ldots,$ x_n are the mortality rates for the national age groups, and $p_1, \ldots, p_n$ are the proportions of the subarea population in the age groups, the mortality rate, x, for the subarea can be estimated by

$$x = x_1 p_1 + \cdots + x_n p_n.$$

To use a regression method one can assume a model

$$x = B_1 p_1 + \cdots + B_n p_n \ (+ \text{ possibly other terms})$$

and then estimate the weights $B_1, \ldots, B_n$ on the basis of past trends or current patterns in a sample of areas. Of course, one can consider variables other than all or some of $p_1, \ldots, p_n$, and the key to good estimates is to use appropriate variables. Noel J. Purcell and Leslie Kish (1979) present an excellent overview of these kinds of methods.

When estimating characteristics or small-area population totals, it is necessary to consider potential circularity problems. If symptomatic data such as school enrollments have been used to estimate total population, say for a state some years after a census, certain population or characteristic estimates for small areas within that state should not be prepared using the ratio-correlation, regression, and other techniques described earlier (or these estimates should be prepared and used only with careful attention to potential circularity problems). As an example, if school enrollments and Medicare registrations have been used to estimate the state population, one should be cautious about using a regression technique on these estimates to project future school age populations in a small area within the state or to estimate the number of persons over age 65 in a given small area (e.g., a county) within the state.

Ranges and Types of Errors. The accuracy of small-area estimates of population may be studied by several approaches, none completely satisfactory. One approach is to make estimates for a national census date and then compare these to the census results. This approach involves either waiting until the next census or else making the estimates retrospectively for a past census date and hoping the accuracy of the result does not diminish over time. Either way, accuracy can be studied for only ten-year (or five-year) time spans, and one can only speculate about accuracy over shorter intervals. In addition, undercounts in the censuses affect the reliability of the comparisons.

Another approach is to compare the estimates with results of special censuses, when such are available. In the United States, hundreds of special census results are obtained annually for a nonrandom selection of areas, and these results can be interpolated or extrapolated over time to be compared with the small-area estimates. Caution must be exercised in inferring accuracy and change in accuracy over time because of the nonrandom selection. Census undercounting also confounds this approach.

A third method is to compare small-area estimates to sample data when the latter are available along with estimates of sampling variance. The differences between the sample data and postcensal estimates can be broken down into sampling error plus error in the postcensal estimates, and judicious use of error models allows inferences to be drawn about the latter error (Ericksen, 1974; U.S. National Research Council, 1980).

A fourth method of evaluation compares the dispersion of several alternative estimates for small areas. As there is rarely a basis for assuming that separate estimates are unbiased (or have independent errors), studying the sample range or variance of the estimates tends to give at best a crude indication of the accuracy of a particular estimate.

Certain findings about the accuracy of postcensal estimates (at least in the United States) are generally accepted. The term "percent error" refers to the error in the postcensal estimate of total population expressed as a percentage of the true total population. Evaluations show that the percent error is a decreasing function of population size and an increasing function of the amount of population change (disregarding direction). For example, errors in estimates of five-year postcensal population change, expressed as a percent of total population, may range from about 3 percent for areas with over 25,000 population to more than 25 percent for areas with under 250 population. For areas with slight change (less than 5 percent) the errors may be under 6 percent, while for areas with rapid change (at least 50 percent) the errors may exceed 20 percent. When expressed as a percent of the population change itself, the errors may range from over 200 for areas with slight change to about 60 or less for areas changing by at least 10 percent (U.S. National Research Council, 1980). While it is generally accepted that the percent error increases with longer time intervals, it is not known whether the error increases gradually and then more rapidly (e.g., exponentially), increases steadily (e.g., linearly), or increases at first rapidly and then only gradually (e.g., logarithmically). It should be noted that the above findings are based on comparisons of postcensal estimates with census results, where it was implicitly assumed that any effects of census undercounting cancelled out.

Examples. The following examples illustrate several questions and problems faced by communities in the United States and the ways in which small-area data estimates were developed to address them.

School enrollment projections. Appleton Regional School District provides public education for elementary and high school students in a growing area fifty miles from a major metropolis. During the mid-1970s a large debate took place over the planned construction of a new high school to serve the district. Enrollment was then running between six and seven hundred. One group, including the school administration, wanted a fifteen-hundred-student plant; another group including vocal representatives from a costly senior citizen condominium complex wanted the smallest possible tax outlays and argued that a plant for seven to eight hundred students would be sufficient.

From small-area data, a set of enrollment projections was developed. Alternate projections through 1985/86 were based on available community and school data and on assumptions concerning community trends such as construction of new homes, births, and nonpublic school enrollment trends. The result was to show continued growth of the high school population into the 1980s followed by a leveling off at about a thousand students. Finally, a high school of that size was constructed after the district voters approved the necessary bond issue.

Tax relief. The Baker Consolidated School District covers a population of about 30,000 in a suburb of a major metropolis where property taxes are high: annual school taxes of $2,500 to $3,000 per single-family home were not unusual in the late 1970s. In the early 1970s the elected school board was concerned about the tax burden on older homeowners living on small incomes. However, with an annually approved school budget (voted on by the district electorate), any reduction in tax levies for a particular subgroup would mean an increase for others. Before going ahead with this tax break for older, low-income citizens, the Baker District school board wanted to calculate, from small-area information, the increased cost to the other taxpayers. The question was "If prop-

erty owners residing in their own home, having an annual income under $5,000, and being 65 or more (or either spouse being 65 if both lived in the home) were allowed a 50 percent reduction in their school taxes, how much additional tax would each other single-family property owner on average have to pay?"

A reasonable answer was available from 1970 census tabulations (available on microfilm) and from local tax records. Census data included (1) individual tabulations by age and by income at the county and township levels (the school district includes nearly all of one township and part of a second township) and (2) township tabulations showing the numbers of persons above and below the poverty level and aged 65 and over. The census tabulation breakpoints for household income and age included $5,000 and age 65, although interpolation would be possible if the age and income categories were not divided at exactly those points. (For further details of 1970 census "Fifth Count" data, see U.S. Bureau of the Census, 1974.) Thus as a first step it was possible to estimate the number of heads of household aged 65 or over with annual income under $5,000. Surprisingly, this number turned out to be only twenty-seven among approximately nine thousand households in the district.

The calculations of the estimated cost to other taxpayers are shown in Table 1. An adjustment was made (upward) to account for households where the head of household might be under 65 but the spouse 65 or older. A second adjustment (downward) was made to account for older low-income families living in housing not occupied by the owner, mostly apartments. Using an estimate of the early 1970s average tax bill for older low-income property owners, the total estimated cost of this tax break was calculated ($5,600). It amounted to an average additional tax between fifty cents and sixty cents per single-family homeowner not eligible for the tax break; the district adopted the program, later raising the eligible maximum income level to $7,200.

Hospital needs. Calhoun County lies in one of the Health Systems Agency (HSA) areas established in the late 1970s under proposed federal guidelines developed by the U.S. Department of Health, Education, and Welfare (HEW) to bring about more rational health planning in the United States. One aspect of this effort is to reduce the number of acute care beds (from the 1977 average of 4.4 to 4.0 beds per 1,000 population); therefore some HSA's attempted to close down smaller and less modern hospitals, since consolidation of hospital facilities is one way to achieve a lower bed-to-population ratio. Local areas, on the other hand, which possess a hospital currently are frequently less than eager to see it closed, even though more comprehensive facilities may exist some distance away.

TABLE 1. *Calculation of the effects of a property tax break for older low-income citizens on other property owners*[1]

1. Number of households with head of household age 65 or over and family income under $5,000	27
2. Adjustment for households where spouse is over 65 but head of household is under 65: $27 \times 1.04 =$	28
3. Adjustment for number of households not in resident owner-occupied home (about one-third of all households in school district are in apartments, and it is assumed that a greater proportion of low-income families reside in apartments): $28 \times .5 =$	14
4. Total cost to be absorbed by other taxpayers; average single-family house tax bill × 50 percent reduction × number of eligible households: $\$800 \times .50 \times 14 =$	$5,600
5. Average cost to other single-family home taxpayers; proportion of total school taxes paid by single-family homeowners (about 60 percent, with remainder paid by apartment and commercial property owners) × total cost to be absorbed ÷ number of single-family homeowners sharing the cost: $\$5,600 \times .60 \div 5,960 =$	$.56

[1]The calculations present the estimated average cost to single-family property owners if resident homeowners aged 65 and over with household income under $5,000 are allowed a 50 percent reduction in their school property taxes.

In 1977 in Calhoun County a substantial part of the population wanted to keep open a particular hospital, whereas the HSA responsible for Calhoun County (and for six other counties in its region) wanted to shut it down. The dispute centered on the need for the hospital in the context of total available facilities in the county. (Although there are other elements besides the "need" criterion, this example is confined to that topic.) To help decide the issue, estimates of the Calhoun County population for 1976 and 1977, with projections to 1980 and 1983, were needed. The HEW-proposed guidelines state that the figure of 4.0 beds per 1,000 population may be exceeded in areas where certain conditions obtain: "in areas where the percentage of elderly people is significantly (more than 33 percent) higher than the national average," and in areas where there is a large seasonal variation in hospital use reflecting vacation patterns (U.S. Health Resources Administration, 1977, p. 48,503). Both of the latter conditions are relevant in Calhoun County; there has been in-migration, particularly of retirement-age persons, and there is a substantial transient summer population. The age 65-and-over group is especially important for the estimation of needed hospital beds; the National Center for Health Statistics has shown

that hospital use (patient-days per 1,000 population per year) in the 65-and-over age group is two and a half times as great as among persons aged 45–64, and four and twelve times as great, respectively, as persons aged 15–44 and 0–14.

Official population estimates for Calhoun County showed an estimated mid-1976 population of 60,800, up by 15 percent from 52,800 in 1970 (census count). The estimate of 60,800 was developed under the joint Federal State Program for Local Population Estimates, and published by the U.S. Bureau of the Census in Current Population Reports, series P-26. In 1970 the proportion of persons aged 65 and over in Calhoun County was 13.1 percent compared with 9.8 percent in the United States as a whole and under 11 percent in the state containing Calhoun County. The first task was to develop a more refined estimate of the mid-1976 population, to use as a base for projections to 1980 and 1983.

Three methods described earlier were used to calculate 1975 population estimates: regression, yielding 61,672; component method II, 59,280; and the administrative-records method, 60,279. It was believed, however, that the assumptions underlying component method II did not apply. All three estimates are "uncontrolled," that is, not adjusted to make the sum of all counties add up to an independent estimate of the state total. In addition to these 1975 estimates, several sets of records were reviewed and used to evaluate and construct alternative estimates of the county population for mid-1976 and later: (1) Social Security records; (2) income tax records; (3) vehicle registration and drivers' licenses; (4) births and deaths; (5) institutional population; and (6) housing and trailer permits, including building permits for single-family homes, multiple-dwelling units, and trailers being issued a permit for the first time.

Table 2 presents the changes in several of these compo-

TABLE 2. *Changes in individual components used to evaluate and construct mid-1976 population estimates for Calhoun County*

1. Persons aged 65 and over receiving Social Security benefits: change 1970–1976	+30%
2. New York State income tax returns filed: change 1970–1976	+17%
3. Motor vehicle registration: change 1971–1976	+30%
4. Drivers' licenses issued: change 1971–1976	+39%
5. Institutional population: estimated change 1970–1977 from new group quarters	+26%
6. Net change in housing stock; reported housing starts and first-time trailer permits 1970–1976 (less loss of housing units to casualty and demolition): change expressed as percentage of households reported in 1970 census	+21%

nents between 1970 and 1976 or 1977. These percentage changes are used to evaluate and, for items 4, 5, and 6, to help construct alternate 1976 population estimates, but each item is not sufficiently refined to permit the calculation of an individual population estimate, nor is it appropriate to average these percentages to obtain an average population growth estimate for the period 1970–1976.

Three mid-1976 population estimates for Calhoun County were prepared. Estimate A used the information on housing and trailer permits, vital statistics, and institutional populations. This estimate began with the April 1970 census count adjusted for an undercount estimated at 1.5 percent. The change resulting from vital events (difference between births and deaths between 1 April 1970 and 30 June 1976) was added, as was the net gain in the institutional population (new group quarters and net addition to college student population resident in the county). The net population gains from housing starts were calculated, using 3 persons per new, single-family home, 2.2 persons per multiple-dwelling unit, and 2.0 persons per first-time trailer permits. Three percent of the population gained from new housing and trailers was subtracted as the proportion moving to replacement housing. These calculations lead to 63,800 as Estimate A, for 1 July 1976.

Estimate B was a slight variation of Estimate A; it allowed for a net gain resulting from owners of second homes becoming permanent residents. This simply assumed that thirty families per year, with 2.0 persons per family, made such a change, raising the estimated mid-1976 population to 64,145. Estimate C was based on the average results of the 1975 regression and administrative-records methods projected to 1976, with allowance for 1.5 percent census undercount and adjustment to a separately estimated state total. It gave 63,172 for mid-1976.

These three estimates were used with the 1970 census figures to calculate average annual rates of growth for 1970–1976, which were projected to 1 January 1983 as seen in Table 3.

Finally, the proportion aged 65 and over was estimated. Using data from Social Security records, and assuming that the proportion of persons aged 65 and over in the county who received Social Security benefits was the same in mid-1976 as was estimated for 1970, the number of persons aged 65 and over as of 1 July 1976

was estimated to be 9,054. Combining this figure with the population projections shown in Table 3 yielded the following estimated proportions as of that same date: for Estimate A, 14.2 percent; for Estimate B, 14.1 percent; and for Estimate C, 14.3 percent. Given the reported general composition of persons moving into Calhoun County (many of them retirees), it was quite reasonable to conclude that the proportion of the population aged 65 and over would rise further, to 15 percent by 1 January 1980. Thus, in early 1978 Calhoun County had in hand a set of age-composition estimates suggesting that in 1980 the proportion of persons 65 and over in the county would be very close to 33 percent above the projected 1980 national average of $11\frac{1}{4}$ percent. (The calculation involves determining the difference between the projected county and national percentages, and dividing this number by the projected national percentage: $.15 - .1125 = .0375$; $.0375 \div .1125 = 33.3$ percent.)

This example also illustrates the difficulties faced by persons charged with making decisions on issues where estimates lie close to the criteria set. Calhoun County's results, if subjected to a small margin of error, would fall below the 33 percent standard. Regulations and guidelines must be written with precise boundaries, such as the use of a different hospital bed-to-population ratio under specified circumstances. But, even with reasonably good data, it is impossible to attain certainty in estimation, however desirable and useful.

Conclusions. Government agencies are working to make small-area data more easily available to users and are also trying to develop better methods for constructing small-area population and characteristics estimates. One example is the U.S. Census Bureau program for local-population estimates noted in the Calhoun County example, a program carried out with cooperating state agencies.

Another important example is the new Neighborhood Statistics Program of the Census Bureau to assist municipalities that have designated subareas "by providing to local officials and neighborhood representatives basic demographic, social, and economic data (from the 1980 census) by neighborhoods" (U.S. Bureau of the Census, 1979). This new program gives cities a chance to request 1980 census statistics for neighborhoods if the neighborhoods met three criteria and the cities had notified the Bureau of the Census by 15 January 1982 that they wished to take part. The criteria were (1) recognition of the neighborhood by law or similar administrative action; (2) clearly defined nonoverlapping neighborhood boundaries; and (3) a mechanism such as a neighborhood council or liaison to the city government through which neighborhood residents can present their views on municipal matters to city officials. The program provides

TABLE 3. *Population projections, Calhoun County*

Estimate	1 July 1976	1 Jan. 1978	1 Jan. 1980	1 Jan. 1983
A	63,800	66,600	70,500	76,800
B	64,100	67,000	71,100	77,600
C	63,200	65,800	69,500	75,300

(beginning in late 1982) statistical tables showing summary data for neighborhoods on education, employment, income, shelter costs, and other subjects.

Specific information about available Census Bureau data for small areas can be obtained from the Data Access and Use Staff, User Services Division, Bureau of the Census, Washington, D.C. 20233. In 1979 the Bureau of the Census published the *Directory of Data Files* (Abramowitz and Aldrich, 1979), a compilation of descriptions of machine-readable data files. Updates are published periodically. The directory contains general information on the Census Bureau statistical programs and related data products and specific information on more than three hundred machine-readable data files.

Robert J. Lapham
Bruce D. Spencer

See also DATA COLLECTION; MACHINE-READABLE DATA FILES.

BIBLIOGRAPHY

Abramowitz, Molly, and Barbara Aldrich. *Directory of Data Files, Bureau of the Census, 1979.* Prepared for the U.S. Bureau of the Census. Washington, D.C.: U.S. Government Printing Office, October 1979.

Ericksen, Eugene P. "A Regression Method for Estimating Population Changes of Local Areas." *Journal of the American Statistical Association* 69(348):867–875, December 1974.

Fay, Robert E., and Roger A. Herriot. "Estimates of Income for Small Places: An Application of James-Stein Procedures to Census Data." *Journal of the American Statistical Association* 74(366, pt. 1):269–277, June 1979.

Purcell, Noel J., and Leslie Kish. "Estimation for Small Domains." *Biometrics* 35(2):365–384, June 1979.

Shryock, Henry S., Jr., Jacob S. Siegel, et al. *The Methods and Materials of Demography.* 2 vols. Prepared for the U.S. Bureau of the Census. Washington, D.C.: U.S. Government Printing Office, 1971 (3d rev. printing, 1975).

United States, Bureau of the Census. *1970 Census Fifth Count for Zip Codes, Counties, and Smaller Areas.* Data Access Descriptions, no. 36. Washington, D.C.: U.S. Government Printing Office, December 1974.

———. "Neighborhood Statistics Program: Notice of Determination." *Federal Register* 44(226):66,862–66,864, 21 November 1979.

———. *Population and Per Capita Money Income Estimates for Local Areas: Detailed Methodology and Evaluation.* Current Population Reports, series P-25, no. 699. Washington, D.C.: U.S. Government Printing Office, June 1980.

United States, Health Resources Administration. "National Guidelines for Health Planning: Notice of Proposed Rulemaking." *Federal Register* 42(185):48,502–48,505, 23 September 1977.

United States, National Research Council. *Estimating Population and Income of Small Areas.* Report of the Panel on Small-area Estimates of Population and Income. Washington, D.C.: National Academy Press, 1980.

SOUTH AMERICA

See LATIN AMERICA.

SOVIET UNION

The Union of Soviet Socialist Republics (USSR), also known as the Soviet Union, has the largest area and the third largest population in the world. Its demographic history has been distinguished by governmental programs to integrate population planning into general state planning, by the long-term effort to employ women fully, by the country's ethnic heterogeneity, and by such exceptional disturbances as World War II.

Location and Description. The Soviet Union covers a large part of both Europe and Asia and extends from the Baltic Sea on the west to the Pacific Ocean on the east. It has a longer border and touches more neighboring countries than any other nation. There are more than one hundred different ethnic groups in the Soviet Union; indeed, the federal system is established along ethnic lines. The country is divided into fifteen "union republics," each named after a major ethnic group and generally located in that group's traditional area of settlement. The Russian Soviet Federated Socialist Republic (Russian SFSR), which extends from European Russia across northern Asia, is by far the largest union republic in area. In the Baltic area are the Estonian Soviet Socialist Republic (Estonian SSR), the Latvian SSR, and the Lithuanian SSR. Occupying the rest of the European region are the Ukrainian SSR, the Belorussian SSR, and the Moldavian SSR. In the Caucasus region are the Armenian SSR, the Georgian SSR, and the Azerbaijani SSR; and in Central Asia, the Kazakh SSR, the Kirghiz SSR, the Uzbek SSR, the Turkmen SSR, and the Tadzhik SSR.

Some other ethnic groups have territories at lower levels of political designation. Below the union republics are twenty "autonomous soviet socialist republics," eight autonomous oblasts (autonomous regions) and ten national circles (national districts). Most of these thirty-eight ethnically linked areas of political designation are located within the Russian SFSR. Members of an ethnic group are not required to live within that group's area of political designation; however, various services and facilities use the native language of the ethnic group within its area of political designation more than elsewhere.

Population. The Soviet Union, with 8,650,000 square miles (22,403,500 square kilometers) of area, covers one-sixth of the world's land area. Preliminary results from the 1979 census show a total population of 262,436,000. This implies an annual growth rate from 1959 to 1970 of

TABLE 1. *Basic characteristics of the population of the Soviet Union, 1959 and 1970*

Characteristics	1959	1970
Population	208,827,000	241,720,000
Persons per square mile	24	28
Women aged 15–49	59,190,000	63,156,000
Labor force (population aged 15–64)	133,184,000	151,929,000
Dependency ratio	57	59

Source of data: Official government statistics, 1959 and 1970 censuses.

1.3 percent and an annual growth from 1970 to 1979 of 0.9 percent. Table 1 shows some basic characteristics of the Soviet population in 1959 and 1970.

Sources and quality of data. A system of tax censuses (*revisii*) was begun in the mid-eighteenth century, and censuses were taken approximately once every ten years until the mid-nineteenth century. These tax censuses counted the number of males and sometimes recorded other information. Vital registration before the Revolution of 1917 appears to be reasonably accurate in the areas of the European parts of the Russian empire that were predominantly Russian Orthodox in religion, but it seems deficient in areas in which other religious groups were significant. The first of a series of censuses of individual large cities was the Saint Petersburg city census of 1869. The only pre-Revolutionary national census was taken in 1897. Other censuses were taken in 1926, 1939, 1959, 1970, and 1979. The 1939 census results were not published at that time but have appeared in various later statistical publications, especially as comparative data in the 1959 census.

It is generally accepted that published Soviet demographic data are correct, subject to the usual types of errors in population data. Data from the non-European parts of the Soviet Union exhibit many characteristics common to data collected in less-developed countries. For instance, since World War II, recorded infant mortality rates in parts of Central Asia rose, although it is certain that living conditions improved there. The increases in recorded infant mortality primarily reflected an improvement in the completeness of registration of infant deaths. Since the early 1960s there has been a series of special surveys on demographic topics, which serve to illuminate many demographic processes in the Soviet Union. For instance, surveys have been conducted of (1) ideal and expected family size (Belova, 1971); (2) reasons given by women seeking abortions for not wanting additional children (Sadvokasova, 1963); and (3) interethnic attitudes about residence and personal relations (Arutiunian, 1969).

Characteristics. Wars, revolution, and the collectivization program have taken a heavy toll of the Soviet popu-

FIGURE 1. *Age-sex pyramid, USSR*

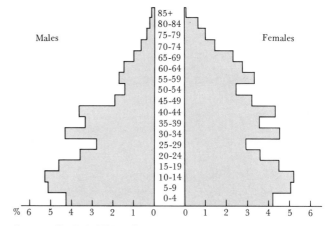

SOURCE: *Naselenie SSSR, 1974,* p. 19.

lation. The 1897 census of the Russian empire revealed a smooth age-sex pyramid without gouges, typical of a country with fairly high fertility and mortality. The age-sex pyramid from the 1970 census (Figure 1) demonstrates the twentieth-century changes in age-sex composition. The male deficit at many ages has made it difficult for many women to marry and has certainly been an additional incentive to the Soviet government to encourage the full employment of women. Also, the large differences in the sizes of adjacent cohorts makes social planning of age-related facilities such as schools very difficult.

Everywhere in the Soviet Union mortality has declined substantially from earlier levels. Table 2 shows expectations of life at birth by sex for 1938/39 through 1971/72. Along with a general long-term improvement in living conditions, some increase in the mortality rate for older males has occurred since 1965/66. Increased mortality rates begin at age 30 and become more pronounced after age 50.

Selected characteristics for the total Soviet Union and four union republics for 1979 are shown in Table 3. The four republics are representative of the diversity in social characteristics and demographic behavior in the fifteen union republics. The population of the Russian SFSR is primarily Slavic and traditionally Orthodox. The people of the Estonian SSR speak a Finnic language, and their

TABLE 2. *Expectation of life at birth, by sex, Soviet Union, 1938/39–1971/72*

Year	Total	Male	Female
1938/39	47	44	50
1958/59	69	64	72
1965/66	70	66	74
1970/71	70	65	74
1971/72	70	64	74

Source of data: Naselenie SSSR, 1973, p. 139.

TABLE 3. *Characteristics of the Soviet Union and selected union republics, 1979*

Characteristics	Soviet Union	Russian SFSR	Estonian SSR	Armenian SSR	Uzbek SSR
Population (thousands)	262,436	137,410	1,464	3,037	15,389
Crude birth rate	18.2	15.8	14.9	22.9	34.4
Crude death rate	10.1	10.8	12.3	5.6	7.0
Natural rate of increase	8.1	5.0	2.6	17.3	27.4
Growth rate per 1,000, 1970–1979	9.0	6.1	8.5	22.0	29.5
% Urban	62	69	70	66	41
People per sq km	11.7	8.0	32.5	101.9	34.4
% Titular ethnic group	—	83	65	90	69
% Russian or Ukrainian	69	85	30	3	12
% Russian	52	83	28	2	11
% Males aged 10+ with incomplete secondary schooling	69	69	68	74	65
% Females aged 10+ with incomplete secondary schooling	60	61	60	69	61
% Workers who are women	51	53	54	46	43
Average family size	3.5	3.3	3.1	4.7	5.5

Sources of data: Narodnoe khoziastvo, 1979; Vestnik statistiki, 1980, nos. 2, 6, 7, and 12.

traditional religion is Lutheran. The people of the Armenian SSR, in the Caucasus, are traditionally a part of the Gregorian (Christian) Eastern Orthodox Church. The Uzbek SSR is the largest Central Asian union republic in population size; Uzbeks are traditionally Muslim and speak a Turkic language. (The Kazakh SSR has a larger population than the Uzbek SSR, but the Kazakh SSR is not considered to be a part of Soviet Central Asia.)

Since mortality levels are low throughout the Soviet Union, the largest demographic differences derive from differences in fertility. The Uzbek SSR, the other Central Asian union republics, and the Azerbaijani SSR tend to have a younger age at first marriage and more universal marriage than has the rest of the Soviet Union. The Caucasus republics, such as the Armenian SSR, have a somewhat older age at marriage. The Baltic republics, such as the Estonian SSR, tend to have the oldest age at marriage. The republics with earlier and more universal marriage also tend to have higher overall fertility, as indicated by the crude birth rates, and less restriction on fertility within marriage.

Age-specific fertility rates and total fertility over time for the Soviet Union and the selected republics are shown in Table 4. Fertility was already quite low in the Baltic area by 1958/59. Fertility in the Russian SFSR, the rest of the European region, and the Georgian SSR had declined greatly by 1958/59. Between 1958/59 and 1977/78 in the Russian SFSR and many other parts of the European region, fertility dropped so much that the net reproduction rate in those areas was at a level that would lead to a decreasing population in the long run. Between 1958/59 and 1977/78 fertility in the Armenian SSR and the Kazakh SSR also dropped considerably, although not to replacement levels. In the Uzbek SSR, the rest of Central Asia, and the Azerbaijani SSR, there was only slight indication of any reduction in fertility between 1959 and 1970. Table 4 shows age-specific fertility rates for the Soviet Union as a whole and for selected union republics. The differences in the crude birth rate shown in Table 3 are further supported by the age-specific rates and the total fertility rates.

Table 5 shows that differences in the level of fertility are strongly related to differences among republics in ideal family size. These differences correspond well with the actual fertility differences in the survey from which these data were taken.

Abortions have been a major form of fertility control in the Soviet Union. In 1958/59 there were approximately 85 abortions per 1,000 women aged 15–49 and in 1972 approximately 120. Survey questions on why women do not want more children elicited as frequent reasons lack of adequate living space, household members busy with work or studies, and no one available to stay home with the child.

Within union republics, higher education is consistently associated with low fertility, as is urban residence. Studies of the relation of income to fertility have yielded mixed results. Differences in socioeconomic factors within

TABLE 4. *Age-specific female fertility and total fertility for the Soviet Union and selected union republics, 1958/59–1978/79*

	15–19	20–24	25–29	30–34	35–39	40–44	45–49	Total fertility rate
Soviet Union								
1958/59	29.2	162.2	164.8	110.1	66.6	24.1	5.0	2.8
1969/70	30.4	163.9	128.7	88.1	48.5	15.3	2.9	2.4
1977/78	36.7	172.8	128.7	76.9	34.0	13.2	1.4	2.3
1978/79	39.4	174.6	125.6	72.1	31.9	11.7	1.6	2.3
Russian SFSR								
1958/59	28.4	157.9	156.4	101.9	57.7	19.9	3.0	2.6
1969/70	28.3	146.9	107.4	69.3	32.2	9.0	1.1	2.0
1977/78	37.0	156.2	106.5	59.2	21.6	6.7	0.4	1.9
1978/79	39.4	174.6	125.6	72.1	31.9	11.7	1.6	2.3
Estonian SSR								
1958/59	20.1	122.3	119.1	72.9	41.9	12.0	0.9	1.9
1969/70	30.1	157.1	130.6	73.0	29.9	7.4	0.5	2.1
1977/78	37.2	164.8	121.4	60.9	24.6	5.7	0.3	2.1
1978/79	41.0	165.2	111.6	55.8	23.4	5.5	0.3	2.0
Armenian SSR								
1958/59	37.6	200.6	264.1	204.4	154.9	68.0	16.4	4.7
1969/70	41.2	213.3	164.2	123.8	67.6	23.8	5.1	3.2
1977/78	41.7	214.8	147.3	73.3	29.8	12.0	1.8	2.6
1978/79	41.3	202.7	144.1	67.9	24.5	10.0	1.4	2.5
Uzbek SSR								
1958/59	38.3	209.9	240.7	206.0	178.6	96.8	38.4	5.0
1969/70	41.7	261.3	265.2	245.6	194.9	91.5	27.0	5.6
1977/78	37.2	282.4	286.3	216.9	141.3	71.9	13.4	5.2
1978/79	35.4	277.3	281.7	210.7	134.7	66.9	12.5	5.1

Sources of data: Vestnik statistiki, 1971, no. 12; 1979, no. 11; 1980, no. 11.

a given union republic and especially within a given ethnic group are not so great as differences among different union republics and especially among different ethnic groups.

Between 1959 and the late 1970s, rates of both marriage and divorce rose. In the Soviet Union as a whole, there were 1.1 divorces per 1,000 population in 1959; in 1976 there were 3.4 divorces per 1,000 population. Divorce rates have increased most markedly for women below age 25, rising from 17.7 per 1,000 married women aged 20–24 in 1966 to 28.2 per 1,000 married women aged 20–24 in 1976. Marriage rates for the Soviet Union as a whole increased for women below age 30 between 1959 and 1976 and decreased slightly for women at older ages. The changes in marriage and divorce patterns by age almost completely counteract each other so that they have virtually no effect on fertility.

Within the union republics, divorce has increased virtually everywhere. Although the divorce rates in Central Asia remain the lowest, the rate of increase in divorce rates in Central Asia has been the highest in the Soviet Union. Even in 1973, the chance that a married woman in the Uzbek SSR would become divorced was only about 48 percent of that for the average married woman in the Soviet Union.

Statements and Actions on Population Matters. Marxist literature has long contended that there is a "socialist population law," to the effect that while capitalism

TABLE 5. *Ideal family size by number of living children,*[1] *Soviet Union, 1969*

	0	1	2	3	4	5	6+	All respondents
Soviet Union	2.7	2.5	2.8	3.3	3.9	4.9	6.8	2.4
Russian SFSR	2.6	2.5	2.7	3.0	3.2	3.6	—[2]	2.2
Estonian SSR	2.5	2.6	2.8	3.1	3.1	—[2]	—[2]	2.3
Armenian SSR	4.1	3.5	3.7	4.1	4.7	5.0	6.1	3.4
Uzbek SSR	3.4	3.1	3.3	4.6	5.5	6.3	8.5	4.3

[1]The sample did not include collective farmers. [2]Too few cases to show results.
Source of data: Belova, 1971.

discourages population growth, socialism is favorable to and compatible with high fertility and growth rates. Since the late 1960s, however, this law has been referred to less frequently in the Soviet demographic literature.

The major legal changes relating to population growth since the 1917 Revolution are summarized in Table 6. It seems likely that one purpose of the 1936 legal changes was to increase the rate of population growth, and an explicit reason for the 1944 changes was to replenish the war-depleted Soviet population. It was hoped that the 1968 changes would decrease the incidence of divorce, and the 1974 legislation was intended to raise fertility. Thus explicit measures have been taken to assist whatever natural tendencies socialism has toward growth.

The concern with declining population growth rates in the Soviet Union as a whole has been sharpened by low growth rates among the European population in the presence of high growth rates among the non-European population. This imbalance of growth among various ethnic groups has not, however, given rise to population policies that are explicitly different for various ethnic groups. Nevertheless, it has been suggested that allowances not be paid for families with more than four children, and such a policy would primarily affect the non-European population. (Although family allowances for children under age 8 were instituted in 1974, the amount

of the allowance is small. The high costs of larger allowances have precluded them; moreover, because of the important role of women in the labor force, the Soviet government has been reluctant to institute programs that might entice them to leave it.)

The imbalance in growth rates of various ethnic groups led to slow population growth in the European parts of the Soviet Union and high rates of population growth in the Caucasus and especially in Central Asia. At the same time industrial labor demands are high in central European Russia. It has a labor shortage while Central Asia has a surplus. Various incentive programs to induce Central Asians to migrate permanently or for long periods of time to central Russia have not been successful. The major interregional migration stream is instead from the European regions of the Soviet Union to Central Asia. It is yet to be seen whether heavy industry will be relocated to any substantial extent in Central Asia.

At the 26th Congress of the Communist Party in Moscow in February 1981, official acceptance of regionally differentiated fertility policies was pronounced. This broke with the earlier policy of treating all regions identically. The first action will probably be to increase maternity benefits in the Far East.

In 1970, there were ten cities in the Soviet Union with over a million inhabitants; and in 1980 there were twenty. Soviet planners have thought it undesirable for population to grow very rapidly in a few large cities. Thus Moscow, Leningrad, Riga, and a number of other metropolises are "restricted residence cities." It is difficult to obtain permission to become a permanent resident in such cities, and new housing construction there has been slight, to try to slow their rates of growth. In order to fill necessary labor needs, retired persons in such cities are allowed to work without losing pension or other retirement benefits.

The Soviet Union has also pursued a variety of ethnic population policies unrelated to growth. One is a policy of respecting the integrity of the languages of the fifteen union republics and using for most purposes the language of the ethnic group for which the union republic is designated. Ethnic groups from the autonomous SSR's, the autonomous oblasts, and the national circles are encouraged to adopt the language of the dominant ethnic group in the union republic in which they are located (chiefly the Russian SFSR). All Soviet citizens are expected to learn Russian at least as a second language. In keeping with this policy, the extent of bilingual schooling available in languages other than that of the union republic's titular ethnic group has generally decreased in the last forty years. During World War II, various minority ethnic groups that were thought to be potentially sympa-

TABLE 6. *Dates of major legislative changes in Soviet population policy*

Date	Legislative changes
1918 & 1926	Secularization of marriage, prohibition of polygamy, freedom of marriage and divorce, equality of men and women in the family, equality of legitimate and illegitimate children
1920	Abortion legalized
1925	Divorced women entitled to support from former spouse, recognition of *de facto* marriages
1936	Abortion illegal, governmental assistance to families with many children, strengthening of penalties against nonpayment of alimony, some restrictions on divorce
1944	More restrictions on divorce, no recognition of *de facto* marriages, no way to legitimatize an illegitimate child
1955	Abortions legalized, more liberal divorce
1965	Divorce liberalized further
1968	More liberal abortion policy, possible ways to legitimatize an illegitimate child, longer wait required before marriage
1974	Family allowance program for children under age 8
1981	Official acceptance of the application of regionally differentiated fertility policies

thetic to the Germans were relocated from European regions and the Caucasus into Asiatic regions. These groups included the Volga Germans, Chechen-Ingush, Balkars, Karachay, and Crimean Tatars. By the late 1960s, the political rights of these ethnic groups were restored and many members had returned to their traditional areas of settlement. The Volga Germans, however, did not regain their former autonomous republic on the Volga and continue to live primarily in Asiatic regions of the Soviet Union.

Scholarly Activities. Before the 1917 Revolution, considerable demographic research was done in European parts of the Russian Empire, and such research continued into the 1920s. Since the 1950s, demographic research and publication in the Soviet Union have increased considerably. Demographic research is done by the Central Statistical Bureau of the U.S.S.R. The journal of the bureau, *Vestnik statistiki,* is published monthly and contains articles and statistical tables on population topics. The Central Statistical bureaus of the union republics also engage in research and publication. *Narodnoe khoziastvo,* the yearbook of the national economy of the Soviet Union, contains demographic information, as do the yearbooks on the national economies of the union republics. The Center for the Study of Population Problems (established in 1965) at Moscow State University conducts research and teaching in population and publishes the quarterly demographic journal *Narodonaselenie* (Population). Historical work on population topics is conducted in the Institute of History of the Estonian Academy of Sciences in Tallin, the Institute of History of the Soviet Academy of Sciences in Moscow, and the Department of History of Moscow State University.

Barbara A. Anderson

See also ASIA.

BIBLIOGRAPHY

Arutiunian, Iu. V. "Konkretno-sotsiologicheskoe issledovanie natsionalnikh otnoshenii" (A Concrete Sociological Study of Ethnic Relations). *Voprosy filosofii* 12:129–139, 1969.

Belova, V. "Obsledovaniye mnenii o nailuchshem i ozhidaenom chisle detey v sem'e" (Survey of Attitudes of the Ideal and Intended Number of Children in the Family). *Vestnik statistiki* 6:23–24, 1971.

Berent, Jerzy. "Causes of Fertility Decline in Eastern Europe and the Soviet Union. Part 1: The Influence of Demographic Factors." *Population Studies* 24(1):35–38, March 1970.

———. "Causes of Fertility Decline in Eastern Europe and the Soviet Union. Parts 2 and 3: Economic and Social Factors, Family Planning and Population Policies." *Population Studies* 24(2):247–292, July 1970.

Biraben, Jean-Noël. "Essai sur l'évolution démographique de l'U.R.S.S." *Population* 13(2):29–62, June 1958.

Coale, Ansley J., Barbara A. Anderson, and Erna Härm. *Human Fertility in Russia since the Nineteenth Century.* Princeton, N.J.: Princeton University Press, 1979.

Heer, David M. "Recent Developments in Soviet Population Policy." *Studies in Family Planning* 3(11):257–264, November 1972.

Lewis, Robert A., Richard H. Rowland, and Ralph S. Clem. *Nationality and Population Change in Russia and the U.S.S.R.: An Evaluation of Census Data, 1897–1970.* New York: Praeger, 1976.

Narodnoe khoziastvo (The Yearbook of the National Economy). Issued annually by the Central Statistical Bureau of the U.S.S.R., Moscow.

Naselenie SSSR: Chislennost, sostav i dvizhenie naselenie (Population of the U.S.S.R.: Number, Composition, and Distribution of the Population). Issued annually by the Central Statistical Bureau of the U.S.S.R., Moscow.

Sadvokasova, E. A. "Nekotorie sotsialno-gigienicheskie aspekti izycheniia aborta: Po materialam spetsialnogo issledovaniia v riade gorodov i selskikh mestnostei RSFSR za 1958–1959 gg." (Certain Social-hygienic Aspects in the Study of Abortions: According to the Data of Special Investigation Carried Out in a Number of Towns and Rural Localities of the RSFSR in 1958–1959). *Sovetskoe zdravookhranenie* 22(3):45–50, 1963.

Vestnik statistiki (Statistical Herald). Issued monthly since 1949 by the Central Statistical Bureau of the U.S.S.R., Moscow.

Weber, Cynthia, and Ann Goodman. "The Demographic Policy Debate in the USSR." *Population and Development Review* 7(2):279–295, June 1981.

SPATIAL DISTRIBUTION

See DISTRIBUTION.

STATISTICAL METHODS

Statistical methods in the field of population studies vary widely. Continuous invention within the field has accompanied extensive borrowing from other disciplines, with little in the way of an organizing principle except description and explanation of the phenomenon of immediate interest. The subject matter addressed can differ greatly, the methods used may be simple or complex, and the intent may be to describe or to analyze. Because the field can only rarely use experimental techniques it relies for explanation chiefly upon observational approaches, and generally uses statistical methods that accept observational data.

Because the methods are so disparate they are presented in this work in separate articles. RATES AND RATIOS gives the basic measures used most generally in the field. LIFE TABLES explains that technique as it is applied to mortality and gives a number of applications to other topics. ACTUARIAL METHODS presents additional methods for analysis of mortality that have been developed in connection with insurance. INDIRECT ESTIMATION OF FERTILITY AND MORTALITY describes a variety of specialized techniques used when data are incomplete or defective.

POPULATION MODELS explains the conceptual structure of numerous efforts at explanation of population processes within the field and discusses the statistical methods that accompany them. MATHEMATICAL DEMOGRAPHY is a general survey of both historical and contemporary quantitative applications.

Investigation of the distribution of a population and the process of urbanization uses many specialized methods; these are covered in DISTRIBUTION, article on DISTRIBUTION, CONCENTRATION, AND DISPERSION. Marriage studies also use special techniques, given in NUPTIALITY INDEXES, as do studies of geographic movement, discussed in MIGRATION MEASUREMENT. A number of interesting statistical methods have been invented or adapted to assess the effect of contraception and of family planning programs; these are presented in FAMILY PLANNING PROGRAMS, articles on MANAGEMENT AND EVALUATION and EFFECTS ON FERTILITY, and in FAMILY PLANNING RESEARCH.

Many statistical methods take their character from the kind of data they use, as illustrated in the three articles that comprise DATA COLLECTION; these are NATIONAL SYSTEMS, which compares surveys, censuses, and vital registration systems, INTERNATIONAL SYSTEMS, and UNITED STATES CENSUS. Survey work has become a mainstay of the field over the last few decades, and a most important aspect of the methodology is discussed in SAMPLING METHODS. A further group of methods that is governed by the data employed is given in SMALL-AREA ANALYSIS.

STATUS OF WOMEN

The "status of women," understood in terms of opportunities for additional education, alternatives to domestic roles, freedom of movement, and related issues, is usually considered by demographers in relation to fertility. A correspondence between higher status and lower fertility is often found, but the causal direction is not always clear: women without children are better able to seek education and to work outside the home, but those who desire school and work are less likely to have children. Although improved female status is often discussed as a way to reduce fertility rates, programs that by whatever means give women closer control over their own fertility thereby affect a powerful determinant of status. The

implications for women of declines in mortality are equally complex. This article examines current demographic and socioeconomic changes for their effects on the position of women in society.

Mortality. If people were power, women would soon rule the world. In the most powerful countries they already outnumber males (e.g., by about a combined 35 million in the United States and the Soviet Union), and they are gaining rapidly in many other nations. Without doubt, increased chances for survival represent women's greatest single gain of the twentieth century. The improvement has not only been spectacular relative to the baseline, but it has in general also been superior to gains made by men. For eighteen developed countries with adequate data between 1900 and 1965, life expectancy at birth increased by 50 percent for males but 54 percent for females. By the mid-1960s the newly born female in these countries could expect to live 5.5 years longer than the average male. The feminine advantage, moreover, seems to be accelerating. Thus, between the late 1950s and late 1960s females in all of seventeen developed countries showed increases in life expectancy at ages 0, 1, 15, and 65; while males showed decreases in up to half of the countries at a number of ages (computed from United Nations, 1973, p. 116). Indeed, in recent years women in some countries have reached a kind of landmark figure that still eludes men. This achievement by American women in 1975 was quietly heralded by the Metropolitan Life Insurance Company, which noted that "their life expectancy [at birth] was, for the first time in the nation's history, equal to their life expectancy at age one" (1976, p. 4).

In the developing countries women have also benefited from the general declines in mortality, but their advantage vis-à-vis males is less clear-cut. In countries as diverse as India, Mexico, and Trinidad, the percentage increases in life expectation for women have not exceeded those for men. In India the female advantage characteristic of the late nineteenth century has been lost and males now enjoy a lead of 1.3 years in life expectancy. The sex ratio has risen from 1,029 (males to 1,000 females) at the beginning of the century to 1,075 in 1971. Indian scholars have shown that this difference cannot be attributed to underenumeration of females, selective migration, or differential sex ratios at birth (Karkal, Kuman, and Roy, 1976). In India, Egypt, Costa Rica, Guatemala, Mexico, Taiwan, Pakistan, and Ceylon, girls under 5 years of age have higher death rates than boys. While causes are obscure, studies in Egypt and Jordan show that infant males are better nourished than females and, therefore, have a lower death rate. Muslim women in rural areas are reported to nurse their sons longer than their daughters (Fullam, 1975).

Nevertheless, it is generally true that women are living longer lives than ever before, meaning that more years can be spent in marriage, reproductive life, and widowhood. Where life expectancy is only twenty-five years, at the time of her marriage a woman can anticipate only another thirty-one years of life; but under modern conditions, a life expectancy of seventy-five years, she can expect fifty-seven years of life after marriage. At the turn of the century an American woman of 21 who married a 23-year-old could expect thirty-one years of joint survival. In 1970 the same couple could expect over forty-two years. Such changes could be expected to strain an institution that is possibly geared to shorter periods of joint survival. Moreover, since life expectancy is now longer than the time necessary for women to bear and rear children, we can anticipate strains on the roles that have traditionally filled much of adult women's years.

Fertility. If women are experiencing a growing liberation from excessive rates of mortality, world trends also suggest a growing freedom from excessive rates of fertility. Between 1950 and 1975, birth rates in the developed countries dropped by 29 percent and in the developing countries by 15 percent. In fourteen developing countries in the Americas the rates declined by a total of 23 percent, in ten developing countries of Asia by 30 percent, and in three African countries by 23 percent.

In the developed countries the combined effect of increased longevity and low fertility has been to drastically reduce the number and proportion of years spent in child care. As just one evidence, over the past eighty years in the United States the number of years between the marriage of the last child and the death of one parent has increased sevenfold, from 1.6 to 12.9 years. In many developed countries this means that increasing numbers of women live more years alone. One-person households have shown dramatic increases: from 5 percent of U.S. households in 1900 to 15 percent in 1960; from 6 percent of British households in 1921 to 15 percent in 1966, and from 3 to 8 percent in Japan between 1955 and 1965. Older women probably represent a disproportionate share of these increases.

In developing countries the situation is different but hardly less difficult for women. The decline in fertility has tended to lag well behind that of mortality, and consequently the major burdens of the demographic gap, usually attributed to the population in general, have fallen disproportionately on the shoulders of women. Who else, after all, could be expected to care for the additional surviving children? For despite the theoretical modernization of family structure as a result of social and economic development, household size has been increasing in a number of developing countries in Latin Amer-

ica and Asia, almost surely a consequence of reductions in infant and child mortality.

For a number of countries there even appears to be a long gap between the inception of decline in fertility and the decline in household size—half a century in Japan, a generation in England. Increasing household size must represent a relatively sudden strain on the household. Thus, during a period when international authorities are urging women to participate more fully in the modernization process, in most of the world they are being burdened with additional surviving children. "Burdened" because these additional household members are not only rarely "needed" in an economic sense, but to a large extent they were not *wanted*. In sixty knowledge, attitude, and practice surveys (KAP surveys) conducted in thirty-nine developing countries, about two-thirds of the rural women with four children wanted no more (Berelson, 1974).

Development. In the twentieth century victories over illiteracy at least match victories over death and birth. In most parts of the world, female gains in primary schooling have been impressive. In the developed countries and in Latin America illiteracy rates are now low for both sexes. But women still lag markedly behind males in Asia, Africa, and the Arab states; and nearly two-thirds of the world's current illiterates are women. More serious are the deficiencies at secondary and higher levels where schooling has the greatest significance for meaningful employment, changes in female roles, fertility, and national development generally. In 1970, males constituted two out of every three secondary school enrollments in Asia and Africa, and about three of every four university enrollments. In the United States the attainment of a college education by white females showed a marked deterioration relative to white males since 1940. In other countries sex segregation or tracking (domestic science, education, and humanities for women) may have in part vitiated otherwise notable educational advances for women.

The long-run trend of female employment in the twentieth century has been upward in the developed countries, and married women have shown striking gains. In Great Britain, half the married women in their early forties were employed in 1966, as contrasted with only 30 percent in 1951. In the United States, the most rapid increases in participation rates during the past quarter of a century have taken place among wives and mothers.

The situation in the developing countries is less clear but is probably less favorable. In Latin America, where rates of female participation in the labor force are low, no substantial changes have occurred during the last twenty years. A United Nations analysis shows that for nineteen of twenty-eight semi-industrialized or agricultural countries female participation rates have been declining since World War II (though less markedly than for males), while in twelve of seventeen industrialized countries their rates have been increasing (United Nations, 1973).

Even in the developed countries, however, the significance for women's roles of increases in female employment is not clear. The degree of sex segregation in the occupational structure may be a more sensitive indicator of the position of women than the extent of female participation in the labor force, and it was shown that sex segregation in the United States has not diminished as female participation in the labor force has grown. Fragmentary evidence from European studies indicates that employment may merely be added to the traditional duties for the woman, rather than diminishing such duties.

J. Mayone Stycos

Demographic determinants and consequences of the status of women are discussed in several entries. The effects of population growth at the family level, specifically for health and education, are discussed in FERTILITY AND DEVELOPMENT. AGE AT MARRIAGE *presents trends toward later marriages and their implications for fertility. The wide range of patterns of female employment among nations is considered in* LABOR FORCE. FERTILITY AND MIGRATION *analyzes changes in women's roles that occur both in the urban place of destination and in the rural area of origin. The effects of marriage disruption and the increase in families headed by females are described in* MARRIAGE AND DIVORCE. *The rights of women to choose the number and timing of births are discussed in* LAW AND FERTILITY REGULATION *and* ETHICS, *and the legal foundations for women's position in the United States in the family and society appear in* FAMILY LAW.

BIBLIOGRAPHY

Berelson, Bernard. "World Population: Status Report 1974." *Reports on Population/Family Planning,* no. 15, January 1974.

Blake, Judith. "The Changing Status of Women in Developed Countries." In *The Human Population,* edited by Scientific American editors, pp. 91–101. San Francisco: Freeman, 1974.

Campbell, Arthur A., et al. (editors). *The Family in Transition.* Fogarty International Center Proceedings, no. 3. Washington, D.C.: U.S. Government Printing Office, 1971.

Dixon, Ruth B. "Women's Rights and Fertility." *Reports on Population/Family Planning,* no. 17, pp. 1–20, January 1975. Excerpted as "Education and Employment: Keys to Smaller Families," *Journal of Family Welfare* 22(2):38–49, December 1975.

Fullam, Maryellen. "Half the World." *People* 2(2), 1975.

Karkal, Molini, Joginder Kuman, and T. K. Roy (editors). *Sex Ratio: Demographic Analysis.* Bombay: International Institute for Population Studies, 1976.

Metropolitan Life Insurance Company. "Longevity Patterns in the United States." *Statistical Bulletin,* no. 57, pp. 3–4, May 1976.

Oppenheimer, Valerie Kincade. *The Female Labor Force in the United States: Demographic and Economic Factors Governing Its Growth and Changing Composition.* Population Monograph Series, no. 5. Berkeley: Institute of International Studies, University of California, 1970.

Tinker, Irene. "The Adverse Impact of Development on Women." In *Women and World Development,* edited by Irene Tinker, Michèle Bo Bramsen, and Mayra Buvinić, pp. 22–34. New York: Praeger, 1976.

United Nations, Department of Economic and Social Affairs. *The Determinants and Consequences of Population Trends.* Volume 1: *New Summary of Findings on Interaction of Demogaphic, Economic, and Social Factors.* Series A, Population Studies, no. 50. New York, 1973.

————. *The Population Debate: Dimensions and Perspective; Papers of the World Population Conference, Bucharest, 1974.* 2 vols. Series A, Population Studies, no. 57 and no. 57–add. 1. New York, 1975. In English, French, and Spanish.

STERILIZATION TECHNIQUES

Sterilization is a permanent form of contraception. It involves either the removal of a portion of the male or female reproductive tract or a blocking or some form of interruption of the continuity of the system so that a sperm is prevented from uniting with an ovum. Sterilization can be accomplished in a number of different ways.

Female Sterilization. In order to block conception the Fallopian tubes can be cut, tied, crushed, burned, or blocked by chemicals or occlusive devices. The tubes can be reached by either a vaginal or an abdominal approach. Transcervical approaches have been used experimentally but to date have not been found sufficiently effective for general clinical use. At present five major operative methods are used for female sterilization: laparotomy, minilaparotomy, colpotomy, and the endoscopic methods, laparoscopy and culdoscopy. These approaches allow occlusion of any part of the Fallopian tube. Hysterectomy, or the removal of the uterus, has largely been replaced by these procedures for the purpose of contraceptive sterilization alone.

It should be noted that although sterilization is considered a highly effective method of permanent contraception, the specific techniques used to accomplish sterilization are not always 100 percent effective. Varying failure rates have been reported for all methods. The failure rate is dependent on the particular method used, the time surgery is performed (postpartum or at a time not related to pregnancy or abortion), patient characteristics, and skill of the operator.

Operative procedures. The type of operative procedure depends on a number of factors: the time of sterilization; whether it is postpartum or interval (done at a time not related to pregnancy or abortion); patient characteristics such as weight and history of prior pelvic surgery or tubal infections; type of anesthesia available; skill of the operator; and availability of sterilization equipment. The major operative approaches for female sterilization are as follows.

1. Laparotomy involves a traditional surgical approach in which a 10-centimeter incision is made into the abdomen in order to reach the Fallopian tubes. This method is considered to be major surgery requiring hospitalization and a general anesthetic.

2. Minilaparotomy has become widely used because it can easily be learned by physicians and paramedical personnel and because it requires a minimum of equipment. It can be done as an inpatient or outpatient procedure using either local or general anesthesia. In performing a minilaparotomy, the tubes are reached through a small 2.5-centimeter abdominal incision, usually slightly below the umbilicus if sterilization is performed in the immediate postpartum period, but slightly above the pubic area for interval sterilization.

3. Colpotomy is performed by making a small incision through the rear vaginal wall into the peritoneal cavity to reach the tubes. It can be done as an inpatient or outpatient procedure under local or general anesthesia.

4. Laparoscopy involves the insertion of an optical instrument called a laparascope through a small incision into the abdominal cavity, which has been distended with a gas, either carbon dioxide or nitrous oxide. The instrument uses fiberoptic light bundles to transmit cold light from an external source into the abdomen so that its contents can be seen. A special instrument either to cut the Fallopian tube or to coagulate it with an electric current is inserted through a tube in the laparoscope. Alternatively, with the two-puncture technique a second incision may be made to insert the instrument. Laparoscopy can be performed as an inpatient or outpatient procedure under either local or general anesthesia.

5. Culdoscopy involves the use of an optical instrument called the culdoscope, which is similar to the laparoscope. It is inserted through the rear wall of the vagina into the peritoneal cavity in order to allow the operator to see the tubes and to perform sterilization. Culdoscopy can be done as either an inpatient or outpatient procedure under local or general anesthesia.

Occlusion techniques. After entrance has been gained to the Fallopian tubes, a number of different techniques can be employed to occlude them. These techniques can be classified as (1) ligation, (2) fulguration, and (3) the application of occlusive devices.

1. There are five major approaches to performing tubal ligation. In simple ligation a nonabsorbable material is used to tie, or ligate, the tube. This is a simple procedure, but it is seldom used because of a failure rate as high as 20 percent (Wortman, 1976, p. C-74). Ligation and crushing, also known as the Madlener technique, involves tying and crushing a portion of the tube. The failure rate varies with the approach, increasing with colpotomy, and ranging from 1 to 2 percent. Ligation, division, and burial involves dividing the tube, tying the cut ends, and burying the stumps into the adjacent uterus. The two most popular techniques of this kind are the Irving and the Wood procedures. They are nearly 100 percent effective but require more skill and operative time to perform than other ligation techniques (Wortman, 1976, p. C-75).

Ligation and resection involves the tying and removal of a portion of the tube. The three most widely used techniques of this kind are salpingectomy, the Pomeroy technique, and fimbriectomy.

Salpingectomy is the removal of the Fallopian tubes. It is rarely performed because it is a more extensive procedure associated with higher morbidity, mainly because of bleeding. The failure rate is 0 to 1.9 percent. The most frequently used ligation method is the Pomeroy technique. This procedure is performed by grasping the middle of the tube to form a loop, tying the base of the loop with absorbable sutures, and then cutting off the top of the loop. The occluded ends of the tube separate as the sutures are absorbed. The failure rate ranges from 0 to .4 percent with some investigators reporting failure rates of 2.5 to 5 percent if it is done at the time of Caesarean section. The reason for this is not known (Wortman, 1976, p. C-77).

Fimbriectomy is the removal of the fimbrial end of the Fallopian tube. It is nearly 100 percent effective, but it is rarely done because it is a complex operation.

Ligation, resection, and burial procedures are complex to perform and involve the tying, or ligation, of the tube, removing a portion, and then burying the stump in an adjacent structure such as the uterus. The two procedures of this type performed today are cornual resection and Uchida technique. Cornual resection has a moderately high failure rate, 2.8 to 3.2 percent, and also the increased risk of complications such as bleeding or adhesions. The Uchida technique is more effective but also much more complicated to perform than other ligation procedures (Wortman, 1976, p. C-78).

2. In fulguration, an electrical current is applied to the Fallopian tubes in order to divide the tube in half (cutting current) or to burn segments of the tube until occlusion occurs (coagulation current). Both types of current can be used individually or in combination with one an-

other. Reports vary as to which method—coagulation, division, or coagulation and division combined—produces the best results in terms of effectiveness and safety. The major risk with this method of sterilization is that heat or sparks from the electrical current may damage other nearby organs in the abdomen. New equipment is being developed to reduce the incidence of burn complications. This method of tubal occlusion can be performed with an endoscope inserted into the abdomen (laparoscopy), the vagina (culdoscopy), or the uterus (hysteroscopy). Hysteroscopic fulguration is performed by introducing a hysteroscope through the cervix and into the uterus. Coagulating current is then applied to each tube at the uterotubal junction. In general, hysteroscopic fulguration has not been found satisfactory because of a high incidence of failure (11 to 35 percent) and morbidity (Wortman, 1976).

3. Occlusive devices, clips or bands of either metal or some other non-tissue-reactive material, can be applied to the tube to close it. These can be applied via the abdomen or the vagina using either traditional surgical methods or endoscopic instruments. Varying rates of effectiveness have been reported for sterilizations performed with occlusive devices. Further study is necessary in order to compare the effectiveness of these devices with other methods of sterilization.

Experimental methods. Numerous experiments are being conducted to develop effective methods of female sterilization that will not require surgical intervention. Several types of chemicals have been used transcervically in attempts to occlude the Fallopian tubes without surgery. Some act as tissue adhesives, which solidify in the tube and form plugs. Others are sclerosing agents, which destroy the inner lining of the tube with subsequent scarring and fibrosis. Experiments have been carried out using quinacrine, silver nitrate, silastic, MCA (methyl-2-cyanoacrylate monomer, a tissue adhesive), and GRF (a gelatin-resorconal formaldehyde, a biodegradable tissue adhesive). Several problems are associated with these chemicals. Many are ineffective after a single application. Some are highly toxic and in instances of intraperitoneal spillage may damage other internal organs. Many require special equipment for administration. The exact dosage to occlude the tube is not always known. Also being conducted are experiments that attempt to occlude the tube by the insertion of a solid plug. A number of different plugs have been developed and are being tested. They are solid silastic intratubal devices, polyethylene plugs, ceramic and proplast plugs, and dacron and teflon plugs. The plugs can be introduced into the tube using surgical or endoscopic techniques. Since very little experimentation with these devices has been done in

humans, it is not possible to state effectiveness rates accurately.

Male Sterilization. Vasectomy, or male sterilization, is a simple, relatively easy operation to perform. It can be done in an outpatient setting under local anesthesia. There are fewer complications associated with vasectomy than with tubal occlusion.

In doing a vasectomy, either one or two small incisions are made into the scrotum; each vas is isolated. The operator then cuts, ties, fulgurates, or ties and fulgurates the ends of both vas to prevent sperm from traveling from the testes to the upper portion of the vas deferens and ultimately into the female reproductive tract. After vasectomy there is still an ejaculate (devoid of sperm) because the bulk of the semen is composed of secretions from the seminal vesicles, the prostate gland, and the bulbourethral glands. A man is not considered sterile immediately after a vasectomy because sperm linger in the upper portion of the vas deferens; he is usually considered sterile after having two negative semen analyses. The number of ejaculations needed to remove the remaining sperm from the male reproductive tract varies from person to person.

Vasectomy has a reported failure of less than one per hundred procedures (Wortman, 1975, p. D-32). Failures are generally due to one of the following factors: spontaneous recanalization (rejoining) of the cut ends of the vas; intercourse before the reproductive tract is devoid of sperm; occlusion or division of a structure other than the vas; or the rare occurrence of more than one vas on one side.

Contra-indications to performing a vasectomy include infection or systemic blood disorders such as hemophilia. Factors that may make surgery more difficult are inguinal hernia, previous surgery for hernia, hydrocele, variocele, preexisting scrotal lesions, or thick, tough scrotal skin (Wortman, 1975, p. D-26).

Experimental methods for occluding the vas deferens involve the application of clips or staples to the vas. Generally two or more staples or clips are applied to the vas in an occluding manner and a portion of the vas may be excised. Low failure rates have been reported with these methods, but further research is needed on their design, their applicators, procedures for their use, and their effect on the vas itself.

Although sterilization is considered an irreversible method of contraception, some men and women, for various reasons, seek reversal of the operation. Experimental procedures using newly developed microsurgical techniques are being tried in an attempt to restore fertility. To date, the results of these procedures, as measured by the achievement of pregnancy, have not been very good. Further research is needed to develop a safe, inexpensive, easily reversible means of sterilization.

Vera Plaskon

See also CONTRACEPTIVE METHODS.

BIBLIOGRAPHY

Bradshaw, Lois E. "Vasectomy Reversibility: A Status Report." *Population Reports,* series D, no. 3, whole issue, May 1976.
Green, Cynthia P. "Voluntary Sterilization: World's Leading Contraceptive Method." *Population Reports,* series M, no. 2, whole issue, March 1978.
Saidi, M. H., and C. M. Zainie. *Female Sterilization: A Handbook for Women.* New York: Garland, 1981.
Sciarra, John J., W. Droegemueller, and Joseph J. Speidel (editors). *Advances in Female Sterilization Techniques.* Hagerstown, Md.: Harper & Row, 1976.
Wortman, Judith. "Vasectomy: What Are the Problems?" *Population Reports,* series D, no. 2, whole issue, January 1975.
———. "Tubal Sterilization: Review of Methods." *Population Reports,* series C, no. 7, whole issue, May 1976.
Wortman, Judith, and Phyllis T. Piotrow. "Vasectomy: Old and New Techniques." *Population Reports,* series D, no. 1, whole issue, December 1973.
Zatuchni, Gerald L., Miriam H. Labbok, and John J. Sciarra. *Research Frontiers in Fertility Regulation.* Hagerstown, Md.: Harper & Row, 1980.

STRUCTURE
See COMPOSITION.

SUB-SAHARAN AFRICA

Forty-nine political units, including forty-five independent states, comprise the region of sub-Saharan Africa, which is defined here to include several islands in the Atlantic and Indian oceans but to exclude the eight countries that are together known as North Africa. With a population estimated to have reached 361 million in mid-1980, sub-Saharan Africa is home to about 8 percent of the world's population. Nigeria alone has about one-fifth of the region's people. Including Nigeria, twenty-seven countries account for 95 percent of the region's population; of the remaining twenty-two countries in the region thirteen had populations under 1 million in 1980.

In this article countries are grouped into four subregions according to United Nations classification: eastern, middle, southern, and western Africa. Table 1 lists the countries of each subregion. Although considerable differences exist among some countries within the subregions, this classification nevertheless illustrates conveniently the general demographic picture; in particular the subregion of southern Africa has relatively lower fertility and mortality rates than the other subregions.

The land mass of sub-Saharan Africa is 21,805,650 square kilometers (8,419,161 square miles), or about 16 percent of the world's total. Many countries are sparsely populated, and overall population density is low compared with that of other regions of the world. Much of the land, however, is not arable, including the Kalahari Steppe and the Namib Desert in southwestern Africa; the Sahara, which extends from Mauritania to the Sudan; and much of the Sahel, a semiarid region below the Sahara extending from Senegal across the continent to Ethiopia. Estimates of average population densities in 1978 ranged from 8 persons per square kilometer (21 per square mile) in middle Africa to 22 (57) in western Africa (United Nations, ECA, 1978). Although these figures are low in comparison to the world average density of 31 persons per square kilometer (80 per square mile), they do not reflect the low capacity of large tracts of arid or depleted land to support predominantly agricultural populations at present levels of technology.

The region has a great diversity of languages; at least eight hundred ethnic groups exist, speaking more than one thousand languages and dialects. European colonial languages, principally English, French, Portuguese, and Dutch, have served at once to unify and to divide African peoples. Most countries designate one of the European languages as the official language, although Amharic is the official language in Ethiopia and Swahili and English have equal status in Tanzania. Swahili is widely spoken in eastern Africa, and Hausa in western and middle Africa, and Arabic has spread across the continent with Islam.

Although demographic statistics in the region must in general still be regarded as approximate, a number of assessments are possible. Sub-Saharan Africa can be characterized by its high birth rates (see Table 2). Subregional estimates for 1980, per 1,000 population, were 48 for eastern Africa, 45 for middle Africa, 39 for southern Africa, and 49 for western Africa. Estimated death rates were very high but are declining: for 1975–1980, per 1,000, 18.3 for eastern Africa, 19.6 for middle Africa, 11 for southern Africa, and 18.8 for western Africa. The overall growth rate for Africa has soared, from about 2 percent in 1950–1955 to an estimated nearly 3 percent in 1980. Because the region is at best just entering the demographic transition, still higher growth rates may lie ahead, as mortality continues to drop faster than fertility.

TABLE 1. *Demographic indicators, sub-Saharan Africa*

Subregion and country	(1) Estimated midyear population (thousands), 1980	(2) Estimated annual growth rate, 1975–1980	(3) Estimated population density per sq km, 1980	(4) Estimated population under 15, 1975	(5) Infant mortality rate, 1980	(6) Life expectancy at birth, 1980 Males	(7) Life expectancy at birth, 1980 Females
Eastern Africa	*133,551*	*2.9*	*21*	*45.4%*	*132*	*46.8*	*50.2*
Br. Indian Ocean Territory	2	0.0	—	—	—	—	—
Burundi	4,512	2.74	154	43.6	140	44.4	47.6
Comoros	335	2.21	160	44.4	148	45.9	49.2
Djibouti	119	2.31	—	—	—	—	—
Ethiopia	32,601	2.50	26	44.9	162	39.4	42.6
Kenya	16,402	3.85	27	49.2	83	53.2	56.8
Madagascar	8,742	2.60	16	43.1	102	46.9	50.2
Malawi	6,162	3.20	47	47.2	142	44.4	47.6
Mauritius	995	1.94	474	37.7	35	66.7	70.3
Mozambique	10,473	2.59	13	43.2	148	46.9	50.2
Réunion	525	1.71	218	40.3	41	64.6	68.2
Rwanda	4,797	3.04	185	46.0	127	44.4	47.6
Seychelles	65	2.28	—	45.0	43	—	—
Somalia	3,645	2.79	6	—	177	44.4	47.6
Tanzania	17,934	3.06	19	45.4	125	47.8	51.2
Uganda	13,201	3.04	56	44.8	120	53.2	56.8
Zambia	5,645	3.20	8	46.6	144	47.8	51.2
Zimbabwe	7,396	3.38	19	46.9	129	54.6	58.2
Middle Africa	*53,094*	*2.55*	*8*	*43.0*	*167*	*45.1*	*48.4*
Angola (incl. Cabinda)	7,078	2.46	6	43.3	203	41.9	45.1
Cameroon	8,444	2.30	15	40.9	157	44.4	47.6
Central African Rep.	2,221	2.25	3	40.2	190	44.4	47.6
Chad	4,524	2.31	3	41.7	165	39.9	43.1
Congo	1,537	2.56	4	42.8	180	46.9	50.2
Equatorial Guinea	363	2.34	12	40.9	165	46.9	50.2
Gabon	551	1.12	2	32.5	178	44.4	47.6
São Tomé & Príncipe	85	1.21	—	—	64	—	—
Zaire	28,291	2.75	12	44.4	160	46.9	50.2
Southern Africa	*33,012*	*2.75*	*12*	*41.9*	*101*	*53.8*	*57.4*
Botswana	821	2.74	1	49.4	97	46.9	50.2
Lesotho	1,341	2.36	42	40.4	111	49.3	52.7
Namibia	1,009	2.85	1	43.6	142	44.4	47.6
South Africa	29,285	2.77	23	41.6	97	54.6	58.2
Swaziland	556	2.82	31	44.9	168	46.9	50.2
Western Africa	*140,973*	*3.06*	*22*	*46.0*	*159*	*44.0*	*47.2*
Benin	3,530	2.97	31	45.7	149	44.4	47.6
Cape Verde	324	1.67	80	40.8	105	53.2	56.8
Gambia	603	2.81	50	44.2	217	40.9	44.1
Ghana	11,679	3.12	48	46.1	115	46.9	50.2
Guinea	5,014	2.54	20	43.1	175	44.4	47.6
Guinea-Bissau	573	1.75	16	37.3	208	41.9	45.1
Ivory Coast	7,973	3.45	17	43.4	154	46.9	50.2
Liberia	1,863	3.37	17	47.1	148	46.9	50.2
Mali	6,646	2.70	5	45.0	190	39.9	43.1
Mauritania	1,634	2.79	1	45.6	187	39.9	43.1
Niger	5,305	2.91	4	46.5	200	39.9	43.1
Nigeria	77,082	3.21	79	47.1	157	44.4	47.6
St. Helena	5	0.75	—	—	—	—	—
Senegal	5,661	2.58	25	44.2	160	40.9	44.1
Sierra Leone	3,474	2.64	47	43.4	136	46.9	50.2
Togo	2,699	2.98	46	45.7	163	44.4	47.6
Upper Volta	6,908	2.57	25	44.2	182	39.4	42.6

Sources of data. Columns 1, 2, and 4: United Nations, 1979. Columns 3, 6, and 7: United Nations, 1975. Column 5: Haub and Heisler, 1980.

626

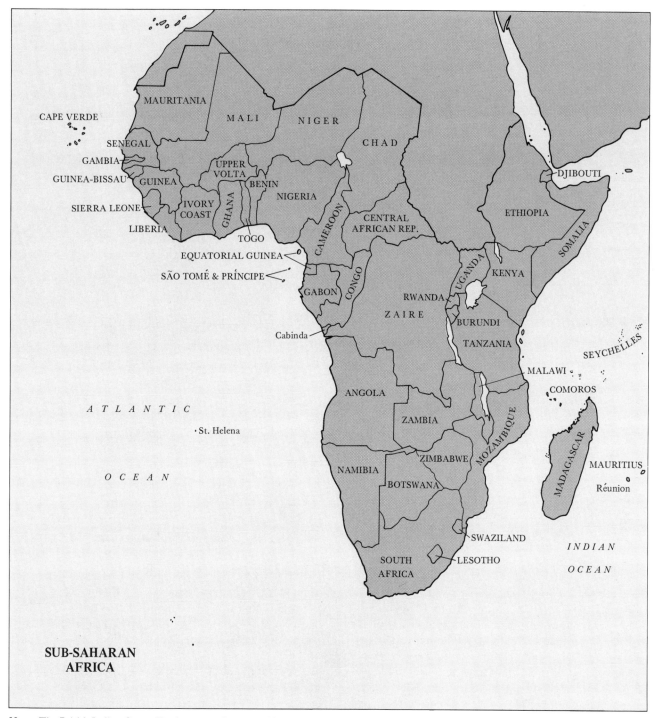

SUB-SAHARAN
AFRICA

NOTE: The British Indian Ocean Territory, not shown on this map, is east of the Seychelles and in 1981 consisted of the group of islands known as the Chagos Archipelago.

Illustrating this situation is Kenya, where in 1977 the estimated crude birth rate was 54 and the crude death rate 14, yielding a rate of natural increase of 4 percent, more than double that of the 1980 worldwide average for less-developed countries, and implying a population that will double in seventeen years (United States, 1980).

(Table 2 figures differ slightly because they are derived from another source.)

Lack of reliable data throughout the region severely impedes the study of demographic trends. Except for small islands such as Mauritius and Réunion, birth registration is very incomplete and death registration proba-

TABLE 2. *Selected mortality, fertility, economic, and educational indicators, sub-Saharan Africa, selected countries*

Subregion and country	(1) Crude birth rate (per 1,000), 1975–1980	(2) Total fertility rate. 1975–1980	(3) Estimated crude death rates (per 1,000) 1950–1955	(4) 1975–1980	(5) GNP per capita, 1979 US$	(6) No. enrolled in primary school as % of age group, 1978[a]	(7) Adult literary rate, 1976[a]
Eastern Africa	*47.6*	*7.1*	*27.8*	*18.3*	—	—	—
Burundi	47.2	6.8	30.5	19.8	$ 180	21%	25%
Ethiopia	49.9	7.3	30.8	24.9	130	38	15
Kenya	50.8	7.9	21.8	12.4	380	99	45
Madagascar	45.0	6.6	30.6	19.0	290	94	50
Malawi	51.1	7.6	31.4	19.1	200	59	25
Mozambique	44.8	6.6	30.1	19.0	250	—	—
Rwanda	49.6	7.5	31.3	19.3	200	64	—
Somalia	48.3	6.6	28.7	20.4	—	44	60
Tanzania	46.3	7.0	25.7	15.8	260	70	66
Uganda	44.8	6.6	23.9	14.4	290	50	—
Zambia	49.2	7.5	28.2	17.2	500	98	39
Zimbabwe	47.3	7.2	22.8	13.6	470	97	—
Middle Africa	*45.1*	*6.5*	*29.4*	*19.6*	—	—	—
Angola (incl. Cabinda)	47.6	6.9	34.4	23.1	440	—	—
Cameroon	42.3	6.1	31.7	19.4	560	101	—
Chad	43.9	6.4	33.4	20.8	110	35	15
Zaire	46.2	6.6	26.3	18.7	260	90	15
Southern Africa	*38.6*	*5.6*	*19.5*	*11.0*	—	—	—
South Africa	37.9	5.5	18.3	10.3	1,720	—	—
Western Africa	*49.0*	*7.3*	*29.6*	*18.8*	—	—	—
Benin	48.8	7.3	30.7	19.1	250	60	—
Ghana	48.4	7.3	28.2	17.2	400	71	—
Guinea	47.1	6.7	31.6	20.7	246	34	20
Ivory Coast	47.6	7.3	30.5	18.3	1,040	71	20
Mali	49.1	7.3	30.5	22.1	140	28	10
Niger	51.4	7.7	31.1	22.4	270	23	8
Nigeria	49.8	7.5	29.0	17.8	670	62	—
Senegal	47.8	7.0	30.9	22.1	430	41	10
Sierra Leone	45.5	6.6	31.1	19.2	250	37	—
Upper Volta	47.8	7.0	30.9	22.1	180	17	—

[a]Data generally are for a variety of years within two years of those specified.
Sources of data. Columns 1, 3, and 4: United Nations, 1979, tables 2-A and 2-B. Column 2: United Nations, 1979; calculations based on table 4. Column 5: World Bank, 1981, table 1. Columns 6 and 7: World Bank, 1981, table 23.

bly even more so. Thus, most observations about African demography are based on limited or old data. Until the 1960s few African countries had taken complete censuses, although in some there is a history of administrative enumerations, or censuses of certain ethnic groups, such as Europeans, or of certain populations, such as urban dwellers. The need for demographic data for national planning purposes soon became evident in the many African countries that gained their independence in the 1960s, and this need coincided with worldwide interest in preparing for the 1974 World Population Year. A 1970s round of censuses was taken, many with financial or technical assistance from the United Nations African Census Programme or from individual countries. A 1980s round of censuses was planned in many countries. Ethiopia and Zaire, two of the largest states in size of population, had yet to take their first census as of 1981. Nigeria, the popu-

lation giant of the region, had no definite date for a new census although it had taken earlier censuses. (For a listing of countries and their census experience or plans during the 1975–1984 decade, see the 1979 *Demographic Yearbook*, p. 3.)

Demographic data for Africa are poor for many reasons. Time trends are generally lacking; age-specific data have been difficult to obtain where birth dates are unknown; tribal groups have been suspicious of attempts to count them; ethnic rivalries have led to double counting in some areas. Some of the concepts that seem important in Western data-gathering cannot be readily translated into local languages. Many censuses and sample surveys that do exist are inadequate because of these factors. Moreover, lack of human and financial resources to carry out censuses and analyze data, poor roads and communications, and unfavorable topography and climate have deterred population counts. Thus, data provided in the accompanying tables are based on expert judgments of available country data, but with few exceptions they are only estimates.

Location and Description. Although sub-Saharan Africa lies entirely within the tropical and subtropical zones, it has great topographic and climatic diversity, ranging from desert, steppe, dry and wooded savannah, and high veld to tropical rainforest and monsoon and temperate subregions.

The area has rich but unevenly distributed mineral resources. Niger has large reserves of uranium; South Africa is the world's largest producer of gold, gem diamonds, and antimony; and Zaire produces two-thirds of the world's cobalt. Nigeria and, to a lesser degree, Gabon are major oil producers and are the sole sub-Saharan members of the Organization of Petroleum Exporting Countries (OPEC). Other principal natural resources include timber and rubber. Ocean and fresh-water fishing and fish processing are major industries in some countries.

The region is largely agricultural; some 264 million (73 percent of the people) are considered rural. Subsistence farming predominates, with shifting cultivation practiced in much of tropical Africa. Staple crops include peanuts (groundnuts), soybeans, rice, maize, and other cereals, cassava, sorghum, and plantain. Many national economies are based on only a few cash crops and little industry and are thus heavily dependent on world market prices as well as on fluctuating weather conditions. Agricultural exports include coffee, cocoa, tea, tobacco, palm products, cotton, sisal, copra, pyrethrum, and gum. Sizable plantations exist in Liberia, Kenya, Tanzania, and Nigeria. Livestock ranching is carried out on a large scale in South Africa, but otherwise much of the region is unsuited to this enterprise because of infestation by the tsetse fly.

Historical Context. Although much of the history of the peoples of sub-Saharan Africa has yet to be reconstructed, it is thought that the human species may have originated there. Three main races developed in the area—Negroid, Khoisan/Hottentot, and Pygmoid—and migrations brought Caucasians and Mongols to northern and eastern Africa as early as the Paleolithic period. Negroid peoples, linguistically classified as Niger-Congo, now dominate the sub-Saharan region; major subgroups speaking Bantu languages pushed the Pygmoid and Khoisan peoples south and nearly eliminated them. Bedouin influences across the Sudanic region in the north, and Arab influences in the east completed the general racial-linguistic picture until the time of European colonial settlement.

Major African empires, including several Sudanic kingdoms, developed in the early centuries A.D., and by the fifteenth century, the city-states of the Guinea coast had been formed, and the Luba-Lunda and Mutapa empires were well organized in the central part of the region. European contacts began in the early fifteenth century, leading to the unsettling demographic effects of the slave trade.

The Atlantic slave trade (estimates in Curtin, 1969) delivered nearly 9.6 million slaves alive into the Americas between 1451 and 1870. Large numbers of Africans were also seized and transported by Arab traders into Zanzibar and to Arab lands in the north. The demographic effects doubtless went beyond the immediate phenomena of forced migration and depleted numbers. Reliable mortality estimates are unavailable (although data are available for certain voyages), but many people undoubtedly died during the raids of the slavers, in captivity, and in transit to the auction block. Since little is known of the sizes of the indigenous African populations, the impact of the slave trade is difficult to place in context. Analysis of the demographic, social, and economic impact of the trade upon African populations has been made but leads to conflicting conclusions. For example, mortality doubtless increased because of diseases carried by Europeans, yet population growth may also have occurred because of the importation of new staple crops that could support larger numbers than previously.

The partition of Africa by European powers was formalized by the 1884 Treaty of Berlin legitimizing spheres of influence established earlier. This treaty set the boundaries for the African nations that became independent after World War II. That the boundaries seldom took into account indigenous linguistic or ethnic patterns remains a prominent factor in current African political, economic, and social life.

With the exception of Dutch and British settlement in the Cape of Good Hope (now South Africa), Rhodesia (now Zimbabwe), and parts of eastern Africa, neither colonial conquests nor more recent migrations led to sizable infusions of nonindigenous peoples, unlike the European migrations into North and South America. South Africa, with about 19 percent of the population classified as whites and Asians in 1976, has the largest proportion of nonindigenous people, followed by Namibia with about 9 percent whites. Nowhere else on the mainland do non-African populations rise above 5 percent, and the proportions for western and middle African countries range from about 0.1 to 1 percent. Despite the post-independence exodus of non-African settlers from many countries, the numbers of non-Africans probably remain about the same in many places because of an increase of temporary foreign residents engaged in business or technical assistance.

Age Composition. The populations of sub-Saharan Africa are young. Estimates for 1975 showed proportions under age 15 ranging from about 40 percent to nearly 50 percent. Only Gabon (at 32.5 percent), Guinea-Bissau (37.3 percent), and Mauritius (37.7 percent) fall below this range, owing to relatively low fertility. The southern African subregion had the lowest estimate at 41.9 percent under age 15. The population momentum that can be expected from the generally high proportions of youth who will enter child-producing years before the end of the century will contribute, other things being equal, to even higher rates of natural increase than now prevail.

Fertility. Fertility is high in sub-Saharan Africa. Estimated 1980 crude birth rates range between 42 and 51 per 1,000 population for most of the region. Exceptions can be found in the traditionally low-fertility area of Gabon (32.7), and in Mauritius and Réunion (25.7 and 24.0, respectively). The Republic of South Africa is also atypical, with the rate estimated at 37.9. The fertility of the black South Africans approximates that of African populations elsewhere, while that of the "Coloured" and Asian populations falls between the high African rates and the lower rates for whites who make up about one-fifth of the populace. Except for southern Africa and several of the islands (notably Réunion and Mauritius), the total fertility rate in the region is thought to exceed six children per woman in many countries, seven in some others, and at least in Kenya to approach eight (see Table 2).

Analyses of survey data from the 1950s, 1960s, and early 1970s by William Brass, Hilary J. Page and Ansley J. Coale, Olukunle Adegbola, and others lead to a better understanding of the variations concealed by these average rates (Brass et al., 1968; Page and Coale, 1972; Adegbola, 1977). Adegbola, who restudied the earlier works and employed refined techniques, found total fertility rates ranging from a low of 2.77 in the Moyen Ogooué region of Gabon (1960–1961), to a high of 9.33 in the Twa area of Rwanda (1970). While he and the other researchers caution using even their careful assessments as anything but plausible estimates, their findings provide a snapshot of the wide variations of fertility found among ethnic groups across the continent. (The key variable is not the ethnic group itself, but the ecological and social conditions in which the group lives.) It has been found that high-, medium-, and low-fertility areas may exist side by side; national averages obscure these often considerable differences.

Recent studies bear out the need to analyze the intermediate determinants of fertility in subgroups of a population in order to clarify the levels that have been observed nationally or in the population as a whole. Page and Lesthaeghe (1981) and their collaborators have amassed considerable evidence on the changing patterns of the components of fertility in Africa (e.g. postpartum amenorrhea, postpartum abstinence) in relation to social, cultural, and economic changes and modernization. They argue that future studies should focus on examining these differentials in the cultural context of a concurrent decline in traditional fertility regulation and the adoption of modern contraceptives.

Throughout the region, high fertility can be explained as a result of African cultural norms, which support large family size. The ideal family size is very large; surveys of knowledge, attitude, and practice (KAP surveys), although evidencing the same intrinsic faults as other African surveys, reveal that urban women on the average desire six or more children, and rural women often seven or more. John C. Caldwell (1975) saw evidence for a recent trend downward among significant portions of urban families (perhaps one-fourth)—greater among elite groups (perhaps one-third)—toward a stated ideal family size of four. In the world context, African fertility remains high and shows little possibility of any early significant decline.

Better fertility data for some countries should be available when results are published for those that have participated in the World Fertility Survey. [*See* WORLD FERTILITY SURVEY.] As of late 1981, Lesotho, Kenya, Benin, Nigeria, Ivory Coast, Cameroon, Ghana, and Senegal had taken part in the survey or were scheduled to do so.

A widespread belt of low fertility extends from the west coast of Gabon and Cameroon through northern Zaire into lower Sudan, and pockets of low fertility are found in western Botswana and parts of Mozambique and Swaziland. Crude birth rates as low as 20 were found in one region of Zaire. Moreover, the proportion of women over 45 who had never conceived ranged up to 45 percent (Romaniuk, 1968). In these and in other areas where women remain childless involuntarily or bear fewer children than are specified by societal norms, infertility is associated with social and economic distress for the woman; it leads to a high probability of divorce and to lack of social security in old age. These conditions have stimulated policy makers and health personnel, especially in the middle African countries of relatively low fertility, to view infertility, not high fertility, as their main priority. In several countries, diagnosis and treatment of infertility are offered by maternal and child health and family planning programs.

If women in many parts of the sub-Sahara region who are less fecund than average were able to give birth to the number of children they desire, the region's already high fertility would rise substantially.

Marriage Patterns and Related Cultural Practices. Considerable heterogeneity exists throughout the region in all aspects of family and social structure that have bearing on fertility. These include inheritance patterns (matrilineal or patrilineal), residence patterns (matrilocal or patrilocal, extended or nuclear), and role differentiation by sex and age. Social practices such as age at marriage, duration of breastfeeding, postnatal sexual abstinence, and child rearing also vary considerably.

The dominant marriage patterns are the universal and early marriage of females, widespread polygyny, and high rates of separation and divorce. Statistics on marriage and on age at marriage are poor, but an analysis of available data for the region suggests that about 55 percent of women aged 15–19 are married. [*See* AGE AT MARRIAGE.] Anatole Romaniuk (1968) noted that the most commonly observed average age at first marriage was approximately 16 years for females. Population Reference Bureau 1980 estimates indicate this low age only in a few Sahelian countries (Mali, Niger, Chad), with 17 indicated for Upper Volta and Togo. Rather high average ages at first marriage seem to occur in Kenya, Congo, Lesotho, and several other countries, reaching 25 in Botswana (perhaps caused in part by migration of men for employment in South Africa).

Age at marriage of females in the Muslim areas appears to be lower than elsewhere. There, in polygynous unions, young women are married to men often ten or more years older than they. Anecdotal and anthropological evidence points to girls as young as 12 being affianced or married in some Muslim Sahelian countries. In these areas as elsewhere in much of traditional Africa, most young women are "circumcised" (the medical term varies according to the procedure used); scarification and infection, which can result, may affect their ability to bear live children and may contribute to maternal mortality and morbidity. Additionally, where poor nutrition and childbearing in early adolescence occur together, obstetrical problems can lead to gynecological problems that result in secondary sterility and may contribute to divorce.

Separation and divorce are common in Africa, and have long been so, according to studies of many traditional tribal cultures. Temporary separation after the birth of a child is common, with the wife usually returning to her family home until the child is weaned, generally a period of twelve to thirty-six months. Although this pattern is breaking down with the effects of modernization and urbanization, it is still common. Subfecundity, whether inability to bear a first child or, in some instances, subsequent children, may be grounds for divorce. In many traditional cultures, marriage cannot be formalized until a woman has proven her fertility by bearing a child. Usually the woman is thought to be the one who is infertile, or her inability to conceive may be attributed to spiritual forces frowning on the marriage.

Mortality. Mortality data for the region are considerably poorer than fertility data, with gross underregistration everywhere except in the small islands and for the white populations of Zimbabwe and South Africa. It is known, however, that mortality rates are higher in the region than in any other world region. They were estimated for 1978 by the U.S. Census Bureau at about 18–20 per 1,000 population for eastern Africa, 19–21 for middle Africa, and 18–21 for western Africa. Only in southern Africa does the rate approach the world average, estimated at around 11–12 deaths per 1,000 population.

Table 2 shows estimated crude death rates for selected countries for two periods, 1950–1955 and 1975–1980. It is probable that a constant although relatively slower decline in mortality has occurred in the region as compared with the rest of the developing world; however, the age-specific pattern of the decline and therefore its magnitude have been questioned by some investigators. Caldwell (1975) points out that data from certain studies show "enormously high toddler mortality . . . [which] might well make any external life tables unusable" for preparation of African projections. (Most population projections for Africa assume declining mortality to the extent that expectation of life at birth increases by one-half year every year. They do not take into account that age-specific mortality rates in much of Africa may not conform to the model life tables because of the higher mortality in the 1–3 age group.)

Infant mortality in the region was estimated for 1980 to range from a low of 35 deaths per 1,000 live births in Mauritius to a high of more than 200 deaths per 1,000 live births in Gambia (see Table 1). The extremely high infant mortality rate (IMR) remaining in most countries compares unfavorably with average IMR's of 20 in developed countries worldwide. Using data for varying years between 1950 and 1971 for twenty-seven countries, Adegbola (1977), in a refinement of Page and Coale's estimates of infant and child mortality, found IMR's ranging from 78 in the Kinshasa province of Zaire (1957) to 356 in the Twa area of Rwanda (1970). Moreover, he found strikingly different rates within countries, even for adjacent territories.

Life Expectancy. In comparison with other world regions, sub-Saharan Africa has the lowest life expectancy at birth. Life expectancy there has not risen so fast as in Latin America, for example; nevertheless, it is thought to have increased by about ten to twelve years between 1950–1955 and 1975–1980, varying somewhat by subregion. Life expectancy is approaching 50 throughout most of the region, and exceeds that in South Africa, where it is close to 59 for men and 62 for women (see Table 1). The average subregional figures obscure substantial differences among countries. In Ethiopia, 1980 life expectancy at birth for men was thought to be only 39.4, and for women 42.6, while in Nigeria, the figures were 44.4 and 47.6, respectively.

Estimates should be regarded with caution, however, and subnational differentials may be considerable. For example, the long Sahelian drought and subsequent famine in the 1970s can be presumed to have adversely affected the area's inhabitants at least in the short term, with the likelihood that excessive deaths have occurred particularly among infants and children but also among the aged. Although recovery to the prefamine levels is expected, and death rates are expected to fall by the end of the century, such conditions as famine and war will change life expectancy estimates for affected populations.

It should be noted as well that the difference between female and male life expectancy at birth in sub-Saharan Africa, about three years, is considerably less than that in industrial, developed countries, where there is an average difference of five to eight years in favor of females. Preferential treatment of male children may account for this in some areas. Male mortality still exceeds female mortality at young ages, but a reversal may occur with maternal mortality and higher female death rates during the reproductive years.

Migration. Although migrations on a substantial scale preceded European colonization, migration within sub-Saharan Africa follows in general the pattern laid out in early colonial times. Other than Europeans, early migrants from outside the continent included Indians into eastern and southern Africa, who were originally brought by the Europeans as laborers. The Dutch brought slaves from their eastern possessions to South Africa. Some 50,000 Chinese impressed laborers were imported into South Africa in 1904 to work the mines. Small but economically active groups of Greeks and of Arab-speaking settlers from Lebanon, Syria, and other West Asian countries became shopkeepers and traders in western Africa.

The migratory movements have been from north to south, and from the inland to the coastal zones, toward the plantations, mines, and towns established by the Europeans. Colonial powers instituted compulsory measures to move African labor to areas where it was needed; heavy taxes that had to be paid in cash compelled further migration for work in the European enterprises. But the terms of the labor contracts and regulations on the place and length of residence were formulated to control the numbers of Africans in European regions, and they prevented migration of families and permanent settlement. These policies still prevail in South Africa and Namibia, where only limited numbers of black Africans are allowed to reside in cities; otherwise they are restricted to black townships and to tribal "homelands." Most of the labor migration was cyclical, with periods of time varying from months to several years spent in wage labor, alternating with return to the home villages and subsistence farms. By the 1930s the supply of voluntary labor had increased, and the great Depression halted most construction projects, resulting in the practical cessation of an international demand for forced labor.

The cyclical, or oscillating, pattern of migration persists in many areas; but accelerated, more permanent migrations out of rural areas since independence have brought about rapid urban growth, causing the governments of several countries to formulate policies to stem the flow from the rural areas. A relatively free movement across colonial frontiers has been somewhat curtailed since independence, but interterritorial migrations are still substantial. Estimates of total labor migrations across frontiers were about 1.25 million in the 1960s, more than 25 percent of the labor force. Among the countries that experienced population outflow, Togo around 1960 had about 12.5 percent of its total population living outside the country, mostly in Ghana. Mozambique, Lesotho, and Botswana export labor. South Africa imports, and most of the other countries do both. Upper Volta is the largest supplier of migrant labor to southern Ghana and to southern and central Ivory Coast. East-west migrations include the Ibo movement into southwestern Nigeria and seasonal migrations from Mali into Senegal and Gambia.

Good data on migration and foreign residence remain elusive, although most recent censuses are designed to provide this information. Because of long, permeable land borders in most but the island countries, immigration departments can usually only count arrivals by air and by sea.

Refugee movements within and across national boundaries and flight from Sahelian droughts and from infestation of disease in some areas have uprooted large numbers of Africans. Political factors caused the flight or expulsion of Asians or nonlocal African populations, or both, from several countries. For example, Ghana expelled about 200,000 aliens from neighboring states and Nigeria in 1965–1970; and Uganda expelled 80,000 Asians in 1971: Ivory Coast (1959, 1966), Kenya (1968–1969), and Zaire (1964) also expelled aliens.

Sub-Saharan Africa has the largest proportion of refugees and displaced persons of any world region, with nearly 5 million estimated in 1980, up from about three-quarters of a million in 1970. Countries of origin of refugees in 1980 were Angola, Burundi, Chad, Equatorial Guinea, Ethiopia, Lesotho, Namibia, Rwanda, South Africa, Sudan, Tanzania, Uganda, Zaire, and Zimbabwe. Ethiopia alone accounted for about half of the total in 1980. Refugees were temporarily settled in twenty-two countries. The main refugee problem in numbers was in the Horn of Africa. Somalia, Ethiopia's neighbor to the southeast, alone had more than 1.5 million registered refugees. Sudan, Ethiopia's western neighbor (considered by United Nations classification to be in North Africa), hosted approximately another half million.

Colonization or resettlement schemes have been attempted to alter the distribution of the population in the interest of economic development. In Ghana, for example, new lands were opened for agriculture through the Volta Dam irrigation program; Kenya's government bought and expropriated large pieces of land especially from white settlers and subdivided them for sale to indigenous colonists; and in Tanzania, scattered farmers have been clustered in villages to promote social and economic development.

The importance of women in agricultural production in much of the region tends to keep them in the rural areas, but there is some recent increase in female migration to the cities, which may be partially the result of changing attitudes toward the role of women. The long prominence of women in urban marketing and retail trade in the Ivory Coast, for instance, appears to encourage female migration. In general, however, young males predominate in the rural-urban movement, as well as in the seasonal rural-rural migrations.

The separation of husband and wife for long periods, as required by cyclical migration, and the disproportionate removal of the population of reproductive age from rural areas are thought to be responsible for lower fertility rates in certain parts of Africa. The repeated return of the migrants and the kinship linking city dwellers and those in farm communities have contributed to social and economic changes, particularly the introduction of the technology and capital for cash cropping and the development of cash retail trade. But the major change associated with migrations today is the rapid growth of the African cities. An important migratory stream in the post–World War II period has been the exodus of the African educated elite, from their home nations to other nations and from Africa to Europe and North America. Another significant, long-term stream has been the pilgrimage of Muslims to Mecca along land routes; the trip sometimes takes years and is broken by periods of settlement. Finally, the nomadic herders of the Sahel, eastern Africa, and southern Africa continue to cross national borders in a seasonal pattern.

Urbanization. Sub-Saharan Africa remains the least urbanized region on earth, despite long histories of cities in some areas. Subregional differences in levels of urbanization by country and within country are considerable. In western Nigeria, people have long resided in towns of substantial size and farmed the surrounding areas, while in large parts of the Sahel the only settlements are the small and temporary ones of nomadic groups of herders.

In 1950 no sub-Saharan city had yet reached 1 million population. Except for the industrial South African cities, Accra (Gold Coast, now Ghana), at 277,000, and Dakar (Senegal), the capital of French West Africa at 260,000, were possibly the largest cities. By 1980, fifteen cities had exceeded the 1 million figure, the largest being Kinshasa, Zaire, and Lagos, Nigeria. Of these, several are expected to double their size during the 1980s and fifteen more are expected to join the ranks of those with 1 million people. According to United Nations estimates, Kinshasa is expected to exceed 5 million, Lagos to exceed 4 million, and Addis Ababa to exceed 3 million by 1990. The Nigerian government, however, estimated that the Lagos metropolitan area already contained 4.5 million in 1980.

In the 1960s and 1970s the regional annual rate of urban growth was estimated at around 5 percent. In western Africa, coastal cities such as Accra and Abidjan exceeded this figure, and Sahelian cities were thought to have had relatively higher rates of growth. In the Sahel, the growth resulted from administrative concentration of power but also from the pressures of drought and famine, which forced nomadic peoples such as the Tuareg into settlements to obtain food and water.

By 1980, the percentage of population in urban areas was estimated as follows: eastern Africa, 16 percent; middle Africa, 34 percent; southern Africa, 46 percent; and western Africa, 22 percent. These figures were, for the most part, lower than the world urban population, estimated to be 41 percent. Important differences between countries were obscured by the subregional percentages: Burundi, 2; Rwanda and Lesotho, 4; Nigeria, 20; Zaire, 40; Mauritius, 52; and Réunion, 54 (United Nations, 1980). As with other African data, these estimates should be interpreted with caution, since definitions of urban population differ from place to place; for example, some countries count towns of 2,000 and others count towns of 5,000 as urban.

Throughout the subcontinent, as in much of the developing world, employment and income opportunities in the modern sector, schools, health facilities, clean piped water, and government social services all tend to be concentrated in urban places. Given the relative wealth of the cities and the deprived circumstances of most rural communities, the cities can be expected to remain magnets for rural migrants.

Literacy and Education. Adult literacy remains low throughout the region, although that in English-speaking eastern African countries tends to be higher than elsewhere. Several countries, most notably Ethiopia, have ambitious campaigns against adult illiteracy. Adult literacy rates and primary school enrollment rates for countries with populations of 1 million or more can be found in Table 2. Wide variations occur in primary school enrollment. A few countries approach near-universal rates. In more than one-third of the countries, however, fewer than half of those of primary school age were in school in the mid to late 1970s.

Enrollment rates at the secondary school level ranged from 5 percent or less (in Upper Volta, Rwanda, Chad, Somalia, Burundi, Malawi, Tanzania, Niger, Uganda, and Mauritania) to 25 percent in Togo, 32 percent in Ghana, and reportedly 69 percent in Congo (although the Congolese figure is improbable). Those enrolled in higher education throughout the region generally numbered less than 1 to only 3 percent of the population aged 20–24. By contrast, comparable enrollment in higher education in industrialized countries ranges from an average of 21 percent in the nonmarket (centrally planned) economy countries, to 37 percent in the market economy countries (World Bank, 1981, table 23).

Economic Development. Twenty-three sub-Saharan countries rank among the thirty-seven countries worldwide designated by the World Bank as having "low income," that is, those with gross national product (GNP) per capita at US$370 or less for 1979. Another nine have per capita income under $700; and only South Africa (at $1,720) lies in the upper range of middle-income countries. (The World Bank provides no data for countries with populations under 1 million.) While South African whites enjoy a "developed" economy, most of the blacks in that country live in poverty, with the Asians and "coloureds" falling somewhere between. Income is unevenly shared in most other sub-Saharan countries as well, so that GNP per capita figures do not mean that most people receive approximately those amounts. Elite groups may be quite wealthy, while the masses of people remain on the fringes of the money economy.

These very low levels of GNP per capita also cannot be said to measure accurately productivity in African countries. Much of the subsistence output, especially food production, is not measured since the product does not enter into national statistics even when sold in a local marketplace. Hence the work, chiefly of African women, who are responsible in most societies for home gardening and the processing, storage, and preparation of food, is not measured as contributing to the national economy. In Lesotho, where men contract as migrant laborers in South Africa for periods of up to two years, many women are solely responsible for maintaining the children, disabled, and elderly, on the basis of their own production and remittances from the men.

A bleak economic picture is predicted by the World Bank for most of sub-Saharan Africa. The bank projects

that under any but the most favorable circumstances, people in the region will be poorer in 1990 than in 1980. The only exceptions may be the few countries that do not depend on oil imports for their energy. Many countries are expected to have economic growth rates of only about 1.8 to 2.4 percent and to experience real declines as population growth outstrips economic growth. In the 1960–1977 period, some of the hardest hit of the poor countries, notably Somalia, Chad, Niger, Madagascar, Ghana, and Senegal, actually experienced declines in GNP per capita, although a few countries' growth rates exceeded 3 percent. Most countries experienced declines in per capita food production between 1969 to 1977, with only a few showing more than modest achievement. Moreover, annual rates of inflation exceeded 10 percent in many countries in the period 1970–1977. The consequences of all this are that few countries will have investment capital to modernize or to improve human services, and many will have to rely on foreign assistance just to maintain the status quo.

Statements and Actions on Population Matters. Explicit government population policies in sub-Saharan Africa are for the most part concerned with reversing flows of rural to urban migration, adjusting urban and rural configurations, dealing with refugee problems, and reducing the high mortality rates. In many countries underpopulation and infertility have caused greater concern than high growth rates. Except in a few countries, governments perceive that growth rates, many among the highest in the world, are presently acceptable. In Kenya, Ghana, Rwanda, Botswana, Lesotho, and Senegal, rates of natural increase and fertility are seen as creating constraints for economic development. However, the Central African Republic, Chad, and Cameroon desire larger populations; among these, the Central African Republic views its population growth rate and fertility rate as too low.

The government of Ghana has developed a strategy of "Growth Poles," to transform characteristically rural regions into a rural-urban continuum; the government's 1973–1978 plan further stipulates a target of reducing the population growth rate from about 3.9 percent in 1970 to 1.8 percent in 2000. Kenya also has an ambitious, demographically oriented program to reduce population growth. However, policies to reduce fertility have had little demographic effect except in Mauritius and Réunion.

Family planning programs have been slow to develop in the region. Historically, English-speaking countries offered family planning services through voluntary private associations before these were available in French-speaking or Portuguese-speaking countries. These colonially influenced differences are now reduced in importance, as increasing support is given in most countries for family planning as an important component of maternal and child health. Ghana and Kenya have nationwide programs, and family planning services are at least nominally available in the rest of the English-speaking countries except for Malawi. Increasingly the French-speaking countries have begun to support the concept of family planning services in the context of maternal and child health, and several have inaugurated pilot family planning projects. Among Portuguese-speaking countries, Mozambique has begun to offer family planning services, but Angola and Guinea-Bissau have not.

Scholarly Activities. The teaching of demography and population expanded greatly in African universities during the 1960s and 1970s, but they started from a low base in 1960. By 1974, at least twenty-five offered population courses in departments of sociology, economics, or geography. Postgraduate training in demography is offered at the universities of Ghana, Dar es Salaam, and Nairobi and in five Nigerian universities [see NIGERIA]. In French-speaking countries, demographic training generally takes place in specialized institutes outside the university program, although the National University of Zaire offers a two-year licentiate degree in demography. The African and Mauritian Institute of Statistics and Applied Economics (IAMSEA) in Rwanda, conducting training and research in French, and the Institute of Statistics and Applied Economics in Kampala, working in English, are regional in character. The French government continues to supply funds for branches of the Office de la Recherche Scientifique et Technique d'Outre-Mer (ORSTOM) in several countries for demographic and other research. Little demographic training occurs in the Portuguese-speaking countries.

The United Nations organized two subregional demographic training centers in the early 1970s: the Regional Institute of Population Studies (RIPS) in Legon, Ghana, which trains in English, and the Regional Institute for Demographic Research (IFORD) in Yaoundé, Cameroon, which trains in French. RIPS publishes the *RIPS Newsletter, African Demography,* and *PIDSA Abstracts* (Population Information and Documentation System for Africa); IFORD publishes *Annales de l'IFORD, Bulletin de liaison,* and *African Population.* Multidisciplinary population studies programs have been organized at the University of Nairobi and the University of Ghana. The Institut du Sahel in Bamako, Mali, also carries out demographic research.

The Population and Statistics divisions of the United Nations Economic Commission for Africa have regional advisory services in the areas of population censuses and surveys. The Statistics Division provides assistance in census planning, data collection, and data processing, while the Population Division assists in the analysis of data. Both have been actively involved in the African Census Programme for the 1970s and 1980s rounds. Publications of the Population Division include the *Demographic Handbook for Africa* (1978), the periodic *African Population Newsletter,* the African Population Studies Series, and papers of the First Joint Conference of African Planners, Statisticians, and Demographers (1980). The joint conference was established by the Conference of Ministers of the Economic Commission for Africa to foster integration of population with development planning.

The Population Association of Africa (PASAF) held its inaugural conference at the University of Ibadan, Nigeria, in 1974. It is open to both African and non-African specialists. Its main journal, *Jimlar mutane,* has appeared occasionally since May 1976. The working languages of PASAF are English and French.

The sub-Saharan region has been the focus of research by many non-African demographers; numerous interested institutions in Europe, the United States, and Australia carry out cooperative research with African collaborators and provide training abroad for African scholars. Important ongoing research activities include the 1980 round of censuses and African Household Survey Capability Programme, assisted by the United Nations, and the World Fertility Survey.

Jeanne Betsock Stillman

BIBLIOGRAPHY

Adegbola, Olukunle. "New Estimates of Fertility and Child Mortality in Africa, South of the Sahara." *Population Studies* 31(3):467–486, November 1977.

Brass, William, Ansley J. Coale, Paul Demeny, Donald F. Heisel, Frank Lorimer, Anatole Romaniuk, and Etienne van de Walle. *The Demography of Tropical Africa.* Princeton, N.J.: Princeton University Press, 1968.

Caldwell, John C. (editor), and Nelson O. Addo, Samuel K. Gaisie, Adenola A. Igun, and P. O. Olusanya. *Population Growth and Socioeconomic Change in West Africa.* A Population Council Book. New York: Columbia University Press, 1975.

Caldwell, John C., and Chukuka Okonjo (editors). *The Population of Tropical Africa.* New York: Columbia University Press, 1968.

Cantrelle, Pierre (editor), and Ahmed M. Bahri, John Blacker, Robert Blanc, William Brass, Kweku T. de Graft-Johnson, James Greig, Léon Tabah, and Bruno Remiche. *Population in African Development.* 2 vols. Dolhain, Belgium: Ordina Editions, 1974.

Curtin, Philip D. *The Atlantic Slave Trade: A Census.* Madison: University of Wisconsin Press, 1969.

Hance, William A. *Population, Migration, and Urbanization in Africa.* New York: Columbia University Press, 1970.

Haub, Carl, and Douglas W. Heisler. "1980 World Population Data Sheet of the Population Reference Bureau." Washington, D.C.: Population Reference Bureau, 1980.

Haupt, Arthur. "The Sub-Saharan Region: Africa Faces New Population Challenges." *Intercom* 8(5):1,12–15, May 1980.

International Review Group of Social Science Research on Population and Development, El Colegio de México. *Social Science Research for Population Policy: Directions for the 1980s.* Mexico City, June 1979.

Page, Hilary J., and Ansley J. Coale. "Fertility and Child Mortality South of the Sahara." In *Population Growth and Economic Development in Africa,* edited by S. H. Ominde and C. N. Ejiogu, pp. 51–66. London: Heinemann, 1972.

Page, Hilary J., and Ron Lesthaege (editors). *Child-spacing in Tropical Africa: Traditions and Change.* New York and London: Academic Press, 1981.

Romaniuk, Anatole. "Infertility in Tropical Africa." In *The Population of Tropical Africa,* edited by John C. Caldwell and Chukula Okonjo, pp. 214–224. New York: Columbia University Press, 1968.

United Nations, Department of Economic and Social Affairs. "Selected World Demographic Indicators by Countries, 1950–2000." Population Working Paper No. 55. New York, 28 May 1975.

United Nations, Department of International Economic and Social Affairs. *World Population Trends and Prospects by Country, 1950–2000: Summary Report of the 1978 Assessment.* Series R, no. 33. New York, 1979.

————. *Demographic Yearbook, 1979.* Series R, no. 9. New York, 1980. In English and French. (United Nations, 1980*a*)

————. *Patterns of Urban and Rural Population Growth.* Series A, Population Studies, no. 68. New York, 1980. (United Nations, 1980*b*)

United Nations, Economic Commission for Africa. *Demographic Handbook for Africa, 1978.* Addis Ababa, November 1979. In English and French.

United Nations High Commissioner for Refugees. *Refugees in Africa: A Country by Country Survey.* New York: United Nations, 1981.

United States, Bureau of the Census. *World Population 1979: Recent Demographic Estimates for the Countries and Regions of the World.* Washington, D.C.: U.S. Government Printing Office, 1980.

World Bank. *World Development Report, 1981.* Washington, D.C., August 1981.

Zachariah, K. C., and Julien Condé. *Migration in West Africa: Demographic Aspects.* New York and London: Oxford University Press, 1981.

SURVEYS

See Data collection, *articles on* national systems *and* united states census; Family planning research; Sampling methods; World fertility survey.

THEORY, DEMOGRAPHIC TRANSITION

See Demographic transition theory.

THEORY, ECONOMIC

See Fertility determinants, *article on* sociological and economic theories.

THEORY, SOCIOLOGICAL

See Fertility determinants, *article on* sociological and economic theories.

THRESHOLD HYPOTHESIS

See Fertility decline, *article on* threshold hypothesis.

TRAINING

See Education.

TRANSITION, DEMOGRAPHIC

See Demographic transition theory.

UNION OF SOVIET SOCIALIST REPUBLICS

See Soviet union.

UNITED NATIONS

The United Nations began its population activities as early as 1946, when the Population Commission was established as a functional part of the Economic and Social Council. The Commission, which meets every two years, consists of twenty-seven representatives of Member States of the United Nations. These are elected by the Economic and Social Council for a term of four years on the basis of equitable geographic distribution and balance in representing the various disciplines covered by the Commission's work. The distribution of seats is as follows: African States, seven members; Asian States, five members; Latin American States, five members; Socialist States of Eastern Europe, three members; Western European and Other States, seven members.

The Population Commission advises the Economic and Social Council on (1) the size and structure of populations and the changes therein; (2) the interplay of demographic factors and economic and social factors; (3) policies designed to influence the size and structure of populations and the changes therein; and (4) any other demographic questions on which either the principal or the subsidiary organs of the United Nations or the specialized agencies may seek advice.

After the 1974 World Population Conference the Commission's mandate was widened: (1) to examine on a biennial basis the results of the continuous process of monitoring the World Population Plan of Action and to bring its findings to the attention of the Council; and (2) to contribute, within its competence, advice for the comprehensive review and appraisal of the progress made toward achieving the goals and recommendations of the World Population Plan of Action and to report its findings to the Council.

Historical Background. In its early years the United Nations was mainly concerned with supplying and interpreting facts on population to United Nations agencies and to governments for use in planning for economic and social development. Because adequate data were lacking for large parts of the world, efforts were at first focused on the improvement of demographic statistics. As the supply and quality of statistical data improved, the United Nations became increasingly concerned with the application of statistical data in analytical studies, and was the pioneer in the preparation of population estimates and projections on a worldwide basis, and in the preparation of technical manuals on demographic methods that could be useful in demographic evaluation and analysis of data, especially in those parts of the world where required data were inadequate or defective.

The 1950s saw the spectacular emergence of new trends in population growth, which were subsequently confirmed by the population censuses taken around 1960. The rate of growth of the world's population, which in the first half of the century had been less than 1 percent annually, doubled to average nearly 2 percent annually in the period between 1950 and 1970. The impact of population growth was far greater, however, in the developing regions of the world where the annual growth rate of population, which had averaged 0.8 percent in the years before 1950, suddenly jumped to 2.2 percent. In the 1960s, with increasing recognition of the implications of these trends for economic and social development, many governments began to consider policies designed to moderate population growth and population matters became a subject for debate in various legislative bodies of the United Nations system.

The role of the United Nations in this field was reviewed and, upon the recommendation of the Population Commission at its thirteenth session in 1965, the Economic and Social Council recommended that the United Nations and its specialized agencies take a more active role in developing population programs, widening the scope of available assistance to governments in all aspects of population questions, including training, collection of basic statistics, research, and action programs.

The United Nations study *World Population Prospects as Assessed in 1963*, published in 1966, drew global attention to the projected acceleration in population growth. (Similar reports on world population prospects are prepared regularly.) Increased awareness of population problems in general and of the need for action by the international community to harmonize trends in population and resources led to a full-scale debate on population problems in the General Assembly at its twenty-first session. Resolution 2211 (XXI), unanimously adopted on 17 December 1966, gave new impetus to the United Nations work on population questions with the emphasis shifting to action-oriented programs. The United Nations Fund for Population Activities (UNFPA) was established in 1967 to allow the United Nations system to broaden its work in the field of population and to expand technical cooperation in such programs.

The World Population Conference held at Bucharest, Romania, in August 1974 marked another turning point in the work of the United Nations in population matters. It was the first global, intergovernmental conference on population convened by the United Nations. (Until then the United Nations had held scientific meetings attended by population experts.) Population questions were considered in a political and developmental context by the 136 States participating. A World Population Plan of Action and other recommendations were adopted by consensus, and these provided a basis for further expansion of the work of the United Nations to allow more specifically for types of analysis that would help governments take demographic factors into account when planning for development.

Following the 1974 Conference, the United Nations reoriented its work program to give greater emphasis to studies designed to promote a clearer understanding of the complex interactions between demographic and socio-economic variables. The study of traditional subjects (fertility, mortality, and migration) was related more closely to development and such factors as food, natural resources, environment, habitat, employment, education, health, income, and consumption came to be included in population studies.

Population Program. The aims of the United Nations population program, reflecting the views of governments and the guidance given by the legislative bodies of the United Nations, are to provide governments, United Nations bodies, institutions, and research workers with analyses of current world population trends and policies, comprehensive demographic estimates and projections, analyses of the relationships between population and socioeconomic development, and review and appraisal of the World Population Plan of Action. The population program also is intended to provide technical assistance (advisory services, training, equipment, etc.) to governments which request it in dealing with their population problems.

At United Nations Headquarters, the Population Division of the Department of International Economic and Social Affairs and the Population Programmes and Projects Branch of the Department of Technical Co-operation for Development carry out the above activities in collaboration with other offices working in population-related areas, such as the Statistical Office, the Office for Development Research and Policy Analysis, the Centre for Social Development and Humanitarian Affairs, as well as with the regional commissions and the specialized agencies. Close collaboration is also maintained with many intergovernmental and nongovernmental organizations with activities in population.

Research. The research program of the United Nations, carried out by the Population Division, is designed to reflect the recognition that population is at the core of the total development process and that solutions to problems involving population growth, structure, fertility, mortality, migration, and urbanization can be found only by understanding and intervening in the relationship between these variables and social and economic development factors.

The Population Division therefore carries out studies on levels and trends of mortality, model life tables, urban and rural population distribution, and demographic aspects of internal and international migration, including volume, trends, and characteristics of migrants. *Trends and Characteristics of International Migration since 1950* dealing with the volume of international migration during the period 1950–1974 was published by the Division in 1979.

A study on levels and trends of mortality, carried out in collaboration with the World Health Organization, was published in 1981. *Patterns of Urban and Rural Population Growth* (1980) documents and interprets the post–World War II history of population change in areas classified as rural and urban.

The Population Division also carries out studies on levels and trends of fertility, the relationship between fertility and other demographic, social, and economic phenomena; on the economic and demographic factors affecting family planning programs; and on methods of measuring the impact of family planning programs on fertility. A comparative analysis of data on the knowledge, attitude, and practice (KAP) of contraception of women in twelve countries of Asia, Africa, and Latin America appeared as *Factors Affecting the Use and Non-use of Contraception* (1979). Comparative analyses at the global and interregional levels of World Fertility Survey data are undertaken by the Division, which also has the role of guiding the program of comparative analysis of WFS data carried out by the regional commissions and the specialized agencies.

In response to the 1974 Conference, the Population Division also analyzes the social and economic consequences of population trends and structure, reviews and appraises population and development models, and carries out studies on income growth and distribution and the relationships among population, resources, environment, and development. The work program includes the preparation of a manual on the integration of demographic factors in development planning, covering such aspects as population, consumption, and production, population and regional planning, and population and sectoral planning.

Population projections prepared by the Population Division are regarded worldwide as a valuable tool for demographic and economic analysis. These projections are internationally comparable and cover every country and territory of the world. Their methods, assumptions, and basic demographic parameters are presented uniformly and are used as official projections by the more than two-thirds of the countries of the world that have never prepared official projections of their own.

In order to assist governments to formulate, implement, and evaluate population policies, the Population Division maintains a population policy data bank, carries out research on the translation of population policies into measures and programs, and provides case studies of political and administrative institutions responsible for the formulation and implementation of population policy. The Division issues a series of reports, by country, entitled "National Experience in the Formulation and Implementation of Population Policy" and also publishes, jointly with the UNFPA, the "Population Policy Compendium," a series of pamphlets giving condensed information for each country's basic demographic data, some nondemographic indicators, and major governmental policies with regard to population.

The monitoring of world population trends, carried out every two years in cooperation with the regional commissions and the specialized agencies, covers the basic demographic variables, namely population growth, mortality, fertility, migration, urbanization, and structural aspects including sex, age, labor-force participation, and groups of special social and economic significance. Some of the more general and interdisciplinary aspects, such as population and food and population and education, have also been included. The monitoring of population policies includes analysis of governmental perceptions and policies with respect to population growth, mortality, fertility, spatial distribution, and international migration.

The first quinquennial review and appraisal of the World Population Plan of Action was undertaken in 1979. The evolution of policies and programs regarding population since the 1974 Conference was examined and attention was given to some key social and economic topics such as education, food, employment, income distribution, and the status of women, resulting in recommendations for action to enhance the effectiveness of the Plan of Action.

As an integral part of its research activities the Population Division provides a forum for discussion of population problems by organizing technical meetings and conferences for exchange of information between groups of specialists or among government officials. Most notable of these, other than the 1974 Conference in Bucharest, were the first and second World Population Conferences held in 1954 and 1965 in Rome and Belgrade, respectively. *Ad hoc* groups of experts, international seminars, and workshops are also convened to discuss various aspects of the work program.

The main results of the research work are published for wide dissemination. The Division's pioneering study, *The Determinants and Consequences of Population Trends,* summarizing the state of knowledge and hypotheses concerning the factors affecting population trends and the influence of these trends on economic and social conditions, was first published in 1953. A 1973 revision of this study, *The Determinants and Consequences of Population Trends: New Summary of Findings on Interaction of Demographic, Economic, and Social Factors,* was distilled from some seven thousand sources in many languages to synthesize the findings of major research on population change throughout the world and on its economic and social correlates.

The United Nations has made significant contributions to the field of demography in the development of model life tables, methodology for evaluation and adjustment of data, population projections, and derivation of basic demographic measures for developing countries, particularly in the use of incomplete and defective data. In addition to the reports on the biennial monitoring of population trends and policies and the quinquennial review and appraisal of the World Population Plan of Action, numerous analytical studies on mortality, fertility, urbanization, migration, and population policies have also been published.

The *Population Bulletin of the United Nations,* published twice a year, presents brief articles selected to meet the interests and needs of governments, international organizations, research institutions, and individuals engaged in social and economic research, as well as the public interested in population matters. Contributions come from other bodies of the United Nations system as well as from scholars.

The Division also issues the *Population Newsletter* twice a year, to disseminate information on program activities of the Population Division and on actions of those legislative bodies of the United Nations having competence in the field of population.

Recognizing the importance of the dissemination and exchange of population information as a major means of strengthening the capacity of countries to deal with their population problems, the United Nations established in 1981 an international population information network (POPIN) as a decentralized network of libraries, clearinghouses, and documentation and information centers to improve the flow of population information.

Technical Cooperation. The 1974 World Population Conference recommended that the United Nations pay particular attention to helping developing countries reinforce their technical capacities in the population field. The United Nations technical cooperation program in population is designed to further self-sufficiency among developing countries in dealing with population matters and in giving full attention to demographic factors in their social and economic planning. This is achieved by three principal means.

1. The program gives direct assistance (advisers, consultants, experts, equipment, and other services) to countries for their national research on population dynamics, including analysis of population census and demographic survey data, population studies, and demographic evaluation of family planning programs. Such direct assistance is also given for building up national capacities to carry out analytical research studies, which are essential for the incorporation of population factors in programs of development planning.

2. The program provides direct assistance for establishing or strengthening national policy-making institutions such as population commissions or councils, which will be responsible for the formulation of population policies (such as national family planning programs and internal migration and human settlement programs). It also assists countries in implementing such policies as a means of improving economic and social development planning and in evaluating their impact on national demographic conditions.

3. Finally, the program offers training in the population disciplines, at United Nations–supported training institutions, in seminars, at institutions abroad, and through assistance for the development of national population training facilities (e.g., demographic units in universities).

The World Population Conference in 1954 recommended that regional training and research centers be established, that teams of demographers be assigned in specified countries and regions, and that the centers—although international—be adapted to regional needs and be of an interdisciplinary nature. Six United Nations–sponsored training centers now give basic courses at the graduate level, as well as advanced courses. The centers are the International Institute for Population Studies (IIPS), Bombay, India; the Centro Latinoamericano de Demografía (CELADE), Santiago, Chile; the Cairo Demographic Centre (CDC), Cairo, Egypt; the Regional Institute for Population Studies (RIPS), Accra, Ghana; the Institut de Formation et de Recherche Démographiques (IFORD), Yaoundé, Cameroon; and the Centre Démographique ONU-Roumanie (CEDOR), Bucharest, Romania. In 1977 an Interregional Training and Research Programme in Population and Development Planning was also established, under joint United Nations–Soviet Union auspices, at the State University of Moscow, offering specialized training in population and development. The regional centers (IIPS, CELADE, RIPS, and IFORD) are backstopped by the regional commissions. These centers train annually a total of more than two hundred students from developing countries, with fellowship support from the United Nations; they also train other students who obtain financial support elsewhere. The Department of Technical Co-operation for Development also administers fellowships in population for qualified, government-nominated personnel for study overseas at other than United Nations–sponsored institutions. More than one hundred such fellowships are awarded each year.

The Population Programmes and Projects Branch provided technical assistance in the preparation of the 1980 round of censuses and for the analysis of the data arising therefrom. *Demographic Evaluation and Analysis of Population Census Data: Aspects of Technical Co-operation* (1980) explains and discusses the type of substantive collaboration given in this area. As the focal point of country and intercountry technical cooperation activities in population, the Branch is involved in the development and formulation of projects, providing advice for project planning and implementation, and the monitoring, backstopping, and evaluation of projects.

Other Population Programs. Programs of other bodies of the United Nations system concerned with population fall into three groups according to the organizational status of the sponsoring body.

1. The five United Nations regional commissions form the first group: the Economic Commission for Europe (ECE), the Economic and Social Commission for Asia and the Pacific (ESCAP), the Economic Commission for Latin America (ECLA), the Economic Commission for Africa (ECA), and the Economic Commission for Western Asia (ECWA). All these are subsidiary organs of the Economic and Social Council. Each one works closely with the national governments within its respective region, as the particular concerns within the regions naturally vary according to their differing population objectives and conditions.

Concerns for population in the program of ECE are quite different from those expressed in other regions since a number of countries in Europe are experiencing rates of population growth near to zero. Current trends of fertility are therefore of special interest and emphasis is given to the integration of population with other aspects of social and economic activities, with particular emphasis on the age distribution.

A significant feature of the ESCAP region is its long-standing concern for the population issue and the directness of its approach. There are quantitative targets in countries of the region for population growth, mortality, and fertility. The innovation and management of family planning programs, including use of communications programs, incentives, and a broad range of other techniques, are highly developed in the area. Special attention is now being given to the reduction of mortality rates and studies on urbanization and spatial distribution.

Within ECLA the regional activities in population are carried out by CELADE (Centro Latinoamericano de Demografía). In addition to its well-established training program and information services, CELADE's demographic analyses emphasize studies on internal and international migration, urban and regional development, and their interrelations with other demographic and nondemographic variables.

In the ECA region, data collection and analysis continue to be matters of primary concern. An event of major importance in the region has been the completion of the African Census Programme in the 1970s. A major component of the regional program is the enhancement of awareness of the relationships between population trends and socioeconomic development. Reduction of mortality rates and population distribution are also areas of primary concern.

In the ECWA region, the view has been expressed that rapid population growth in the area does not necessarily constitute an obstacle to socioeconomic development. The issues of greatest concern in the region are internal and international migration. Emphasis is also given to the collection and analysis of population and manpower data.

2. Five offices and programs comprise a second group of United Nations organizations that sponsor population programs: the United Nations Environment Program (UNEP), the United Nations Industrial Development Organization (UNIDO), the United Nations Childrens' Fund (UNICEF), the United Nations Fund for Population Activities (UNFPA), and the United Nations Institute for Training and Research (UNITAR). These vary greatly of course in their primary mandates, and they generally shape their population programs to be consistent with their own areas of specialty. The UNFPA plays a major general role in the field by providing financial assistance to developing countries in carrying out their population programs.

Within the framework of its general strategy UNEP participates in further investigation of the interacting relationships between population, resources, and the environment. The activities of UNIDO in the population program are linked with economic aspects such as industrialization, better utilization of available raw materials, and specifically the utilization of facilities in developing countries to help them to become more self-reliant in their population programs.

UNICEF's population activities arise from its concern for the health, welfare, and development of children, with assistance in family planning added as part of its maternal and child health services at the request of governments, and as part of other social services benefiting children and women. Population activities are undertaken by UNITAR in pursuing its mandate to enhance, by means of training and research, the effectiveness of the United Nations in achieving the major objectives of the organization, "in particular the maintenance of peace and security and the promotion of economic and social development."

3. Finally, the six specialized agencies of the United Nations sponsoring population programs are the International Labour Organisation (ILO), the Food and Agricultural Organization of the United Nations (FAO), the United Nations Educational, Scientific, and Cultural Organization (UNESCO), the World Health Organization (WHO), and the International Bank for Reconstruction and Development (IBRD), more generally known as the World Bank. Each of these specialized agencies works within its own province, and each contributes according to its particular character and area of competence.

One of the principal long-term objectives of the population and labor policies program of ILO is to increase knowledge and understanding of the interrelationships between employment, income distribution, labor, poverty, and changes in population size, structure, and location. The objectives of the population activities undertaken by FAO stem from its basic responsibility for raising rural living levels.

UNESCO's population program is carried out in accordance with the principle that the true goals of population policies go beyond the purely demographic aspects and are linked to major world concerns such as the quality of life and human rights in relation to education, information, and the sociocultural and natural environment.

WHO's population activities relate to its primary responsibility in the field of public health. Priority is given to the monitoring, review, and appraisal of national population trends and prospects with particular emphasis on neonatal, infant, childhood, and maternal morbidity and mortality and changes in fertility patterns.

The World Bank provides financial assistance to countries for a wide range of activities relevant to an effective population program—e.g., financing construction of physical facilities (health centers, clinics, nursing colleges, paramedical schools, family planning training centers, and so forth) and financing training, research, and fellowships, as well as equipment and supplies.

Coordination among all the bodies of the United Nations system involved in population is effected through *ad hoc* group meetings, usually under the chairmanship of the Director of the Population Division, organized under the auspices of the United Nations Administrative Committee on Coordination. Particular attention is given to the coordination of selected areas of work such as the monitoring of world population trends and policies, population and development, and population, resources, environment, and development. Another good example of coordination is in the area of demographic projections. Better use is now made of statistical inputs from the regional commissions and one standard classification scheme has been agreed upon for presenting United Nations population estimates and projections.

Each component of the population program of the United Nations system is aimed at assisting governments to assess their demographic situations and identify population problems, make policy decisions, and implement programs in the light of their political, social, cultural, religious, and economic conditions.

Léon Tabah
Frances Zainoeddin

See also UNITED NATIONS FUND FOR POPULATION ACTIVITIES.

BIBLIOGRAPHY

"National Experience in the Formulation and Implementation of Population Policy." Series R, Population Studies. New York: United Nations, 1977. A series of reports, usually covering the period 1960–1976, issued by the Department of International Economic and Social Affairs. Reports have been issued on Chad, Cuba, Ghana, Guinea, Indonesia, Madagascar, Malaysia, Mali, Mexico, Nepal, Oman, Panama, Peru, Saudi Arabia, Tanzania, Thailand, Trinidad and Tobago, and Yemen.

Population Bulletin of the United Nations. Issued twice yearly by the Department of International Economic and Social Affairs of the United Nations, New York.

"Population Policy Compendium." New York: United Nations, undated. A series of unnumbered reports issued jointly by the Department of International Economic and Social Affairs, Population Division, and the United Nations Fund for Population Activities. Reports have been issued on Argentina, Bolivia, Burma, Cuba, the Dominican Republic, El Salvador, Indonesia, Mexico, Mongolia, Nepal, Pakistan, Panama, Peru, Sri Lanka, and Thailand.

United Nations, Department of Economic and Social Affairs. *World Population Prospects as Assessed in 1963.* Series A, Population Studies, no. 41. New York, 1966.

———. *The Determinants and Consequences of Population Trends.* Rev. ed. 2 vols. Volume 1: *New Summary of Findings on Interaction of Demographic, Economic, and Social Factors.* Volume 2: *Bibliography and Index.* Series A, Population Studies, no. 50 and no. 50–add. 1. New York, 1973.

———. *Manual VIII: Methods for Projections of Urban and Rural Population.* Series A, Population Studies, no. 55. New York, 1974.

———. *The Population Debate: Dimensions and Perspectives; Papers of the World Population Conference, Bucharest, 1974.* 2 vols. Series A, Population Studies, no. 57 and no. 57–add. 1. New York, 1975. In English, French, and Spanish.

———. *Methods of Measuring the Impact of Family Planning Programmes on Fertility: Problems and Issues.* Series A, Population Studies, no. 61. New York, 1978.

———. *Trends and Characteristics of International Migration since 1950.* Series A, Demographic Studies, no. 64. New York, 1979.

———. *World Population Trends and Policies: 1977 Monitoring Report.* 2 vols. Volume 1: *Population Trends.* Volume 2: *Population Policies.* Series A, Population Studies, no. 62 and no. 62–add. 1. New York, 1979.

United Nations, Department of International Economic and Social Affairs. *Demographic Transition and Socio-economic Development: Proceedings of the United Nations/UNFPA Expert Group Meetings, Istanbul, 27 April–4 May 1977.* Series A, Population Studies, no. 65. New York, 1979.

———. *Factors Affecting the Use and Non-use of Contraception: Findings from a Comparative Analysis of Selected KAP Surveys.* Series A, Population Studies, no. 69. New York, 1979.

———. *Manual IX: The Methodology of Measuring the Impact of*

Family Planning Programmes on Fertility. Series A, Population Studies, no. 66. New York, 1979.

———. *Prospects of Population: Methodology and Assumptions.* Series A, Population Studies, no. 67. New York, 1979.

———. *Review and Appraisal of the World Population Plan of Action.* Series A, Population Studies, no. 71. New York, 1979.

———. *Concise Report on the World Population Situation in 1979: Conditions, Trends, Prospects, and Policies.* Series A, Population Studies, no. 72. New York, 1980.

———. *Patterns of Urban and Rural Population Growth.* Series A, Population Studies, no. 68, New York, 1980.

———. *World Population Trends and Policies: 1979 Monitoring Report.* 2 vols. Volume 1: *Population Trends.* Volume 2: *Population Policies.* Series A, Population Studies, no. 70 and no. 70–add. 1. New York, 1980.

United Nations, Department of Technical Co-operation for Development. *Demographic Evaluation and Analysis of Population Census Data: Aspects of Technical Co-operation.* Series E, no. 22. New York, 1980.

UNITED NATIONS FUND FOR POPULATION ACTIVITIES

The United Nations Fund for Population Activities (UNFPA) is a subsidiary organ of the United Nations General Assembly with aims and purposes, outlined in 1973 by the Economic and Social Council, as follows:

a) To build up, on an international basis, with the assistance of the competent bodies of the United Nations system, the knowledge and the capacity to respond to national, regional, interregional and global needs in the population and family planning fields; to promote co-ordination in planning and programming, and to co-operate with all concerned; b) To promote awareness, both in developed and in developing countries, of the social, economic and environmental implications of national and international population problems; of the human rights aspects of family planning; and of possible strategies to deal with them, in accordance with the plans and priorities of each country; c) To extend systematic and sustained assistance to developing countries at their request in dealing with their population problems; such assistance to be afforded in forms and by means requested by the recipient countries and best suited to meet the individual country's needs; d) To play a leading role in the United Nations system in promoting population programmes and to co-ordinate projects supported by the Fund.

History of the Fund. When the United Nations Fund for Population Activities began operations in 1969, after two years as a Trust Fund, population as a field of multilateral assistance was still new for most of the member states of the United Nations. Although prior to this time considerable work had been done within the United Nations in promoting technical cooperation in demographic

activities, there was limited experience in the delivery of assistance in population. The first few years of the Fund's work were therefore devoted to creating awareness of the importance of population factors in development and to building up the capacity of the United Nations organizations to deliver population assistance to countries in need, at their request. During this period understanding the dimensions of the population problem and finding the proper and suitable forms of delivery and assistance were of primary importance.

The work of the Fund developed markedly after the General Assembly, in 1972, placed the Fund under the Assembly's authority and decided that the Governing Council of the United Nations Development Programme should be its governing body under the policy guidance of the Economic and Social Council, which defined the Fund's aims and purposes in 1973. Thereafter, the Fund assumed its own distinct identity. Going beyond awareness and institutional effectiveness, the work of the Fund emphasized the delineation of a core program of population assistance, more adequate conceptualization of its goals and purposes, more effective modes and procedures of delivering assistance, and improvement of developing countries' manpower and institutional capacity to solve their particular population problems. In December 1979, the General Assembly confirmed the UNFPA as a subsidiary organ of the assembly.

In 1969, the Fund was engaged in 12 projects. By the end of 1980, the UNFPA was assisting 1,831 projects; 1,135 had been completed. Projects range in size from $100 million (India) to a few thousand dollars, for example, allocated for a one-time regional conference on demographic training methods.

The Fund began its operations with $2.5 million in 1969; by the end of 1980 its cumulative resources totaled $726.4 million. The cumulative number of donors totaled 119. In 1979 the Fund's governing body, the Governing Council of the United Nations Development Programme, authorized the UNFPA to allocate $138 million for its assistance programs in 1980, $147 million for 1981, and $144 million for 1982. The UNFPA is now the largest multilateral source of direct assistance for population activities in developing countries. [*See* INTERNATIONAL POPULATION ASSISTANCE.] More than a quarter of total global population aid to developing countries, currently estimated at over $500 million, is channeled through it annually.

In 1980, family planning projects, including those integrated with maternal and child health projects, received the major share of the $150.5 million in project allocations, 41.7 percent. Communication and education projects closely related to family planning added another 11.6 percent. Projects in basic data collection represented 19.2 percent of allocations. Population dynamics, which involves the utilization of collected data, creation of awareness of the uses of research, and training of researchers, as well as support for research and its application, accounted for 11.4 percent of the Fund's 1980 project allocations. Assistance to the development of more effective national population policies and their integration with development planning absorbed 5.0 percent. Support for the implementation of national policies having an impact on fertility and other demographic factors, yet going beyond family planning proper, received 1.0 percent. Special programs received 1.6 percent of allocations in 1980; these included programs aimed at increased participation of women and youth in national population and development-related activities and programs addressed to the problems of aging, as well as programs designed to promote social mobility. The remaining 8.5 percent of UNFPA project allocations in 1980 went to multisectoral activities, including support for multidisciplinary and interdisciplinary research, expenses for UNFPA field staff, and population infrastructure support to relevant organizations of the United Nations system.

In terms of geographic areas, during the period 1969–1979, the Asia and Pacific region received the largest amount of UNFPA assistance, $184.2 million, primarily for family planning; the Latin America and Caribbean region, $100.5 million, for family planning as well as basic data collection; the sub-Saharan African region, $69.4 million, primarily for basic data collection; and the Middle East, the Mediterranean region, and Europe, $64.4 million, for basic data collection and family planning. Interregional and global population projects accounted for $128.9 million.

The work of the Fund became universal in its first decade. The Fund has assisted population projects in 121 member states of the United Nations and in 14 other countries and territories. Its worldwide role has been furthered by voluntary contributions from many member states.

Demands for population assistance, however, have continued to exceed available resources by far. The success of the World Population Year in 1974 and the World Population Conference held in Bucharest in 1974 brought in such heavy requests by developing countries to the UNFPA for assistance for population activities that the Fund found it necessary to institute a priority system regarding the future allocation of its resources. It developed a set of general principles to carry out its work. These principles, which were endorsed by the Economic and Social Council and the General Assembly in 1976, are (1) to promote population activities proposed in international strategies, particularly the World Population Plan of Action; (2) to meet the needs of developing countries that have the most urgent need for assistance in the area of population activities, in view of their population problems; (3) to respect the sovereign right of each nation to formulate, promote, and implement its own population policies; (4) to promote the recipient countries' self-reliance; and (5) to give special attention to meeting the needs of disadvantaged population groups.

Priority countries for UNFPA population assistance on an urgent basis were selected by applying a set of demographic indicators for which data are generally available. Economic conditions of countries were also taken into consideration by including per capita income as an additional qualifying factor. As a result, forty countries were designated "priority countries" for population assistance. A goal of two-thirds of total program resources available to the UNFPA for population activities at the country level was established for assistance to these countries as a group.

Conferences and Educational Activities. The Fund has sponsored or taken an active part in a variety of conferences in recent years designed for leaders and opinion makers to ensure that understanding of population issues reaches people everywhere. For example, the UNFPA, in cooperation with the United Nations Economic Commission for Latin America and other regional institutions, cosponsored the Latin American Conference on Population and Development Planning, held in Cartagena, Colombia, in May 1979, the first regional conference of its kind for planning ministers. It provided funds for the preparatory colloquium for the United Nations Conference on Science and Technology for Development, the World Conference of the International Women's Year in 1975, and the follow-up Mid-Decade Conference in 1980, as well as for a variety of other meetings.

In 1979, the Fund cosponsored with the Inter-Parliamentary Union an International Conference of Parliamentarians on Population and Development in Colombo, Sri Lanka. The Conference provided interested parliamentarians from 58 countries an opportunity to discuss the main population and related development problems facing the world, to acquaint themselves with current demographic trends, and to define areas of action in which they, as representatives of the people, could supplement and enhance population efforts of governments. In 1980, the UNFPA convened a conference, in Rome, of national planning officials from thirty-one countries and mayors and community leaders of forty-one rapidly growing cities that are projected to have populations of 5 million or more by the year 2000. The Conference had three objectives—to increase the awareness and understanding of population factors in urban planning at local and national levels; to bring to the attention of planners, policymakers, and administrators the result of recent research and experience on urban issues and problems; and to provide a forum where all the parties involved in urban management could share problems and possible solutions, identify areas that have hitherto been neglected, and formulate ideas and proposals for future action.

The UNFPA publishes a quarterly, *Populi;* a monthly newsletter; an annual *Inventory of Population Activities in Developing Countries Around the World;* and an *Annual Review of Population Law* (available for individual years, 1977–1980); as well as annual reports of its own activities. A partial list of other publications includes the following: *Guide to Sources of International Population Assistance* (issued every three years); *Survey of Laws on Fertility Control;* "Population Policy Compendium" (a series of reports on seventeen nations); and *Population in the Arab World: Problems and Proposals,* by Abdel-Rahim Omran. *Population Profiles* have been published on nations and regions as well as on issues such as *Law and Population; Population and Mutual Self-reliance; Women, Population, and Development;* and *Labour and Population.* Conference reports include the *Report on Latin American Conference on Population and Development Planning* (see above); *Report of International Conference of Parliamentarians on Population and Development* (see above); and *Report of the International Conference on Population and the Urban Future* (see above). *Population Facts at Hand* provides basic data on global and national population as well as data on historical trends in population in a convenient index card format.

Conclusions. The goals set for the Fund in its first decade have been largely accomplished. This achievement has been mainly the result of the three basic approaches of the Fund's operations: (1) neutrality in its policies through responding to each country's perception and formulation of its own population policy, (2) flexibility in the conceptualization and implementation of programs, and (3) innovation in its managerial operations. Some of the innovations, unique within the United Nations system, include the direct execution of population projects by recipient countries; enlistment of nongovernmental organizations as executing agents; and a four-year "rolling plan" approach to budgeting of resources, in which the UNFPA requests its Governing Council to authorize the total approval authority shown in the first year of the Fund's Work Plan submitted, and portions of the approval authority shown in the Work Plan for the second and third years, in order to permit multiyear programming; other innovations include budget support for local costs, when required, and the employment of national experts in local projects, when appropriate.

The Fund's most important contribution may lie in its efforts to overcome political and cultural sensitivities on population assistance. By 1980, almost all developing countries had population policies and programs as part of their development plans. The debates that used to be heard on the acceptance or nonacceptance of population policies have become progressively muted in tone and no longer becloud the issues. Instead, discussions on the subject have become more focused on the feasibility of programs to be implemented under the varying national interpretations of population policies.

In the 1980s, the UNFPA, as the largest source of multilateral population assistance, plans to adapt its policies and operations to the foreseeable changing needs of countries. Priorities will be to consolidate the gains made and to maintain the momentum of programs that have proven effective in influencing population trends. This course will entail strengthened efforts at applying the concepts and goals of the World Population Plan of Action, adopted by the World Population Conference in Bucharest in 1974, concerning the relationships between population and development as well as adopting a broader outlook in the interpretation of the Fund's mandate in regard to its operational guidelines.

Rafael M. Salas

See also INTERNATIONAL POPULATION ASSISTANCE; UNITED NATIONS.

BIBLIOGRAPHY

Hauser, Philip M. (editor). *World Population and Development: Challenges and Prospects.* Syracuse, N.Y.: Syracuse University Press, 1979.
Salas, Rafael M. *International Population Assistance: The First Decade; A Look at the Concepts and Policies Which Have Guided the UNFPA in Its First Ten Years.* Elmsford, N.Y.: Pergamon Press, 1979. Also published in Arabic, French, Japanese, and Spanish editions.
———. *People: An International Choice; The Multilateral Approach to Population.* Elmsford, N.Y.: Pergamon Press, 1976. Also published in Arabic, Chinese, French, Japanese, and Spanish editions.

UNITED STATES

This article describes the demographic characteristics of the population of the United States around 1980. It also summarizes some of the information on the United States given in various other articles in this work.

The United States of America is the fourth largest country of the world in population. Its approximately 230 million people occupy a land area of 3,540,023 square miles (9,168,660 square kilometers) divided into forty-eight contiguous states and the states of Hawaii, in the Pacific Ocean, and Alaska, which borders on northwestern Canada. In 1977, 73 percent of the population was urban, and three-quarters of this urban population lived in cities of more than 500,000. Thirty-five metropolitan areas had more than 1 million people, and three had more than 8 million. This highly industrialized country has scarcely 3 percent of its labor force in the agricultural sector.

Early settlement of the territory by the British, the French, the Dutch, and the Spanish; importation of slaves from Africa; and continual immigration from all parts of the world throughout most of its history have given the United States its characteristic ethnic and racial diversity. In 1978, 12 percent of the population was classified as black, while at least 12 percent was of Hispanic origin, with the Hispanic proportion of the population increasing every year. Overall population growth has slowed in recent years to about 0.8 percent per year.

Population Characteristics. The history of fertility and mortality trends in the United States has been, in general, like that of the western European countries. Declines were gradual to the late nineteenth century and, with some fluctuations, became more rapid to the present time. The crude birth rate was 28.5 per 1,000 population in 1917, around 18.4 in the Depression years of the 1930s, and at a peak of 26.6 in 1947 after World War II. The crude birth rate remained high at around 25 throughout the baby boom, which added nearly 42 million births in the 1955–1964 decade. As shown in Figure 1, the long-term trend toward lower fertility was back on course by the early 1970s and was relatively stable at a general fertility rate of about 65 births per 1,000 women aged 15–44 by the end of the decade.

Fertility rates are below replacement level (i.e., a couple in 1980 would, on the average, produce 1.8 children) but the upsurge in fertility from 1947 to 1964 produced enough prospective parents to increase the numbers of annual births throughout the 1980s, even if fertility rates remain low. By 1985, there will be 20.5 million women aged 20–29 in the United States, 2.5 million more than in 1978, and 8 million more than in 1965. [*See* FERTILITY TRENDS.]

The mortality experience in the United States has also been one of continual decline, interrupted in this century only by the influenza pandemic of 1918–1919. The crude death rates and age-adjusted death rates shown in Figure 2 illustrate the effects of the changing age composition of the United States. The crude death rates are declining only moderately because, as a consequence primarily of lowered fertility rates, a larger proportion of the population is at older ages, when death rates are always high. The age-adjusted rates indicate the gains that have been made in preventing death at younger ages. Life expectancy at birth for the total population in 1977 reached a record high of 73.2 years—a continuation of a general upward trend over the past several decades, as shown in Figure 3. Recent gains in life expectancy have been greater for females than for males. [*See* EPIDEMIOLOGIC TRANSITION, *article on* UNITED STATES.]

Racial differentials in death rates and life expectancy that are characteristic of the United States have narrowed somewhat in the last decade. Expectation of life at birth for nonwhites in 1977 was 64.6 for males and 73.1 for females, compared to 70.0 and 77.7 respectively for whites. Increases in life expectancy from 1940 to 1977 for nonwhites were approximately 12 years for males and 18 for females, while the increase for white males was 7

FIGURE 1. *Live births and fertility rates, United States, 1910–1978*[1]

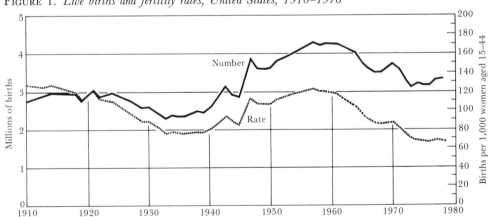

[1]Trend lines for 1910–1959 are based on live births adjusted for underregistration and for 1959 onward on registered live births; 1959 itself was calculated both ways, with trivial difference.
SOURCE: United States, NCHS, 1980, p. 1.

FIGURE 2. *Crude and age-adjusted death rates, United States, 1930–1977*

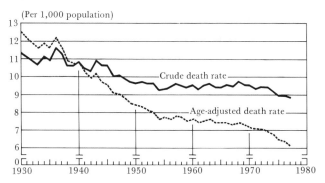

SOURCE: United States, NCHS, 1979, p. 1.

years, and for white females 10 years. The difference in life expectancy between the total white population and all other races in 1977 was 5 years.

Racial differentials in infant mortality rates have also diminished. In 1977, the overall infant mortality rate was 14.1 per 1,000 infants born that year, 12.3 for white infants and 21.7 for nonwhite. In 1960, the national figure was 26; 22.9 for white infants and 43.2 for nonwhite.

The aging of the United States population has brought about a 2.4 percent increase in the population aged 65 and over in the short period from 1975 to 1978. The age group from 5 to 17 declined during that period by 1.6 percent, and the group under 5 years declined by 1.1 percent. The median age of the population was 29.6 in 1978. [*For an examination of implications of the shift in the ratio of working-age persons to retirement-age persons, see* AGING POPULATION.]

Migration. The size of the U.S. population, its ethnic and racial diversity, the distribution of people across the land, and, to an extent, its economic growth and the role it plays on the international scene all reflect immigration and a high degree of internal mobility. While the great

FIGURE 3. *Life expectancy by sex, United States, 1930–1977*

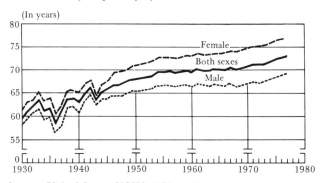

SOURCE: United States, NCHS, 1979, p. 3.

waves of immigrants (6.3 million from 1900 to 1910 alone) dwindled by the end of the 1920s, net civilian legal immigration still adds about 400,000 to 500,000 to the population each year. This accounts for approximately 20 to 25 percent of the annual population growth. Estimates of undocumented immigration vary widely but are in the millions, although many undocumented migrants are known to be temporary residents. No longer do most immigrants come from Europe. From 1971 to 1977, 32 percent of legal immigrants came from Asia, 45 percent from Canada, Central and South America, and Caribbean countries, and about 20 percent from Europe. [*See* IMMIGRATION POLICY; INTERNATIONAL MIGRATION.]

About 18 percent of the U.S. population changes residence every year, although many of these moves are of short distance. The major flow in this century was from the farm to the cities and from the south to the north. In 1900, 60 percent of the population were on farms or in small towns. By 1970, that figure had declined to 26 percent in a long, solid trend toward urbanization that created large, virtually unbroken metropolitan areas on both east and west coasts. The 1970s brought an apparent reversal of that trend. The largest metropolitan areas especially have either lost population or stopped growing, and the nonmetropolitan counties are registering population gains from either natural increase, migration, or both. The earlier net flow from the southern states to the north has also reversed direction. [*See* INTERNAL MIGRATION, *article on* UNITED STATES.]

The population is still highly concentrated on the eastern and western coasts. Average density in 1978 was 61.7 persons per square mile of land area, but regional density varied from 367.1 in the middle Atlantic states to 12.0 in the western mountain states. Individual states show even greater diversity. New Jersey had 974.2 persons per square mile, while Wyoming had 4.4, and Alaska 0.7.

The American Family. Age at marriage in the United States has been increasing since the 1960s to an average in 1979 of 22.1 years for women and 24.4 years for men. Some reasons offered for this change are the rising educational attainment that tends to delay marriage; economic uncertainty and high unemployment; and ideological changes regarding early marriage and even the need to marry. An additional cause might be the increase in the number of couples living together outside of marriage, a number that was estimated at 1.3 million in 1979. Never-married women aged 25 to 29 increased by more than 100 percent from 1960 to 1979.

Marital disruption is also in an upward trend. There were about 92 divorced persons per 1,000 intact marriages in 1979, a 96 percent increase from 1970. Remarriage rates are high, but there has been a marked increase in single-person households and in the proportion of families headed by women. Nearly one child in five was living with only one parent in 1979. [*These changes in the American family are discussed in* MARRIAGE AND DIVORCE. *See also* FAMILY LAW.]

Population Policy. The United States does not have an explicit policy regarding the growth and distribution of the population. As in many other countries, however, there are policies and programs on various social and economic subjects that together amount to a population policy. The Commission on Population Growth and the American Future was established by Congress in 1970 to examine existing policies related to population in the United States, and to recommend action by the government. The commission, in 1972, issued its final report, Population and the American Future, accompanied by seven volumes of research papers on subjects such as the effects of population growth on federal programs, on the educational systems, on the labor force, and the implications of population change for the status of women and children. A Select Committee on Population of the U.S. House of Representatives was established in 1975 to continue studying these issues. [*See* POPULATION POLICY, *article on* UNITED STATES.]

The United States laws intended to regulate fertility behavior have restricted access to contraceptive methods. The so-called Comstock laws passed by Congress in 1873 prohibited the importation, transportation in interstate commerce, and mailing of contraceptives, and anything having to do with abortion. Almost one hundred years later, virtually all of the states had laws making abortion, except to save the life of a woman, a criminal offense. It was only in the 1960s and 1970s that regulation of one's own fertility was recognized as a constitutional right. In 1970 the Family Planning Services and Population Research Act (Title X of the Public Health Services Act) brought the federal government into the development of family planning programs. Three years later, the Supreme Court struck down as unconstitutional a Texas law that made abortion a crime except to save the life of a woman (*Roe* v. *Wade*, 410 U.S. 113, 1973). In 1980, however, the Court found that federal and state laws restricting the public funding of abortions were constitutional. [*See* LAW AND FERTILITY REGULATION, *article on* UNITED STATES.]

Family Planning. In the 1960s family planning became a legitimate part of regular medical services. The approximately 5,000 public and nonprofit family planning clinics in the United States in 1980 were largely subsidized by various federal and state financing authorities. About three-fourths of the funds for organized family planning programs in 1977 came from federal sources.

In 1977, more than 4.2 million women went to public and nonprofit clinics for family planning services. Most of them had low or marginal incomes, and about 1.3 million were adolescents. The pill and surgical sterilization were the main methods used. Approximately 1.4 million abortions (or 27.5 per 1,000 women of reproductive age) were performed in the United States in 1978. [*See* ABORTION; CONTRACEPTIVE USE; FAMILY PLANNING PROGRAMS, *article on* UNITED STATES.]

Sources of Data. The census of population has been taken regularly every ten years since 1790. It was one of the first to be established in modern times and is now an inventory of many of the personal, social, and economic characteristics of the American people. The Bureau of the Census also conducts the Current Population Survey, a regular monthly series on employment, marital status, households and families, and related demographic and social data, with periodic supplements on fertility and other special topics. There are also data of demographic interest in the censuses of housing and agriculture. [*See* DATA COLLECTION, *article on* UNITED STATES CENSUS.]

Surveys to collect data of demographic interest are now conducted by state and local governments and private survey organizations are working in this field as well. Several of these organizations are based in universities.

In the United States, the registration of births, deaths, marriages, and divorces has been the responsibility of the states and a few cities. Qualification for inclusion in the national system, the Birth and Death Registration Areas, requires that 90 percent of the births and deaths be registered—standards that were met by all of the present states except Alaska by 1933, and by Alaska, Puerto Rico, and the Virgin Islands by 1950.

Scholarly Activities. The teaching of population in the United States is generally the responsibility of university sociology departments. More than forty graduate programs are listed as emphasizing demography by the Population Association of America (PAA). The PAA, with a predominantly American membership, was formed in 1931 to promote research with respect to human population and to publish research results. This is now done primarily through its journal, *Demography*. [*See* POPULATION ASSOCIATION OF AMERICA.]

Other periodicals in the field of population include the bibliographical journal *Population Index*, published by the Office of Population Research at Princeton University; *Population Bulletin*, published by the Population Reference Bureau; *Population Reports*, by the Population Information Program at Johns Hopkins University; *Family Planning Perspectives*, by the Alan Guttmacher Institute; and *Studies in Family Planning* and the *Population and Development Review*, published by the Population Council.

Regina McNamara

BIBLIOGRAPHY

Berelson, Bernard (editor). *Population Policy in Developed Countries*. A Population Council Book. New York: McGraw-Hill, 1974.

Monthly Vital Statistics Report. Issued by the U.S. National Center for Health Statistics, Hyattsville, Md.

United States, Bureau of the Census. *Statistical Abstract of the United States, 1979.* 100th ed. Washington, D.C.: U.S. Government Printing Office, 1979.

United States, Commission on Population Growth and the American Future. *Population and the American Future.* Washington, D.C.: U.S. Government Printing Office, 1972. New York: New American Library (Signet), 1972.

———. *Research Reports.* 7 vols. Washington, D.C.: U.S. Government Printing Office, 1972.

United States, National Center for Health Statistics. *Monthly Vital Statistics Report* 28(1), supplement, 11 May 1979. (United States, NCHS, 1979)

———. *Monthly Vital Statistics Report* 29(1), supplement, 28 April 1980. (United States, NCHS, 1980)

Vital Statistics of the United States. Issued annually by the U.S. National Center for Health Statistics, Hyattsville, Md.

URBANIZATION

1.
OVERVIEW

By the year 2000 about one half of the world population will be living in cities, an increase from about two-fifths in 1980. Because the term "city" or "urban area" can refer to concentrations of as few as 1,000 people, depending on national definitions, urbanization in the late twentieth century may perhaps be more powerfully illustrated by the changes that are taking place in the largest cities rather than only by the proportion of the population that is counted as urban.

The ten largest urban clusters in 1950 and at intervals to 2000 are listed in Table 1 (on the following page). At the present rate of in-migration and natural increase, Mexico City could be the largest city, with a population of more than 30 million, by 2000; that city did not appear in the first ten in 1950 but was the third largest in 1975. London, second largest in 1950, will not be among the first ten by 1990, according to these predictions by the

United Nations (1980). The cities of the more developed countries, where urban growth is now not so rapid and there are even some declines, will in general fall behind those of developing countries when they are ranked by size. Environmental and social constraints may prevent cities of the magnitude that is projected, but it is likely that at least twenty-five cities of more than 10 million will exist by the year 2000 as compared with seven of that size in 1975.

Some urban areas cover extensive regions of linked cities and towns, called "megalopolises." Table 1 refers, for example, to "Chicago/northwestern Indiana" and "Tokyo/Yokohama." The northeastern region of the United States, from southern Maine to southern Virginia, varies in density of population, but economically and socially it constitutes an almost unbroken urban strip extending 600 miles along the Atlantic coast.

Overall, about 1,650 million people are expected to be added to the world's urban population before the year 2000, and 80 percent of this increase will be in developing countries. Latin America is already relatively highly urbanized, with about 65 percent of the population counted as urban in 1980. Sub-Saharan Africa, with the most rural of the world's populations, is urbanizing the most rapidly. Some observers and analysts believe that "overurbanization" is occurring, and that developing countries are unable to handle the stresses that accompany rapid urban growth. Others view urbanization as a necessary and desirable step toward economic development and the rational use of resources in developing countries. Control of this growth, and balanced geographic distribution of the population, are major policy issues in many countries.

Regina McNamara

See also DISTRIBUTION.

BIBLIOGRAPHY

Chandler, Tertius, and Gerald Fox. *Three Thousand Years of Urban Growth.* New York and London: Academic Press, 1974.

Mumford, Lewis. *The City in History: Its Origins, Its Transformations, and Its Prospects.* New York: Harcourt Brace & World, 1961. Reissued in paperback by Harcourt Brace Jovanovich, New York, in 1968.

Thomlinson, Ralph. *Population Dynamics: Causes and Consequences of World Demographic Change.* 2d ed. New York: Random House, 1976.

United Nations, Department of International Economic and Social Affairs. *Patterns of Urban and Rural Population Growth.* Series A, Population Studies, no. 68. New York, 1980.

TABLE 1. *Ten largest agglomerations in the world, ranked by size, 1950–2000 (population in millions)*

Rank	1950 Population	1975 Population	1990 Population	2000 Population
1.	New York/northeastern New Jersey 12.3	New York/northeastern New Jersey 19.8	Tokyo/Yokohama . . . 23.4	Mexico City 31.0
2.	London 10.4	Tokyo/Yokohama . . . 17.7	Mexico City 22.9	São Paulo 25.8
3.	Rhein/Ruhr 6.9	Mexico City 11.9	New York/northeastern New Jersey 21.8	Tokyo/Yokohama . . . 24.2
4.	Tokyo/Yokohama . 6.7	Shanghai 11.6	São Paulo 19.9	New York/northeastern New Jersey 22.8
5.	Shanghai 5.8	Los Angeles/ Long Beach 10.8	Shanghai 17.7	Shanghai 22.7
6.	Paris 5.5	São Paulo 10.7	Peking 15.3	Peking 19.9
7.	Greater Buenos Aires 5.3	London 10.4	Rio de Janeiro 14.7	Rio de Janeiro 19.0
8.	Chicago/north-western Indiana . 4.9	Greater Buenos Aires . 9.3	Los Angeles/ Long Beach 13.3	Greater Bombay 17.1
9.	Moscow 4.8	Rhein/Ruhr 9.3	Greater Bombay 12.0	Calcutta 16.7
10.	Calcutta 4.4	Paris 9.2	Calcutta 11.9	Jakarta 16.6

SOURCE: United Nations, 1980, p. 58; reprinted by permission.

2.

DEVELOPING COUNTRIES

Large transfers of population from rural to urban areas are occurring throughout the developing world. These transfers are being superimposed upon rates of natural increase that are very high by historical standards in both rural and urban areas. The result of these twin processes is a rate of urban growth that appears to many observers to have attained frightening proportions, carrying with it problems of labor absorption, public service provision, excessive congestion, depletion of rural work forces, social dislocation, and political unrest. The term "urban crisis" is often used to denote the many problems posed by rapid urban growth. Governments themselves are usually acutely aware of the problems of urban growth and of rural-urban distribution. They cite them as among the most serious demographic problems that their countries face.

Urban Growth. In discussing the demography of urban areas, it is essential to distinguish between two related but conceptually distinct processes. "Urban growth" refers to the proportionate growth rate of urban areas themselves: annual net additions to urban population divided by the size of the urban population. "Urbanization," on the other hand, is the process of growth in the proportion of the population living in urban areas. It is usually measured as the rate of change per unit of time (e.g., per year). Urban growth can be very rapid, but if rural areas are growing equally rapidly, no urbanization will be occurring because the urban proportion will be constant through time.

A recent study by the United Nations has estimated the magnitude of urbanization in developing countries and regions (United Nations, 1980). The regional results are presented in Table 1. This table shows that, for less-developed regions as a whole (Latin America, Africa, and Asia except Japan, Turkey, Israel, and Cyprus), the percent that was urban grew from 16.7 in 1950 to 28.0 in 1975, or by 11.3 percentage points over a span of twenty-five years. Over the same period, the urban percentage grew somewhat faster in more-developed regions (15.0 percentage points). Such a comparison is in some ways misleading because the more-developed countries began from a higher base. It is useful therefore to examine the rate of urbanization in the developed regions at a time when they had a comparable urban percentage. John V. Grauman (1977) has estimated the urban percentage for these countries to have been 17.2 in 1875 and 26.1 in 1900. Thus, there is little difference between the estimated rate of urbanization in less-developed regions today and that in more-developed regions seventy-five years earlier, when they had comparable levels of the urban proportion.

The same rate of urbanization may of course mask profound differences in the nature of urbanization. In particular, it has been pointed out that developing countries tend to have a much lower percentage of their labor force in manufacturing or industrial activities than did developed countries at equivalent levels of the urban proportion (e.g., Hoselitz, 1953). Thus, it is argued, urbanization in less-developed countries is "supported" by a less substantial manufacturing base. The developing countries have larger fractions in the service sector to compensate for the deficit in the manufacturing sector. Some view work in the service sector as less productive than manufacturing work, while others point out that productivity is best measured by wages and that workers accumulate in the service sector because for many it affords better wage opportunities than does manufacturing. However, for workers in government activities or in activities subject to government wage control, wages may be inadequate as indicators of productivity. Thus, inflation of the service sector may be serious cause for concern, particularly in capital cities with large government bureaucracies. Whatever the merits of the service sector as a locus of economic activity, it is worth noting that its role in the urbanization process changed little during the period between 1950 and 1975. On the average, each man-

ufacturing job "supported" about two city dwellers in developing countries in 1975, just as it did in 1950. In other words, the growth of manufacturing jobs has about kept pace with the growth of urban areas. A major regional exception to this finding is Latin America, where urban growth has outstripped manufacturing growth and where service-dominated economies have begun to appear much as they have in the more-developed world.

Rural-Urban Transfers. The major cause of urbanization, in the demographic sense at least, is net transfer of population from areas classified as rural to areas classified as urban. Without such transfers, the growth rates of urban and rural areas would be virtually identical in developing countries. Rural areas typically have some-

TABLE 1. *Percentage of population living in urban areas in major world regions, 1950–1975*

Area/region	1950	1960	1970	1975
WORLD TOTAL	28.95	33.89	37.51	39.34
More-developed regions	52.54	58.73	64.68	67.49
Less-developed regions	16.71	21.85	25.82	28.03
Africa	14.54	18.15	22.85	25.67
Eastern Africa	5.50	7.54	10.69	13.20
Middle Africa	14.57	18.10	25.16	29.66
Northern Africa	24.51	29.77	36.61	40.12
Southern Africa	37.27	41.70	43.76	44.81
Western Africa	10.15	13.48	17.27	19.58
Latin America	41.18	49.45	57.37	61.21
Caribbean	33.51	38.22	45.08	48.62
Middle America	39.75	46.71	53.88	57.37
Temperate South America	64.77	72.74	77.87	80.16
Tropical South America	36.29	46.36	56.05	60.70
Northern America	63.84	67.09	70.45	71.99
East Asia	16.72	24.71	28.61	30.70
China	11.00	18.60	21.60	23.29
Japan	50.20	62.40	71.30	75.08
Other East Asia	28.61	36.31	47.46	53.43
South Asia	15.65	17.80	20.45	22.02
Eastern South Asia	14.83	17.52	20.02	21.38
Middle South Asia	15.59	17.19	19.40	20.77
Western South Asia	23.38	32.52	44.48	50.45
Europe	53.70	58.42	63.94	66.45
Eastern Europe	41.48	47.90	53.26	56.26
Northern Europe	74.32	76.73	81.28	83.32
Southern Europe	41.01	46.15	52.90	56.25
Western Europe	63.92	69.20	74.38	76.25
Oceania	61.24	66.22	70.77	73.35
Soviet Union	39.30	48.80	56.70	60.90

SOURCE: United Nations, 1980, p. 16; reprinted by permission.

what higher birth rates, but they also tend to have higher death rates.

Rural-urban transfers of population take two forms. The most important is a physical change in residence from a rural to an urban area. The second, which accounts for a highly variable and largely unknown fraction of urbanization, is a reclassification of areas from rural to urban. A person can become a city dweller not only by moving to an urban area but also by having the area in which he lives reclassified as urban. The definition of what constitutes an urban place varies from country to country. Usually, it consists of one or more of three components: size of population, density of inhabitation, and percentage of the labor force in nonagricultural activities. These features change in the course of time for a particular area and its classification will correspondingly change. Another source of reclassification is, of course, a change in the urban definition itself. Figures in Table 1 and elsewhere in this discussion have been adjusted for such "nuisance" changes. On the average, reclassification may account for 10–30 percent of the urbanization occurring in developing countries.

The dominant factor in urbanization is physical movement from rural to urban areas. Surveys of rural-urban migration in developing countries indicate that the most important motive for movement is economic advancement; important secondary reasons are better social services in urban areas and family reunification (e.g., Yap, 1977; Findley, 1977). Aggregate-level studies of migration flows usually also point towards the dominance of economic concerns. Surveys of migrants who remain in urban areas usually indicate a high level of satisfaction with the outcome of the move (e.g., Findley, 1977). The sketchy information available on migrants who return to rural areas suggests that they have fared no more poorly than those who remain. Other studies point out that migrants do not inevitably remain in marginal employments and residences even though they often begin there but frequently filter rapidly into more attractive social locations.

On an international level, the rural-urban migration process does not appear to be unstructured and chaotic but to have marked regularities. Rural-urban migration rates, expressed over the base of the rural population, tend to be quite constant from period to period in a particular country. Countries that experience the fastest rates of rural-urban migration are in general those that are more advanced economically and that already have a higher urban percentage. Thus, annual net rural out-migration rates in Puerto Rico, Argentina, Chile, and Venezuela have in recent years exceeded 25 per 1,000 rural population, whereas they have fallen below 8 per 1,000 in Paraguay, Ghana, Guatemala, Bangladesh, India, and Indonesia. In other words, the rural exodus tends to be fastest in countries that are economically best positioned to accommodate the flow. Such a tendency is clearly difficult to reconcile with popular accounts that view absolute deprivation in rural areas as the principal force driving multitudes to the city.

Urban and City Growth. Although urbanization is produced almost exclusively by rural-urban population transfers, the major source of urban growth is to be found not in migration or reclassification but in the natural increase of city residents themselves, that is, in the excess of their births over their deaths. This conclusion is based upon demographic analysis of the most recent intercensal population changes in twenty-nine countries whose data could support such an analysis (United Nations, 1980). In twenty-four of these countries, including the largest countries examined (India, Indonesia, and Brazil), natural increase contributed more to urban growth than did rural-urban transfers. The mean percentage of urban growth attributable to urban natural increase for the twenty-nine countries was 60.7, and the average was still higher among the poorest countries. These calculations pertain to a moment in time and exclude the long-term demographic impacts of migration and of natural increase.

Estimated rates of urban growth by region are shown in Table 2. The figures indicate an average annual rate of growth of 3.95 percent in less-developed countries as a whole between 1970 and 1975, a rate that is sufficient to double urban populations every seventeen years. The rate is highest in Africa, very nearly 5 percent per year. Africa is just at the beginning stages of its urban revolution; although the urban percentage grew at about an average speed for a developing region between 1950 and 1975, this growth was being applied to a relatively low urban base.

Perhaps more informative than a tabulation of growth rates for all areas classified as urban is an examination of the factors that seem to be associated with the rate of growth of specific cities (Preston, 1979). Obviously, many factors unique to a city have an important influence on its growth rate: annexation practices, topography and geography, the health of industries in which the city specializes, productivity trends in the rural hinterland, government investment patterns and redistribution policies, rural-urban income and employment disparities, possibilities for accommodating marginal settlements, and so on. Despite the undoubted importance of these individual factors, it is possible to form some solidly based generalizations about more readily measured variables that discriminate among the growth rates of individual cities. The results reported further on are based primarily upon an examination of growth rates of the 1,212 cities in the

TABLE 2. *Average annual growth rates of urban areas in major world regions, 1950–2000*

Area/region	1950–60	1960–70	1970–75	1975–80	1980–90	1990–2000
WORLD TOTAL	3.35	2.91	2.84	2.93	2.93	2.81
More-developed regions	2.44	2.05	1.75	1.68	1.50	1.20
Less-developed regions	4.68	3.94	3.95	4.06	4.02	3.76
Africa	4.42	4.85	4.97	5.10	5.00	4.56
Eastern Africa	5.37	6.06	6.95	6.87	6.39	5.59
Middle Africa	4.07	5.71	5.56	5.40	5.04	4.40
Northern Africa	4.33	4.71	4.57	4.59	4.40	3.74
Southern Africa	3.52	3.38	3.17	3.62	3.84	3.94
Western Africa	4.97	4.87	5.10	5.34	5.43	5.21
Latin America	4.57	4.21	4.01	3.86	3.56	3.06
Caribbean	3.22	3.62	3.44	3.43	3.24	2.84
Middle America	4.68	4.62	4.46	4.42	4.22	3.73
Temperate South America	3.08	2.26	2.01	1.90	1.65	1.27
Tropical South America	5.44	4.83	4.49	4.21	3.74	3.12
Northern America	2.29	1.80	1.33	1.45	1.47	1.19
East Asia	5.46	3.09	3.06	3.03	2.82	2.67
China	6.84	3.15	3.17	3.32	3.29	3.25
Japan	3.36	2.37	2.29	1.95	1.29	0.87
Other East Asia	4.16	5.20	4.52	4.00	3.33	2.36
South Asia	3.37	3.91	4.01	4.33	4.47	4.27
Eastern South Asia	3.92	3.99	4.02	4.31	4.49	4.34
Middle South Asia	2.98	3.66	3.80	4.22	4.46	4.33
Western South Asia	5.80	6.12	5.74	5.22	4.50	3.63
Europe	1.78	1.80	1.52	1.45	1.36	1.19
Eastern Europe	2.33	1.69	1.73	1.68	1.48	1.28
Northern Europe	0.77	1.15	0.91	0.85	0.76	0.66
Southern Europe	2.41	2.53	2.36	2.29	2.14	1.81
Western Europe	1.73	1.69	1.08	0.93	0.90	0.78
Oceania	3.00	2.70	2.67	2.63	2.37	1.84
Soviet Union	3.91	2.75	2.42	2.23	1.87	1.35

SOURCE: United Nations, 1980, p. 13; reprinted by permission.

world (excluding China) that had reached 100,000 in population at the earliest of the two most recent observations. In most instances, the observations derive from successive national population censuses.

City Size and City Growth. The general relation between city size and city growth rates in developing regions is U-shaped. Cities in two size classes between 100,000 and 500,000 are growing at an average of about 3.9 percent annually. In three size classes between 500,000 and 4 million, the average growth rate has declined to 3.1–3.2 percent. For the cities in developing regions larger than 4 million, growth rates again reach the level of 3.9 percent. There are only ten such cities, however—2 percent of the total number of cities and about 11 percent of the total urban population of developing countries—so that the predominant relation between city size and city growth rates is negative. It is also negative, though somewhat irregular, in developed regions. For all cities, the correlation between growth rates and the log of city size is negative, a modest −0.083. These results are consistent with studies showing economic gains from city growth to decline after a size of 100,000 to 300,000 is reached, although they do not suggest that city size is a dominant influence on city growth rates.

The slight negative association between city size and city growth may be surprising. The reason is probably that so many calculations of urban growth patterns present tabulations based not on individual cities but on size classes. Under the latter format, the set of cities within a particular size class changes over time as cities graduate into and out of the limits that define the class. Under conditions of rapid population growth, it typically happens that no cities devolve out of the highest size class, while many graduate into it. The result is that the highest size class of cities experiences by far the most rapid growth. For example, between 1965 and 1975 it is estimated that the population in cities over 4 million in developing regions grew from 55.9 to 120.6 million, or at the very rapid annual rate of 7.7 percent. But almost half of this growth resulted from the fact that the number of cities in this class grew from nine to seventeen, so that 32 million were added to this size class through graduation.

The basic relation between city size and city growth rates remains negative when other variables are controlled. When size of city increases by a factor of 4 above 100,000, annual city growth rates decline on average by about 3 per 1,000. There is evidence, however, that, apart from the absolute size of a city, its position in a country's urban hierarchy influences its growth rate. In particular, national capitals grow at an average annual rate of 0.6 percent, or 6 per 1,000, faster than would otherwise be expected. And if a city is the largest in a country, it grows at an annual rate of 3 per 1,000, faster than otherwise would be expected. The results are thus consistent with the view that spatial patterns of government expenditure bias patterns of city growth toward capital cities and toward the largest city in a country. Whatever economic advantages pertain to size of city should be captured in the variable directly measuring its size. But being the largest city in a country or a capital confers a sizable additional growth increment.

National Growth. The rate of population growth in the nation in which a city is located also has a powerful effect on a city's growth rate. The simple correlation between growth rates in these 1,212 cities and rates of population growth in their respective nations is +0.516. This is by far the strongest correlate of a city's growth rate. An appreciation for the dominance of this factor can be gained from a simple cross-tabulation of city growth rates by city size and by national population growth rates, presented in Table 3. Without exception, cities in a particular size class experience faster average growth as their country's population growth rate increases in increments of 1 percent. All of the categories in which average city growth rates exceed 4.5 percent occur within the group of nations in which population growth exceeds 3 percent. Within a particular category of national growth rates, the relation between city size and city growth tends to be flat and somewhat irregular, certainly not as systematic as the relation with national population growth rates. Regression results also suggest that, other things being equal, an increment of 1 percent in national population growth rates is associated with an increment of 1.002 percent in city growth rates. Nothing could indicate more clearly that cities draw from the same sources of growth as nations.

In addition to a city's size and administrative status and to national rates of population growth, national economic indicators are also associated with its growth rate. Other things being equal, nations at higher levels of gross national product (GNP) per capita and with faster rates of economic growth have faster growing cities. A gain of $1,000 in GNP per capita is associated with a rise of 3.3 per 1,000 in annual rates of city growth, and 1 percent faster annual growth in gross domestic product is associated with a gain of 2.4 per 1,000 in city growth rates. These results thus support those cited above (based on a different data set and estimation procedures) suggesting

TABLE 3. *Average annual city growth rates between latest two censuses as a function of city size and growth rate of the country in which city is located (number of cities in parentheses)*

	Population growth rate of country			
Size of city	0–.0099	0.01–.0199	0.02–.0299	0.03+
4 million+	0.0123 (8)	0.0324 (7)	0.0404 (4)	0.0577 (1)
2–3.999 million	0.0092 (11)	0.0210 (10)	0.0419 (10)	0.0 (0)
1–1.999 million	0.0112 (36)	0.0252 (23)	0.0339 (11)	0.0412 (4)
500–999,999	0.0189 (71)	0.0248 (38)	0.0377 (25)	0.0454 (9)
250–499,999	0.0166 (130)	0.0312 (72)	0.0351 (64)	0.0519 (22)
100–249,999	0.0192 (349)	0.0311 (199)	0.0382 (176)	0.0532 (58)
All cities	0.0178 (605)	0.0298 (349)	0.0375 (290)	0.0517 (94)

SOURCE: United Nations, 1980, p. 43; reprinted by permission.

that rural-urban migration is faster in countries at higher economic levels and with faster economic growth.

The results just described pertain to all cities of the world, including those in developed and less-developed countries alike. There is no evidence, however, that relations differ among the regions, with one major exception: cities in Latin America are in general growing faster than could be predicted based upon their national economic levels, rates of national population growth, and other factors just mentioned. The "excess" in their growth rates amounts to an average of 6 per 1,000 annually. Latin America appears deviant in other respects as well. Latin America has a more top-heavy size distribution of cities than other regions (more very large cities of 2 million and above relative to the number of small and medium-size cities); city growth rates in Latin America are persistently positively related to city size, contrary to relations elsewhere and reinforcing the top-heavy distribution; and occupational structures in Latin America show a remarkably large concentration of nonagricultural activities in cities, without their normal pattern of dispersion into rural areas. That such regional peculiarities exist is indicative of the complexity of urban growth processses in developing countries. International reviews are useful for pointing out general tendencies, but they are no substitute for intensive analysis of the factors operative in a specific context.

Samuel H. Preston

See also DISTRIBUTION, *article on* DISTRIBUTION, CONCENTRATION, AND DISPERSION; INTERNAL MIGRATION.

BIBLIOGRAPHY

Findley, Sally E. *Planning for Internal Migration: A Review of Issues and Policies in Developing Countries.* Prepared for the U.S. Bureau of the Census. Washington, D.C.: U.S. Government Printing Office, 1977.

Grauman, John V. "Orders of Magnitude of the World's Urban Population in History." In *Population Bulletin of the United Nations, No. 8, 1976,* pp. 16–33. New York: United Nations, 1977.

Hoselitz, Bert F. "The Role of Cities in the Economic Growth of Underdeveloped Countries." *Journal of Political Economy* 61(3):195–208, June 1953.

Preston, Samuel H. "Urban Growth in Developing Countries: A Demographic Reappraisal." *Population and Development Review* 5(2):195–215, June 1979.

United Nations, Department of International Economic and Social Affairs. *Patterns of Urban and Rural Population Growth.* Series A, Population Studies, no. 68. New York, 1980.

United Nations, Economic and Social Council. *Concise Report on Monitoring of Population Policies: Report of the Secretary-General.* New York, 22 December 1978.

Yap, Lorene Y. L. "The Attraction of Cities: A Review of Migration Literature." *Journal of Development Economics* 4(3):239–264, September 1977.

3.
DEVELOPED COUNTRIES

Urbanization trends in the second half of the twentieth century are often described as divergent. Variations in rates and patterns among countries and among the world's major regions have apparently widened during recent years and produced a polarization of trends into accelerated urban growth, typical of the less developed countries, and metropolitan contraction, observed in most of the highly urbanized countries. This recent experience has called for a reassessment of urban and population models, as well as settlement policies at national and regional levels.

Basic Patterns. Since the beginning of the 1970s the population of Standard Metropolitan Statistical Areas (SMSA) in the United States has been growing at rates lower than the rates for nonmetropolitan areas (0.8 as compared to 1.2 percent annually). The latter areas have recorded a net migration gain of some 0.4 million people per year (Beale, 1977). This development contrasts with past experience, although the trend toward convergence and turnaround of the rates of population growth for metropolitan versus nonmetropolitan areas started a few decades earlier. According to calculations by Charles L. Leven (1981), during 1940–1950 the Standard Metropolitan Statistical Areas grew at 3.3 times the non-SMSA rate; in the following two decades this ratio had gradually diminished to 2.4 and 1.8, respectively, and during the 1970–1980 period it fell to 0.64. Within the metropolitan areas, the central cities consistently showed slower population growth compared to metropolitan rings during the whole period of 1940–1980, until they reached the stage of contraction in the last decade. Within the group of large SMSAs, with central cities of more than 1 million inhabitants, however, absolute decline started as early as in the 1950s.

Data for Europe show a path of urban change basically similar, although less pronounced than in the United States. A comparison of urban growth rates versus total population growth rates for the 1950s, 1960s, and 1970s reveals no substantial changes, except for a marked decrease in variation; over the whole period, mean annual urban growth rates were roughly double the corresponding figures for the total population. In those countries that are over 70 percent urban, however, the ratio of urban to rural population has stabilized since 1970. As an increasing number of countries approach a state in which a minimum share of their population remains in the agricultural sector, the major population shifts become inevitably contained within urban areas.

During the 1950s, the large cities grew faster than the total urban population. This pattern changed by the 1960s, when most of the cities in the 500,000-and-above category recorded growth rates below the corresponding figures for urban population as a whole. This trend is found irrespective of the proportion of the total population of a given country that lives in large urban centers.

All except a few of the urban cores with populations over 1 million experienced a decline of growth rates in the 1960s as compared to the 1950s, and for nearly half of these cities the latter decade brought an absolute decline in terms of population size. For middle-sized urban cores, the patterns of population change were highly diversified, ranging from very rapid growth to contraction. Some core areas will inevitably grow to become large urban cores, thus increasing the number of the latter. The overall picture for the highly urbanized countries, however, is one of irregular, albeit pronounced, deconcentration within urban areas, and from larger to smaller settlements.

Urban Expansion and Decline. Substantial variations occur in patterns of spatial population change among countries with comparable levels of urbanization and economic development indicators, as well as among different regions within individual countries. In Western Europe, for example, population has declined in the London and Ruhr regions, remained basically stable in the Randstad region (the heavily urbanized western part of the Netherlands, including that country's largest cities of Amsterdam, Rotterdam, Utrecht, and the Hague), made slight gains in the Paris region and expanded substantially in the Munich region. All of these regions except Munich have recorded net migration losses. Areas with the highest migration gains still cluster around the largest urban agglomerations, yet those peripheral regions that have recorded a recent population gain still suffer a high net outflow of young and educated people. These variations are aptly summarized in a United Nations publication:

During the latter part of the period studied (i.e., 1950–1975) the beginning of the movement away from metropolitan cities can be discerned in those countries in which urbanization had progressed furthest. While the trend in some countries may reflect mainly the movement from large cities to the suburbs, in others it appeared to indicate a growing preference for residence in non-metropolitan cities. In the latter countries, urban growth seemed to be taking place more and more in towns of intermediate size and in the hinterland of industrial centers. (1979, p. 273.)

Although the observed patterns of urban change display considerable variations over space, it is fair to state that limits to urban-metropolitan growth are evident at present, at least in the developed countries, and that "posturbanization" phenomena deserve extensive research into both their underlying forces and consequences. As to forces, the importance of popular demand,

such as environmental preferences, has been emphasized by many authors. Leven (1978), however, asserts that demand tends to be dominated by economic opportunity, which varies according to geographic location. Following Leven, we can speak of three main groups of determinants of urban change, namely (1) economic and technological, (2) demographic, and (3) policy-related.

Economic and technological determinants. The category of economic and technological determinants attributes the relatively poor performance of large cities, in terms of population growth rates, to structural shifts between various sectors and to changes in the location of economic activity. Locational changes are explained by a steady decline in economic advantages offered by both large-scale production and concentration of industries within large urban complexes. (These advantages are referred to in the economics literature as scale and agglomeration economies.) Such a decline is partly explained by the increasing ubiquity of transportation and communication and the adaptability of a growing number of industries to small urban settings. Furthermore, increasing drawbacks associated with concentration of people and industry in large cities tend to impair the traditional functions of metropolitan areas as "incubators" for new industries.

Demographic determinants. The demographic roots of urban change have not been explored until recently; however, they may be of special interest because of their universal nature. The phenomena of metropolitan stability and contraction may thus be attributed to long-standing population trends, in particular to decline in fertility, changing age composition, and related evolution of migration patterns. Subject to a particular national context, migration contributes highly varying proportions of total net population change in large metropolitan areas of the urbanized countries. Such proportions, however, will probably tend to decline.

The out-migration potential of nonmetropolitan areas is dwindling, especially when national declines in the birth rate are superimposed on the specific age and sex structures of the local populations that result from past out-migration and recent in-migration patterns. Hence urban growth is no longer associated with in-migration from those rural areas within commuting radius or from peripheral regions representing migration pools on a national scale but rather, to an increasing degree, with the balance of urban-to-urban flows. When natural increase is small and migration is more frequently from city to city, a growing percentage of cities and urban agglomerations may experience more out-migration than in-migration. Thus, the shrinking absolute size of the rural population, together with a change in socioeconomic incentives in favor of medium-size cities may further thin out population flows toward large urban agglomerations in the near future. So far, the predominant pattern of urban-to-urban migrations, in Europe at least, has been movement from smaller to larger cities, but such trends have been more recently replaced by less regular patterns of population flows among cities of various size.

Policy-related determinants. The present trends in population and employment distribution have been influenced by planning measures that follow either from explicit national urban policies, or from implicit ones embedded within overall socioeconomic policies. Settlement policy in many countries, including those countries that now exhibit clear symptoms of large-city decline, have for at least two decades been concerned with excessive population concentration in their main urban agglomerations and with the thinning out of the population in peripheral regions. This applies equally to countries with strong urban primacy (defined as the dominance of the largest city) and to countries with a balanced urban hierarchy (that is, having several cities of considerable importance and located in various regions, as well as a number of medium-sized cities). Depending on socioeconomic conditions, some countries have plans that emphasize economic goals (for example, Sweden, which stresses public services), and some have plans that emphasize environmental goals (Great Britain and the Netherlands, for example, which are concerned with urban containment).

Recognition of the negative effects of large urban agglomerations—their encroachment upon agricultural land and their traffic, pollution, and other social costs—has been persistent. Prevailing policies have been aimed at dispersing population from metropolitan to peripheral regions on the national scale and, in some instances, from urban cores to marginal zones on a local scale. This has been true even though priorities have changed over time, focusing more recently mainly upon balanced employment.

Few studies have attempted to measure the actual impact of settlement policies in quantitative terms, but this impact is believed to be of a considerable magnitude. In Great Britain, for example, the transfer of 325,000 jobs from the conurbations (aggregations of urban communities) to the development areas between 1960 and 1976 is attributed to direct policy measures. In Poland, the effectiveness of policies limiting large-city growth, carried out during the 1960s, can be measured by a shift in the annual rate of employment expansion in the city of Warsaw, from 50 percent above the national average during 1960–1964 to 40–50 percent below the average by the late 1960s.

The empirical evidence of a slowdown in urban growth and, occasionally, an absolute metropolitan contraction has prompted refocusing of policies from control of growth to generation of growth. The importance of policy as a factor governing urban change should be underscored, although the scope of such policies varies considerably depending upon socioeconomic conditions. Moreover, because policies tend to adjust to changing economic, technological, and demographic factors, they cannot be treated as a fully independent force of urban change.

Consequences of Urban Change. Since causes and consequences of urban change are mutually interdependent, one can identify a number of outcomes for each of the three determinants listed above. Undesirable consequences of metropolitan contraction include deterioration of the economic and financial bases of the major cities, which results in the decline of such aspects of the quality of life as the level of services and environmental conditions. Other undesirable effects are the rapid growth in energy costs associated with decentralization and the mismatch between the distribution of economic opportunities and the skills of city residents.

Taking a more general perspective, one can expect that slow population growth is associated with a number of difficulties that are quite different from those prevailing during periods of rapid growth. A low rate and a high selectivity of immigration tend to produce changes in the age and sex structure, which in turn influence the amount, distribution, and composition of public services rendered to the local population. These changes also have pronounced effects on the levels of income, productivity, and investment. Urban redevelopment and rehabilitation, a problem typical of all large urban areas, also represents a different dimension in a situation of stability or decline when compared to previous conditions of sustained growth.

During the decades of rapid metropolitan development, the slowing down of its momentum was looked upon as a means of improving the quality of urban life. Once the slowdown occurred, however, such a positive change did not seem to follow. Population decline in large urban areas has not been accompanied by improvement of working and living conditions.

Problems associated with the patterns of urban change differ in terms of the political level at which action may be taken. Some problems must be dealt with at the national level, for example, adjusting to changing foreign trade relations and overall demographic trends. Other problems pertain to the changing allocation of resources between regions with the resulting interregional flows of capital and migrants. Yet other aspects of urban change apply to the local level, for example, the difficulties faced by large urban areas in adjusting their physical structures to evolving economic, technological, and social requirements. Turning the argument around, it can be claimed that patterns of urban change are not without effects upon national economic and demographic development, as well as upon relations among regions and between urban cores and the hinterlands. Thus, a comprehensive study of the determinants and consequences of urban change should not bypass any of these levels.

Urban Development and Settlement Structures. One of the failures of analyses of metropolitan growth and contraction is insufficient recognition of the changing role of large cities within regional and national contexts. Neither the stability nor the rapid growth of metropolitan areas should be viewed only in terms of dependence and impact on national and intraurban trends, but also in terms of the evolving urban hierarchy. Such an evolution entails shifts in the nature and location of specialized (nonlocal) versus local functions and growing interdependence among urban agglomerations as well as between their cores and hinterland areas.

Many authors, for example Harry W. Richardson (1973), have pointed out that no systematic statistical relations exist between the distribution of a country's cities by size and its economic level. Nevertheless, the highest indexes of urban primacy are associated with less-developed countries, especially when a sample is limited to larger countries. In fact, planners in both the developed and the developing countries have consistently identified urban primacy as a problem area and have devised a variety of measures aiming at diminishing the gap between the dominant city (typically a nation's capital) and the other cities, if such a gap was found to exist. Among the best-known examples of such policies are the French concept of *métropoles d'équilibre*, the Hungarian policy of developing five major cities as countermagnets to Budapest, and the corresponding attempts by Irish planners to promote nine centers of secondary growth, which would offset the excessive concentration of population and economic power in the Dublin area and keep the growth of the capital region at a level corresponding to the natural increase of its resident population.

Arguments in favor of a balanced urban hierarchy characterized by the existence of several major cities can readily be assembled. First, the services of a metropolitan center can be provided within different regions. Second, the country will have better economic and cultural integration. Third, the processes of cultural innovation and diffusion may prove more effective starting from several points of origin rather than radiating through the so-called neighborhood effect, that is, spread from the unique origin outward.

The recent trends in developed countries lead toward an evening-out of the disparities of size and rank among cities and thus to the decline of the role played by the largest cities, although the role change may lag behind changes in their proportion of the population. Such

trends are evidently congruent with the objectives of settlement policies mentioned earlier. At the same time, they give rise to new policy issues. These include the underuse of existing capital resources within urban areas and the mismatch between geographic patterns of labor supply and demand, as well as rapid and often unpredictable shifts in the distribution of economic activity as individual industries and other economic enterprises perceive the advantages of new locations.

Another characteristic of observed urban trends is that they are not adequately explained by the existing theory of settlement. Most of the concepts available in this research area support the notion of continuous and unhampered expansion of large urban agglomerations, while alternative interpretations, based on the concept of "urban transition" (Klaassen and Paelinck, 1979) have been proposed only very recently and are still in an early formulation stage. According to this concept, a city undergoes repetitive cycles of growth, stability, and decline, which are attributable to its internal transformations, such as replacement of residential use of land in the core (central) districts by commercial use, and expansion of the urban ring.

Thus the question of whether the trend toward urban deconcentration is likely to be sustained or temporary cannot be easily answered at present. The growing concern over resources, and in particular energy conservation, would rather support a trend toward concentration. Once started, however, the processes of deconcentration of population may not easily lose their momentum, at least during the next few decades. Demographic change seems to point in this direction.

Piotr Korcelli

BIBLIOGRAPHY

Beale, Calvin L. "The Recent Shift of United States Population to Nonmetropolitan Areas, 1970–75." *International Regional Science Review* 2(2):113–122, Winter 1977.

Boudeville, Jacques R. "Les regions de villes en l'Europe." In *Le structure urbaine en Europe occidentale: Faits, theories, modelles,* edited by Jean H. P. Paelinck. Westmead, England: Saxon House, 1978.

Gordon, Peter, and Jacques Ledent. "Modeling the Dynamics of a System of Metropolitan Areas: A Demoeconomic Approach." *Environment and Planning A* 12(2):125–133, February 1980.

Klaassen, L. H., and Jean H. P. Paelinck. "The Future of Large Towns." *Environment and Planning A* 11:1095–1104, 1979.

Lasuén, José R. "Urbanization and Development: The Temporal Interaction between Geographical and Sectoral Clusters." *Urban Studies* 10(2):163–188, June 1973.

Leven, Charles L. "The Emergence of Maturity in Metropolis." In *The Mature Metropolis,* edited by Charles L. Leven, pp. 3–20. Lexington, Mass.: Lexington Books, 1978.

———. "Regional Shifts and Metropolitan Reversal in the U.S." Paper presented at the Conference on Urbanization and Development, Laxenburg, Austria, 1–4 June 1981.

Mosely, Malcolm J. *Growth Centres in Spatial Planning.* Oxford and New York: Pergamon Press, 1974.

Pred, Allan R., and Gunnar E. Törnqvist. *Systems of Cities and Information Flows: Two Essays.* Lund Studies in Geography, series B, no. 38. Lund, Sweden: Gleerup, 1973.

Richardson, Harry W. *The Economics of Urban Size.* Westmead, England: Saxon House, 1973. Lexington, Mass.: Lexington Books, 1973.

United Nations, Economic Commission for Europe. *Labour Supply and Migration in Europe: Demographic Dimensions 1950–1975 and Prospects.* Economic Survey of Europe in 1977, part 2. New York, 1979.

4.
MEASUREMENT

The definition of what constitutes an urban area and the procedures for demarcating such areas vary considerably among the nations of the world and at times even within individual countries. Similarly, a large number of different techniques exist for measuring various aspects of urbanization. This article discusses some of these techniques and their advantages and disadvantages in terms of (1) the data needed for their computation, (2) the ease with which they can be calculated, (3) the dimension of urbanization actually measured, and (4) the ease with which the measures can be interpreted.

Measures of the degree and changes in the degree of urbanization are presented first because together they are the basic dimensions of the process that must be quantified if the phenomenon of urbanization is to be studied statistically. The measures presented give the most objective procedures for monitoring and tracking the process consistently over time and from country to country. Since urbanization is strongly influenced by the various components of urban population change, the final section of this article focuses upon the breaking down of change into its components, permitting the reclassification of areas, natural change, and net migration.

Because the measurement of urbanization can be affected by different definitions of the boundaries of cities, particular attention should be given to what is taken for the limits of a city. Are the boundaries administrative, or is the actual city larger than its administrative limits? When should the rural and suburban population close to the city be considered part of a metropolitan area? These questions could be answered differently in every country or in a single country at different times. The practices followed affect comparisons of urban data.

Finally, classification of the population as urban or rural, or sometimes suburban, should not be considered sufficient information. In all instances it is preferable to have detailed information about component elements of the urban complex and about the various types of rural populations, such as farm, nonfarm, nomadic, seminomadic, and sedentary.

Degree of Urbanization. The phrase "degree of urbanization" usually refers to the absolute or relative number of people who live in what are defined as urban places. Two kinds of indexes have been developed for measuring the degree of urbanization of a country: those based only on the proportion of people living in places defined as urban and those that also take into account the size of the cities of a country.

Urban percentage. The percentage of population in urban places has been the most commonly used index for measuring the degree of urbanization. This index is popular because it is easy to calculate and interpret and because of the relative availability of the needed data. When the percentage of the population that is urban is used to measure the degree of urbanization, particularly in historical or international comparisons, the definition of "urban" and of what constitutes the boundaries of a city must be taken into account. Nevertheless, once a definition of urban is adopted, the urban continuum is transformed into a dichotomous phenomenon.

Currently most countries record information about the size of their principal cities, and a better urban comparison can be made by looking at the populations living in cities of similar size. Instead of comparing the people in urban areas as defined in censuses, it makes more sense to compare the people living in cities of 10,000 and over, of 20,000 and over, or some other standard figure. Measuring the degree of urbanization either by using census definitions of urban or by using the population living in localities over a particular size could give different results in an international comparison. When historical or international comparisons are made, constant categories of city size should be used.

Urban-rural ratio. Although seldom used as an index of urbanization, the ratio of urban to rural population measures another aspect of the urbanization process. This index is as simple as the percentage of the total population that is urban and is closely related to it in that it tells how many city dwellers there are for each rural person in a country. In symbols the urban-rural population ratio may be expressed as

$$RA = U/R, \tag{1}$$

where RA is the urban-rural ratio, and U and R are the urban and rural populations.

This index has a lower limit of 0 when the whole population is rural. It is 1 when 50 percent of the population is rural, thus indicating one city dweller for each rural person. In theory the upper limit is infinite when a country has no rural population. In the few instances where this might occur it can be assumed that there is one rural person, thereby making the upper limit of the index equal to the total size of the population minus one.

Like urban percentages, the urban-rural ratio is affected by changes and differences in the definition of "urban." For historical comparisons, however, it is probably the best index for measuring the tempo of urbanization.

Residence of the median inhabitant. Another index establishes the size of the locality where the median inhabitant lives. The concept is similar to that of median age except that the index uses the size of cities rather than age. That is, if the population of a country is ordered according to the size of localities where people live, from the largest to the smallest, or vice versa, and a rank is assigned to each inhabitant from number one to the total population number, the index represents the size of the locality inhabited by the person occupying the fiftieth percentile, that is, with the rank equal to one half of the population of the country (or the inhabitant who divides the population in half).

When interpreting this index it is assumed that the larger the city size of the median inhabitant, the greater the degree of urbanization. Thus, unlike the indexes previously discussed, this measure of urbanization takes into account the actual size of a locality and allows it to be an indicator of the degree of urbanization. As the distribution of population by city size approaches a continuous distribution, the calculation and interpretation of this index is improved. Nevertheless, the value of the index can vary over time or between countries solely because of the city-size distribution. Among countries with just a few cities, historical changes in this index do not reflect actual changes in the degree of urbanization.

Moreover, in countries where the rural population is greater than 50 percent and no classification of rural localities exists, this index cannot be calculated unless some hypothesis about the distribution of rural localities is made. Finally, we may note that this index has two limits; it will be 1 if more than 50 percent of the population is dispersed, and it will equal the total population when all people are concentrated in a city.

Mean city population size. Another way to measure the degree of urbanization is to obtain an average of the size of cities. The statistical concept of this index is the expected value of the locality of residence of the population. According to the statistical concept of expected value, mean city population size is expressed as

$$MC = E(C_i) = \sum p_i v_i, \qquad (2)$$

where $E(C_i)$ represents the expected value of the size of the cities, p_i is the probability that a randomly selected person lives in city C_i, and v_i is the size of the city. The probability p_i is equal to the population living in the particular city C_i divided by the total population of the country, P. Since the population living in a particular city is also the size of the city, both the variable value and the city population are the same and can be represented by the same symbol, C_i. Therefore, since

$$v_i = C_i \qquad \text{and} \qquad p_i = C_i/P,$$

$$MC = \frac{\sum_{i=1}^{m} C_i^2}{P}, \qquad (3)$$

where C_i is the population of city i, P is the total population of the country, and m is the total number of localities.

Another way of understanding what this index measures is to think of it as a weighted average of the sizes of the cities. As in the previous index a parallel with the mean age of a population can be drawn. For instance, the calculation of the mean age of a population is made by multiplying the age by the population at each particular age and dividing by the total population. In the instance of the mean city population size, instead of age, size of locality is used and instead of population at each particular age, population in each particular locality is used. The value of this index, practically speaking, does not change when, instead of using all localities, as in equation (3), only the urban localities over a particular city size are used in its calculation.

The lower limit of this index (approaching 1) would be obtained when the population of the country is completely dispersed over the territory without constituting any cities. The upper limit (the total population size) is reached when the country's entire population lives in a single city. Although the lower limit is the same for any population, the upper limit would differ depending upon a country's total population size.

This index may also be used for analyzing the urbanization process of particular groups (e.g., ethnic, religious, income, or professional). Although for such purposes the concept of the index remains the same, the equation for each particular group is obtained by using the size of the city population where a group resides weighted by the population of the particular group.

This index has the advantage of not being significantly affected by changes in the city population distribution or by the definition of the term "urban" used in a particular country. Also the index can be broken down into two factors: the proportion that is urban and the mean city population size of the urban population. This fact offers the possibility of analyzing the contribution of each aspect of urbanization to the change of the degree of urbanization. This index, however, is affected by the delimitation of city boundaries. Since the population of each city is weighted by its own size, the index is sensitive to whether or not metropolitan areas are considered in the calculation and to where the actual boundaries of cities are established. If the administrative boundaries are smaller than the actual size of the city, or if cities are used instead of metropolitan areas, the index will yield an underestimate of the degree of urbanization.

Tempo of Urbanization. The concept of tempo of urbanization refers to change in the degree of urbanization during a period of time. If the degree of urbanization is measured by the percentage of population living in urban places, by the urban-rural ratio, by the city size of the median inhabitant, or by the mean city population size, the speed of urbanization would be the change registered in these indexes over a period of time. Since a change in urbanization can be referred to different periods of time, annual changes can be calculated and compared. Presented here are only those methods for calculating the annual change of each index that are most frequently used or most generally recommended.

Change in the urban percentage. When the degree of urbanization has been measured in terms of the percentage that is urban, the tempo can be calculated either as the absolute change in percentage points or as the annual rate of change in the percentage of urban population between two dates. In the first situation, the estimation consists of dividing the difference of the urban percentage at the two dates by the number of years between such dates. For instance, if the urban proportion increased from 35 percent to 48 percent between 1961 and 1972 respectively, the difference of 13 percent should be divided by the time (11 years). In this instance, the tempo would be an increase of 1.2 percent per year.

The annual rate of change of the urban percentage is a better measurement, and the following equation is recommended:

$$TR = \frac{1}{n}\left(\ln \frac{PU^{t+n}}{PU^t}\right), \tag{4}$$

where TR represents the tempo, n is the length of the period in years, "ln" stands for "natural logarithm," and PU^t and PU^{t+n} are the urban percentages at dates t and $t + n$, respectively. If the tempo is measured by this procedure, it can be proven that TR represents the difference between annual exponential growth rates of the urban and total populations, or r_u and r_t, respectively. That is,

$$TR = r_u - r_t. \tag{5}$$

When the degree of urbanization has been measured by the urban percentage and the tempo by the difference between urban and total annual population growth

rates, once the population becomes 100 percent urban, the tempo becomes 0, in spite of the fact that the cities may continue growing. Since the population would be 100 percent urban, both growth rates, those of both the urban and the total populations, would be the same. This is one of the disadvantages of measuring the degree of urbanization as the urban percentage.

Change in the urban-rural ratio. If the degree of urbanization has been measured by the urban-rural ratio, absolute or relative annual changes in this index constitute the tempo of urbanization, whether positive or negative. The annual absolute change of this index would indicate (on the average) the annual increase or decrease in the number of city dwellers per rural inhabitant.

If the tempo of urbanization is measured by the annual rate of change of the urban-rural ratio, an interesting result is obtained:

$$TU = \frac{1}{n}\left(\ln \frac{RA^{t+n}}{RA^t}\right), \tag{6}$$

where n is the duration of the interval (in years) and RA^t and RA^{t+n} are the urban-rural ratios for dates t and $t + n$, respectively. In this instance, it can also be proven that

$$TU = r_u - r_r, \tag{7}$$

where r_u and r_r are the annual growth rates of the urban and rural populations, respectively, during the considered interval. In words, the tempo of urbanization in this instance is the difference between the growth rates of the urban and rural populations. The tempo measured in this way would not necessarily approach zero as the population approaches 100 percent urban. On the contrary, the tempo, in that particular situation, would be equal to the urban population growth rate.

Observation indicates that the proportion that is urban tends to follow an **S** curve, or logistic curve, through time. The growth rate of such a logistic trend would be the difference between the urban and rural population growth rates or the tempo of urbanization.

Change in median inhabitant residence. If the degree of urbanization was measured by the index of place of residence of the median inhabitant, the tempo of urbanization is taken to be the average annual rate of exponential change in that index:

$$TMI = \frac{1}{n}\left(\ln \frac{MI^{t+n}}{MI^t}\right). \tag{8}$$

Since changes in the index of the place of residence of the median inhabitant may merely reflect changes in the distribution of localities, this index of tempo must always be interpreted with caution, and it is not recommended.

Change in the mean city population size. If the degree of urbanization was measured by the index of the mean city population size, the tempo will be the average annual rate of exponential change in this index:

$$TMC = \frac{1}{n}\left(\ln\frac{MC^{t+n}}{MC^t}\right). \qquad (9)$$

The tempo of urbanization measured in this way will not be affected by changes in the definition of "urban," but it will be affected by improper city boundaries.

A second advantage of measuring the tempo of urbanization as change in the mean city size is that this index can be broken down into two components: the percentage of population taken as urban and the size of the localities considered urban. Since the index of mean city population size is the product of these two components, the product can be transformed in addition of the logarithms of each component and hence the contribution of each component can be easily analyzed.

Components of Urban Population Growth. A change in the urban population during a given period has at least two dimensions: (1) the localities within which change may occur and (2) the growth components that act within these localities. The "locality" and "component" dimensions of urban population change can be summarized in a two-way table, as shown in Figure 1. Types of localities designate columns, and the components of population growth designate rows. The two-way tabular format isolates the role of each factor in determining total urban population change. When each of the eight cells in the table is filled, adding the appropriate row will give the component of urban population change due to natural change, migration, or the reclassification of the people. Adding the columns will yield the components of urban growth by type of locality.

Contribution of localities. The procedure for calculating the contribution of each kind of locality to urban population change will depend upon the available informa-

FIGURE 1. *Two-story tabular format for analyzing factors responsible for urban population growth*

COMPONENTS OF CHANGE	TYPE OF LOCALITY		
	Same urban localities	Localities that have been reclassified	Localities or areas that have been annexed to other urban areas
Natural change			
Migration			
Reclassified population	Not applicable		

tion. If there is a list of all localities at the beginning and at the end of the period with data on the size and rural-urban status of each, and if it is possible to determine which rural areas have been annexed to previous urban areas, then urban population change can be broken down into three components.

First, the contribution to total urban growth made by localities that have been urban during the entire period is calculated by taking the differences between the ending and starting populations of cities that have remained such throughout the period. In calculating this contribution, no annexations should be included. It is important, of course, to be alert for boundary changes no matter what unit (city, urban, or metropolitan area) is being studied.

Second, the contribution of annexation to total urban growth is estimated by determining the total population living in those areas that were annexed during the period of analysis.

Finally, the contribution of the reclassification of localities to total urban population growth can be calculated by subtracting from the total population of those localities that have been reclassified from rural to urban, the total population of those localities that have been reclassified from urban to rural.

The magnitude of the effect of reclassification of localities on total urban population growth is sometimes overlooked. In general, the longer the period of time under observation, the more important this component will tend to be.

Population growth components. The population growth of localities that have been urban during the whole period (column 1 of the two-way table) is broken down into two parts, natural change (row 1) and migration (row 2). The procedure depends on whether or not vital statistics for each particular locality are available. If they are, natural change is the difference between the births and deaths that have occurred during a specific period in the locality. The difference between total city growth and natural change then constitutes net migration.

When vital statistics are not available, the two components must be measured by indirect procedures. This usually involves assumptions about the natural growth rate of localities or about the amount of net migration during the period. If an estimate of net migration is made using the survival ratio method by age or by using census information about place of birth, the natural growth figure can be obtained by subtracting the net migration estimate from the total change. If, however, an estimate of the natural growth rate of the urban population is used, some additional considerations should be taken into account. For instance, a distinction might be drawn between the natural growth contributed by the population resident at the beginning of the period and the natural growth contributed by net migrants.

In most instances the information needed to break down the combined effect into the number of migrants and their natural effect is not available. Then assumptions have to be made about the demographic characteristics of migrants (sex, age, fertility, and mortality) if their natural increase is to be estimated.

The growth of the urban population resulting from the reclassification of localities (column 2 of the two-way table) can be analyzed by considering the natural growth of the population of localities that have been changed from rural to urban (row 1), the migration to localities that have been changed from rural to urban (row 2), and the population that was living in reclassified localities (row 3) at the beginning of the period, year t. The third component can be calculated if there is a list of the population of localities with their urban or rural status at the beginning and at the end of the period. When this list is available, the contribution of the population that has been reclassified is the total population at time t in all those localities changing from rural to urban during the period minus the population at time t in all those localities changing from urban to rural during the period.

A similar breakdown into natural increase, migration, and reclassification of population can be made for those localities that have been annexed (column 3).

Summary. Several indexes have been presented for measuring the degree of urbanization, each of which allows analysis of one particular aspect of the phenomenon. The index selected will depend primarily upon the purposes of the particular study. The simplest and the most common, the percentage of population in urban areas, indicates how many city dwellers there are per 100 inhabitants in a particular population. While this index reveals nothing about the size of cities in which the urban population is located, it can be refined by calculating the percentage of population by categories of city size. Another index of the degree of urbanization, the ratio of urban to rural population, measures the number of city dwellers per rural inhabitant; but neither does this index take into account the size of cities. This index, however, has advantages over the urban percentage when the tempo of urbanization is being analyzed.

Since city size is also a distinctive urban characteristic, its inclusion is frequently desirable in the measurement of the degree of urbanization. The index of size of locality of residence of the median inhabitant meets this purpose. In general, it indicates the size of the city above which 50 percent of the population lives. This index, however, is affected by the particular boundaries of the city-size cate-gories used. The last method discussed for measuring the degree of urbanization uses a weighted average of the size of cities where the population resides. The index of mean city population size can be considered the product of the proportion of urban localities and the mean city population size of the urban localities. This index has the advantage of not being affected by different definitions of urban population.

In general, the tempo of urbanization is measured by comparing the level of urbanization at two different times. Therefore, it implicitly involves the advantages and disadvantages of the indexes used to measure the degree of urbanization. The tempo of urbanization measured as changes in the percentage of urban population tends toward zero when the urban percentage approaches 100. This disadvantage is avoided when tempo is measured as changes in the other three indexes of the degree of urbanization. Particular caution should be exercised, however, when tempo is measured as changes in the size of the locality of residence of the median inhabitant, since this index may be affected by the city-size categories chosen for its calculation. Measuring urbanization tempo as changes in the urban-rural ratio has the advantage of simplicity because tempo is then calculated by taking the difference in urban and rural annual population growth rates; but this procedure could be affected by changes in the definition of "urban." When tempo is measured by changes in the mean city population size, it can be broken down into the change resulting from the urban proportion and that resulting from the size of cities.

As a first step in analyzing the demographic causes of urban population growth within any country, the total change of the urban population between two points in time must be broken down into the components of growth. These processes can be studied from two perspectives. One analyzes urban growth in terms of the localities that contribute to it, that is, localities that have been reclassified (from rural to urban or vice versa) and localities or areas that have been annexed to other urban areas. The second perspective analyzes urban population growth in terms of three different demographic components: natural growth, migration, and the reclassification of population (from rural to urban or vice versa) in the absence of migration. The cross-classification of the demographic components with the types of localities generates eight possible sources or components of urban population growth.

It is important to emphasize that no single index can measure all aspects of the urbanization process. Each particular index measures specific aspects of each facet. The selection of a particular index should be made taking into account (1) what is to be measured, (2) what the index actually measures, and (3) the possible interpretation of the index value.

Eduardo E. Arriaga

See also DISTRIBUTION, *article on* DISTRIBUTION, CONCENTRATION, AND DISPERSION; MATHEMATICAL DEMOGRAPHY.

BIBLIOGRAPHY

Arriaga, Eduardo E. "A New Approach to the Measurements of Urbanization." *Economic Development and Cultural Change* 18(2):206–218, January 1970.
————."Selected Measurements of Urbanization." In *The Measurement of Urbanization and Projection of Urban Population,* edited by Sidney Goldstein and David F. Sly, pp. 19–87. Dolhain, Belgium: Ordina Editions, 1975.
Davis, Kingsley. "The Urbanization of the Human Population." In *Cities,* edited by Scientific American editors, pp. 3–24. New York: Knopf, 1966.
Duncan, Otis Dudley. "The Measurement of Population Distribution." *Population Studies* 11(1):27–45, July 1957.
Goldstein, Sidney. "An Overview of the World Urbanization." In *International Population Conference, Liège, 1973,* vol. 1, pp. 177–190. Liège, Belgium: International Union for the Scientific Study of Population, 1973. In English and French.

USSR

See SOVIET UNION.

VALUE OF CHILDREN

Studies of the value of children encompass both the satisfactions provided by children and the costs entailed in rearing them. Such satisfactions and costs have social, economic, and psychological dimensions. The value of children to parents varies across cultures, socioeconomic groups, communities, and individuals.

Knowledge about the value of children can take several forms and can be derived from quite different research approaches. In macrolevel models, the value of children is often inferred on the basis of proxy measures, such as children's education or participation in the labor force. Community-level studies usually include direct observation of children's economic contributions and collection of information about their social and familial roles. Studies based on survey interviews collect a wide range of data dealing mainly with attitudes toward children in the context of parents' needs and desires.

These diverse research approaches have in common a functional view of children. However, there is no common perspective on the processes by which the values and costs of children are linked to fertility behavior. At issue, for example, is the extent to which childbearing reflects planned choices or decisions. This topic tends to be treated differently in the various disciplinary and theoretical perspectives on fertility.

Theoretical and Empirical Foundations. Since the early 1970s, extensive research on the value of children has been conducted in each of the world's major geographic and cultural areas. The impetus for this work stems from several sources (see Fawcett, 1972, 1977). Writings on the demographic transition, both historical and contemporary, frequently include discussion of changes in the value of children related to economic development. The focus in this perspective is on reduced economic benefits and higher costs of children as a result of the shift from a rural, agricultural society to an urban, industrialized one. Also considered in transition theory are the impacts of changing family structure and higher levels of education, with concomitant development of personal goals and aspirations that are incompatible with large families. Such social trends are often reinforced by the emergence of public programs, such as pension schemes, that provide substitutes for some of the functions traditionally fulfilled by children.

The broad historical perspective of demographic transition theory has been complemented by theoretical approaches linked to analysis of contemporary fertility trends and differentials. In the sociological literature, for example, the utility of children and their costs are viewed as a function of institutional structures that prescribe certain roles, especially for women (Blake, 1971). This structural approach is shared by some anthropologists, who have also been concerned about the culturally defined functions of children and their roles in household production (Nag, White, and Peet, 1978). Economists have analyzed the value of children in the context of household decision making. From this perspective, the utility to be gained from having children is weighed against competing alternatives, within a framework of allocation of limited resources, including the parents' time (Schultz, 1973). Psychologists have also taken a decision-making approach and have emphasized the diverse needs of parents that are fulfilled by having children, with particular attention to life cycle changes in the motivational context for childbearing (Fawcett, 1970; Hoffman and Hoffman, 1973; Hoffman, Thornton, and Manis, 1978).

A substantial body of empirical research has accompanied each of these theoretical perspectives. This article touches briefly upon community studies, which have an anthropological emphasis, then focuses on survey research that reflects a psychological perspective.

Community-level studies designed explicitly to assess the value of children are few in number, are concentrated in Asia and Africa, and are primarily descriptive (Cain, 1977; Hull and Hull, 1977; Nag, White, and Peet, 1978; Ruzicka, 1977; Ware, 1978). Such studies have, however, provided an important contextual understanding of the role of children in the economy of rural households.

In a number of communities data have been collected on the tasks actually performed by children, including farm chores as well as household tasks, such as cooking and care of younger children. Several studies have classified these activities according to age and sex of the child and have computed the economic value of the child's contribution to the household.

Rural children typically are assigned useful tasks at an early age, no later than age 5 or 6. Tasks are allocated according to sex-role distinctions, which become more pronounced with age as boys take on increased responsibilities as productive workers and girls devote greater time to household maintenance. By the early teens, both boys and girls are doing work roughly equivalent to an adult in many societies.

These patterns show cultural variation, of course, and are affected by other factors such as socioeconomic status of the household, type of crop production, and extent of compulsory schooling. But the evidence for a net economic value of children in some rural settings is clear, especially when viewed from the perspective of lifetime return to parents. Children may be net producers by their late teens, and even more important they are often the only source of old-age security for their parents. In the context of the parents' life cycle, the costliness of young children is frequently outweighed by the expectation of crucial long-term benefits.

Community studies thus illuminate linkages between household economy in a life-cycle context and economic contributions of children. Some attitudinal surveys have also focused on economic dimensions (e.g., Mueller, 1972), but more often the attitudinal approach has incorporated diverse emotional, social, and economic aspects of the satisfactions and costs of children. A limitation of attitudinal surveys is that they are never fully convincing with respect to cause-and-effect relationships; however, causal inferences can be made with some confidence when attitudinal studies include cross-cultural comparisons and when their findings are supported by evidence from community-level studies.

Many fertility surveys have incorporated questions on the benefits and costs of children, and in recent years a number of studies have adopted this topic on a central focus. Broadest in scope is a cross-national study known as the Value of Children (VOC) Project, in which comparable interview data have been collected from more than twenty thousand men and women in ten countries. Although this study is based on a psychological framework, the findings have been interpreted with reference to other orientations, particularly transition theory and microeconomic approaches (Arnold et al., 1975; Bulatao, 1979a). The VOC project is the primary source for the discussion that follows.

Conceptual Framework. A useful contribution of research on the value of children has been the formulation of conceptual schemes that distinguish among different types of satisfactions and costs. These have taken several forms, with each proving useful for different analytic purposes (see Bulatao, 1979a; Fawcett et al., 1974; Hoffman and Hoffman, 1973; Townes et al., 1977). Following is a classification of fifteen types of values derived from analysis of cross-national data in the VOC project.

Positive general values
- *Emotional benefits.* Happiness, love, companionship, fun; also viewed in reverse as relief from strain and avoidance of boredom or loneliness.
- *Economic benefits and security.* Benefits from children's help in the house, business, or farm, from care of siblings, and from sharing of income; old-age security for the parents, including economic support, physical care, and psychological security.
- *Self-enrichment and development.* Learning from the experience of childbearing; becoming more responsible and mature; deriving incentives and goals in life from having children; being viewed as an adult, a grown woman or man; self-fulfillment; feeling competent as a parent; being needed and useful.
- *Identification with children.* Pleasure from watching growth and development of children; pride in children's accomplishments; reflection of self in children.
- *Family cohesiveness and continuity.* Children as a bond between husband and wife; fulfillment of marriage; completeness of family life; continuity of family name and traditions; producing heirs; possible future grandchildren.

Negative general values

- *Emotional costs.* General emotional strains; concern about discipline and moral behavior of children; worry over health; noise and disorder in household; children as a nuisance.
- *Economic costs.* Expenses of childrearing; educational costs.
- *Restrictions or opportunity costs.* Lack of flexibility and freedom; restrictions on social life, recreation, travel; lack of privacy; restrictions on career or occupational mobility; no time for personal needs and desires.
- *Physical demands.* Extra housework, caring for children; loss of sleep; general weariness.
- *Family costs.* Less time with spouse; disagreements over rearing of children; loss of spouse's affection.

Large-family values

- *Sibling relationships.* Desire for another child to provide companionship for existing children; enriching the lives of children; avoiding an only child.
- *Sex preferences.* Specific desire for a son or a daughter; desire for a certain combination of sexes among children.
- *Child survival.* Concern that existing children may die; desire for more children to have enough survive to adulthood.

Small-family values

- *Maternal health.* Concern that too many pregnancies, or pregnancies when the mother is beyond a certain age, are bad for the mother's health.
- *Societal costs.* Concern about overpopulation, belief that another child would be a burden to society.

In psychological research on the value of children, dimensions such as these are incorporated in a conceptual framework that emphasizes the choices to be made between children and alternative means of meeting particular needs or desires. This individual-level paradigm provides a central focus. However, it is recognized that individual choices are made within a socioeconomic context that may facilitate or constrain action, and that perceptions of children and alternatives are conditioned by the background of the individual. In addition, childbearing is a function of influences other than the desire for children, such as the factors determining natural fertility and the availability of contraception. Thus, a focus on the value of children must be viewed as but one part of a larger model that would encompass the different influences on fertility. In an expanded microeconomic model, for example, perceptions of children would fit under the rubric of "demand factors," which interact with supply and cost factors to influence decisions about another child and completed family size.

Selected Research Findings. Data from studies of the value of children have been used in a number of ways, ranging from simple descriptive analysis of motivational patterns to complex multivariate analyses in which indexes of the value of children are related to diverse antecedent and consequent variables. In this brief review, selected research findings are presented under three headings: comparative theoretical analyses; social stratification differences; and gender differences and life cycle patterns. The first section uses VOC data in a macroanalytic framework, where countries are the unit of analysis; the second section uses an intermediate level of aggregation, based on social class; and the last section is microanalytic, focusing on individuals and couples.

Comparative theoretical analyses. Comparative data on the value of children have been used to test hypotheses about the demographic transition (Bulatao, 1979a). Changes in specified values are predicted to be associated with fertility decline, and cross-national comparisons are made to seek confirming or disconfirming evidence for particular hypotheses.

This type of analysis has shown evidence for a decrease in the perceived economic value of children with lower fertility levels. By contrast, emotional values, such as love and companionship, show an increase in salience at lower fertility levels, as do perceived opportunity costs of chil-

FIGURE 1. *Perceived economic advantages and security from children by fertility level*

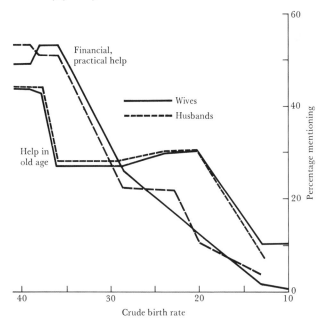

Source of data. Data in Figures 1–4 were derived from VOC surveys in Indonesia, Philippines, Singapore, South Korea, Taiwan, Thailand, Turkey, and the United States. Curves were smoothed by taking medians of three successive values.

SOURCE: Bulatao, 1979a, p. 37; reprinted by permission.

FIGURE 2. *Perceived emotional advantages of children by fertility level*

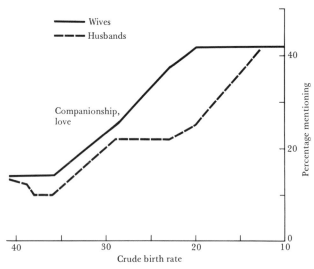

SOURCE: Bulatao, 1979a, p. 74; reprinted by permission.

FIGURE 3. *Perceived restrictions of childrearing by fertility level*

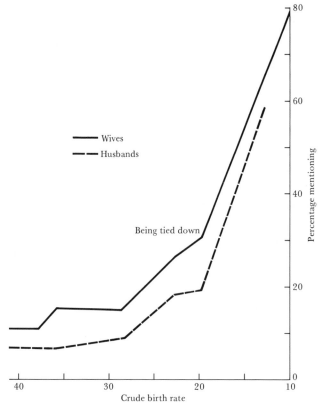

SOURCE: Bulatao, 1979a, p. 50; reprinted by permission.

dren (see Figures 1, 2, 3). Perceived economic costs of children have been found to be relatively unchanging across fertility levels (see Figure 4), perhaps reflecting the tendency of parents with few children to invest more resources per child to have children of higher quality.

Results from this comparative analytic approach have shown sufficient consistency across countries to allow interpretation within the context of a theory of the transition of the value of children (Bulatao, 1979b, p. 1), in which it is concluded, "First, children are liberated from having to contribute to the labors of their families; then parents are liberated from the burden of caring for many children." In the early stages of the value-of-children transition, going from high to moderate levels of fertility, a major factor is the decline in economic productivity of children. And, as childhood mortality is reduced, parents tend to make greater psychological investments in each child. Special care and status are given to children, and emotional relationships between parents and children gain in significance.

At a later stage of the transition, the reliance on children for old-age support declines, and children become wanted almost exclusively for the psychological gratifications they provide. At the same time, however, childrearing becomes more psychologically costly and parents develop aspirations that compete with children. These factors depress fertility further, from moderate to low levels. Parents find satisfactions in having fewer children of high quality, while pursuing goals that provide nonfamilial sources of gratification.

Attitudinal data on the value of children have thus portrayed a trend that is consistent with the tenets of demographic transition theory. Although based on cross-sectional analyses in a limited number of countries, the observed patterns provide convincing evidence of changes that occur over time as societies undergo socioeconomic development.

Social stratification differences. Trends shown in cross-national comparisons by fertility level are similar in many respects to differentials appearing in within-country analyses. The more educated, urbanized segment of society views children in ways differing markedly from the traditional, agricultural population. Such differentials have been shown in a number of countries (Arnold et al., 1975; Fawcett et al., 1974).

Parents who are more educated, particularly those who live in cities, emphasize the emotional and interpersonal benefits connected with the rearing of children. By contrast, rural parents are much more concerned with the practical contributions that children can make to the welfare of the family, including farm work, help in the household, and, in the long run, old-age support and care for the parents.

Parents of all social classes are aware of the purely

FIGURE 4. *Perceived economic disadvantages of children by fertility level*

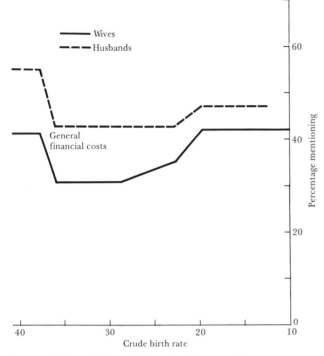

SOURCE: Bulatao, 1979*a*, p. 65; reprinted by permission.

TABLE 1. *Most important advantages and disadvantages of having children, by social class, Taiwan, selected variables (percentages of respondents)*

	Urban middle class	Urban lower class	Rural agricultural
Advantages			
Happiness, love, companionship	62%	39%	19%
Economic benefits, security	3	9	36
Disadvantages			
Financial costs	17	35	49
Restrictions	25	14	9

SOURCE: Arnold et al., 1975; reprinted by permission.

economic costs of childrearing, although the components of such costs may vary. For example, those who have higher aspirations for their children are more concerned about costs of education. As would be expected, parents with lower incomes and larger families are most sensitive to the economic burden of children. Middle-class urbanites are especially sensitive to the restrictions on their freedom that stem from childcare responsibilities; depending on the cultural setting, this concern may include the conflict between childrearing and the wife's work or career.

The nature and extent of social class differences in the perceived value of children are illustrated in Table 1, with data from a survey in Taiwan. Clearly, the parents' background, their position in society, and their economic situation have a substantial impact on the importance attached to various benefits and costs of children. Studies in many countries have confirmed the existence of such class differentials and have established connections with fertility preferences. Expectations for economic benefits from children have been shown to be a particularly strong factor in the desire for large families.

Gender differences and life cycle patterns. In different societies, different values are ascribed to sons and daughters, and perceptions of children vary according to the sex of the parent. Moreover, the relative importance of

certain values changes as parents move through the life cycle, owing in part to the experiences associated with childrearing. These patterns are complex and are subject to social and cultural variation (see, e.g., Bulatao and Arnold, 1977; Williamson, 1978). Some generalizations are possible, however, and these provide useful insights into the motivational aspects of childbearing decisions.

Sons are especially valued in many developing countries for long-term economic benefits, including old-age security. Sons are also wanted for their role in continuing the family name and lineage; this motivation is linked more to cultural values than to level of development, and it is present to some degree in most countries. Daughters tend to be valued for the practical help they provide in the household rather than for long-term economic utility, although they are sometimes looked to for care and comfort in the parents' old age. Daughters are also wanted to provide companionship for the mother and because girls are perceived as having more appealing personalities than boys.

These preferences related to gender of children are largely a reflection of sex-role differences in the society at large, which also have an effect on the differential perceptions of children by men and women. For example, women are more likely than men to emphasize the emotional stress and physical weariness connected with childrearing, a finding consistent with the fact that women usually have primary responsibility for child care. Men, on the other hand, tend to be more concerned with the financial burden of children, presumably because of the man's role as family breadwinner.

Concerning positive values, men and women share a broadly similar orientation toward children. However, some consistent differences have been found, mainly reflecting the interaction between sex of the parent and sex of the child. Men, for example, are more concerned about the value of sons for perpetuating the family name.

(In most societies, it is the father's name that is continued.) Fathers are likely to cite the companionship value of sons, whereas mothers give more emphasis to emotional relationships with daughters. These gender-related preferences become especially important in the dynamic context of family formation, as the pattern of sex composition among children emerges with each successive birth. Gender is one of several dimensions of the value of children that vary in relation to parity (Bulatao, 1981; Fawcett, 1978).

In the early stages of marriage and childbearing, values attached to children are heavily emotional, and a strong commitment to parenthood is reflected in young parents' statements about caring for and loving children. The first child is often viewed as a means of strengthening the marital bond and may signify the attainment of adulthood for the parents. On the other hand, distinctive costs are associated with early childbearing: these are mainly opportunity costs, such as loss of freedom, less time with spouse, and interference with the wife's work.

After the first child, different motivational forces emerge. Particularly potent is the desire for a second child as a companion for the first, that is, a desire to avoid having an only child. Gender preferences also become more salient at this stage, although the nature of such preferences varies by cultural setting. Where preference for a son is strong, for example, this motivation will be heightened if the first child is a daughter. Even where preference for a particular gender is weak, however, the desire for a balance of sons and daughters in the family may result in a gender-specific motivation for the second child. Because of such factors, the motivation for another child is usually at peak strength after the first birth.

For third- and higher-order births, the picture becomes more complex. Gender preference may still be significant, depending on the intensity of this value and the sex of earlier children. Economic and practical benefits of children become increasingly salient as family size increases, partly because of selectivity factors. (Parents with strong economic motives are more likely than others to have large families.) Life cycle elements are also relevant: as firstborn children grow older, their economic contributions to the family increase, thus reinforcing this dimension; and as parents grow older, they become more sensitive to the need for old-age security. The economic burden of children also becomes more salient with the birth of each successive child, however, and this factor is usually cited as most important in the decision to limit family size.

Summary. Research on the value of children thus confirms the notion that economic considerations are significant in fertility decisions, both influencing the desire for large families and creating pressures to stop having children. But motivational processes are complex and economic factors do not operate independently of social and emotional considerations. People want children for many reasons, and childrearing entails diverse kinds of costs. Even though prospective parents may not be able to anticipate fully the personal impact of such benefits and costs, they are generally aware of them. And, as experience is gained after the first birth, attitudes toward children become anchored more firmly in reality. Ongoing research on the value of children is directed toward further explication of the life cycle linkages between attitudes toward children and the behaviors that determine family size.

James T. Fawcett

See also FERTILITY AND DEVELOPMENT; FERTILITY DECLINE; FERTILITY DETERMINANTS; HOUSEHOLD AND FAMILY DEMOGRAPHY.

BIBLIOGRAPHY

Arnold, Fred, et al. *The Value of Children: A Cross-national Study.* Volume 1: *Introduction and Comparative Analysis.* Honolulu: East-West Center, 1975.

Blake, Judith. "Reproductive Motivation and Population Policy." *BioScience* 21(5):215–220, March 1971.

Bulatao, Rodolfo A. *On the Nature of the Transition in the Value of Children.* Papers of the East-West Population Institute, no. 60-A. Honolulu: East-West Center, 1979. (Bulatao, 1979a)

———. *Further Evidence of the Transition in the Value of Children.* Papers of the East-West Population Institute, no. 60-B. Honolulu: East-West Center, 1979. (Bulatao, 1979b)

———. "Values and Disvalues of Children in Successive Childbearing Decisions." *Demography* 18(1):1–25, February 1981.

Bulatao, Rodolfo A., and Fred Arnold. "Relationships between the Value and Cost of Children and Fertility: Cross-cultural Evidence." In *Proceedings of the International Population Conference, Mexico City, 1977,* pp. 141–156. Liège, Belgium: International Union for the Scientific Study of Population, 1977.

Cain, Mead T. "The Economic Activities of Children in a Village in Bangladesh." *Population and Development Review* 3(3):201–227, September 1977.

Fawcett, James T. *Psychology and Population: Behavioral Research Issues in Fertility and Family Planning.* New York: Population Council, 1970.

Fawcett, James T. (editor). *The Satisfactions and Costs of Children: Theories, Concepts, Methods.* Honolulu: East-West Center, 1972.

Fawcett, James T. "The Value and Cost of Children: Converging Theory and Research." In *The Economic and Social Supports for High Fertility,* edited by Lado T. Ruzicka, pp. 91–114. Canberra: Australian National University and Development Studies Center, 1977.

———. "The Value and Cost of the First Child." In *The First Child and Family Formation,* edited by Warren B. Miller and

Lucile F. Newman, pp. 244–265. Chapel Hill, N.C.: Carolina Population Center, 1978.

Fawcett, James T., et al. *The Value of Children in Asia and the United States: Comparative Perspectives.* Papers of the East-West Population Institute, no. 32. Honolulu: East-West Center, July 1974.

Hoffman, Lois Wladis, and Martin L. Hoffman. "The Value of Children to Parents." In *Psychological Perspectives on Population,* edited by James T. Fawcett, pp. 19–76. New York: Basic Books, 1973.

Hoffman, Lois Wladis, Arland Thornton, and Jean Denby Manis. "The Value of Children to Parents in the United States." *Journal of Population* 1(2):91–131, Summer, 1978.

Hull, Terence H., and Valerie J. Hull. "The Relations of Economic Class and Fertility: An Analysis of Some Indonesian Data." *Population Studies* 31(1):43–57, March 1977.

Mueller, Eva. "Economic Motives for Family Limitation: A Study Conducted in Taiwan." *Population Studies* 26(3):383–403, November 1972.

Nag, Moni, Benjamin N. F. White, and R. Creighton Peet. "An Anthropological Approach to the Study of the Economic Value of Children in Java and Nepal." *Current Anthropology* 19(2):293–306, June 1978.

Ruzicka, Lado T. (editor). *The Economic and Social Supports for High Fertility.* Canberra: Australian National University and Development Studies Center, 1977.

Schultz, Theodore W. "The Value of Children: An Economic Perspective." *Journal of Political Economy* 81(2, pt. 2): 52–53, 1973.

Townes, Brenda D., Lee R. Beach, Frederick L. Campbell, and Donald C. Martin. "Birth Planning Values and Decisions: The Prediction of Fertility." *Journal of Applied Social Psychology* 7(1):73–88, January/March 1977.

Ware, Helen. *The Economic Value of Children in Asia and Africa: Comparative Perspectives.* Papers of the East-West Population Institute, no. 50. Honolulu: East-West Center, 1978.

Williamson, Nancy E. "Boys or Girls? Parents' Preferences and Sex Control." *Population Bulletin* 33(1), whole issue, January 1978.

VALUES

See ETHICS.

VITAL STATISTICS

See DATA COLLECTION; RATES AND RATIOS.

WZ

WORK FORCE

See LABOR FORCE.

WORLD FERTILITY SURVEY

The World Fertility Survey (WFS) is an international research program designed to assist countries, particularly in the developing world, to carry out scientifically designed sample surveys of human fertility behavior. The project was undertaken with the collaboration of the United Nations and in cooperation with the International Union for the Scientific Study of Population (IUSSP). Officially announced in 1972, WFS is administered by the International Statistical Institute (ISI) and is financed principally by grants from the United Nations Fund for Population Activities (UNFPA) and the United States Agency for International Development (USAID), with supplements from other countries, notably Canada, France, Japan, and the United Kingdom.

The primary aim of the World Fertility Survey has been to provide participating countries with accurate demographic data describing and interpreting the fertility of their populations. The availability of such data is intended to facilitate national efforts in social, economic, health, and population planning. Ancillary objectives are (1) to enhance capabilities in developing countries for undertaking fertility and other demographic survey research and (2) to provide researchers in participating countries and in the world at large an opportunity to make international comparison of data on fertility levels and differentials, family-size ideals, and knowledge and practice of fertility regulation.

The WFS consists of national surveys carried out by agencies of the local government with technical and (in developing nations) financial assistance. Each survey uses similar core questionnaires and optional questionnaire modules that permit international comparisons of data. The first national survey in the WFS program was conducted in Fiji in 1973-1974. By December 1980 about 400,000 women had been interviewed in forty-three developing countries and twenty developed countries, and the WFS had become the largest social science research project ever undertaken. Developed countries have participated under the coordination of the United Nations Economic Commission for Europe in close collaboration with WFS, but without external financial support.

Survey Materials. The WFS has developed a set of materials to aid and guide countries in carrying out their surveys. These include the household schedule for the screening interview, the individual questionnaire, various modules that can be incorporated into the individual or household questionnaires, and manuals for national project directors and their staffs.

The household schedule is a flexible instrument that can perform various functions, depending on the survey design. In the majority of countries, the design calls for interviewing all eligible women encountered in sample households. In these countries, the household schedule may serve three purposes. First, it provides the listing of household members that is essential to identifying eligible respondents for the individual questionnaire. Second, by gathering data on such matters as age, sex, and marital status of household members, it provides the denominators necessary for calculating certain demographic statistics as well as the opportunity to analyze nuptiality. Third, it provides the possibility of collecting useful contextual data on factors that may relate to fertility, such as ownership of modern objects, membership in cultural or ethnic groups, and housing conditions. In countries lacking good systems of vital registration, the household schedule may also serve to gather data on fertility.

The recommended individual, or core, questionnaire of the WFS consists of seven sections of questions presented in twenty-one pages: (1) respondent's background, (2) maternity history, (3) contraceptive knowledge and use, (4) marriage history, (5) fertility regulation, (6) work history, and (7) current (or last) husband's background.

As an aid to countries wishing to investigate certain topics in greater depth than that afforded by the core questionnaire, various modules or sets of questions have been developed. Each module consists of a series of questions on a particular topic and can be added, either in part or in total, to the core questionnaire. The modules deal with two kinds of variables: those that affect fertility directly and those that may affect fertility indirectly. Variables that affect fertility directly are mainly covered in six modules: (1) fertility regulation, (2) family planning, (3) abortion, (4) factors other than contraception affecting fertility, (5) community-level variables, and (6) general mortality.

Processing and Analyzing Surveys. The principal function of the WFS headquarters professional staff, based in London, is to assist developing countries to carry out and analyze their fertility surveys. Assistance is provided at all stages, including questionnaire and sample designs, interviewer training, fieldwork, coding and editing, data processing, and report writing.

Two stages of data processing must be completed before a "first country report" can be written. The first is data editing, or cleaning; the second is the production of statistical tables. For years the least-developed phase of processing social surveys has been data editing. Fortunately, at about the time the WFS recognized a need for the development of a general purpose editing package for computer use, the Centro Latinoamericano de Demografía (CELADE) was developing just such a package, named CONCOR (for CONsistency and CORrection). The WFS has worked closely with CELADE in adapting

and improving the various components of CONCOR. As a result of the use of CONCOR, the interval between the end of fieldwork and the start of tabulation can be significantly reduced. Since CONCOR is a generalized system, once installed in a country it can be used for cleaning other survey and census data.

To produce tables to be included in country reports, the WFS recommends using COCENTS (for CObol CENsus Tabulation System), a tabulation package developed by the U.S. Bureau of the Census. Major advantages of COCENTS are its adaptability to many different computers and its ability to produce camera-ready copy for offset printing. A major disadvantage in comparison with more sophisticated packages is the amount of programming required for even the simplest tables. As an answer to this problem, the WFS developed a program called COCGEN (for COCENTS GENerator), which permits the preparation of tables in a much simplified form and prepares the parameters for later use of the COCENTS program. As a result, the time required for programming and running tabulations has been cut, for some countries, to as little as two months.

As a further contribution to the state of the art and as an aid to analysts in interpreting survey results (or, more precisely, to help them avoid attributing significance to insignificant results), the WFS has developed a program for the calculation of sampling errors and associated statistics. Named CLUSTERS (for Computation and Listing of Useful STatistics on ERrors of Sampling), the program has powerful recoding routines, is easy to set up, and can be run on relatively small computers. Country reports now contain, as a standard element, an appendix presenting detailed sampling error calculations.

To ensure adequate use and application of the survey data, WFS has encouraged countries to undertake further analysis based on their data, and to assist the countries in this work. Twelve topics were identified for illustrative analyses. The topics selected, with the country supplying data to be analyzed in each case, were

1. Fertility levels and trends estimated from birth history data (Sri Lanka),
2. Evaluating fertility levels and trends (Colombia),
3. Life table analysis of birth intervals (Colombia),
4. The analysis of nuptiality (Sri Lanka and Thailand),
5. Contraceptive sterilization and births averted (Panama),
6. Socioeconomic determinants of the use of contraceptives (Thailand),
7. Breastfeeding and its impact on fertility (Pakistan),
8. Socioeconomic determinants of fertility preferences (Sri Lanka),

9. Use of contraception as related to fertility preferences (Colombia),
10. Family structure and fertility (Bangladesh and Sri Lanka),
11. Socioeconomic differentials in cumulative fertility (Sri Lanka), and
12. Levels and differentials of infant and child mortality (Colombia).

WFS country data converted into a standard recode tape are stored in the WFS offices in London along with the necessary documentation. The data belong to the country concerned but can be released to organizations or individuals for bona fide research work with the permission of, and subject to the conditions specified by, that country. By the time the surveys in all the participating countries are completed, WFS will have assembled for the first time ever a set of internationally comparable data on reproductive behavior and attitudes collected within a relatively narrow span of time from about sixty-five countries of the world.

Some Substantive Findings. By 1980 results were available from the first fifteen developing countries to complete their national surveys. These were nine coun-tries in Asia and the Pacific (Bangladesh, Fiji, Indonesia, Malaysia, Nepal, Pakistan, South Korea, Sri Lanka, and Thailand) and six countries in Latin America (Colombia, Costa Rica, the Dominican Republic, Mexico, Panama, and Peru). In Costa Rica and Panama, the women surveyed were aged 20–49; in all other countries, 15–49.

Fertility trends. This first analysis of the WFS indicated a noticeable decline in fertility levels under way in many parts of the developing world. Among the fifteen countries studied there were only three possible exceptions: Bangladesh, Nepal, and Pakistan. In the other twelve countries fertility was clearly declining. Figure 1 shows the results of comparing the number of children women aged 45–49 have had in their lives, representing past fertility, with the current total fertility rate (TFR), both as estimated from the survey data. The TFR essentially indicates what completed family size will be if the fertility rates now prevailing among women of all ages are maintained. Some caution is necessary, as the TFR is based on all women while the other figures are based on ever-married women, but in most countries 98 percent or more of women aged 45–49 have been married. In some countries—Sri Lanka, Thailand, Mexico, Panama, and Peru, where about 95 percent of women aged 45–49 have

FIGURE 1. *Past and current fertility levels in fifteen developing countries with published World Fertility Survey reports*[1]

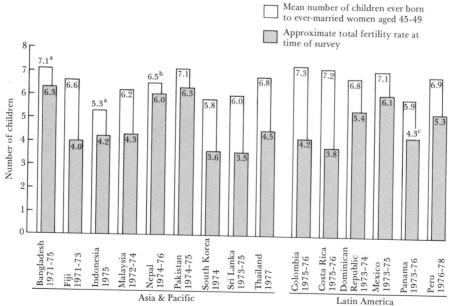

[1]The mean number of children ever born to ever-married women aged 45–49 (white bars) is based on the number of ever-married women, while the total fertility rate (shaded bars) is based on all women, except as noted. Thus, to the extent that fewer than all women marry, the fertility decline is exaggerated. [a]Figure for women aged 45–49 lower than for women aged 40–44; latter shown. [b]Figure for mean number of children corrected after publication of country report. [c]For women aged 20–49.
SOURCE: Kendall, 1979, p. 75; adapted by permission.

been married, and Costa Rica, where about 90 percent have been married—the difference in denominators exaggerates somewhat the extent of the fertility decline.

The most dramatic, sustained, and appreciable fertility decline shown in Figure 1 was in Costa Rica. There, the mean number of live births to ever-married women 45 to 49 years old was 7.2 in 1979, while the current total fertility rate was just 3.8. Almost as impressive are the figures for Colombia and Thailand, 7.3 and 6.8 compared with 4.2 and 4.5, respectively. The WFS has also gathered evidence of fertility declines in countries where such declines had not been identified previously. For the Dominican Republic the respective figures are 6.8 and 5.4, and for Peru, where family planning until recently was positively discouraged and where there is still no national family planning program (even though the use of traditional contraceptive methods has been widespread), the figures are 6.9 and 5.3. The existence of family planning programs does not seem to be a prerequisite for the onset of a fertility decline in situations like that of Peru, although clearly such programs have played an important role in lowering fertility in countries like Costa Rica and South Korea and might have made possible an even more rapid decline in Peru had they existed there.

Fertility preferences. Changes in fertility preferences are also documented in WFS data. Of the currently married fecund women who were questioned, about half want no more children. This figure ranges from more than 60 percent in South Korea, Sri Lanka, Colombia, Panama, and Peru to about 30 percent in Nepal. Even more significant may be the number of currently married women with at least one birth or currently pregnant who did not want their last child or current pregnancy. Where data are available they show that, except in Indonesia, more than one quarter of these women did not want their last child or current pregnancy.

The desire for no more children is substantial in all socioeconomic groups, including the rural and the least educated. Of course, rural and uneducated women tend to have large families, and this is indeed one reason they want no more children. Among currently married fecund women with four living children, the difference between urban and rural women, between educated and uneducated women, and between women whose husbands hold high-level and low-level jobs is in most cases less than 10 percentage points. These results appear to support the conclusion that desire for no more children may be less influenced by socioeconomic development than by practical recognition of the burdens of supporting a large family under difficult circumstances.

While nowhere in the developing world is the two-child family yet the established norm, there are indications that large numbers of women in some countries are coming to view this family size as their target. In South Korea, Sri Lanka, Thailand, Colombia, and Peru, half or more of the nonpregnant, fecund, married women with two children—one son and one daughter—state that they want no more. In another five countries more than 30 percent of such women want no more children. The real exceptions to this pattern are Malaysia and Nepal, where more than three quarters either want more or express no preference.

The preference for sons over daughters still very much characterizes a large part of Asia. In Bangladesh, South Korea, and Nepal, more than 95 percent of women with one living son and one living daughter who want another child and state a sex preference would prefer the next to be a boy. The only exception in the Asian countries analyzed is Indonesia, where roughly half of the women do not care one way or the other. In Latin America, the more traditional societies of Mexico and Peru prefer sons, but not to the same extent as in most of Asia. In Panama there is some degree of preference for daughters.

Marital unions. In WFS reports, age at marriage is calculated for women aged 25 or more at interview who married before age 25. The results show that such women in most areas of Asia and the Middle East marry earlier than women in Latin America and that women with secondary education marry, on the average, about two years later than women with only primary school education.

A comparison of the cohorts, or age groups, of women now aged 25–29 and 40–44 shows that in many countries the mean age at which women first marry, whether legally or consensually, is rising. This is especially true for societies characterized by early entrance into matrimony, like Bangladesh, with a mean age of 12.5 years. It is also true in those Asian societies where women tend to marry late, such as South Korea and Sri Lanka, with mean ages of 19.9 and 18.7 years, respectively. The most dramatic change has occurred in South Korea, where age at marriage for those marrying before age 25 has risen from 18.6 to 21.6 years, with smaller changes taking place in many of the other Asian countries. In Latin American countries, with the sole exception of Panama, mean age at marriage has changed very little.

Overall, however, these data on mean age at marriage are not a sensitive indicator of recent trends, since the analysis is restricted to women over age 25 at interview who first married before the age of 25. For even the youngest age group in such an analysis, those currently aged 25–29, the data refer to an event that happened, on the average, eight or nine years before the survey; for those now aged 45–49, to an event occurring almost thirty years prior to the survey. Even if recollection is accurate, such analyses will not give a true picture of very recent changes. In Bangladesh, for example, although nearly 80 percent of married women in their late twenties who were surveyed had been married by age 15, among the women aged 15 at the time of the household survey only 47 percent were married. To study recent trends, attention should be directed to complete birth cohorts (age groups) of women, both married and single. Trends are detected by examining, for successive cohorts, the proportion who first married prior to a given age, for example, 15, 20, or 25.

Nevertheless, recent and rapid changes in age at first marriage are detectable from WFS data in a number of countries. In Sri Lanka and Malaysia, for example, where age at first marriage has averaged less than 19 years, currently the percentage of women aged 20–24 who have ever entered into a marital union is only 39 percent and 50 percent, respectively. Quite obviously, by the time this cohort reaches the age of 50 their mean age at first marriage will be several years higher than the current mean of under 19 years.

The degree of stability of marital unions varies considerably across countries, but the total amount of time that women spend in marital unions is much more uniform. Figures on the percentage of ever-married women who have been married more than once vary from a low of 4 percent for South Korea, Pakistan, and Sri Lanka to a high of 32 percent for Indonesia and the Dominican Republic. Where separation and divorce are most common, remarriage is also the rule. Hence the proportion of elapsed time spent in marital union since date of first marriage varies much less across countries and across social groups within countries than do the figures on the number of times married.

In countries in which only 4 percent of women have been married more than once, women have, on the average, spent 97 percent of the elapsed time since first marriage in marital union. For the three countries where separation and remarriage are most common (Indonesia, the Dominican Republic, and Panama), women have spent 88 percent of the elapsed time in marital union. Since the total time spent in marital union is a measure of the exposure of women to the risk of childbearing, and inasmuch as it generally varies by less than 10 percent across groups within societies and across societies themselves, it is not surprising that fertility bears little relationship to marital stability.

There are interesting variations in the timing of fertility with respect to the date of marriage, both among countries within regions and among regions. The percentage of premarital conceptions among first births varies from presumably zero in Bangladesh, Nepal, and Pakistan to well over 20 percent in some Latin American countries. In the same way, the mean number of children born either before or within the five years following the

date of first marriage varies from 0.9 for Nepal to 2.4 for Costa Rica. The average for the nine Asian countries is 1.5; for the six Latin American countries it is 2.2.

Dividing the Asian and Latin American regions each into two groups based on age at marriage, it becomes clear that high fertility early in marriage is associated with an older age at marriage. In Latin American countries characterized by late marriage (mean age of 19.1 years) women have an average of 2.3 births in the first five years, whereas in the early-marrying Asian countries (mean age of 15.2) women have an average of 1.2 births in the first five years. Thus although an increase in age at marriage would be expected to lower completed fertility by reducing the number of years that women are exposed to the risk of childbearing, this is partly compensated for by a tendency of late-marrying women to have more children in the first four years of marriage.

Contraceptive use. In all but one of the fifteen countries surveyed, three quarters or more of ever-married women have heard of at least one contraceptive method and in ten of them this figure is 90 percent or higher. Only in Nepal, where a mere 22 percent have heard of a method of contraception, has the message not come across. In all but three countries, the best-known method is the pill, followed by sterilization and intrauterine devices (IUD's). Traditional methods such as withdrawal and abstinence are cited by less than half of the women in most countries.

There is much more intercountry variability when it comes to the percentage of ever-married or currently married women who have actually used a contraceptive at some time. The figure for ever-married women varies from a low of 4 percent in Nepal to a high of 82 percent in Costa Rica. The most startling contrasts between knowledge and use occur in Bangladesh and Pakistan. In both countries 70 percent or more of currently married, fecund women say that they have heard of contraception, but only 15 percent and 10 percent, respectively, report ever having used a method.

On the whole, countries with strong family planning programs show the highest levels of knowledge about and practice of family planning. Figures on the current use of contraception by women exposed to the risk of pregnancy show the same pattern of variation among countries as do the figures on ever-use. Costa Rica and Panama exhibit the highest current-use rates (78 percent and 65 percent, respectively), while in Nepal, Pakistan, and Bangladesh, 10 percent or fewer of exposed women are currently using a method. In general, the figures for Latin America are higher than for Asian countries.

The picture changes somewhat when attention is directed to the current use of "modern," or effective, methods. On the average, across all countries, three quarters of current users are using a modern method. But in Peru and Sri Lanka, with identical figures on current use (41 percent), only 15 percent and 24 percent, respectively, of exposed women (currently married, fecund, nonpregnant) are using a modern method. By contrast, Indonesia, Thailand, the Dominican Republic, and Mexico, with about the same level of overall use as Peru and Sri Lanka, show more than 30 percent of exposed women using a modern method.

One of the most striking findings in the area of contraceptive use is the high incidence of male or female sterilization for contraceptive purposes. The proportion of exposed women who have been sterilized for contraceptive purposes—or whose husbands have been sterilized—is 11 percent in Thailand; about 15 percent in Sri Lanka, the Dominican Republic, and Costa Rica; 22 percent in Fiji; and 26 percent in Panama. Indeed, contraceptive sterilization has displaced the pill as the most popular modern method of contraception in four of these six countries and is the second most used modern method, after the pill, in Malaysia, Thailand, and Costa Rica.

An important application of WFS data is to determine the extent of unmet need for family planning services. The most conservative definition and measurement uses a base, or denominator, of all currently married women and a numerator of women who are exposed *and* want no more children *and* are not using an efficient modern method. Unmet need calculated in this manner runs from a high of 47 percent in Bangladesh and over 30 percent in South Korea, Sri Lanka, and Peru to a low of 12 percent in Costa Rica and Fiji.

Measured in a different way, as a percentage of all exposed women who want no more children, the percentage not using modern methods of family planning is considerably higher—in fact, on the average more than twice as high. In Nepal, Bangladesh, and Pakistan, for example, the percentage of exposed women wanting no more children who are not using modern means of family planning is close to 90 percent. In most of the other countries, it is well above 50 percent.

A further insight into family planning use is provided by looking at the practices of women who do not desire more children but are using family planning to space births. In eleven of the fifteen countries, more than 20 percent of the women who desire future births are using some form of family planning. In both Costa Rica and Panama, the figure is higher than 50 percent. It is lowest in Nepal, Pakistan, and Bangladesh. Not surprisingly, the pill is the favorite method for spacing births in all countries except Sri Lanka and Peru, where rhythm is most widely used, and Pakistan and Bangladesh, where the condom is most common. The IUD ranks second in

Indonesia, Sri Lanka, Thailand, Colombia, the Dominican Republic, Mexico, and Panama.

Publications. The variety of substantive results reflected in the above findings is shown much more extensively in the summaries of country reports and in other publications of the WFS. The main categories of publications generated by the WFS are as follows:

- *Annual progress reports:* detailed information of WFS work, including a list of analysis projects based on WFS data.
- *Basic documents:* ten basic survey instruments, such as questionnaires, manuals, guidelines, and so on.
- *Technical bulletins:* selected techniques for analysis of WFS data.
- *Scientific reports:* results of substantive analyses carried out by participating countries, by the WFS, and by others; illustrative analyses are also included in this series.
- *Comparative studies:* cross-national summaries on selected topics and results of both methodological and substantive work in the area of comparative analysis.
- *Occasional papers:* background materials and other materials relevant to the WFS.
- *Summaries of country reports:* salient findings of the First Report published by each participating country.

The proceedings of the WFS conference held in London in July 1980 are scheduled for publication and will include invited papers and a record of the discussions.

Maurice G. Kendall
V. C. Chidambaram

BIBLIOGRAPHY

First Country Reports, usually published by government agencies or national organizations of participating countries, are available in bound copies or on microfiche from the Publications Office, International Statistical Institute, 428 Prinses Beatrixlaan, P.O. Box 950, 2270 AZ Voorburg, Netherlands.

Casterline, John B., and D. S. Whitelegge (editors). *Proceedings of the World Fertility Survey Conference, 1980.* Voorburg, Netherlands: International Statistical Institute, forthcoming.

Grebenik, Eugene. *The World Fertility Survey and Its 1980 Conference.* Voorburg, Netherlands: International Statistical Institute, 1981. Includes a complete list of WFS publications as of mid-1981.

Kendall, Maurice G. "The World Fertility Survey: Current Status and Findings." *Population Reports,* series M, no. 3, whole issue, July 1979.

World Fertility Survey. "Individual Country Reports: A Summary of Findings." Voorburg, Netherlands: International Statistical Institute, 1977–. A series of reports including the salient findings of the First Reports of the countries participating in the World Fertility Survey program. Reports have been issued on Bangladesh, Belgium, Colombia, Costa Rica, Czechoslovakia, the Dominican Republic, Fiji, Guadeloupe and Martinique, Guyana, Haiti, Hungary, Indonesia, Jamaica, Japan, Jordan, Kenya, Lesotho, Malaysia, Mexico, Nepal, the Netherlands, Pakistan, Panama, Peru, the Philippines, Senegal, South Korea, Spain, Sri Lanka, Thailand, and Turkey.

WORLD POPULATION

Estimates in 1981 ventured that world population had reached 4.4 billion during 1980. The recent rates of population growth generating these billions have been unprecedented. Although much of the doomsaying of the 1960s and early 1970s about a "population bomb" has subsided, the historical import of such rapid population growth remains undisputed.

The time line depicting this historical population trajectory (see Figure 1) underscores both the uniqueness and magnitude of the recent surge in population. Despite the uncertainty surrounding the date of man's origin and the reliance on conjecture to reconstruct our earliest history, a distinctive growth pattern emerges. This pattern, grossly simplified, consists of a very long period of slow growth interspersed with occasional brief spans of decline, followed by a relatively short period of contrastingly rapid growth.

The slow-growth era extends from man's nascence, conservatively estimated to be about 300,000 B.C. with

the first *Homo sapiens,* to roughly A.D. 1650, which marked the beginnings of accelerated growth. A paucity of data concerning this early era makes speculation inevitable. It is generally agreed, however, that exceedingly harsh conditions militated against man's survival, resulting in high mortality rates and thus slow population growth. More specifically, this earliest of demographic experiences is typified by sporadic periods of slight growth interrupted by declines due to the vagaries of weather, food supply, and disease, both endemic and epidemic. Although women were most likely reproducing close to their biological capacity, the prevailing high death rate allowed for only marginal population growth.

Hence, world population augmented slowly, bolstered from time to time when man could wrest slightly greater control from the inhospitable environment. After thousands of years of hunting and gathering, the development of agriculture led to a more reliable food supply and more stable forms of social organization, but the shift to settlement from a nomadic way of life did not significantly reduce the prevailing high mortality, although it may have increased life expectancy from around 18–20 years to 25–30 years. Agricultural settlements in turn led to the development of urban civilizations, first in Mesopotamia, then in Egypt, Crete, India, China, and Peru, wherein populations could flourish to a greater extent. Beginning around 8000–6000 B.C., with the emergence of agrarian societies, world population increased steadily, growing from an estimated 5–10 million to perhaps 300 million by A.D. 1, and rising to about 500 million by 1650, although these figures are highly conjectural. The growth pattern of the period was not,

FIGURE 1. *World population growth through history*

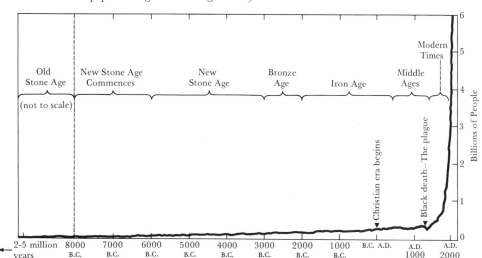

SOURCE: van der Tak, Haub, and Murphy, 1979, p. 2; reprinted by permission.

however, without interruption, as evidenced by one of its best-documented setbacks, the notorious black death of 1348, which is thought to have reduced the European population by one quarter.

In contrast, the short time span from 1650 to the present was characterized by a rapid increase in population as a result of an accelerating growth rate. This surge in population growth coincided with the social, economic, industrial, geographic, and intellectual revolutions heralding what is referred to as the modern age. Lowered mortality, and, to a much lesser extent, increased fertility, resulting from improved nutrition, disease control, and sanitation efforts, were hallmarks of this era. The falling death rate, a consequence of advances attributed to the modern age, was largely responsible for the consequent exceedingly rapid population growth.

During this period, around 1800, world population climbed to 1 billion. One hundred and thirty years later, a world population of 2 billion was attained, followed by successively shorter intervals of thirty years for the third billion and fifteen years for the fourth. The 4.4 billion people alive in 1980 constituted a population larger than all persons born during the entire Paleolithic age of approximately 258,000 years.

A particularly significant upturn in the growth rate occurred with the end of World War II as the developing world experienced mortality declines, mostly through intensive application of medical and public health technology. The sharp upward trend continued, peaking at an annual rate of global increase of about 2 percent by the early 1960s. A gradual turnabout began around 1965, resulting in a decline to a rate of approximately 1.8 percent by 1980 with a continued fall to perhaps 1.5 percent predicted by the year 2000. Notably, this reduction in the overall rate of increase represents the first decline from a historic high in about 400 years.

The global rate, derived using rates from both developed and developing countries, masks the considerable differences between them. Whereas the developing world exhibited a rate of 2.2 percent as of 1980, the developed world's rate was 0.6 percent. Moreover, regional rates tend not to reflect the extremes between countries, with the developing world, for example, experiencing country rates varying from about 1 to 3.5 percent.

Demographers and development planners have sought to quantify scenarios of possible futures through population projections. The Population Division of the United Nations has prepared a set of such long-range projections based on the assumption that the world as a whole is experiencing a modified version of the demographic transition. [See PROJECTIONS; DEMOGRAPHIC TRANSITION THEORY.] The resulting medium variant assessment shows world population reaching 6.2 billion in the year 2000,

9.8 billion in 2050, and stabilizing eventually at about 10.5 billion. According to these projections, Europe and North America have already undergone the transition and East Asia is heading toward completion of its final phases, meaning that birth rates are falling to become in concert with lowered death rates. Africa, South Asia, and West Asia are expected to follow this demographic trend as well, although varying as to when they experience its denouement.

Regional variation in population size as well as in growth rates is considerable. The Third World, composed of Africa, Asia (excluding Japan), Latin America, and Oceania (excluding Australia and New Zealand), is estimated to have had 3.3 billion people in 1980, or three-quarters of the world's population. Figure 2 shows world population by region for 1980 and projected to the year 2100. (The regional breakdowns used in Figure 2 vary slightly from those used elsewhere in this work.) A few points are especially salient. China, which has by far the world's largest population, approximately 980 million at the end of 1980, has a relatively slow rate of population growth and thus tends to depress estimates of composite Third World growth. In contrast, Africa is predicted to experience the most rapid growth, with its 1980 population of 470 million reaching 2.2 billion by 2100. Although Asia is not considered likely to have the highest growth rates, it will account for most of the increase in global population since it possesses the largest base, nearly 60 percent of the world's present population. From a 1980 population of 2.6 billion, Asia is projected to expand in 2100 to 5.9 billion. South Asia's population, expected to encounter growth rates similar to Latin America, is predicted to grow to 4.1 billion in 2100 from a base of 1.4 billion in 1980. Concurrently, the percent-

FIGURE 2. *Distribution of the world population by major areas, medium variant, 1980 and 2100*

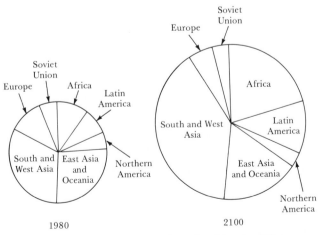

1980   2100

SOURCE: United Nations, 1981, p. 14; reprinted by permission.

age of world population in the developed world is expected to decrease from 27 percent in 1980 to about 13 percent by 2100.

Projections of future world and regional population growth, however, are only quantitative indicators and as such cannot be interpreted out of their social and political context. It would be presumptuous to construe population figures as being intrinsically salutary or deleterious. Even environmentally speaking, surmises of the earth's carrying capacity have not gelled to consensus, making definitive judgments hazardous as to what number, if any, constitutes too many. Since neither the causes nor consequences of population growth are isolated phenomena divorced from the existent political and social reality, interpretation of world population data begs a humane and balanced perspective.

Lynn Collins

BIBLIOGRAPHY

Cook, Robert C. "How Many People Have Ever Lived on Earth?" *Population Bulletin* 28(1):1–17, February 1962. Issued by the Population Reference Bureau, Washington, D.C.

United Nations, Department of International Economic and Social Affairs. "Long-range Global Population Projections, Based on Data as Assessed in 1978." Population Working Paper No. 75. New York, August 1981.

van der Tak, Jean, Carl Haub, and Elaine Murphy. "Our Population Predicament: A New Look." *Population Bulletin* 34(5), December 1979. Issued by the Population Reference Bureau, Washington, D.C.

Westing, Arthur H. "A Note on How Many Humans That Have Ever Lived." *BioScience* 31(7):523–524, July/August 1981.

WORLD POPULATION CONFERENCE

See ETHICS; UNITED NATIONS.

WOMEN, STATUS OF

See STATUS OF WOMEN; LAW AND FERTILITY REGULATION.

ZERO POPULATION GROWTH

See RESOURCES AND POPULATION.

Directory of Contributors
and Reviewers

Contributors

George T. Acsádi
Consultant, New York
PALEODEMOGRAPHY

B. Kwaku Adadevoh
Professor, College of Medical Sciences, University of Maiduguri, Nigeria
CONTRACEPTIVE METHODS, *overview article*

John S. Aird
Chief, Foreign Demographic Analysis Division, U.S. Bureau of the Census, Washington, D.C.
CHINA

Mohiuddin Alamgir
Research Director, Bangladesh Institute of Development Studies, Dacca
BANGLADESH

Francisco Alba
Researcher and Professor, El Colegio de México
MEXICO

Barbara A. Anderson
Associate Professor, Department of Sociology and Population Studies and Training Center, Brown University
SOVIET UNION

Eduardo E. Arriaga
Special Assistant for International Demographic Methods, International Demographic Data Center, U.S. Bureau of the Census, Washington, D.C.
DISTRIBUTION, *article on* DISTRIBUTION, CONCENTRATION, AND DISPERSION; URBANIZATION, *article on* MEASUREMENT

Roderic Beaujot
Assistant Professor of Sociology, University of Western Ontario
CANADA

Nancy Birdsall
Economist, World Bank, Washington, D.C.
FERTILITY AND DEVELOPMENT

John Bongaarts
Associate of the Center for Policy Studies, The Population Council, New York
FERTILITY DETERMINANTS, *article on* PROXIMATE DETERMINANTS

Thomas K. Burch
Professor of Sociology, University of Western Ontario
HOUSEHOLD AND FAMILY DEMOGRAPHY

Elizabeth W. Cecelski
Project Officer for Energy and Rural Women's Work, International Labour Office, Geneva
RESOURCES AND POPULATION

Chang Chih-Ye
Professor and Vice Director, Institute of Zoology, Academia Sinica, Beijing
CONTRACEPTIVE METHODS, *overview article*

Murray Chapman
Professor of Geography, University of Hawaii, and Research Associate, East-West Population Institute, Honolulu
CIRCULATION

V. C. Chidambaram
Deputy Director for Data Analysis, World Fertility Survey/International Statistical Institute, London
WORLD FERTILITY SURVEY

Robert L. Clark
Associate Professor, North Carolina State University at Raleigh
AGING POPULATION, *article on* UNITED STATES

Lynn Collins
Assistant Editor, International Encyclopedia of Population, *Center for Population and Family Health, and Research and Teaching Assistant, Sociology Department, Columbia University*
WORLD POPULATION

Katherine F. Darabi
Assistant Professor of Public Health, Columbia University
ADOLESCENT FERTILITY; EDUCATION, *article on* SEX EDUCATION

Léa Melo da Silva
Centro de Desenvolvimento e Planejamento Regional, Belo Horizonte, Brazil
BRAZIL

Frances Dennis
Director of Information and Public Relations, International Planned Parenthood Federation, London
INTERNATIONAL PLANNED PARENTHOOD FEDERATION

Joy G. Dryfoos
Consultant, Hastings-on-Hudson, New York
FAMILY PLANNING PROGRAMS, *article on* UNITED STATES

Arthur J. Dyck
Mary B. Saltonstall Professor of Population Ethics, School of Public Health; member of the faculty of the Divinity School; and Co-director, Kennedy Interfaculty Program in Medical Ethics, Harvard University
ETHICS

Patricia E. Elwell
Research Assistant, Hispanic Research Center, Fordham University
REFUGEES

Ruth S. J. Farmer
Senior Lecturer in Geography and Associate of the Population Studies Centre, University of Waikato, Hamilton, New Zealand
OCEANIA

James T. Fawcett
Research Associate, East-West Population Institute, Honolulu
VALUE OF CHILDREN

Sally E. Findley
Demographic Consultant, Population Studies and Training Center, Department of Sociology, Brown University
FERTILITY AND MIGRATION; INTERNAL MIGRATION, *articles on* DETERMINANTS *and* EFFECTS

Kathleen Ford
Assistant Professor, Department of Population Dynamics, Johns Hopkins University
CONTRACEPTIVE USE, *article on* UNITED STATES SINCE 1970

James R. Foreit
Research Associate, Center for Population and Family Health, Columbia University
FAMILY PLANNING PROGRAMS, *article on* NONCLINICAL PROGRAMS

Jacqueline Darroch Forrest
Director of Research, Alan Guttmacher Institute, New York
ABORTION, *article on* UNITED STATES

Ronald Freedman
Roderick D. McKenzie Professor of Sociology and Associate Director of the Population Studies Center, University of Michigan–Ann Arbor
FERTILITY DECLINE, *article on* THEORIES

Tomas Frejka
Associate, The Population Council, New York
MOMENTUM; PROJECTIONS

Moye Wicks Freymann
Professor, University of North Carolina at Chapel Hill
PUBLIC HEALTH

Dov Friedlander
Professor of Demography and Statistics, Hebrew University of Jerusalem
NORTH AFRICA AND SOUTHWEST ASIA, *article on* ISRAEL

Halvor Gille
Deputy Executive Director, United Nations Fund for Population Activities, New York
INTERNATIONAL POPULATION ASSISTANCE

Calvin Goldscheider
Professor of Demography and Sociology, Hebrew University of Jerusalem
NORTH AFRICA AND SOUTHWEST ASIA, *article on* ISRAEL

Martin E. Gorosh
Associate Professor, Center for Population and Family Health, Columbia University
FAMILY PLANNING PROGRAMS, *articles on* NONCLINICAL PROGRAMS *and* MANAGEMENT AND EVALUATION

Richard Hankinson
Editor, Population Index, *Office of Population Research, Princeton University*
PUBLICATIONS, *article on* SERIALS AND REFERENCE WORKS

Amos H. Hawley
(Kenan) Professor Emeritus, University of North Carolina at Chapel Hill
ECOLOGY

Donald F. Heisel
Coordinator, World Population Conference Implementation, Population Division, United Nations, New York
INTERNATIONAL MIGRATION

Alice Henry
Staff Research Associate, Johns Hopkins University
AGE AT MARRIAGE

Albert I. Hermalin
Professor of Sociology and Director, Population Studies Center, University of Michigan–Ann Arbor
FAMILY PLANNING PROGRAMS, *article on* EFFECTS OF FERTILITY

Kenneth Hill
Senior Research Associate, National Research Council, Washington, D.C.
INDIRECT ESTIMATION OF FERTILITY AND MORTALITY

Stephen L. Isaacs
Assistant Director and Assistant Professor, Center for Population and Family Health, Columbia University
LAW AND FERTILITY REGULATION, *article on* UNITED STATES

Anrudh K. Jain
Senior Associate, The Population Council, New York
INDIA

Gavin W. Jones
Executive Director, Development Studies Centre, Australian National University
FERTILITY DETERMINANTS, *article on* SOCIOLOGICAL AND ECONOMIC THEORIES; INDONESIA

Virginia Josephian
Editor, Demographic Yearbook, Statistical Office, United Nations, New York
DATA COLLECTION, *article on* INTERNATIONAL SYSTEMS

John Frederick Kantner
Professor, Department of Population Dynamics, Johns Hopkins University
POPULATION ASSOCIATION OF AMERICA

Louise Kantrow
Population Affairs Officer, Population Programmes and Projects Branch, Department of Technical Co-operation for Development, United Nations, New York
HISTORICAL DEMOGRAPHY

Charles B. Keely
Associate, Center for Policy Studies, The Population Council, New York
IMMIGRATION POLICY; REFUGEES

Maurice G. Kendall
Project Director (Retired), World Fertility Survey/International Statistical Institute, London
WORLD FERTILITY SURVEY

Nathan Keyfitz
Andelot Professor of Sociology and Demography, Harvard University, and Lazarus Professor of Social Demography, Ohio State University
MATHEMATICAL DEMOGRAPHY; POPULATION THEORY

Maurice Kirk
Senior Lecturer, Department of Social Policy, University of Leeds
EUROPE

Leslie Kish
Professor and Research Scientist, University of Michigan–Ann Arbor
SAMPLING METHODS

John Knodel
Professor, Department of Sociology and Population Studies Center, University of Michigan–Ann Arbor
BREASTFEEDING; FERTILITY DECLINE, *article on* EUROPEAN TRANSITION

Piotr Korcelli
Research Scholar, International Institute for Applied Systems Analysis, Laxenburg, Austria
URBANIZATION, *article on* DEVELOPED COUNTRIES

Juanita Kreps
James B. Duke Professor Emeritus, Duke University
AGING POPULATION, *article on* UNITED STATES

Karol J. Krótki
Professor of Sociology, University of Alberta
NORTH AFRICA AND SOUTHWEST ASIA, *article on* REGIONAL SURVEY

Robert J. Lapham
Study Director, Committee on Population and Demography, National Academy of Sciences, Washington, D.C.
SMALL-AREA ANALYSIS

Donald Lauro
Assistant Director, Center for Population and Family Health, Columbia University
COMPOSITION

Marc Lebrun
Assistant Executive Secretary, International Union for the Scientific Study of Population, Liège, Belgium
INTERNATIONAL UNION FOR THE SCIENTIFIC STUDY OF POPULATION

Barbara D. Levine
Health Services Representative, American Red Cross, New York
CONTRACEPTIVE USE, *article on* UNITED STATES OVERVIEW

Larry H. Long
Senior Research Associate, Center for Demographic Studies, U.S. Bureau of the Census, Washington, D.C.
INTERNAL MIGRATION, *article on* UNITED STATES

Katherine Ch'iu Lyle
Field Staff–China, The Rockefeller Foundation, Beijing
CHINA

Sheila Macrae
United Nations Consultant Demographer, South Pacific Commission, Nouméa, New Caledonia
OCEANIA

W. Parker Mauldin
Senior Scientist, The Rockefeller Foundation, New York
FERTILITY AND POPULATION GROWTH

Peter McDonald
Research Fellow, Department of Demography, Australian National University
EDUCATION, *article on* TEACHING DEMOGRAPHY

Robert T. McLaughlin
Director of Program Coordination, International Planned Parenthood Federation, Western Hemisphere Region, New York
BRAZIL

Regina McNamara
Associate Editor, International Encyclopedia of Population, Center for Population and Family Health, Columbia University
CARIBBEAN REGION; DEMOGRAPHIC TRANSITION THEORY; DISTRIBUTION, *article on* DISTRIBUTION POLICY; INFANT AND CHILD MORTALITY; INFANTICIDE; INTERNAL MIGRATION, *article on* MODELS; MIGRATION MEASUREMENT; MORTALITY TRENDS, *article on* HISTORICAL TRENDS; NORTH AMERICA; URBANIZATION, *overview article*

Geoffrey McNicoll
Senior Associate, Center for Policy Studies, The Population Council, New York
POPULATION AND DEVELOPMENT

John A. McWilliam
Evaluation Officer, United Nations Fund for Population Activities, New York
NIGERIA

Jane Menken
Assistant Director, Office of Population Research, and Professor of Sociology, Princeton University
REPRODUCTION, *article on* MODELS

Morvan de Mello Moreira
Fundacão de Informacãos para o Desenvolvimento de Pernambuco, Recife, Brazil
BRAZIL

Minoru Muramatsu
Director, Department of Public Health Demography, Institute of Public Health, Tokyo
JAPAN

Pearila Brickner Namerow
Assistant Professor of Public Health, Center for Population and Family Health, Columbia University
ADOLESCENT FERTILITY; EDUCATION, *article on* SEX EDUCATION

Dorothy L. Nortman
Associate, Center for Policy Studies, The Population Council, New York
CONTRACEPTIVE USE, *article on* DEVELOPING COUNTRIES

Abdel R. Omran
Professor of Epidemiology, School of Public Health, University of North Carolina at Chapel Hill
EPIDEMIOLOGIC TRANSITION, *articles on* THEORY *and* UNITED STATES

Susan Kingsley Pasquariella
Head Librarian, Center for Population and Family Health, Columbia University
PUBLICATIONS, *article on* BIBLIOGRAPHIC RESOURCES

Eve W. Paul
Vice-President for Legal Affairs, Planned Parenthood Federation of America, New York
LAW AND FERTILITY REGULATION, *article on* UNITED STATES

John M. Paxman
Chief, Population Policy Division, The Pathfinder Fund, Chestnut Hill, Massachusetts
LAW AND FERTILITY REGULATION, *article on* WORLDWIDE PERSPECTIVES

Susan Gustavus Philliber
Associate Professor, Center for Population and Family Health, Columbia University
ADOLESCENT FERTILITY; EDUCATION, *article on* SEX EDUCATION

Harriet F. Pilpel
Senior Partner, Greenbaum, Wolff & Ernst, New York
LAW AND FERTILITY REGULATION, *article on* UNITED STATES

Phyllis T. Piotrow
Director, Population Information Program, Johns Hopkins University
AGE AT MARRIAGE

Vera Plaskon
Consultant, Center for Population and Family Health, Columbia University
ABORTION, *article on* MEDICAL TECHNIQUES; STERILIZATION TECHNIQUES

John H. Pollard
Professor, Macquarie University, North Ryde, Australia
MORBIDITY AND LONGEVITY

Ian Pool
Professor and Director, Population Studies Centre, University of Waikato, Hamilton, New Zealand
OCEANIA

Samuel H. Preston
Chairman, Graduate Group in Demography, University of Pennsylvania
URBANIZATION, *article on* DEVELOPING COUNTRIES

Ronald G. Ridker
Senior Fellow, Resources for the Future, and Senior Economist, World Bank, Washington, D.C.
RESOURCES AND POPULATION

Allan Rosenfield
Professor of Obstetrics-Gynecology and Public Health and Director, Center for Population and Family Health, Columbia University
CONTRACEPTIVE METHODS, *article on* ORAL CONTRACEPTIVES AND INTRAUTERINE DEVICES

John A. Ross
Editor in Chief, International Encyclopedia of Population, Center for Population and Family Health, Columbia University
ACTUARIAL METHODS; FAMILY PLANNING RESEARCH; GENETICS; LIFE TABLES; RATES AND RATIOS

Judith S. Rowe
Associate Director, Princeton University Computer Center
MACHINE-READABLE DATA FILES

Norman B. Ryder
Professor, Princeton University
FERTILITY TRENDS

Rafael M. Salas
Executive Director, United Nations Fund for Population Activities, and Under-Secretary-General, United Nations, New York
UNITED NATIONS FUND FOR POPULATION ACTIVITIES

Janet E. Sceats
Epidemiologist and Medical Demographer, Waikato Hospital, Hamilton, New Zealand
OCEANIA

Sheldon J. Segal
Director, Population Sciences, The Rockefeller Foundation, New York
CONTRACEPTIVE METHODS, *overview article*

William Seltzer
Chief, Demographic and Social Statistics Branch, Statistical Office, United Nations, New York
DATA COLLECTION, *article on* NATIONAL SYSTEMS

Nasra M. Shah
Research Fellow, East-West Population Institute, Honolulu
PAKISTAN

Henry S. Shryock, Jr.
Professorial Lecturer, Kennedy Center for Population Research, Georgetown University
DATA COLLECTION, *article on* UNITED STATES CENSUS

Catherine H. Siener
Deputy Director for Legislative Analysis, New York City Health and Hospitals Corporation
INTERNATIONAL CLASSIFICATION OF DISEASES

O. J. Sikes
Chief, Population Education and Communication Section, United Nations Fund for Population Activities, New York
EDUCATION, *article on* POPULATION EDUCATION

David P. Smith
Assistant Professor, School of Public Health, University of Texas Health Science Center at Houston
SEX SELECTION

Peter C. Smith
Research Associate, East-West Population Institute, Honolulu
NUPTIALITY INDEXES

Kathryn H. Speert
Senior Consultant, Center for Population and Family Health, Columbia University
ASSOCIATION FOR POPULATION/FAMILY PLANNING LIBRARIES AND INFORMATION CENTERS—INTERNATIONAL

Bruce D. Spencer
Assistant Professor, School of Education, Northwestern University
SMALL-AREA ANALYSIS

Joseph J. Spengler
Professor Emeritus, Duke University
AGING POPULATION, *article on* UNITED STATES

K. Sivaswamy Srikantan
Professor, Gokhale Institute of Politics and Economics, and Head, Population Research Centre, Pune, India
FERTILITY DECLINE, *article on* THRESHOLD HYPOTHESIS; POPULATION MODELS

Guy Standing
Senior Economist, International Labour Office, Geneva
LABOR FORCE

Zena A. Stein
Chief of Psychiatric Research, New York State Psychiatric Institute
REPRODUCTION, *article on* MALNUTRITION AND FAMINE

Jeanne Betsock Stillman
Associate Editor, International Encyclopedia of Population, Center for Population and Family Health, Columbia University, and Staff Associate, The Population Council, New York
AGING POPULATION, *overview article;* BIRTH CONTROL MOVEMENT; MORBIDITY; SUB-SAHARAN AFRICA

George J. Stolnitz
Professor of Economics, Indiana University, Bloomington
MORTALITY TRENDS, *article on* POST–WORLD WAR II TRENDS

J. Mayone Stycos
Director, International Population Program, and Professor of Sociology, Cornell University
LATIN AMERICA; POPULATION POLICY, *overview article;* STATUS OF WOMEN

Mervyn Susser
Gertrude H. Sergievsky Professor of Epidemiology and Director, Gertrude H. Sergievsky Center, Columbia University
REPRODUCTION, *article on* MALNUTRITION AND FAMINE

James A. Sweet
Professor of Sociology, University of Wisconsin at Madison
MARRIAGE AND DIVORCE

Léon Tabah
Director, Population Division, United Nations, New York
UNITED NATIONS

Michael S. Teitelbaum
Senior Associate, Carnegie Endowment for International Peace, New York
POPULATION POLICY, *article on* UNITED STATES

Christopher Tietze
Senior Consultant, The Population Council, New York
ABORTION, *article on* INDUCED ABORTION.

Etienne van de Walle
Director, Population Studies Center, and Professor of Demography, University of Pennsylvania
FERTILITY DECLINE, *article on* EUROPEAN TRANSITION; HISTORICAL DEMOGRAPHY

Pravin Visaria
Professor, Sardar Patel Institute of Economic and Social Research, Ahmedabad, India
INDIA

Walter B. Watson
Senior Research Associate, Center for Population and Family Health, Columbia University
ASIA; FAMILY PLANNING PROGRAMS, *article on* DEVELOPING COUNTRIES

Judith Wilkinson
Assistant Librarian, Center for Population and Family Health, Columbia University
DIRECTORIES

Yeun-chung Yu
Statistician, Statistical Office, United Nations, New York
DATA COLLECTION, *article on* NATIONAL SYSTEMS

Frances Zainoeddin
Associate Population Affairs Officer, Population Division, United Nations, New York
UNITED NATIONS

Hania Zlotnik
Research Associate, National Research Council, Washington, D.C.
INDIRECT ESTIMATION OF FERTILITY AND MORTALITY

Ruth Jane Zuckerman
Judge, Family Court of the State of New York
FAMILY LAW

Reviewers

James Allman
Research Associate, Center for Population and Family Health, Columbia University

Jan Breman
Department of Social Economic Sciences, Bogor Agricultural University, Bogor, West Java

John C. Caldwell
Professor, Department of Demography, Research School of Social Sciences, Australian National University

Pat Caldwell
Department of Demography, Research School of Social Sciences, Australian National University

Arthur L. Caplan
Associate for the Humanities, The Hastings Center, Hastings, New York, and Associate for Social Medicine, College of Physicians and Surgeons, Columbia University

Katherine F. Darabi
Assistant Professor of Public Health, Center for Population and Family Health, Columbia University

Kathleen Ford
Assistant Professor, Department of Population Dynamics, Johns Hopkins University

Gwen P. Gentile
Assistant Professor, Downstate Medical Center, State University of New York

Sidney Goldstein
George Hazard Crooker University Professor, Professor of Sociology, and Director, Population Studies and Training Center, Brown University

Martin E. Gorosh
Associate Professor, Center for Population and Family Health, Columbia University

Donald F. Heisel
Coordinator, World Population Conference Implementation, Population Division, United Nations, New York

Donald W. Helbig
Associate Professor, Downstate Medical Center, State Univerity of New York

Stephen L. Isaacs
Assistant Director and Assistant Professor, Center for Population and Family Health, Columbia University

John Frederick Kantner
Professor, Department of Population Dynamics, Johns Hopkins University

Zifa William Kazeze
Regional Demographic Adviser, Economic Commission for Africa, United Nations, Addis Ababa

Donald Lauro
Assistant Director, Center for Population and Family Health, Columbia University

John J. Macisco, Jr.
Professor of Sociology, Fordham University

Deborah Maine
Editor, Center for Population and Family Health, Columbia University

James Clyde Mitchell
Official Fellow, Nuffield College, University of Oxford

Pearila Brickner Namerow
Assistant Professor of Public Health, Center for Population and Family Health, Columbia University

Leo A. Orleans
China Specialist, Library of Congress, Washington, D.C.

Susan Kingsley Pasquariella
Head Librarian, Center for Population and Family Health, Columbia University

Susan Gustavus Philliber
Associate Professor, Center for Population and Family Health, Columbia University

Joanne E. Revson
Assistant Professor, Center for Population and Family Health, Columbia University

Allan Rosenfield
Professor of Obstetrics-Gynecology and Public Health and Director, Center for Population and Family Health, Columbia University

Irving Sivin
Senior Associate, Center for Biomedical Research, The Population Council, New York

David G. Stillman
Program Coordinator, Department of Technical Co-operation for Development, United Nations, New York

Jeremiah M. Sullivan
Associate Professor, University of North Carolina at Chapel Hill

William Seltzer
Chief, Demographic and Social Statistics Branch, Statistical Office, United Nations, New York

Walter B. Watson
Senior Research Associate, Center for Population and Family Health, Columbia University

Eugene Weiss
Research Associate, Center for Population and Family Health, Columbia University

Acknowledgments

The editors gratefully acknowledge permission to adapt, use, or reprint materials from previously published sources. Details are given in the following listing.

ABORTION, *article on* INDUCED ABORTION. Table 2 is reprinted from Christopher Tietze and Sarah Lewit, "Life Risks Associated with Reversible Methods of Fertility Regulation," *International Journal of Gynaecology and Obstetrics* 16(6):456–459, May/June 1979, by permission of the editor.

ABORTION, *article on* UNITED STATES. Tables 1 and 2 are reprinted from Stanley K. Henshaw, Jacqueline Darroch Forrest, Ellen Sullivan, and Christopher Tietze, "Abortion in the United States, 1978–1979," *Family Planning Perspectives* 13(1):6–18, January/February 1981, by permission of The Alan Guttmacher Institute, New York.

AGE AT MARRIAGE. Based on Alice Henry and Phyllis T. Piotrow, "Age at Marriage and Fertility," *Population Reports*, series M, no. 4, whole issue, November 1979. Used by permission of the Population Information Program, Johns Hopkins University, Baltimore, Maryland.

AGING POPULATION, *article on* UNITED STATES. Based on Robert L. Clark, Juanita Kreps, and Joseph J. Spengler, "Economics of Aging: A Survey," *Journal of Economic Literature* 16(3):919–962, September 1978. Used by permission of the American Economic Association, Nashville, Tennessee.

BRAZIL. Based on Morvan de Mello Moreira, Léa Melo da Silva, and Robert T. McLaughlin, *Brazil,* Country Profiles (New York: Population Council, May 1978). Used by permission of the publisher.

BREASTFEEDING. Based on John Knodel, "Breastfeeding and Population Growth," *Science* 198(4322):1111–1115, 16 December 1977. Copyright 1977 by the American Association for the Advancement of Science, Washington, D.C. Used by permission of the publisher. Figure 2 is reprinted from John Knodel and Hallie Kintner, "The Impact of Breastfeeding Patterns on the Biometric Analysis of Infant Mortality," *Demography* 14(4):391–409, November 1977, by permission of the Population Association of America, Washington, D.C.

CANADA. Table 1 is reprinted from Roderic Beaujot, "Canada's Population: Growth and Dualism," *Population Bulletin* 33(2), whole issue, April 1978, by permission of the Population Reference Bureau, Washington, D.C.

CHINA. Opinions expressed in this article are the sole responsibility of the authors and do not necessarily reflect the policies or judgments of the agencies with which they are affiliated.

CIRCULATION. Table 1 is reprinted from R. Mansell Prothero, "Disease and Mobility: A Neglected Factor in Epidemiology," *International Journal of Epidemiology* 6(3):259–267, September 1977, by permission of Oxford University Press. Table 2 is reprinted from Graeme J. Hugo, "New Conceptual Approaches to Migration in the Context of Urbanization: A Discussion Based on Indonesian Experience," a paper prepared for the Seminar on New Conceptual Approaches to Migration in the Context of Urbanization, organized by the IUSSP Committee on Urbanization and Population Distribution, Bellagio, Italy, 30 June–3 July 1978, by permission of the International Union for the Scientific Study of Population, Liège, Belgium.

COMPOSITION. Figure 1 is reprinted from Ronald Freedman and Bernard Berelson, "The Human Population," *Scientific American,* September 1974, by permission of W. H. Freeman and Company, San Francisco. Copyright 1974 by Scientific American, Inc. All rights reserved. Figure 2 is reprinted from Mario E. Fernandez et al., *La población de Costa Rica,* Instituto de Investigaciones Sociales—CICRED (San José: Editorial

Universidad de Costa Rica, 1976), p. 56, by permission of the author. Figure 3 is reprinted from Robert W. Gardner and Eleanor C. Nordyke, *The Demographic Situation in Hawaii,* Papers of the East-West Population Institute, no. 31 (Honolulu: East-West Center, June 1974), by permission of the publisher.

CONTRACEPTIVE METHODS, *overview article.* Based on Sheldon J. Segal, B. Kwaku Adadevoh, and Chang Chih-Ye, "Reproduction, Fertility Regulation and Infertility," in *World Population and Development: Challenges and Prospects,* edited by Philip M. Hauser (Syracuse, N.Y.: Syracuse University Press, 1979), pp. 174–210. Used by permission of the publisher.

CONTRACEPTIVE USE, *article on* DEVELOPING COUNTRIES. Figure 4 is reprinted from Dorothy L. Nortman and Ellen Hofstatter, *Population and Family Planning Programs: A Compendium of Data through 1978,* 10th ed. (New York: Population Council, 1980), by permission of the publisher.

CONTRACEPTIVE USE, *article on* UNITED STATES SINCE 1970. Table 2 is reprinted from Kathleen Ford, "Contraceptive Use in the United States, 1973–1976," *Family Planning Perspectives* 10(5):264–269, September/October 1978, by permission of the author and The Alan Guttmacher Institute, New York. Table 3 is reprinted from Melvin Zelnik and John F. Kantner, "Sexual and Contraceptive Experience of Young Unmarried Women in the United States, 1976 and 1971," *Family Planning Perspectives* 9(2):55–71, March/April 1977, by permission of the authors and The Alan Guttmacher Institute, New York.

DATA COLLECTION, *article on* NATIONAL SYSTEMS. Opinions expressed in this article are the sole responsibility of the authors and do not necessarily reflect the policies or judgments of the agency with which they are affiliated.

DATA COLLECTION, *article on* INTERNATIONAL SYSTEMS. Opinions expressed in this article are the sole responsibility of the author and do not necessarily reflect the policies or judgments of the agency with which she is affiliated.

DEMOGRAPHIC TRANSITION THEORY. Figure 1 is reprinted from Nathan Keyfitz, *Applied Mathematical Demography* (New York: John Wiley & Sons, 1977), by permission of the publisher.

DISTRIBUTION, *article on* DISTRIBUTION, CONCENTRATION, AND DISPERSION. Based on Eduardo E. Arriaga, "Selected Measurements of Urbanization," in *The Measurement of Urbanization and Projection of Urban Population,* edited by Sidney Goldstein and David F. Sly (Dolhain, Belgium: Ordina Editions, 1975), pp. 19–87. Used by permission of the publisher. Opinions expressed in this article are the sole responsibility of the author and do not necessarily reflect the policies or judgments of the agency with which he is affiliated.

EDUCATION, *article on* POPULATION EDUCATION. Opinions expressed in this article are the sole responsibility of the author and do not necessarily reflect the policies or judgments of the agency with which he is affiliated.

EPIDEMIOLOGIC TRANSITION, *article on* UNITED STATES. Based on Abdel R. Omran, "Epidemiologic Transition in the United States: The Health Factor in Population Change," *Population Bulletin* 32(2), whole issue, May 1977; updated reprint, May 1980. Used by permission of the Population Reference Bureau, Washington, D.C. Table 2 is adapted from Abdel R. Omran, "A Century of Epidemiologic Transition in the United States," *Preventive Medicine* 6(1):30–51, March 1977, by permission of Academic Press, New York.

FAMILY PLANNING PROGRAMS, *article on* NONCLINICAL PROGRAMS. Based on James R. Foreit, Martin E. Gorosh, Duff G. Gillespie, and C. Gary Merritt, "Community-based and Commercial Contraceptive Distribution: An Inventory and Appraisal," *Population Reports,* series J, no. 19, whole issue, March 1978. Used by permission of the Population Information Program, Johns Hopkins University, Baltimore, Maryland.

FAMILY PLANNING PROGRAMS, *article on* UNITED STATES. Table 2 is adapted from Alan Guttmacher Institute, *Data and Analyses for the 1980 Revision of the DHHS Five-year Plan for Family Planning Services* (New York, July 1981), by permission of The Alan Guttmacher Institute. Figure 2 is reprinted from Aida Torres, Jacqueline Darroch Forrest, and Susan Eisman, "Family Planning Services in the United States, 1978–1979," *Family Planning Perspectives* 13(3):132–141, May/June 1981, by permission of the authors and The Alan Guttmacher Institute, New York.

FERTILITY AND DEVELOPMENT. Based on Nancy Birdsall, "Analytical Approaches to the Relationship of Population Growth and Development," *Population and Development Review* 3(1/2):63–102, March/June 1977. Used by permission of The Population Council, New York.

FERTILITY DECLINE, *article on* THEORIES. Based on Ronald Freedman, "Theories of Fertility Decline: A Reappraisal," *Social Forces* 58(1):1–17, September 1979. Copyright © The University of North Carolina Press, Chapel Hill. Used by permission of the author and the publisher.

FERTILITY DECLINE, *article on* EUROPEAN TRANSITION. Based on John Knodel and Etienne van de Walle, "Lessons from the Past: Policy Implications of Historical Fertility Studies," *Population and Development Review* 5(2):217–245, June 1979. Used by permission of The Population Council, New York. Figure 3 is reprinted from Ansley J. Coale and Roy C. Treadway, "A Summary of Changing Fertility in the Provinces of Europe," a paper prepared for the Summary Conference on European Fertility, Princeton, New Jersey, 23–27 July 1979, by permission of the authors.

FERTILITY DETERMINANTS, *article on* SOCIOLOGICAL AND ECONOMIC THEORIES. Figure 1 is reprinted from Ronald Freedman, *The Sociology of Human Fertility: An Annotated Bibliography,* A Population Council Book (New York: Irvington Publishers, 1975), p. 15, by permission of the author.

HISTORICAL DEMOGRAPHY. Opinions expressed in this article are the sole responsibility of the authors and do not necessarily reflect the policies or judgments of the agencies with which they are affiliated.

HOUSEHOLD AND FAMILY DEMOGRAPHY. Based on Thomas K. Burch, "Household and Family Demography: A Bibliographic Essay," *Population Index* 45(2):173–195, April 1979. Used by permission of the Office of Population Research, Princeton University, Princeton, New Jersey.

INDIA. Based on Pravin Visaria and Anrudh K. Jain, *India,* Country Profiles (New York: Population Council, May 1976). Used by permission of the publisher.

INFANT AND CHILD MORTALITY. Table 2 is reprinted from Tim Dyson, "Levels, Trends, Differentials, and Causes of Child Mortality: A Survey," *World Health Statistics Report* 30:282–311, 1977, by permission of the World Health Organization. Figure 1 is reprinted from Hugo Behm, "Socioeconomic Determinants of Mortality in Latin America," a paper presented at the World Health Organization meeting on Socioeconomic Determinants and Consequences of Mortality, Mexico City, June 1979, by permission of the World Health Organization.

INTERNAL MIGRATION, *article on* MODELS. Figure 1 is reprinted from Everett S. Lee, "A Theory of Migration," *Demography* 3(1):47–57, 1966, by permission of the Population Association of America, Washington, D.C.

INTERNAL MIGRATION, *article on* UNITED STATES. Opinions expressed in this article are the sole responsibility of the author and do not necessarily reflect the policies or judgments of the agency with which he is affiliated.

INTERNATIONAL MIGRATION. Opinions expressed in this article are the sole responsibility of the author and do not necessarily reflect the policies or judgments of the agency with which he is affiliated.

INTERNATIONAL POPULATION ASSISTANCE. Opinions expressed in this article are the sole responsibility of the author and do not necessarily reflect the policies or judgments of the agency with which he is affiliated.

LABOR FORCE. Based on Guy Standing, *Labour Force Participation and Development* (Geneva: International Labour Office, 1978). Copyright 1980 by the International Labour Organisation, Geneva. Used by permission of the publisher. Responsibility for opinions expressed in this article rests solely with the author, and its publication does not constitute an endorsement by the International Labour Office of the opinions expressed in it.

MARRIAGE AND DIVORCE. Based on James A. Sweet, "Demography and the Family," *Annual Review of Sociology,* vol. 3, pp. 363–405, 1977. Copyright © 1977 by Annual Reviews, Inc., Palo Alto, California. Used by permission of the author and Annual Reviews, Inc. Table 2 is reprinted from Heather L. Ross and Isabel V. Sawhill, *Time of Transition: The Growth of Families Headed by Women* (Washington, D.C.: Urban Institute, 1975), app. 4, p. 207, by permission of The Urban Institute.

MATHEMATICAL DEMOGRAPHY. Based on Nathan Keyfitz, "Mathematical Demography: A Bibliographic Essay," *Population Index* 42(1), January 1976. Used by permission of the Office of Population Research, Princeton University, Princeton, New Jersey.

MORBIDITY AND LONGEVITY. Based on John H. Pollard, "Factors Affecting Mortality and the Length of Life," in *Population Science in the Service of Mankind: Conference on Science in the Service of Life, Vienna, 1979* (Liège, Belgium: International Union for the Scientific Study of Population, 1979), pp. 53–79. Used by permission of the publisher.

NIGERIA. Opinions expressed in this article are the sole responsibility of the author and do not necessarily reflect the policies or judgments of the agency with which he is affiliated. Table 1 is reprinted from P. O. Olusanya, "Population

Growth and Its Components: The Nature and Direction of Population," in *Population Growth and Socioeconomic Change in West Africa,* edited by John C. Caldwell (New York and London: Columbia University Press, 1975), pp. 236–253, by permission of the publisher.

NUPTIALITY INDEXES. Based on Peter C. Smith, "Indexes of Nuptiality: Asia and the Pacific," *Asian and Pacific Census Forum* 5(2):1–3,6, November 1978.

POPULATION AND DEVELOPMENT. Figure 1 is reprinted from Samuel H. Preston, *Mortality Patterns in National Populations: With Special Reference to Recorded Causes of Death* (New York: Academic Press, 1976), by permission of the author and the publisher.

POPULATION POLICY, *overview article.* Based on J. Mayone Stycos, "Population Policy and Development," *Population and Development Review* 3(1/2):103–112, March/June 1977. Used by permission of The Population Council, New York.

POPULATION THEORY. Based on Nathan Keyfitz, "Population Theory and Doctrine: A Historical Survey," in *Readings in Population,* edited by William Petersen (New York: Macmillan, 1972). Used by permission of the author and the publisher.

PROJECTIONS. Based on Tomas Frejka, "Future Population Growth," in *Handbook of Futures Research,* edited by Jib Fowles (Westport, Conn.: Greenwood Press, 1978), pp. 533–550. Used by permission of Greenwood Press, a division of Congressional Information Service, Inc., Westport, Connecticut.

REPRODUCTION, *article on* MALNUTRITION AND FAMINE. Figure 1 is adapted from Zena Stein, Mervyn Susser, Gerhart Saenger, and Francis Marolla, *Famine and Human Development: The Dutch Hunger Winter of 1944–1945* (New York: Oxford University Press, 1975), by permission of the publisher.

RESOURCES AND POPULATION. Based on Ronald G. Ridker and Elizabeth W. Cecelski, "Resources, Environment, and Population: The Nature of Future Limits," *Population Bulletin* 34(3), whole issue, August 1979. Used by permission of the Population Reference Bureau, Washington, D.C.

SMALL-AREA ANALYSIS. The authors of this article, Robert J. Lapham and Bruce D. Spencer, wish it to be known that their names are listed in alphabetical order.

STATUS OF WOMEN. Based on J. Mayone Stycos, "On the Demographic Progress and the Status of Women," *International Population Conference, Mexico, 1977* (Liège, Belgium: International Union for the Scientific Study of Population, 1978), vol. 3, pp. 445–461. Used by permission of the publisher.

UNITED NATIONS. Opinions expressed in this article are the sole responsibility of the authors and do not necessarily reflect the policies or judgments of the agency with which they are affiliated.

UNITED NATIONS FUND FOR POPULATION ACTIVITIES. Opinions expressed in this article are the sole responsibility of the author and do not necessarily reflect the policies or judgments of the agency with which he is affiliated.

URBANIZATION, *overview article.* Table 1 is reprinted from United Nations, Department of International Economic and Social Affairs, *Patterns of Urban and Rural Population Growth,* Series A, Population Studies, no. 68 (New York, 1980), by permission of the United Nations.

URBANIZATION, *article on* DEVELOPING COUNTRIES. Based in part on Samuel Preston, "Urban Growth in Developing Countries: A Demographic Reappraisal," *Population and Development Review* 5(2):195–215, June 1979. Used by permission of the Population Council, New York. Tables 1, 2, and 3 are reprinted from United Nations, Department of International Economic and Social Affairs, *Patterns of Urban and Rural Population Growth,* Series A, Population Studies, no. 68 (New York, 1980), by permission of the United Nations.

URBANIZATION, *article on* DEVELOPED COUNTRIES. Based on Piotr Korcelli, "Urban Change: An Overview of Research and Planning Issues," Working Paper 80–30, International Institute for Applied Systems Analysis, Laxenburg, Austria, March 1980.

URBANIZATION, *article on* MEASUREMENT. Based on Eduardo E. Arriaga, "Selected Measurements of Urbanization," in *The Measurement of Urbanization and Projection of Urban Population,* edited by Sidney Goldstein and David F. Sly (Dolhain, Belgium: Ordina Editions, 1975), pp. 19–87. Used by permission of the publisher. Opinions expressed in this article are the sole responsibility of the author and do not necessarily reflect the policies or judgments of the agency with which he is affiliated.

VALUE OF CHILDREN. Figures 1, 2, 3, and 4 are reprinted from Rodolfo A. Bulatao, *On the Nature of the Transition in the Value of Children,* Papers of the East-West Population Institute, no. 60-A (Honolulu: East-West Center, 1979), by permission of the publisher. Table 1 is reprinted from Fred Arnold et al., *The Value of Children: A Cross-national Study,* volume 1, *Introduction and Comparative Analysis* (Honolulu: East-West Center, 1975), by permission of the publisher.

WORLD FERTILITY SURVEY. Based on Maurice G. Kendall, "The World Fertility Survey: Current Status and Findings," *Population Reports,* series M, no. 3, whole issue, July 1979. Used by permission of the Population Information Program, Johns Hopkins University, Baltimore, Maryland.

WORLD POPULATION. Figure 1 is reprinted from Jean van der Tak, Carl Haub, and Elaine Murphy, "Our Population Predicament: A New Look," *Population Bulletin* 34(5), December 1979, by permission of the Population Reference Bureau, Washington, D.C. Figure 2 is reprinted from United Nations, Department of International Economic and Social Affairs, "Long-range Global Population Projections, Based on Data as Assessed in 1978," Working Paper No. 75 (New York, August 1981), by permission of the United Nations.

The editors wish further to acknowledge the gracious administrative support given, during the several years of preparation of this encyclopedia, by Matilde Dominguez, Alice Capozzi, John Ramirez, Hussein Elmeshad, Jean Thomas, and Susan Kistler. We and our secretary, Irene Steger, are grateful for the assistance with typing so generously given by Marie Delgado, Nina Gray, Leslie Grigg, Adelaide Hirscheimer, Alina Martin, Carol Neu, Nancy Ortiz, Sydney Spero, Annette Topilow, and Gloria Wall of the Center for Population and Family Health. Marvin Walton and Wayne Horace cheerfully copied and mailed the many manuscripts, and Peggy Demarrais was very helpful in the library. Mary Anderson and Lynn S. Millard were invaluable at critical times when extra typing had to be done. For additional help with typing we thank Susan Carter, Edith Chartier, Kathy Charton, Rose Guistra, Robert J. Schwarz, and Alexandra Smyth. We also thank Pi Yu Ting for the computerized listings of our articles and contributors that helped us keep track of so many details.

Editorial and Production Staff

Claude Conyers, *Senior Project Editor*

BIBLIOGRAPHY DEPARTMENT

Lynn S. Millard, *Director of Research*
Mary Jane Chase, *Researcher*
Charlotte H. Hamlin, *Researcher*
Daniel Ostrow, *Researcher*
William P. Wilkinson, *Researcher*

COPY DEPARTMENT

Susan Converse Winslow, *Chief Copy Editor*
David J. Conti, *Editorial Assistant*
Edward J. Cripps, *Editorial Assistant*
Phyllis Korper, *Editorial Assistant*
Frances P. Long, *Editorial Assistant*
Tatiana Lupenko, *Editorial Assistant*

Severy Bruce Bumby, *Managing Editor*

Gail Liss, *Indexer*

Joan Greenfield, *Book Designer*

J & R Studio, *Illustrators*

Winston Sukhnanand, *Production Manager*

Topical Outline of Contents

The eleven major categories of classification are given in full-size capital letters; subcategories are shown in small capitals. Titles of core entries are indicated by italics.

Index

Both proper names and topics appear in this index as main entries in a single alphabetical order. Article titles are printed in capital letters (as are certain names of data indexes and archives). All subentries in this index are article titles (often shortened), showing contexts in which names and topics are mentioned or discussed. Cross-references connect related entries, clarify synonymous terms, and explain wording inverted for alphabetical order. Acronyms and abbreviations head each alphabetical listing.

A

ADQ
  see Association des Démographes du Quebec
AFDC
  see Aid to Families with Dependent Children
AGI
  see Alan Guttmacher Institute
AICIP
  see Asociación Interamerica de Centros de Información de Población
APLIC
  see Association for Population/Family Planning Libraries and Information Centers—International
ASEAN
  see Association of South East Asian Nations

Aaron, Henry, 34, 36
Abbasi, Nasreen, 509
Abbey, Helen, 341
Aborigines, 499–500, 501

ABORTION, 1–15

INDUCED ABORTION, 1–8
MEDICAL TECHNIQUES, 8–11
UNITED STATES, 11–15

adolescent fertility, 20
age at marriage, 22, 23, 25, 26
Asia, 48, 49
Brazil, 69
Canada, 81
Caribbean region, 86
contraceptive use: U.S. overview, 121–122
ethics, 186
Europe, 197
family planning programs: developing countries, 209, 210, 213–214
family planning programs: United States, 225
fertility and population growth, 253
fertility decline: theories, 262
fertility determinants: proximate, 278
India, 321
international population assistance, 381
Japan, 388
Latin America, 403
law and fertility regulation: United States, 413, 414–416, 419
law and fertility regulation: worldwide, 409–411
marriage and divorce, 431
Nigeria, 475
North Africa and Southwest Asia: Israel, 490, 491
North Africa and Southwest Asia: regional survey, 485
Oceania, 503
Pakistan, 511
population policy: United States, 534
public health, 557
reproduction: malnutrition and famine, 585, 586
sex selection, 605
Soviet Union, 615, 616
United States, 648
Abortion rates, 2–5, 12–13
  adolescent fertility, 20
Abortion ratios, 2–5, 577
Abridged life table, 421, 422
Abramowitz, Molly, 614
Abstinence
  family planning programs: developing countries, 209
  India, 318
  Indonesia, 336

701

B

D

F

H

J

M

N

O

S

law and fertility regulation: worldwide, 407, 408, 409
machine-readable data files, 428
nuptiality indexes, 495, 497
projections, 545
urbanization: developed countries, 657
Swedish Data Archive, Institute of Political Science, University of Göteborg, 428
Swedish International Development Agency, 323
Swedlund, A. C., 513
Sween, Joyce A., 250
Sweet, James A.

contributor: Marriage and divorce, 429–436

Swindell, K., 96
Switzerland
birth control movement, 61
education: teaching demography, 170
Europe, 195–196
fertility and population growth, 253
international migration, 367, 368, 370
Symptomatic data, 608, 609, 610
Synopsis Nosologiae Methodicae, 365
Synthetic method, 610
Syphilis, 177
Syria
international migration, 370
North Africa and Southwest Asia: regional survey, 478, 480, 481, 482, 483, 484, 485
Systematic random selection of elements, 603
Systems Development Corporation, 573, 574
Szilágyi, János, 512

T

Tabah, Léon

contributor: United Nations, 637–643

population and development, 524
Tabbarah, Riad G., 246
Tabulating machine for censuses, 144
Tabulation of census data, 144
Tadzhik, 42
Taeuber, Conrad, 175
Taeuber, Irene B., 175
Taichung experiment, Taiwan, 211
Taiwan
age at marriage, 24, 25
Asia, 42, 43, 44, 45, 46–47, 49
breastfeeding, 75, 76
contraceptive use: developing countries, 114, 116
education: sex, 167
epidemiologic transition: theory, 175

family planning programs: developing countries, 206, 210, 211, 212, 213
fertility and development, 243
fertility decline: theories, 261, 262, 263
household and family demography, 302
international migration, 367
law and fertility regulation: worldwide, 411
migration measurement, 449
mortality trends: post–World War II, 468
nuptiality indexes, 497
population models, 527
status of women, 620
Talon, Jean, 77–78
Tamil Nadu, India, 316, 317, 320, 322
Tangier
North Africa and Southwest Asia: regional survey, 478
Tanner, J. M., 586
Tanzania
age at marriage, 27
distribution: distribution policy, 156
internal migration: determinants, 344
public health, 558
sub-Saharan Africa, 629, 632, 633
Taussig, Michael, 34, 36
Tax relief, 611
Taylor, Henry Longstreet, 588
Taylor, Howard C., Jr., 213
Te-Hsiung Sun, 302
Teaching of demography, 168–171
see also Scholarly activities
Technical Advisory Committee, U.S. Bureau of the Census, 525
Technology advances and population, 161–162, 520
mortality trends: post–World War II, 463
see also Fertility and development; Population and development
Technology and resources, 591, 593, 596–597, 598
Teenage childbearing
see Adolescent fertility
Teenage contraceptive use
contraceptive use: United States since 1970, 125, 126
population policy: United States, 534
Teitelbaum, A., 455
Teitelbaum, Michael S.

contributor: Population policy, *article on* United States, 533–536

fertility decline: theories, 259
Tel Aviv, Israel, 489
Telephone "hot line" information service, 210
TEMPO demographic-socioeconomic model, 527
Tempo of urbanization, 661–662, 663
Terhune, Kenneth W., 244
Territoriality, 542
Tetanus, 554
Texas, 534

Texas, University of, 567, 569
Thai Auxiliary Midwife Project, 211
Thailand
age at marriage, 24, 25
Asia, 42, 45, 47, 49
breastfeeding, 74, 75, 76
contraceptive use: developing countries, 114
education: sex, 167
family planning programs: developing countries, 209, 211, 213
family planning programs: nonclinical, 216, 219
fertility and development, 244
fertility and migration, 251
fertility and population growth, 255
fertility decline: theories, 260, 263
international population assistance, 378
law and fertility regulation: worldwide, 407
nuptiality indexes, 498
refugees, 580
World Fertility Survey, 675, 676, 678
Theoretical effectiveness, 236, 237
Theoretical Population Biology (journal), 437, 562
Theory of ——
see under subject of the theory, such as Demographic transition theory
Thesauri, 567–568
Third World
see Developing countries; *specific countries*
Thomas, Dorothy Swaine, 361
Thomas, R. N., 249
Thornton, A. D., 434–435
Thornton, Arland, 666
Three Mile Island, 597
Threshold hypothesis, 266–268
Thromboembolic disease, 110, 111
Thrush, 177
Tianjin, China, 89
Tietze, Christopher

contributor: Abortion, *article on* induced abortion, 1–8

abortion: United States, 12, 13
contraceptive use: U.S. overview, 121
family planning research, 237
Tilly, Charles, 524
Time series analysis, 439
Time-use surveys, 392
Title IV-A of the Social Security Act, 415
Title V of the Social Security Act, 415
Title X of the Public Health Services Act, 220, 223, 224, 414–415, 418, 536, 648
Title XIX of the Social Security Act
see Medicaid program
Title XX of the Social Security Act, 415, 418
Tobin, J. D., 457
Todaro, Michael P.
internal migration: determinants, 344
internal migration: models, 352
population and development, 522

V

W